LINUX TCP/IP
NETWORKING FOR EMBEDDED SYSTEMS
SECOND EDITION

LIMITED WARRANTY AND DISCLAIMER OF LIABILITY

THE CD-ROM THAT ACCOMPANIES THE BOOK MAY BE USED ON A SINGLE PC ONLY. THE LICENSE DOES NOT PERMIT THE USE ON A NETWORK (OF ANY KIND). YOU FURTHER AGREE THAT THIS LICENSE GRANTS PERMISSION TO USE THE PRODUCTS CONTAINED HEREIN, BUT DOES NOT GIVE YOU RIGHT OF OWNERSHIP TO ANY OF THE CONTENT OR PRODUCT CONTAINED ON THIS CD-ROM. USE OF THIRD-PARTY SOFTWARE CONTAINED ON THIS CD-ROM IS LIMITED TO AND SUBJECT TO LICENSING TERMS FOR THE RESPECTIVE PRODUCTS.

CHARLES RIVER MEDIA, INC. ("CRM") AND/OR ANYONE WHO HAS BEEN INVOLVED IN THE WRITING, CREATION, OR PRODUCTION OF THE ACCOMPANYING CODE ("THE SOFTWARE") OR THE THIRD-PARTY PRODUCTS CONTAINED ON THE CD-ROM OR TEXTUAL MATERIAL IN THE BOOK, CANNOT AND DO NOT WARRANT THE PERFORMANCE OR RESULTS THAT MAY BE OBTAINED BY USING THE SOFTWARE OR CONTENTS OF THE BOOK. THE AUTHOR AND PUBLISHER HAVE USED THEIR BEST EFFORTS TO ENSURE THE ACCURACY AND FUNCTIONALITY OF THE TEXTUAL MATERIAL AND PROGRAMS CONTAINED HEREIN. WE HOWEVER, MAKE NO WARRANTY OF ANY KIND, EXPRESS OR IMPLIED, REGARDING THE PERFORMANCE OF THESE PROGRAMS OR CONTENTS. THE SOFTWARE IS SOLD "AS IS" WITHOUT WARRANTY (EXCEPT FOR DEFECTIVE MATERIALS USED IN MANUFACTURING THE DISK OR DUE TO FAULTY WORKMANSHIP).

THE AUTHOR, THE PUBLISHER, DEVELOPERS OF THIRD-PARTY SOFTWARE, AND ANYONE INVOLVED IN THE PRODUCTION AND MANUFACTURING OF THIS WORK SHALL NOT BE LIABLE FOR DAMAGES OF ANY KIND ARISING OUT OF THE USE OF (OR THE INABILITY TO USE) THE PROGRAMS, SOURCE CODE, OR TEXTUAL MATERIAL CONTAINED IN THIS PUBLICATION. THIS INCLUDES, BUT IS NOT LIMITED TO, LOSS OF REVENUE OR PROFIT, OR OTHER INCIDENTAL OR CONSEQUENTIAL DAMAGES ARISING OUT OF THE USE OF THE PRODUCT.

THE SOLE REMEDY IN THE EVENT OF A CLAIM OF ANY KIND IS EXPRESSLY LIMITED TO REPLACEMENT OF THE BOOK AND/OR CD-ROM, AND ONLY AT THE DISCRETION OF CRM.

THE USE OF "IMPLIED WARRANTY" AND CERTAIN "EXCLUSIONS" VARIES FROM STATE TO STATE, AND MAY NOT APPLY TO THE PURCHASER OF THIS PRODUCT.

LINUX TCP/IP
NETWORKING FOR EMBEDDED SYSTEMS
SECOND EDITION

THOMAS F. HERBERT

CHARLES RIVER MEDIA
Boston, Massachusetts

Copyright 2007 Career & Professional Group, a division of Thomson Learning, Inc.
Published by Charles River Media, an imprint of Thomson Learning Inc.
All rights reserved.

No part of this publication may be reproduced in any way, stored in a retrieval system of any type, or transmitted by any means or media, electronic or mechanical, including, but not limited to, photocopy, recording, or scanning, without prior permission in writing from the publisher.

Cover Design: Tyler Creative

CHARLES RIVER MEDIA
25 Thomson Place
Boston, Massachusetts 02210
617-757-7900
617-757-7969 (FAX)
crm.info@thomson.com
www.charlesriver.com

This book is printed on acid-free paper.

Thomas F. Herbert. *Linux TCP/IP Networking for Embedded Systems, Second Edition.*
ISBN: 1-58450-481-1
ISBN-13: 978-1-58450-481-8

All brand names and product names mentioned in this book are trademarks or service marks of their respective companies. Any omission or misuse (of any kind) of service marks or trademarks should not be regarded as intent to infringe on the property of others. The publisher recognizes and respects all marks used by companies, manufacturers, and developers as a means to distinguish their products.

Library of Congress Cataloging-in-Publication Data
Herbert, Thomas F.
  Linux TCP/IP Networking for Embedded Systems / Thomas F. Herbert. -- 2nd ed.
       p. cm.
  Rev. ed. of: Linux TCP/IP stack. 2004.
  ISBN 1-58450-481-1 (pbk. with cd : alk. paper)
 1. Linux. 2. Operating systems (Computers) 3. TCP/IP (Computer network protocol) 4. Embedded computer systems. I. Herbert, Thomas F. Linux TCP/IP stack. II. Title.

  QA76.73.O63H47 2006
  004.16--dc22

2006033957

Printed in the United States of America
06 7 6 5 4 3 2 First Edition

CHARLES RIVER MEDIA titles are available for site license or bulk purchase by institutions, user groups, corporations, etc. For additional information, please contact the Special Sales Department at 800-347-7707.

Requests for replacement of a defective CD-ROM must be accompanied by the original disc, your mailing address, telephone number, date of purchase and purchase price. Please state the nature of the problem, and send the information to CHARLES RIVER MEDIA, 25 Thomson Place, Boston, Massachusetts 02210. CRM's sole obligation to the purchaser is to replace the disc, based on defective materials or faulty workmanship, but not on the operation or functionality of the product.

Contents

Acknowledgments		vii
1	**Data Communication and Linux TCP/IP**	1
	A Few Beginning Words	1
	Introduction	3
	The Linux TCP/IP Source Code	4
	A Brief History of Data Communication	5
	The OSI Seven-Layer Network Model	11
	Connection-Oriented and Connectionless Protocols	13
	Packets and Frames	13
	Broadband Networking versus Local Area Networking	14
	The Digital Data Rate Hierarchy in the Public Network	36
	Networking Standards	37
	Summary	39
2	**TCP/IP in Embedded Systems**	41
	Introduction	41
	How We Got Here	42
	A Few Words on TCP/IP Implementation	42
	TCP/IP and the OSI Reference Model	43
	TCP/IP in Embedded Systems	54
	TCP/IP Standards, Numbers, and Practical Considerations	57
	Summary	58

3 Linux Network Interface Drivers — 59

- A Few Words — 59
- Introduction — 60
- Network Interface Devices — 61
- The Network Device Structure, `struct net_device` — 61
- Network Device Initialization — 70
- Linux Network Interface Driver Facilities — 89
- Receiving Packets — 95
- Transmitting Packets — 100
- `Notifier` Chains and Network Interface Device Status Notification — 103
- Summary — 107

4 Linux Sockets — 109

- A Few Words — 109
- Introduction — 110
- What is a Socket? — 110
- `Socket`, `sock`, and Other Data Structures for Managing Sockets — 111
- Socket Layer Initialization — 124
- The Transport Layer Interface and the Socket Application Programming Interface — 133
- Packet, Raw, Netlink, and Routing Sockets — 143
- Security and Linux `Capabilities` — 146
- A Note About the Socket API and IPv6 — 147
- Implementation of the Socket API System Calls — 149
- Creation of a Socket — 157
- `Netlink` and `Rtnetlink` — 165
- Summary — 170

5 The Linux TCP/IP Stack — 171

- A Few Words — 171
- Introduction — 172
- Glue and Infrastructure — 173
- Linux TCP/IP Stack Initialization — 175
- Kernel Threading — 180
- Packet Queuing Layer and Queuing Disciplines — 186
- Receiving Packets in Packet Queuing Layer, `NET_RX_SOFTIRQ` — 193
- Transport Layer De-Multiplexing and Internal Packet Routing — 201
- Cache Rich — 205
- `In_device` Structure for IPv4 Address Assignment, Multicast, and Configuration — 232
- Security, Stackable Destination, and XFRM — 236
- Some Practical Considerations — 237
- Summary — 238

6 Socket Buffers and Linux Memory Allocation — 239

- A Few Words — 239
- Introduction — 240
- Requirements for TCP/IP Memory Allocation — 241
- Traditional Memory Allocation Schemes — 242
- Slab Allocation — 247
- Linux Socket Buffers — 252
- Socket Buffers, Fragmentation, and Segmentation — 260
- Socket Buffer Allocation and Lists — 264
- Socket Buffer Utility Functions — 266
- Some Practical Considerations — 274
- Summary — 274

7 Sending the Data from the Socket through UDP and TCP — 275

- A Few Words — 275
- Introduction — 276
- Socket Layer Glue — 276
- Transport Layer Socket Initialization — 286
- Initiating a Connection at the Transport Layer — 290
- Sending Data from a Socket via UDP — 297
- Sending Data from a Socket via TCP — 307
- TCP Output — 317
- Some Key TCP Data Structures — 322
- TCP Timers — 334
- Summary — 348

8 The Network Layer, IP — 349

- A Few Words — 349
- Introduction — 350
- Routing Theory — 350
- IPv4 Routing, Routing Cache, and the Routing Policy Database — 351
- IP Protocol Initialization — 353
- The Route Cache — 354
- The RPDB, the FIB, and the FIB Rules — 369
- Routing Input Packets — 395
- Routing Output Packets — 407
- Internet Peers and the IP Header ID Field — 418
- The Address Resolution Protocol — 419
- The Internet Control Message Protocol (ICMP) — 431
- Sending ICMP Packets — 438
- Multicast and IGMP — 440
- Sending Packets from IP — 448
- Receiving Packets in IP — 450
- Summary — 458

Contents ix

9 Receiving Data in the Transport Layer, UDP, and TCP 459

A Few Words 459
Introduction 459
Receive-Side Packet Handling 460
Receiving Data in TCP 472
TCP Receive State Processing 486
Processing Data Segments in Established State 495
The TCP TIME_WAIT State 503
TCP Socket-Level Receive 510
Summary 520

10 A Protocol Family Implementation 521

A Few Words 521
Introduction 522
The AF_NADA Protocol Family 523
Address Family Initialization 525
Module Initialization 527
Socket Layer Interface 529
Receiving Packets in the AF_NADA Family 539
Sending Packets from the Socket Layer 543
The Test Setup for AF_NADA 548
Summary 551

11 Internet Protocol Version 6 (IPv6) 553

A Few Words 553
Introduction 554
Facilities in IPv6 554
IPv6 Addressing 555
IPv6 Packet Format 560
The IPv6 Implementation in Linux 562
IPv6 Socket Implementation 568

IPv6 Fragmentation and De-Fragmentation	571
IPv6 Output	575
IPv6 Input	577
IPv6 UDP	581
IPv6 TCP	584
The ICMP Protocol for IPv6, ICMPv6	588
IPv6 Neighbor Discovery	591
The Multicast Listener Discovery Protocol	596
Auto Configuration	598
Routing and the IPv6 FIB	598
Summary	602

Appendix A: RFCs — 603

Appendix B: About the CD-ROM — 605

Bibliography — 609

Index — 613

Acknowledgments

I wish to dedicate this book to the memory of my late parents, George and Dorothy Herbert. My father is my main inspiration. He was a self-taught and very intelligent man with a strong, life-long interest in learning, literature, and writing. He brought me up in a house filled with books, and at a very young age, I came to see the value of the printed word. Both my father and my mother always told me that I could do anything and accomplish anything I put my mind to. Whenever I stumble along the way, I remember my mother's advice that with hard work, courage, and creativity, I can achieve any goal in which I believe.

Also, I wish to thank the staff at Thomson Learning for their patience and consideration. Particularly, Executive Editor of Charles River Media, Jenifer Niles, who in particular has given me gracious encouragement during this effort. This book is a second edition, and as is often the case with many projects, the amount of effort to update this book was greater than anticipated. In addition to the new chapter, many changes were made because of changes in the 2.6 kernel. There were also formatting and heading updates intended to give the book a better index, making it more useful for readers.

I owe enormous gratitude to the many people who have helped me along my career path, which led to this book, in particular the people of the embedded development community, which has been my profession and source of income for most of the last 25 years.

I am extremely grateful to all of the people involved in the open-source community and the Linux development project. The open-source movement grows in strength all the time and has defined a new way of doing business in our industry. It is opening markets around the world and proving to be an effective counterweight to the monopolistic practices of some major players in our industry. I am indebted to pioneers in the open-source movement, such as Richard Stallman, who begin the Free Software Foundation and first used the term *free software*, meaning freedom to create, modify, and improve. I am particularly indebted to Linux Torvalds, the original developer of the Linux kernel.

In addition, there are all the people involved in the long development and improvement of TCP/IP, beginning with the late Jon Postel, who was the editor of the RFCs for many years. He authored many of the early RFCs, specifying how the protocols written about in this book actually work. For more information about Jon Postel, go to the Postel Center at the University of Southern California, *www.postel.org/postel.html*. I also am grateful to the late W. Richard Stevens, author of definitive works about the functioning and implementation of TCP/IP. In this second edition, I hope I am approaching the high standard he has created. I also extend my thanks to the many contributors to the Linux TCP/IP implementation.

I wish to thank my friends and colleagues. Many of them have suffered my absences and lack of attention to other important matters during the creation of this book. Finally, my family made the greatest sacrifices while I toiled away, hopefully not altogether inattentive to their needs.

1 Data Communication and Linux TCP/IP

In This Chapter

- A Few Beginning Words
- Introduction
- The Linux TCP/IP Source Code
- A Brief History of Data Communication
- The OSI Seven-Layer Network Model
- Connection-Oriented and Connectionless Protocols
- Packets and Frames
- Broadband Networking versus Local Area Networking
- The Digital Data Rate Hierarchy in the Public Network
- Networking Standards

A FEW BEGINNING WORDS

This book is about the Linux implementation of TCP/IP. Certainly, some of you are eager to dive headfirst into the Linux TCP/IP source code. If this is your wish, don't linger here but go straight to the later chapters. Start with Chapter 3, "Linux Networking Interfaces and Device Drivers," and proceed from there. It is in Chapter 3 that we begin to dive deep into the details of the Linux TCP/IP implementation.

It is difficult to discuss any networking topic, especially TCP/IP, without first building a common basis of discussion, which is the goal of these first two chapters. This book has two primary goals: first, we build a foundation; second, we show that although it is a complex system, Linux TCP/IP is amazingly robust. Linux is a versatile implementation suitable for both desktop-based systems, high-volume servers, and, of course, embedded systems, the primary emphasis in this work.

In this chapter we cover some computer networking theory and introduce a few beginning concepts. Mostly throughout the book, we assume a general background in data communications. This chapter provides background in data communications and shows how modern implementations of TCP/IP, such as Linux, evolved over many years. The next chapter provides a general discussion of the TCP/IP stack and how it is organized. Then, starting in Chapter 3, our approach to covering the Linux TCP/IP is more practical, and we take a developer's point of view. We show how Linux TCP/IP is at the apex of the evolution of data communications even as standards and practice adapt to market needs. Thanks to the open source movement and the foresight of Linus and the Linux developers, the popularity and flexibility of the Linux operating system makes it one of the best platforms to implement data communications in many types of systems. TCP/IP has been around for more almost 25 years, and the Linux implementation is already more than 10-years old. We will see how the strength of TCP/IP comes from its maturity and how it has evolved to meet modern needs.

The general approach in this book is to follow the data as it flows through the networking protocols. We follow a packet as it is sent from a networking application running in a Linux host and continue to follow it as the packet flows through the stack and out the wire. We observe while the packet is received by a peer host system, and we see what happens when the data is extracted from the packet as the packet is posted to the application program. Along the way, we will see how the bits work, how packets are routed, how TCP connection states are maintained, and how the socket interface works.

In this chapter, we show how the Linux sources are organized. All Linux source code discussed in this book is included in the CD-ROM. Next, we provide background in data communication and computer networking protocols. Then we go into data communication in more detail and discuss some significant networking. Although the protocols in this chapter are not directly related to TCP/IP, the discussion will help to build the background needed for the detailed information in later chapters.

Next, Chapter 2, "TCP/IP in Embedded Systems," discusses TCP/IP from the standpoint of the embedded systems engineer. After some general background on network interfaces, Chapter 3 concentrates on Linux network interface drivers and how to interface them to the Linux TCP/IP stack. The socket library is the primary means for application programs to send and receive data using the TCP/IP protocols, so Chapter 4, "Linux Sockets," covers sockets, how they are implemented in Linux, and how applications exchange data with protocols in the kernel by way of the socket API. Chapter 5, "The Linux TCP/IP Stack," covers basic elements of the Linux TCP/IP stack including the OS facilities that are the framework that holds the stack together. Information about general kernel utilities and functions are included where they are used by TCP/IP. Next, Chapter 6, "Socket Buffers and Linux Memory Allocation," includes some background on memory allocation for network systems, the Linux slab cache memory allocation system, and the specific slab caches used by TCP/IP for networking data and protocols. In addition, Chapter 6 explains the socket buffer structure because socket buffers are the containers that hold the packets as they flow through the system.

Chapter 7, "Sending the Data from the Socket through UDP and TCP," covers the transport protocols, TCP and UDP, and follows the flow of outgoing data packets through the transport layer. Chapter 8, "The Network Layer, IP," is about the network layer, and in this chapter we will see how IP handles both incoming and outgoing packets. We see how an outgoing packet is received from TCP or UDP and how it is handed off to the network interface driver. Also, we see how IP receives an incoming packet from the network interface driver and queues it to the transport layer protocols. Along the way, Chapter 8 includes information about routing tables and how routing decisions are made. Chapter 9, "Receiving Data in the Transport Layer, UDP, and TCP," covers the receive side of UDP and TCP. It follows a packet as it is received from IP and is queued up to the socket for reading by the application code.

In Chapter 10, "A Protocol Family Implementation, " we introduce a sample network protocol implementation that doesn't really do anything useful. Instead our goal in Chapter 10 is to walk though code showing how the infrastructure of a protocol family is implemented for a new protocol. We don't actually implement the semantics of the protocol, but instead show the framework elements and interfaces. The source code introduced in Chapter 10 is included in the CD-ROM. Finally, Chapter 11, "Internet Protocol Version 6 (IPv6)," examines IPv6 and which facilities IPv6 shares with IPv4 and where the infrastructure for IPv6 is unique.

For the convenience of the reader, copies of all the referenced RFCs are provided in the companion CD-ROM along with all source code introduced or discussed in this book. All the referenced RFCs are also listed in Appendix A.

INTRODUCTION

The Linux operating system was originally conceived and written by Linus Torvalds with the assistance of many people all over the world. It was intended to be an open source replacement for Unix and is compatible with Unix in almost every respect. The TCP/IP stack is implemented as part of the Linux kernel. It is also compatible with all the applicable Posix standards. Almost all application programs written for Unix readily port to Linux without modification. Like the rest of the operating system, the TCP/IP stack was specifically designed for compatibility. In addition, it is completely interoperable with other TCP/IP implementations. It provides a socket interface that is compatible with Berkeley sockets. The code in Linux TCP/IP is very stable, and this is demonstrated by how few changes there are to the TCP/IP code in recent revisions.

In this chapter, we show how the Linux sources are organized and where in the kernel source tree the TCP/IP sources can be found. Next, we introduce a brief history of data communication and the OSI seven-layer model, which is the basis for examining networking protocols of all types. We discuss connection-oriented and connectionless protocols. Following this is a discussion of the difference between Local Area Networks (LANs) and broadband or Wide Area Networks (WANs). We will talk about networking standards and provide a guide for navigating among the various standards bodies. Finally, we discuss a number of communication protocols in historical use or in common use today.

THE LINUX TCP/IP SOURCE CODE

The sources in this book are based on the 2.6.16.20 kernel release. Linux kernels are best found at kernel.org. For the 2.6 kernels, *http://www.kernel.org/pub/linux/kernel/v2.6/*. All sources discussed in this book are covered by the GNU Public License (GPL). For a copy of the license, refer to the CD-ROM included with this book or Appendix B, "About the CD-ROM." Copies of the GNU public license can also be obtained at *www.gnu.org/copyleft/gpl.html*.

The 2.6.16.20 kernel was the most recent stable 2.6 kernel version available at publication time. Also, we should pause to mention that in addition to the Linux kernel development team, much credit is deserved by the USAGI project where the majority of Linux IPv6 development activity, occurred generating much of the IPv6 code in the Linux kernel. A copy of the kernel source tree covered in this book is also provided on the CD-ROM.

Generally in the book, when we refer to pathnames, we use the term linux to mean the top-level directory containing the Linux source tree. For example, if the 2.6 kernel sources are placed in the traditional place for Linux kernels, /usr/src, in our case, linux would expand to /usr/src/linux-2.6.16.20. In this book, we are concerned primarily with the source and header files related to networking and TCP/IP. The TCP/IP sources are in the linux/net directory. Most of the core networking source files that are not specific to either IPv4 or IPv6 are in the linux/core directory, which contains fundamental networking infrastructure definitions and functions used by both IPv4 and IPv6 and other protocols. The directory linux/net/ipv4 contains IPv4 sources and the protocols TCP and UDP. The IPv6 files are in linux/net/ipv6. Finally, the network interface drivers are in linux/drivers/net. In some cases where the drivers are complex, a separate directory is in linux/drivers/net for each specific network interface hardware type. Most drivers like the tunnel pseudo-driver tun.c, are found directly in linux/net/. Also, not all core network functions are in the core directory. For example, the generic device initialization functions and definitions in net_init.c are in linux/net/drivers as well.

The companion CD-ROM does not include all the drivers in the Linux source tree but does have sources for the drivers discussed in this book.

A BRIEF HISTORY OF DATA COMMUNICATION

The original purpose of data communication was to transport symbolic or abstract information across distances too great for physical travel. Of course, over time, this has evolved with the need to transport great quantities of information over short distances as well. The early beginnings of information transmission go back a long way. From the beginning of written history and even before, humans have been working on ways to transmit information across great distances. The early methods used visible smoke or light flashes that could be observed by people watching from a distance. From the start, communication methods required ways to represent information as signals or messages that could be understood by both the transmitter and receiver of the information. From the beginning, all the formal ways of encoding messages involved breaking down the information into some sort of easy-to-represent pattern. Of course, these early patterns were not transmitted electrically. Instead, the messages were transmitted as timed bursts of smoke or flashes of light that could be easily observed. However, despite the simplicity, we can see that this was the beginning of the evolutionary process leading to modern electronic and optical data communication. Along the path of evolution, each method of data communication improves something lacking in an earlier method but introduces new problems or challenges. Attempts to find solutions to these problems lead to innovations that are incorporated in the next generation of protocols. Recent data communication methods are the result of an evolutionary process that can be traced back to early and primitive nonelectrical methods.

The Evolution of Data Communication Methods

Modern data transmission methods actually evolved from primitive methods of signaling used since the earliest days of written history. However, the first common example of the use of electrical data communications was the telegraph. The early telegraphs consisted of a simple on and off modulation of a continuous DC current. This simplest method was often called make or break. The telegraph operator's key was a simple switch forming a complete circuit all the way between the sending operator and the receiving operator. Pressing the key connected the circuit, and releasing the key disconnected the circuit. Pressing the key for alternating short and long lengths of time form what was known as "dots" and "dashes." The dot was a short duration current, and the dash was a longer duration current [WIKIPEDa]. This system was invented by Samuel Morse in 1832 and came to be known as

Morse Code. All methods of data communication in use at that time involved manual intervention. Telegraph operators were trained to key messages onto the wire as fast as possible and to interpret received messages just as quickly. Eventually, though, it became obvious that there was a need for even more rapid interpretation of the telegraphed information.

Coded Transmission and the Printing Telegraph

After telegraph lines began to stretch from town to town, all over the continent and beyond, there was a need for faster and more reliable message transmission. Most of these improvements involved, in one form or another, what was known as a *Printing Telegraph.* There were various systems for printing telegraph messages that were tried throughout the mid- and late-nineteenth century. The early printing telegraphs actually printed the dots and dashes on paper as a sequence of lines that could be read by the human eye, but only an experienced telegrapher was able to interpret the printouts.

We recall from an earlier section how a telegraph made use of a simple single circuit for each message. At first, the need for printing seemed that it was going to make things quite a bit more complex. Most of the early methods used in printing telegraphy required either the use of multiple circuits or multiple current directions, or in some cases, a combination of the two. In those early days, the theoretical advantages of different encodings or of using current directions could not be realized easily by the technology of the time. The methods were not practical because the grounding problems inherent in single-wire circuits prevented the transmission of multiple current levels. In general, printing telegraphy demonstrated the need for increasing message capacity while efficiently utilizing the current system of individual circuits. Printing telegraphs needed more capacity but were hampered by the scarcity and expense of multiple wires. In particular, inter-urban wiring was expensive and required at least one separate physical wire for each circuit. These limitations, along with the need to interpret the messages quickly, inspired the search for a completely automatic mechanism for data communication. Refer to Table 1.1 for a chronology of some of the key events in the early history of data transmission. For excellent source materials and information about the history of telecommunications, visit the North American Data Communications Museum, *http://www.nadcomm.com/* [HOUSE].

Character Coded Transmission

In 1874, the French inventor Baudot devised a method of transmitting the characters directly over the circuit rather than having a skilled human operator key the transmissions. He came up with what was the first system of encoding Roman characters directly in a telegraph transmission. A skilled telegraph operator would

TABLE 1.1 Events in the History of Data Communication

Year	Protocol	Technology	Purpose
1844	Telegraph	Modulated continuous character	Transmission of messages from operator to operator [Newton98a].
1871	Baudot	5-bit code—Represents alphanumeric data	Automate printing telegraph.
1910	Telex	Network of automatic printing telegraph	Automatic message transmission [WIKIPEDc].
1962	EBCDIC	8-bit character encoding	Used originally on IBM mainframes such as the 360/370 series [WIKIPEDd].
1964	ASCII	8-bit character encoding	Used for encoding human-readable characters in digital transmission.
1960s	PCM	Modulation	Digitized voice transmission used in North American T-1 and other digital carriers [NEWTON98b].
1968	IBM Bisync	Half duplex synchronous	Data transmission [NEWTON98c].
1973	Ethernet	LAN	Local data transmission. Originally invented by Bob Metcalf at the Xerox Palo Alto Research Center [GALENETa]. Standardized as [IEEE802.3].
1974	IBM SNA	Layered protocol network based on synchronous transmission	Networking and data transmission among IBM computers and remote peripherals. This layered networking architecture dominated computer networking before more modern WAN and LAN standards [CISCOa].
1976	X.25	Layered protocol based on synchronous transmission	Interconnect customer equipment through Public Switched Network (PSN) [X.25].

no longer be needed to interpret the dots and dashes in the message. His idea, with a few variations, dominated data communications for almost 100 years. The invention consisted of a 5-bit code called *Baudot* code. The code used five bits to represent 26 uppercase letters, plus the characters SPACE, CR (Carriage Return), LF (Line Feed), BELL, and 14 punctuation characters. Out of the five bits, two are designated as shift bits, which are used by the receiving machine to differentiate among groups of characters. They are used to differentiate between letters, control characters, and numbers depending on the value represented by the two shift bits. In the first implementations, the *Baudot* code was punched into paper tape at the sending machine prior to transmission. On the receiving machine, it could be directly punched into paper tape and converted into printed text later using a paper tape reader. The tape was punched with holes where a hole represented a digital one and an absence of a hole known as a space represented a digital zero [WIKIPEDe].

The earliest methods of automatic data synchronization required *Baudot* or some other similar character-coding scheme. When it was transmitted, the *Baudot* bit code was preceded by a start bit and followed by a stop bit. These bits were the first system of synchronizing the sending and receiving machine. They were called *start* and *stop bits* because the receiving machine was a mechanical device that would start interpreting bits when the start bit was received and end its interpretation when the stop bit was received. Transmission of each character was separate, and the receiving machine had to wait for the start bit to arrive before beginning to decode the character and would end the decoding of the character when the stop bit was received. On later machines called *teletype*s, the reading of the character from the transmission line was done with an electro-mechanical system. This device consisted of a rotating wheel connected by an electrical clutch to a continuously rotating motor. When a start bit was received, the clutch would engage, the wheel would start rotating, and it would "read" each bit until the stop bit was received, at which point the clutch would disengage. The machine would sit idly humming away waiting for the beginning of the next character. This method became known as asynchronous data transmission. Some readers who have actually seen an old teletype machine will notice that the data rate is slow enough that the character reception can be physically seen by watching the spinning of the wheel. Notice that the wheel starts rotating with the beginning of the train bits and stops at the end. As each bit is interpreted, the machine aligns a group of electromagnets to rotate the print wheel to the correct position to print the received character after the stop bit is received and the wheel stops turning.

Measuring Data Communication Speeds

For many years, data communication speed was measured in baud rate rather than bits or words per second. The origin of this word has an interesting history. The word baud is actually short for Baudot, who invented the 5-bit code that became known as Baudot code, and this code was used for many years for various purposes in data transmission. Also named after this inventor is the term *baud rate,* which is a way of measuring the speed of asynchronous (character-oriented) data transmission. People often incorrectly use baud rate as if it were synonymous with character transmission rate provided by any type of data transmission. Baud rate is actually the number of 0 to 1 state transitions per second. This concept does not directly calculate out as characters per second in that characters per second can't be determined precisely by dividing the baud rate by the number of bits per character. This is because baud rate includes overhead due to the presence of start and stop bits. To translate baud rate to character rate, you take into account the total number of bits used to encode each character in the data transmission stream. For example, data transmission was at one time limited to at most 110 baud, which was the fastest rate at which the electromechanical teletypewriters could receive the transmission. However, the maximum character rate was far less than 10 characters per second because the 110 baud number includes overhead for the start and stop bits in addition to the 8-bit characters.

Data Transmission over the Telephony Voice Network

The telegraph was in common use for less than 20 years when the telephone was invented in 1876. Then, for more than 100 years from 1876 until at least 1976, the primary user of long-distance bidirectional information exchange of any type was voice telephony. The familiar system of telephones and voice transmission is known as the Plain Old Telephone System (POTS), in which the voice signal is transmitted by analog modulation of a carrier tone. This system is based on assigning a pair of wires to a physical circuit or in modern times, a virtual circuit, at the start of each telephone call and maintaining the circuit while the call is in progress. The system of creating the circuit before a call, and removing the circuits afterward is called signaling. In the earliest systems, these circuits were actual twisted pairs of wires from the bundle or trunk, and the circuits were established by a human operator in the telephone company central office, who would physically connect the phones based on the request of the caller [WIKIPEDb].

Late in the nineteenth century and early in the twentieth century, the number of telephones started to grow rapidly. There were too many simultaneous phone calls active to establish each connection by hand. A faster method was needed to construct the circuit connecting the phones engaged in the call. The improved method was a mechanism to make and break the circuit repeatedly, the dial or pulse generator. When a caller dials the phone, a sequence of pulses is emitted called *dial pulses.* Now, instead of patch panels, the circuit can be created automatically by electromechanical equipment at each switching point between the two phones. This switching point is called a *central office.* The request to construct the circuit begins at the central office nearest to the phone initiating the call. Relays at the central office forward the request to the next switching station by coupling the input circuit to a specific outgoing circuit, extending the circuit to the next switching station, and eventually to the called party. The first telephone switch was known as the *Strowger Switch* after its inventor, Almon Strowger [RBHILL].

Multiplexing Data Communication Channels

As mentioned earlier, throughout the evolution of data communications, the predominant concern has been maximizing the use of copper wires to reduce the numbers of wires. We have seen how multiplexing was foreseen as a way to expand the capacity of a circuit as early as the mid-nineteenth century. Before discussing multiplexing techniques, it is interesting to point out how developments in nineteenth-century mathematics form a basis for twentieth-century data communications theory. There really isn't one single event out of those presented earlier in Table 1.1 that leads to multiplexing. Instead, what we have is an evolutionary process leading to mid-twentieth-century developments in data communication based on earlier mathematical theory. The theory shows that a waveform can be thought of as a periodic continuous function. This complex waveform or function can be represented by a series of trigonometric functions called the *Fourier series*. The nineteenth-century French mathematician, Joseph Fourier (1768–1830), developed this idea during his search for a solution for a partial differential equation describing heat diffusion. This is called the *Fourier* series and allows a continuous function or waveform to be thought of as a composite of sinusoidal functions. The Fourier transform is what converts the complex function into its components. Application of Fourier transform allows the breaking up of available bandwidth of a carrier to individual components or channels [GALENETb].

Eventually, as technology progressed, voice traffic was aggregated onto common lines called trunks, named after the cables of bundles of twisted pairs of wires. These new trunks used Frequency Division Multiplexing (FDM), a method of multiplexing. With the FDM method, an analog broadband carrier is modulated with separate bands of 3-kHz voice channels with a 1-kHz separation between the channels. Along with FDM came automatic switching equipment that instead of using electromechanical relays could electronically switch circuits using Dual-Tone Multi-Frequency (DTMF) tones generated by "touch-tone" phones.

As computers and peripheral equipment became more spread out geographically, there was increasing interest in communications not only for voice, but for pure data. In a way, this is a return to the earlier days of telegraphy where all messages were encoded data. Nevertheless, a need arose for a method of data transmission that could use the ordinary and ubiquitous POTS lines used to carry voice. If telephone lines could be used for data transmission, data could be sent from or received anywhere there was an available telephone connection. At that time, telephones were almost ubiquitous in the developed world. The first modems developed in the late 1960s modulated the 3-kHz voice band with digital data. Modems permitted digital data to be transmitted through long distance lines with inductive loading characteristics. The digital signals could then be sent over lines originally intended only for transmission of analog voice signals. The first commercially available modems for use with POTS could transmit at only 300 baud. Modems got their name because they originally were responsible for the modulation and demod-ulation of the analog frequency with digital data. Modems modulate the voice band with data that is encoded as sequences of 8-bit characters. This encoding could be in various methods, but in modern use generally used ASCII, which is similar to the 5-bit Baudot code discussed earlier and used since the telegraph era [ITUTTV21].

Later in this chapter, we include more detail about synchronous and asynchronous data communication methods. We will see how asynchronous data transmission could be sent digitally directly across carriers without the overhead necessary to convert it into an analog signal and back to analog. However, because for many years direct digital lines were not available everywhere, modems continued to be widely used. In addition, new modem standards became available and allowed for faster transmission of data.

It is interesting to note how in the evolutionary process of data communication, things often come full circle. Ironically, analog modulations in the form of Digital Subscriber Lines (DSL) came back into wide use making far more effective use of the available bandwidth in a poorly conditioned twisted pair, and now DSL is one of the main method of digital transmission over copper in the last mile.

THE OSI SEVEN-LAYER NETWORK MODEL

The Open System Interconnect (OSI) seven-layer model [OSI7498] was first specified in the early 1980s. Although neither traditional nor modern networking protocols fit neatly into this model, it has been the common framework to discuss and explain networking protocols for more than 20 years. The layered model is often called a *stack* because each layer in the sending computer in effect has a logical relationship with the corresponding layer in the receiving machine. See Table 1.2 for an illustration of the seven-layer model.

The OSI Lower Layers

The lowest layer, Layer 1, is the physical layer. It is concerned with the lowest level of detail about data transmission. This layer worries about issues such as how to indicate

TABLE 1.2 The OSI Seven-Layer Model

Layer Number	Layer Name
7	Application
6	Presentation
5	Session
4	Transport
3	Network
2	Data Link
1	Physical

the presence of a one bit versus a zero bit on the physical media. It also deals with electrical signal levels and other details related to physical transmission. The next layer up, Layer 2, is the data link layer. The data link layer is primarily responsible for establishing and maintaining connections or providing connectionless service. It is concerned with how the two endpoints will establish a communication. It also deals with framing or how to differentiate user or payload data from control data. It contains a way for machines to identify each other, generally called station IDs or Media Access Control (MAC) addresses. The next layer up, Layer 3, is the network layer. It is responsible for how nodes on the network are named or addressed. It is concerned with network topology and how to route packets from one node to another. As with the data link layer, the network layer has address information, too. However, network addresses are more abstract; they have to do with network topology and, at least theoretically, are not tied to a particular physical interface. The next layer up, Layer 4, or the transport layer, provides a way for data to be collected or aggregated for passage across the network. In addition, the transport layer provides a simple programming interface to users at higher layers so they don't have to deal with the network details of Layer 3 or lower. In the world of TCP/IP, we think of the transport layer interface as providing two types of interfaces. The first is a streaming interface where the user can send and receive data as a continuous stream of bytes. The other interface provides a chunked or datagram interface to the user where the user must break up the data into discrete packets before sending.

The OSI Upper Layers

The higher layers are often thought to be part of the application. Layer 5, the session layer, is primarily about managing access and session control of a user on one machine who wants to access another machine. Layer 6, the presentation layer, is for abstract data representation. Data in network representation is mapped to the user's view so the application need not worry how the data looks when it is stored on a different machine. Architectural details of data representation particular to a machines architecture are removed at this layer. The uppermost layer, Layer 7, is the application layer. Only pure OSI-compliant networking protocols think of this as a separate layer. It is important to point out that the upper layers—Layers 5, 6, and 7—are not part of the TCP/IP stack. (See Chapter 2 for a discussion of the upper layers and their relation to the TCP/IP stack.)

CONNECTION-ORIENTED AND CONNECTIONLESS PROTOCOLS

WAN or broadband protocols are typically connection oriented. Connection oriented means that they emulate an end-to-end circuit much like the physical pairs we discussed earlier. WANs evolved from desire to exploit spare capacity in the Public Switched Telephone Network (PSTN). As discussed in earlier sections, the public network was originally intended to carry voice traffic; therefore, the connections are actually virtual circuits that were intended to provide a path with guaranteed characteristics for transmission of voice traffic between telephones. Before individual packet-switching service was available, each transmission between two machines required a provisioned connection to be set up first. These connections used in broadband networks are called Virtual Circuits (VCs). There are two types of VCs: the first type, Permanent Virtual Circuits (PVCs) are provisioned and maintained as static connections; The second type, Switched Virtual Circuits (SVCs) are set up through signaling between the end systems when a call or connection is requested and before data is transmitted. In the TCP/IP stack, the connection-oriented concept is incorporated in the transport layer rather than in the data link layer.

PACKETS AND FRAMES

When discussing computer networking, we can get confused whether a chunk of data is a *packet* or a *frame*. Often, when IP-based networking is discussed over Ethernet, the difference between these two terms is blurred. There is a difference, though. When discussing data transmission at the data link layer or the physical layer, the term *frame* is used to describe a unit of data. A frame is consists of a beginning sequence of characters or bits for the start followed by a sequence of characters or bits containing the payload data and terminated by a sequence of characters or bits defining the end of the frame. In contrast, when discussing data transmission at the network layer or above, we consider the unit of data transmission a packet. A packet is a data chunk preceded by a header, and we think of the header as encapsulating the data. The header typically includes a length field because packets are generally variable length. Another way to think of it is that a frame is often closer to the hardware, and a packet is processed by software.

BROADBAND NETWORKING VERSUS LOCAL AREA NETWORKING

For the purposes of this book, the term *broadband* is used synonymously with the term *wide area network* (WAN). In both the popular press and the engineering press, the term *broadband* is generally used to differentiate the slower POTS-based dial-up line from a faster Digital Subscriber Line (DSL) or cable modem. There is one important differentiating factor between LANs and WANs. Every machine on a LAN can see every other machine. However, on WANs, the connections are virtual circuits and are set up either as point-to-point connections between two machines or as multicast connections of one-to-many. LANs and WANs can also be differentiated by the role played by the data link layer of the OSI model. Later in this chapter, we discuss the OSI model in more detail, and Chapter 2 shows how the OSI model fits in with the TCP/IP protocol. The Data Link (DL) layer for a LAN need only worry about framing, transmission, and receiving. The data link layer for a WAN is far more complex and is concerned with connection negotiation and management as well as providing configurable degrees of reliability or speed.

Local Area Networks

LANs are newer than WANs. The concept of LANs was developed about 20 years ago. On a LAN, each machine can see every other machine. Some type of low-level machine identification scheme is used to identify each computer. In addition, LANS include a method of arbitrating among machines that attempt simultaneous access to the network. The first and still the most popular LAN is Ethernet. From the standpoint of TCP/IP and some other data communication stacks, the link layer is far simpler in Ethernet and other LANs than it is for WANs. This is because there is no requirement for connection-oriented service. However, if the particular network configuration includes packet filtering, bridging or switching, or address translation, these capabilities will add quite a bit of complexity to the data link layer. Almost always, the data link layer for Ethernet consists only of a framing layer and the MAC header. All of Ethernet's complexity is hidden in the physical layer (PHY). It is at the physical layer where error detection and collision avoidance occur.

Generally, most LAN reception and transmission is handled at the device driver level. Incoming packets are written directly in a circular buffer by the DMA capability of the Ethernet interface. Outgoing packets are queued at the Ethernet chip for transmission. There are more complex LANs such as WIFI 802.11. Although these protocols are more complex than Ethernet, the details are hidden in the physical layer, and the data link layer provides a fairly simple Ethernet-compatible interface. Of course, authentication and authorization complicates the picture, but when a user is validated, the interface presents a simple LAN type interface where each machine on the immediate LAN can see all the other machines.

LANs are newer than WANs. The first and still the most popular LAN is Ethernet. The link layer is far simpler in Ethernet than it is in the broadband protocols discussed later in this chapter. For example, a basic Ethernet Layer 2 interface consists only of a framing layer and the Media Access Control (MAC) header. In its simplest form, the MAC header contains the source address, the destination address, and the protocol number of the payload. Most of the complexity of the LANs is hidden in the physical layer (PHY) and is not visible to software. Of course, for completeness, we must note that modern GB capable interfaces do have programmable PHYs and can be quite a challenge. In LANs, each machine can see the transmission from all other machines that are directly reachable. There is no allocated bandwidth or channels. Instead, LAN protocols provide a way to negotiate access to the network by allowing only one machine to transmit at a time. There have been various schemes, and we don't intend to cover them all here, but the most popular LAN, Ethernet, uses Carrier Sense Multiple Access with Collision Detect (CSMA/CD.) In CSMA/CD, each machine waits for a clear carrier before transmitting a packet. Each machine also generates a Frame Check Sequence (FCS) code, and the recipient machine will drop the packet if the FCS is bad.

With most Ethernet interfaces, the data link layer is responsible for receiving the incoming packets, which are placed directly in a circular buffer by the Direct Memory Access (DMA) capability of the Ethernet interface. Incidentally, many Linux Ethernet network interfaces place the packets arriving sequentially in noncontiguous locations known as scatter-gather capability. When available, Linux makes use of scatter-gather by minimizing expensive copying of packets received from Ethernet interfaces. Similarly, outgoing packets are queued at the Ethernet chip for transmission, and if the interface has scatter-gather capability, these packets are transmitted directly from a linked list so they don't have to be copied separately by software into a separate buffer.

Most other LAN protocols including wireless protocols, although they might be far more complex than Ethernet, present a fairly simple Ethernet-compatible interface at the data link layer. This type of interface is specified by the ISO 8802 series or IEEE 802.x.

Wide Area Networks

In this book, we look at things from the viewpoint of TCP/IP. Essentially, we consider protocols other than TCP/IP from two points of view. First, we see how some historical protocols contributed essential technology to TCP/IP; second, we see how some protocols commonly used for WAN data transmission are interfaced to TCP/IP.

As discussed in earlier sections, WANs are concerned with using capacity on the public carrier networks. Many methods exist to interface computers to WANs, from simple modems, DSL, and cable modems, up to high-speed optical interfaces such as OC192. Essentially, however, there are two types of WAN interfaces. The first is a direct point-to-point connection through a dedicated or private link. An example would be a dedicated physical twisted pair or a leased line. These links are interfaced to a network interface driver, which provides support for the interface hardware. A second more complex type of WAN interface involves a complete separate protocol suite capable of managing negotiated bandwidth, various classes of data traffic, and Quality of Service (QoS) These protocols are for use in a public network where data streams from individuals are merged with other rate-payer's traffic or where data packets are sub-modulated on a shared carrier along with voice traffic. Examples include Frame Relay or ATM. Interfacing protocols such as these to TCP/IP involves one or more network interfaces without low-level hardware support since the low-level interface is managed by the WAN protocol and not directly by TCP/IP. Examples of these interfaces might be IP over Frame Relay, or Classical IP over ATM (CLIP). Some examples of WAN data communication protocols are discussed in more detail in the following sections.

Asynchronous versus Synchronous Data Transmission

To fully understand data communication, we must differentiate between asynchronous and synchronous methods. In comparing to synchronous methods, asynchronous data transmission has more overhead and doesn't scale to higher rates. The primitive methods discussed earlier in this chapter are examples of asynchronous and involved sending sequences of characters in a linear fashion. Each and every character transmitted adds additional overhead because each character has framing bits before and after the character, and these extra bits add to the total amount to be transmitted. Additionally, no synchronizing external clock sources are used, and no synchronizing pulses are embedded within the data stream. Each character is separately framed with start and stop bits so the receiving station must resynchronize on each character, effectively limiting the maximum transmission speeds.

In contrast to asynchronous methods, synchronous data transmission doesn't include start and stop bits with each character. Instead, the characters are grouped together into frames, and the frames are transmitted as a stream. Each frame consists of a sequence of beginning bits or characters, followed by a data payload and then followed by a terminating sequence of bits or characters. Compared to asynchronous methods where the overhead can be as high as 25 percent, the overhead is far lower for synchronous data transmission methods. The overhead for synchronous protocols is far lower and could be as little as 5 percent depending on the frame or cell size and the type of framing.

Flow Control and Reliable Transmission

Flow control and reliable transmission are really two separate topics. In this section, we discuss these topics in the context of data transmission at the lower layers. At the lower layers, we are concerned with how to acknowledge received frames to implement error recovery and reliable sequenced delivery of the information. The transmitter maintains queues to accumulate data waiting to be sent and to provide an even flow of information.

> *Note that TCP/IP does not require either reliable or sequenced packet delivery service. TCP/IP is designed to work with LANs that don't implement retransmission in the case of dropped packets at the lower layers.*

The method of low-level flow control is different with simple character-oriented protocols than when used with faster synchronous-oriented protocols. Character-oriented protocols in their simplest form provide the most basic method of flow control. The sending station must wait for an Acknowledge (ACK) from the receiving station before sending the next character. This is known as *stop and wait acknowledgment*. With this method, it is not possible to fully use the channel's bandwidth because the transmitting station must waste time and send empty sync characters while waiting to receive an acknowledgment of an earlier frame from the receiving station. This problem is solved with bit-synchronous protocols by using a technique called *sliding windows*, which as we will see is far more efficient. The sliding windows technique has less overhead by using multiple acknowledgments where one ACK can collectively acknowledge multiple incoming frames. After sending the first frame, the sending station can continue to send additional frames without stopping to wait for the receiving station to acknowledge the first frame. An example of sliding windows is explained in more detail later in this chapter.

> *Note that the TCP protocol also implements a version of sliding windows, and Chapter 7 shows how sliding windows is implemented in Linux.*

The data link layer typically provides a link status indication to be used with flow control. Queues of frames waiting for transmission are maintained below the network layer but above the data link layer. When the higher layer has a packet ready, it is added to the end of the queue. When the lower layer is ready to transmit a packet, it removes the next packet from the bottom of the queue. This ensures that higher layers continue processing independently from the lower layer link status.

Synchronous Data Transmission

In the previous section about asynchronous data transmission, we discussed how higher overhead is associated with asynchronous character-oriented methods. As discussed earlier, with synchronous forms of data transmission, the overhead is far lower. Instead of sending each byte of data as an individual transmission, the data is gathered into frames and transmitted together as either a stream of bits or a stream of characters.

Synchronous Character-based Data Transmission

Because of the lower overhead, synchronous methods are better suited for high-speed transmission. However, to understand the more recent high-speed methods, it is important to take a moment and look at an earlier method. The first binary synchronous protocol in common use was developed by IBM and was known as BISYNC, or BSC. This protocol was the basis of what was to become the Systems Network Architecture (SNA) protocol suite. Although it was only available as part of IBM's product line at the time, SNA was an early attempt for diverse computers and telecommunications equipment to exchange data using one basic standard.

As with asynchronous character-oriented protocols, BISYNC has a specific character coding. The data is framed by using special characters called control characters, which are used to indicate the start of a frame, the header and control information, and the end of a data frame. Table 1.3 shows the specific control characters used with the BISYNC protocol. Table 1.4 shows the framing used with BISYNC and how the control characters are used for framing. The start of a frame is indicated by two consecutive syn characters, and the stx character in the data stream indicates the beginning of payload data. The etx character is used to terminate the frame. The coding method used with BISYNC was called EBCDIC. Other character-oriented protocols used American Standard Characters for Information Exchange (ASCII). The ASCII character set is still the basis of almost all 8-bit character representations used for representing European languages.

The Data Transparency Problem

One of the problems with character-oriented protocols is the lack of data transparency. Character sets like ASCII and EBCDIC character have only enough bits for a subset of all the bit combinations in one. Originally, the character-coding schemes were only intended to represent actual characters for printed text. Unfortunately, not all transmitted data can be represented within this subset, and there is usually a need to exchange unrestricted binary data. Therefore, data must be encoded as hex characters or some other method using only characters from within the subset. Character-oriented protocols use a scheme called escaping and include an escape character for this purpose. The escape used in EBCDIC was the DLE character and

TABLE 1.3 BISYNC Control Characters

Character	Name	Purpose	ASCII Value in Hex
ack	Acknowledge	Acknowledges a frame.	06
etb	End of data block	Terminates a block of data.	17
etx	End of text	Terminates a block of data.	03
eot	End of transmission	Indicates end of transmission.	04
enq	Enquiry used for polling by controlling station	Used by polling station to query for a response.	05
nak	Negative acknowledge	Acknowledges a frame to indicate errors were received.	15
dle	Escape	Tells receiving station that next character is a control character.	10
syn	Synchronous idle	Maintains synchronization without sending data.	16
soh	Start of header	Indicates start of the header.	01
stx	Start of text	Indicates the end of the header and the start of the data.	02

TABLE 1.4 BISYNC Frame

| SYN | SYN | SOH | Header | STX | data... | ETX | Block Check |

in ASCII, it is the familiar Escape character still found on everyone's keyboard today. The escape tells the receiving station that the byte immediately following the escape is to be interpreted as data and not as a control character. This prevents the receiving station from dropping the connection or when it encounters a byte in the data stream corresponding to a control. If the receiving station gets two escape characters in sequence, it interprets these as a single escape.

Count-Oriented Synchronous Protocols

Count-oriented protocols have another way to solve the data transparency discussed in the previous section. The count-oriented protocols solve the problem by inserting a length field before the payload data. In this way, all possible binary types of data could be included in the user payload data. Overhead is reduced because, unlike character-oriented methods, the transmitting station does not have to sift through all the data in the transmission inserting escapes before each occurrence of a binary data character. Count-oriented protocol frames include a length field. This type of framing used is the most popular and forms the basis for most modern data framing techniques used in electrical transmission. As we will see in Chapter 2, "TCP/IP in Embedded Systems," TCP/IP makes extensive use of this framing technique. A side effect of the count-oriented protocols is that since they have a header containing a length field, they can have variable-length frames, where the other methods in this section have fixed-length frames.

Bit-Oriented Synchronous Transmission

In this section, we discuss a family of protocols that are closer to the WAN protocols used in modern electrical and, to some lesser degree, in modern optical networks today. The growth in demand for bandwidth in the late 1970s and 1980s necessitated the need for better data communication protocols. Both count-oriented protocols and character-oriented protocols have disadvantages when they are used with higher-speed data transmission. Both types of protocols required the use of a character encoding scheme along with the escaping technique discussed earlier. Both count-oriented and character-oriented protocols were inherently slow and not suitable for implementing in hardware. One of the earlier protocols that used bit-oriented data transmission is called Synchronous Data Link Control (SDLC). SDLC eventually replaced BISYNC as the basis for SNA. SDLC is also called a link control protocol and could be considered a member of the family of the High Level Data Link protocols, (HDLC). Of course, these protocols aren't really *high level*. Today, we consider anything below the network layer low-level protocols, but at the time HDLC was first envisioned, most data communication techniques were very low level in that they didn't use any framing techniques at all. SDLC and other link control protocols are widely used with bit-oriented synchronous transmission methods.

Bit Stuffing

Bit-oriented transmission methods addressed the performance issue by using a technique called *bit stuffing*. Bit stuffing provides a more efficient method for the receiving station to differentiate between flags marking the beginning of a frame, flags for the end of a frame, errors, and user payload data. Bit-oriented protocols indicate the start and end of a frame with a sequence of six 1 bits or a hex 7E. In the payload part of the frame, the transmitting machine inserts a single 0 bit after every sequence of five 1 bits. While it is processing the received data, if the receiving station receives five 1 bits and then sees a 0 bit, it simply removes the 0 bit from the data frame. If it encounters five 1 bits followed by a sixth 1 bit, it interprets these as the start or end of a frame because it is equivalent to a hex 7E. If the receiving station sees between seven and fifteen 1 bits in order, it flags this as an error condition. When more than 15 consecutive 1 bits are received in sequence, the receiving station interprets this as an idle channel.

The X.25 Protocol

As discussed in earlier sections, at one time a data communication methods in common use was SNA, widely used with IBM mainframes. SNA was used in private links and there was a need for a communication protocol that would make use of the spare bandwidth in the PSTN and X.25 was developed for this purpose. X.25 is an International Telecommunications Union (ITU) specification. It was originally limited to 2 MB per second and is no longer used very much in public networks. However, because of its robust nature and error-correcting capability, it is still in wide use today over slow but unreliable terrestrial radio connections. X.25 is important to include in our discussion of foundational data communication protocols because it is the first example of a truly layered protocol for use in the public network. X.25 actually incorporates the first three layers of the OSI model, the PHY, the link layer, and network layer. It was designed for low-quality transmission lines, so it has error control and correction at both the link and network layers. This error checking is redundant for reliable modern optical or electrical transmission lines. Currently, X.25 is only used to provide reliable data delivery for low-quality wireless links for certain specialized aviation and military communications applications.

X.25 was the first protocol to introduce the concept of a virtual circuit (VC) for data transmission. The purpose of VCs is to connect customer equipment in one location across the common carrier's PSTN to customer equipment at another location by using negotiated connections that are analogous to voice circuits. VCs can be multiplexed by combining many separate streams of data packets into a single stream over the public network. The X.25 protocol defines a service access point where the common carrier's equipment and the customer equipment meet. X.25 hides the internal function of the PSTN from the customer's equipment. The carrier's equipment is called data communications equipment (DCE), and the customer's equipment is called data terminal equipment (DTE).

The top layer or network layer of X.25 is called the packet layer. The job of this layer is to manage either connections of switched virtual circuits (SVCs) or Permanent Virtual Circuits (PVCs). The packet layer is responsible for establishing and breaking down these connections, and this connection negotiation is also termed call management or signaling.

It is interesting to point out that the terms signaling and call management come from voice telephony. Earlier in this chapter, we discussed the evolutionary nature of data communication and how it evolved from telegraphy and voice telephony.

The packet layer supports two types of packets: control packets and data packets. The control packets are used for call management: and the data packets contain user payload data. X.25 also provides an individual packet or datagram delivery service. This service consists of transmitting individual user datagram packets without doing connection negotiation to establish a connection or circuit before transmission. Figure 1.1 illustrates the layers of X.25.

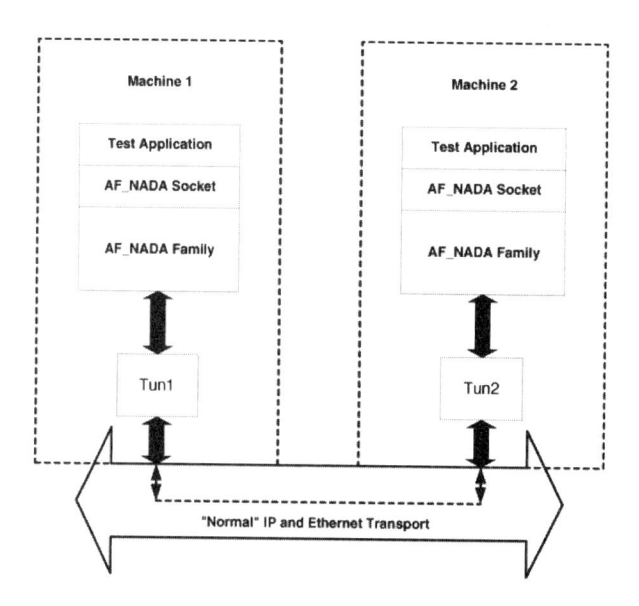

FIGURE 1.1 The X.25 protocol.

In terms of the OSI model, the middle layer in the X.25 protocol stack is the equivalent of Layer 2, the link layer. It incorporates a protocol called Link Access Protocol Balanced (LAPB). LAPB is another variant of HDLC. The types of HDLC are described in more detail in the next section. In the X.25 protocol stack, the link layer provides both a connection-oriented service and a user datagram service. Even though X.25 contains its own network layer when TCP/IP is interfaced to X.25, the entire stack sits under TCP/IP's network layer and appears as a Layer 2 interface implemented as a Linux network interface driver.

> *The Linux kernel contains an implementation of X.25. It can be found in* linux/net/x25. *We won't cover X.25 in detail in this book, but the sources can be found in the CD-ROM. Also, in Chapter 11, we discuss the implementation of a generic protocol family in Linux and sources for that sample implementation are provided in the CD-ROM.*

High Level Data Link Protocol

As discussed in the previous section, X.25 was the first protocol suite to incorporate a generic Layer 2 protocol for its link layer definition called LAPB. The family of generic Layer 2 protocols are called High Level Data Link Protocols (HDLCs). It is called high level because originally, when layered protocols were new, anything more abstract than the electrical details of physical transmission were considered to be high level. HDLC is still the basis of many data communication protocols in common use today including PPP. A few variants on the basic theme of HDLC exist, and most of these variants are governed by ISO standards. However, there are also a few HDLC-type protocols specified by ITU and IEEE standards ISO 3300 and ISO 4335. See Table 2.3 for a list of various HDLC derivative protocols. It is important to point out that although these HDLC variants are similar in the way they work, they do not expect interoperation between variants because the framing details are different.

TABLE 1.5 HDLC Protocol Variants

HDLC flavor	Name	Purpose or Use
LAPB	Link Access Protocol—Balanced	X.25
LAPM	Lank Access Protocol—Modem	Used with V.42 compression protocols in modems
AHDLC	Asynchronous HDLC	PPP over asynchronous links
BHDLC	Bit synchronous HDLC	PPP over synchronous links
802.2 LLC	Logical Link Control	Basis of Data Link Provider Interface in STREAMS
LAPD	Link Access Protocol—D channel.	ISDN
SDLC	Synchronous Data Link Control	IBM SNA
LAPF	Q.922 Link Access Protocol for Frame Relay	Frame Relay Bearer Service

HDLC Types and Configurations

This section shows the HDLC protocol in more detail. All the variants of HDLC are functionally similar. They might differ in the precise lengths of the address, control, or FCS fields, but generally are similar. In general, HDLC supports three types of stations and two types of configuration. The three types of stations are as follows:

- Primary—Controlling station on the link
- Secondary—Slaves to primary stations
- Combined—Act as either primary or secondary stations

In addition to the three types of stations, HDLC specifies two types of configurations. The configurations can be thought of as modes of service. The two types of configurations are shown below:

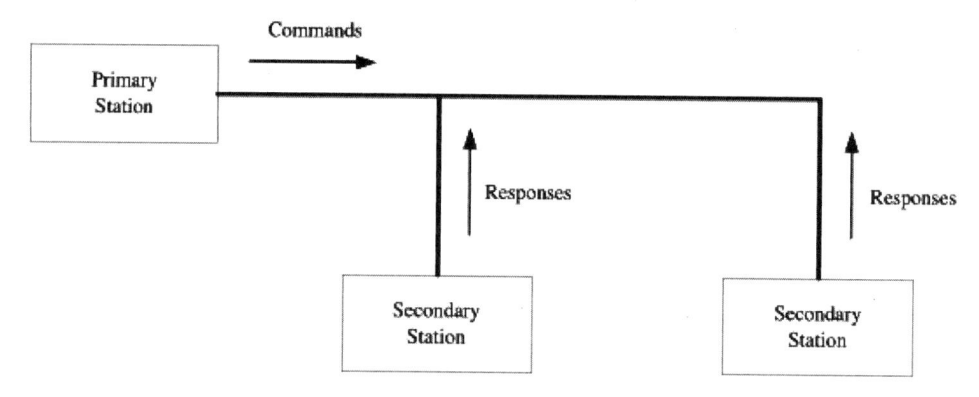

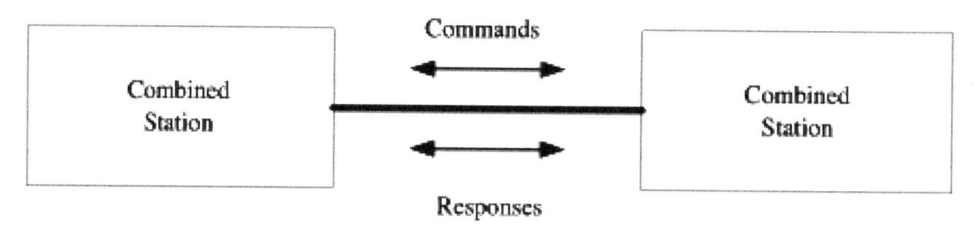

- Balanced: In a balanced configuration, two stations are connected with a point-to-point link. In this configuration, each station acts as a combined station.
- Unbalanced: With the unbalanced configuration, there are two or more stations. One station acts as a primary station. Two or more other stations act as secondary stations.

Figure 1.2 illustrates the unbalanced configuration, and Figure 1.3 shows the balanced configuration. With the balanced configuration, the stations are peers. Each station can send both commands and responses. The balanced configuration is used primarily for point-to-point links. In contrast, with the unbalanced configuration, the primary station is the controlling station on the link and the secondary stations are slaves. The primary station is the only one that can send commands, and the secondary stations answer with responses.

FIGURE 1.2 HDLC unbalanced configuration.

FIGURE 1.3 HDLC balanced configuration.

HDLC Framing

As we have seen, there are many variants of HDLC. The HDLC framing detailed in this section shows framing that is generally common to all of the HDLC variants. Table 1.6 shows HDLC framing that applies to most of the variants. Three types of formats are in an HDLC frame:

- Information format for carrying user data
- Supervisory format for control functions
- Unnumbered format for control and management

TABLE 1.6 General HDLC Framing

Field	Flag	Address	Control	Information	FCS	Flag
Field Value or Purpose	7E	Variable	See Tables 2.5, 2.6, or 2.7.	Payload Data	Frame Check Sequence	7E
Field Length	8 bits	8 bits	8 or 16 bits	Variable	8 or 16 bits	8 bits

The primary distinguishing factor for each type of frame is the control field. The control field has different values for each type of framing, which is determined by the first 2 bits in the control field. In the 8-bit control format, bit 5 is the poll/final bit. It is treated as the poll bit if it is part of a frame sent by the primary station, and it is called the final bit if it is encountered in a frame sent by the secondary station. Although the HDLC variants are similar, the specific use of the control field is somewhat different for each type of HDLC. For example, Section 2.9 on PPP shows a specific variant of HDLC called LAPB where the control field can be either 8 or 16 bits in length. Tables 1.7 through 1.11 show the format of the Control field for each type of frame.

Table 1.7 shows the information format. This format is used to transmit user data. The "I" type frames or information frames are sequenced or numbered frames for providing a connection-oriented service. The transmitted frames include sequence numbers, and the response frames include expected sequence numbers.

TABLE 1.7 Information Format

1	2	3	4	5	6	7	8
0	n(s)			p/f	n(r)		

Table 1.8 shows the supervisory format. This format is for control functions only, primarily acknowledgment and requests for retransmissions. Outgoing information frames are not sequenced but the n(r) field might contain the number of an acknowledged frame.

TABLE 1.8 Supervisory Format

0	1	2	3	4	5	6	7
1	0	sc		p/f	n(r)		

The format for commands used with the supervisory format is shown in Table 1.9.

TABLE 1.9 Supervisory Format Commands

Command	sc Field Value	Name
RR	0	Receive ready
REJ	1	Reject
RNR	2	Receive not ready
SREJ	3	Selective reject

Table 1.10 shows the unnumbered format of HDLC. This format is used for control functions and management functions such as link establishment. Table 1.11 shows some key unnumbered format commands.

TABLE 1.10 Unnumbered Format

0	1	2	3	4	5	6	7
1	1	un		p/f	un continued		

Sliding Windows

One of the important functions of data link protocols is to provide a connection-oriented or reliable transmission service. A reliable service guarantees ordered packet delivery by doing retransmission of lost or damaged packets. Elsewhere in this chapter, we discuss several data communication protocols. Some of these protocols are used to carry IP datagrams, and as such, they are interfaced to IP at the link layer.

TABLE 1.11 Unnumbered Format Commands

Command	Response	un Field Value	Command Name	Name Response	Purpose
UI	UI	0	Unnumbered information	Unnumbered information	I field contains datagram for connectionless service
SNRM		1	Set normal response mode		
DISC	RD	2	Disconnect	Request Disconnect	
UP		4	Unnumbered poll		
	UA	6	Unnumbered acknowledge		
	FRMR	11		Frame reject	
SARM	DM	18	Set asynchronous response mode	Disconnect mode	Also used by secondary station to say it is off-line
RSET		19	Reset		n(s) and n(r) are reset
SABM		1c	Set asynchronous balanced mode		Set mode where stations are equals.

Note that TCP/IP does not require connection-oriented service at the link layer. The TCP transport protocol actually includes its own version of sliding windows, which in theory works almost identically to the protocol described in this section. In the later chapters, we will see that the TCP state machine is far more complex. In addition, we will see that Linux TCP has many enhancements, which originated with HDLC.

Sliding windows provides a means of recovering from lost, erroneous, or out-of-sequence frames. As discussed previously, more primitive protocols used a system called start-and-stop acknowledgment to manage the integrity of the connection. This system wasted bandwidth because the sending station had to wait for an acknowledgment before sending another frame. In contrast, sliding windows provides a better mechanism for acknowledging transmissions. The receiving station sends an accumulative acknowledgment. This is more efficient because a response from the receiving station can acknowledge multiple packets from the sending station, and the sending station need not wait for the ACK frame before sending more frames. When used in conjunction with packet queuing, this method can provide an excellent mechanism for flow control. Most modern communication protocols use a method that is in some way fundamentally derived from sliding windows.

The sliding windows method uses a window size determined by the size of the sequence number n(s) and the acknowledgment number n(r) fields of the particular HDLC variant. The window size becomes the number of unacknowledged transmit frames that can be sent before receiving an ACK frame. Originally, HDLC reserved 3 bits for the sequence and acknowledgment fields in the information format frame and supervisory format frames, which allows for a window size of 7. Later variants of HDLC increased this field width, subsequently increasing the window size. Figure 1.4 demonstrates a typical sequence for HDLC sliding windows. In each transmitted frame, the n(s) field is set to a consecutive sequence number. The sending station responds by sending acknowledgment frames with n(r) set to the next expected value of n(s) in a received frame.

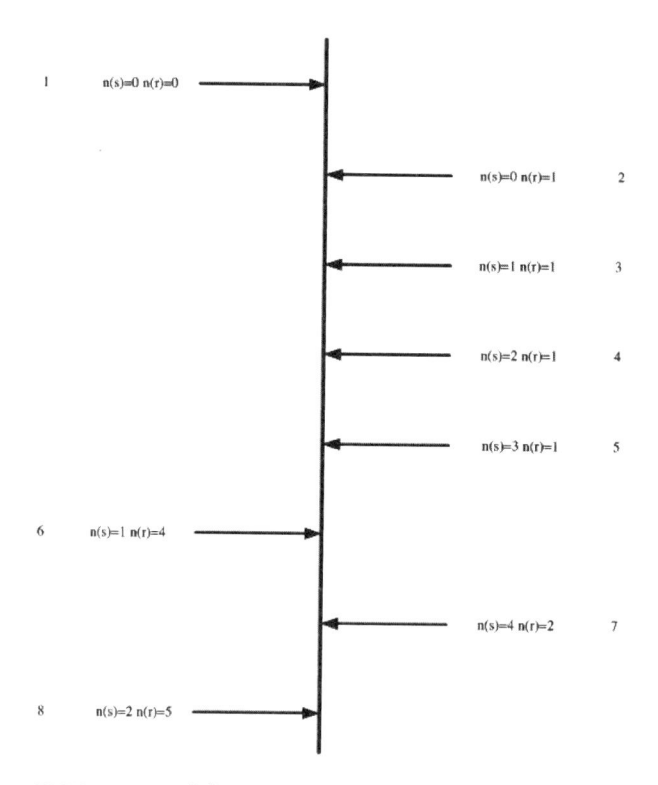

FIGURE 1.4 Sliding windows.

Frame Relay Bearer Service

As discussed earlier, X.25 has a performance disadvantage in that it has multiple layers with error correction. The Frame Relay Bearer Service (FR) eventually replaced X.25 for most data traffic over public networks. This was because X.25 was intended for low-quality physical links where its redundant error checking and correction at both Layers 2 and 3 is appropriate. Frame Relay eliminates the extra layer of error correction; it is intended for PHYs with far greater intrinsic reliability than the early copper-based transmission circuits that were predominant when X.25 was first used. The elimination of extra error correction makes FR more suitable than X.25 for high data rates such as those found in fast optical links up to OC-3. It is important to point out that TCP/IP traffic does not require a reliable link layer. The TCP/IP protocol has its own error checking and correction as part of the TCP protocol at the transport layer.

The PHY for Frame Relay includes support for DS0, DS1, DS3, E1, or E3. (These rate classes are shown in Table 1.15.) FR's framing layer uses Link Access Protocol Frame Relay (LAPF), which is similar to the HDLC framing used in X.25 but somewhat simpler. See Figure 1.5 for the framing details for all three types of frames used in FR. As in HDLC framing, the FR frame is preceded by a flag consisting of a 0 bit followed by five consecutive 1 bits, which is a value of 0x7e. This flag is used to indicate the frame start. The frame is also terminated with a similar flag having the same value of 0x7e. The reason for 0x7e is that it used to differentiate control data, payload data, and detected errors similar to the bit stuffing technique used in HDLC. Earlier in this chapter we covered HDLC and bit stuffing. Table 1.12 shows the frame format for FR.

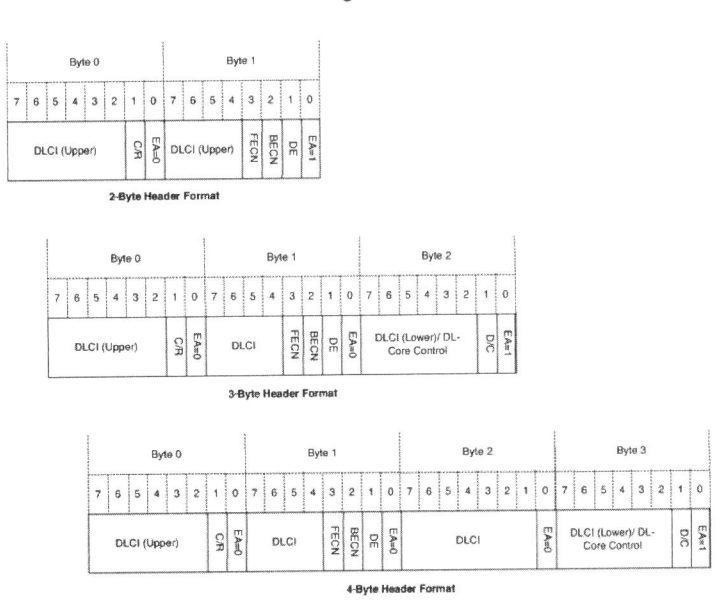

FIGURE 1.5 Frame Relay header formats.

TABLE 1.12 Framing Details for Frame Relay Bearer Service

Flag	Header	User Data	Frame Check Sequence	Flag
0x7E	Table n	Payload Data	FCS	0x7E
1 byte	2, 3 or 4 bytes	Variable	2 or 4 bytes	1 byte

FR allows multiple virtual circuits to be multiplexed across the same physical link. The virtual circuits are differentiated by the FR header field. which contains a field known as Data Link Connection Indicator (DLCI). This field is used by FR routers to determine how to send a frame to its destination. There are four different DLCI lengths: 10, 16, 17, or 23 bits. The values of the D/C and EA bits determine the type of DLCI field. Because of the varying DLCI field, three different header formats exist for HR: 2 byte, 3 byte, and 4 byte. The multiplexing techniques make use of a field in the DLCI header. The function of the DLCI field is to be a virtual circuit identifier. This is similar to the address field in a LAN network packet. FR packets are switched among channels by the FR routers based on the value of the DLCI field. Specific descriptions of each of the fields in the Frame Relay header format are shown in Table 1.13.

TABLE 1.13 Explanation of Fields in Frame Relay Header

DLCI	Data Link Connection Indicator	The identifier of the SVC or PVC to which this Frame Belongs
C/R	Command or Response bit	Not used by the Core Frame Relay Protocol.
EA	Extended Address	Allows for multiple DLCI or address lengths. 0 indicates that another header byte is to follow. 1 means that this header byte is the last.
FECN	Forward Explicit Congestion Notification	Used for Congestion Avoidance and Traffic Control.
BECN	Backward Explicit Congestion Notification	Used for Congestion Avoidance and Traffic Control.
DE	Discard Eligible	Discardable packets are marked with this bit if Congestion exceeds a threshold.
D/C	DLCI or DL-Core Indicator	1 indicates that DLCI bits in last byte are used for DL-Core functions. 0 means that DLCI bits in lowest byte extends the DLCI address space.

Frame Relay includes a signaling protocol for managing SVCs, but FR service can be provided over PVCs as well. The frames that actually do the negotiation to control the SVCs don't travel in the same link as the frames carrying data traffic. This signaling method is called *out-of-band signaling* when the signaling frames are transmitted over a special channel. In addition, signaling frames use a different form of the header than the header format for data frames. The signaling protocol used with FR is ITU standard Q.931.

As discussed earlier, the mechanism for reliable service used in X.25 was based on HDLC and its sliding windows protocol. FR does not provide reliable or connection-oriented service or a specific mechanism for flow control at Layer 2; instead, it provides a mechanism called *traffic engineering*. FR establishes a Committed Information Rate (CIR) for each channel based on the nominal amount of available bandwidth. The traffic engineering is provided by the use of three fields in the CR frame header. Frames with the DE bit set to 1 can be discarded if the transmission rate during a burst period exceeds the CIR. The Forward Explicit Congestion Notification (FECN) field indicates to the sender that there is congestion on the network. Likewise, the Backward Explicit Congestion Notification (BECN) field indicates to a receiving station that there is congestion on the network. A node on the network can start flow control if it detects the FECN or BECN bits in a frame. The flow can be maintained until adjacent nodes have time to clear out the congestion.

> *TCP also incorporates some of these concepts including congestion avoidance. However, the argument about whether TCP/IP has sufficient traffic management for QoS still continues. It is somewhat difficult for TCP to approximate all of the features inherent in WAN protocols such as FR and ATM. Refer to Chapter 5 for more details.*

Asynchronous Transmission Mode (ATM)

In the 1980s, the telephone companies were looking for a way to deliver differentiated digital services to customers using the PSTN. They came up with a suite of protocols called Integrated Services Digital Network (ISDN) that specified how a user would interface to the PSTN to access various services with different speeds, capacities, and degrees of reliability. ATM evolved from ISDN and was originally called Broadband ISDN (B-ISDN). It had the ability to specify available services on bit rates higher than what was available with ISDN. ATM is scalable from a single DS0 all the way to OC192. It defines a complete complex protocol stack and can provide telephony-type voice circuits as well as connectionless data services. It can provide different needs for quality of data transmission (QoS). In the 1990s, it was thought that ATM would replace TCP/IP for most data transmission because of its ability to support Quality of Service (QoS). However, with the low cost of available bandwidth, TCP/IP is very capable of providing sufficient bandwidth for many voice and video applications.

Refer to Chapter 8, "The Network Layer, IP," where you will see how Linux IP can be configured to provide QoS, although the QoS is never guaranteed like it is with ATM.

ATM has similarities to both Frame Relay Bearer Service and X.25. ATM is a complex protocol, so we will not be able to discuss it in detail here. It provides the basic infrastructure for the modern PSTN although Passive Optical Networks (PON) and various Ethernet schemes are gaining acceptance. ATM is designed to deal with transmitting data, voice, and video simultaneously. Instead of being based on frames or packets, it is implemented with a small Protocol Data Unit (PDU) called a *cell*. The ATM cell is 53 bytes and includes a 5-byte header and a 48-byte payload. This particular cell size is used because it is the optimum size for individual sub-modulation of the carriers used with the digital data hierarchy found in all the public networks of the world, North America, Europe, and Asia. The small cell size is sufficient to maintain a digitally modulated voice channel at the DS0 speed but is scalable to far higher data rates. Because of the small cell size and high speeds, header manipulation and cell switching are done in hardware or firmware instead of in slower software. However, because of the small cell size and 5-byte header, it has more than 10 percent overhead, higher than many other protocols.

The ATM Stack

The ATM stack defines both User-to-Network Interfaces (UNI) and Network-to-Network Interfaces (NNI). It includes a signaling protocol for negotiating connections and provides a management interface to allow for provisioning of PVCs and gathering of cell-level statistics. The UNI specification includes definitions of classes of service and how to specify service types at a particular QoS when interfacing to an ATM network. The different service classifications are provided for video, voice, and data.

Because of the complexity of ATM, it is shown in a layered model similar to OSI but is three-dimensional, with separate planes for data, management, and control. ATM is interfaced to Linux IP through network interface drivers. Several drivers are supplied for ATM Adaption Layer 5 (AAL5) interfaces including IP over ATM (IPoA), bridged protocol interface [RFC2684] and others. AAL5 packets are generated by a Segmentation and Reassembly (SAR) layer. The SAR layer, which is part of AAL builds larger IP packets from the smaller incoming ATM cells and to break up outgoing IP packets into cells for transmission. Refer to Figure 1.6 for a picture of the ATM stack showing how it interfaces to IP.

> *Linux includes a complete ATM stack that is quite robust and reliable. It can be found in the Linux source code in* `linux/net/atm`*. Drivers for various low level ATM optical and copper interfaces are found in* `drivers/net/atm`*. For your convenience, all sources discussed or referenced in this book are provided in the included CD-ROM.*

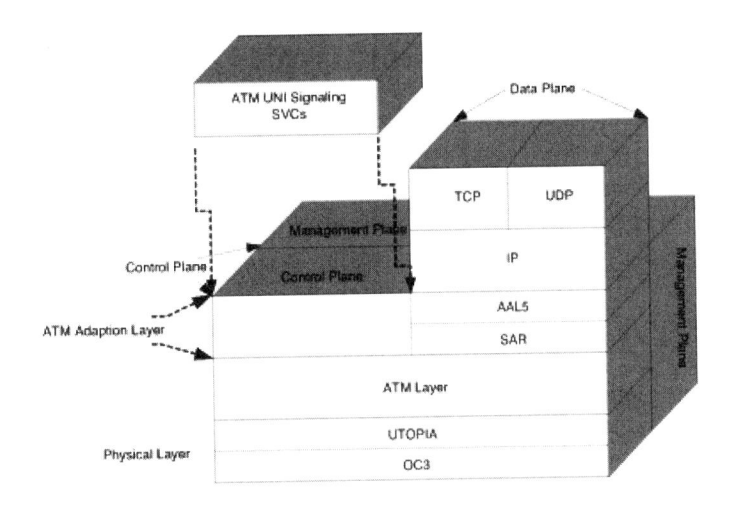

FIGURE 1.6 The ATM stack.

The ATM Physical Interface (PHY)

The lowest layer in the ATM stack is the PHY. It is divided into upper and lower sublayers. The lower sublayer handles the physical transmission details for the optical or electrical interface and generally consists of an interface to the Universal Test and Operations PHY Interface (UTOPIA) bus, which is a parallel interface that hides the implementation details of the TDM multiplexing from the PHY layer of ATM. The upper sublayer in the PHY is the Transmission Convergence (TC) sublayer, and there are TCs defined for each of the supported PHYs, DS1, DS3, up to OC3. The TC layer maps individual ATM cells onto a TDM data stream.

ATM Network Interfaces

The next higher layer in the ATM stack is the ATM layer. This layer is responsible for differentiating among the different types of cells during routing and switching. There are two types of ATM layers: one implements the NNI, and the other implements the UNI. The NNI ATM layer is actually a switch that moves individual ATM cells from one or more input data stream ingress points to one or more output data stream egress points. The NNI ATM switch is also known as an *Intermediate System* (IS); it controls the circuit connections from ingress point to egress point. In the IS, cells are switched on an individual level because cells are individually multiplexed among different virtual channels depending on the type of channels and cells. The switching needs to be very fast to handle the high data rates and, therefore, is usually implemented in hardware called an ATM *switching fabric*. The ATM switches or ISs include the management plane, but they don't include the AAL layer.

ATM is connection oriented; therefore, before any cells can be transmitted, an endpoint-to-endpoint connection must be established. As in other protocols discussed earlier, each connection becomes a VC. Each VC is full duplex or bidirectional. The circuits are built by the ISs in the network by building two end-to-end chains of connections. A connection for each direction is built from Virtual Channel Links (VCL) and Virtual Path Links (VPL). See Figure 1.7 for a picture of the ATM UNI cell format. Figure 1.8 shows the ATM NNI cell format.

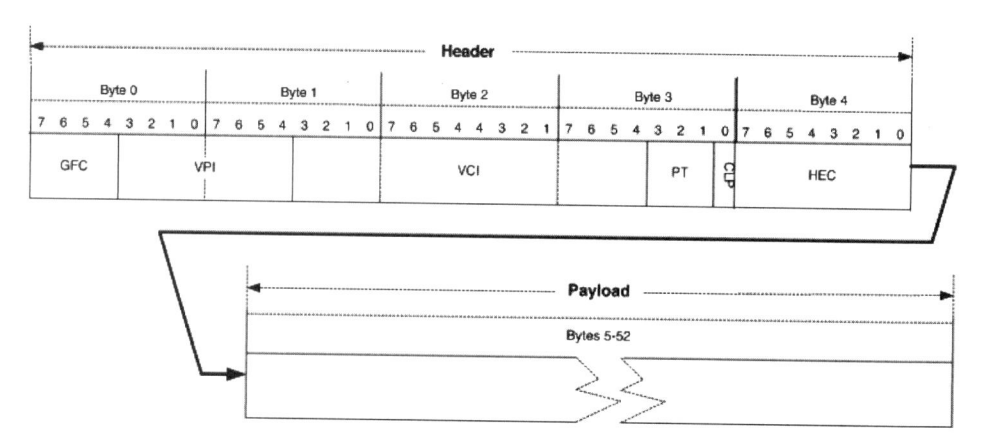

FIGURE 1.7 ATM UNI.

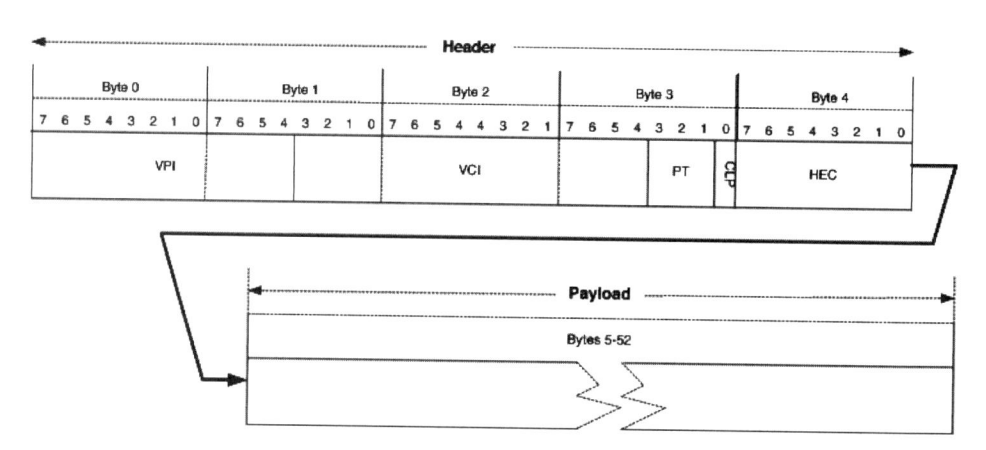

FIGURE 1.8 ATM NNI.

ATM UNI Service Class Definitions

The UNI, also known as an End System (ES), includes the ATM Adaption Layer (AAL). The ES also has an ATM layer but it is simpler than the ATM layer in the IS.

AAL is defined as five sublayers: AAL1 through AAL5. The AAL is further subdivided into a Service Specific Convergence Function (SSCF) and Service Specific Convergence Sublayers (SSCS). The SAR firmware looks at the cell headers and subdivides the cells by class and passes them to the ATM stack through a specific SSCS, depending on the service class and which AAL level interface is required for each service class. Refer to Table 1.14 for a summary of the ATM UNI traffic class definitions.

- **VBR:** Variable Bit Rate
- **CBR:** Constant Bit Rate
- **CO:** Connection Oriented
- **CL:** Connectionless
- **FR:** Frame Relay
- **IPoA:** Classical IP over ATM
- **Rt-VBR:** Real-time VBR

TABLE 1.14 ATM UNI Traffic Class Definitions

Class	Sender – Receiver synchronization	bit rate	Connection	AAL	Content type
A	Yes	CBR	CO	1	Voice circuits
B	Yes	Rt-VBR	CO	2	time critical packets, voice signaling, video
C	No	VBR	CL	3,4,5	Packet data, FR
D	No	VBR	CL	5	IPoA

As shown in Table 1.14, four classes are defined to carry each of the traffic types carried in ATM cells. In addition to the four traffic classes, there are two types of bit rates and two connection types. Each of the five sublayers corresponds to different service classes and traffic types to provide either constant or variable bit rate and streaming or bursty traffic. Like Frame Relay, ATM contains mechanisms for congestion control based on a concept called Available Bit Rate (ABR). ABR is defined for traffic engineering and is not explicitly defined as part of the UNI service definition.

As can be seen, the ATM protocol is very complex. Some IP-based data such as Voice over IP (VoIP) and other applications demanding specific QoS must interface to the ATM stack in more complex ways. However, for most pure data applications, the actual interface from IP to ATM is fairly simple conceptually. It consists of the AAL5 layer and the SAR. The internal implementation of the SAR is complicated, but in most applications it is implemented in firmware or hardware as part of a PHY chip.

THE DIGITAL DATA RATE HIERARCHY IN THE PUBLIC NETWORK

Most of the protocols in this chapter are for transmitting data across the public network. As discussed earlier, the public network evolved from early hardwired voice circuits and evolved over many years to be able to provide a variety of services and different rates. As discussed earlier in this chapter, in the beginning of electronic data communications, a separate pair of wires implemented each voice channel. We also discussed how voice channels were multiplexed using analog multiplexing and modulation techniques such as FDM. Almost 25 years ago, it became apparent that it was not the most efficient use of broadband channel capacity. FDM required expensive switching equipment in the telephone company's switching stations and, therefore, was not scalable to ever-increasing demands for increased circuit carrying capacity [EDWAR00a].

Therefore, in the late 1970s and early 1980s, the public network was converted from analog to digital. Voice phone calls were transmitted over individual channels modulated using pulse code modulation (PCM) over a base band carrier. With this method, the voice information is travels across an analog line but is combined into digital carriers at the phone company's Central Office (CO) using Time Division Modulation (TDM) techniques. Each channel requires 3 kHz of bandwidth and it works out that 64 K bits per second was required for audible voice quality. Therefore, the fundamental unit of bandwidth for the public network is 64 KB, and all digital data rates are calculated in units of 64 KB of capacity. Table 1.15 shows the hierarchy of digital channel capacity carried across electrical networks in North America. Table 1.16 shows the equivalent hierarchy in use in Europe. Table 1.17 shows the Sonet and SDH Optical Hierarchy [MCDYSO20a].

TABLE 1.15 TDM Digital Hierarchy in North America

Name	Multiplexing Level	Number of Voice Channels	Rate in Bits per Second
DS0	0	1	64 K
DS1	1	24	1.544 M
DS2	2	96	6.312 M
DS3	3	672	44.376 M

TABLE 1.16 TDM Digital Hierarchy in Europe

Name	Multiplexing Level	Number of Voice Channels	Rate in Bits per Second
E0	0	1	64 K
E1	1	30	2.048 M
E2	2	120	8.448 M
E3	3	480	34.368 M

TABLE 1.17 Sonet and SDH Optical Hierarchy

SONET	SDH	Line Rate in Mbits per Second
OC-1		51.84
OC-3	STM-1	155.52
OC-12	STM-4	622.08
OC-48	STM-16	2488.32
OC-192	STM-64	9953.28

The availability of data rates greater than 64 KB began when carriers also provided specially provisioned twisted pairs to customers for carrying digital data. Each of these lines, called *leased lines*, carried more than the 64 KB of bandwidth that was typical for voice. Originally, there was no standard to determine the bandwidth and capacity for these leased lines. Eventually, these non-regulated channels were replaced with standard channels based on available standard rates as shown earlier in Table 1.15.

NETWORKING STANDARDS

Software engineers working in the networking area have two major frustrations. One is that networking has far more acronyms than most other engineering disciplines. The other frustration is caused by trying to navigate among the different standards bodies and committees that publish computer networking standards. Engineers working with broadband networking standards or general data communications must work with various international standards as well. In this section, the various standards bodies are discussed and what types of standards they each govern.

Of course, most of us who are working with Linux TCP/IP are primarily interested in the standards governing the TCP/IP protocol suite. Most of these standards are published by the Internet Engineering Task Force (IETF) in the form of Request For Comments (RFCs).

In this book, all RFCs referenced are provided in Appendix A and in the companion CD-ROM.

In general, standards for protocols at the data link layer and below for either LANs and Metropolitan Area Networks (MANs) are governed by the Institute of Electrical and Electronics Engineers (IEEE). Standards having to do with interoperation and interfacing of equipment to the PSTN are specified by the International Telecommunications Union (ITU.) The ITU standards include X.25, Frame Relay, Integrated Services Digital Network (ISDN), and ATM. Table 1.18 shows a list of standards bodies and what types of standards they govern. In addition, ATM & MPLS Theory and Applications [MCDYSO20b] contains an excellent summary of most networking and telecommunication standards for local area networks, broadband, and ATM and Multi Protocol Label Switching (MPLS.)

TABLE 1.18 Standards Bodies

Name	Full Name	Purpose
ITU	International Telecommunications Union	International inter-networking standards started for interoperable telephony and telegraph.
ISO/IEC	Joint Technical Committee (JT) of the Standards Organization (ISO) and the International Electrotechnical Commission (IEC)	Information Technology standards for global markets, *www.jtc1.org*.
ETSI	European Telecommunications Technical Institute	European telecommunications standards, *www.etsi.org*.
ANSI	American National Standards Institute	Communications standards usually published jointly as ISO/IEC JTC, *www.ansi.org*.
IETF	Internet Engineering Task Force	Internet standards. IETF publishes RFCs for management standards, TCP/IP, and interoperability with TCP/IP-based networks, *http://ietf.org*.

Name	Full Name	Purpose
ATMF	ATM Forum	Industry group publishing ATM standards, most of which became ITU standards, *http://www.atmforum.com*.
ANSI T1	American National Standards Institute T1 Subcommittee	Standards for synchronization in subsystems, *www.t1.org*.
IEEE	Institute of Electrical and Electronic Engineers Standards Association	LAN and MAN standards, including bridging, switching, MAC definition, Layer 2 and PHY protocols, *http://standards.ieee.org*.

SUMMARY

In this chapter, we gathered some basic concepts and history to help build a basis of understanding of data communication, and TCP/IP in particular. We presented an introduction to data communication including some of its early implementations. We learned how modern data communication was inspired by this early history, and we saw how the technology evolved as a series of steps up to modern high-speed optical switched networking. We covered some specific non-TCP/IP standards that form the basis for modern data communications. We learned how the OSI model serves as a basic framework to discuss computer networking. We also discussed some WAN protocols including X.25, FR, and ATM. In Chapter 2, we will apply this knowledge to TCP/IP, and in Chapters 3, 4, and 5 we cover the Linux TCP/IP infrastructure in detail.

2 TCP/IP in Embedded Systems

In This Chapter

- Introduction
- How We Got Here
- A Few Words on TCP/IP Implementation
- TCP/IP and the OSI Model
- TCP/IP in Embedded Systems
- TCP/IP Standards, Numbers, and Practical Considerations

INTRODUCTION

Before examining TCP/IP, we should discus a few dominant trends that affect what we do. The first is that TCP/IP is the dominant protocol suite in modern networking. This is true even though TCP/IP is far from new technology; its origins go back to the 1970s. The second trend is the popularity of the Linux Operating System (OS). The predominance of Linux is the result of an evolutionary process that dates back to the 1970s. The third trend is the growth in embedded systems. These three trends have merged, causing Linux to become one of the most popular operating systems in general use on our earth and even in outer space. A major advantage of Linux is that it comes bundled with a mature and stable implementation of its TCP/IP stack. Linux TCP/IP has made Linux one of the most successful platforms for modern networked devices. This chapter builds on Chapter 1 by exploring the TCP/IP protocol stack and discussing aspects of the TCP/IP of particular importance to embedded systems engineers and other people who care about the internal implementation of this software. We shall see in the following section how the ubiquity of Linux and the maturity of TCP/IP makes the combination an excellent platform for embedded devices.

HOW WE GOT HERE

To understand the events that led up to the current popularity and near dominance of the Linux implementation of TCP/IP, it is important to divert our attention a little to the history of the protocol suite, the open source movement, and the Linux operating system. TCP/IP networking goes back to earlier days of government-funded, computer-related research in the 1970s. Academic and research institutions scattered across the United States were using computers that needed to talk to each other, and researchers looked into new open protocols to exchange generic information. This research led to the development of the first protocols in the TCP/IP suite. At the time of development of TCP/IP, the Unix system was in wide use as an alternative to proprietary operating systems in common use. These proprietary OSs were only available from computer manufacturers such as DEC and IBM and ran only on the respective vendor's hardware architecture. The first version of Unix was developed by AT&T Bell Labs as a platform for developments in telephony. In the late 1970s and early 1980s, the University of Berkeley Computer Systems Research Group (CSRG) began distributing a version of Unix available for DEC hardware called BSD (Berkeley Software Distribution).

During this time, ARPANET, the forerunner of the TCP/IP protocol suite, was already in use at United States Defense Advanced Research Projects Agency (DARPA) funded research labs. DARPA contracted with BBN to have TCP/IP integrated into the BSD OS as part of a government contract. Since the BSD OS was already being distributed to universities in source form, TCP/IP suddenly became available in source form to students, researchers, and engineers. It quickly became an accepted industry standard and was ported into all sorts of small and embedded systems running proprietary OSs. In the meantime, various Unix derivatives were in use in embedded systems, and these OSs were the first ones to introduce TCP/IP to the embedded systems engineer.

A FEW WORDS ON TCP/IP IMPLEMENTATION

It is important to draw a distinction between the actual networking protocol and its implementation in software and hardware. The networking protocol is a specification for an exact sequence of exchanges of data between computers. Let's look at a simple example without specifying any particular OS. In Figure 2.1, machine A broadcasts a packet requesting the address of machine B in order to send a packet directly to B. A server on the network, Q responds to the request from A with a packet containing the address of B. A then sends a packet directly to B.

The implementation of the protocol defines how the software, or hardware, performs the protocol functions and steps in a given computer and OS. For example, consider the steps that are executed internally in the TCP/IP stack in the generic example protocol in Figure 3.1. An application constructs a buffer for a packet to send. The buffer is passed to the User Datagram Protocol (UDP) input routine, which copies it into an internal buffer and then passes it to IP. The buffer is queued up at the Ethernet network interface when the IP output routine calls the driver's send function. The driver makes a call to the address resolution function to get the destination MAC address. The address resolution function checks the ARP cache to see whether there is already an entry for the destination IP address. In this example, ARP doesn't find an entry, so it makes a request by broadcasting an ARP request packet called a *who-has*. When and if the response packet is received, the ARP cache is updated, and the destination hardware or Media Access Control (MAC) address is returned to the caller. The driver then takes the MAC address, puts it in the hardware header, and transmits the packet.

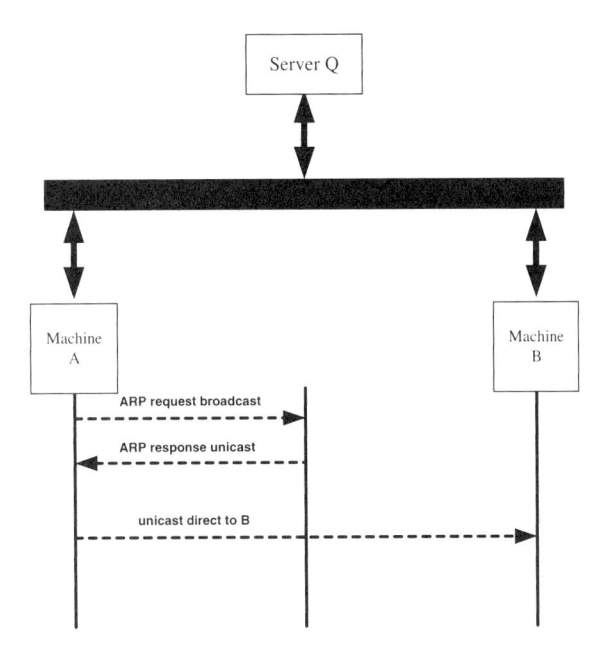

FIGURE 2.1 Simple protocol example.

TCP/IP AND THE OSI REFERENCE MODEL

In this book, as in most publications about networking, the TCP/IP protocols or *stack* are described in terms of the OSI (Open System Interconnect) reference model. Refer to Chapter 1, "Linux, TCP/IP, and Data Communication," for more about networking fundamentals and the OSI model. In this chapter, we will see how the OSI model fits in with TCP/IP. The OSI model was specified in the 1970s by the International Standards Organization (ISO) to promote interoperability between widely diverse computer architectures and OSs. The reference model describes a seven-layer architecture. At the time the OSI model was specified, TCP/IP was already established, so not all the components of TCP/IP fit neatly within the OSI layered definition. However, the OSI model remains the best framework to explain network protocols in general and the TCP/IP stack in particular. After the original Berkeley version of TCP/IP was distributed and widely used, it came to be discussed in terms of the OSI model. The TCP/IP stack in terms of the model is shown in Figure 2.2.

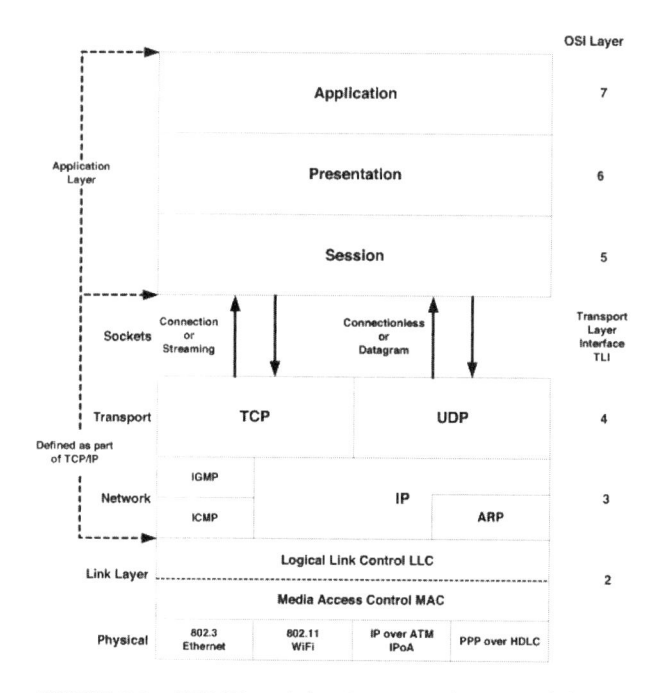

FIGURE 2.2 TCP/IP and the OSI seven-layer model.

At one time many architectures were battling for market share, but only two main architectures survived, *little endian* and *big endian* both of which use 8-bit bytes and 4-byte words expressed as a multiple of 8-bit bytes. In ancient times when the OSI model was specified, things were much more complicated. It was like the Wild West in that there was no order, no coordination, and a jumble of incompatible computers. Different manufacturers of computers used different byte and word lengths, as well as different bit and byte ordering. A well-defined method to implement computer protocols was sorely needed.

Two guiding principles allow protocol stacks to be implemented as shown in the OSI model: *information hiding* and *encapsulation*. Each layer hides its implementation details from the adjacent layers above and below. In addition, as two machines communicate, each layer in the transmitting machine has a peer-to-peer relationship with the same layer in the receiving machine. Encapsulation is the primary mechanism that allows the layers to hide information from the layers above and below. As the data being readied for transmission travels down the stack, each layer puts its header in front of the data it receives from the layer above. In the receiving machine, each layer strips its header off after receiving the data from the layer below.

Layer 1, the Physical Layer

The physical layer (PHY) is responsible for the modulation and electrical details of data transmission. An example of a PHY used in LANs is Ethernet. Ethernet uses a technique called Carrier Sense Multiple Access with Collision Detect (CSMA/CD). Another example of a PHY is a T1 interface, which is used in WANs. Refer to Chapter 1, for more information about WANs. Each machine has a unique physical address that is usually called a Media Access Control address (MAC) on LANs or a station ID on WANs.

> **NOTE** *In the Linux sources, MAC addresses are usually called hardware headers or simply* hh.

The MACs can support several addressing modes, including unicast, multicast, and broadcast. Unicast is the transmission of a frame to a specific single recipient; multicast is the transmission of a frame or packet to a specific group of recipients; and broadcast is the sending of it to all the machines that can be physically reached from the sending machine.

Layer 2, the Data Link Layer

In the simplest terms, the purpose of the data link layer is to isolate the network layer above from the electrical transmission details in the physical layer below. Another of the responsibilities of the data link layer is to provide an error-free transmission channel known as Connection Oriented (CO) service. In TCP/IP, CO service at the data link layer is not required because TCP/IP assumes that the lower layers do not have any type of error recovery. If a user requires reliable transmission, she should use SOCK_STREAM type sockets, which transmit and receive data using the TCP protocol. In the TCP/IP suite, TCP provides reliable service at the transport layer. However, in real-world systems, there are some cases in which CO or reliable delivery service at the data link layer is used. When we use the CO service underneath IP, the network interface driver is not for hardware support. Instead, it interfaces IP to another complete protocol stack. The best example is Point-to-Point Protocol (PPP). PPP presents a common example of a reliable link because it contains several layers of control protocols that must negotiate a reliable connection before it is ready to carry IP packets. In examples such as PPP where IP runs over a reliable link, often the purpose of the link is to forward IP across a public carrier-based network of some sort. Examples of public carrier networks are X.25 or ATM.

In most TCP/IP stack implementations, a filtering layer exists where incoming packets or frames can be intercepted before being passed up to IP. This filtering occurs at Layer 2 in terms of the OSI model. Linux is no exception, and an example of filtering would be `netfilter`. For more details about `netfilter`, refer to Chapter 4, "Linux Sockets." Linux also includes AF_PACKET sockets, raw sockets, and other mechanisms for intercepting raw packets. Actually, the simplest form of filtering occurs automatically at the PHY. The PHY receives packets where its own MAC address matches the destination field, multicast packets, and broadcast packets. (An exception is made when the PHY is in promiscuous mode, discussed later in this chapter.) Another function of the link layer is to establish the type of framing to be used when the IP packet is transmitted. For example, if the incoming packet is from an Ethernet interface, it can have two types of framing. One is often called Ethernet Type II framing; the other, used for Ethernet, is 802.3 type framing. The length field in the 802.3 packet is at the same displacement as the type field in the Ethernet type II frame. See Figure 2.3 for an illustration of Ethernet Type II framing and Figure 2.4 for an illustration of 802.3 type framing. The 802.3 type framing also has a type field that contains the protocol number carried by the frame. Table 2.1 shows the protocol numbers commonly used for IPv4 networking. Later in this chapter, we include more specific information about Internet standards and protocol numbers.

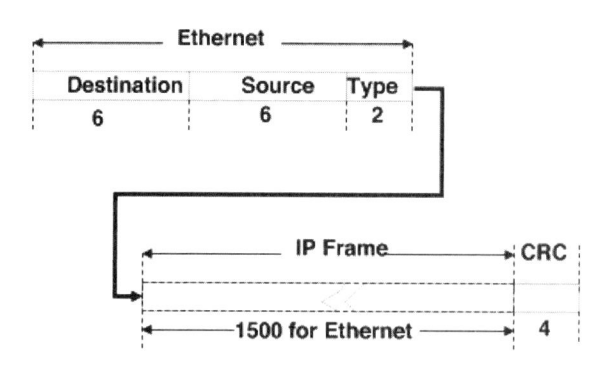

FIGURE 2.3 Ethernet framing.

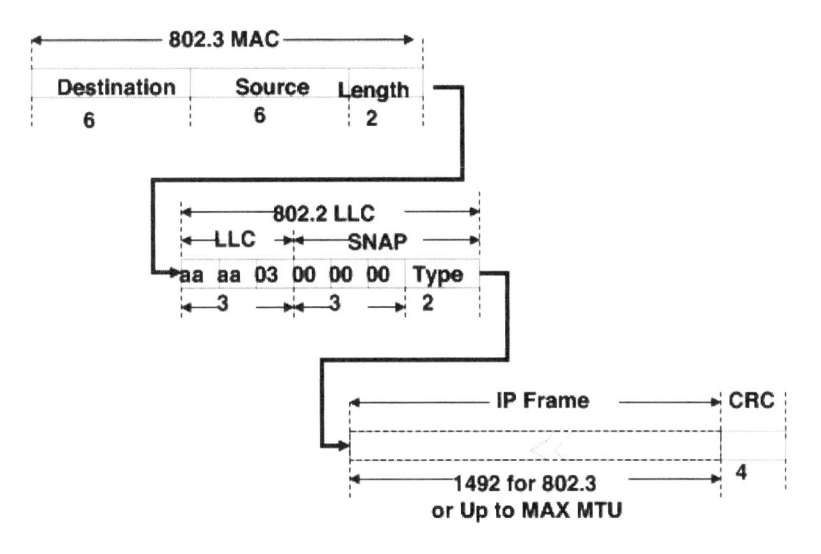

FIGURE 2.4 802.3 framing.

TABLE 2.1 Protocol Types for Type Field in Ethernet MAC Header

0x0800	IP
0x0806	ARP
0x8035	RARP

Layer 3, the Network Layer

The network layer in the TCP/IP protocol suite is called IP, for Internet Protocol [RFC 791]. This layer contains the knowledge of network topology. It includes the routing protocols and understands the network addressing scheme. Although the main responsibility of this layer is routing of packets, it also provides fragmentation to break large packets into smaller pieces so they can be transmitted across an interface that has a small Maximum Transmission Unit (MTU). Another function of IP is the capability to multiplex incoming packets destined for each of the transport protocols. See Figure 2.5 for an illustration of the IP header.

IP Addressing

This book does not attempt to duplicate the work of many excellent books available about TCP/IP network configuration and administration. Instead, we concentrate

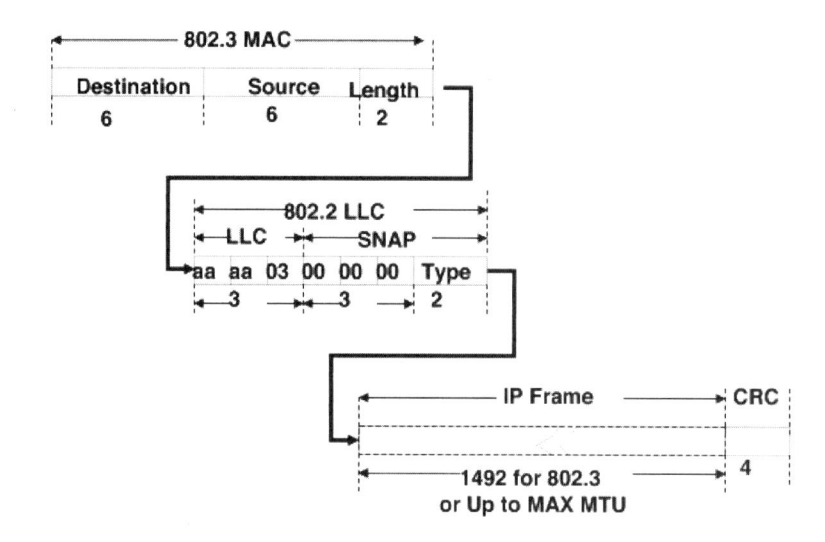

FIGURE 2.5 IP header.

on the internal implementation of Linux TCP/IP. Before diving into IP routing in later chapters, it is necessary to introduce the IP addressing scheme. Differentiating among the classes of addresses is a significant function of the IP layer. The three fundamental types of IP addresses are unicast addresses for sending a packet to an individual destination, multicast addresses for sending data to multiple destinations, and broadcast addresses for sending packets to everyone within reach.

It is conventional to express IP addresses in dotted decimal notation in which each byte of the address is written as a decimal number. The IP addresses are divided into classes. The first three bits of the IP address determine the class [RFC796]. The class of address determines the size of the network; it defines what portion of the address is the network portion and what portion is the host portion. The network portion is the higher order side of the address, and the host portion is the right part of the address. See Table 2.2 for a layout of the IP addressing scheme. Class A and B addresses were once used widely in an enterprise for all the hosts on the network. After a while, as the popularity of the Internet increased, A and B addresses became used less often because they allow too many hosts on a network. Routers became more prevalent so an enterprise could implement multiple smaller networks at lower cost than what was once possible. Therefore, class C addresses became more common; however, the problem with class C addresses is that they don't have enough hosts.

In modern times, available network address space on the Internet is extremely limited. An organization is typically assigned only one or very few addresses, and all the traffic destined to an organization is directed to addresses within this group. This is called Classless Interdomain Routing (CIDR) [RFC 1519]. Internally, orga-

TABLE 2.2 IP Addressing

Class	Lower Bound of Network	Upper Bound of Network	Lower Bound of Host	Upper Bound of Host
Default Route Is all zeros	0.0.0.0	0.0.0.0	0.0.0.0	0.0.0.0
A- 8 bits net 24 bits host	0.0.0.0	126.0.0.0	126.0.0.0	126.255.255.255
Loopback	127.0.0.0	127.0.0.0	127.0.0.0	127.x.x.x
B-16 bits net 16 bits host	128.0.0.0	191.255.0.0	128.0.0.0	128.0.255.255
C-24 bits net 8 bits host	192.0.0.0	223.255.255.0	192.0.0.0	192.0.0.255
Multicast	224.0.0.0			239.255.255.255

nizations can translate incoming and outgoing packets from the external address to an internal address space. The internal network addresses are subdivided by using subnets [RFC917].

The *netmask* can be used to separate the network portion of the address from the host portion, but the dividing point is not necessarily on one of the class boundaries shown in Table 2.2. This is called *subnetting*. Netmasks are usually shown as hex numbers, particularly in systems that have a Unix heritage such as Linux. The subnet mask subdivides the host portion of the address into a subnet identifier and a host identifier. For example, a network ID might be 191.254.0.0 and the subnet could be 0xffffff80. This would give 128 host IDs within the network identified by 191.254.0.0.

Address Resolution Protocol

The Address Resolution Protocol (ARP) determines how physical addresses such as Ethernet hardware addresses map to network layer IP addresses. It is sometimes thought of as being in the link layer, but for the purposes of this explanation, it will be placed in the network layer alongside IP. As we will see later in Chapter 3, the Linux IP layer hands over its packet to the interface driver when the IP portion of the header is complete, but IP has no way of knowing the physical transmission details needed to determine the hardware address. The driver or network interface knows how to form the hardware or MAC address but doesn't know the address associated with the specific destination for this packet. The network interface driver checks the destination address to see whether it is known or not by looking at the cached hardware header associated with the current open socket structure if there is one.

If the destination address is not already known, the resolve function in the ARP module has to find out the destination address. If the ARP cache contains an entry for the physical address, the address resolve function can be retrieved immediately, and the resolve function returns. Otherwise, the ARP module sends out a broadcast packet to locally connected hosts called a *who-has* to see whether anybody knows the MAC address associated with this IP address. When a reply to the *who-has* is received, a new entry is created in the ARP cache. Later, the network interface driver can access the address from the local ARP cache. As we shall see in later chapters, Linux manages the ARP cache in a somewhat more complex way. The ARP cache is created from the generic destination cache. A pointer to the destination cache entry is placed in the packet before it is handed off for transmission. Later when the packet is being transmitted, the MAC header can be retrieved quickly from the cache if the address has been resolved. If not, the packet is passed to ARP where it is queued while ARP gets the destination address.

Layer 4, the Transport Layer

The transport layer in TCP/IP consists of two major protocols. It contains a connection-oriented reliable service otherwise known as a streaming service provided by the TCP protocol. In addition, TCP/IP includes an individual packet transmission service known as an unreliable or datagram service, which is provided by UDP. Since, historically, it was the function of the data link layer to provide an end-to-end connection-oriented service that includes error checking and recovery, one wonders why there is a need for a reliable delivery method at the transport layer. The reason why TCP/IP evolved this way is that it was designed to be carried over Ethernet and other LAN protocols, which don't provide a connection-oriented service at the link layer.

UDP, the User Datagram Protocol

UDP is used where there is a need to send individual packets or datagrams. Each packet is sent as an individual transmission—no sequencing of packets and no error detection and recovery mechanism retry transmitting lost packets. UDP does not provide a means of ordering the packets. It is possible that packets could arrive at the destination in an order different from the one in which they were sent. Application code using UDP should make no assumptions that packets will arrive in order or arrive at all. It is necessary for applications using UDP to code in their own acknowledgment scheme if reliability is a concern. UDP provides a simple interface to the socket layer above and to the IP layer below. Figure 2.6 shows the UDP header format.

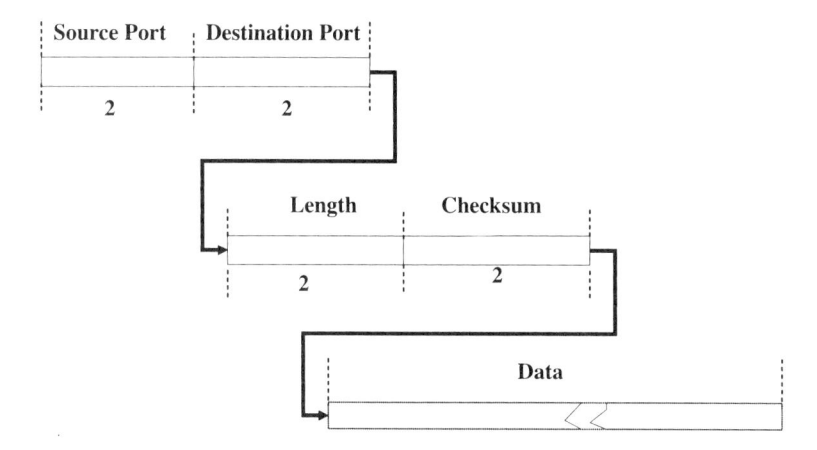

FIGURE 2.6 UDP header.

TCP, the Transmission Control Protocol

TCP is used where an application requires a reliable or streaming service. Its internal implementation details are almost completely invisible to applications using TCP. To the application program, it looks like a stream of bytes. Most of the well-known and common applications used in the modern connected world use TCP such as FTP and Telnet. The most common of these is the HTTP protocol used by Web browsers. TCP guarantees that each byte will arrive in sequence, and if an intermediate packet was dropped or errors are detected, the protocol handles retransmission of dropped or erroneous packets. See Figure 2.7 for the fields in the TCP header.

TCP is quite complex and is covered much more in depth in Chapter 7, "Sending the Data from the Socket through UDP and TCP," where we delve into the internals of the Linux implementation of the TCP. In this section, we will talk about some fields in the TCP header that are needed to illustrate the basic function of TCP. In Chapter 1, "Data Communication and Linux TCP/IP," we discussed the sliding windows algorithm, and a similar algorithm is used by TCP. Sliding windows are used by the TCP protocol to transmit a sequenced stream of data, necessary for reliable and ordered exchange of information. The window size, sequence number, and acknowledgment number fields are used by TCP to implement sliding windows. TCP divides the data stream into segments. The sequence number and acknowledgment number fields are byte pointers that keep track of the position of the segments within the data stream. The flag bits are used to maintain the state of the connection. See Figure 2.8 for more detail on the other TCP header fields used to maintain the connection state.

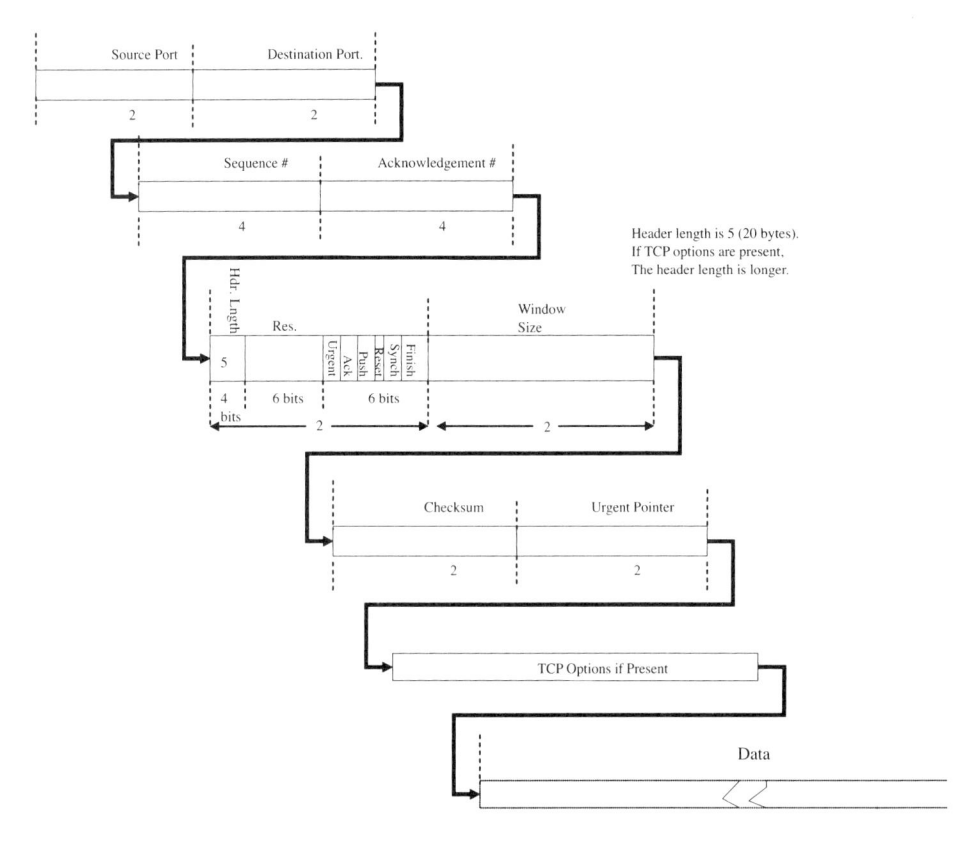

FIGURE 2.7 The TCP header.

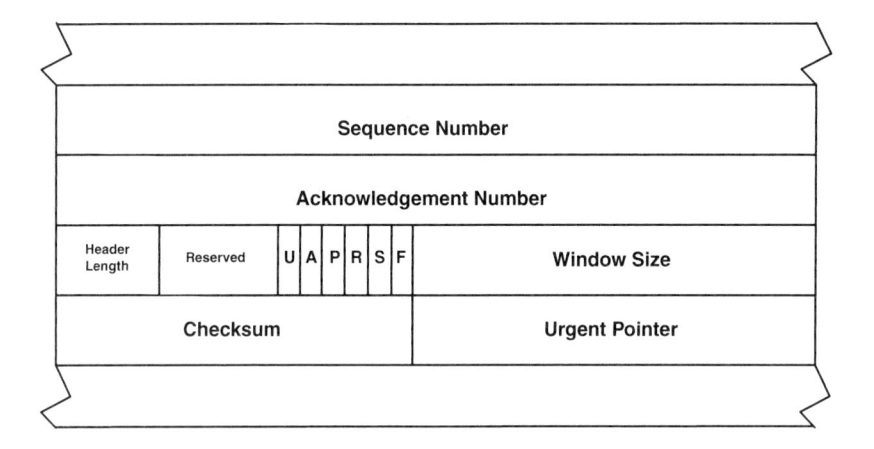

FIGURE 2.8 TCP segments.

Sockets, and the Transport Layer Interface (TLI)

The socket API is probably one of the most widely used APIs in software development. It is a very versatile and well understood interface. The socket interface supports both UDP (SOCK_DGRAM) and TCP (SOCK_STREAM). The most common socket standard is known as BSD sockets. Almost all socket implementations conform to the BSD sockets, and Linux is no exception. Application code that uses the socket API can be ported to Linux with virtually no changes. The socket API, fundamental to client-server programming, is the underlying basis of Web services, XML, JSP, or many other common Web-based programming paradigms. In Chapter 5, "Linux Sockets," we walk through the socket API. We show how sockets work internally and how the socket API works with TCP, UDP, and other protocols. In addition, we show how sockets can be used to access configuration items specific to the Linux operating system. For a complete and comprehensive explanation of socket programming from the applications perspective, refer to *Unix Network Programming* by W. Richard Stevens [STEV98].

A main advantage of Linux (as well as other legacy Unix like OSs) is that the socket is treated as a file descriptor, and all the standard IO functions work on sockets in the same way they work on a local file. This increases code portability and decreases software development costs. Quite recently, this characteristic was rare in many commercial OSs sold in the embedded market. The fundamental mode of programming sockets, particularly TCP or streaming sockets, is called *client-server programming*. The basic difference between a client and a server is that the server listens for a connection on a socket, and the client initiates the connection to the server through a socket.

Application Layer Protocols

The OSI model discussed in Chapter 1 defines seven layers. The TCP/IP specification only defines Layers 3 and 4, the network and transport layers. Therefore, the TCP/IP protocol suite specification does not specifically concern itself with anything above the socket interface. From the viewpoint of TCP/IP, the upper layer protocols can be grouped and considered application layer protocols. It is useful, however, to discuss the upper layers briefly to create a complete picture of how TCP/IP fits into the seven-layer ISO model.

Layer 5, Session

In a way, the session layer is similar to the signaling protocols in traditional telephony. The purpose of the session layer is to exchange information between endpoints about how to set up for a data transmission and how to terminate the association after the transmission is complete. The session layer was originally used for terminal emulation in which multiple users were logged in to a central terminal server simultaneously in what used to be called time-sharing. This was a common practice with early Unix systems when most people accessed a computer through dumb terminals. After Graphical User Interfaces (GUIs) became the normal mode of interaction with computers, the use of session layer protocols for this purpose is not as critical. One widely used session layer protocol is the Telnet protocol, which has been used for many years for virtual terminal access to remote systems [RFC853]. In the TCP/IP world, it is implemented as an application layer protocol over SOCK_STREAM (TCP) sockets. A good example of a session layer protocol in modern use is the Session Initiation Protocol (SIP) [RFC 3261]. This protocol is for controlling the creation and maintenance of sessions between two or more participants for voice calls and for controlling multimedia exchange and distribution.

Layer 6, Presentation

Even though presentation is defined as Layer 6 of the OSI model, as with the session layer, from the viewpoint of TCP/IP the presentation layer is not part of the stack in the kernel, it is the application programmer's responsibility. The purpose of the presentation layer is to provide a user with a view of data that is independent from its implementation details on any particular computer architecture and independent from details about how the data is transmitted over a network. The presentation layer generally consists of a data description language of some sort to specify the format of the information to be exchanged between endpoints. Many data description languages are in use. One common example, originally intended for use with the OSI protocol stack, is Abstract Syntax Notation (ASN.1). ASN.1 is now commonly used as the basis of the Structure of Management Information (SMI), used to represent manageable objects in the Simple Network Management Protocol (SNMP). Other examples of presentation layer protocols could include systems such as Common Object Request Broker Architecture (CORBA) or Extensible Markup Language (XML) because their primary interest is to provide an implementation-independent way to view varying data resources and to share that data among dissimilar systems.

TCP/IP IN EMBEDDED SYSTEMS

Before TCP/IP came to be widely used in embedded systems, it was common for embedded applications to run in systems without any OS at all. Sometimes embedded engineers would use a minimal OS containing no interface to integrate a networking stack, and most embedded engineers would use in-house designed operating systems if they had any OS at all. However, as the cost of hardware and memory decreased, computers for embedded applications needed to support software with increased complexity, so commercial embedded OS vendors moved into the market. The first commercial or outside operating systems consisted of small multitasking kernels that advertised high efficiency and low memory requirements. These OSs, however, didn't have any standard IO interfaces and didn't support file systems, TCP/IP, or any other networking interfaces. In the meantime, embedded systems became more and more widely used, and they were incorporated in just about any machine or device that is controllable, configurable, or programmable. As the complexity of embedded applications increased, there was an increasing need for more features in the operating systems such as file systems and TCP/IP networking. Commercial vendors filled the need, selling operating system software that included TCP/IP as a built-in component. These vendors collected royalties on each target system. As hardware became cheaper, the royalty became a more significant factor in the cost of the end product. Therefore, more and more embedded systems engineers are now looking for an open source solution for their embedded OS and TCP/IP networking stack.

Originally, Unix was too big and complex for most embedded applications. Now with cheaper memory and faster cheaper processors, the memory requirements of the OS is less significant a factor in the overall design. Therefore, Linux becomes increasingly practical for embedded systems. Along with Linux, embedded systems designers get a robust implementation of TCP/IP with complete source code. Quite a few years ago, the lack of source code was a major impediment in projects particularly if a vendor stack wasn't documented or supported very well. Engineers would sell body parts if they had to for access to complete source code. In addition, as the popularity of Linux increases, it gets used more widely for desktop and server applications This wide acceptance outside the smaller embedded community makes it easier to get support or find components, tools, and information. The combination of the Linux OS with a stable TCP/IP stack has become the primary choice for many embedded systems and a powerful factor when used in many diverse embedded networked applications.

Specific Requirements for an Embedded OS

The later chapters of this book illustrate the Linux implementation of TCP/IP in detail. An important focus of this book is embedded systems so before digging much deeper, we will take the time to discuss the requirements for a generic embedded system for hosting a TCP/IP stack. We compare these requirements with specific Linux capabilities to see how Linux compares with its competitors as a choice for an embedded OS and how well it is suited to support an embedded system's networking needs. The TCP/IP stack, like all networking protocols, is asynchronous. The stack implementation is event oriented rather than linear. This is because processing is invoked whenever a packet becomes available at a given layer. Each packet travels through the stack as a separate thread independent of other packets. In addition, concurrent activities are needed to keep track of time-related events required by the protocol specifications. In the light of these general requirements, the following is a brief list of specific facilities that every embedded OS should have for hosting a TCP/IP stack:

- **Timer facility:** All protocols require timers for retransmissions and timeouts. Some simple OSs used for embedded systems either lack this simple facility or do not have a consistent interface. For an example of the use of timers by Linux TCP/IP, See Chapter 7 for a discussion about the use of timers in the TCP protocol.
- **Concurrency and multitasking:** The socket API (or equivalent) should allow for multiple simultaneous users. The TCP/IP stack should be multithreaded. Of course, concurrency requires locking of resources and critical code sections. At the simplest level, buffer contention can be avoided by having semaphore protection at the buffer level. Chapter 5, "The Linux TCP/IP Stack," discusses Linux kernel threading and how kernel threads are used within TCP/IP.
- **Buffer management:** TCP/IP and most communication protocols are the most efficient when they are provided with a fixed-length buffer system. In earlier TCP/IP implementations and particularly in embedded systems, the buffer pool was pre-allocated at boot-up time. This system avoids problems with heap fragmentation but is limited in how it can adapt to changing needs because the maximum number of buffers is fixed. Buffers are assigned dynamically from the pool when a new incoming packet arrives at the network interface device or a new outgoing packet is created at the socket layer. As we will see in Chapter 7, "Sending Data from the Socket through UDP and TCP," Linux networking buffers are called socket buffers. Socket buffers are allocated from a slab cache, which also solves the fragmentation problem. Another advantage of the slab cache is scalability and that there is no preconfigured upper bound.
- **Link layer facility:** Complex protocol implementation requires a way to add layers and sometimes complete protocols in the sliver below IP but above the network interface drivers. In general, it is good to have a facility and framework to add protocols such as Network Address Translation (NAT), Point-to-Point Protocol (PPP), software-implemented bridging, or switching capability without having to alter either the IP source code or alter the network interface driver sources. As we shall see in Chapter 3, Linux provides a network interface driver facility. These devices can either be real devices with interrupt capability or can be pseudo-devices for interface TCP/IP with an underlying protocol stack like IP over ATM (IPoA.) In addition, as discussed in later chapters, Linux provides a queuing layer between the network interface drivers to the network layer to handle specific requirements for multiple traffic classes.

There are also a few other examples where Linux can be differentiated from other real-time OSs used for embedded applications. Standard Linux like other earlier Unix implementations is a nonpre-emptable implementation of the OS kernel. However, since TCP/IP is part of the Linux kernel, it can make use of the `softirq` kernel threading facility. We will see how this works in Chapter 5, "The Linux TCP/IP Stack." Linux has the capability of deferring interrupt-level work to kernel threads to decrease latency problems.

- **Low latency:** The operating system should not add any more latency than necessary for the minimum amount of processing required at interrupt time for the physical reception and transmission of a frame. The goal of the OS should be to minimize context switches while a packet is processed by the stack. Linux uses `softirqs` to handle most of the internal processing. In addition, as we will see in later chapters, fast paths are provided for packet transmission and reception to reduce the amount of overhead.
- **Minimal data copying:** It is advantageous for embedded systems to minimize the amount of copying necessary to move a packet of data from the application, down through the stack to the transmission media. Embedded applications are performance sensitive and should have a TCP/IP stack implementation that has no buffer copying at the device driver level and allows for the option of eliminating buffer copying at the socket level. Typically, the Ethernet chip or hardware networking PHY device places the packet directly in memory via DMA. Linux provides scatter-gather DMA support where the socket buffers are set up to allow for the direct transmission of lists of TCP segments. In addition, at the user level, when data is transferred through a socket, copying can be avoided and data can be mapped directly into the user space from the kernel space.

TCP/IP STANDARDS, NUMBERS, AND PRACTICAL CONSIDERATIONS

As discussed in Chapter 1, the bodies responsible for the standards that govern the Internet are the Internet Engineering Task Force (IETF), *www.ietf.org,* and the Internet Architecture Board (IAB). These bodies are part of the Internet Society (ISOC), *www.isoc.org.* The Internet standards are published as Request for Comments (RFCs). Many websites provide databases of RFCs; one of the best at the time of writing is *http://www.faqs.org/rfcs/.* For the reader's convenience, all RFCs referenced in this book are included in Appendix A and in the companion CD-ROM.

Throughout this book are tables of values for stuffing in various function arguments and structure fields. Tables in each chapter show some of these values, and many of the values are actually officially assigned numbers. In some places, the lists of numbers might not be entirely complete because of new protocols that are registered from time to time. Much of what makes the Internet function is based on these agreed-upon numbers. The numbers include the protocol fields in the link layer or Ethernet header, the protocol numbers in the IP header, well-known transport layer port numbers, and many others. Figures 2.3 and 2.4 illustrate the link layer headers, and Table 2.1 shows the protocol fields for the IPv4 Ethernet MAC header. These number assignments at one time were specified by RFCs that were re-issued from time to time as new protocols were defined. The last of these RFCs that defined protocol numbers was RFC 1700. Now, as of RFC 3232 in early 2002, the responsibility of maintaining assigned numbers was removed from the RFC editor. The assigned numbers are now maintained in a database by the Internet Assigned Number Authority (IANA) *www.iana.org/assignments*.

SUMMARY

This first part of this chapter introduced the origins of TCP/IP and the history of its implementation in Linux. Later, the TCP/IP protocol stack was laid out in terms of the OSI seven-layer model. We explored each major component of TCP/IP and how it fits into the conceptualized OSI networking model. In this chapter, some issues specific to embedded systems were discussed relative to the use and implementation of TCP/IP. We showed how Linux is an excellent platform for networking either in embedded systems or any other networking-oriented computing application. Now that you have a basic understanding of data communication protocols and the TCP/IP stack, let's delve into some of the infrastructure in the Linux implementation of TCP/IP.

3 Linux Network Interface Drivers

In This Chapter

- A Few Words
- Introduction
- Network Interface Devices
- The Network Device Structure, `struct net_device`
- Network Device Initialization
- Linux Network Interface Driver Facilities
- Receiving Packets
- Transmitting Packets
- `Notifier` Chains and Network Interface Device Status Notification

A FEW WORDS

In Chapter 1, "Data Communication and Linux TCP/IP," we discussed networking in general and how to build on basic networking concepts and introduced some networking protocols that either incorporated significant concepts of data communications or are often interfaced to TCP/IP. Chapter 2, "TCP/IP in Embedded Systems," covered the TCP/IP protocol and its implementation in general terms. This chapter begins the detailed discussion of the Linux by starting with Linux network interfaces. Some very good books on Linux device drivers are available, and we won't attempt to replicate that work here. However, we will discuss in detail the aspects of device drivers that are utilized in Linux network interface drivers. In general, a good understanding of the Linux TCP/IP stack necessitates a discussion of network interface drivers both in how they function in Linux and how they interface to IP and other network layer protocols.

INTRODUCTION

In this chapter, we show the internal structure of Linux network interface drivers. Later chapters continue this discussion by showing the infrastructure of Linux above the network interface drivers and how the drivers are interfaced to IP and other network layer protocols. Much of the Linux internal kernel implementation is not completely documented. Several good reference books for writers of Linux device drivers include [Rubini00], which is excellent but does not discuss the networking interface drivers as much as other drivers and the details of how the drivers interface to the TCP/IP stack. This chapter does not attempt to duplicate other works and, therefore, will not provide a complete discussion about writing Linux device drivers. Instead, the intent of this book is to discuss the networking interface drivers and in particular, their internal data structures and how data packets flow into and out of the TCP/IP stack. It is quite possible to construct a device driver by using an existing device driver as sample code. This is often the quickest way to approach a development task. However, it is helpful for driver writers, and kernel diggers in general, to have a good understanding of how the network interface driver is structured, and that is the approach we will take in this chapter.

We discuss the network driver initialization and registration process and the programming interface required by network drivers for the driver to function properly in the OS. In other Unix-like operating systems, the interface functions are often called the driver entry points, but in Linux, these driver interface functions are called network interface service functions. We will discuss these functions, the packet queuing layer, and how the packets are transmitted and received. Some aspects of how packets are routed through the queuing layer are discussed in other chapters including the multiple queuing disciplines and traffic class-based schedulers, which are discussed along with IP routing. The Linux networking interface drivers are similar to network drivers used with other Unix-like operating systems, and the device driver details are hidden from the network layer implementation. The TCP/IP stack provides a registration mechanism between the device drivers and the layer above, to allow the output routines in the networking layer, whether IP or something else, to invoke a network interface driver's transmit function for a specific interface instance without needing to know the driver's internal details or details about the hardware. Another similarity between the Linux approach and other operating systems is that network interface drivers only interface to other parts of the Linux kernel. There is no direct API with which code outside the kernel can make direct calls to the network driver. Unlike other Linux drivers, network interface drivers are not accessed via standard IO through file descriptors. Instead, packets are transmitted and received by Layer 3 protocols, which are connected to the driver via a registration mechanism. Moreover, network interface driver configuration is not done via direct IO; instead, driver configuration is done either with `ioctl` calls through the socket API or via the `sysctl` interface.

NETWORK INTERFACE DEVICES

Each network interface device must have a driver, and the driver provides initialization functions that are called at kernel startup or module load time. The driver also includes tables that allow the device to work with the Linux kernel. All Linux network interface devices can be associated with the kernel in two different ways: either at kernel build time or later by loading after the kernel is up and operating. In addition, a Linux network interface driver can be implemented as a module so it is not necessary to statically link it into the kernel, and generally, it is preferable to implement the driver as a module. If the driver is a module, it does not preclude it from being statically linked with the kernel. Whether modules are statically linked into the kernel is specified at kernel configuration time. Driver modules can be loaded dynamically at boot time or later using the `insmod(8)` command. Whether the driver is written as a module or is statically linked, the driver must provide an initialization function that is called by the kernel before the network interface device is ready to receive and transmit packets. Although primarily about kernel versions before 2.6, [Rubini00a] has a good discussion of how to implement kernel modules. The network driver initialization function sets up the driver's internal data structures; the driver is introduced to the Linux kernel; and the send and receive queues are connected to the TCP/IP stack. The main driver structure is the `net_device` structure. Although many different types of network interface drivers exist, they each have one thing in common: they must initialize an instance of the net device structure. The initialization sequence for a driver for a PCI bus device is explained later in the text.

THE NETWORK DEVICE STRUCTURE, STRUCT NET_DEVICE

The net device structure, defined in file `linux/include/linux/netdevice.h`, is the data structure that defines an instance of a network interface. It tracks the state information of all the network interface devices attached to the TCP/IP stack. The structure might seem longer and more complex than is necessary, but it contains fields for implementing devices that have been added after the more generic network interfaces were originally defined. In our description of the `net_device` structure, the fields that are of most interest to network interface driver writers contain explanations. We also include explanations of the things needed to connect the network interface driver to the TCP/IP stack. In general, we concern ourselves only with the public part of the driver's data structure, but some key fields in the private part of the driver's data structure are important for PCI devices. This is because they must be initialized with a pointer to the PCI card's configuration space, and this pointer is dereferenced later when the driver allocates buffer space for Ethernet DMA that is mapped into PCI device space. However, most of the discussion in this section pertains to the public part of the structure contained within the net device structure.

```
struct net_device
{
```

This first field, name, is the beginning of the visible part of this structure. It contains the string that is the name of the interface. By visible, we mean that this part of the data structure is generic and doesn't contain any private areas specific to a particular type of device. This is the part that is initialized by the linux/drivers/net/Space.c file, which contains the generic probe functions for each device type. hlist_node is the list head for the hash bucket containing the net device structure. Linux provides an extensive series of list handling functions in linux/include/linux/list.h where the hlist_node structure and other list related facilities are described.

```
char              name[IFNAMSIZ];
struct hlist_node name_hlist;
```

mem_end is the pointer to the end of the device-specific shared memory area, and mem_start is the pointer to the beginning of the area.

```
unsigned long     mem_end;
unsigned long     mem_start;
```

Base_addr is the device I/O address used primarily by x86 processors and other architectures that do memory mapped I/O. IRQ is the device's Interrupt number, also used by x86 processors.

```
unsigned long     base_addr;
unsigned int      irq;
```

Both of the following fields are used by some types of hardware but are generally specified by the file, linux/drivers/net/Space.c, which holds the initial configuration information for various classes of devices.

```
unsigned char     if_port;
unsigned char     dma;
```

This field, `state`, holds the network device state. These values are private to the queuing layer and are not used anywhere else. They are shown in Table 3.1.

```
unsigned long      state;
```
next is a pointer to the next device on the list.
```
struct net_device  *next;
```

TABLE 3.1 Network Queuing Layer Device State

State	Value	Description
__LINK_STATE_XOFF	0	Device queue turned off
__LINK_STATE_START	1	Device queue turned on
__LINK_STATE_PRESENT	2	Device ready to be scheduled
__LINK_STATE_SCHED	3	
__LINK_STATE_NOCARRIER	4	
__LINK_STATE_RX_SCHED	5	Device placed on poll list

init is the pointer to the device's initialization function. This function is called only once. This is the last field that is pre-initialized by the probe functions in linux/drivers/net/Space.c. features has bits set for hardware device capabilities. These are maintained so Linux can make optimum use of the various hardware speedups available in many Ethernet and other drivers. The bits and their meanings are shown in Table 3.2.

```
int            (*init)(struct net_device *dev);
unsigned long  features;
```
ifindex is the interface index, and iflink is the unique device identifier.
```
int            ifindex;
int            iflink;
```

The next field, net_device_stats, is a pointer to the driver's function for returning the network interface statistics including the various counters. iw_statistics is for wireless devices and returns a set of interface statistics specific for wireless interfaces.

```
struct net_device_stats* (*get_stats)(struct net_device *dev);
struct iw_statistics*    (*get_wireless_stats)(struct net_device
                           *dev);
```

TABLE 3.2 Linux Network Interface Device Features

Name	Value	Purpose
NETIF_F_SG	1	Device is capable of hardware assisted chained DMA known generally in Linux as scatter-gather IO.
NETIF_F_IP_CSUM	2	Device can support hardware checksums but only for TCP and UDP running over IPv4.
NETIF_F_NO_CSUM	4	This device does not require a checksum. It is probably a pseudo-device such as the loopback device.
NETIF_F_HW_CSUM	8	Device's can generate checksums for all types of packets.
NETIF_F_HIGHDMA	32	Device can DMA into high memory. This really applies to legacy PC non-linear architectures.
NETIF_F_FRAGLIS	64	This flag pertains to scatter-gather IO and indicates that the chained pieces are in an attached list of fragments. See Chapter 6 for more about fragment lists.
NETIF_F_HW_VLAN_TX	128	This device supports transmit VLAN hardware acceleration.
NETIF_F_HW_VLAN_RX	256	Device is capable of receive VLAN acceleration.
NETIF_F_HW_VLAN_FILTER	512	Device is capable of receive side VLAN filtering.
NETIF_F_VLAN_CHALLENGED	1024	Device cannot handle VLAN packets at all.
NETIF_F_TSO	2048	Device can do TCP segmentation in hardware. See Chapters 7 and 9 for more about TCP segments.
NETIF_F_LLTX	4096	This flag says that upper layers can call the device's transmit function without acquiring the lock.
NETIF_F_UFO	8192	Device can offload a large UDP packet on send. This is useful for VOIP and other streaming UDP type applications.

The next field points to a list of functions to handle device extensions that are specific to wireless network interface drivers. The file iw_handler.h has more details of these functions, which are an alternative to using ioctl. wireless_data points to instance data used by the wireless handlers.

```
struct iw_handler_def     *wireless_handlers;
struct iw_public_data     *wireless_data;
struct ethtool_ops        *ethtool_ops;
```

Now we have come to the end of the visible part of the net_device structure. All the fields that follow are internal and might change in future revisions of the kernel; therefore, device driver implementers should not count on the following fields.

The next few fields can be used for auto-power down code. Trans_start is the timestamp in jiffies of the last transmitted packet, and last_rx is the timestamp of the last received packet. Jiffies contains the current time in ticks.

The next field, flags, contains the BSD style interface flags.

```
unsigned short     flags;
unsigned short     gflags;
```

This field, priv_flags, is like flags but is private so it is used internally by various network interface drivers and will never show up at the user level.

```
unsigned short     priv_flags;
unsigned short     padded;
```

Mtu contains the interface's Maximum Transmission Unit (MTU) value. The next field, type, is the interface hardware type.

```
unsigned           mtu;
unsigned short     type;
```

hard_header_len is the size of the link layer header (sometimes called the hardware header in the Linux sources) for this network interface. master is the pointer to the master device for this device's group.

```
unsigned short     hard_header_len;
struct net_device  *master;
```

The next two fields contain the interface specific link layer address information. perm_addr is where the interface driver stores the hardware address, and addr_len is the length of the hardware address. This is 14 bytes for Ethernet, and the maximum address length is 32 bytes. perm_addr is used by the ethtool(1) utility to access Ethernet interface addresses.

```
unsigned char      perm_addr[MAX_ADDR_LEN];
unsigned char      addr_len;
```

mc_list is the list of the network interface's link layer or MAC multicast addresses, and mc_count is the number of multicast addresses on the list. If set to TRUE, the field promiscuity indicates that promiscuous mode is set for this interface. In promiscuous mode an interface can see all packets on the wire.

```
struct dev_mc_list  *mc_list;
int                 mc_count;
int                 promiscuity;
int                 allmulti;
```

The next few fields are protocol-specific pointers. atalk_ptr is a pointer to AppleTalk-specific data, and ip_ptr is a pointer to IPv4-specific data. dn_ptr is for DECnet-specific data, and ip6_ptr is for IPv6 data. Finally, ec_ptr is Econet-specific, and ax25_ptr is specific to the AX.25 protocol.

```
void                *atalk_ptr;
void                *ip_ptr;
void                *dn_ptr;
void                *ip6_ptr;
void                *ec_ptr;
void                *ax25_ptr;
```

The next field, poll_list, is a pointer to the list of queued packets. This field and the next group of fields are used by the queuing layer so multiple queuing disciplines can be used with the network interface device. poll is a pointer to the driver's polling function. Quota is used by the backlog device (blog_dev) for input queuing, and weight is the backlog weight also used by blog_dev for input packets.

```
struct list_head    poll_list;
int                 (*poll) (struct net_device *dev, int *quota);
int                 quota;
int                 weight;
```

The next field, last_rx, is the time of the last transmission through this network interface. It is generally set to jiffies, the current time when a packet is transmitted. Hardware addresses can be tweaked in modern Ethernet cards, and dev_addr is a more volatile hardware address. It is used by the eth_type_trans() function to get the protocol number of incoming packets. broadcast contains the hardware broadcast address for this type of interface.

```
unsigned long      last_rx;
unsigned char      dev_addr[MAX_ADDR_LEN];
unsigned char      broadcast[MAX_ADDR_LEN];
```

queue_lock is the device queue's mutex lock, and qdisc is the queue discipline that is used for this network interface. qdisc_sleeping points to the list of registered queue disciplines used with this network interface device. tx_queue_len is the maximum number of output packets allowed for this device queue. The next field, ingress_lock, is for ingress path synchronization, and disc_ingress is the queuing discipline for input packets.

```
spinlock_t         queue_lock ____cacheline_aligned_in_smp;
struct Qdisc       *qdisc;
struct Qdisc       *qdisc_sleeping;
struct Qdisc       *qdisc_list;
unsigned long      tx_queue_len;
spinlock_t         ingress_lock;
struct Qdisc       *qdisc_ingress;
```

The next few fields are used with the devices to transmit capability. xmit_lock is the spinlock for synchronizing the driver's transmit function when used with multiple CPU applications. xmit_lock_owner is the CPU ID of the holder of the lock. The next field, hard_start_xmit, points to the driver's actual transmit function.

```
spinlock_t         xmit_lock ____cacheline_aligned_in_smp;
int                xmit_lock_owner;
int                (hard_start_xmit) (struct sk_buff *skb,
                       struct net_device *dev);
```

The following fields are for a watchdog timer, if one is used by this interface. trans_start contains the time when the last packet was transmitted.

```
unsigned long      trans_start;
int                watchdog_timeo;
struct timer_list  watchdog_timer;
```

refcnt contains the number of references to this device.

```
atomic_t           refcnt ____cacheline_aligned_in_smp;
```

todo_list is for delayed device registration and unregistration, and reg_state is the state machine for delayed registration and unregistration.

```
struct list_head    todo_list;
enum { NETREG_UNINITIALIZED=0,
```

Register_netdevice has been called.

```
NETREG_REGISTERING,
```

Registration is completed.

```
NETREG_REGISTERED,
```

Unregistration has begun.

```
NETREG_UNREGISTERING,
```

Unregistration is completed.

```
NETREG_UNREGISTERED,
```

The function free_netdev is called to free the net_device structure.

```
NETREG_RELEASED,
} reg_state;
```

This function uninit is called after the device is detached from network, and destructor is called after the last user reference is removed.

```
void            (*uninit)(struct net_device *dev);
void            (*destructor)(struct net_device *dev);
```

Next in the net_device structure, we have the pointers to the service routines for the network interface device. These functions are discussed in detail later in this chapter.

```
int             (*open)(struct net_device *dev);
int             (*stop)(struct net_device *dev);
int(*hard_header)       (struct sk_buff *skb,
                         struct net_device *dev,
                         unsigned short type,
                         void *daddr,
```

```c
                              void *saddr,
                              unsigned len);
    int                 (*rebuild_header)(struct sk_buff *skb);
#define HAVE_MULTICAST
    void                (*set_multicast_list)(struct net_device *dev);
#define HAVE_SET_MAC_ADDR
    int                 (*set_mac_address)(struct net_device *dev,
                              void *addr);
#define HAVE_PRIVATE_IOCTL
    int                 (*do_ioctl)(struct net_device *dev,
                              struct ifreq *ifr, int cmd);
#define HAVE_SET_CONFIG
    int                 (*set_config)(struct net_device *dev,
                              struct ifmap *map);
#define HAVE_HEADER_CACHE
    int                 (*hard_header_cache)(struct neighbour *neigh,
                              struct hh_cache *hh);
    void                (*header_cache_update)(struct hh_cache *hh,
                              struct net_device *dev,
                              unsigned char *  haddr);
#define HAVE_CHANGE_MTU
    int                 (*change_mtu)(struct net_device *dev, int
new_mtu);

#define HAVE_TX_TIMEOUT
    void                (*tx_timeout) (struct net_device *dev);

    void                (*vlan_rx_register)(struct net_device *dev,
                              struct vlan_group *grp);
    void                (*vlan_rx_add_vid)(struct net_device *dev,
                              unsigned short vid);
    void                (*vlan_rx_kill_vid)(struct net_device *dev,
                              unsigned short vid);

    int                 (*hard_header_parse)(struct sk_buff *skb,
                              unsigned char *haddr);
    int                 (*neigh_setup)(struct net_device *dev, struct
neigh_parms *);
#ifdef CONFIG_NETPOLL
    struct netpoll_info *npinfo;
#endif
#ifdef CONFIG_NET_POLL_CONTROLLER
    void                    (*poll_controller)(struct net_device *dev);
#endif
```

The next field, `br_port`, is for implementing Layer 2 bridging.

```
struct net_bridge_port    *br_port;
```

This field, `divert`, is used by a `rt_netlink` packet diversion facility that allows user space processing of network packets.

```
#ifdef CONFIG_NET_DIVERT
    struct divert_blk  *divert;
#endif /* CONFIG_NET_DIVERT */
```

The next field, `class_dev`, contains device class information, including the class, net, and name. See `linux/include/linux/device.h` for more information

This file is part of the Linux source tree and is included on the companion CD-ROM.

```
    struct class_device class_dev;
}
```

NETWORK DEVICE INITIALIZATION

Network device initialization begins when the Linux kernel "discovers" a device of a certain type by calling a probe function looking for a match of a particular hardware interface with its associated driver.

After a match is discovered, the driver's specific initialization function is called. This function is generally typed __devinit or __init, both of which are defined in file `linux/include/linux/init.h`. When the network interface driver's initialization or probe function is called, the first thing it does is allocate the driver's private data structure, which also contains the generic `net_device` structure, covered previously. Next, it must set a few key fields in the structure, the first of which is the name field, which is used later to register the network interface device. Name is generally set to a string of characters that identifies the class of device. For example, in Ethernet devices, the name field begins with the string "eth". The last characters in the name field should be set to the format string %d. Later, when the device is registered, the formatting string is replaced with a number from 0 to 99. These initialization steps can be done in one of least three ways. The first method is generally used by drivers for non-Ethernet devices. These drivers set up the data structure directly in the driver's probe function by calling `kmalloc` to allocate the structure, calling `dev_alloc_name` to set up the name string, and then directly initializing the other device-specific fields in the `net_device` structure. See Figure 3.1 for an illustration of three initialization methods of the net device structure used by various network interface drivers.

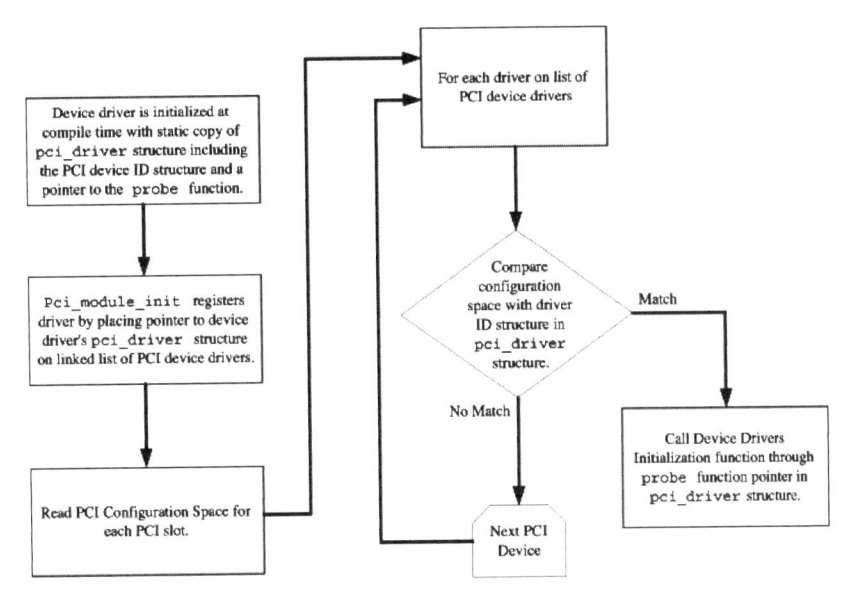

FIGURE 3.1 Network interface driver registration sequence.

Linux provides some generic device allocation and initialization functions for the convenience of writers of network interface drivers. Most of these are found in linux/net/net_init.c, except for some functions that are specific for Ethernet devices. For example, we will look at the initialization sequence for an Ethernet network interface device, shown in Figure 3.1. This sequence uses an allocation method provided specifically for Ethernet drivers. The function alloc_etherdev defined in linux/net/ethernet/eth.c and declared in file linux/include/linux/etherdevice.h, does both structure allocation and name string initialization. Under the covers, alloc_etherdev calls alloc_netdev and passes it a pointer to a setup function as the second argument. This function used to be ether_setup in earlier kernel versions. At this point, the function netdev_boot_setup actually saves any boot time settings in an instance of the netdev_boot_setup structure. Later, these settings are put into the net_device structure by calling

netdev_boot_setup_check.

At this point in the initialization sequence, the net_device structure is initialized with the name, the irq, base address, and bounds of the IO mapped memory.

However, for most devices, more initialization must be done before the network interface can be registered. Interrupt hardware must be set up, and any device-specific information is read from the device's registers and PCI configuration space if applicable. After this is complete, the initialization function sets up spin locks and some additional hardware-specific information. If these steps don't generate an error, the field `priv` is set to point back to the private part of the data structure, and buffers are allocated for transmit and receive space from memory that is accessible by DMA. Next, pointers to the driver's service routines are set in the `net_device` structure. The most important service routines to support are the `open`, `hard_start`, `stop`, `get_stats`, `set_multicast_list`, and `do_ioctl` functions. The network interface service routines are discussed in more detail later in this chapter. Next, the `features` field of the net device structure is filled in to indicate device abilities. Drivers for network interface devices that have hardware speed-up capabilities, such as the ability to calculate IP checksums, will be indicated in this field.

Initialization of the `net_device` Structure

Each network driver provides an initialization function, which is called after any module housekeeping and PCI device ID matching is complete. PCI device initialization is discussed in detail later. As we shall see, in the case of PCI network interface devices, the driver's initialization function is called by de-referencing the `probe` field in the `pci_driver` structure. The initialization function in each driver must allocate the `net_device` structure, which is used to connect the network interface driver with the network layer protocols. Typically, most drivers have unique hardware-specific data to maintain, so the driver will allocate a larger private structure, which in turn contains the `net_device` structure. For example, Ethernet drivers can call the function `alloc_etherdev`, declared in the file `etherdevice.h` and defined in `linux/net/ethernet/eth.c`. This function is provided by the Linux kernel as a support routine for network device structure allocation and initialization. Alternatively, as we discussed earlier, non-Ethernet device drivers may call `kmalloc` directly to allocate the data structure and then initialize it manually. For an example of Ethernet interface initialization, look at the following code example where we show the initialization function from the e100 Ethernet driver, called `e100_probe`, found in file `linux/drivers/net/e100.c`. It allocates the public dev structure and the driver's private data structure at the same time by calling `alloc_etherdev`, which sets the `priv` field in the `net_device` to point to an instance of struct `nic`, the driver's private structure. Next, the probe function sets the network service function entry points in the dev structure.

```
static int __devinit e100_probe(struct pci_dev *pdev, const struct
pci_device_id *ent)
```

```
    {
        struct net_device *netdev;
        struct nic *nic;
        int err;
```

The structure `nic` is declared in the top of the source file, linux/drivers/net/e100.c, and alloc_etherdev is one of several allocation functions provided for different classes of network devices. The argument to alloc_etherdev is the size of the private structure, but alloc_etherdev also allocates enough space for the net_device structure, too. It sets the priv field in the net_device structure to point to the private structure, struct nic.

```
        if(!(netdev = alloc_etherdev(sizeof(struct nic)))) {
            if(((1 << debug) - 1) & NETIF_MSG_PROBE)
                printk(KERN_ERR PFX "Etherdev alloc failed, abort.\n");
            return -ENOMEM;
        }
```

Here, we set pointers to the service functions into the net_device structure.

```
        netdev->open = e100_open;
        netdev->stop = e100_close;
        netdev->hard_start_xmit = e100_xmit_frame;
        netdev->get_stats = e100_get_stats;
        netdev->set_multicast_list = e100_set_multicast_list;
        netdev->set_mac_address = e100_set_mac_address;
        netdev->change_mtu = e100_change_mtu;
        netdev->do_ioctl = e100_do_ioctl;
        SET_ETHTOOL_OPS(netdev, &e100_ethtool_ops);
        netdev->tx_timeout = e100_tx_timeout;
        netdev->watchdog_timeo = E100_WATCHDOG_PERIOD;
        netdev->poll = e100_poll;
        netdev->weight = E100_NAPI_WEIGHT;
#ifdef CONFIG_NET_POLL_CONTROLLER
        netdev->poll_controller = e100_netpoll;
#endif
```

Here we set up pointers to the PCI device structure and prepare to enable the PCI interface. We must remember that this function is called when the PCI probe discovers a match in the PCI space.

```
        strcpy(netdev->name, pci_name(pdev));
```

```c
nic = netdev_priv(netdev);
nic->netdev = netdev;
nic->pdev = pdev;
nic->msg_enable = (1 << debug) - 1;
pci_set_drvdata(pdev, netdev);

if((err = pci_enable_device(pdev))) {
    DPRINTK(PROBE, ERR, "Cannot enable PCI device, aborting.\n");
    goto err_out_free_dev;
}

if(!(pci_resource_flags(pdev, 0) & IORESOURCE_MEM)) {
    DPRINTK(PROBE, ERR, "Cannot find proper PCI device "
        "base address, aborting.\n");
    err = -ENODEV;
    goto err_out_disable_pdev;
}

if((err = pci_request_regions(pdev, DRV_NAME))) {
    DPRINTK(PROBE, ERR, "Cannot obtain PCI resources, aborting.\n");
    goto err_out_disable_pdev;
}
if((err = pci_set_dma_mask(pdev, DMA_32BIT_MASK))) {
    DPRINTK(PROBE, ERR, "No usable DMA configuration, aborting.\n");
    goto err_out_free_res;
}

SET_MODULE_OWNER(netdev);
SET_NETDEV_DEV(netdev, &pdev->dev);
```

This is where we map our PCI space so our device registers are accessible.

```c
nic->csr = ioremap(pci_resource_start(pdev, 0), sizeof(struct csr));
if(!nic->csr) {
    DPRINTK(PROBE, ERR, "Cannot map device registers, aborting.\n");
    err = -ENOMEM;
    goto err_out_free_res;
}

if(ent->driver_data)
    nic->flags |= ich;
else
    nic->flags &= ~ich;

e100_get_defaults(nic);
```

These spinlocks must be initialized before the hardware is turned on when concurrent operations start

```
spin_lock_init(&nic->cb_lock);
spin_lock_init(&nic->cmd_lock);
spin_lock_init(&nic->mdio_lock);
```

`pci_set_master` sets up pci bus mastering, essential for any DMA device. However, first we reset our own hardware to make sure that we are in an initialized state and the interrupt handler is registered before turning on bus mastering.

```
e100_hw_reset(nic);

pci_set_master(pdev);
```

Here we initialize timers and watchdogs.

```
init_timer(&nic->watchdog);
nic->watchdog.function = e100_watchdog;
nic->watchdog.data = (unsigned long)nic;
init_timer(&nic->blink_timer);
nic->blink_timer.function = e100_blink_led;
nic->blink_timer.data = (unsigned long)nic;

INIT_WORK(&nic->tx_timeout_task,
    (void (*)(void *))e100_tx_timeout_task, netdev);
```

We allocate our local pci accessible space. This function mostly allocates the memory for DMA, but it also initializes some fields in the private data structure, `nic`.

```
if((err = e100_alloc(nic))) {
    DPRINTK(PROBE, ERR, "Cannot alloc driver memory, aborting.\n");
    goto err_out_iounmap;
}
```

Now, we load the device-specific `eeprom` and initialize our PHY.

```
if((err = e100_eeprom_load(nic)))
    goto err_out_free;

e100_phy_init(nic);
```

```
memcpy(netdev->dev_addr, nic->eeprom, ETH_ALEN);
memcpy(netdev->perm_addr, nic->eeprom, ETH_ALEN);
if(!is_valid_ether_addr(netdev->perm_addr)) {
    DPRINTK(PROBE, ERR, "Invalid MAC address from "
        "EEPROM, aborting.\n");
    err = -EAGAIN;
    goto err_out_free;
}
```

Check whether `wol` is enabled on the EEPROM. `wol` is the automatic wakeup facility used with many Ethernet devices.

```
if((nic->mac >= mac_82558_D101_A4) &&
    (nic->eeprom[eeprom_id] & eeprom_id_wol))
    nic->flags |= wol_magic;

/* ack any pending wake events, disable PME */
err = pci_enable_wake(pdev, 0, 0);
if (err)
    DPRINTK(PROBE, ERR, "Error clearing wake event\n");
```

This is where the base string is set for the device name. Later, as devices are discovered and initialized at boot time, the `%d` will be replaced with the device instance number.

```
strcpy(netdev->name, "eth%d");
```

After the `net_device` structure is initialized, we can register it. This is where the network interface driver is hooked to the TCP/IP stack. This registration function and other utility functions for network interface registration are discussed later in this chapter.

```
if((err = register_netdev(netdev))) {
    DPRINTK(PROBE, ERR, "Cannot register net device, aborting.\n");
    goto err_out_free;
}

DPRINTK(PROBE, INFO, "addr 0x%lx, irq %d, "
    "MAC addr %02X:%02X:%02X:%02X:%02X:%02X\n",
    pci_resource_start(pdev, 0), pdev->irq,
    netdev->dev_addr[0], netdev->dev_addr[1], netdev->dev_addr[2],
    netdev->dev_addr[3], netdev->dev_addr[4], netdev->dev_addr[5]);

return 0;
```

Next, we have various returns. If things didn't work, we make sure to exit cleanly.

```
err_out_free:
    e100_free(nic);
err_out_iounmap:
    iounmap(nic->csr);
err_out_free_res:
    pci_release_regions(pdev);
err_out_disable_pdev:
    pci_disable_device(pdev);
err_out_free_dev:
    pci_set_drvdata(pdev, NULL);
    free_netdev(netdev);
    return err;
}
```

Device Discovery and Dynamic Network Interface Driver Initialization

We don't attempt to explain every type of hardware supported by the Linux operating system. However, it is useful to see how a network interface driver is automatically configured and how a device is matched by PCI ID to the correct driver. We have glimpsed a little of that in our discussion of the e100_probe function earlier. We use a PCI device as an example because most common network interface devices including Ethernet chips are implemented as PCI devices. This section explains what happens for one method of discovering a PCI device. We examine how a PCI device is matched and the driver's initialization function is called. In general, a device is detected on the PCI bus by matching the vendor and device IDs in the PCI configuration space and on the PCI card with an internally stored value in the network device driver. The main match is on the PCI device ID and vendor codes, both of which are 16-bit numbers, but the PCI vendor and class can be matched, as well.

Recent versions of the Linux 2.6 kernel have added generic driver and bus handling in a way that is more friendly to SMP. These new structures clean up unloading modules, clean up bus structures, and generalize bus registration capabilities. Most of these capabilities are not specific to network interface drivers in that they are generic to all Linux device drivers. We will touch on some of these structures here but only to the extent necessary to explain what happens when our network interface driver is loaded and initialized.

For example, we will use the IDs for one of the Intel Ethernet chips handled by the e100 driver. These values are shown in Table 3.3. We will describe the things that happen when a device is matched. Figure 3.2 shows a typical initialization sequence for a network interface driver module for a PCI hardware device.

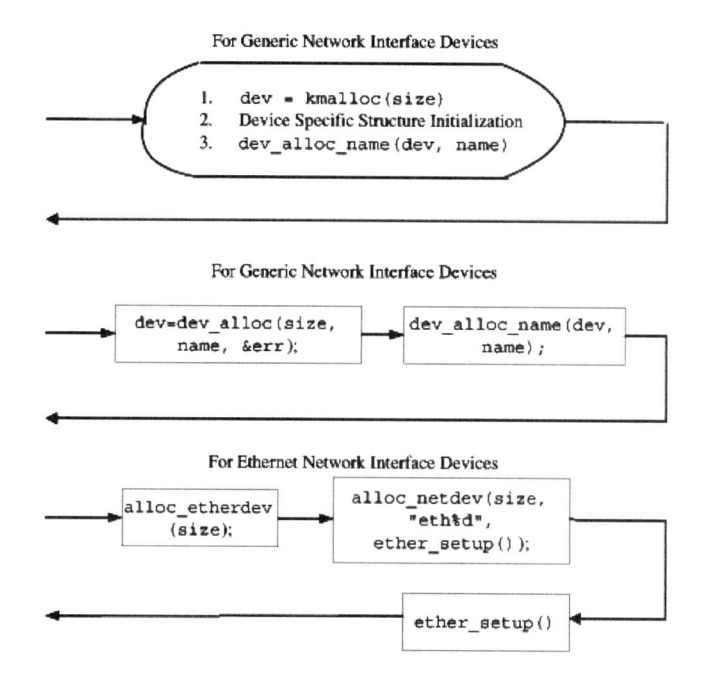

FIGURE 3.2 PCI device driver initialization sequence.

TABLE 3.3 PCI Device ID Structure for an Ethernet Chip

Field	Purpose	Example	Example Description
vendor	Vendor ID	0x8086	Intel
device	Device ID	0x1229	Intel 82556 Ethernet chip
subvendor	Optional Vendor ID	0xffff	PCI_ANY_ID
subdevice	Optional Device ID	0xffff	PCI_ANY_ID
class	Class ID	0x0	
class_mask	Class mask	0x0	

Let's begin with the module initialization before the hardware is discovered. Each network driver, implemented as a module, must contain a driver-specific module initialization function, which is called when the kernel loads the network driver module either at boot time or later. For example, we will be using the e100 Ethernet driver. We will look at the module initialization function e100_init_module in the file linux/drivers/net/e100/e100_main.c. To begin the initialization process, if the e100 driver is statically linked into the kernel, e100_init_module is called by the kernel. However, if the driver is a module, this function is called when the insmod(8) or modprobe(8) utilities are run to install the module. In our example, the driver name is initialized to "e100". id_table is initialized to e100_id_table, and probe to the function e100_probe. e100_probe is the function that actually does the PCI device match, and it is discussed in detail earlier in this chapter.

```
static int __init e100_init_module(void)
{
    int ret;
```

The first thing we do is call the generic function, pci_module_init, which is defined as pci_register_driver, and is the function that does most of the actual work of registering the PCI device.

```
    ret = pci_module_init(&e100_driver);
        if(((1 << debug) - 1) & NETIF_MSG_DRV) {
                printk(KERN_INFO PFX "%s, %s\n", DRV_DESCRIPTION,
                    DRV_VERSION);
                printk(KERN_INFO PFX "%s\n", DRV_COPYRIGHT);
        }
    return ret;
}
```

pci_register_driver is defined in linux/include/linux/pci.h. It places a pointer to this particular PCI driver on a linked list of PCI drivers, and this is how the device driver registers both the PCI device ID and the vendor code with the Linux kernel. Later, the ID and vendor are matched when a PCI device is discovered or plugged in (if it is hot-pluggable).

```
static inline int pci_register_driver(struct pci_driver *driver)
{
    return __pci_register_driver(driver, THIS_MODULE);
}
```

As we can see, the only thing this function does is call __pci_register_driver, defined in the file linux/drivers/pci/pci_driver.c to register the driver, initialize the common fields in the pci_driver structure, and add the driver to the list of registered drivers. __pci_register_driver returns the number of PCI devices that are claimed by the driver during registration, and even if its function returns a zero, the driver remains registered.

```
pci_register_driver(struct pci_driver *drv)
{
    int error;
```

We initialize the common fields in the `pci_driver` structure including the driver name string and bus type, which is PCI, of course.

```
drv->driver.name = drv->name;
drv->driver.bus = &pci_bus_type;
```

Just in case, the driver didn't set the PCI shutdown function, we do it here. PCI driver writers should use the generic PCI shutdown function `pci_device_shutdown`.

```
if (!drv->driver.shutdown)
    drv->driver.shutdown = pci_device_shutdown;
else
    printk(KERN_WARNING "Warning: PCI driver %s has a struct "
        "device_driver shutdown method, please update!\n",
        drv->name);
drv->driver.owner = owner;
drv->driver.kobj.ktype = &pci_driver_kobj_type;
spin_lock_init(&drv->dynids.lock);
INIT_LIST_HEAD(&drv->dynids.list);
```

Most of the work of actual driver registration is generic and not specific to PCI bus. Therefore, we call `driver_register` defined in `drivers/base/driver_register.c` to do the generic work of device registration, such as setting the probe function.

```
    error = driver_register(&drv->driver);
    if (!error)
        error = pci_create_newid_file(drv);
    return error;
}
```

Next, we will take a quick look at the function `driver_register`, which does some of the work of driver registration that is not specific to PCI bus. This function can be found in file `linux/drivers/base/driver.c`.

```
int driver_register(struct device_driver * drv)
{
    if ((drv->bus->probe && drv->probe) ||
        (drv->bus->remove && drv->remove) ||
        (drv->bus->shutdown && drv->shutdown)) {
```

```
        printk(KERN_WARNING "Driver '%s' needs updating - please use
        bus_type methods\n", drv->name);
    }
```

Now, we update the list of kernel resources.

```
    klist_init(&drv->klist_devices, klist_devices_get,
    klist_devices_put);
```

When a driver is de-instantiated, unloaded is called. init_completion and other functions and structures for handling generic device and resource completion is defined in the file linux/include/linux/completion.h.

```
    init_completion(&drv->unloaded);
```

The function bus_add_driver, in file linux/drivers/base/bus.c is called to do most of the heavy lifting because at this point we are dealing with bus-specific structures.

```
    return bus_add_driver(drv);
}
```

Now, let's take a close look at the PCI data structure, pci_driver. Since the first edition of this book, much of the capabilities previously associated with PCI have been generalized for cleaner and more integrated support of other busses. Therefore, the pci_driver structure mostly contains pointers to service functions specific to PCI. The ID matching tables that are specific to the PCI probing are defined in this data structure. Also, this is where the probe function is defined. We will recall that the probe function for our sample driver, e100 pointed to the function e100_probe, which is explained earlier in this chapter. A driver's probe function is called when a nic is newly discovered or in a hotplug enabled system when the nic is inserted.

```
    struct pci_driver {
        struct list_head node;
```

name is the driver name string. id_table is the pointer to the PCI configuration space information and must not be NULL for the probe function to be called. One example of the id_table entry for one of the Ethernet chips supported by our e100 driver is shown in Figure 3.2. Probe points to the function that is called when a matching device is discovered or, if the device is hot-pluggable, when it is inserted. Remove must not be NULL for hot-plug devices.

```
char *name;
const struct pci_device_id *id_table;
int    (*probe)  (struct pci_dev *dev, const struct pci_device_id *id);
```

The next function, remove, is called when a hot-swap capable device is removed from the PCI bus. Suspend is called when a device is suspended, and resume is called when a device is awakened.

```
void (*remove) (struct pci_dev *dev);
int  (*suspend) (struct pci_dev *dev, pm_message_t state);
int  (*resume) (struct pci_dev *dev);
```

The next field, enable_wake, points to the function that enables or disables the wake_up event.

```
int (*enable_wake) (struct pci_dev *dev, pci_power_t state,
int enable);
void (*shutdown) (struct pci_dev *dev);

struct pci_error_handlers *err_handler;
struct device_driver  driver;
struct pci_dynids dynids;
};
```

In most drivers, the pci_driver structure is initialized as a static structure. Here we show that the e100 module initializes each of the fields in the pci_driver structure. This initialization code can be found in the file linux/drivers/net/e100.c.

```
MODULE_DEVICE_TABLE(pci, e100_id_table);
static struct pci_driver e100_driver = {
    name:              "e100",
    id_table:          e100_id_table,
```

We can see that the probe field is initialized to e100_probe, which is called when the device is discovered or plugged in (if it is hot-pluggable).

```
    .probe =                e100_probe
    .remove =               __devexit_p(e100_remove)
#ifdef CONFIG_PM
    .suspend =              e100_suspend,
    .resume =               e100_resume,
#endif
    .shutdown =             e100_shutdown,
};
```

Network Interface Registration

After all the initialization of the net device structure and the associated private data structure is complete, the driver can be registered as a networking device. Network device registration consists of putting the driver's net device structure on a linked list. The file linux/net/core/dev.c provides utility functions to do the registration and perform other tasks. Most of the functions involved in network device registration use the name field in the net_device structure. This is why driver writers should use the dev_alloc_name function to ensure that the name field is formatted properly. The list of net devices is protected by the netlink mutex locking and unlocking functions, rtnl_lock and rtnl_unlock. The list of devices should not be manipulated without locking. If the locks are not used, it is possible for the device list to become corrupted or for two devices to try to register in parallel and be assigned the same name. The device interface utility functions for manipulating the list of network devices are shown later in this section. Each function we describe takes a mutex lock so it is safe to call. There are safe and unsafe versions of each of these functions. The unsafe ones in linux/net/core/dev.c (in most cases) can be used, but only if the caller takes the netlink semaphore. The unsafe versions generally have the same name but proceeded by a double underscore with the exception of the register function, which has an unsafe version called register_netdevice. Also, for reference, the network interface driver registration sequence was shown earlier in this chapter in Figure 3.1.

To perform the last step of network interface registration, the driver's initialization function calls register_netdev, also in the file linux/net/core/dev.c.

```
int register_netdev(struct net_device *dev)
{
    int     err;
```

We lock by taking the netlink semaphore.

```
    rtnl_lock();
```

dev_alloc_name is called to substitute the formatting string, %d, in the device name with a number. The number selected is the total number of devices registered so far for the particular type supported by this driver minus one. For example, the first Ethernet device will be called eth0; the second one will be eth1; and so on.

```
    if (strchr(dev->name, '%')) {
        err = dev_alloc_name(dev, dev->name);
        if (err < 0)
            goto out;
    }
```

This is a backward-compatibility hook for implicit allocation of old Ethernet devices and may be deprecated. By the time this function is called, the name field in the `net_device` structure should be initialized to the base name plus the formatting character.

```
if (dev->name[0]==0 || dev->name[0]==' ')
{
    err = dev_alloc_name(dev, "eth%d");
    if (err < 0)
        goto out;
}
```

We call `register_netdevice` to do the heavy lifting associated with network interface registration. If the caller knows that the device name is already set up properly, `register_netdevice` can be called directly, but only if the `netlink` semaphore is taken first.

```
err = register_netdevice(dev);
out:
```

Since this function is the safe version, we must unlock before returning.

```
    rtnl_unlock();
    return err;
}
```

Linux provides a number of multiple queuing disciplines and class-based scheduling methods for drivers that would benefit from a performance increase. These are used in conjunction with traffic shaping. See Chapter 5 for a detailed discussion on the queue disciplines and packet scheduling mechanisms. The `netlink` layer is an internal message-based communication facility and is discussed in Chapter 4, "Linux Sockets." It allows application programs to use the socket API to set and get information about each of the attached protocols. Chapter 4 includes a discussion of how to use the `netlink` type sockets to control and configure the protocols from the application layer. Next, the default packet scheduler and queue disciplines are set for this device by calling `dev_init_scheduler` declared in the file `linux/net/sch_generic.h` and defined in `linux/net/sched/sch_generic.c`. The function `dev_init_scheduler` sets the `qdisc` field of the net device structure to point to the default queue discipline, `noop_qdisc`. A driver can change the queue discipline later when the driver's `open` function is called, but in the meantime, the `qdisc` and `qdisc_sleeping` fields are set to point to this default queuing discipline when the net device structure is initialized.

> *Theoretically, although this isn't done very often, the packet scheduler and queue disciplines could be changed at any time as long as the driver is offline and the appropriate lock mutexes are taken.*

Network Device Registration Utility Functions

Earlier in this chapter when we discussed the initialization code for a network interface, we saw how there are a series of utility functions for network device registration. In this section, we will dive into some of the more significant of these functions in more detail. All of the functions in this section are declared in the file linux/include/linux/netdevice.h. All of the functions in this section are also included in the Linux source tree found on the companion CD-ROM.

dev_get_by_name

The first function, dev_get_by_name, finds a device by matching the device name string against all the members in the list of network interface drivers. It can be called from any context because it does its own locking. It returns a pointer to a net_device based on the string name. The reference count field in net_device is incremented before the function returns.

```
struct net_device *dev_get_by_name(const char *name);
```

register_netdev and *register_netdevice*

```
int        register_netdev(struct net_device *dev);
```

register_netdev registers a network interface device driver. This version of the function acquires the lock. The function register_netdevice can also be used, but it requires the caller to hold the rtnl lock.

```
int        register_netdevice(struct net_device *dev);
```

An important responsibility of register_netdevice is to place the net device structure on the list of network device drivers maintained in the Linux kernel. Before doing this, it checks a global variable called dev_boot_phase, set at compile time to indicate that no devices are initialized too soon. Next, it initializes the device's queue_lock and xmit_lock fields. If the network interface driver has an init function, that function is called to complete driver and device initialization.

> *For more details about the queuing layer, see Chapter 5.*

A unique ifindex is assigned to the device, and this number is set in the ifindex field of the netdevice. Next, the state field is set to __LINK_STATE_PRESENT, which indicates that the device is present and ready to be scheduled.

unregister_netdev and unregister_netdevice

These two functions, unregister_netdev and unregister_netdevice, remove the device, dev, from the list of devices. The first of these functions, unregister_netdev, is the safe version. In this routine, we take the rt_netlink semaphore and then call the internal unsafe version, unregister_netdevice.

```
int unregister_netdevice(struct net_device *dev)
{
    struct net_device *d, **dp;

    BUG_ON(dev_boot_phase);
    ASSERT_RTNL();
```

We must protect against being called with a device that has never been registered by checking the registration state, the reg_state field in the net_device structure.

```
if (dev->reg_state == NETREG_UNINITIALIZED) {
    printk(KERN_DEBUG "unregister_netdevice: device %s/%p never "
        "was registered\n", dev->name, dev);
    return -ENODEV;
}

BUG_ON(dev->reg_state != NETREG_REGISTERED);
```

Next, we check for IFF_UP in the flags of the network device structure to see whether the device is running. If the device is running, we call the network interface generic function, dev_close to stop the device.

```
if (dev->flags & IFF_UP)
    dev_close(dev);
```

Next, we remove the pointer to the net_device structure from the linked list of devices and shut down the device's queues for the particular queuing discipline in effect by calling dev_shutdown.

```
for (dp = &dev_base; (d = *dp) != NULL; dp = &d->next) {
    if (d == dev) {
        write_lock_bh(&dev_base_lock);
        hlist_del(&dev->name_hlist);
```

```
                hlist_del(&dev->index_hlist);
                if (dev_tail == &dev->next)
                    dev_tail = dp;
                *dp = d->next;
                write_unlock_bh(&dev_base_lock);
                break;
            }
        }
        if (!d) {
            printk(KERN_ERR "unregister net_device: '%s' not found\n",
                   dev->name);
            return -ENODEV;
        }
        dev->reg_state = NETREG_UNREGISTERING;
```

The list of network interface devices is on an RCU list, so packet processing routines don't have to acquire a lock. The function synchronize_net is called to do any synchronization and locking.

```
        synchronize_net();
        dev_shutdown(dev);
```

We send a notification message to any interested protocols that this device is about to be destroyed by calling the function notifier_call_chain, which is discussed later in this chapter.

We flush the list of multicast addresses from the device.

```
        dev_mc_discard(dev);
            if (dev->uninit)
                dev->uninit(dev);
```

This is a check of the notifier chain. It makes sure that our driver has been detached from the master device in the notifier group. The function free_divert_blk has to do with the netlink divert facility, which allows packets to be diverted into user space for processing outside of the kernel.

> **NOTE** *We will discuss this* netlink *facility and other aspects of* netlink *and* rtnetlink *in Chapter 5.*

```
        BUG_TRAP(!dev->master);

            free_divert_blk(dev);
```

In Linux 2.6, device registration is asynchronous. We call `net_set_todo` because work on device registration and unregistration can be deferred if a device is busy.

```
net_set_todo(dev);
synchronize_net();
```

Finally, we check the reference count in the `refcnt` field of the `net_device` structure by calling `dev_put`. If it is one or higher, a reference to the device must be active, and, therefore, it is okay to decrement the reference count.

```
dev_put(dev);
    return 0;
}
```

To complete the discussion on network device registration, we will discuss some functions that Linux provides for the convenience of network interface driver writers. We saw how some of these functions are used in our discussion of the `e100` sample driver earlier in this chapter.

Functions for Searching and Retrieving Devices

In this section, we will list a few functions Linux provides to retrieve a device. Each of these functions returns a `net_device` structure based on various criteria such as type, hardware address, `flags`, or `ifindex`.

```
struct net_device      *dev_getbyhwaddr(unsigned short type,
                                        char *hwaddr);
struct net_device      *__dev_getfirstbyhwtype(unsigned short type);
struct net_device      *dev_getfirstbyhwtype(unsigned short type);
struct net_device      *dev_get_by_flags(unsigned short flags,
                                         unsigned short mask);
struct net_device      *__dev_get_by_flags(unsigned short flags,
struct net_device      *dev_get_by_index(int ifindex);
```

Functions for Allocating `net_device` *Structure or* `name` *String.*

Several functions exist for allocation of a device structure. There are also functions that allocate a device name string only. We will discuss some of these functions in this section. The first function, `dev_alloc_name`, checks for a valid format in `name`. It appends a digit 1 to 99 to the name and returns the number appended to the name. `name` should be a string followed by the formatting characters, %d.

```
int dev_alloc_name(struct net_device *dev, const char *name);
```

The next function, `alloc_etherdev`, allocates a complete `net_device` structure specifically for an Ethernet device.

```
struct net_device *alloc_etherdev(int sizeof_priv);
```

The next function in this group, `alloc_netdev`, is generally not called directly. Instead, it is usually called by one of the functions that are specific to the device type, such as `alloc_etherdev`. Alloc_netdev allocates the private data area and the net device structure. It also initializes the name field in the `net_device` structure to the base string for the name such as "eth".

```
struct net_device *alloc_netdev(int sizeof_priv, const char *mask,
                                void(*setup)(struct net_device *));
```

Finally, we look at the function, `netdev_boot_setup`, provided to all driver writers, not just writers of network interface drivers. This function is particularly useful for setting fields in the `net_device` structure from boot time parameters. This allows some device and driver initialization from `grub(8)` or firmware boot loaders such as redboot.

```
int __init netdev_boot_setup(char *str);
```

LINUX NETWORK INTERFACE DRIVER FACILITIES

Linux provides some other facilities for writers of network interface drivers. These facilities include a set of generic entry points for network interface drivers called network interface service functions. As discussed earlier in this chapter, the service functions are set in the dev structure during driver initialization. Each of the service functions is associated with generic versions implemented in the file `linux/net/core/dev.c` but can be overridden by functions specific to a particular network interface driver. They can also be overwritten by a function for a particular network interface device type such as Ethernet. The service functions are not called directly by application code or by any protocols in the TCP/IP suite. Instead, they are called by de-referencing the corresponding pointers in the net device structure.

Network Interface Driver State Flags

Most of the functions affect the state of the network interface, whether it is up, down, or in some other state. The state is maintained in the flags field in the net device structure, and most of the interface service functions will change the flags. The values for the network interface flags are shown in Table 3.4.

TABLE 3.4 Network Interface Flags

Flag	Value	Purpose
IFF_UP	0x1	The interface is up.
IFF_BROADCAST	0x2	The broadcast address is valid.
IFF_DEBUG	0x4	Turns on debugging.
IFF_LOOPBACK	0x8	The interface is a loopback interface.
IFF_POINTOPOINT	0x10	Interface is a point-to-point link.
IFF_NOTRAILERS	0x20	Avoid the use of trailers.
IFF_RUNNING	0x40	The interface is running and resources allocated.
IFF_NOARP	0x80	The ARP protocol is not supported on this interface.
IFF_PROMISC	0x100	The interface is in promiscuous mode. It receives all packets.
IFF_ALLMULTI	0x200	The interface receives all multicast packets.
IFF_MASTER	0x400	Master of a load balancer.
IFF_SLAVE	0x800	Slave of a load balancer.
IFF_MULTICAST	0x1000	The interface supports multicast.
IFF_VOLATILE	(IFF_LOOPBACK| IFF_POINTOPOINT| IFF_BROADCAST| IFF_MASTER| IFF_SLAVE| IFF_RUNNING)	
IFF_PORTSEL	0x2000	Media type can be set on this interface.
IFF_AUTOMEDIA	0x4000	The auto media select is active.
IFF_DYNAMIC	0x8000	Interface is a dial-up device with changing addresses.

Network Interface Driver Service Functions

During driver initialization, the entry points are set to generic functions or to NULL. In most cases driver writers can use generic functions. However, in some cases a driver writer may want to set one or more entry points to functions defined with her driver. In this section, we discuss the specific functions defined within a driver. We also discuss the associated generic functions provided by Linux to see what actually happens when the function is called. These generic functions are important because much of the work that actually glues the driver to the TCP/IP stack is done in the generic function.

Common Network Interface Service Functions

In this section, the more common network interface service functions are described. The functions described in this section must be implemented by all device drivers.

open and dev_open

```
int (*open) (struct net_device *dev);
```

The driver's specific open function is called by the generic dev_open function in linux/net/core/dev.c so we will look at dev_open in more detail.

```
int dev_open(struct net_device *dev)
```

First, dev_open checks to see whether the device has already been activated by checking for IFF_UP in the flags field of the net_device structure and if the driver is already up, we simply return a zero. Next, it checks to see wehther the physical device is present by calling netif_device_present, which checks the link state bits in the state field of the network device structure. If all this succeeds, dev_open calls the driver through the open field in the net_device structure.

```
if (dev->flags & IFF_UP)
    return 0;
if (!netif_device_present(dev))
    return -ENODEV;
```

Most drivers use the open function to initialize their internal data structures prior to accepting and transmitting packets. These structures may include the internal queues, watchdog timers, and lists of internal buffers. Next, the driver generally starts up the receive queue by calling netif_start_queue, defined in linux/include/linux/netdevice.h, which starts the queue by clearing the __LINK_STATE_XOFF in the state field of the net_device structure.

> **NOTE** *The states are listed in Table 3.1 and are used by the queuing layer to control the transmit queues for the device. Later in this chapter, we will show how the packet queuing layer works in more detail. As discussed earlier in this chapter, right up to the point where the queuing is started, the driver can change the device's queuing discipline. Chapter 5 has more detail about Linux's capability to work with multiple queuing disciplines for packet transmission queues.*

After the driver's `open` returns, `dev_open` does a little bit more housekeeping. If the driver's `open` function encounters an error, `dev_open` returns `ENODEV` right away. If everything is okay, the flags field is set to `IFF_UP`, and the state field is set to `LINK_STATE_START` to indicate that the network link is active and ready to receive packets.

```
set_bit(__LINK_STATE_START, &dev->state);
if (dev->open) {
    ret = dev->open(dev);
    if (ret)
        clear_bit(__LINK_STATE_START, &dev->state);
}
if (!ret) {
    dev->flags |= IFF_UP;
```

Next, `dev_open` calls the `dev_mc_upload` to set up the list of multicast addresses for this device. Finally, `dev_open` calls `dev_activate`, defined in file `linux/net/sched/sch_generic.c`, which sets up a default queuing discipline for the device, typically `pfifo_fast` for hardware devices and `none` for pseudo- or software devices.

```
    dev_mc_upload(dev);

    dev_activate(dev);
    notifier_call_chain(&netdev_chain, NETDEV_UP, dev);
}
return ret;
}
```

set_multicast_list

The `set_multicast_list` driver service function is specific to the network interface driver. It pertains to drivers that have link layer multicast support. If needed, the driver would provide this function to allow the list of multicast addresses to be downloaded directly into the driver's memory. `set_multicast_list` is not used for most network interface drivers such as Ethernet, because for TCP/IP, multicast is handled at the IP layer, not in the link layer.

```
void    (*set_multicast_list)(struct net_device *dev);
```

hard_start_xmit

The `hard_start_xmit` network interface service function starts the transmission of an individual packet or queue of packets.

```
int     (*hard_start_xmit) (struct sk_buff *skb, struct net_device
                             *dev);
```

This function is called from the network queuing layer when a packet is ready for transmission. Later in this chapter, we provide more information on the packet queuing layer. The first thing the driver must do in `hard_start_xmit` is ensure that hardware resources are available for transmitting the packet and that a sufficient number of buffers are available. If buffers are available, it enables transmission for the hardware's PHY chip. For a typical Ethernet driver, we would simply enable the Ethernet chip for transmission and return. If no hardware buffers are available, the packet is re-queued. If the driver is a pseudo-driver, it would have no transmission hardware and no separate transmission queue within the driver, so the buffer can be removed from the queue for processing immediately. If the packet can't be transmitted for some reason, the queuing layer is informed by calling `netif_stop_queue`.

uninit

The `uninit` network interface service function is responsible for any device-specific cleanup when the device is unregistered.

```
void    (*uninit)(struct net_device *dev);
```

`Uninit` is called from the `unregister_netdevice` function in `linux/net/core/dev.c`, covered earlier. Generally, only pseudo-device drivers that have protocol functionality will implement this function. In our example, the e100 driver, we do not implement `uninit`; generally, Ethernet or similar device drivers will not need to provide this network service function. In addition, if the device driver is a new style device that implements the destructor service function, it could be relied on to do some of the cleanup.

stop

The `stop` network interface service function could be thought of as the `close` function for the device and is called when the kernel wants to tell the driver to terminate packet transmission.

```
int (*stop)(struct net_device *dev);
```

In our example, the e100 driver, the `stop` service function is set to `e100_close`. It turns off transmission interrupts (if applicable) and cleans up any open internal transmission buffers. An internal `close` flag (in the private part of the driver's data structure) is used in many drivers to keep track of its open or closed state. Generally, this function will check to see whether the driver is up by checking the IFF_UP flag in the flags field of net_device. If so, the queuing layer is told to stop queuing packets by calling netif_stop_queue.

change_mtu

The change_mtu network interface service function is to change the Maximum Transmission Unit (MTU) of a device.

```
int (*change_mtu)(struct net_device *dev, int new_mtu);
```

Since the MTU is generally fixed for a particular device type, this function is rarely used. However, in some circumstances, such as when working with VLAN, network administrators may want to tweak the MTU of a network interface device. As is the case of several of the calls covered in this section, it is not necessary that this field is initialized in net_device driver's initialization function.

get_stats

get_stats returns a pointer to the network device statistics.

```
struct net_device_stats* (*get_stats)(struct net_device *dev);
```

Generally, network interface drivers will keep the network device statistics in the private part of the network interface driver's data structure, so this function is provided to retrieve them. The net_device_stats structure is defined in file linux/include/linux/netdevice.h. This structure contains counters for the number of packets received and transmitted, the number of bytes received and transmitted, the number of dropped packets, and other statistics.

do_ioctl

do_ioctl implements any device-specific socket IO control (ioctl) functions.

```
int (*do_ioctl)(struct net_device *dev, struct ifreq *ifr, int cmd);
```

Not all network interface drivers will implement do_ioctl. In most cases, socket-layer ioctl calls are handled by the generic device layer function, dev_ioctl in linux/net/core/dev.c. When dev_ioctl can't handle the request and the do_ioctl service function entry is defined for the specific device, the driver's do_ioctl entry point is called. It is not required that the network interface driver initialize this function pointer. The socket IO controls are defined in the file linux/include/linux/sockios.h.

destructor

The destructor isn't technically a service function.

```
void (*destructor)(struct net_device *dev);
```

We include it in this section because as is the case with the service functions, destructor is an entry point in the driver called through the net_device structure as defined in linux/include/linux/net_device.h. destructor does any final cleanup, including de-allocating the net_device structure. Not all network interface drivers need to implement this function. In many cases, the destructor field of net_device points to free_netdev defined in linux/net/core/dev.c.

RECEIVING PACKETS

The first step in packet processing occurs when the device responds to an interrupt from the network interface hardware, and this begins a complex chain of events. With Ethernet drivers including our example driver, e100, after DMA of an incoming packet is complete, the network interface driver's interrupt handler is called. It is in the interrupt handler that we first detect the cause of the interrupt. We determine whether the interrupt is valid, and if so, whether it is a transmit or a receive interrupt. If we detect a receive interrupt, we know that a received packet is available for processing so we can begin to perform the steps necessary for packet reception. One of the first things we must do is gather the buffer containing the raw received packet into a socket buffer known in Linux as a socket buffer (sk_buf). Most efficient drivers for real hardware will avoid copying the data at this step, but instead rely on the hardware DMA engine to move the data. In Linux, the socket buffers, despite the confusing name, are the containers for containing network data packets, and they can be set up to point directly to the DMA space. Chapter 6 covers socket buffers in detail. Generally, in the network interface driver, we maintain a list of sk_buffs in our private data structure sometimes called struct nic. When the interrupt indicates that input DMA is complete, we can place the socket buffer containing the new packet on a queue of packets ready for processing by the higher level protocol's input function.

Network Queuing Layer

For efficiency, we generally want network interface drivers to return from the interrupt as soon as possible. While we are processing an interrupt, all other processes are suspended; therefore, we want to do as little as possible while we are in the interrupt service routine. Typically, we queue up the packet for further processing in the `softirq` context to offload as much processing as possible from the interrupt service routine. Table 3.5 shows functions used to control the device state shown earlier in Table 3.1. Each of these inline functions are used by network interface drives to control the queues of input packets. Most of these functions are defined as inlines in the file `linux/include/linux/netdevice.h`.

TABLE 3.5 Network Queuing Layer Functions

Function	Arguments	Returns	Purpose
netif_start_queue	struct net_device *	void	Starts the queue.
netif_receive_skb	struct sk_buff *	int	Packet receive function. Netif_receive_skb is called in the case of congestion to try to process backlog.
netif_schedule	struct net_device *	void	This function schedules output queue processing.
netif_wake_queue	struct net_device *	void	Restarts transmission.
netif_stop_queue	struct net_device *	void	Turns off transmission of output queue.
netif_queue_stopped	struct net_device *	int	Checks state of transmission link to see whether transmission is turned off.
netif_running	struct net_device *	int	Checks to see if transmission is in the start state.

In most network interface drivers, the interrupt handler is where the first processing is done when a packet is received. Typically, it does some internal hardware management for mapping and unmapping device space, maintaining device state, setting up for the next DMA transfer, and ensuring that a sufficient number of socket buffers are available for subsequent DMA transfers. When these internal procedures are complete, the interrupt handler sets the packet type in the socket buffer by setting the protocol field to the type in the Ethernet packet header. It also adjusts the socket buffer to make sure that there is sufficient tail room for the packet size by calling `skb_put`. Refer to Chapter 6 for a description of `skb_put` and the other socket buffer utility functions. The `netif_rx` function declared in file `linux/include/linux/netdevice.h` is called by the ISR to invoke the input side of packet processing and queue up the packet for processing by the packet receive softirq, NET_RX_SOFTIRQ.

Chapter 5 includes a detailed description of the packet queuing layer and the softirq capability. The netif_rx function returns a value indicating the amount of network congestion detected by the queuing layer or whether the packet was dropped altogether. Table 3.6 shows the return values for netif_rx.

TABLE 3.6 Queuing Layer netif_rx Return Values

NET_RX_SUCCESS	No congestion
NET_RX_CN_LOW	Low congestion
NET_RX_CN_MOD	Moderate congestion
NET_RX_CN_HIGH	High congestion
NET_RX_DROP	Packet was dropped

Network Queueing Layer Functions

In much of this book, we make a point of describing how network interface drivers are not necessarily associated with any hardware. In this section, we will look at various functions used by drivers' IRQs and by pseudo-drivers to queue packets for further processing.

netif_rx_ni

In light of this fact that not all drivers have IRQs, it is interesting to take a close look at netif_rx_ni defined in file linux/include/linux/netdevice.h and implemented in linux/net/core/dev.c. This function is provided to queue up input packets from a non-interrupt context. This function reschedules the softirq after queuing up the incoming packet. It also returns the values described in Table 3.6.

```
int netif_rx_ni(struct sk_buff *skb)
{
    int err;
    preempt_disable();
    err = netif_rx(skb);
    if (local_softirq_pending())
        do_softirq();
    preempt_enable();
    return err;
}
```

netif_rx

netif_rx is the main function called from interrupt service routines in conventional network interface drivers. It is defined in the file linux/net/core/dev.c. netif_rx is passed a pointer to a socket buffer holding the new received packet.

```
int netif_rx(struct sk_buff *skb)
{
    struct softnet_data *queue;
    unsigned long       flags;
```

netpoll_rx is part of a low-level network console used for debugging. If the debugger claims the packet, we drop it.

```
    if (netpoll_rx(skb))
        return NET_RX_DROP;
```

First, we call net_timestamp to set the tstamp filed in the sk_buff with the timestamp of when the packet was received.

```
    if (!skb->tstamp.off_sec)
        net_timestamp(skb);
```

The code in this function is written so the execution path is shortest when the CPU is congested. We get a pointer to the queue from the current softnet_data structure.

The code in this function is written so the execution path is shortest when the CPU is congested. We get a pointer to the queue from the current softnet_data structure.

```
    local_irq_save(flags);
    queue = &__get_cpu_var(softnet_data);
    __get_cpu_var(netdev_rx_stat).total++;
```

We check for backlog by seeing whether the input packet queue is longer than the constant value set in the netdev_max_backlog global variable defined in linux/net/core/dev.c.

```
    if (queue->input_pkt_queue.qlen <= netdev_max_backlog) {
```

If there is room on the queue, we go ahead and attempt to queue up the packet.

```
                if (queue->input_pkt_queue.qlen) {
enqueue:
                        dev_hold(skb->dev);
                        __skb_queue_tail(&queue->input_pkt_queue, skb);
                        local_irq_restore(flags);
                        return NET_RX_SUCCESS;
                }
```

We call `netif_rx_schedule` to add the interface to the tail of the poll list. This effectively reschedules the interface for later processing when the `softirq` executes.

```
                netif_rx_schedule(&queue->backlog_dev);
                goto enqueue;
```

If there is no room on the queue, we drop the packet; there is not much to do—increment the statistics, free the `skb`, and indicate to the caller the congestion indication, which, of course, is `NET_RX_DROP`.

```
        __get_cpu_var(netdev_rx_stat).dropped++;
        local_irq_restore(flags);

        kfree_skb(skb);
        return NET_RX_DROP;
}
```

softnet_data

We can't talk about the queuing layer input side without including some discussion of a data structure essential to the queuing layer. This data structure is `softnet_data`, and it is defined in the file `linux/include/linux/netdevice.h`. Starting with Linux version 2.4, this structure includes a copy of a pseudo-net device structure called `blog_dev`, otherwise known as the backlog device.

```
    struct softnet_data
    {
        struct net_device       *output_queue;
        struct sk_buff_head     input_pkt_queue;
        struct list_head        poll_list;
        struct sk_buff          *completion_queue;

        struct net_device       backlog_dev;
    };
```

`Backlog_dev` is used by the packet queuing layer to store the packet queues for most non-polling network interface drivers. The `blog_dev` device is used instead of the real `net_device` structure to hold the queues, but the actual device is still used to keep track of the network interface from which the packet arrived as the packet is processed by the upper layer protocols. As we have seen, many fields are defined in the net device structure. However, the only fields used in `blog_dev` are `poll_list`, `quota`, `state`, `weight`, `poll`, and `refcnt`.

TRANSMITTING PACKETS

Packet transmission is controlled by the upper layers, not by the network interface driver. To understand what happens when a packet is transmitted, we examine what happens between the time the network layer protocol such as IP decides to transmit a packet and the time the driver's transmit function is started. Earlier, we described the `hard_start_xmit` network service function, which does the actual packet transmission. That function is actually called from the packet queuing layer when one or more packets are in a socket buffer ready to transmit. In most drivers, when it is called from the queuing layer, `hard_start_xmit` will put the `sk_buff` on a local queue in the driver's private data structure and enable the transmit available interrupt. After the interrupt is enabled, the actual transmission will happen as the interrupt service routine executes. Earlier in this chapter, we covered how the `hard_start_xmit` function is implemented in `e100`, our example Ethernet network interface driver.

A complex body of code is involved with queuing the packet to the driver for transmission. The functional details of this series of steps are described in detail in Chapter 5. As we shall see in that chapter, Linux allows multiple queuing disciplines to be used with packet transmission and includes a mechanism where these queuing disciplines can be loaded and registered with the kernel. However, in this section we will describe the process of transmitting packets from the protocol's output function using the default scheduler and default queuing discipline. The default queuing discipline used for hardware drivers is `pfifo_fast`, and for software or pseudo drivers, it is `noop_qdisc`. Both of these are implemented in the file `linux/net/sched/sch_generic.c`.

`dev_queue_xmit` Function

The queuing layer function for transmitting a packet is `dev_queue_xmit`, which is defined in the file `linux/net/core/dev.c`. `dev_queue_xmit` is a generic function, independent of both the network layer protocol and from any particular queuing discipline used in a particular transmission path.

```
int dev_queue_xmit(struct sk_buff *skb)
{
    struct net_device  *dev = skb->dev;
    struct Qdisc       *q;
    int                rc = -ENOMEM;
```

First, we check the features flag, NETIF_F_FRAGLIST, to see whether the skb is split into a list of fragments. In addition, we check for the flag NETIF_F_SG to see whether the device supports *scatter gather IO*. Scatter gather IO is the term for doing DMA to or from noncontiguous memory regions.

> **NOTE** *Later, in Chapter 6, we will learn more about socket buffers and see how a segmented socket buffers consists of a single IP header and a list of fragments that all use the same shared header info. If the packet is fragmented, but the device does not have the scatter gather capability, then the packet must be linearized, which means that the IP header and data portion of the packet is gathered into a single linear skb.*

```
if (skb_shinfo(skb)->frag_list &&
    !(dev->features & NETIF_F_FRAGLIST) &&
    __skb_linearize(skb, GFP_ATOMIC))
        goto out_kfree_skb;
```

Next, we check to see whether we need to complete the checksum calculation. This is a complicated and hairy part of the code that has changed quite a bit over years since this book's first edition. There are many circumstances too numerous to mention that have to be checked. Essentially, the features field is checked for various flags to see whether the device supports hardware assisted checksum and the checksum has not been calculated already. One of these flags is NETIF_F_HW_CSUM, which tells us that the device has the capability of calculating a checksum in hardware. In addition, it checks to see whether the packet already has a checksum. If the device can't calculate the checksum in hardware, and the packet doesn't already have a checksum, we call skb_checksum_help to calculate the checksum in software.

```
if (skb->ip_summed == CHECKSUM_HW &&
    (!(dev->features & (NETIF_F_HW_CSUM | NETIF_F_NO_CSUM)) &&
    (!(dev->features & NETIF_F_IP_CSUM) ||
     skb->protocol != htons(ETH_P_IP))))
        if (skb_checksum_help(skb, 0))
            goto out_kfree_skb;
```

At this point, we may re-queue the packet, or we might send it directly to the driver depending on the queue discipline that is in effect for this device driver, the state of the queue, and the traffic class scheduler in use. We get the device queue discipline from the qdisc field of the net_device structure. If we have a queue available, we put the packet on the queue.

```
spin_lock_prefetch(&dev->queue_lock);
```

Here we stop the softirq. Updates of the queue discipline list are controlled by the lock, queue_lock. The queue discipline list has been converted to an RCU list as with many other Linux kernel lists. Therefore, any frees of a qdisc will be deferred until all references are removed.

```
local_bh_disable();
q = rcu_dereference(dev->qdisc);
#ifdef CONFIG_NET_CLS_ACT
    skb->tc_verd = SET_TC_AT(skb->tc_verd,AT_EGRESS);
#endif
```

When the packet is queued, we schedule the queue discipline for execution.

```
if (q->enqueue) {
    spin_lock(&dev->queue_lock);
    rc = q->enqueue(skb, q);
    qdisc_run(dev);
    spin_unlock(&dev->queue_lock);
    rc = rc == NET_XMIT_BYPASS ? NET_XMIT_SUCCESS : rc;
    goto out;
}
```

Some devices don't have a queue such as pseudo-drivers, loopback devices, and tunnel devices for VLANs.

```
if (dev->flags & IFF_UP) {
    int cpu = smp_processor_id(); /* ok because BHs are off */
    if (dev->xmit_lock_owner != cpu) {
        HARD_TX_LOCK(dev, cpu);
        if (!netif_queue_stopped(dev)) {
```

We check netdev_nit, a global variable to see whether there are any listeners of outgoing packets on this interface. If so, dev_queue_xmit_nit will send the outgoing packet to the promiscuous listeners before transmission out the interface.

```
if (netdev_nit)
    dev_queue_xmit_nit(skb, dev);
rc = 0;
```

Here is where we call the network interface driver's transmit routine.

```
            if (!dev->hard_start_xmit(skb, dev)) {
                HARD_TX_UNLOCK(dev);
                goto out;
            }
        }
        HARD_TX_UNLOCK(dev);
```

Finally, we check for rate limiting and packet recursion. Packet recursion occurs when a listener such as a virtual device is set up to listen to its own transmit routine. It is theoretically possible so we use rate limiting to prevent it.

```
            if (net_ratelimit())
                printk(KERN_CRIT "Virtual device %s asks to "
                       "queue packet!\n", dev->name);
        } else {
            if (net_ratelimit())
                printk(KERN_CRIT "Dead loop on virtual device "
                                 "%s, fix it urgently!\n", dev->name);
        }
    }
    rc = -ENETDOWN;
    local_bh_enable();
out_kfree_skb:
    kfree_skb(skb);
    return rc;
out:
    local_bh_enable();
    return rc;
}
```

See Chapter 5 for more detail about queue disciplines and Chapter 8 for how the queue disciplines are used for routing and traffic class based scheduling.

NOTIFIER CHAINS AND NETWORK INTERFACE DEVICE STATUS NOTIFICATION

Linux provides a mechanism for device status change notification called `notifier` chains. It is based on a generic `notifier` facility that can be used by modules anywhere in the kernel for various purposes. In the TCP/IP stack, the `notifier` chains are used to pass changes in network device status or other events to any protocols, modules, or devices that register themselves with the facility. The `notifier` chains are for passing changes in status to any function that is registered with the `notifier` facility. Table 3.7 shows the predeclared `notifier` events that are used currently in the Linux kernel. These values are declared in file the linux/include/linux/notifier.h. The `notifier` chain is actually a very simple construct and isn't much more than a linked list of functions to call for event notification.

TABLE 3.7 Pre-Declared Net Device Notification Events

Name	Value	Purpose
NETDEV_UP	0x0001	Network device up notifier
NETDEV_DOWN	0x0002	Network device down notifier
NETDEV_REBOOT	0x0003	Tells a protocol that a network interface detected a hardware crash and restarted
NETDEV_CHANGE	0x0004	Notification of device state change
NETDEV_REGISTER	0x0005	Notification of a network device registration event
NETDEV_UNREGISTER	0x0006	Notification of a network device unregistration event
NETDEV_CHANGEMTU	0x0007	Network device MTU change notifier
NETDEV_CHANGEADDR	0x0008	Network device address change notifier
NETDEV_GOING_DOWN	0x0009	Notification that a network device is going down
NETDEV_CHANGENAME	0x000A	Notify that a network device has changed its name
NETDEV_FEAT_CHANGE	0x000B	Notification that a network interface device has been programmed with new features

Each location in the linked list of notifiers is defined by an instance of the `notifier_block` structure. This structure is generally initialized at compile time by the code that wants to use the notification facility.

```
struct notifier_block
{
```

The first field in this structure, `notifier_call`, is the event notification function. This field is initialized statically.

```
        int (*notifier_call)(struct notifier_block *self, unsigned long,
        void *);
```

next is not allocated statically. A module that expects to receive event notification must declare an instance of `notifier_block` and set the next field to NULL so that field can be filled in later when the `notifier` block is registered.

```
        struct notifier_block *next;
        int priority;
};
```

Generic Event Notification Functions

Linux provides a set of generic functions for event notification. These functions are available to network interface driver writers and protocol writers so they can handle various device status change events as described in Table 3.7

`notifier_chain_register`

The first of the event notification functions is `notifier_chain_register`, which registers a `notifier_block` with the event notification facility.

```
        int notifier_chain_register(struct notifier_block **list, struct
        notifier_block *n);
```

When using this function, the parameter n should be set to point to the `notifier_block`, and list to point to the `notifier` event chain.

`notifier_chain_unregister`

To unregister with the event notification facility, the `notifier` unregistration function is called.

```
        int notifier_chain_unregister(struct notifier_block **nl, struct
        notifier_block *n);
```

If the event notification facility is used in a module, `notifier_chain_unregister` must be called before the module is unloaded. There is no protection of the notification call chains. Once registered, the function pointed to by the `notifier_call` field in `notifier_block` cannot be reused or altered until after the unregistration is complete.

notifier_call_chain

To pass an event into the notification call chain, the function `notifier_call_chain` is called with a pointer to the `notifier_block` list, n; an event value, val; and an optional generic argument, v.

```
int notifier_call_chain(struct notifier_block **n, unsigned long val,
    void *v);
```

netdev_chain, a Specific Notifier Chain

In the previous section, we looked at the generic Linux notification event facility. There is also a specific event notification facility for network interface devices called the `netdev_chain` used in the file linux/net/core/dev.c. The `netdev_chain` is used widely throughout the Linux TCP/IP protocol family, and its main purpose is to inform protocols when network devices are brought up and down. Through this facility, recipients are notified of a number of predefined events related to network interface device status, shown in Table 3.7. The functions provided to register and un-register with the `netdev_chain` are also implemented in the file linux/net/core/dev.c and have prototypes defined in the file linux/include/linux/netdevice.h. As is the case with the generic facility, a user registers a `notifier_block`, and neither the block nor the function in it can be reused until the function is un-registered. To use this facility, we create a `notifier_block` instance usually at compile time. The block contains a pointer to the function that is to be called when the event occurs.

register_netdevice_notifier

To register with the call chain, we call the registration function `register_netdevice_notifier` with a pointer to the `notifier_block`.

```
int register_netdevice_notifier(struct notifier_block *nb);
```

The caller to this function doesn't pick or choose which events it will see.

notifier_call

A notification function will be called through the `notifier_call` field in nb for all the event types in Table 3.7.

```
int (*notifier_call)(struct notifier_block *self, unsigned long, void *);
```

This function should explicitly check for the types of events it wants to process. The first argument, self, will point back to the `notifier_block`; the second argument will be one of the event types from Table 3.7; and the third argument will be a pointer to a `net_device` structure indicating the device that caused the event.

unregister_netdevice_notifier

To un-register with the net device `notifier` chain, we call `unregister_netdevice_notifier` to remove the `notifier_block` from the call chain.

```
int unregister_netdevice_notifier(struct notifier_block *nb);
```

SUMMARY

In this chapter, we discussed Linux network interfaces to provide a foundation for more detailed discussion in later chapters on the internals of Linux socket buffers and the network and transport protocols. We covered the network interface drivers and Linux TCP/IP features that are directly related to network interfaces and discussed the interface between network interface drivers and the queuing layer. In addition, the driver's network interface driver service functions were discussed. We covered the registration and unregistration process for network interfaces, and the `netdev_chain` event notification facility. We explained the `net_device` structure along with a description of all the important fields. The reader should leave this chapter with a good understanding of how Linux network interface drivers work and how they interface to the TCP/IP stack.

4 Linux Sockets

In This Chapter

- A Few Words
- Introduction
- What Is a Socket?
- `Socket`, `sock`, and Other Data Structures for Managing Sockets
- Socket Layer Initialization
- The Transport Layer Interface and the Socket Application Programming Interface
- Packet, Raw, Netlink, and Routing Sockets
- Security and Linux Capabilities
- A Note About the Socket API and IPv6
- Implementation of the Socket API System Calls
- Creation of a Socket
- `Netlink` and `Rtnetlink`

A FEW WORDS

The socket interface originally was developed as part of the BSD operating system. Sockets provide a standard protocol-independent interface between the application-level programs and the TCP/IP stack. As discussed in Chapter 1, the OSI model serves us well as a framework to explain networking protocol stacks. It defines all seven layers, including the three layers above the transport layer—session, presentation, and application. As we know, TCP/IP does not define these three upper layers. As a matter of fact, it does not define anything above the transport layer. From the viewpoint of TCP/IP, everything above the transport layer is part of the application. Linux is similar to traditional Unix in the sense that the TCP/IP stack lives in the kernel, sharing memory space with the rest of the kernel. All the network functions performed above the transport layer are done in the user application space. Linux provides an API and sockets, which are compatible with Unix and many other systems. Applications use this API to access the networking facilities in the kernel.

INTRODUCTION

The original intent of Linux was to create an OS that is functionally compatible with the proprietary versions of Unix that were popular at the time Linux was originally developed. The socket API is the best known networking interface for Unix application and network programming. Linux has not disappointed us in that it has provided a socket layer that is functionally identical to traditional Unix and other OSs. Almost every type of TCP/IP-based networking application has been successfully ported to Linux over many years including applications used in the smallest embedded system to the largest servers. Many excellent books on Unix network programming do a great job of explaining the socket API and Unix network layer programming; see [STEV98] for an excellent book. In this book, we will not duplicate earlier efforts by providing elaborate explanations of application layer protocols. Instead, our intent is to explain the underlying structure of Linux TCP/IP. Therefore, although the socket API will be discussed, the emphasis is on the underlying infrastructure, the way things are put together in the kernel to make sockets work.

As we stated previously, the Linux socket API conforms to all applicable standards, and application layer protocols and other code are generally entirely portable to Linux from other flavors of Unix and many other OSs. However, the underlying infrastructure of the socket layer implementation is unique to Linux and differs greatly from BSD. In this chapter, we discuss `netlink` sockets and other ways that an application programmer can use sockets to interact with the protocols and layers in the TCP/IP stack. We discuss the definition of a socket, and provide a detailed discussion of the `sock` and `socket` structure and the socket API. In addition, we show how the socket API functions are mapped to equivalent functions for network IO and file operations. We also cover how sockets can be used with a new protocol and how the `netlink` mechanism allows applications to control the operations of the internal protocols in TCP/IP.

WHAT IS A SOCKET?

One definition of the socket interface is that it is the interface between the transport layer protocols in the TCP/IP stack and all protocols above. However, the socket interface is also the interface between the kernel and the application layer for all network programming and maintenance functions. Almost all control functions for the TCP/IP stack pass through the socket interface. As we discussed in the early chapters, the TCP/IP stack itself does not include any protocols above the transport layer. Upper layer protocols run in the application or user space and for this purpose,, Linux and most other operating systems must provide a standard interface for these protocols. In Linux and most other OSs, the interface is sockets. The socket interface is really TCP/IP's window on the world. In most modern systems incorporating TCP/IP—and this includes Linux—the socket interface is the only way that applications make use of the TCP/IP suite of protocols. Sockets can also be used by protocol families other than TCP/IP and we will examine some of the socket registration mechanisms that make this possible.

Overall sockets can be thought of as having three fundamental purposes. These are to transfer data, manage connections for TCP, and control or tune the operation of the protocols in the kernel. The socket interface is an elegant and simple design and this is probably the primary factor leading to the wide acceptance of the TCP/IP protocol stack by application programmers over many years. Sockets are generic; they have the capability of working with protocol suites other than TCP/IP, including the internal process-to-process communication, AF_UNIX. The protocol family types supported by Linux sockets are listed in Table 4.1. The complete list of official protocol families is part of the assigned numbers database that is currently maintained by the Internet Assigned Numbers Authority (IANA) [IAPROT03].

TABLE 4.1 Supported Protocol and Address Families

Name	Value	Protocol
AF_UNSPEC	0	The address family is unspecified.
AF_UNIX	1	Unix domain sockets.
AF_LOCAL	1	The same as AF_UNIX address family.
AF_INET	2	Internet, the TCP/IP protocol family.
AF_AX25	3	Amateur radio AX.25 protocol.
AF_IPX	4	IPX protocol sockets.
AF_APPLETALK	5	AppleTalk DDP sockets.
AF_NETROM	6	NET/ROM sockets.
AF_BRIDGE	7	Multiprotocol bridge sockets.
AF_ATMPVC	8	ATM PVX sockets.
AF_X25	9	X.25 sockets.
AF_INET6	10	IP version 6.
AF_ROSE	11	Amateur radio X.25 PLP.
AF_DECnet	12	Reserved for DECnet sockets.

→

Name	Value	Protocol
AF_NETBEUI	13	Reserved for 802.2LLC project.
AF_SECURITY	14	Security callback pseudo address family.
AF_KEY	15	Sockets for PF_KEY key management API.
AF_NETLINK	16	Netlink protocol sockets. Message passing between applications and kernel. See Section 5.9.
AF_ROUTE	16	Alias to emulate 4.4BSD routing sockets. Same as AF_NETLINK in Linux.
AF_PACKET	17	Packet family sockets.
AF_ASH	18	Ash sockets.
AF_ECONET	19	Acorn Econet sockets.
AF_ATMSVC	20	ATM SVC sockets.
AF_SNA	22	Linux SNA sockets.
AF_IRDA	23	IRDA sockets.
AF_PPPOX	24	PPPoX sockets.
AF_WANPIPE	25	Wanpipe API sockets.
AF_LLC	26	Linux LLC sockets.
AF_BLUETOOTH	31	For Bluetooth sockets.
AF_MAX	32	Currently, only 32 address families are supported.

The socket API actually has two parts. It consists of a set of functions specifically for a network. It also contains a way of mapping standard Unix I/O operations so application programmers using TCP/IP to send and receive data can use the same calls that are commonly used for file I/O. Instead of open, the socket function is used to open a socket. However, after the socket is open, generic I/O calls such as read and write can be used to move data through the open socket.

SOCKET, SOCK, AND OTHER DATA STRUCTURES FOR MANAGING SOCKETS

Sometimes the choice of names for data structures and functions can be confusing, and this is definitely the case when we discuss sockets in Linux. As with other operating systems, Linux uses similar names or terms to describe functionally different data structures. For example, several data structures for sockets can be confused with each other. In Linux, the three different data structures each have the letters s-o-c-k in them: socket buffers, sock structures, and socket structures.

The first of the three structures is the socket buffer. It is defined in `linux/include/linux/sk_buff.h`. Socket buffers are structures to hold packet data; they don't necessarily have anything directly to do with sockets; and they may or may not be created at a socket interface. Socket buffers are covered in detail in Chapter 6. In the Linux source code, socket buffers are often referred to by the variable `skb`.

```
struct sk_buff *skb;
```

The next two data structures are covered in this chapter. The second of these is the `socket` structure defined in `linux/include/linux/net.h`. The `socket` structure is not specific to TCP/IP. Instead, it is a generic structure used primarily within the socket layer to keep track of each open connection with an application program and as a vehicle to pass information about these connections among the API functions of the socket layer. Generally, each instance of a socket structure corresponds to an open socket that was open with the `socket` API system call. Sockets are also implicitly referenced in the application code by the file descriptor returned by `socket`. In most places in the Linux sources, the `socket` structure is usually referenced by a variable called `sock`.

```
struct socket *sock;
```

The third data structure is also a structure that we will discuss in detail in this chapter. It is called the `sock` structure and is defined in the file `linux/include/net/sock.h`. It is a more complex structure used to keep state information about open connections. It is accessed throughout the TCP/IP protocol but mostly within the TCP protocol. It is usually referenced through a variable called `sk`.

The `sock` and Related Structures

Earlier we discussed how Linux has several structures having to do with sockets. The first structure we will discuss is `sock` and some related structures. This structure is of fundamental importance to the TCP/IP suite and is referenced everywhere in the sources. In earlier versions of the kernel, the `sock` structure was much more complex. In 2.6, it has been greatly simplified in two ways. The structure is preceded with a common part that is generic to all protocol families. The other way it is different is that in Linux 2.6, instances of the `sock` structure are allocated from protocol-specific slab caches instead of a generic cache. Following the generic part of the structure there is an IPv4 and IPv6 specific part that contains the `prot_info` structure for each of the member protocols in the protocol family. We show the protocol specific portion in a later section as part of the discussion of socket creation.

The sock_common Structure

The first part of the sock structure is kept in a structure called sock_common, found in the file linux/include/net/sock.h.

```
struct sock_common {
```

The first field in the structure is skc_family, which contains the network address family, such as AF_INET for IPv4. skc_state is the connection state, and skc_reuse holds the value of the SO_REUSEADDR socket option.

```
unsigned short          skc_family;
volatile unsigned char  skc_state;
unsigned char           skc_reuse;
```

The next field, skc_bound_dev_if holds the index for the bound network interface device. If there is a connection or route associated with this socket, this would be the device through which traffic destined for this socket would flow.

```
int                     skc_bound_dev_if;
```

The next two fields hold hash linkage for the protocol lookup tables. Finally, skc_refcnt is the reference count for this socket.

```
struct hlist_node       skc_node;
struct hlist_node       skc_bind_node;
atomic_t                skc_refcnt;
unsigned int            skc_hash;
```

This field, skc_prot is used by IPv6 for the protocol definition.

```
struct proto            *skc_prot;
};
```

The sock Structure

Now we will look at the sock structure itself also found in the file linux/include/net/sock.h.

```
struct sock {
```

The first thing in the sock structure must be sock_common, described previously. Sock_common is first because tcp_w_bucket structure and perhaps other structures also have sock_common as the first part. This is to allow the same list processing and queuing functions to be used on both kinds of structures.

```
        struct sock_common    __sk_common;
```

Here we have some defines to make it easier to find the fields in the common part.

```
#define sk_state         __sk_common.skc_state
#define sk_reuse         __sk_common.skc_reuse
#define sk_bound_dev_if  __sk_common.skc_bound_dev_if
#define sk_node          __sk_common.skc_node
#define sk_bind_node     __sk_common.skc_bind_node
#define sk_refcnt        __sk_common.skc_refcnt
#define sk_hash          __sk_common.skc_hash
#define sk_prot          __sk_common.skc_prot
```

The next field is used with the RCV_SHUTDOWN and SEND_SHUTDOWN socket options. As we will see in later chapters, when the SEND_SHUTDOWN option is set, in TCP, an RST will be sent when closing the socket.

```
        unsigned char     sk_shutdown : 2;
```

Next, sk_no_check contains the value of the SO_NO_CHECK socket option and indicates whether to disable checksums.

```
                          sk_no_check : 2,
```

sk_userlocks holds the SO_SNDBUF and SO_RCVBUF socket option settings which are used to set the buffer sizes for receive and send buffers.

```
                          sk_userlocks : 4;
```

The following field, sk_protocol, holds the protocol number for this socket within the AF_INET family. It is the same as the 1-byte protocol field in the IP header.

```
        unsigned char     sk_protocol;
```

The next field, sk_type, holds the socket type such as SOCK_STREAM or SOCK_DGRAM. These indicate whether this socket is using TCP or UDP and corresponds with the type field in the socket call, socket(2), which was used to create this socket.

```
        unsigned short    sk_type;
```

The next field, sk_rcvbuf, holds the actual size of the receive buffer in bytes and is set from the SO_RCVBUF socket option.

```
int                sk_rcvbuf;
```

sk_lock is the individual socket lock used for socket synchronization. Sk_sleep is the sock wait queue, and sk_dst_cache is the pointer to the destination cache entry.

```
socket_lock_t      sk_lock;
wait_queue_head_t  *sk_sleep;
struct dst_entry   *sk_dst_cache;
```

This field is used with the Security Policy Database (SPD) and is used to hold policy information for Internet Key Exchange (IKE), IP Security (IPSec), and related protocols. See Chapter 5 for more information.

```
struct xfrm_policy  *sk_policy[2];
```

sk_dst_lock is a lock for destination cache options and primarily used by the IPv6 protocol family

```
rwlock_t           sk_dst_lock;
```

In the next two fields are for queuing, sk_rmem_alloc is the number of committed bytes in the receive packet queue, and sk_wmem_alloc is the transmit queue committed length. The next field, sk_omem_alloc, is the number of optional committed bytes.

```
atomic_t           sk_rmem_alloc;
atomic_t           sk_wmem_alloc;
atomic_t           sk_omem_alloc;
```

sk_receive_queue is the head of the receive queue. sk_write_queue is the head of the transmit queue for this socket.

```
struct sk_buff_head  sk_receive_queue;
struct sk_buff_head  sk_write_queue;
```

sk_wmem_queued is the persistent write queue size.

```
int                sk_wmem_queued;
```

sk_forward_alloc is the number of bytes in pre-allocated pages attached to this socket. These are used to make connection-oriented transfers more efficient. sk_allocation is the allocation mode.

```
int                sk_forward_alloc;
gfp_t              sk_allocation;
```

The next field, sk_sndbuf, holds the actual size of the send buffer in bytes and is set from the SO_SNDBUF socket option. sk_route_caps has to do with the capabilities, capabilities(7), associated with the cached route associated with this socket if there is one.

```
int                sk_sndbuf;
int                sk_route_caps;
```

sk_flags contains the values of the socket options SO_BROADCAST, SO_KEEPALIVE, and SO_OOBINLINE. The value of sk_lingertime is set to TRUE if the SO_LINGER socket option is set. Sk_hashent contains a hash entry for several tables. The value of sk_lingertime is set to TRUE if the SO_LINGER socket option is set.

```
unsigned long      sk_flags;
unsigned long      sk_lingertime;
```

This structure, sk_backlog, is the socket backlog queue. It is always used with the individual socket lock held. It requires low latency access.

```
struct {
    struct sk_buff *head;
    struct sk_buff *tail;
} sk_backlog;
struct sk_buff_head  sk_error_queue;
```

sk_prot_creator is the value of the skc_prot field of the original socket creator. This field is necessary for IPv6.

```
struct proto       *sk_prot_creator;
```

This lock, sk_callback_lock, is for the six callback functions at the bottom of the sock structure. sk_err is the last error on this socket, and sk_err_soft are for errors that don't cause complete socket failure, such as when the connection associated with this socket times out.

```
rwlock_t           sk_callback_lock;
int                sk_err,
                   sk_err_soft;
```

The next two fields are for the current listen backlog and the maximum backlog set in the `listen` call. The field `sk_priority` holds the value of the `SO_PRIORITY` socket option.

```
unsigned short      sk_ack_backlog;
unsigned short      sk_max_ack_backlog;
__u32               sk_priority;
```

The `sk_peercred` field is not used for TCP/IP. It is for passing file descriptors using Berkeley-style credentials. After that, the next three fields hold the value of the `SO_RCVLOWAT`, `SO_RCVTIMEO`, and the `SO_SNDTIMEO` socket options.

```
struct ucred        sk_peercred;
int                 sk_rcvlowat;
long                sk_rcvtimeo;
long                sk_sndtimeo;
```

`sk_filter` is for socket filtering.

```
struct sk_filter    *sk_filter;
```

`sk_protinfo` is a private area. It is not used when sockets are allocated from the slab cache and, therefore, is not used with TCP/IP. `sk_timer` is the sock cleanup timer.

```
void                *sk_protinfo;
struct timer_list   sk_timer;
```

`sk_stamp` is the timestamp of the most recent received packet. `sk_socket` points to the socket structure for this socket.

```
struct timeval      sk_stamp;
struct socket       *sk_socket;
void                *sk_user_data;
struct page         *sk_sndmsg_page;
struct sk_buff      *sk_send_head;
__u32               sk_sndmsg_off;
int                 sk_write_pending;
void                *sk_security;
```

The following five fields point to callback functions for this socket. The first field, `sk_state_change`, is called when the state of this `sock` is changed, and the next field, `sk_data_ready`, indicates that there is data available to be processed. `sk_write_space` is called when there is buffer space available for sending. `sk_error_report` is called when there are errors to report and is used with MSG_ERRQUEUE. sk_backlog_rcv is called to process the socket backlog in conjunction with socket queue management.

```
void            (*sk_state_change)(struct sock *sk);
void            (*sk_data_ready)(struct sock *sk, int bytes);
void            (*sk_write_space)(struct sock *sk);
void            (*sk_error_report)(struct sock *sk);
int             (*sk_backlog_rcv)(struct sock *sk,
                    struct sk_buff *skb);
void            (*sk_destruct)(struct sock *sk);
```

Finally, the last field is the destructor function for this sock instance. It is called when all the references are gone, when refcnt becomes zero.

```
};
```

The inet_sock Structure

When a sock instance is allocated from the slab, space is reserved after the sock for another structure called the inet_sock structure. inet_sock contains specific protocol information for IPv6 and IPv4. It is found in the file linux/include/net/inet_sock.h.

```
struct inet_sock {
    struct sock         sk;
#if defined(CONFIG_IPV6) || defined(CONFIG_IPV6_MODULE)
    struct ipv6_pinfo   *pinet6;
#endif
```

These first few fields in inet_sock are for socket layer de-multiplexing of incoming packets. Daddr is the peer IPv4 address, and rcv_saddr is the bound local IPv4 address. Dport is the destination port, num is the local port, and saddr is the source address.

```
    __u32               daddr;
    __u32               rcv_saddr;
    __u16               dport;
    __u16               num;
    __u32               saddr;
```

The uc_ttl field is for setting the time-to-live field in the IP header. The cmsg_flags field is used by setsockopt and getsockopt to communicate network layer IP socket options to the IP protocol layer. In addition, opt points to the values associated with the options set in the cmsg_flags field.

```
      __s16                   uc_ttl;
      __u16                   cmsg_flags;
      struct ip_options       *opt;
```

sport is the source port number, the destination port field in the transport header. The next field, id, contains the counter for identification field in the IP header. This field is used by the receiving machine for re-assembling fragmented IP packets.

```
      __u16                   sport;
      __u16                   id;
```

tos is for setting the type of service field in the IP header.

```
      __u8                    tos;
```

This field, mc_ttl is the multicasting time-to-live. pmtudisc indicates whether MTU discovery should be performed on this interface. MTU discovery involves sending special ICMP packet to determine the size of the MTU of the interface.

```
      __u8                    mc_ttl;
      __u8                    pmtudisc;
      __u8                    recverr:1,
                              is_icsk:1,
                              freebind:1,
```

hdrincl is for raw sockets. It states that the IP header is included in the packet delivered to the application level. The next field, mc_loop indicates whether multicast packets should be looped back. mc_index is the index for the output network interface used for transmission of multicast packets, and mc_addr is the source address used for outgoing packets sent to a multicast address.

```
                              hdrincl:1,
                              mc_loop:1;
      int                     mc_index;
      __u32                   mc_addr;
```

This field, mc_list, points to the list of multicast address groups to which the interface has subscribed. Refer to the IGMP protocol for more information. Implementation of IGMP and multicast routing is covered in later chapters about the IP layer.

```
      struct ip_mc_socklist *mc_list;
```

The following structure keeps information about the IP options needed to build an IP header on each outgoing IP fragment. Since all the fragments have almost identical headers, the options are kept here to speed the process of building IP headers on consecutive fragments. It is called `cork`, because the socket is said to be corked, while it is waiting for all fragments of the total IP datagram to be transmitted.

```
struct {
    unsigned int        flags;
    unsigned int        fragsize;
    struct ip_options   *opt;
    struct rtable       *rt;
```

This field, `length`, is the total length of the packet including all frames in the fragmented IP datagram.

```
    int             length;
    u32             addr;
    struct flowi    fl;
} cork;
};
```

The socket and Related Structures

The structures discussed in this section are the highest level kernel structures defined for the Transport Layer Interface (TLI) or socket API. Sockets are functionally equivalent to the Berkeley sockets invented almost a generation ago. The main purpose of these data structures is to contain mappings between the traditional Berkeley API and the internal Linux implementation of the socket layer. The data structures in this section are defined in `linux/include/linux/net.h`.

The socket Structure

The `socket` is the general structure that holds control and states information for the user-to-kernel transport layer interface otherwise known as sockets. Its main purpose is to support the BSD-type socket interface and map the socket flags and value arguments used with the BSD socket API to the internal Linux implementation. The definition of the socket structure can be found in the file `linux/include/linux/net.h`.

```
struct socket {
```

The first field, `state` contains the state of the socket and is set to one of the socket state values shown later in Table 4.8. The socket `flags` are in the next field and they represent the socket wait buffer state information containing values such as SOCK_ASYNC_NOSPACE.

```
socket_state        state;
unsigned long       flags;
```

ops points to the protocol-specific operations for the socket. prot_ops is discussed in more detail immediately after the socket structure.

```
struct proto_ops    *ops;
```

The next field, fasync_list, points to the wake-up list for asynchronous file calls. For more information, see fsync(2). File points to the file structure for this socket. We need to keep a pointer here to facilitate garbage collection.

```
struct fasync_struct *fasync_list;
struct file         *file;
```

sk points to the sock structure for this socket which is shown in detail earlier in this chapter. wait is the socket wait queue.

```
struct sock         *sk;
wait_queue_head_t   wait;
```

type is the socket type, corresponding to the type argument in the socket(2) system call. For TCP/IP, it is generally is SOCK_STREAM, SOCK_DGRAM, or SOCK_RAW.

```
short               type;
};
```

The proto_ops Structure

The proto_ops structure contains the operational functions for a particular protocol family. It contains the family type and the specific internal functions for that address family's particular set of socket operations. There is an instantiation of proto_ops for each address family defined for Linux. For IPv4, it will contain AF_INET and pointers to the functions for IPv4 operations. Later, during the discussion on socket initialization we will see how this structure is initialized and how a pointer to an instance is set in the ops field of the socket structure.

```
struct proto_ops {
```

`family` is the address family. It is equivalent to the `domain` argument in the `socket(2)` system call. It is set to `AF_INET` for IPv4. `owner` is the module that owns this socket.

```
int                     family;
struct module           *owner;
```

Each of the following fields corresponds to a socket call. They are all pointers to the function implementing the protocol-specific operations for the protocol family defined in `family`.

```
int             (*release)    (struct socket *sock);
int             (*bind)       (struct socket *sock,
                                struct sockaddr *myaddr,
                                int sockaddr_len);
int             (*connect)    (struct socket *sock,
                                struct sockaddr *vaddr,
                                int sockaddr_len, int flags);
int             (*socketpair)(struct socket *sock1,
                                struct socket *sock2);
int             (*accept)     (struct socket *sock,
                                struct socket *newsock, int flags);
int             (*getname)    (struct socket *sock,
                                struct sockaddr *addr,
                                 int *sockaddr_len, int peer);
unsigned int    (*poll)       (struct file *file, struct socket *sock,
                                struct poll_table_struct *wait);
int             (*ioctl)      (struct socket *sock, unsigned int cmd,
                                unsigned long arg);
int             (*listen)     (struct socket *sock, int len);
int             (*shutdown)   (struct socket *sock, int flags);
int             (*setsockopt)(struct socket *sock, int level,
                                int optname, char __user *optval,
                                int optlen);
int             (*getsockopt)(struct socket *sock, int level,
                                int optname, char __user *optval,
                                int __user *optlen);
int             (*sendmsg)    (struct kiocb *iocb, struct socket
                                *sock,
                                struct msghdr *m, int total_len);
int             (*recvmsg)    (struct kiocb *iocb, struct socket
                                *sock,
                                struct msghdr *m, int total_len,
                                int flags);
```

```
        int         (*mmap)      (struct file *file, struct socket *sock,
                                  struct vm_area_struct * vma);
        ssize_t     (*sendpage)  (struct socket *sock, struct page *page,
                                  int offset, size_t size, int flags);
};
```

SOCKET LAYER INITIALIZATION

In this section, we will explore how Linux initializes the socket layer for the TCP/IP protocol family. Each supported protocol suite has an address family that is registered with the socket layer so the API can be used with the member protocols in diverse protocol suites and these address families are listed in Table 4.1. In this book, we are primarily interested in TCP/IP and its address family, AF_INET. AF_INET is registered during kernel initialization, and the internal hooks that connect the AF_INET family with the TCP/IP protocol suite are done during socket initialization. However, it is possible to register new protocol families dynamically with the socket layer. Chapter 5 includes more information about the general Linux kernel initialization mechanism, and Chapter 11 shows how a completely new address family can be introduced as a module into the Linux kernel. However, in this section, we are mainly concerned about the initialization of the AF_INET address family. As part of this initialization process we shall see how each of he member protocols in TCP/IP are also registered with the socket layer.

The sock_init Function

The socket layer, like any other Linux kernel facility, has an initialization function called during kernel initialization. This function, sock_init, is defined in the file linux/net/socket.c. Note that initialization functions can be quickly found because they are all typed __init. sock_init is called before Internet protocol registration because basic socket initialization must be done before each of the TCP/IP member protocols can register with the socket layer.

```
    void __init sock_init(void)
    {
```

The first thing we do is call sk_init to initialize the slab cache for the sock data structure. This data structure, discussed earlier, contains all of the internal socket state information. Next, sock_init calls skb_init to set up the slab cache for socket buffers, or sk_buffs. Chapter 6 includes more detailed information about Linux slab memory allocation and socket buffers.

```
        sk_init();
        skb_init();
```

Now, we build the pseudo-filesystem for sockets, and the first step is to set up the socket `inode` cache. Linux, like other Unix operating systems, uses the `inode` as the basic unit for filesystem implementation.

```
        init_inodecache();
```

Next, a pseudo-filesystem is created for sockets called `sock_fs_type` by calling `register_filesystem`. Linux, like many operating systems, has a unified IO system, so that IO calls are transparent whether they are accessing devices, files, or sockets. We must register with the filesystem to use the IO system calls to read and write data through open sockets. Later in this chapter we discuss the IO system call mapping in more detail. When the socket file system is built, we can mount it in the kernel.

```
        register_filesystem(&sock_fs_type);
        sock_mnt = kern_mount(&sock_fs_type);
```

The remaining part of protocol initialization is done later when the function `do_initcalls` in main.c is executed. The last thing that `sock_init` does is initialize `netfilters` if they have been configured into the kernel.

```
        #ifdef CONFIG_NETFILTER
            netfilter_init();
        #endif
            return 0;
        }.
```

Family Values and the Protocol Switch Table

When we look at this initialization process, it is important to remember that the socket layer has many functions and can be used for multiple simultaneous protocol families. The socket layer is used to interface with multiple protocol families and multiple protocols within a protocol family. After incoming packets are processed by the protocol stack, they eventually are passed up to the socket layer to be handed off to an application layer program. The socket layer must determine which socket should receive the packet, even though there may be multiple sockets open over different protocols. This is called *socket de-multiplexing,* and the protocol switch table is the core mechanism. This mechanism functions very much like the BSD operating system. It is from BSD that the term *protocol switch table* was derived.

Much TCP/IP member protocol initialization is discussed in Chapter 5 for IPv4 and Chapter 11 for IPv6.

126 Linux TCP/IP Networking for Embedded Systems

> *Chapter 10 includes source code that shows how a completely new protocol family may be created as a module.*

However, socket layer registration is discussed here because it is closely related to socket layer de-multiplexing. Linux makes a distinction between permanent and nonpermanent protocols. For example, permanent protocols include protocols such as UDP and TCP, which are a fundamental part of any functioning TCP/IP implementation. Removal of permanent protocols is not allowed; therefore, UDP and TCP can't be unregistered. However, other protocols can be added to the protocol switch table dynamically, and these protocols are considered nonpermanent. Figure 5.1 illustrates the registration process. It shows how the `inet_protosw` structure is initialized with `proto` and `proto_ops` structures for TCP/IP, the `AF_INET` family.

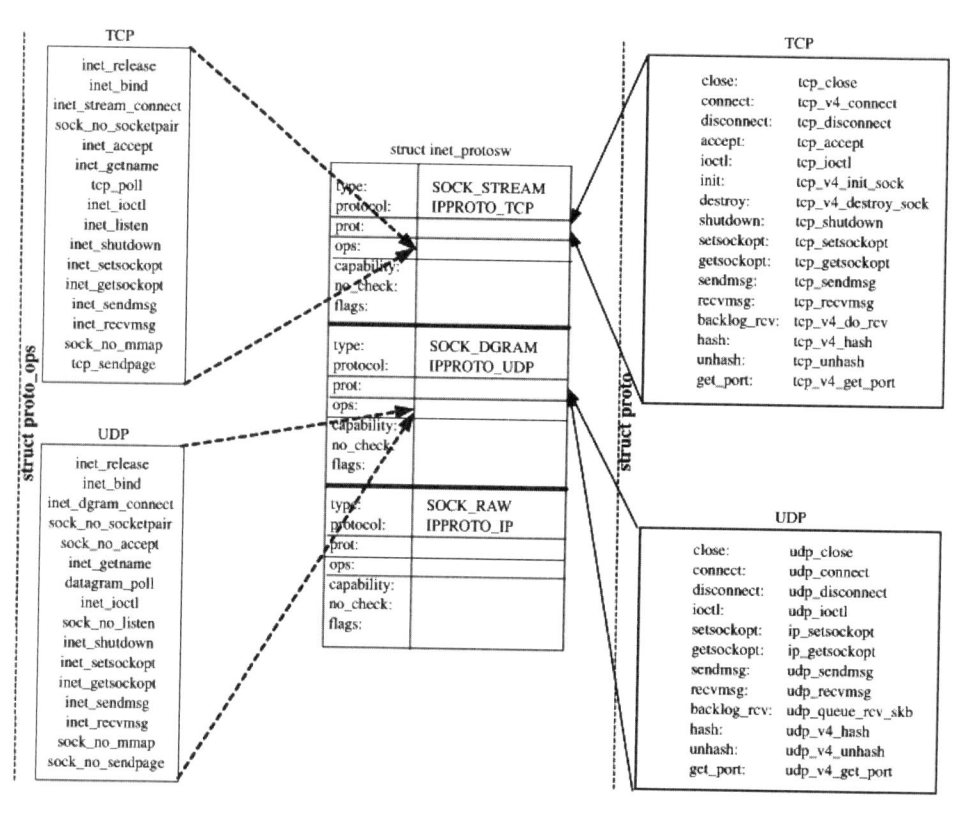

FIGURE 4.1 AF_INET protocol family and socket calls.

Protocol Switch Registration

The protocol switch registration mechanism consists of two functions and a data structure for maintaining the registered protocols. One of the functions is for registering a protocol, and the other function is for unregistration. Each of the registered protocols is kept in a table called the *protocol switch table*. Each entry in the table is an instance of the `inet_protosw` data structure.

The `inet_register_protosw` Function

The registration function, `inet_register_protosw`, puts the protocol described by the argument p into the protocol switch table. This function is defined in file linux/net/ipv4/af_inet.c, and it is declared in the file linux/include/net/protocol.h.

```
void inet_register_protosw(struct inet_protosw *p);
```

The `inet_unregister_protosw` Function

The unregistration function, `inet_unregister_protowsw`, removes the protocol described by the argument p from the protocol switch table.

```
void inet_unregister_protosw(struct inet_protosw *p);
```

The `inet_protosw` Structure

Each protocol instance in the protocol switch table is an instance of the `inet_protosw` structure, defined in the file linux/include/protocol.h.

```
struct inet_protosw {
```

The first two fields in the structure, `list` and `type`, form the key to look up the protocol in the protocol switch table. `type` is equivalent to the type argument of the socket call, and the values for this field are shown in Table 4.2. These values are defined in the file linux/include/linux/net.h.

```
    struct list_head    list;
    unsigned short      type;
```

The next field, `protocol`, corresponds to the well-known protocol argument of the socket call. This field is set to one of the following values, the protocol number for TCP, UDP, another protocol number, or zero for raw. It is the protocol number for the protocol that is being registered. For more information, refer to the socket call in the socket API discussion later in this chapter.

```
    int                 protocol;
```

TABLE 4.2 Values for Socket Types

Name	Value	Purpose
SOCK_STREAM	1	Streaming sockets. For connection-oriented or TCP sockets.
SOCK_DGRAM	2	Datagram sockets. For connectionless or UDP sockets.
SOCK_RAW	3	Raw socket. Provides application layer with direct access to network layer protocols.
SOCK_RDM	4	Reliable Delivery Message (RDM) socket.
SOCK_SEQPACKET	5	Sequential packet socket.
SOCK_PACKET	10	Sockets for direct packet access at the network device level.

The field prot points to the protocol block structure. This structure is used when a socket is created. This structure is used to build an interface to any protocol that supports a socket interface. The next field, ops, points to a protocol-specific set of operation functions for this protocol. The proto_ops structure is discussed earlier in this chapter. It has the same definition as the ops field in the socket structure.

```
struct proto        *prot;
struct proto_ops    *ops;
```

Capability is used to determine if the application layer program has permission for a socket operation. The appropriate level of permission is required for some socket operations with raw sockets. This is to prevent security attacks because raw socket operations can get access to internal operations of TCP/IP. See the section on Linux capabilities later in this chapter for more information.

```
int                 capability;
```

The next field, no_check, tells the network interface driver not to perform a checksum.

Finally, the last field, flags, is defined as one of two values also defined in the same file.

```
#define INET_PROTOSW_REUSE      0x01
#define INET_PROTOSW_PERMANENT  0x02
#define INET_PROTOSW_ICSK       0x04
```

If `flags` is set to `INET_PROTOSW_PERMANENT`, the protocol is permanent and can't be unregistered. In this case, the unregistration function prints an error message and returns. For example, UDP and TCP have flags set to `INET_PROTOSW_PERMANENT`, and for raw sockets, the (`SOCK_RAW`) flags value is set to `INET_PROTOSW_REUSE`. The flag `INET_PROTOSW_ICSK` indicates that this is a connection oriented protocol namely TCP.

```
        unsigned char      flags;
};
```

Member Protocol Registration and Initialization in IPv4

In this section, we will discuss how the individual `AF_INET` member protocols such as UDP and TCP register with the socket layer, Chapter 6 contains a complete discussion of the initialization steps for IPv4. Here, we will only look at socket layer registration. In the previous section, we made a distinction between permanent protocols and other protocols. Now we will look at how the permanent calls are registered with the protocol switch table.

The Function `inet_init`

The permanent protocols in IPv4 are registered by the function `inet_init`, defined in the file `linux/net/ipv4/af_inet.c`. We are only including a code snippet here because we are primarily concerned with protocol switch registration.

```
static int __init inet_init(void)
{
```

The code in this function actually registers the protocols after they have been placed into an array.

```
. . .
    for (r = &inetsw[0]; r < &inetsw[SOCK_MAX]; ++r)
        INIT_LIST_HEAD(r);

    for (q = inetsw_array; q < &inetsw_array[INETSW_ARRAY_LEN]; ++q)
        inet_register_protosw(q);
. . .
}
```

In the preceding code snippet, we can see that `inet_init` calls `inet_register_protosw` for each of the protocols in the array, `inetsw_array`. The protocols in the array are UDP, TCP, and raw.

Initialization of `inet_protosw` Structure

The values for each protocol are initialized into the `inet_protosw` structure at compile time as shown here. This initialization is done in the file linux/net/ipv4/af_inet.c.

```
static struct inet_protosw inetsw_array[] =
{
        {
```

The first protocol is TCP, so type is SOCK_STREAM, and flags is set to permanent and INET_PROTOSW_ICSK to show that this is a connection oriented protocol.

```
            {
                    .type =         SOCK_STREAM,
                    .protocol =     IPPROTO_TCP,
                    .prot =         &tcp_prot,
                    .ops =          &inet_stream_ops,
                    .capability =   -1,
                    .no_check =     0,
                    .flags =        INET_PROTOSW_PERMANENT |
                                    INET_PROTOSW_ICSK,
        },
        {
```

The second protocol is UDP, so type is SOCK_DGRAM, and flags is also set to permanent also.

```
            {
                    .type =         SOCK_DGRAM,
                    .protocol =     IPPROTO_UDP,
                    .prot =         &udp_prot,
                    .ops =          &inet_dgram_ops,
                    .capability =   -1,
                    .no_check =     UDP_CSUM_DEFAULT,
                    .flags =        INET_PROTOSW_PERMANENT,
        },
```

The third protocol is "raw," so type is SOCK_RAW, and flags is also set to reuse. Notice the protocol value is IPPROTO_IP, which is zero, and indicates the "wild card," which means that a raw socket actually can be used to set options in any protocol in the IF_INET family. This corresponds to the fact that the protocol field is typically set to zero for a raw socket.

```
        {
                .type =         SOCK_RAW,
                .protocol =     IPPROTO_IP, /* wild card */
                .prot =         &raw_prot,
                .ops =          &inet_sockraw_ops,
                .capability =   CAP_NET_RAW,
                .no_check =     UDP_CSUM_DEFAULT,
                .flags =        INET_PROTOSW_REUSE,
        }
};
```

When this registration is complete, other protocols usually implemented as modules may still add themselves to the protocol switch table at any time by calling `inet_register_protocols`. We will see how this is done in more detail in Chapter 10.

Registration of Protocols with the Socket Layer

This section is about important family values; that is, the registration of protocol families such as the IP family. In this section, we cover the registration of an entire protocol family, which includes an entire suite of protocols, and how it is associated with one of the protocol families listed in Table 5.1. In Chapter 5 we discuss the various mechanisms for protocol registration other than the socket layer specifically for Linux TCP/IP. Also, in Chapter 5, we will include a detailed discussion of the sequence of steps performed for Internet protocol initialization.

Protocol Family Registration

The name of the protocol family for TCP/IP is `AF_INET`. The protocol family registration step is necessary so the application programmer can access all the protocols that are part of the TCP/IP protocol family through the socket API functions. The socket layer family registration facility provides two functions and one key data structure. The functions discussed in this section are in the file `linux/net/socket.c` and declared in the file `linux/include/linux/net.h`.

All files referenced in this chapter are part of the Linux source tree and can be found in the companion CD-ROM.

The sock_register Function

This function registers the protocol family with the socket layer.

```
int sock_register(struct net_proto_family *fam);
```

The family is passed in as a pointer to the `net_proto_family` structure, which is shown later in this chapter. `Sock_register` checks the `family` field in the `net_proto_` family structure pointed to by `fam` to make sure that it is one of the family types listed in Table 4.1. If `family` is within range, it copies the argument `fam` into a location in the global array `net_families` which is indexed by the family value.

```
static struct net_proto_family *net_families[NPROTO];
```

Later, in this chapter, we will see how the `net_families` array is used to look up the protocol family associated with the domain for the requested socket.

The sock_unregister Function

The second function, `sock_unregister`, is the protocol family unregistration function.

```
int sock_unregister(int family);
```

In this function, `family` is the value of the protocol family, such as AF_INET. Sock_unregister reverses the registration process by setting the element in the array indexed by the parameter `family` to NULL. It only makes sense to use this function in a module that implements a nonpermanent protocol family. Protocol families can be written as modules, and this is why Linux provides an unregistration function. However, since IPv4 is generally statically compiled in to the kernel, sock_unregister will never be called for IPv4, the AF_INET family. IPv4 is almost always used with the Linux kernel, and it would be unusual to configure a Linux kernel without it. When protocol families are implemented as modules, the un-registration should be done from the exit function (typed __exit). See Chapter 5 for more about modules in Linux.

> **NOTE**
> *Chapter 10 includes sample source code showing how to write a complete protocol family. All sources discussed in this chapter and other chapters are included in the companion CD-ROM.*
>
> **ON THE CD**

The net_proto_family Data Structure

The data structure `net_proto_family` contains information about the protocol family we are registering. It is defined in the file `linux/include/linux/net.h`. As discussed earlier, it is passed as a parameter to the `sock_register` function.

```
struct net_proto_family
{
```

The first field, `family`, corresponds to one of the protocol families listed in Table 4.1, such as AF_INET.

```
            int       family;
```

The `create` field is a function pointer to the specific socket creation function for the protocol family specified by `family`.

```
            int             (*create)(struct socket *sock, int protocol);
```

This structure contains a few counter fields for security support that aren't widely used.

```
            short           authentication;
            short           encryption;
            short           encrypt_net;
```

Finally, `owner` points to the module that owns this protocol family.

```
            struct module   *owner;
    }
```

THE TRANSPORT LAYER INTERFACE AND THE SOCKET APPLICATION PROGRAMMING INTERFACE

The socket API functions are described in this section. Sockets are the fundamental basis of client server programming. Generally, socket programming follows the client-server model. At the risk of over-simplifying, we will define the server as the machine that accepts connections. In contrast, a client is the machine that initiates connections. This book won't pretend to duplicate the work of other authors on network application programming; instead, refer to [STEV98]. However, in the interest of a complete description of how the socket interface functions in Linux, the socket API functions are provided with a description of the purpose of each call. Later in this chapter, we will see what happens under the covers when each of the functions described in this section is invoked.

IP Address and Sockets

Before we proceed with listing the API functions, we will discuss how IP and other addresses are passed through sockets. In general, when using the socket API, network addresses are stored in a `sockaddr` structure defined in the file `linux/include/linux/in.h`. This structure holds different forms of address information.

```
struct sockaddr_in
{
Sin_port is the port number for the socket.
    in_port_t sin_port;
Sin_addr is the IP address.
    struct in_addr sin_addr;
};
```

We use the `sockaddr_in` structure with the socket API because sockets are generic and intended to work with a variety of protocol families and a variety of address formats, not just IPv4 with its well-known but limited 32-bit address format. This is why the `sockaddr` structure can vary in length depending on the format of the address it contains.

It is important to note that the terms *port* and *socket* are not synonymous. The port, along with the IP address, identifies the destination address for a packet. However, the socket is the identifier that the application uses to access the connection to the peer machine. Linux, like most Unix operating systems, provides a complete set of functions for Internet address and port manipulation.

Like most Unix operating systems before it, Linux provides a variety of IP address conversion functions for manipulation of Internet addresses. Included are functions to convert addresses between character strings and binary numbers. An example is `inet_ntoa`, which converts a binary IP address to a string. The Linux functions are compatible with the traditional BSD functions for network programming that have been used for many years. These conversion functions are just about indispensable for doing any type of network application programming and are too numerous to list in this section. However, you can consult the Linux manual, page `inet(3)` for a detailed list.

The socket API

The socket API deals with addresses and ports, and it is important to note that TCP/IP, like other network protocols, always considers ports and Internet addresses passed through the socket API to be in network byte order. Network byte order is the same as big endian or what used to be known as Motorola byte order. Linux, like other Unix-compatible OSs, provides a set of conversion functions to convert integers of various lengths between host byte order and network byte order. For a list of these functions, see the Linux manual, page `byteorder(3)`.

One more thing should be mentioned before exploring the socket API functions. There are two types of sockets, one for individual datagrams and another for a streaming sequence of bytes. These two types of sockets reflect the difference between connectionless and connection-oriented service. The UDP protocol provides the connectionless or datagram service and is accessed through sockets of type

SOCK_DGRAM. The TCP protocol is accessed through sockets of type SOCK_ST..
which provide connection-oriented service. Most of the socket calls can be used
with either socket type. However, one of the socket calls, connect, has slightly different semantics depending on the socket type, but connect is more commonly
used with TCP. Two of the socket calls, accept and listen, are not used for UDP at
all. In addition, recv, recvfrom, recvmsg, send, sendto, and sendmsg are usually used
only with UDP. Generally, TCP servers and clients use write and read to move data
to and from the sockets.

The socket API Functions

Now we will look at the socket API functions, the first and most important of which
is socket, which opens up a new connection.

The socket *Function*

```
int socket(int domain, int type, int protocol);
```

Socket must be called first, before the application can use any of the networking functions of the operating system for any purpose. socket returns an identifier
also known as a socket. This identifier is essentially a file descriptor and can be
used in the same way as the file descriptor returned by the open system call. In
other words, read and write calls can be done by specifying the socket.

The first argument to the socket call, domain, specifies which protocol family
will be accessed through the socket returned by this call. It should be set to one of
the protocol families used in Linux (shown in Table 4.1), and for us it is generally
AF_INET. In Linux generally, and everywhere in this book, we use the terms *protocol
family* and *address family* interchangeably. The BSD derived socket implementations make a distinction between these two, but Linux does not. For compatibility
with BSD, the protocol family is defined with names preceded by PF_, and the address families have names that begin with AF_, but the numerical values corresponding to each are identical. Type is generally set to one of three values for Linux
TCP/IP. It is set to SOCK_STREAM if the caller wants reliable connection-oriented service generally provided by the TCP transport protocol. Type is specified as
SOCK_DGRAM for connectionless service via the UDP transport protocol, or SOCK_RAW
for direct network access to underlying protocols below the transport layer. The
access to lower-layer protocols is generally referred to as "raw network protocol"
access. The allowed values for type are shown in Table 4.2.

Finally, the protocol argument to the socket call is typically set to zero when
sockets are open for conventional UDP or TCP packet transmission. In some cases,
though, the protocol field is used internally by the socket layer code to determine

which protocol the socket accesses if the `type` field is insufficient. For example, to get raw protocol access to ICMP, `protocol` would be set to `IPPROTO_ICMP`, and `type` is set to `SOCK_RAW`.

The `bind` Socket Call

The next socket API call, `bind`, is called by applications that want to register a local address with the socket. The local address generally consists of the port number and is referred to as the `name` of the socket. Applications that are sending UDP packets or datagrams don't have to call `bind`. If they want the peer to know where the packets came from, they should call `bind`.

```
int bind(int sockfd, struct sockaddr *my_addr, socklen_t addrlen);
```

`bind` is usually used by application servers to associate an endpoint or port and address combination with a socket. Applications will call `bind` if they want the socket layer to know the port on which they will be receiving data. The port number and the local IP address are specified in `myaddr` in the form of the `sockaddr` structure.

The `listen` Socket Call

The `listen` API function is called by a `SOCK_STREAM` or TCP server to let the socket layer know that it is ready to receive connection requests on the socket, s.

```
int listen (int s, int backlog );
```

`backlog` specifies the length of the queue of pending connection requests while the server is waiting for the `accept` call to complete.

The `accept` Call

`accept` is called by the application when it is ready to accept a connection request. It returns a new socket for the accepted connection. The address of the peer requesting the connection is placed in the `sockaddr` structure pointed to by `addr`. `addrlen` should point to a variable containing the size of `struct sockaddr` before calling `accept`. After the function call returns, `addrlen` points to the length of the new address in `addr`.

```
int accept (int s, struct sockaddr *addr, socklen_t *addrlen);
```

The `connect` Xall

The socket call, `connect`, is primarily used by a client application to establish a connection-oriented or `SOCK_STREAM` type connection with a server using the TCP protocol.

```
int connect (int s const struct sockaddr *serv_addr, socklen_t addrlen);
```

Serv_addr specifies the address and port of the server with which the caller wants to make a connection, and addrlen is set to the length of struct sockaddr. When used with TCP, connect actually causes TCP to initiate the connection negotiation between peers. Connect may also be used with SOCK_DGRAM, but in this case, it does not actually cause a connection; instead, it only specifies the peer address information so the send call can be used through the socket, s.

The socketpair Call

The socket call, socketpair, is not used for TCP/IP so it will not be discussed here. It is used for AF_UNIX domain sockets for inter-process communication within a system. We will see later as we discuss the internal structure of the socket layer that quite a bit of the complexity of sockets is due to the fact that they must support AF_UNIX based inter-process communication.

The send, sendto, and sendmsg Calls

These three calls are for passing an individual datagram. and we will take a closer look at these next three calls because of the added complexity. These three socket calls, send, sendto, and sendmsg—each transmit data from socket s to a peer socket. send is used only with a socket that has been connected, either as a server or client by having previously called connect. Sendto is used with any open SOCK_DGRAM socket because it includes the arguments to and tolen, which specify the address of the destination.

The send and sendto Functions

```
int send(int s, const void *msg, size_t len, int flags);
int sendto (int s, const void *msg, size_t len, int flags,
            const struct sockaddr *to, socklen_t tolen);
```

Normally, these calls will block until there is sufficient buffer space to receive the packet of the specified length.

The flags Argument

The flags argument for the three calls can contain any of the values shown in Table 4.3.

The sndmsg Call

```
int sendmsg (int s, const struct msghdr *msg, int flags);
```

Table 4.3 Socket API Function Values for Flags

Flag	Value	Purpose
MSG_OOB	1	Request out-of-bound data.
MSG_PEEK	2	Returns data from the head of the receive queue without removing it.
MSG_DONTROUTE	4	Don't route this message. Often used when sending ICMP packets as in the ping utility.
MSG_TRYHARD	4	Not used by TCP/IP. Synonym for MSG_DONTROUTE.
MSG_CTRUNC	8	For SOL_IP internal control messages.
MSG_PROBE	0x10	For MTU discovery.
MSG_TRUNC	0x20	Truncate message.
MSG_DONTWAIT	0x40	Set if the caller wants nonblocking IO.
MSG_EOR	0x80	End of record.
MSG_WAITALL	0x100	Wait for the full length of requested data before returning.
MSG_FIN	0x200	TCP FIN field in TCP header.
MSG_SYN	0x800	TCP SYN field in TCP header.
MSG_CONFIRM	0x800	Confirm the validity of the path before transmitting packet.
MSG_RST	0x1000	TCP RST
MSG_ERRQUEUE	0x2000	Requests that messages be read from the error queue.
MSG_NOSIGNAL	0x4000	Don't generate SIGPIPE signal when a connection is determined to be broken.
MSG_MORE	0x8000	Set to indicate that sender will send more data.

This function is often used to for internal communication between the kernel and the user layer. Messages are passed between application layer control programs and the protocols themselves. sendmsg is used widely with netlink sockets, PF_KEY sockets, and other internal mechanisms.

The msghdr Structure

The sendmsg call is used for a wide variety of functions, and the argment msg is defined to allow almost anything to be passed to the kernel with this call. The msg argument is a pointer to an instance of the msghdr structure.

```
struct msghdr {
```

msg_name contains the name of the socket. This is the destination IP address and port number for this message. msg_namelen is the length of the address pointed to by msg_name.

```
void            * msg_name;
socklen_t       msg_namelen;
```

msg_iov is an array of buffers of data to be sent or received. It is often referred to as the "scatter gather array," but it is not used only for DMA operations. msg_iovlen is the number of buffers in the array pointed to by msg_iov.

```
struct iovec * msg_iov;
size_t         msg_iovlen;
```

The following two fields are used for Posix 1003.1g ancillary data object information. The ancillary data consists of a sequence of pairs of cmsghdr and cmsg_data pairs. Msg_control is used to support the cmsg API function to pass control information to the underlying protocols. See the Linux manpage cmsg(3) for more information.

```
void            * msg_control;
socklen_t       msg_controllen;
```

msg_flags contains flags for the received message.

```
int             msg_flags;
};
```

For more information about how this is used see the last section in this chapter which discusses details about the rtnetlink and netlink address family and how these are used to pass control information to underlying protocols.

The iovec Structure

The iovec structure is used in the msghdr structure described earlier. It is defined in the file linux/include/linux/uio.h. The purpose of iovec is to set up memory for address translation between kernel and user space.

```
struct iovec
{
```

iov_base is a pointer to the buffer's base address. In BSD implementations, the field is typed caddr_t.

```
                void            *iov_base;
```

Size of the buffer.

```
                __kernel_size_t iov_len;
        };
```

The recv, recvfrom and recvmsg Calls

The next three socket calls, recv, recvfrom, recvmsg receive a message from a peer socket. As is the case with the socket call, send, recv is generally used with a connected socket, but recvfrom can be used to fetch a datagram from any machine.

```
int recv (int s, void *buf, size_t len, int flags);
int recvfrom ( int s, void *buf, size_t len, int flags, struct sockaddr
*from, socklen_t *fromlen);
int recvmsg ( int s, struct msghdr *msg, int flags);
```

Normally, these calls block until data is available of the specified length. Each call returns the length of the data read from the socket. After recvfrom returns, the parameters from and fromlen contain the sender's address and length. Often, these three calls are used with select to let the caller know when data is available. The argument flags may have one or more values from the list in Table 4.3. All the socket flags are shown with their values in Table 4.3.

The getsockopt and sendsockopt Calls

The two socket calls getsockopt and setsockopt are provided so the caller can access options or settings in the underlying protocols.

```
int getsockopt ( int s, int level, int optname, void *optval, socklen_t
*optlen );
int setsockopt ( int s, int level, int optname, const void *optval,
socklen_t optlen );
```

level should be set to one of the values from Table 4.4, each of which has the same values as the 1-byte protocol field in the IP header or the next header field of the IPv6 header. Generally, these values correspond with the 1-byte assigned numbers in the IANA database for IP protocol numbers. However, there are three exceptions: SOL_SOCKET, SOL_RAW, and SOL_IP. The value SOL_SOCKET indicates that the options settings refer to internal settings in the socket layer itself. SOL_RAW and SOL_IP indicate settings for IP internal protocols. See the first two chapters more about Internet number assignments.

TABLE 4.4 Values for Level Argument in setsockopt and getsockopt System Calls

Name	Value
SOL_IP	0
SOL_SOCKET	1
SOL_TCP	6
SOL_UDP	17
SOL_IPV6	41
SOL_ICMPV6	58
SOL_RAW	255

The optname argument is set to one of the values shown in Table 4.5. For the x86 architecture, these values are defined in the file linux/include/asm-i386/socket.h. Before the socket layer allows certain option values to be set, it checks to ensure that the user process has the appropriate level of permissions. These permissions are called capabilities and are described later in this chapter.

TABLE 4.5 Values for optname in getsockopt and setsockopt Calls

Name	Value	Purpose
SO_DEBUG	1	This option enables socket debugging. The option is only valid when the calling program has the CAP_NET_ADMIN capability. For more information on Linux capabilities, see the section on Linux capabilities later in this chapter.
SO_REUSEADDR	2	This option is set to allow reuse of local addresses with bind socket call.
SO_TYPE	3	This option is used with getsockopt call. When this option is used, the socket type is returned.
SO_ERROR	4	This option is also used with getsockopt call. It is for getting and clearing the current socket error.
SO_DONTROUTE	5	When this option is set, packets are not routed. They are sent only to internal destinations and hosts that are directly connected.

→

Name	Value	Purpose
SO_BROADCAST	6	This option is only used with UDP. When set, it allows packets to be sent to or received from a broadcast address.
SO_SNDBUF	7	This option and the next option are used to set the maximum size for the socket send or receive buffers. See Chapter 6 for the related sysctl values.
SO_RCVBUF	8	See the SO_SNDBUF option above.
SO_KEEPALIVE	9	Generally used by TCP. Setting this option keeps socket connections alive by sending keep-alive probes. See Chapter 9 for more details.
SO_OOBINLINE	10	This option is primarily used by TCP. It controls how out-of-band (OOB) data is handled. If the option is set, the OOB data is included in the data stream instead of being passed when the MSG_OOB flag is set.
SO_NO_CHECK	11	This flag is an undocumented flag that can be used to turn off checksums on UDP packets. It is not recommended for use by the average application program. The option is set to UDP_CSUM_DEFAULT, which enables all checksums; UDP_CSUM_NOXMIT, which disables transmit checksums; or UDP_CSUM_NORCV, which disables checksum calculation on received UDP packets.
SO_PRIORITY	12	This option is used to set the IP Type-of-Service (TOS) flags for outgoing packets.
SO_LINGER	13	This option is used with TCP. When set, a close(2) or shutdown(2) call on this socket will block until all queued messages have been sent and received by the peer or the number of seconds specified in the timeout has elapsed.
SO_BSDCOMPAT	14	This option is used by UDP. It specifies that ICMP errors received on this socket will not be passed to the application via this socket.
SO_PASSCRED	16	Used for passing file descriptors via control message. Not generally used by AF_INET-type sockets.
SO_PEERCRED	17	This option is only used for AF_UNIX-type sockets.

→

Name	Value	Purpose
SO_RCVLOWAT	18	This and the next option are used with `getsockopt`. They obtain the size of the buffer necessary before data is passed to TCP. In Linux, they are always set to 1 byte.
SO_SNDLOWAT	19	See SO_RCVLOWAT option.
SO_RCVTIMEO	20	These two options specify the amount of time to wait before receiving or sending an error.
SO_SNDTIMEO	21	See SO_RCVTIMEO option.
SO_SECURITY_AUTHENTICATION	22	Security levels in IPv6.
SO_SECURITY_ENCRYPTION_TRANSPORT	23	Security levels in IPv6.
SO_SECURITY_ENCRYPTION_NETWORK	24	Security levels in IPv6.
SO_BINDTODEVICE	25	This option is available if CONFIG_NETDEVICES is set in the kernel. It provides a method of gaining socket access directly to network interface devices for configuration.
SO_ATTACH_FILTER	26	Attach a socket filter. Socket filters are similar to Berkeley Packet Filters (BPF).
SO_DETACH_FILTER	27	Dettach a socket filter.
SO_PEERNAME	28	Retrieve the "name" of a peer for a connected socket.
SO_TIMESTAMP	29	
SCM_TIMESTAMP	29	Same as SO_TIMESTAMP.
SO_ACCEPTCONN	30	Sets the socket to listen mode. It is not clear how this is to be used.
SO_PEERSEC	31	Retrieve the peer socket security state.

PACKET, RAW, NETLINK, AND ROUTING SOCKETS

To complete any discussion of socket application layer programming, we must include information about Linux's special sockets. These sockets are for internal message passing and raw protocol access. Netlink, routing, packet, and raw are all types of specialized sockets. Netlink provides a socket-based interface for communication of messages and settings between the user and the internal protocols. BSD-style routing sockets are supported by Linux netlink sockets. This is why, as shown in Table 4.1, AF_ROUTE and AF_NETLINK are identical. AF_ROUTE is provided for source code portability with BSD Unix. Rtnetlink includes extensions to the messages used in the regular netlink sockets. Rtnetlink is for application-level management of the neighbor tables and IP routing tables. Chapter 5 includes more details about the internal implementation of netlink and rtnetlink sockets and how they interface to the protocols in the AF_INET family.

Packet Sockets

Packet sockets are accessed by the application when it sets AF_PACKET in the family field of the socket call. See packet(7) for more information about packet sockets.

```
ps = socket (PF_PACKET, int type, int protocol);
```

type is set to either SOCK_RAW or SOCK_DGRAM. Protocol has the number of the protocol and is the same as the IP header protocol number or one of the valid protocol numbers.

Raw Sockets

Raw sockets allow user-level application code to receive and transmit network layer packets by intercepting them before they pass through the transport layer. This type of socket is generally not used for link or physical layer access because the link layer headers are stripped from received packets before delivering them to the socket.

```
rs = socket ( PF_INET, SOCK_RAW, int protocol);
```

protocol is set to the protocol number that the application wants to transmit or receive. A common example of the use of raw sockets is the ping command, ping(8). Ping is an application that accesses the ICMP protocol, which is internal to IP and does not register directly with the socket layer. The ping command sends ICMP echo request packets and listens for echo replies. When the ping application code opens the socket, it sets the protocol field in the socket call to IPPROTO_ICMP. Ping and other application programs for route and network maintenance make use of a Linux utility library call to convert a protocol name into a protocol number, getprotent(3).

Netlink Sockets

Netlink sockets are accessed by calling socket with family set to AF_NETLINK.

```
ns = socket (AF_NETLINK, int type, int netlink_family);
```

The `type` parameter can be set to either `SOCK_DGRAM` or `SOCK_STREAM`, but it doesn't really matter because the protocol accessed by is determined by `netlink_family`, and this parameter is set to one of the values in Table 4.6. The `send` and `recv` socket calls are generally used with `netlink`. The messages sent through these sockets have a particular format. See `netlink(7)` for more details. There is quite a bit more complexity to using the `netlink` sockets than we are describing in this section. Later in this chapter, we will discuss the internal structure of `netlink` in more detail while we see how the `netlink` mechanism interfaces to the protocols in TCP/IP.

Routing Sockets

Routing sockets are specified by the `AF_ROUTE` address family. In Linux, routing sockets are identical to `netlink` sockets.

TABLE 4.6 Values for the `Netlink_family` Argument

Name	Value	Purpose
NETLINK_ROUTE	0	Routing or device hook
NETLINK_W1	1	
NETLINK_USERSOCK	2	Reserved for future user-mode socket protocols
NETLINK_FIREWALL	3	Hook for access to firewalling hook
NETLINK_INET_DIAG	4	AF_INET socket monitoring
NETLINK_NFLOG	5	Netfilter and iptables user logging
NETLINK_XFRM	6	For use by IPSec protocols
NETLINK_SELINUX	7	For Secure Linux event monitoring.
NETLINK_ISCSI	8	For the open source I-SCSI implementation.
NETLINK_AUDIT	9	For auditing
NETLINK_FIB_LOOKUP	10	For lookups in the Forwarding Information Base (FIB)
NETLINK_CONNECTOR	11	
NETLINK_NETFILTER	12	For the netfilter subsystem of netlink.
NETLINK_IP6_FW	13	IPv6 Forwarding
NETLINK_DNRTMSG	14	DECnet routing messages
NETLINK_KOBJECT_UEVENT	15	For passing kernel messages to user space.
NETLINK_GENERIC	16	

rtnetlink

rtnetlink extends netlink sockets by appending netlink type messages with some additional attributes. Rtnetlink sockets are most often used for application layer access to the routing tables.

More information about rtnetlink and the other special socket types can be found in the man pages. Refer to the Linux manpages netlink(7), rtnetlink(7), packet(7), and raw(7) for more information.

SECURITY AND LINUX CAPABILITIES

Linux capabilities are similar to Access Control Lists (ACL) on other systems. If there were no security mechanism, the special sockets discussed in the previous section could be used by programmers to gain almost complete access to underlying kernel structures including the internals of the TCP/IP stack. In the wrong hands, this rich set of functions could be a vehicle for security violations. We want to prevent unauthorized users from engaging in Denial-of-Service (DoS) and other attacks. It is very easy to sabotage a system by deleting routes or rerouting sockets. capabilities are the mechanism in Linux to prevent unauthorized access to these powerful low-level features and are used in recent versions of the kernel for defining levels of access. Traditional Unix systems had two levels of access, either root or user. After a user gained root access, anything could be done. More recently, however, Linux capabilities is compliant with the POSIX.1e Draft Capabilities. It divides the complete set of root-level privileges into subsets. We won't go into a detailed discussion of all the features of Linux capabilities, because it isn't relevant to TCP/IP, but we will cover how Linux capabilities are used to control access to sockets. For more information, refer to the Linux manpage capabilities(7) for more details

Capabilities are important because it stores the user-level permissions that are checked by the socket layer before allowing raw or netlink socket access. To perform these checks, Linux provides an internal function, capable, defined in the file linux/include/linux/capability.h for checking capabilities against the currently executing user-level process.

```
extern int capable(int cap);
```

Starting with Version 2.4, Linux provides a set of data structure and macros in the file linux/include/capability.h to hold and manipulate the capabilities. If security is configured into the kernel, CONFIG_SECURITY, the capable function points to an operation that is part of a loaded capability module, which is a plug-in to the

Linux 2.6 security framework. If not, the function `capable` calls a dummy function, `dummy_capable`, which returns the effective capabilities of the current process, the one that is making the user-level socket call.

```
static int dummy_capable (struct task_struct *tsk, int cap)
{
    if (cap_raised (tsk->cap_effective, cap))
        return 0;
    return -EPERM;
}
```

In Linux, the global variable `current` always points to the currently executing process. The kernel capabilities are stored in a 32-bit integer, `kernel_cap_t`. Current stores the following three types of capabilities.

```
kernel_cap_t   cap_effective, cap_inheritable, cap_permitted;
```

In the socket layer code, we only actually check the `cap_effective` capabilities because we are interested in the capabilities of the current application process making the socket call. See the file `linux/include/linux/capability.h` for a list of all the POSIX capabilities and the numerical values associated with each.

A NOTE ABOUT THE SOCKET API AND IPV6

Chapter 11 covers the Linux IPv6 protocol, how it is implemented, and how it compares to the IPv4 implementation. However, in this section, we will mention the address family used with the IPv6 and a few changes that were made to the 2.6 kernel socket API to accommodate the protocol suite. IPv6 introduces a new address family, `AF_INET6`, which is defined in `linux/include/socket.h` along with the other address families.

IPv6 Sock Address Type, `sockaddr_in6`

To support IPv6 addressing, Linux provides a separate socket address type for IPv6, `sockaddr_in6`, defined in the file `linux/include/linux/in6.h`.

```
struct sockaddr_in6 {
```

The first two fields look very much like the `sockaddr_in` structure. The following field, `sin6_family`, is set to the value `AF_INET6` or 10.

```
unsigned short intsin6_family;
```

This field, sin6_port, is the port number for either UDP or TCP. The next field, sin6_flowinfo, is the IPv6 flow information. See Chapter 11 for more information about this IPv6 flow.

```
__u16                sin6_port;
__u32                sin6_flowinfo;
```

The next field, sin6_addr, is the actual IPv6 address defined as a union. The last field is the scope ID, which defines the scope of the address. We discuss this structure in more detail and the IPv6 address scope in Chapter 11.

```
struct in6_addr      sin6_addr;
__u32                sin6_scope_id;
};
```

IPv6 sockets are backward compatible with IPv4. IPv6 specifies that data can be sent either via IPv4 or IPv6 through any open IPv6 socket. The socket API is defined so that application code that transmits data over IPv6 will also be compatible with IPv4 without modification. Underneath the covers, the actual 128-bit IPv6 address has a subtype that includes the 32-bit IPv4 address. In Chapter 11, we examine IPv6 addressing in more detail.

Address Conversion Functions

To aid programmers in writing code that is independent of either protocol type, Linux provides API library functions. These functions convert addresses between the IPv4 and IPv6 formats.

The getaddrinfo Function

The first function, getaddrinfo(3), is for network address and service translation.

```
int getaddrinfo (const char *node, const char *service, const struct
addrinfo *hints, struct addrinfo **res);
```

It is a generic function that combines the functionality of three other functions: getipnodebyaddr(3), getservbyname(3), and getipnodebyname(3). Getaddrinfo creates either IPv4 or IPv6 type address structures for use with the bind or connect socket calls. If not NULL, hints specifies the preferred socket type. It points to an instance of addrinfo, the fields of which determine the socket type. Either or both of the next two parameters, node or service, may be specified, but only one of them can be NULL. Node specifies an address in IPv4 format, an address in IPv6 format, or a hostname. Service specifies the port number. Getaddrinfo supports multiple addresses and multihoming; therefore, the result res is a linked list of addrinfo structures. This structure is defined in the getaddrinfo(3) manual page.

The addrinfo Structure

The data structure, addrinfo, is used in both the hints and result for the getaddrinfo(3) library function. If used for hints, addrinfo specifies the preferred address family AF_INET, AF_INET6, or AF_UNSPECIFIED.

```
struct addrinfo {
    int             ai_flags;
    int             ai_family;
    int             ai_socktype;
    int             ai_protocol;
    size_t          ai_addrlen;
    struct sockaddr *ai_addr;
    char            *ai_canonname;
    struct addrinfo *ai_next;
}
```

The freeaddrinfo Function

This function frees the addrinfo structure pointed to by res.

```
void freeaddrinfo (struct addrinfo *res );
```

The getnameinfo Function

The last function that we will show is getnameinfo(3).

```
int getnameinfo (const struct sockaddr *sa, socklen_t salen, char
*host, size_t hostlen, char *serv, size_t servlen, int flags);
```

This structure can be either sockaddr_in or sockaddr_in6 getnameinfo is really a generalized function for address to node name translation that can work with the address formats in both IPv4 and IPv6. It converts numerical address to and from text host names in a way that is independent of IPv4 and IPv6.

IMPLEMENTATION OF THE SOCKET API SYSTEM CALLS

Many operating systems designed for embedded systems are implemented in a flat memory space. These operating systems were originally designed for CPUs that don't have a MMU that maps physical memory to virtual memory. In these systems, which are generally smaller, the operating system kernel functions can be called directly from application-level programs without doing any memory address translation. In contrast, Linux is a virtual memory operating system. It requires a processor with an MMU. In a virtual memory operating system, each user process runs in its own virtual address space. The socket API functions are included in the system calls. These system calls are different from ordinary library calls because they can be used in nonblocking mode so that the calling user process does not have to wait while the operating system completes the processing of the request. In addition, arguments in the function call are in the memory space of the user process and must be mapped into kernel space before they can be accessed by any kernel-level code. In our case, these arguments point to data to be sent and received through the TCP/IP protocol stack.

The socket API supports other protocol families besides AF_INET or TCP/IP, and all the protocol families supported by Linux are shown in Table 4.1. In addition, Linux provides the capability of defining a new module containing an unknown protocol family. Because of this, several steps are involved with directing each application layer socket call to the specific protocol that must respond to the request. This is a complex process and has several steps. First, any address referenced in the call's arguments must be mapped from user space to kernel space. A complete discussion of the Linux virtual memory architecture is beyond the scope of this book. However, in Chapter 6 we do discuss the Linux slab cache system of memory allocation as part of the examination of socket buffers. Next, the functions themselves must be translated from generic socket layer functions to the specific functions for the protocol family. Finally, the functions must be translated from the protocol family generic functions to the specific functions for the member protocol in the family.

As we shall see in this section, each of the socket API calls is mapped to a set of corresponding calls in the kernel with a sys_ in front of the name, and each of these calls are defined in the file linux/net/socket.c. Most of these functions don't do much other than call the address family-specific function through the ops field in the socket structure. Sys_socket is discussed separately in another section, because it is quite complex in that it creates a new socket and sets up the structures to allow the other socket API functions work.

Earlier in this chapter, we covered each of the socket API functions, but in this section, we will see what happens under the hood when the socket API functions are called. Figure 4.1 shows how the application layer socket calls are mapped to the corresponding protocol-specific kernel functions. When any of the socket API functions are called, it causes an interrupt to the kernel's syscall facility, which in turn calls the sys_socketcall function in the file linux/net/socket.c. In many CPU architectures such as the Intel x86 family, pointers to the system call's arguments are passed to the kernel in one or more CPU registers. The implementation of the socket call itself is discussed separately in this chapter. However, the implementation of the other socket function is covered in this section.

The Socket Multiplexor

The purpose of the socket multiplexor is to unravel the socket system calls. This mechanism is implemented in the file `linux/net/socket.c`.

The `sys_socketcall` Function

The function that does most of the work of socket call mapping is `sys_socketcall`. This function maps the addresses in the arguments from the user-level socket function to kernel space and calls the correct kernel call for the specified protocol.

```
asmlinkage long sys_socketcall(int call, unsigned long __user *args);
```

The first thing `sys_socketcall` does is map each address from user space to kernel space. It does this by calling `copy_from_user`. Next, `sys_socketcall` invokes the system call function that corresponds to a user-level socket call. For example, when the user calls `bind`, `sys_socketcall` maps the user-level `bind` to the kernel function, `sys_bind`, and `listen` is mapped to `sys_listen`. Each of these socket system call functions is also defined in the file `linux/net/socket.c`. Each of these functions returns a file descriptor (`fd`). The file descriptor is also referred to as a socket. To support standard IO, sockets and file descriptors are treated as the same thing from the IO call's point of view. The `fd` serves as a handle to reference the open socket. Each socket API function includes the file descriptor for the open socket as the first parameter. When a socket API function is called, in the kernel, we use `fd` to fetch a pointer to the socket structure that was originally created when the socket was opened. When we have a pointer to the socket structure, we retrieve the function specific to the address family and protocol type through the open socket. To do this, we call the protocol-specific function through a pointer in the structure pointed to by the `ops` field of the `socket` structure. The socket structure is discussed earlier in this chapter, and the `proto_ops` structure is also covered in detail in the beginning of this chapter.

Mapping of Socket Calls, `sys_send` and Other Functions

For an example of how the socket calls are mapped, we will look at the specific socket API call, `send`. When the application calls `send`, the kernel translates this call to `sys_send`, which calls `sys_sendto` with the peer destination address set to NULL. `sys_sendto` calls `sock_sendmsg`, which in turn calls `__sock_sendmsg`. and that function calls the `sendmsg` function for the protocol by dereferencing the `proto_ops` structure in the socket. Figure 4.1 shows this sequence for all the socket calls.

```
         return sock->ops->sendmsg(iocb, sock, msg, size);
```

sys_bind, sys_listen, and sys_connect do little other than call the function specific to the address family. In addition, sys_getname and sys_getpeername both map to the address family's function for the open socket, fd.

sys_recv calls sys_recvfrom, and Sys_recvfrom calls the socket layer function. sock_recvmsg and sock_recvmsg calls the protocol layer specific recvmsg function through the ops pointer in the sock structure.

```
         return sock->ops->recvmsg(iocb, sock, &msg, size);
```

The sys_setsockopt and sys_getsockopt Functions

sys_setsockopt and sys_getsockopt check the level argument. If level is set to SOL_SOCKET, one of the socket layer functions, sock_setsockopt or sock_getsockopt is called. If level is anything else, the respective protocol-specific function is called through the proto_ops structure accessed by the ops field of the socket structure.

The sys_shutdown Function

sys_shutdown also calls the corresponding protocol specific function through the shutdown field in the proto_ops structure.

The sys_sendmsg and sys_recvmsg Functions

sys_sendmsg and sys_recvmsg have a bit more work to do than the other socket functions. They must verify that the iovec buffer array contains valid addresses first. Each address is mapped from kernel to user space later when the data is actually transferred, but the addresses are validated now. After completing the validation of the iovec structure, sock_sendmsg and sock_recvmsg functions are called, respectively.

The sys_accept Function

Sys_accept is a bit more complicated because it has to establish a new socket for the new incoming connection. The first thing it does is call sock_alloc to allocate a new socket. Next, it has to get a name for the socket by calling the function pointed to by the getname field in the ops field in the socket structure. Remember that the "name" of a socket is the address and port number associated with the socket. Next, it calls sock_map_fd to map the new socket into the pseudo-socket filesystem. Early in this chapter, we can see how the sys_accept mechanism works because it does something very similar to the socket call.

Implementation of Socket Layer Internal Functions

In the previous section, we showed how the application layer calls translate into the socket system calls. Next, we discussed how these calls get resolved to the internal socket layer functions. Now, we will look at some of these internal functions in more detail. Figure 4.1 shows a simplified view of how the mapping of functions occurs in the socket layer.

The `sock_sendmsg` and `sock_recvmsg` Functions

The first two functions in the socket layer, `sock_sendmsg` and `sock_recvmsg`, will be discussed briefly. They are called from `sys_sendmsg` and `sys_recvmsg`, respectively. These two functions are implemented in the socket layer to allow user-level applications to send and receive individual datagrams. The `AF_UNIX` address family makes heavy use of these calls for interprocess communication. This is really beyond the scope of this book, but `AF_UNIX` also includes a Unix-compatible method of passing file descriptors among user-level applications.

File IO Functions

The file IO functions are handled differently from the socket system calls. Refer to the later section on IO system calls to see how the file structure is initially de-referenced. In this section we will describe what the socket level IO calls do and how they call the underlying protocol family's send and receive functions.

The Functions `sock_read` and `sock_write`

Next, we will discuss the functions `sock_read`, and `sock_write`. These functions are also defined in file `linux/net/socket.c` and are actually socket layer implementations of the IO system calls. To extract the `msg_flags` from the `file` structure and then call `__sock_recvmsg` and `__sock_sendmsg`, respectively. This function in turn calls the protocol specific `recvmsg` function as follows.

```
return sock->ops->recvmsg(iocb, sock, msg, size, flags);
```

The functions `sock_close` and `sock_ioctl` are similar to the file IO functions. These functions are also defined in file `linux/net/socket.c` and are actually socket layer implementations of the IO system calls.

The `sock_ioctl` Function

`sock_ioctl` is called with a file pointer in the argument `file`. First it extracts the `sock` structure from the private area of the `file` structure. Next it checks for `ioctls` that can be handled at the socket layer. Any unknown `ioctls` are passed directly to the device or lower layers. Earlier in this chapter, we saw how the file IO system calls are mapped to sockets.

The sock_readv and sock_writev Functions

The functions sock_readv and sock_writev set up an iovec type msghdr structure before calling __sock_recvmsg and __sock_sendmsg, respectively.

The sock_setsockopt and sock_getsockopt Functions

sock_setsockopt and sock_getsockopt are implemented in the file linux/net/core/sock.c. They are called from the equivalent system call, sys_setsockopt, for example if level is set to SOL_SOCKET. The purpose of these functions is to set values in the sock structure according to the options that were passed as a parameter by the application layer. The system-level functions sys_setsockopt and sys_getsockopt call these socket layer functions before any protocol-specific settings are altered.

sock_setsockopt gets a pointer to the sock structure from the sk field of the socket structure, which was passed as an argument. Next, it sets options in the sock structure based on the values pointed to by the optname and optval arguments. In an earlier section in this chapter, we discussed the sock structure in detail. If SO_DEBUG is set in optname, the debug option is set, sk_reuse is set to the value of SO_REUSEADDR, and the flags field is set to the appropriate values. In addition, rcvtstamp is set to the value of SO_TIMESTAMP, and rcvlowat is set to the value of SO_RCVLOWAT. If SO_SNDBUF or SO_RCVBUF are set, sk_ndbuf or sk_rcvbuf are set to the minimum value or the value in optval times two—whichever is greater. The sk_priority field is set to optval if SO_PRIORITY is set.

A few other fields in sk are handled specially in the sock_setsockopt function. If SO_KEEPALIVE is set in optname, and the protocol field in sk is equal to IPPROTO_TCP, tcp_set_keepalive is called with the value in optval to set the keepalive value for the TCP connection.

NOTE: Chapters 7 and 9 cover the TCP protocol in depth including many aspects of TCP state and connection management, including keepalives, slow start congestion avoidance, and other factors.

The protocol field of the sock structure is used to determine that this socket is a TCP socket. That protocol value originally came from the protocol argument in the socket function that created this socket. If the SO_LINGER option is present, the linger field is set and the value of the lingertime field is calculated from optval.

Sock_getsockopt is the inverse of the function sock_setsockopt. It retrieves certain values from the sock structure for the option socket and returns them to the user. Refer to the earlier section on the sock structure to see which fields hold values for the socket options. A few options deserve special attention because they don't have a corresponding action in `sock_setsockopt`. For example, if `SO_ERROR` is used to extract current recoverable errors such as connection timeouts. If the this option is set in `optname`, the current socket error is retrieved from the `sk_err_soft` field in the `sock` structure, and the `sk_err_soft` field is cleared. If the `SO_TYPE` option is set, the value of the `type` field is returned. This field corresponds to the original setting of the `type` field in the socket call that created this socket. We will recall that `type` indicates whether this is a datagram socket, a streaming socket or a raw socket.

Implementation of Protocol Internal Socket Functions

Most of the behavior specific to the member protocols in the `AF_INET` family is described in later chapters. In this section, we will complete the discussion of how each member protocol communicates with the socket layer. As shown in Figure 4.2, the file descriptor, `fd` is used to map each socket API call with a function specific to each protocol. The mechanism that sets up this mapping was described earlier for the socket system calls and for the IO system calls. In addition, we also saw how each of the protocols registers itself with the protocol switch table. We recall that when the socket structure is initialized, the `ops` field was set to the set of protocol-specific operations from the entry in the protocol switch table.

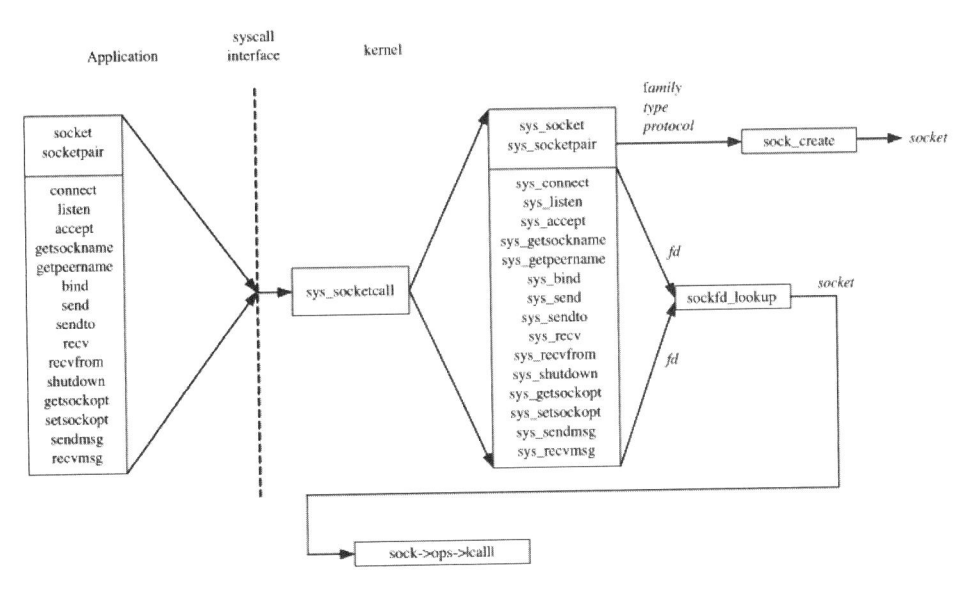

FIGURE 4.2 Mapping of socket calls.

When all the complex initialization is done as described in other sections, the actual mapping is quite simple. In most cases, the "sys_" versions of the socket functions simply call `sockfd_lookup` to get a pointer to the socket structure and call the protocol's function through the ops field. The function `sys_getsockname` in the file linux/net/socket.c can provide us with a simple example. This function is called in the kernel when the user executes the `getsockname` socket API function to get the address (name) of a socket.

```
asmlinkage long sys_getsockname(int fd, struct sockaddr *usockaddr, int *usockaddr_len)
```

`fd` is the open socket. After returning, `usockaddr` will point to the address for the socket. `usockaddr_len` points to the length of the socket address.

```
{
    struct socket *sock;
    char address[MAX_SOCK_ADDR];
    int len, err;
    sock = sockfd_lookup(fd, &err);
```

This is where the protocol-specific function is called. The ops field contains the socket functions for each protocol. The protocols are UDP for SOCK_DGRAM and TCP for SOCK_STREAM.

```
    if (!sock)
        goto out;
```

Recent versions of the 2.6 kernel have centralized the security processing in the kernel. A security framework is created that can intercept all system calls checking for permissions and other restrictions. We call this function `security_socket_getsockname` to ensure that the caller has the `capability` to get the local name of the socket.

```
    err = security_socket_getsockname(sock);
    if (err)
        goto out_put;
```

This is where the protocol-specific function is called. The ops field contains the socket functions for each protocol. The protocols are UDP for SOCK_DGRAM and SOCK_STREAM for TCP.

```
    err = sock->ops->getname(sock, (struct sockaddr *)address, &len, 0);
    if (err)
        goto out_put;
```

Here the return values are mapped into user space.

```
    err = move_addr_to_user(address, len, usockaddr, usockaddr_len);
out_put:
```

This bumps the use count on the open file associated with the socket, fd.

```
    sockfd_put(sock);
out:
    return err;
}
```

CREATION OF A SOCKET

Before the user can perform any operations with the TCP/IP stack, she creates a new socket by calling the socket API function. Sockets are generic and not necessarily associated with TCP/IP, so quite a few things happen before any code in the TCP/IP stack itself gets called. Sockets can be created for many protocol types other than TCP/IP. This section will describe what happens under the hood in the Linux kernel when the system call, socket, is executed.

The sys_socket Function

Early in the chapter, we discussed how the system calls map to kernel implemented functions. It is through this mapping that the sys_socket function executes an AF_INET specific function for the TCP/IP protocol family. sys_socket is defined in the file linux/net/socket.c. Primarily, the socket layer is responsible for activities that are not specific to a particular protocol family such as AF_INET. After the generic initialization is complete, socket creation will call the socket creation function for the protocol-specific family. After we discuss the generic socket creation, we will discuss what happens during socket creation for TCP/IP, the AF_INET protocol family.

The sock_create Function

sock_create initiates the creation of a new socket. It is defined in the file linux/net/socket.c and is called from sys_socket.

```
    int sock_create(int family, int type, int protocol, struct socket **res);
```

`sock_create` only calls `__sock_create`, which does the real work. First, `__sock_create` verifies that `family` is one of the allowed family types shown in Table 4.1. Then, it checks capabilities through the security framework by calling `security_socket_create`. If this check passes, it allocates a new socket by calling `sock_alloc`, which returns a new socket structure, `sock`. Earlier in this chapter, we included a detailed discussion of the socket structure.

The `sock_alloc` Function

`sock_alloc`, called from `sock_create`, returns an allocated socket structure. The socket structure is actually part of an `inode` structure, created when `sock_alloc` calls `new_inode`. It is necessary to have an `inode` for all Linux IO system calls to work with sockets. In an earlier section, we explored the IO system call mapping in more detail. Most of the fields in the `inode` structure are important only to real filesystems; however, a few of them are used by sockets. The fields in the `inode` structure that are used for sockets are listed in Table 4.7. The `inode` structure is defined in the file linux/include/linux/fs.h.

TABLE 4.7 Inode Structure Fields Used by Sockets

Field	Prototype	Purpose
i_dev	kdev_t	Set to device. This is always NULL for a socket inode.
i_mode	umode_t	Set to indicate IO permissions and interface type.
i_uid	uid_t	Set to the UID of the current user process that is opening the socket.
i_gid	i_gid	Set to the GID of the current user process that is opening the socket.
i_fop	struct file_operations *	In a socket type `inode`, points to file operations for sockets.

After the `inode` is created, `sock_alloc` retrieves the socket structure from the `inode`. Then, it initializes a few fields in the socket structure. The `i_mode` field is set to allow user, group, and other access for read, write, and execute permissions. We have seen elsewhere how the security framework makes sure that the caller has the appropriate permissions to use any of the socket features. The `i_uid` and `i_gid` fields are also set to corresponding user and group IDs from `current`, the caller's user process.

The Socket State

Sockets maintain a state related to whether an open socket represents a connection to a peer or not. These states are maintained in the field in the socket structure called, state, which is initialized to SS_UNCONNECTED when the socket is created. See Table 4.8 for a description of the socket states. These states are defined in the file linux/include/linux/net.h.

TABLE 4.8 Socket State

State Name	Value	Description
SS_FREE	0	Socket is not allocated yet.
SS_UNCONNECTED	1	Unconnected to another socket.
SS_CONNECTING	2	Socket is in the process of connecting.
SS_CONNECTED	3	Connected to another socket.
SS_DISCONNECTING	4	Socket is in the process of disconnecting.

It is important to emphasize that sockets are not just for TCP/IP. The states maintained in the socket structure do not contain all the same states as TCP, which is quite a bit more complicated. See Chapters 7 and 9 for a complete discussion of TCP. In contrast to TCP, the socket state really only reflects whether there is an active connection because sockets support other protocol families and must be generic. The internal logic to manage the protocol attached to a new socket will be maintained in the protocol itself, and TCP is no exception. However, since the socket layer must support several protocols, it requires some internal connection management logic in addition to what is in the internal TCP implementation.

The sock_alloc_inode Function

sock_alloc_inode is called from sock_alloc indirectly. A pointer to this function is set in the file ops for the socket inode type. sock_alloc_inode also sets some of the socket specific fields. It sets the ops field to NULL. Later, when the family member protocol-specific create function is called, ops will be set to the set of protocol-specific operations. Sock_alloc_inode initializes a few more fields before returning. The flags field is initialized to zero because no flags are set yet. Later, the application will specify the flags by calling one of the send or receive socket API functions. Table 4.3 contains a description of the flags used with the socket API. Finally, two other fields, sk and file, are initialized to NULL, but they both deserve a little attention. The first of these fields, sk, will be set later to point to the internal sock structure by the protocol-specific `create` function. `File` will be set to a file pointer allocated when `sock_map_fd` is called. The file pointer is used to maintain the state of the pseudo file associated with the open socket.

After returning from the `sock_alloc` call, `sock_create` calls the `create` function for the protocol family. It accesses the array `net_families` to get the family's `create` function. For TCP/IP, `family` will be set to `AF_INET`.

Creation of an `AF_INET` Socket

The `create` function for the TCP/IP protocol family `AF_INET` is `inet_create`, defined in the file `linux/net/ipv4/af_inet.c`. It is called through the create field in the `net_proto_family` structure for the `AF_INET` suite of protocols.

```
static int inet_create(struct socket *sock, int protocol);
```

`inet_create` is defined as static because it is not called directly. It is called from `sock_create` when `family` is set to `AF_INET`. First, `inet_create` searches the protocol switch table to look for a match with the family member protocol with the `protocol` field in the socket call. If it can't find a match, it tries to load the appropriate module. After getting the result from the search of the protocol switch table, the capability flags are checked against the capabilities of the current process, and if the caller doesn't have permission to create this type of socket, the user level socket call will return the EPERM error.

Next, assuming a match is found, we create a new `sock` structure pointed to by `sk`. The new `sock` structure is allocated from the slab cache. We call `sk_alloc` to allocate the `sock` structure from the slab cache that is specific to the protocol for this socket.

```
sk = sk_alloc(PF_INET, GFP_KERNEL, answer_prot, 1);
```

Now, `inet_create` sets a few fields in the new `sock` data structure, however, Many fields are pre-initialized when allocation is done from the slab cache. The field `sk_family` is set to `PF_INET`. The `sk_protocol` field is set to the protocol value. `No_check` and `ops` are set according to their respective values in the protocol switch table. If the type of the socket is `SOCK_RAW`, the `num` field is set to the protocol number. As will be shown in later chapters, this field is used by IP to route packets internally depending on whether there is a raw socket open. The `sk_destruct` field of `sk` is set to `inet_sock_destruct`, the `sock` structure destructor. The `sk_backlog_rcv` field is set to point to the protocol-specific backlog receive function. Also, some fields in the protocol family-specific part of the `sock` structure are initialized. As discussed earlier in this chapter, the `sock` structure is followed by a protocol-specific portion for each of the two protocol families, IPv4 and IPv6, and this part is accessed through a macro, inet_sk.

The default time-to-live field, mc_ttl is initialized because this value will be used in the time-to-live IP header field for multicast packets. Even though these values are initialized here, the application may change the values in these fields later through the setsockopt call.

Finally, inet_create calls the protocol-specific initialization function through the init field in the protocol block structure, proto, defined in the file linux/include/net/sock.h.

The proto Structure

    struct proto {

Most of the fields in this structure point to the protocol-specific operations. We will explain a few of these functions in a little more detail.

    void   (*close)(struct sock *sk,
                            long timeout);
    int   (*connect)(struct sock *sk,
                            struct sockaddr *uaddr,
                            int addr_len);
    int   (*disconnect)(struct sock *sk, int flags);
    struct sock *   (*accept) (struct sock *sk, int flags, int
    *err);
    int   (*ioctl)(struct sock *sk, int cmd,
                            unsigned long arg);

init points to the protocol's specific initialization function. This function is called when a socket is created for this protocol. Destroy points to the destructor function for this protocol. The destructor is executed when a socket for this protocol is closed.

    int   (*init)(struct sock *sk);
    int   (*destroy)(struct sock *sk);
    void   (*shutdown)(struct sock *sk, int how);
    int   (*setsockopt)(struct sock *sk, int level,
                            int optname, char *optval, int
                            optlen);
    int   (*getsockopt)(struct sock *sk, int level,
                            int optname, char *optval,
                            int *option);

```
int                     (*sendmsg)(struct kiocb *iocb, struct sock *sk,
                                   struct msghdr *msg, int len);
int                     (*recvmsg)(struct kiocb *iocb, struct sock *sk,
                                   struct msghdr *msg,
                                   int len, int noblock, int flags,
                                   int *addr_len);
int                     (*sendpage)(struct sock *sk, struct page *page,
                                    int offset, size_t size, int flags);
int                     (*bind)(struct sock *sk,
                                struct sockaddr *uaddr, int addr_len);
int                     (*backlog_rcv) (struct sock *sk,
                                        struct sk_buff *skb);
```

The following three functions are for keeping track of sock structures, looking them up, and getting the port number associated with the sock, respectively.

```
void                    (*hash)(struct sock *sk);
void                    (*unhash)(struct sock *sk);
int                     (*get_port)(struct sock *sk, unsigned short
                                    snum);
```

The following fields are for memory pressure. Memory pressure is a method used by a monitoring process can observe the rate at which memory is released by tasks. See linux/documentation/cpusets.txt for more information.

```
void                    (*enter_memory_pressure)(void);
atomic_t                *memory_allocated;
atomic_t                *sockets_allocated;
int                     *memory_pressure;
int                     *sysctl_mem;
int                     *sysctl_wmem;
int                     *sysctl_rmem;
int                     max_header;
kmem_cache_t            *slab;
unsigned int            obj_size;
atomic_t                *orphan_count;
struct request_sock_ops *rsk_prot;
struct timewait_sock_ops *twsk_prot;
struct module           *owner;
char                    name[32];
```

inuse indicates whether this sock structure is being used. For SMP implementations, there is one per CPU.

```
    struct {
        int         inuse;
        u8          __pad[SMP_CACHE_BYTES - sizeof(int)];
    } stats[NR_CPUS];
};
```

Socket Lockets—Individual Socket Locks

Each open socket has a locking mechanism to eliminate contention problems between the kernel main thread and the "bottom half," or the various `tasklets`, timers, and interrupt handlers. As we know from earlier discussion, each open socket contains an instance of the `sock` structure. The individual socket lock is in the `sk_lock` field of the `sock` structure.

The `socket_lock_t` Structure

The lock field is defined as type `socket_lock_t`, in the file `linux/include/linux/sock.h`. The field, `slock`, is the actual `spinlock`. `owner` is set to the `iocb` for the owner process when the socket is locked and set to `NULL` when the socket is unlocked. `wq` is the queue of waiting tasks.

```
typedef struct {
    spinlock_t          slock;
    struct sock_iocb    *owner;
    wait_queue_head_t   wq;
} socket_lock_t;
```

The `lock_sock` and *release_sock* Functions

Generally, the lock is activated with the function `lock_sock`.

```
lock_sock(sk)
```

The socket lock is released by calling the macro `release_sock`.

```
release_sock(sk)
```

Both macros are defined in `linux/include/linux/sock.h`. When the socket is locked, incoming packets are blocked from being put on the receive queue. Instead, they are placed in the backlog queue for later processing. This backlog queue and other aspects of receiving packets are described fully in Chapter 3.

IO System Calls and Sockets

Linux is a Unix-compatible operating system. Like other similar Unix operating systems, Linux has a unified IO facility. All IO system calls are implementation independent; they work with devices, files, or sockets transparently. For most applications, no distinction is necessary. This has a major advantage in that the Linux application programmer does not have to remember three sets of API functions—one set for files, another for device IO, and a third for network protocols. This section discusses how file IO works with sockets and what is done in the socket layer itself to make this possible.

All IO devices, files, and other entities have a file descriptor. This file descriptor references an object in the file system called an inode, and all objects with file system-like behavior all have inodes. The inode allows the sockets to be associated with a Virtual File System (VFS). The inode structure is accessed with each IO system call such as read, write, fcntl, ioctl, and close. When an IO call is performed on an open socket, a pointer to the socket structure is retrieved from the inode. Remember that the open system call can't be used to create a socket; instead, sockets must be created with the socket API function. After a socket is created, the IO calls work the same way with sockets as they do for files or devices.

The inode is created and initialized by the sock_alloc_inode call defined in the file linux/net/socket.c. As discussed earlier in this chapter, sock_alloc is called from sock_create. Sock_alloc actually creates both a socket structure and an inode structure from the socket inode slab cache.

After the inode is created, the socket layer can map the IO system calls. In linux/net/socket.c, a file_operations structure, socket_file_ops, is created and initialized with pointers to socket versions of each of the IO system calls.

```
struct file_operations socket_file_ops = {
    .owner =        THIS_MODULE,
```

llseek is set to the generic "no" version of the socket call because it is not supported for sockets, and the error return is OK.

```
    .llseek =       no_llseek,
    .aio_read =     sock_aio_read,
    .aio_write =    sock_aio_write,
    .poll =         sock_poll,
    .unlocked_ioctl= sock_ioctl,
    .mmap =         sock_mmap,
```

The open call is not supported for sockets. Open is set to sock_no_open to disallow opening a socket via the /proc file system. It returns an ENXIO error.

```
        .open =         sock_no_open,
        .release =      sock_close,
        .fasync =       sock_fasync,
        .readv =        sock_readv,
        .writev =       sock_writev,
        .sendpage =     sock_sendpage
};
```

NETLINK AND RTNETLINK

`netlink` is an internal communication protocol. It mainly exists to transmit and receive messages between the application layer and various protocols in the Linux kernel. `netlink` is implemented as a protocol with its own address family, AF_NETLINK. It supports most of the socket API functions. `rtnetlink` is a set of message extensions to the basic `netlink` protocol messages. The most common use of `netlink` is for applications to exchange routing information with the kernel's internal routing table.

netlink Sockets

`netlink` sockets are accessed like any other sockets. Both socket calls and system IO calls will work with `netlink` sockets. For example, the `sendmsg` and `recvmsg` calls are generally used by user-level applications to add and delete routes. Both these calls pass a pointer to the `nlmsghdr` structure in the `msg` argument.

The nlmsghdr Structure

This `nlmsghdr` structure is defined in the the file linux/include/linux/netlink.h.

```
struct nlmsghdr
{
```

`nlmsg_len` is the length of the message including the header. The field, `nlmsg_type`, indicates the message content.

```
        __u32           nlmsg_len;
        __u16           nlmsg_type;
```

The next field, `nlmsg_flags`, contain the flags for the request. The values for `nlmsg_flags` are defined in Table 4.9. The next field, `nlmsg_seq`, is the sequence number for the message.

```
        __u16           nlmsg_flags;
        __u32           nlmsg_seq;
```

TABLE 4.9 Values for Netlink Message Flags

Name	Flags Values	Purpose
NLM_F_REQUEST	1	This is a request message.
NLM_F_MULTI	2	This is a multipart message terminated by NLMSG_DONE.
NLM_F_ACK	4	The recipient should reply with an acknowledge, a zero, or an error code.
NLM_F_ECHO	8	The recipient should echo this request.
		Modifiers to get request.
NLM_F_ROOT	0x100	Specify tree root.
NLM_F_MATCH	0x200	Return all matching entries.
NLM_F_ATOMIC	0x400	This is an atomic get.
NLM_F_DUMP	(NLM_F_ROOT| NLM_F_MATCH)	These values are modifiers to the new request.
		Modifiers to new request.
NLM_F_REPLACE	0x100	Replace an existing entry.
NLM_F_EXCL	0x200	Check to see whether an entry already exists.
NLM_F_CREATE	0x400	Create a new entry if it does not exist.
NLM_F_APPEND	0x800	Add entry to the end of list.
		Mapping of BSD 4.4 commands to the Linux netlink flags values.
BSD 4.4 Add	NLM_F_CREATE| NLM_F_EXC	Adds a new entry.
BSD 4.4 Change	NLM_F_REPLACE	Replace an existing entry.
BSD 4.4 Append	NLM_F_CREATE	Create a new entry if it does not exist.
BSD 4.4 Check	NLM_F_EXCL	Check to see if an entry already exists.

nlmsg_pid is the sending Process Identification (PID) if the process is a user-level process, and zero if not.

```
        __u32       nlmsg_pid;
};
```

The `netlink` protocol is implemented in the file `linux/netlink/af_netlink.c`. It is like any other protocol in the TCP/IP protocol suite, except that it is for exchanging messages between user-level processes and internal kernel entities. It is similar to UDP or TCP in that it defines a `proto_ops` structure to bind internal calls with socket calls made through the `AF_NETLINK` address family sockets.

The `netlink_ops`

The bindings are shown in the `netlink_ops` declaration also in the file `linux/netlink/af_netlink.c`.

```
struct proto_ops netlink_ops = {
```

The address family type is `PF_NETLINK`.

```
.family:        PF_NETLINK,
.owner:         THIS_MODULE,
```

The protocol defines `release`, `bind`, and `connect` functions. Most of the other functions are not defined because they are not relevant to this internal protocol family.

```
.release=       netlink_release,
.bind=          netlink_bind,
.connect=       netlink_connect,
.socketpair=    sock_no_socketpair,
.accept=        sock_no_accept,
.getname=       netlink_getname,
.poll=          datagram_poll,
.ioctl=         sock_no_ioctl,
.listen=        sock_no_listen,
.shutdown=      sock_no_shutdown,
.setsockopt=    netlink_setsockopt,
.getsockopt=    netlink_getsockopt,
```

`sendmsg` and `recvmsg` are the main functions used to send and receive messages through `AF_NETLINK` sockets.

```
.sendmsg=       netlink_sendmsg,
.recvmsg=       netlink_recvmsg,
.mmap=          sock_no_mmap,
.sendpage=      sock_no_sendpage,
};
```

Just like other protocols, such as UDP and TCP that register with the socket layer, `netlink` address family declares a global instance of the `net_proto_family` structure in the file `linux/net/netlink/af_netlink.c`.

```
struct net_proto_family netlink_family_ops = {
    .family = PF_NETLINK,
    .create = netlink_create,
    .owner = THIS_MODULE,
};
```

The `netlink_proto_init` Function

The `netlink` module also provides an initialization function for the protocol `netlink_proto_init`.

```
static int __init netlink_proto_init(void);
```

This function registers the `netlink` family operations with the socket layer by calling `sock_register`.

The `rtnetlink` Extensions for Routing

In later chapters in this book we will see how the routing tables and the neighbor cache are structured. In this section, we will show how the `sendmsg` and `recvmsg` functions are used with `rtnetlink` to pass requests for updates to the routing and the neighbor tables. All the operations break down to one of two fundamental operations: either retrieve the content of the table or post an update to the table.

The `rtnetlink_link` Structure

To support the extensions for control of the routing tables, `rtnetlink` provides a structure defined in the file `linux/include/linux/rtnetlink.h`, called `rtnetlink_link`. This structure only contains only function pointers.

```
struct rtnetlink_link
{
    int (*doit)(struct sk_buff *, struct nlmsghdr*, void *attr);
    int (*dumpit)(struct sk_buff *, struct netlink_callback *cb);
};
```

Defined in the same file, rtnetlink also defines a global of instances of the preceding structure called `rtnetlink_links`. There are up to 32 of these instances, defined by NPROTO in which each corresponds to a protocol type.

```
struct rtnetlink_link * rtnetlink_links[NPROTO];
```

To see how `rtnetlink` is used, let's look at an example. If a utility running at the application layer wants to add a route to a internal routing table, it calls `recvmsg` with a pointer to an `nlmsghdr` passed as an argument and with the `nlmsg_type` field set to `RTM_NEWROUTE`. The socket layer will gather the message into an `sk_buff` structure and send it to the `netlink` protocol, which in turn will queue it to the receive queue of a `PF_NETLINK` socket.

rtnetlink Socket Registration

The function `netlink_rcv` in the file `linux/net/core/rtnetlink.c` will get the message when it is de-queued from the socket. `netlink` uses a special "lite" socket for `netlink`. `netlink` member protocols such as `rtnetlink` register with `netlink` address family and messages are exchanged with the user through this special socket. This mechanism is similar to the regular registration mechanism for normal sockets. However, `rtnetlink` registers its receive function `rtnetlink_rcv` with the `AF_NETLINK` family by calling `netlink_kernel_create`. In this code snippet from the initialization function in the file `linux/net/core/rtnetlink.c`, we can see how the `rtnetlink` initialization function registers with the `netlink` "lite" socket.

```
rtnl = netlink_kernel_create(NETLINK_ROUTE, RTNLGRP_MAX,
rtnetlink_rcv,
                             THIS_MODULE);
```

The netlink_rcv Function

`netlink` is completely asynchronous so the `netlink_rcv` function removes all incoming messages in the `netlink` socket. It calls `rtnetlink_rcv_msg` to do the real work.

```
static void rtnetlink_rcv(struct sock *sk, int len)
{
    unsigned int qlen = 0;
    do {
        rtnl_lock();
        netlink_run_queue(sk, &qlen, &rtnetlink_rcv_msg);
        up(&rtnl_sem);
        netdev_run_todo();
    } while (qlen);
}
```

Using rtnetlink from a User Program

As stated earlier in this chapter, the fundamental purpose of rtnetlink is to allow a routing application to retrieve and set routes in the routing database in the Linux kernel. For detailed information about how to right such an application refer to the rtnetlink(3) manual page. It involves instantiating a nlmsghdr structure with specific fields set so the rtnetlink kernel module will be triggered when the message is sent through a netlink socket. There is actually a little more to this process because rtnetlink uses an attached rtmsg structure that includes more information about the routing protocol so we know which routing table to access. There is more information about the aspects that are specific to IPv4 routing in Chapter 8 and IPv6 routing in Chapter 11.

SUMMARY

In this chapter, we explored Linux sockets and their implementation. We introduced sockets and discussed how Linux sockets are entirely compatible with the Posix standards and the socket implementations in other operating systems. We discussed how the socket layer is initialized and how the protocol families and their individual member protocols register with the socket layer. We discussed the socket API and included information about Linux special sockets. We introduced Linux capabilities, which are used to enforce restricted access to internal modifications.

Also in this chapter, we discussed the internal implementation of the socket layer and demonstrated what happens under the hood when one of the socket API functions is called from the application code. Finally, we discussed the netlink protocol and the rtnetlink extensions and how these are used to maintain the routing table and the destination cache.

5 The Linux TCP/IP Stack

In This Chapter

- A Few Words
- Introduction
- Glue and Infrastructure
- Linux TCP/IP Stack Initialization
- Kernel Threading
- Packet Queuing Layer and Queuing Disciplines
- Receiving Packets in Packet Queuing Layer, `NET_RX_SOFTIRQ`
- Transport Layer De-Multiplexing and Internal Packet Routing
- Cache Rich
- Structures and Functions for Address Assignment, Multicast, and Configuration
- Security, Stackable Destination, and XFRM
- Some Practical Considerations

A FEW WORDS

In the first two chapters we discussed basics of networking and a general background on TCP/IP implementations. As we recall, from those earlier discussions, each layer in a network protocol stack is independent from the layers above and the layers below. Each layer maintains its own logical relationship between the sending and receiving machines. Primarily, the layers are kept logically separate through a mechanism called encapsulation and the infrastructure associated with any TCP/IP stack provides functions and macros to extract headers, add headers, and combine and merge packets. However, in addition to these functions, the kernel must provide other facilities for TCP/IP to function. These facilities needed by the stack include timers, kernel threads or tasks, protocol registration facilities at the transport and network layers, a network driver interface, and a buffering scheme. Chapter 3, "Linux Network Interface Drivers," explored specifics of the network device driver interface, and Chapter 4, "Linux Sockets," discussed the socket API. In this chapter, we build on the earlier material by exploring parts of the underlying structure of the Linux implementation of TCP/IP that don't fit neatly into later chapters on the protocols themselves. These facilities include general caching and queuing facilities provided by the kernel so protocol implementations can function efficiently.

INTRODUCTION

Over the years, Linux has evolved into an excellent and stable OS with generally readable and sometimes well-commented source code. Although it has been improved with the 2.6 kernel, there are some inconsistencies in the naming conventions used in comments, variables, functions, and subsystems. There are strong similarities among TCP/IP implementations, and Linux reflects some of the implementation history in its names, conventions, and implementation choices. Some of these inconsistencies are found in the parts of the stack covered in this chapter. As we proceed, to minimize confusion, we will try to clarify some of these naming irregularities. Although they are actually separate facilities, the terms `bottom half`, kernel `tasklets`, and `softirqs` are often used interchangeably. Another example is that the network layer protocols are called *packet handlers*, but the registration facility for the packet handlers is sometimes referred to as *device registration*. Sometimes, the names of files are unrelated to their contents. For example, the file `linux/net/core/dev.c` doesn't just contain device-related information. It also contains the protocol management and registration functionality. Another example is the file `linux/include/linux/if_ether.h`, which contains the definitions for the protocol field in the Layer 2 headers for all Layer 2 headers, not just Ethernet.

In this chapter, we examine the various queuing, hashing, and registration functions that provide the glue between the layers and protocols in TCP/IP as implemented in Linux. We will see how Linux has evolved into a complex system with the capability to add entire protocol families and specific member protocol components. Protocol families can be implemented as modules or compiled into the kernel itself. We will see how the 2.6 version of the kernel has simplified some of the function's data structures and eliminated some of the redundant fields.

The TCP/IP protocol is complex, and it is the subject of much study. TCP is the most complex of the two transport protocols in the `AF_INET` or TCP/IP family, and the IP layer itself is also very complex. It may seem that most of the complexity in the Linux TCP/IP stack implementation should be in the TCP and IP protocols themselves, but this is not entirely the case. Most modern OSs have a modular framework for networking so that the infrastructure can be separate from the protocols themselves, so in this book we try to differentiate the network protocol from any particular implementation or implementation framework for the protocol. With most other TCP/IP implementations, and Linux is no exception, the framework is independent from the protocol and generally includes at least a device-independent interface between the network layer and the data link layer so multiple protocols can run simultaneously. The framework also provides a device-independent mechanism for network to physical address translation. Although Linux does not explicitly refer to its networking infrastructure as a "framework," it is there nonetheless. While other chapters talk about how the protocols work in Linux, in this chapter we will examine some key components in the Linux networking framework.

GLUE AND INFRASTRUCTURE

Linux provides a method for protocols to dynamically register their input functions so they will receive incoming packets from the network interface device drivers. Linux also provides registration mechanisms in which the protocols at each layer can register with the layer above and with the socket layer. Like other protocol stack implementations, Linux must have a way for each layer to hide information and implementation details from the layers above and below. We will discuss some of these facilities in later sections, but in this section, we discuss the glue that connects the network interface drivers to the network layer. We discuss how protocols receive packets from the network interfaces. Linux provides a dispatch mechanism so a network interface driver can pass an incoming packet up to the next layer based on the protocol number.

For example, after the data link layer, or Layer 2, is done processing incoming data, the packet must be efficiently dispatched for handling by any protocol that has registered to receive the particular packet type, be it IP, ARP, or IPv6 or something else. This is a de-multiplexing, and the decisions are made based on the 2-byte protocol field in the link layer header. Table 5.1 shows most of the protocols in the 2-octet field in the protocol field in the data link layer, which are defined in the file linux/include/linux/if_ether.h. Some of the numbers in Table 5.1 are not official protocol numbers. For the official numbers, refer to the Internet Assigned Number Authority (IANA) [IAPROTO3].

TABLE 5.1 Link Layer Protocol Field Values

Protocol	Value	Description
ETH_P_LOOP	0x0060	Ethernet loopback packet
ETH_P_PUP	0x0200	Xerox PUP packet
ETH_P_PUPAT	0x0201	Xerox PUP Addr Trans packet
ETH_P_IP	0x0800	Internet Protocol
ETH_P_X25	0x0805	CCITT X.25
ETH_P_ARP	0x0806	Address Resolution Protocol (ARP)
ETH_P_BPQ	0x08FF	G8BPQ AX.25 Ethernet packet. This protocol number is not official.
ETH_P_IEEEPUP	0x0a00	Xerox IEEE802.3 PUP packet
ETH_P_IEEEPUPAT	0x0a01	Xerox IEEE802.3 PUP Addr Trans packet
ETH_P_DEC	0x6000	DEC assigned proto
ETH_P_DNA_DL	0x6001	DEC DNA Dump/Load
ETH_P_DNA_RC	0x6002	DEC DNA Remote Console
ETH_P_DNA_RT	0x6003	DEC DNA Routing
ETH_P_LAT	0x6004	DEC LAT
ETH_P_DIAG	0x6005	DEC Diagnostics
ETH_P_CUST	0x6006	DEC Customer use
ETH_P_SCA	0x6007	DEC Systems Comms Arch
ETH_P_RARP	0x8035	Reverse Addr Res packet
ETH_P_ATALK	0x809B	AppleTalk DDP
ETH_P_AARP	0x80F3	AppleTalk AARP
ETH_P_8021Q	0x8100	802.1Q VLAN extended header
ETH_P_IPX	0x8137	IPX over DIX
ETH_P_IPV6	0x86DD	IPv6
ETH_P_WCCP	0x883E	Web Cache Co-ordination Protocol
ETH_P_PPP_DISC	0x8863	PPPoE Discovery messages
ETH_P_PPP_SES	0x8864	PPPoE Session messages
ETH_P_MPLS_UC	0x8847	MPLS Unicast Traffic
ETH_P_ATMMPOA	0x884c	MultiProtocol over ATM
ETH_P_ATMFATE	0x8884	Frame-based ATM transport over Ethernet
ETH_P_AOE	0x88A2	ATA Over Ethernet
ETH_P_TIPC	0x88CA	Transparent Inter Process Communication Protocol

LINUX TCP/IP STACK INITIALIZATION

The initialization of the Linux TCP/IP stack is a complex process, and part of this initialization is the protocol registration. The internal registration of the protocols of the stack really consists of three parts. The first part involves registering the network layer protocols (often called `packet handlers`) so they receive packets from the network interface drivers. The second part of the registration process is registering the transport layer protocols with the network layer, IP, so the appropriate transport layer such as UDP or TCP will be dispatched. The third part, which consists of registering the protocols with the socket layer, is discussed in detail in Chapter 5. Later in this chapter, we include detailed information about transport layer protocol de-multiplexing and how the transport layer protocols tell IPv4 that they want packets of certain types, and Chapter 4 contains a detailed discussion of the driver registration process, the network device structure and the sequence of events that occur with packet reception and transmission. The next section discusses the registration of network protocols.

Because of the structure of the Linux TCP/IP stack, it is difficult to separate basic TCP/IP initialization from the socket layer initialization. The initialization steps directly related to the socket layer are covered in Chapter 4, but the more general initialization mechanism of the TCP/IP protocol family is covered in this section. As discussed in Chapter 4, socket layer initialization occurs before the TCP/IP stack is initialized because the socket layer must be in place before the address family, AF_INET, can be registered with the socket layer, allowing any IP packets to be transmitted or received. Remember that AF_INET is another name for the TCP/IP protocol suite. It is used by the socket layer to direct the socket API calls to TCP/IP.

The meat of TCP/IP initialization is done by `inet_init`, which is defined in the file `linux/net/ipv4/af_inet.c`. Chapter 5 describes the registration with the socket layer in detail. In function `inet_init`, after the socket registration is complete, we call the initialization functions for each of the protocols in TCP/IP. The first of these is `arp_init`, which we call to initialize the ARP protocol followed. Next, we call `ip_init` to initialize the IP protocol, followed by a call to `tcp_v4_init` to set up the slab cache for TCP. This is followed by a call to `icmp_init`. If multicast routing is configured, its initialization function, `ip_mr_init`, is called next. See Chapter 8, for more information on multicast routing.

One of the things done at initialization time is to create the entries in the `/proc` pseudo-file system for each of the protocols. In a later section in this chapter, we present more information about the `/proc` file system and other facilities provided by Linux for TCP/IP stack debugging and determining the status and statistics for the member protocols.

Packet Handler Initialization and Registration

According to the OSI layered network model, a network layer protocol deals with the semantics of network addressing and packet routing. However, some OSs and TCP/IP stack implementations define a network layer protocol as anything that receives incoming packets from the network interface drivers. Linux defines all protocols that receive packets from network interface drivers as *packet handlers*. The protocol management and registration facility provided by Linux is called the Packet Handler Registration Facility. Sometimes, in Linux, we refer to the packet handlers as *taps*, and this term is probably more accurate because not all packet handlers do packet processing but just receive copies of incoming packets.

Packet Handler Registration and De-registration

Linux provides two functions for registering and unregistering packet handlers. The registration function is called by a packet handler's initialization routine so it can set itself up to receive incoming packets. Registration is by type, so the packet handler will receive only incoming packets it is supposed to get. When packets arrive, they are de-multiplexed and dispatched to the packet handlers based on the type field of the link header. Here, we will introduce the two functions and the de-multiplexing process is described in more detail later.

The packet handler registration and unregistration functions and arguments are declared in the file linux/include/linux/netdevice.h. The functions are defined in file linux/net/core/dev.c.

The packet_type Structure

Both functions accept a pointer to a packet type structure, packet_type, as an argument.

```
struct packet_type {
```

The first field, type, is the same as the protocol type, which corresponds to the type field in the Ethernet header in network byte order. Table 5.1 shows the list of protocol types.

```
    __be16              type;
```

This field, dev, is a pointer to the net device structure for the network interface from which we want to receive the packet. If it is NULL, we will receive packets from any network interface.

```
    struct net_device   *dev;
```

The next field, func, points to the protocol's handler function for this protocol type. This function is called by the network queuing layer when the protocol type field is matched. af_packet_priv points to a private area generally used by the AF_PACKET protocol family which is for grabbing packets in user space. It generally is set to point to the sock structure.

```
int                 (*func) (struct sk_buff *,
                    struct net_device *,
                    struct packet_type *,
                    struct net_device *);
void                *af_packet_priv;
```

list points to the list of packet handlers. This field is filled in when the packet handler is registered.

```
    struct list_head    list;
};
```

The dev_add_pack Function

The first of the two functions, dev_add_pack, registers a packet handler. It is defined in the file linux/net/core/dev.c and declared in linux/include/linux/netdevice.h.

```
void dev_add_pack (struct packet_type *pt);
```

The argument, pt, is a pointer to the packet_type structure earlier. The type field of pt is set to one of the packet types shown in Table 5.1. The type would be ETH_P_ALL, 0x0003, if the caller wants to receive all packets promiscuously. If the handler is promiscuous, pt is placed on the list of promiscuous handlers, pointed to by ptype_all; otherwise, pt is placed in the hash table, ptype_base.

The dev_remove_pack Function

This function unregisters a packet handler by removing the packet_type pointed to by pt from the registration list.

```
void dev_remove_pack(struct packet_type *pt);
```

Packet Handler Lists and Pseudo Protocol Types

Packet handlers are kept on a linked list because multiple protocols can register handlers to receive the same packet type. Because several protocol handlers may receive the same packet type, none of them should alter the packet contents without cloning them first. As we will see in Chapter 6, Linux provides packet copying and cloning functions so if a packet handler needs to modify the packet, it can do it on a safe copy. We need this because the same skb is passed to each protocol handler on the list in sequence. In multiple CPU implementations of Linux, several protocols registering for a particular packet_type could receive the skb simultaneously while executing in different CPUs. However, the internal locking mechanisms in the kernel prevent any contention problems.

Not all handlers actually receive packets from the external world. Packets are routed internally for various reasons. The protocol type fields for an Ethernet packet are shown in Table 5.1, but Table 5.2 also lists pseudo-packet types used for internal packet routing. ETH_P_ALL is set in the packet_type structure if the handler wants to receive all packets no matter what their type. In most conventional cases, there will only be one protocol handler for each packet type.

TABLE 5.2 Nonofficial and Pseudo Protocol Types

Type	Value	Description
ETH_P_802_3	0x0001	Dummy type for 802.3 frames.
ETH_P_AX25	0x0002	Dummy protocol ID for AX.25.
ETH_P_ALL	0x0003	Every packet. Promiscuous handlers register this type.
ETH_P_802_2	0x0004	802.2 type framing.
ETH_P_SNAP	0x0005	Internal only.
ETH_P_DDCMP	0x0006	DEC DDCMP: Internal only.
ETH_P_WAN_PPP	0x0007	Dummy type for WAN PPP frames.
ETH_P_PPP_MP	0x0008	Dummy type for PPP MP frames.
ETH_P_LOCALTALK	0x0009	Localtalk pseudo type.
ETH_P_PPPTALK	0x0010	Dummy type for Atalk over PPP.
ETH_P_TR_802_2	0x0011	802.2 frames.
ETH_P_MOBITEX	0x0015	Mobitex (kaz@cafe.net).
ETH_P_CONTROL	0x0016	Card-specific control frames.
ETH_P_IRDA	0x0017	Linux-IrDA.
ETH_P_ECONET	0x0018	Acorn Econet.
ETH_P_HDLC	0x0019	HDLC Frame type.
ETH_P_ARCNET	0x001A	ARCnet.

Packet Handler List

Each protocol or packet handler must have three components: a receive function, which is registered by calling `dev_add_pack`; an initialization function; and a declaration of the `packet_type` structure, discussed previously. The protocol type field in the `packet_type` structure corresponds to the type field in the Ethernet packet or the type field in other MAC layer headers. Each protocol initializes an instance of the `packet_type` structure with the protocol number in the `type` field and a pointer to the packet handler's receive function in the `func` field. This initialization is usually done at compile time. The network protocol's initialization function does the registration of the handler.

```
static struct list_head *ptype_all = NULL;
```

The linked list of handlers for specific protocol types is built as a 16-slot hash table for fast dispatch of the packet handler function.

```
static struct list_head*ptype_base[16];
```

There is some overlap in the hash because there is a large number of defined protocol types and the hash has only 16 slots. However, the hashing function provides a much faster dispatch than could be obtained from a simple linear traversal of the list of packet types. Dispatching of each packet handler actually occurs within the context of the `NET_RX_SOFTIRQ`. The kernel threading mechanism, `softirqs`, and the specific kernel threads used for packet reception and transmission are discussed in detail in later in Chapter 5. Specifically, when the tasklet `NET_RX_SOFTIRQ` is scheduled, it calls the function `net_rx_action`, which walks through the input packet queues and dispatches the packet hander functions.

IP Packet Handler Registration and `ip_packet_type`

Most of the packets we receive from the network interface drivers are IP packets. For an example, let's look the packet handler function for the IP protocol. IP is discussed in much more detail in Chapter 8, "The Network Layer, IP," but in this section, we examine how the IP registers its packet handler. In file `net/ipv4/af_inet.c`, the IP protocol initializes `ip_packet_type` with the protocol type set to 0x0800 (IP) and initializes the `func` field to point to `ip_rcv` at compile time.

```
static struct packet_type ip_packet_type =
{
    type = __constant_htons(ETH_P_IP),
    func = ip_rcv,
};
```

The IP initialization function, also in the same file, is `inet_init`.

```
static int __init inet_init(void)
{ . . .
```

This is how the IP `packet_type` structure is registered.

```
dev_add_pack(&ip_packet_type);. . .
```

KERNEL THREADING

In this book, we don't go into a theoretical discussion of multithreading models, nor will we examine the design of the Linux scheduler design in detail. However, we will discuss how Linux kernel threads are used with TCP/IP. We have discussed how Linux provides a special thread to execute the registered packet handlers. This thread is separate from the network interface drivers' Interrupt Service Routines (ISR) in order to off-load work as possible from the interrupt handlers. This thread runs concurrently with the interrupt handlers in the networking interface drivers. We know from studying real-time systems that interrupt handlers can consume a complete CPU. Moreover, even though packet handling within the stack is often faster than reading packets from the input device, we still need to minimize the time spent in interrupt handlers.

Especially with today's fast networks and network interface hardware, it is important to spend as little time as possible in the interrupt handler, or the whole system will bog down. In addition, TCP/IP, like other networking protocols, is asynchronous in nature. The amount of time needed to process a packet and hand it off to the application layer is dependent on the transport protocol and many other factors. Linux TCP/IP provides buffering at various layers so one component will not bog down the entire stack. Because of these factors, it is far preferable to allow the TCP/IP stack to process incoming packets independently from the driver. Some primitive TCP/IP implementations are intended for small footprint-embedded environments where memory utilization is more critical than processing time. These TCP/IP implementations complete the entire input packet processing in the context of the interrupt handler. However, modern operating systems used in all but the smallest embedded systems—and Linux is no exception—provide multitasking OSs, or at least several internal kernel threads or execution contexts.

The Bottom Line on the Bottom Half

Historically, Linux had a concept called the `bottom half`, which was responsible for all low-level processing. We will see how it got its name. Device drivers are generally thought of as consisting of a top part and a bottom part. The bottom part includes the interrupt handler, and the top part interfaces with the rest of the operating system. Earlier versions of the Linux kernel had a kernel threading facility called Bottom Half (BH). The name Bottom Half was chosen because it is analogous to the bottom part of a device driver, its interrupt service routine. In earlier versions of the Linux kernel, the Bottom Half was a lightweight pseudo-interrupt that does work deferred from hardware IRQs after re-enabling interrupts. The early Bottom Half typically did work that can be done while interrupts are re-enabled but couldn't wait for a heavier kernel task or user-level process to get scheduled. Earlier versions of Linux relied exclusively on bottom halves to provide kernel threads for TCP/IP packet processing. However, now we need a more complex model to describe the bottom halves, because recent versions of Linux are designed to run on multiple CPU hardware. Linux is Symmetric Multiprocessing (SMP) aware, so a group of CPUs can share the same memory space. The old bottom-half mechanism was not SMP-aware and had to go. This is because the bottom-half mechanism would hold off the other CPUs in a multi-CPU computer. When the bottom half was executing, all CPUs other than the one running the BH must be stopped. In the next section, we will see how tasklets and softIRQs solve this problem in recent versions of Linux. For an excellent discussion of Linux kernel threading, see Matthew Wilcox's paper presented at Linux Conference Australia in 2003 [WILC03].

Tasklets, SoftIRQs, and Timers

Newer versions of Linux include a multithreading facility called *tasklets*. Bottom halves still exist, but they have been converted into tasklets, which are SMP-aware. In addition to tasklets, the Linux kernel also provides timers for use by device drivers and protocols. The discussion on kernel threads in this book is limited to the threading model used internally in the TCP/IP stack and the network interface drivers. However, Bovet, and Cesati include a complete discussion of Linux kernel threads [BOVET02]. In addition, for a complete examination of the art of using Linux kernel threads in device drivers, see [RUBINO00].

SoftIRQs

The general Linux kernel threading facility is called softIRQs. Linux also has special softIRQs that only execute other kernel threads called tasklets. Theoretically, it is possible to have up to 32 softIRQs in the kernel. However, Linux does not provide an interface for dynamically creating softIRQs directly, and it is not possible to add a softIRQ without modifying the source. However, adding more softIRQs to the kernel is neither necessary nor encouraged for the network protocol or device driver developer. Instead, the kernel provides tasklets that can be allocated dynamically, and Linux provides a predefined softIRQ to run the tasklets. The tasklet facility has its own set of interface functions and is quite sufficient for most kernel threading requirements needed by both protocol and driver developers.

One of the predefined softIRQs is specifically for executing special high-priority tasklets. Two of these softIRQs are used by the queuing layer in TCP/IP. One of the softIRQs is for receive-side packet processing, and the other softIRQ is for transmit-side packet processing. Table 5.3 lists each type of softIRQ. These are defined in the file linux/include/linux/interrupt.h.

TABLE 5.3 SoftIRQs

SoftIRQ	Purpose
HI_SOFTIRQ	For high-priority tasklets.
TIMER_SOFTIRQ	
NET_TX_SOFTIRQ	Transmission-side packet processing from link layer and network layer protocols. This one is used by TCP/IP.
NET_RX_SOFTIRQ	Reception-side packet processing from network interface drivers, and this one is used by TCP/IP, too.
BLOCK_SOFTIRQ	Used by block drivers.
TASKLET_SOFTIRQ	For running tasklets.

Tasklets

Tasklets are ideal for implementing mini-jobs to do high-priority work that is deferred from device driver ISRs but can be done with interrupts enabled. Tasklets are used widely in the TCP/IP stack. For example, they are used by the neighbor cache facility, which is a device—and protocol—independent address translation facility to map network layer IP addresses to link layer MAC addresses. Tasklets are defined by the structure `tasklet_struct`, which is declared in the file linux/include/linux/interrupt.h.

```
struct tasklet_struct
{
```

The field, `next`, is so the `tasklet_struct` instances can be put in a list.

```
struct tasklet_struct *next;
```

State is the scheduling state of the tasklet.

```
unsigned long state;
```

The next field, count, must be equal to zero for the tasklet to be scheduled.

```
atomic_t count;
```

func points to the routine that is executed when the tasklet is scheduled.

```
void (*func)(unsigned long);
unsigned long data;
};
```

Utility Functions for Tasklets

The interface functions for controlling the operation of tasklets is also in the file linux/include/linux/interrupt.h.

The tasklet_init Function

The first of these functions is tasklet_init, which initializes the tasklet_struct instance pointed to by t.

```
void tasklet_init(struct tasklet_struct *t,
                  void (*func)(unsigned long), unsigned long data);
```

The tasklet_kill Function

The next function is tasklet_kill, which we call when we want to stop the tasklet from executing.

```
void tasklet_kill(struct tasklet_struct *t);
```

The tasklet_schedule function.

The function tasklet_schedule prepares a tasklet for scheduling.

```
void tasklet_schedule(struct tasklet_struct *t);
```

The tasklet_disable Function

tasklet_disable prevents a tasklet from being scheduled by incrementing the count field in the structure pointed to by t.

```
void tasklet_disable(struct tasklet_struct *t);
```

The `tasklet_enable` Function

Finally, the last function in this group, `tasklet_enable`, allows a tasklet to be scheduled by decrementing the `count` field in `tasklet_struct`.

```
void tasklet_enable(struct tasklet_struct *t);
```

Macros for Controlling Tasklets

Several macros are provided to aid in establishing tasklets. These macros are also in `linux/include/linux/interrupt.h`.

The DECLARE_TASKLET and DECLARE_TASKLET_DISABLE Macros

The first macro, `DECLARE_TASKLET`, fills in the fields of the tasklet structure.

```
DECLARE_TASKLET(name, func, data)
```

The macro `DECLARE_TASKLET_DISABLED` declares a tasklet but leaves it disabled by initializing the count to zero.

Timers

A third kernel facility, called `timers`, is used by TCP/IP. Timers are not threads. They run at interrupt level, so the timer functions should not do any elaborate processing. If more extensive processing is required, it should be done in a tasklet because tasklets can be pre-empted by interrupts. Linux timers are dynamic; they can be added or deleted at any time. The timer API functions are defined in `linux/include/linux/timer.h`.

The timer_list Structure

A timer is created with a `timer_list` structure.

```
struct timer_list {
```

The first field, `entry`, is used internally for maintaining the list of timers.

```
    struct list_head entry;
```

The next field, `expires`, is the time when the timer goes off. As is generally the case within the Linux kernel, the value is in ticks.

```
    unsigned long expires;
```

The `function` field points to the routine that is executed when the timer goes off.

```
void (*function)(unsigned long);
```

The value in the next field, `data`, is passed as an argument to function when it is called.

```
    unsigned long data;
    struct tvec_t_base_s *base;
};
```

The `TIMER_INITIALIZER` *Macro*

A kernel module may define a timer by declaring a static `timer_list` structure and initializing a few fields. This is usually done with a macro `TIMER_INITIALIZER` also defined in the file `linux/include/linux/timer.h`.

```
TIMER_INITIALIZER(_function, _expires, _data)
```

Linux Kernel Timer API

The API for Linux timers is fairly straightforward. It includes functions for initializing timers, adding them and deleting them from the list of timers, and resetting the time when they go off. All of these function definitions are also found in the file `linux/include/linux/timer.h`.

The `init_timer` *Function*

The first interface function, `init_timer`, is provided to initialize the next and previous pointers in the list field in the `timer_list` to NULL.

```
void fastcall init_timer(struct timer_list * timer);
```

The `add_timer` *Function*

This function activates the timer by adding it to the list of timers to be scheduled. `Init_timer` should be called before `add_timer` is called.

```
static inline void add_timer(struct timer_list *timer)
{
    BUG_ON(timer_pending(timer));
    __mod_timer(timer, timer->expires);
}
```

The `del_timer` Function

This function, `del_timer`, removes the timer from the list. It returns a zero if the timer was pending and a one if the timer was not pending.

```
extern int del_timer(struct timer_list * timer);
```

The `mod_timer` Function

Another function, `mod_timer`, updates the `expires` field of an active timer.

```
extern int mod_timer(struct timer_list *timer, unsigned long expires);
```

It returns zero if the timer was pending. If the timer was not pending, it creates a new timer using the value in `expires` and returns the value one.

The Global Variable `jiffies`

Last but not least, Linux maintains the current time in a global variable, which is used all over the kernel. The variable is called `jiffies` and contains the current time in ticks. `jiffies` is defined in `linux/include/linux/jiffies.h`. The amount of time in each tick is dependent on the processor architecture and for embedded systems, the Board Support Package (BSP). The value `HZ` determines the timer interrupt frequency and is defined in the same file.

PACKET QUEUING LAYER AND QUEUING DISCIPLINES

In this section, we examine one part of the Linux framework for networking, the *queuing layer*. Most of the functionality of the packet queuing layer is implemented in the file `linux/net/core/dev.c` and declared in `linux/include/linux/netdevice.h`.

We will see how packets are sent to the network interface driver from the network layer protocols. The primary purpose for the queuing layer is to provide independence and buffering between the device drivers and the network layer protocols. Another purpose is traffic shaping. To perform traffic shaping, multiple queue disciplines are provided to allow packet transmission decisions to be based on Quality of Service (QoS) and other factors. For a complete explanation of practical applications for Linux traffic shaping, see "Linux Advanced Routing & Traffic Control HOWTO," in Chapter 9 of *Queuing Disciplines for Bandwidth Management* [HUBHOW02]. The queuing layer is actually a separate entity from both the network interfaces and IP; it is a sliver between the device drivers and the network layer protocols. Although predominantly for transmission, the queuing layer includes facilities for both packet reception and transmission.

The final step for the IP layer is to transmit the packet when it is done processing including the fragmenting, checsums, header field calculations, etc. This final step is after IP has already decided to whom to send the packet for the next hop. At this point, on the output side of IP, we might think there would be a simple handoff to the network interface driver to transmit the packet. In addition, on the input side, we might think that once a device driver completes the reception of an incoming packet, it should be a simple matter to pass the packet to IP's input route. However, things are quite a bit more involved. There is a series of steps between IP and the network interface device driver. These steps are performed by the queuing layer, which is the piece of framework that lives between the network layer protocols or packet handlers and the network interface drivers. The queuing layer has many responsibilities. On the input side, it starts and manages the softIRQs that does the processing of input packets received from the network interface driver. On the output side, the queuing layer takes over the transmission from the network layer protocols' output functions once they are ready to transmit the packet. This layer also contains the infrastructure to support multiple queue disciplines and multiple traffic-based scheduling methods for packet transmission. It is through the use of the queuing layer that Linux provides traffic-shaping capability.

Linux version 2.2 introduced the softIRQs, which first introduced kernel threads that provide a separate context for protocol handlers to execute independently from the drivers' interrupt service routines. In contrast, earlier versions of the Linux kernel, as is the case with many other OSs used with embedded systems, almost the entire input packet processing is done in the driver's interrupt context. Most of the initial processing done by the softIRQs is part of the queuing layer. In this section, we discuss the input side of the packet queuing layer and how it gets an incoming packet from the network interface driver's receive-side interrupt handler. We also discuss how the queuing layer handles transmitted packets. To facilitate traffic shaping, the transmit side of the packet queuing layer includes multiple queuing disciplines and multiple traffic classes when making decisions about transmitting a packet. We will examine how this is done.

Input Side Packet Processing, `NET_RX_SOFTIRQ`

As discussed earlier, Linux has two preconfigured softIRQs that provide the execution context for the most of the TCP/IP stack. One of these threads is the receive-side thread, `NET_RX_SOFTIRQ`. This softIRQ continues the packet processing after the network interface driver's receive interrupt is done. `NET_RX_SOFTIRQ` handles queuing and multiplexing of received packets. It schedules the receive-side functions of all the protocols that have registered to receive packets. The receive-side thread decides which of the registered protocols will receive an input packet, handles input packet queues, and determines whether there is internal network congestion. In Chapter 3, we learned how a network interface driver's ISR calls `netif_rx` to queue the input packet for processing by the network layer protocols. For hardware network interface drivers, `netif_rx` generally runs in interrupt context so it must run quickly. Essentially, it queues up the packet and starts the receive softIRQ thread, `NET_RX_SOFTIRQ`, by calling `cpu_raise_softIRQ`, which causes the softIRQ's action function `net_rx_action` to be scheduled.

Output Side Packet Processing, `NET_TX_SOFTIRQ`

The other softIRQ, `NET_TX_SOFTIRQ`, handles packet transmission once the network protocols' output functions are ready to hand off packets for transmission. This softIRQ handles flow control, packet queuing, and multiple queue disciplines. It also does the network interface driver level de-multiplexing to determine which driver should get the output packet.

The queuing layer provides congestion handling and flow control for received packets. It reschedules the protocol's input function if the protocol is too busy to receive a packet when the network interface driver's interrupt handler has it ready. Essentially, this is a layer of insulation between the protocol's input function such as IP and the network device driver. As discussed earlier, our goal is to offload processing from the interrupt service routines in the network device drivers. If it is not possible to re-queue packets, they will be dropped. However, in most cases, the packet is simply either put on the input queue, which generally has enough elasticity to absorb input packets waiting for processing.

Input Packet Queues and the `Softnet_data` Structure

The packet queuing layer has the capability to handle both hard device drivers with interrupt service routines and soft drivers, such as Layer 2, bridging code or packet forwarding engines. The packet queuing layer consists of an internal data structure called `softnet_data`.

```
struct softnet_data
{
```

`output_queue` is a list of `net_device` structures for network interface drivers ready to transmit packets. The output queue works with any queue discipline that is installed in Linux's list of queue disciplines for the particular driver.

```
    struct net_device   *output_queue;
```

`softnet_data` contains pointers to both reception and transmission queues. The `input_pkt_queue` field is for handling received packets. It points to the head of a list of packets or `sk_buffs` ready to be passed up to the network layer protocols. Packets are put in this queue by the `netif_rx` function.

```
struct sk_buff_head    input_pkt_queue;
```

`poll_list` is a list of network interfaces to be processed. It is used by backlog processing.

```
struct list_head       poll_list;
```

`output_queue` is a list of net_device structures for network interface drivers ready to transmit packets. The output queue works with any queue discipline that is installed in Linux's list of queue disciplines for the particular driver.

```
struct net_device      *output_queue;
struct sk_buff         *completion_queue;
```

A pseudo net_device structure is used for queue maintenance; only a few flags and fields are used. This field, `backlog_dev` is used as a default device for maintaining flow control.

```
struct net_device      backlog_dev;
};
```

`softnet_data` instances are in an array indexed by CPU number to support separate queues on each CPU for SMP configurations. In addition to the `softnet_data` structure, the queuing layer includes several queue processing functions that are independent of the queue discipline installed for a particular network interface driver, and these functions are described in detail in Chapter 4.

Queuing Layer Initialization

As we have seen throughout our discussion, often the best way to understand how something works or how it is put together is to look at the sequence of initialization steps.

The Function `net_dev_init`

The queuing layer is initialized by the function `net_dev_init`, defined in the file `linux/net/core/dev.c`. This function is called during the boot phase, which is single threaded.

```
static int __init net_dev_init(void)
{
int i, rc = -ENOMEM;
```

net_dev_init is called from the network registration function when the very first network interface device is registered. For more details about network interface device registration, see Chapter 4. It makes sure that it is only called once by checking the static variable dev_boot_phase as soon as it begins executing. dev_boot_phase is reset when the initialization is completed.

```
BUG_ON(!dev_boot_phase);
if (dev_proc_init())
    goto out;
if (netdev_sysfs_init())
    goto out;
```

We initialize the list of promiscuous packet handlers.

```
INIT_LIST_HEAD(&ptype_all);
for (i = 0; i < 16; i++)
    INIT_LIST_HEAD(&ptype_base[i]);
for (i = 0; i < ARRAY_SIZE(dev_name_head); i++)
    INIT_HLIST_HEAD(&dev_name_head[i]);
for (i = 0; i < ARRAY_SIZE(dev_index_head); i++)
    INIT_HLIST_HEAD(&dev_index_head[i]);
```

We initialize the input packet queue, completion queue and backlog device for each CPU.

```
for_each_cpu(i) {
    struct softnet_data *queue;
    queue = &per_cpu(softnet_data, i);
    skb_queue_head_init(&queue->input_pkt_queue);
    queue->completion_queue = NULL;
```

Next, we initialize the poll_list.

```
    INIT_LIST_HEAD(&queue->poll_list);
    set_bit(__LINK_STATE_START, &queue->backlog_dev.state);
    queue->backlog_dev.weight = weight_p;
    queue->backlog_dev.poll = process_backlog;
    atomic_set(&queue->backlog_dev.refcnt, 1);
}
dev_boot_phase = 0;
```

Now, we start up the two softIRQs for transmit and receive. These were discussed in an earlier section in this chapter.

```
open_softIRQ(NET_TX_SOFTIRQ, net_tx_action, NULL);
open_softIRQ(NET_RX_SOFTIRQ, net_rx_action, NULL);
hotcpu_notifier(dev_cpu_callback, 0);
```

Here, we initialize the destination cache and the multicast routing and multicast address list facility.

```
    dst_init();
    dev_mcast_init();
    rc = 0;
out:
    return rc;
}
```

Queuing Transmitted Packets

In this section, we discuss how an output packet is prepared for transmission through the network interface driver.

The `ip_output` and Associated Functions

For an example, we will use the output function in the IPv4 protocol, `ip_output`, defined in the file linux/net/ipv4/ip_output.c.

```
int ip_output(struct sk_buff *skb);
```

Before it can transmit a packet, the IP protocol must build the IP header, fill in the destination address, and determine the next-hop recipient for an output packet. When it is ready to transmit, the output function is called with a pointer to a socket buffer containing the packet. We will not describe everything IPv4 does to ready a packet for transmission. Refer to Chapter 9 for details about the IPv4 protocol implementation in Linux. In this section, we focus on the last few steps performed by IPv4's output function, `ip_output`. Actually the steps described here are shared between `ip_output`, `ip_finish_output`, and `ip_finish_output2`, all of which are in the same file,. The mechanism we describe shows how the IPv4 protocol or any other network layer protocol transmits a packet by de-referencing generic pointers in the destination cache so it does not need to know how the packet is going to be transmitted or whether it is transmitted at all.

The output function looks at the destination cache entry for this packet to see if it is supposed to transmit the packet or if the packet is to be sent to an internal destination. We check for a valid destination by looking at the destination cache entry to see whether it is a nonzero value. If there is an entry in the destination cache, we check to see whether the destination is resolved. We know it is resolved if there is a hardware header cache entry, `hh`. If `hh` is not zero, we call the function pointed to by the `hh_output` field of the `hh_cache` entry with a pointer to the `sk_buff`. At this point, the `sk_buff` holds the packet ready for transmission.

For destination cache entries that resolve to external destinations, `hh_output` will be set to `dev_queue_xmit`, and this is the function that we call from IP to send the packet.

The `dev_queue_xmit` Function

```
int dev_queue_xmit(struct sk_buff *skb);
```

This function is the primary device independent packet transmit function. References to this function are all over TCP/IP and other networking code. Before the `ip_output` routine calls the transmit function through the destination cache, the destination cache entries that resolve to external destinations, `hh_output` must be set to point to some output function, and this is how `dev_queue_xmit` gets called in the `ip_output` step.

The first thing we do in `dev_queue_xmit` is to check the integrity of the `skbuff` to be transmitted. We also check to see whether the `skbuff` is broken up into a list of fragment buffers. If the output device does not support scatter-gather DMA, we must gather together up the buffers; this step is called linearization..

Next, we check to see whether the device has a registered queue discipline. Most drivers for Ethernet devices and other conventional hardware network interfaces use output queuing. However, pseudo-devices—devices without an interrupt handler—such as IP tunnels, the loopback device, or other specialized Layer 2 interfaces don't use a queue discipline. The queue discipline is determined by checking the `qdisc` field in the net device structure to see whether it is initialized. If the device has a queue discipline, the enqueue function for the queue discipline associated with the device is called. For Ethernet devices, the default queue discipline is `pfifo_fast`. For pseudo-devices—devices that don't have an interrupt service routine—the default queue discipline is set to `none`. The packet gets placed on the end of the queue. Then `dev_queue_xmit` will execute when the queue is scheduled. In `dev_queue_xmit`, we call `qdisc_restart` to remove the packet from the queue and check to see if the driver's transmitter is busy. If it is busy, the packet is re-queued. If not, the driver's `hard_start_xmit` service function is called. For an illustration of the flow of the transmitted packet, see Figure 5.1.

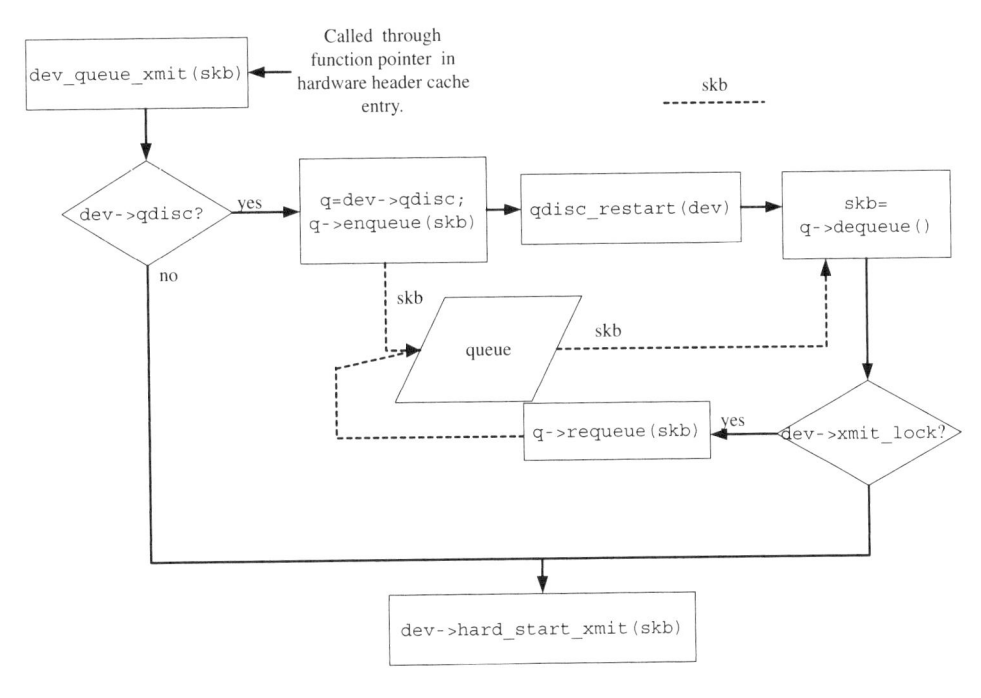

FIGURE 5.1 Transmit packet sequence.

RECEIVING PACKETS IN PACKET QUEUING LAYER, NET_RX_SOFTIRQ

From the discussion in the earlier chapters, we know that each network interface driver's interrupt service routine calls a generic function to queue up incoming packets for further processing. We recall from Section 6.4 that Linux TCP/IP provides a softIRQ kernel thread, NET_RX_SOFTIRQ, to process the queued up input packets. Actually, the kernel thread (softIRQ) does most of the packet processing in the TCP/IP stack, including the transport protocols UDP and TCP. In general, the purpose of this thread is to remove each packet from the input packet queue and execute the packet handling function for any packet handler whose type matches the protocol field in the link layer packet header. The packet handlers can be any protocol modules that expect to receive an incoming packet and have registered with the packet queuing layer (see Figure 5.2).

As we know from earlier sections in this chapter, each softIRQ has an action function. The action function associated with the network receive thread, NET_RX_SOFTIRQ, is net_rx_action, defined in the file linux/net/core/dev.c. The essential activity of this

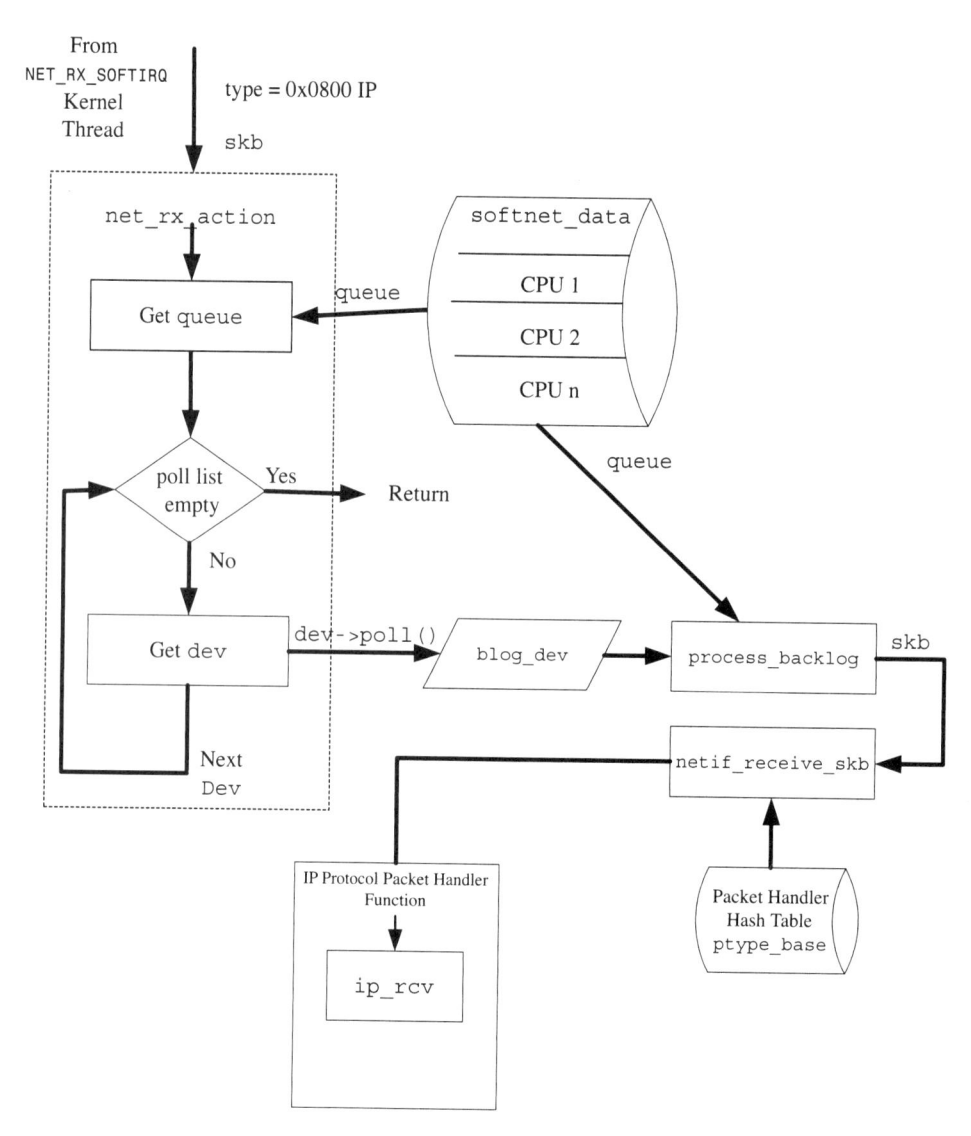

194 Linux TCP/IP Networking for Embedded Systems

FIGURE 5.2 Receive packet sequence.

function is to process the packets on the input packet queue, pointed to by the `input_pkt_queue` field of the `softnet_data` structure described earlier. As discussed in Chapter 4, packets were put on the input packet queue earlier when each network driver calls the `netif_rx` function. It is the job of the function `net_rx_action` to remove the packets from the queue and call the packet handlers. However, it does not actually remove the packets directly. Instead, it calls each driver's poll function through the poll field in the `net_device` structure for the input network interface from which the packets came. Actually, most networking device drivers don't have poll functions. Usually, poll functions are used with pseudo-drivers that don't have interrupts. However, we also have a fake device called the backlog device, `backlog_dev`. As shown earlier, `backlog_dev` is initialized when the `softnet_data` is created, and its poll function, `process_backlog`, does most of the real work of removing the input packets from the queue and calling the various protocols' packet handling routines.

The `net_rx_action` Function

The function `net_rx_action` runs in the context of the `NET_RX_SOFTIRQ`. It walks through the poll list of all the attached input network interfaces and executes the function pointed to by the `poll` field in the `net_device` structure for each driver if there is one.

```
static void net_rx_action(struct softIRQ_action *h)
{
```

The `softnet_data` structures are actually in an array indexed by CPU number for SMP configurations, and `get_cpu_var` returns the queue for the correct CPU.

```
    struct softnet_data *queue = &__get_cpu_var(softnet_data);
    unsigned long start_time = jiffies;
```

`netdev_max_backlog` is a `sysctl` constant that determines the maximum number of packets that can be queued up.

```
    int budget = netdev_max_backlog;
    void *have;
    preempt_disable();
    local_irq_disable();
```

Here we get each interface driver on the `poll_list`. One of these will be the pseudo-device, `backlog_dev`.

```
    while (!list_empty(&queue->poll_list)) {
        struct net_device *dev;
        if (budget <= 0 || jiffies - start_time > 1)
            goto softnet_break;
        local_irq_enable();
        dev = list_entry(queue->poll_list.next,
                    struct net_device, poll_list);
        have = netpoll_poll_lock(dev);
```

Here is where we call poll functions for each network interface driver, dev. If dev points to the backlog pseudo-device, backlog_dev, process_backlog, is the function we actually call through the poll pointer. The poll function returns zero if it successfully processed all the packets on the input queue and returns a negative one if the quota was exceeded.

```
            if (dev->quota <= 0 || dev->poll(dev, &budget)) {
                netpoll_poll_unlock(have);
                local_irq_disable();
                list_del(&dev->poll_list);
                list_add_tail(&dev->poll_list, &queue->poll_list);
                if (dev->quota < 0)
                    dev->quota += dev->weight;
                else
                    dev->quota = dev->weight;
            } else {
                netpoll_poll_unlock(have);
                dev_put(dev);
                local_irq_disable();
            }
        }
out:
    local_irq_enable();
    br_read_unlock(BR_NETPROTO_LOCK);
    return;
softnet_break:
    __get_cpu_var(netdev_rx_stat).time_squeeze++;
    __raise_softIRQ_irqoff(NET_RX_SOFTIRQ);
}
```

The process_backlog Function

As discussed earlier, the backlog device provides flow control for incoming packet processing, and the packet input processing posts incoming packets to the input packet queue in the backlog device. The poll field of the backlog device points to the function that does the next step of processing the input packets. This function is process_backlog. It is defined in the file linux/net/core/dev.c.

```
static int process_backlog(struct net_device *backlog_dev, int *budget)
{
    int work = 0;
    int quota = min(blog_dev->quota, *budget);
```

We must get the queue instance from `softnet_data` for the current CPU. This will point to a list of devices containing queues of packets for processing.

```
struct softnet_data *queue = &__get_cpu_var(softnet_data);
unsigned long start_time = jiffies;
```

This function loops until all the packets on the backlog devices input packet queue are processed. However, it will not entirely take over the CPU in which it is running if there are a large number of packets to process. Therefore, the number of packets to process is controlled by the parameter budget. This mechanism will help prevent the kernel from robbing all the bandwidth in the current CPU from other high-priority tasks.

```
for (;;) {
    struct sk_buff *skb;
    struct net_device *dev;
```

We must disable hardware interrupts to protect the `input_pkt_queue` because the packets were put on this queue by network interface drivers' ISRs.

```
local_irq_disable();
skb = __skb_dequeue(&queue->input_pkt_queue);
if (!skb)
    goto job_done;
local_irq_enable();
```

Here we get the real interface device from the `skb` and remove the device from the queue. `netif_receive_skb` is called to process the receive packet.

```
dev = skb->dev;
netif_receive_skb(skb);
dev_put(dev);
work++;
if (work >= quota || jiffies - start_time > 1)
    break;
```

We drop through to this point if we run out of time before we process all the input packets. A nonzero return tells the caller, `net_rx_action`, that we didn't finish our work. The caller's budget is adjusted.

```
blog_dev->quota -= work;
*budget -= work;
return -1;
```

We jump here once we have successfully processed all packets on the queue.

```
job_done:
    blog_dev->quota -= work;
    *budget -= work;
    list_del(&blog_dev->poll_list);
    smp_mb__before_clear_bit();
    netif_poll_enable(backlog_dev);
```
We re-enable interrupts before we exit.
```
    local_irq_enable();
    return 0;
}
```

The `netif_receive_skb` Function

This function is called from the `process_backlog` function, described in the previous section. `Netif_receive_skb`, found in the file `linux/net/core/dev.c` processes each packet on the input packet queue.

```
int netif_receive_skb(struct sk_buff *skb)
{
```

`ptype` and `pt_prev` are used to go through the list of `packet_type` structures. These list entries point to network layer protocols that have registered receive handler functions with the queuing layer.

```
    struct packet_type *ptype, *pt_prev;
    struct net_device  *orig_dev;
    int ret = NET_RX_DROP;
```

We set the arrival time for each incoming packet in the `stamp` field of the `skb`. The receive statistics are also incremented.

```
    unsigned short type;
    if (skb->dev->poll && netpoll_rx(skb))
        return NET_RX_DROP;
    if (!skb->tstamp.off_sec)
        net_timestamp(skb);
    if (!skb->input_dev)
        skb->input_dev = skb->dev;
    orig_dev = skb_bond(skb);
    __get_cpu_var(netdev_rx_stat).total++;
```

At this point, we are in an early stage of packet processing; network layer processing hasn't happened yet, and the skb still contains the packet headers. Therefore, the skb field data points to the beginning of the header information so we update the raw header pointers to point to the header start.

```
        skb->h.raw = skb->nh.raw = skb->data;
        skb->mac_len = skb->nh.raw - skb->mac.raw;
        pt_prev = NULL;
        rcu_read_lock();
#ifdef CONFIG_NET_CLS_ACT
        if (skb->tc_verd & TC_NCLS) {
            skb->tc_verd = CLR_TC_NCLS(skb->tc_verd);
            goto ncls;
        }
#endif
```

This loop is for promiscuous packet handling. The variable ptype_all is the start of the list of protocols that have requested promiscuous packet reception.

```
        list_for_each_entry_rcu(ptype, &ptype_all, list)
            if (!ptype->dev || ptype->dev == skb->dev) {
                if (pt_prev)
```

deliver_skb updates the use count in the skb and calls the protocol's packet handler function through the func field of pt_prev.

```
                    ret = deliver_skb(skb, pt_prev, 0);
                pt_prev = ptype;
            }
        }
#ifdef CONFIG_NET_CLS_ACT
    if (pt_prev) {
        ret = deliver_skb(skb, pt_prev, orig_dev);
        pt_prev = NULL; /* noone else should process this after*/
    } else {
        skb->tc_verd = SET_TC_OK2MUNGE(skb->tc_verd);
    }
    ret = ing_filter(skb);
    if (ret == TC_ACT_SHOT || (ret == TC_ACT_STOLEN)) {
        kfree_skb(skb);
        goto out;
```

```
        }
        skb->tc_verd = 0;
ncls:
#endif
```

Linux has an option called the frame diverter to allow for fast hardware assistance packet handling at this layer before packets are passed to the protocols for processing. The function `handle_diverter` will check to see whether the packet `skb` should be diverted.

```
        handle_diverter(skb);
```

Next, we see whether bridging has been implemented. Remember from earlier chapters that bridging is fundamentally a packet copy at Layer 2. Bridging consumes the incoming packet, so if it is bridged, we have no need for further processing.

```
        if (__handle_bridge(skb, &pt_prev, &ret))
            goto out;
```

Here we find the protocols that have registered to receive the packets of a specific type, such as IPv4 packets, where the type is 0x800. We use the same function we used for promiscuous handlers earlier in this function. However, in this case, `deliver_skb` is called for each `packet_type` instance on the list of registered handlers that matches the protocol in the incoming packet. For example, the IP protocol's registered packet handler function is `ip_rcv`, since it is set in the `func` field of the packet handler structure for packets having the type 0x0800.

```
        list_for_each_entry_rcu(ptype, &ptype_base[ntohs(type)&15], list) {
            if (ptype->type == type &&
                (!ptype->dev || ptype->dev == skb->dev)) {
                if (pt_prev)
```

This is where we call the protocol's packet handler function.

```
                    ret = deliver_skb(skb, pt_prev, 0);
                pt_prev = ptype;
            }
        }
        if (pt_prev) {
            ret = pt_prev->func(skb, skb->dev, pt_prev);
        } else {
```

```
        kfree_skb(skb);
        ret = NET_RX_DROP;
    }
out:
    rcu_read_unlock();
    return ret;
}
```

TRANSPORT LAYER DE-MULTIPLEXING AND INTERNAL PACKET ROUTING

Transport layer de-multiplexing is the process of deciding which transport layer protocol will receive an incoming IP packet when IP processing is complete. When IPv4 is done with a received packet, it must pass the protocol up to a transport layer protocol or one of the protocols internal to IPv4 such as ICMP and IGMP. The protocol field in the IP header determines which member protocol in the AF_INET family will receive the packet. Each of the protocols registered at initialization time to receive the packets of the type specified by the 1-byte protocol field in the IP header. We recall that the protocol field is not the same as the protocol field in the Ethernet MAC header. Link layer and IPv4 Header encapsulation is discussed earlier in Chapter 2.

The inet_protos Array

The protocols are registered by the inet_init function when the kernel is initialized in the file linux/net/ipv4/af_inet.c. As part of this initialization, pointers to each of the protocols are placed in an array of pointers called inet_protos. This array is declared in the file linux/net/ipv4/protocol.c. The data structure net_procol is declared in the file linux/include/net/protocol.h.

```
struct net_protocol *inet_protos[MAX_INET_PROTOS];
```

The net_protocol Structure

Each protocol declares an instance of the structure net_protocol.

```
struct inet_protocol
{
```

handler points to the protocol's input function, and err_handler points to the protocol's error function if one is defined. Later, we show how these fields are initialized for the higher-layer protocols in TCP/IP.

```
int         (*handler)(struct sk_buff *skb);
void        (*err_handler)(struct sk_buff *skb, u32 info);
```

The last field has no use in IPv4. It corresponds to a field in IPv6 that determines the security association policy for the protocol.

```
    int         no_policy;
};
```

Each protocol is placed in the hash array called inet_protos. The array can hold up to up to 255 protocols. Four locations in the array are filled when the four protocols are added that are the basic part of the IPv4 protocol suite: UDP, TCP, ICMP, and IGMP. This is done during AF_INET family initialization. Protocols are put in the inet_protos hash table by calling inet_add_protocol. After initialization, protocols can be added dynamically.

Initialization of AF_INET Family Member Protocols

This is how net_protocol instances are initialized for the three permanent protocols in the IPv4 protocol suite: TCP, UDP, and ICMP. IGMP is shown also, because this protocol is configured if multicast routing is configured into Linux at kernel build time.

```
#ifdef CONFIG_IP_MULTICAST
static struct inet_protocol igmp_protocol = {
    handler =   igmp_rcv,
};
#endif
static struct inet_protocol tcp_protocol = {
    handler =   tcp_v4_rcv,
    err_handler =tcp_v4_err,
    no_policy = 1,
};
static struct inet_protocol udp_protocol = {
    handler =   udp_rcv,
    err_handler =udp_err,
    no_policy = 1,
};
static struct inet_protocol icmp_protocol = {
    handler =   icmp_rcv,
};
```

Adding and Removing Protocols from the `inet_protos` Array

Two functions, defined in the file linux/include/net/protocol.h, are provided by Linux to add or delete protocols from the hash table. The first of these functions is net_add_protocol, which registers a new protocol by adding prot to the hash table of protocols, inet_protos.

The `inet_add_protocol` Function

```
void inet_add_protocol(struct inet_protocol *prot);
```

The `inet_del_protocol` Function

```
int inet_del_protocol(struct inet_protocol *prot);
```

inet_del_protocol removes prot from the hash table.

The protocols are accessed with a 1-byte hash index, and since there is only a 1-byte protocol field in the IPv4 header, there aren't likely to be any hash collisions.

Protocol Registration and the Protocol Switch Table

So far we have been covering the protocol registration facility in the Linux networking framework. There is another similar facility called the protocol switch table and it is important to differentiate the protocol registration facility from the protocol switch table protosw. The mechanism we have been discussing is for protocol registration, but the protocol switch table is for socket layer de-multiplexing. There is a separate set of interface functions associated with the protocol switch table, and they were previously discussed in Chapter 4.

The Transport Protocol Dispatch Process and Protocol De-Multiplexing.

Conceptually, the dispatch of the transport layer protocol is simple, IP gets the protocol field value, calculates the hash, indexes into inet_protos, obtains the net_protocol instance, and dispatches the transport layer protocol's receive function through the handler field. This is a summary of what ultimately happens, but the actual implementation is quite a bit more complicated.

IPv4 receive processing is covered in more detail in Chapter 8. In this chapter, we will confine our discussion to the part of the initialization process that involves the inet_protos array. During the processing of input packets, once the IP layer is finished processing, it proceeds to pass the packets up to the transport layer protocols. This hand-off from IP to the transport layer uses the packet routing facility, the same mechanism used for routing of external packets. Internal routing involves the destination cache discussed later in this chapter, the routing table,

The IP Receive Routine, `ip_rcv`

We begin by looking at the IPv4 receive routine. The receive routine, `ip_rcv` is passed a packet in a socket buffer in the parameter `skb`. The `ip_rcv` routine can be found in the file `linux/net/ipv4/ip_input.c`.

```
int ip_rcv(struct sk_buff *skb, struct net_device *dev, struct
packet_type *pt, struct net_device *orig_dev);
```

We check the `dst` field in `skb` that points to the destination cache entry to differentiate between packets we are supposed to transmit and packets that must be internally routed. If `dst` is not NULL, it means that that IP already knows where to send this packet. If `dst` is NULL, we must find a route, either internal or external, for the packet. To do this, the `skb` is passed to the IP router to determine the route and whether it is an external route or an internal destination. `Ip_route_input` fills in the destination field, in the `skb`. As part its processing, the IP router checks the `type` field in the routing result structure, `fib_result`.

The `fib_result` Structure

```
struct fib_result
{
    unsigned char    prefixlen;
    unsigned char    nh_sel;
    unsigned char    type;
    unsigned char    scope;
#ifdef CONFIG_IP_ROUTE_MULTIPATH_CACHED
    __u32            network;
    __u32            netmask;
#endif
    struct fib_info *fi;
#ifdef CONFIG_IP_MULTIPLE_TABLES
    struct fib_rule *r;
#endif
};
```

If `type` is set to RTN_LOCAL, the packet is sent to the transport layer protocol by setting the destination cache's input field to `ip_local_deliver`. In addition, if the entry in the routing table entry has the flag RTCF_LOCAL set, we know we must route this packet locally. Since the `ip_local_deliver` is set in the destination cache entry, it will be executed when the packet is sent. Later, when `ip_local_deliver` is called, it calculates a hash value from the protocol field in the IP header. This hash value is used to find an entry in the `inet_protos` table to select the transport protocol that is the destination for this packet. Finally, the destination transport protocol's input function is called through the handler field of the entry in `inet_protos`.

CACHE RICH

Linux contains several important cache facilities all of which are utilized by the routing and address translation code. One of these caches is the routing table cache and contains the cached entries for the recently used routes. Another cache is the neighbor cache which in IPv4 is commonly called the ARP cache. The ARP cache contains the mapping of the IP address at Layer 3 with the link layer address used at Layer 2.

Routing at OSI Layer 3 and address translation at OSI Layer 2 are conceptually very different. Layer 3 is the network layer. Its cache is really a front end for a complete routing table used to facilitate decisions about which next-hop machine to send packets. The Layer 2 cache is for address translation and essentially is a lookup table where IP addresses can be mapped into hardware addresses. However, if a route in the table points to a reachable destination, there probably already is an ARP cache entry for the next-hop destination for that route. In an optimized system, we want to avoid multiple table lookups during processing of packets, therefore, we have the route entry reference the ARP cache entry. In any real-world protocol implementation such as Linux TCP/IP, these two functions are closely related. There is a benefit for some of the underlying data structures to be shared.

Both the route cache and the ARP facilities generally cache entries for performance reasons, because a cache provides for fast lookup without having to traverse many entries. In addition, they both require timeouts that are associated with each of the table entries. Linux implementation stresses performance, so IP uses some shared infrastructure to implement both caches. As the reader will know from Chapter 3, ARP is the protocol commonly used for address translation in IPv4. In some other TCP/IP stack implementations, ARP is implemented with a separate table in memory called the ARP cache. Each entry in the ARP cache contains a destination IP address and a corresponding physical address, and the destination physical address is inserted into the destination field of the MAC header when a packet is transmitted. All TCP/IP implementations supporting Ethernet must implement the ARP protocol. Earlier implementations tended to hard code their implementations for ARP and Ethernet and don't provide any type of general address translation facility. In contrast, Linux has a flexible mechanism to do address translation independent of Ethernet or any other specific MAC addressing scheme and independent of the ARP protocol. An advantage of using a generic mechanism is that the same infrastructure can be used for IPv4, IPv6, ARP, and other protocols.

The Three Caches

Three interacting mechanisms are involved in network address translation. The first is the *destination cache*. It is a generic holder for destination addresses and functions in a form independent of the specific protocol. The second mechanism, the *hardware header cache* (HH), holds the MAC layer header and pointers to functions to manipulate the header. The third cache is called the *neighbor cache*. It maintains information about all locally reachable nodes on the network.

The neighbor cache is used primarily by neighbor discovery in IPv6 [RFC 2461] but is also used by ARP in IPv4 and is available for use by other address resolution protocols besides ARP.

These three caches are part of a complex mechanism that might seem hard to sort out at first. Together, the three caches do most of the work of address translation. They provide a framework for any protocol to maintain its address translation table, and allow device drivers to easily access the link layer header information. It is a very flexible system but might seem to be a complicated way to do a simple job. Extensive use of hashing techniques makes address translation quite efficient so packet processing speed is not impacted.

The detailed discussion of IP routing is in Chapter 9. However, in this chapter we will show important fields in the data structures and explain the primary functionality for address translation. Next, we will walk through the transmission sequence to show how the data structures are used to do address translation.

Destination Cache

The destination cache entry contains all the information for a resolved route. The destination can be an internal destination for incoming packets or can resolve to a specific hardware address for an external machine. It is through this structure that the link layer header is obtained for transmitted packets. This facility is generic and protocol independent; it is not just used by IP.

The destination cache is really a library of generic functions and structures that serves as part of the framework for Linux. Specific implementations of the destination cache can be found in the ARP protocol for IPv4 and the ND protocol for IPv6.

The `dst_entry` Structure

The `dst_entry` structure defines an individual entry in the destination cache. This data structure is defined in the file `linux/include/net/dst.h`.

```
struct dst_entry
{
```

Most of the important fields are explained except those related to the internal hash processing. The first field, next, is a pointer to next dst_entry on the list. A routing table cache entry (described in more detail in Chapter 8) can also point to a dst_entry structure, so either type of structure can be treated identically.

```
        struct dst_entry    *next;
```

The following field contains the reference count for the entry in the destination cache __refcnt. When the destination cache entry is freed, the reference count is decremented. A zero value means garbage collection can be performed on this entry. A nonzero value keeps the cache entry from being deleted if it is still being referenced. The destination cache entry structure must be locked before changing these two fields. The next field, __use, is the use count. It is incremented when a route is being used.

```
        int                 flags;
        atomic_t            __refcnt;
        int                 __use;
        struct dst_entry    *child;
```

Dev points to either an input network interface device or an output network interface device depending on whether this destination is internal or external. The next field, obsolete, indicates that this entry is no longer used. If the value is greater than one, it means that the entry has been returned to the slab cache.

```
        struct net_device   *dev;
        int                 obsolete;
```

flags is set to the flags for this destination entry.

```
        int                 flags;
```

The field, flags can contain the following four values.

```
#define DST_HOST          1
#define DST_NOXFRM        2
#define DST_NOPOLICY      4
#define DST_NOHASH        8
#define DST_BALANCED      0x10
```

lastuse is set to the time in ticks that this entry was allocated. It indicates the age of cache entry. Expires is the time when this cache entry ages out. It is used by the garbage collection facility to determine which entries are obsolete. For example, when these entries are used for routing cache, expires indicates which routes have aged out.

```
unsigned long      lastuse;
unsigned long      expires;
```

The following two fields indicate that space needs to be reserved in packets sent via this route.

```
unsigned short     header_len;    unsigned short    trailer_len;
u32                metrics[RTAX_MAX];
struct dst_entry   *path;
```

The next two fields are for rate limiting of the ICMP protocol.

```
unsigned long      rate_last;
unsigned long      rate_tokens;
int                error;
```

The next field, neighbour, is a pointer to neighbor cache entry that is used for address resolution. For more information, the neighbor cache is discussed later in this section. If not NULL, hh points to the hardware header cache for this destination. If the destination cache entry is for a packet with an internal destination, hh will be NULL. For output packets, hh will be used to get the link layer header.

```
struct neighbour   *neighbour;
struct hh_cache    *hh;
```

The next field, xfrm_state, points to a transformation instance for the Security Policy Database (SPD).

```
struct xfrm_state  *xfrm;
```

The next two fields, input and output, point to functions that are called when a packet is processed using a particular destination cache entry. input is the default input function. When dst_entry is first created, this field is initialized to dst_discard_in. For example, for cache destinations used in routing input packets intended for local consumption, this field points to the function ip_local_deliver. output is the default output function. This function is called by the protocol's output function if `hh` and `neighbour` are NULL. When a destination cache entry is created, output is initialized to `dst_discard_out`. For example, when destination cache entries indicate that IPv4 output packets should be routed, output will point to `ip_forward`.

```
int               (*input)(struct sk_buff*);
int               (*output)(struct sk_buff*);
```

`tclassid` contains traffic classes and is used for traffic shaping. It is defined if the class-based routing option is configured into the Linux kernel.

```
#ifdef CONFIG_NET_CLS_ROUTE
    __u32              tclassid;
#endif
```

The next field, `ops`, is the set of operation functions for the destination cache. This structure is initialized to a set of functions specific to a network layer protocol. They are usually statistically defined when the network layer protocol is initialized. For example, IPv4 initializes `dst_ops` to `ipv4_dst_ops` in the file `linux/net/ipv4/route.c`. This is how the generic destination cache is adapted as a specific cache for the AF_INET family of protocols.

```
    struct   dst_ops      *ops;
    struct   rcu_head     rcu_head;
    char                  info[0];
};
```

The `dst_init` function.

Although it has an initialization function, the destination cache is instantiated when it is used as part of ARP or ND. The initialization function, `dst_init`, is defined in the file `linux/net/core/dst.c`.

```
void __init dst_init(void)
{
```

The only thing we do in this function is register the destination cache with the network device notifier so destination cache entries will be automatically removed when a network interface device goes down or is disconnected.

```
    register_netdevice_notifier(&dst_dev_notifier);
}
```

The `dst_dev_notifier` Block

The notifier block, `dst_dev_notifier`, consists of only one function, `dst_dev_event`, which is discussed later in this chapter.

```
struct notifier_block dst_dev_notifier = {
    dst_dev_event,
    NULL,
    0
};
```

The Destination Operation Structure, `dst_ops`

The destination operation structure contains pointers to operation functions for the destination cache entry. It is largely through this structure that the destination cache takes on its personality as the ARP cache or neighbor discovery cache. The `dst_ops` structure is accessed through the `ops` field in the `dst_entry` described previously. The `dst_ops` instance effectively is a protocol independent way of defining an entry in the destination cache.

```
struct dst_ops
{
```

The first field, `family`, is the address family for this cache entry, such as AF_INET. The next field, `protocol`, is the same as the link layer header protocol field value. For example, if this entry were for IP, `protocol` would be ETH_P_IP.

```
    unsigned short          family;
    unsigned short          protocol;
```

`gc_thresh` is the garbage collection threshold value. If the destination cache entry is doubling as a routing cache entry, this field is equal to the size of the routing cache hash table plus one. Garbage collection is the mechanism by which stale routes or cache entries are aged out.

```
    unsigned                gc_thresh;
```

`gc` is the garbage collection function for this entry, and `check` is a pointer to the function to check the validity of this cache entry.

```
    int                     (*gc)(void);
    struct dst_entry        *(*check)(struct dst_entry *, __u32 cookie);
```

The next field, `destroy` points to the destructor function for this entry. Again, since this is protocol independent, each protocol family can define a destructor function that makes sense for that protocol. The destructor function will get called when the entry is obsolete or aged out and generally the destructor function will de-allocate the entry.

```
void                    (*destroy)(struct dst_entry *);
```

The next field is the negative advice function pointer, `negative_advice`, which is called when we receive a redirect ICMP packet that negates this entry in the destination cache. `link_failure` is a pointer to a function that says that a previously good entry is no longer valid because of a dropped link. `update_pmtu` is called if the route Maximum Transmission Unit (MTU) has changed. The route MTU can be negotiated between endpoints to reduce fragmentation.

```
struct dst_entry        *(*negative_advice)(struct dst_entry *);
void                    (*link_failure)(struct sk_buff *);
void                    (*update_pmtu)(struct dst_entry *dst, u32 mtu);
```

This field, `get_mss` points to a function to be called to obtain the MSS (Maximum Segment Size) for this route.

```
int                     (*get_mss)(struct dst_entry *dst, u32 mtu);
```

`entry_size` is the size of the destination cache entry. `entries` contains the number of entries in a particular destination cache implementation and is atomically incremented and decremented. `kmem_cachep` is the pointer to the slab cache from which destination cache entries are allocated.

```
    int                 entry_size;
    atomic_t            entries;
    kmem_cache_t        *kmem_cachep;
};
```

Destination Cache Utility Functions

There are a few important utility functions associated with the destination cache. Several of these functions are called directly by users of the destination cache, and some of them are generic functions for manipulating entries that are initialized in the destination cache entry when it is created. The functions are defined in file `linux/net/core/dst.c`.

The dst_alloc Function

Destination cache entries are allocated with dst_alloc.

```
void * dst_alloc(struct dst_ops * ops)
{
```

In this function, we allocate an instance of a dst_entry structure. In most cases, the callers will have initialized an instance of a dst_ops structure at compile time. Then, we are called with a pointer to the dst_ops instance each time a new destination cache entry is requested.

```
struct dst_entry * dst;
```

We check that entries in dst_ops is greater than the garbage collection threshold, gc_thresh. By checking the values in the destination operations, in effect we are checking the values specific to the destination cache user.

```
if (ops->gc && atomic_read(&ops->entries) > ops->gc_thresh) {
```

If the threshold is exceeded, it calls the cache garbage collection function through the gc field of dst_ops.

```
        if (ops->gc())
            return NULL;
}
```

We allocate the entry from the slab cache pointed to by kmem_cachep in the dst_ops structure.

```
dst = kmem_cache_alloc(ops->kmem_cachep, SLAB_ATOMIC);
if (!dst)
    return NULL;
memset(dst, 0, ops->entry_size);
atomic_set(&dst->__refcnt, 0);
```

Then it sets the ops field to the dst_ops pointer passed in as a parameter. It sets lastuse to the current time, jiffies, and atomically increments entries. It sets input to dst_discard_in and output to dst_discard_out.

```
dst->ops = ops;
dst->lastuse = jiffies;
dst->path = dst;
```

```
    dst->input = dst_discard_in;
    dst->output = dst_discard_out;
#if RT_CACHE_DEBUG >= 2
    atomic_inc(&dst_total);
#endif
    atomic_inc(&ops->entries);
    return dst;
}
```

The dst_free Function

Destination cache entries are freed by calling dst_free, an inline function defined in file linux/include/net/dst.h.

```
static inline void dst_free(struct dst_entry * dst);
```

First, dst_free locks the entry. If __refcnt is zero, the entry is immediately destroyed. If not, it re-initializes dst_entry and places it on the garbage collection list, dst_garbage_list, to be destroyed when the garbage collection timer executes.

The dst_destroy Function

dst_destroy immediately removes a cache entry.

```
void dst_destroy(struct dst_entry * dst);
```

The first thing we do in dst_destroy is check to see if there is an attached neighbor cache entry. If so, we free the neighbor. Then, we check for a hardware cache entry, and if there is one, we free it. Before calling kmem_cache_free to return dst to the slab cache, we call the higher-level destroy function by de-referencing the destroy function pointer referenced in the ops field of dst_entry.

The dst_hold and dst_clone Functions

These two functions, both automatically increment the reference count in the __refcnt field. Both of these functions check that the argument dst is not NULL, but dst_hold assumes that the argument is valid. These functions are inlines defined in linux/include/net/dst.h.

```
static inline struct dst_entry * dst_clone(struct dst_entry * dst);
static inline void dst_hold(struct dst_entry * dst);
```

The `dst_confirm` Function

`dst_confirm` calls `neigh_confirm`, passing it the value in the `neighbour` field. Neighbor confirmation verifies that the neighbor entry is reachable. `dst_confirm` is an inline defined in `linux/include/net/dst.h`.

```
static inline void dst_confirm(struct dst_entry *dst);
```

The `dst_link_failure` and `dst_negative_advice` Functions

The two functions `dst_link_failure` and `dst_negative_advice` call the higher-level `negative_advice` and `link_failure` functions through the respective pointers in the `ops` field of `dst_entry`. Of course, they each could theoretically call different functions depending how `ops` is initialized.

```
static inline void dst_link_failure(struct sk_buff *skb);
static inline void dst_negative_advice(struct dst_entry **dst_p);
```

Destination Cache Garbage Collection

The purpose of Garbage Collection (GC) is to implement a generic cache aging mechanism. When a cache entry or route times out, there must be a way to remove this entry to allow the memory and other resources to be re-used for other entries. The GC must be implemented in a way to minimize heap fragmentation. In this section, we discuss how the destination cache GC works. In addition to the default GC, the higher-level users of the destination cache may also have a separate garbage collection capability with a GC function reached through the `gc` field of the `dst_ops` structure. This is how the facility for aging out cached routes works; explicit garbage collection of cached routes is covered in Chapter 8. Here, we discuss generic low-level destination garbage collection, implemented in the file `linux/net/core/dst.c`. In addition, we also show how device status change events are handled for network interface devices.

The Destination Cache State Lock, `dst_lock`

The state that governs garbage collection of dead destination cache entries is protected by a lock, `dst_lock`, accessible to all functions within the destination cache facility.

```
static DEFINE_SPINLOCK(dst_lock);
```

The destination cache maintains a garbage collection list for stale entries. Entries may be placed on the garbage collection list either in a bottom-half context or by a higher-level kernel facility. However, the garbage collection function itself executes in the bottom-half context by the garbage collection timer. dst_lock protects entries while they are being added to the garbage collection list. The garbage collection timer is called dst_gc_timer, and it is defined in the file linux/net/core/dst.c.

```
static DEFINE_TIMER(dst_gc_timer, dst_run_gc, DST_GC_MIN, 0);
```

DST_GC_MIN is the minimum expiration time for an entry. It is never less than one second because we never would have route cache entries time out that fast. The timer expiration values are altered so the timer execution is somewhat randomized, and so does not self-synchronize and cause a large number of routes to age out at once.

The dst_run_gc Function

The timer function, dst_run_gc, executes when the garbage collection timer expires.

```
static void dst_run_gc(unsigned long dummy);
```

dst_run_gc is not a complex function, and most of what we do involves calculating a new timer expiration value. The first thing we do is to try the lock, dst_lock, to see whether the GC list is locked. If so, we simply call mod_timer to restart the timer and return. If it survives this test, we delete the existing timer and then walk through the garbage collection list, dst_garbage_list, and call the dst_destroy function pointer in dst_ops for each entry on the list.

We saw earlier that the destination cache registers with the netdevice_notifier when it is initialized. This is because the destination cache will want to post all entries associated with the interface for GC.

The dst_dev_event Function

The function that will receive device notification events is dst_dev_event, which is also in the file linux/net/core/dst.c.

```
static int dst_dev_event(struct notifier_block *this, unsigned long
event, void *ptr);
```

The parameter this points to the notifier_block. Event contains the event type we are looking for. We actually are interested in two event types, NETDEV_DOWN and NETDEV_UNREGISTER. The third argument, ptr, is actually the net_device structure pointer back to the device that is telling us about the event. In dst_dev_event, we walk through the garbage collection list to see which entries refer to the device that is sending the event. If we are receiving the NETDEV_DOWN event, we set the input field of the `dst_entry` to `dst_discard_in` and the `output` field to `dst_discard_out`. This is to ensure that any transmit or receive packets queued up for the device will be discarded. If we are receiving the `NETDEV_UNREGISTER` event, we set the device to point to the loopback device, `loopback_dev`.

The Neighbor System

As discussed earlier, the ARP protocol is implemented using the Linux generic destination cache. In addition, we know that we have a generic destination cache facility to allow the same data structures to be used for the Neighbor Discovery (ND) protocol [RFC 2461] for IPv6. The destination cache is used by the neighbor system to provide a precalculated fast path for output packets once a destination address has been resolved. This provides faster packet processing for connected TCP sockets. Since many packets are going to the same destination, we want to be able to quickly build the packet from known information and avoid time-consuming searches of the routing table and ARP cache for each packet. If a destination is connected, the fast path is used and the protocol's output packet will be internally routed in such a way that the packet's destination address can be quickly prepended to the packet.

A neighbor table instance consists of a list of neighbor cache entries accessed through hash tables. Each neighbor table is specific to an address resolution protocol. In this section, we will discuss the neighbor cache entry, the neighbor parameters, and the neighbor table.

The `neigh_table` Structure

The neighbor system includes a few key data structures. The most fundamental one is the neighbor table, `neigh_table`, defined in the file `linux/include/net/neighbour.h`.

```
struct neigh_table
{
```

Each address resolution protocol such as ARP will create one instance of the `neigh_table`. The table contains a slab cache from which neighbor cache entries are allocated. It also contains pointers to the individual neighbor cache entries and a hash table for quick access to the entries. The neighbor tables are put on a list and the field next points to the next table instance in the list. A neighbor cache entry can be accessed by multiple tables, so a specific cache entry can be used for both IPv4 and IPv6. Family contains the address family associated with this particular neighbor table instance.

The first field in the `neigh_table`, next, points to the next neighbor cache entry in the list. `family` is the address family for this neighbor cache implementation, and for TCP/IP, it will be set to `AF_INET`.

```
struct neigh_table  *next;
int                 family;
int                 entry_size;
int                 key_len;
```

The hash field points to a hash calculation function. For example, ARP sets this field to the function arp_hash. neigh_table includes callback functions, constructor, pconstructor, pdestructor, and proxy_redo. When a neighbor table instance is created, these function pointers are initialized to point to protocol-specific functions. constructor is for creation of a neighbor cache entry, and pconstructor is for creation of a neighbor proxy entry. In general, the fields beginning with a "p" are used for proxy cache entries. The proxy fields are used for proxy ARP.

```
__u32       (*hash)(const void *pkey, const struct
                net_device *);
int         (*constructor)(struct neighbour *);
int         (*pconstructor)(struct pneigh_entry *);
void        (*pdestructor)(struct pneigh_entry *);
void        (*proxy_redo)(struct sk_buff *skb);
char        *id;
```

parms points to the neighbor table parameters, discussed later in this section. Along with each table are a GC task and a garbage collection timer. The neighbor table system uses GC as a generic mechanism for aging out cache entries. The fields beginning with "gc" are used by the garbage collection.

```
struct neigh_parms   parms;
int                  gc_interval;
int                  gc_thresh1;
int                  gc_thresh2;
int                  gc_thresh3;
unsigned long        last_flush;
struct timer_list    gc_timer;
struct timer_list    proxy_timer;
struct sk_buff_head  proxy_queue;
int                  entries;
rwlock_t             lock;
unsigned long        last_rand;
kmem_cache_t         *kmem_cachep;
struct neigh_statistics stats;
```

The two fields, hash_buckets and phash_buckets, are used with hash functions for quick access to the neighbor and proxy neighbor cache entries for this particular neigh_table instance. It is possible, at least theoretically, for a particular neighbour to be accessed through two different neigh_tables instances.

```
    struct neighbour    **hash_buckets;
    unsigned int        hash_mask;
    __u32               hash_rnd;
    unsigned int        hash_chain_gc;
    struct pneigh_entry **phash_buckets;
#ifdef CONFIG_PROC_FS
    struct proc_dir_entry *pde;
#endif
};
```

The neigh_parms Structure

In addition to the neigh_table, there is a structure that contains parameters for manipulating neighbor table cache entries. These are used with the sysctl (System Control) mechanism, if sysctl is configured into the Linux kernel. Therefore, entries in the neighbor table cache can be added or deleted.

Along with the other data structures, the neighbor cache system neighbor parameters structure, neigh_parms, is defined in the file linux/include/net/neighbour.c.

```
struct neigh_parms
{
```

Each entry in the neighbor cache has an associated neigh_parms accessed through the parms field in the neighbor cache entry. neigh_parms includes configurations items, reachability information, and timeouts for a neighbor cache entry. The values in neigh_parms are set differently for each address resolution protocol.

```
    struct  neigh_parms *next;
    int     (*neigh_setup)(struct neighbour *);
    struct  neigh_table *tbl;
    void    *sysctl_table;
    int     dead;
    atomic_t refcnt;
    struct  rcu_head rcu_head;
    int     base_reachable_time;
    int     retrans_time;
    int     gc_staletime;
    int     reachable_time;
    int     delay_probe_time;
    int     queue_len;
```

```
        int     ucast_probes;
        int     app_probes;
        int     mcast_probes;
        int     anycast_delay;
        int     proxy_delay;
        int     proxy_qlen;
        int     locktime;
};
```

Functions Used with the `neigh_parms` Structure

The neighbor system also provides several functions for creation and removal of neighbor cache entries. Most of these functions are defined in the file `linux/net/core/neighbour.c`.

The `neigh_parms_alloc` Function

The first of these functions, `neigh_parms_alloc`, allocates an instance of the `neigh_parms` structure.

```
struct neigh_parms *neigh_parms_alloc(struct net_device *dev,
                                      struct neigh_table *tbl);
```

In this function, the first thing we do is allocate the structure with `kmalloc`. There is no slab cache associated with neighbor parameters because there is one for each protocol that neighbor does discover, which is not likely to be very many. Next, we initialize the reachability timer to a random value. Next, `neigh_parms_alloc` puts the `neigh_parms` structure on the linked list pointed to by `parms` in the `neigh_table`.

The `neigh_parms_release` Function

The next function, `neigh_parms_release`, removes the `neigh_parms` structure from the list in the `parms` field of `neigh_table`.

```
void neigh_parms_release(struct neigh_table *tbl, struct neigh_parms
*parms);
```

The `neighbour` Structure

So far, we have not discussed the neighbor cache entry and the neighbor parameter structure. Now we will look at the neighbor cache entry itself. Each neighbor table consists of a hash table of neighbor cache entries.

Each neighbor cache entry is contained by the `neighbour` structure.

```
struct neighbour
{
```

Each entry is implemented on a list, and next is the pointer to the next entry. tbl is a pointer back to the particular neighbor table, neigh_table, which includes this entry.

```
struct neighbour    *next;
struct neigh_table  *tbl;
```

Next, parms is a pointer to the neighbor parameters described earlier, and dev points to the network interface for this entry.

```
struct neigh_parms  *parms;
struct net_device   *dev;
unsigned long       used;
unsigned long       confirmed;
unsigned long       updated;
__u8                flags;
```

nud_state contains the Neighbor Unreachability State (NUD), the values of which are shown later in Table 5.4. It is initialized to NUD_NONE when a neighbor cache entry is created.

```
__u8        nud_state;
__u8        type;
__u8        dead;
atomic_t    probes;
rwlock_t    lock;
```

The next two fields, ha and hh, contain the hardware header cache used to access the link layer header for an output packet. hh points to the hardware header cache entry. Hh is not NULL when this neighbor cache entry is resolved to an external destination.

```
unsigned char    ha[(MAX_ADDR_LEN+sizeof(unsigned long) 1)
                    &~(sizeof(unsigned long)-1)];
struct hh_cache  *hh;
```

refcnt is incremented for each reference to this neighbor cache entry.

```
atomic_t         refcnt;
```

output points to the function for transmitting a packet when the hardware header is resolved. It is initialized to neigh_blackhole, which causes the packet to be discarded when the neighbor cache entry is first created but not fully operational.

```
int               (*output)(struct sk_buff *skb);
```

If this neighbor cache entry is for the ARP protocol, arp_queue is the queue of packets waiting for address resolution to be completed. Using a queue is preferable to forcing all packets to wait because it does not tie up the output device while waiting for ARP responses. ops is a list of protocol-specific functions used for this neighbor cache entry.

```
    struct sk_buff_head arp_queue;
    struct timer_list   timer;
    struct neigh_ops    *ops;
    u8                  primary_key[0];
};
```

Neighbor System Initialization

The neighbor system supports multiple instantiation; there are no static data structures. This is because we want each protocol family to have its own separate neighbor table. For example, take IPv4. The AF_INET address family includes ARP, the address resolution protocol [RFC 826]. ARP initializes an instance of the neighbor table when it is initialized. After looking at the generic neighbor table initialization functions, we look specifically at what ARP does when it creates a neighbor table.

The neigh_table_init Function

The function that ARP and other resolution protocols call for neighbor table instance creation is neigh_table_init. This function is defined in the file linux/net/core/neighbour.c.

```
void neigh_table_init(struct neigh_table *tbl)
{
```

Now is the current time. Neighbor discovery protocols require messages to be sent out at random intervals. To accomplish this, reachable_time in the neigh_parms structure is set to a random value calculated from the seed, base_reachable_time.

```
    unsigned long now = jiffies;
    unsigned long phsize;
    atomic_set(&tbl->parms.refcnt, 1);
```

```
        INIT_RCU_HEAD(&tbl->parms.rcu_head);
        tbl->parms.reachable_time = neigh_rand_reach_time(tbl >
parms.base_reachable_time);
```

We create a slab cache entry from which neighbor table entries will be created.

```
        if (tbl->kmem_cachep == NULL)
            tbl->kmem_cachep = kmem_cache_create(tbl->id,
                                            (tbl->entry_size+15)&~15,
                                            0, SLAB_HWCACHE_ALIGN,
                                            NULL, NULL);
        if (!tbl->kmem_cachep)
            panic("cannot create neighbour cache");
        tbl->stats = alloc_percpu(struct neigh_statistics);
        if (!tbl->stats)
            panic("cannot create neighbour cache statistics");

#ifdef CONFIG_PROC_FS
        tbl->pde = create_proc_entry(tbl->id, 0, proc_net_stat);
        if (!tbl->pde)
            panic("cannot create neighbour proc dir entry");
        tbl->pde->proc_fops = &neigh_stat_seq_fops;
        tbl->pde->data = tbl;
#endif
        tbl->hash_mask = 1;
        tbl->hash_buckets = neigh_hash_alloc(tbl->hash_mask + 1);
        phsize = (PNEIGH_HASHMASK + 1) * sizeof(struct pneigh_entry *);
        tbl->phash_buckets = kmalloc(phsize, GFP_KERNEL);
        if (!tbl->hash_buckets || !tbl->phash_buckets)
            panic("cannot allocate neighbour cache hashes");
        memset(tbl->phash_buckets, 0, phsize);
        get_random_bytes(&tbl->hash_rnd, sizeof(tbl->hash_rnd));
        rwlock_init(&tbl->lock);
```

Next, garbage collection is initialized. `neigh_periodic_timer` recalculates the reachability time from a random value. This function provides the context for the execution of the garbage collection functions.

```
        init_timer(&tbl->gc_timer);
        tbl->gc_timer.data = (unsigned long)tbl;
        tbl->gc_timer.function = neigh_periodic_timer;
        tbl->gc_timer.expires = now + tbl->gc_interval +
                                tbl->parms.reachable_time;
        add_timer(&tbl->gc_timer);
```

The proxy timer is used for proxy cache entries.

```
init_timer(&tbl->proxy_timer);
tbl->proxy_timer.data = (unsigned long)tbl;
tbl->proxy_timer.function = neigh_proxy_process;
skb_queue_head_init(&tbl->proxy_queue);

tbl->last_flush = now;
tbl->last_rand = now + tbl->parms.reachable_time*20;
write_lock(&neigh_tbl_lock);
```

This neighbor table instance is placed on a linked list of neighbor tables.

```
tbl->next = neigh_tables;
neigh_tables = tbl;
write_unlock(&neigh_tbl_lock);
}
```

ARP and the Neighbor Table

We will look at how the ARP sets up the neighbor system in the file linux/net/ipv4/arp.c. In this section we show how the initialization steps specifically for the ARP protocol in IPv4 correspond to the generic neighbor system and destination cache systems described in previous sections.

ARP Initialization of the `neigh_table` Structure

Before calling the neighbor table initialization function, ARP creates the ARP cache by defining an instance of the neigh_table structure.

```
struct neigh_table arp_tbl = {
    .family      =   AF_INET,
    .entry_size  =   sizeof(struct neighbour) + 4,
    .key_len     =   4,
    .hash        =   arp_hash,
    .constructor =   arp_constructor,
    .proxy_redo  =   parp_redo,
    .id          =   "arp_cache",
    .parms = {
        .tbl                =   &arp_tbl,
        .base_reachable_time = 30 * HZ,
        .retrans_time       =   1 * HZ,
        .gc_staletime       =  60 * HZ,
        .reachable_time     =  30 * HZ,
```

```
                .delay_probe_time =    5 * HZ,
                .queue_len =           3,
                .ucast_probes =        3,
                .mcast_probes =        3,
                .anycast_delay =       1 * HZ,
                .proxy_delay =         (8 * HZ) / 10,
                .proxy_qlen =          64,
                .locktime =            1 * HZ,
        },
        .gc_interval =  30 * HZ,
        .gc_thresh1 =   128,
        .gc_thresh2 =   512,
        .gc_thresh3 =   1024,
};
```

The Function `arp_init`

The initialization function for ARP is `arp_init`. This function is found in the file linux/net/ipv4/arp.c.

```
void __init arp_init(void)
{
```

We initialize a neighbor table for the ARP cache by calling `neigh_table_init`. The other two steps here are important but discussed in more detail in other chapters. We confine our discussion here to the utilization of the neighbor cache system by the ARP implementation.

```
    neigh_table_init(&arp_tbl);
    dev_add_pack(&arp_packet_type);
    arp_proc_init();
```

Here we are registering `neigh_parms` with the `sysctl` (System Control) mechanism if `sysctl` is configured into the Linux kernel.

```
    #ifdef CONFIG_SYSCTL
        neigh_sysctl_register(NULL, &arp_tbl.parms, NET_IPV4,
                              NET_IPV4_NEIGH, "ipv4");
    #endif
```

Finally, we register with the `net_device` notifier, so ARP will be told when a network interface has a change in status.

```
    register_netdevice_notifier(&arp_netdev_notifier);
}
```

Neighbor System Utility Functions

Linux provides a group functions to create and remove neighbor cache entries, resolve addresses, and check the reachability state of a neighbor cache entry. These functions are defined in the file linux/net/neighbour.c.

The neigh_lookup Function

```
struct neighbour *neigh_lookup(struct neigh_table *tbl, const void
*pkey,
                              struct net_device *dev);
```

For IPv4, generally, pkey will be an IP address.

The __neigh_lookup Function

The next function, __neigh_lookup, also finds a neighbor cache entry. It is an inline function implemented in linux/include/net/neighbour.h.

```
struct neighbour *__neigh_lookup(struct neigh_table *tbl,
                                const void *pkey,
                                struct net_device *dev, int creat);
```

It returns a pointer to the neighbor cache entry if it finds one. If not, it creates a new neighbor cache entry if the parameter created is nonzero.

The neigh_create Function

The next function, neigh_create, creates a new neighbor cache entry in neigh_table using pkey and dev. As with neigh_lookup, pkey is a lookup key, and for IPv4, it is generally an IP address.

```
struct neighbour * neigh_create(struct neigh_table *tbl,
                               const void *pkey,
                               struct net_device *dev);
```

The neigh_destroy Function

This function, neigh_destroy, deletes all resources used by a neighbor cache entry, neigh.

```
void neigh_destroy(struct neighbour *neigh);
```

It frees all references to the link layer header in the `hh` field of `neighbour` and removes all socket buffers from the ARP queue, `arp_queue`.

The `neigh_event_send` Function

The `neigh_event_send` inline function is for sending an event based on the entry's NUD state. It is defined in the file linux/include/net/neighbor.h.

```
int   neigh_event_send(struct neighbour *neigh, struct sk_buff *skb);
```

The exact event depends on the protocol. For example, if the neighbor table is an ARP cache, it could be an ICMP message or an ARP who-has request depending on the current NUD state.

The `neigh_release` Function

The next function, `neigh_release`, releases a neighbor cache entry.

```
void neigh_release(struct neighbour *neigh);
```

We release the entry by atomically decrementing the reference count. If the count is zero, we call `neigh_destroy`.

The `neigh_confirm` Function

The next function, `neigh_confirm`, updates the neighbor cache entry.

```
void neigh_confirm(struct neighbour *neigh);
```

It marks the entry with the current time.

The `neigh_is_connected` Function

This function checks to see whether the NUD state is connected.

```
int neigh_is_connected(struct neighbour *neigh);
```

The `neigh_clone` Function

The `neigh_clone` function clones a neighbor cache entry.

```
struct neighbour * neigh_clone(struct neighbour *neigh);
```

It does not copy the entry; it just increments the reference count.

The `neigh_update` Function

This function updates the neighbor cache entry.

```
int neigh_update(struct neighbour *neigh, const u8 *lladdr, u8 new,
                 u32 flags);
```

The parameter override says to update the entry even if the link layer address in `lladdr` is different from the one in the existing entry.

The Function `neigh_resolve_output`

This function, `neigh_resolve_output`, resolves a neighbor cache entry.

```
int  neigh_resolve_output(struct sk_buff *skb);
```

It is for resolving a destination address and sending an event if it needs to.

The Functions `neigh_connected_output` and `neigh_compat_output`

These two functions are both output functions.

```
int  neigh_connected_output(struct sk_buff *skb);
int  neigh_compat_output(struct sk_buff *skb);
```

The `neigh_add` and `neigh_delete` Functions

These two functions, `neigh_add` and `neigh_delete`, are for creating and deleting neighbor cache entries in response to user requests. They are called from the netlink internal messaging protocol.

```
int neigh_delete(struct sk_buff *skb, struct nlmsghdr *nlh, void *arg);
int neigh_add(struct sk_buff *skb, struct nlmsghdr *nlh, void *arg);
```

The Function `neigh_dump_info`

The next function, `neigh_dump_info`, dumps the neighbor cache table.

```
int neigh_dump_info(struct sk_buff *skb, struct netlink_callback *cb);
                    struct netlink_callback *cb)
```

It calls the function pointed to by `cb`.

Proxy Neighbor Cache Functions

Linux also provides a corresponding set of functions to manipulate the proxy neighbor cache entries.

The `pneigh_lookup` and `pneigh_delete` Functions

The first two, `pneigh_lookup` and `pneigh_delete`, are similar to the non-proxy versions.

```
struct pneigh_entry * pneigh_lookup(struct neigh_table *tbl,
                                    const void *pkey,
                                    struct net_device *dev, int creat);
int pneigh_delete(struct neigh_table *tbl,
                  const void *pkey, struct net_device *dev);
```

The Function, `pneigh_enqueue`.

This proxy function queues the `skb` on the proxy queue and sets the proxy timer.

```
void pneigh_enqueue(struct neigh_table *tbl, struct neigh_parms *p,
                    struct sk_buff *skb);
```

We call `pneigh_enqueue` if we want the packet to wait for a response from the proxy ARP request.

Transmitting Packets Using the Caches

In the next few sections, we look at how the destination and neighbor caches are utilized by the packet output routines in various protocols..

Sending Packets Using the Destination Cache

In the next few sections, we look at how the destination cache is used to transmit packets. We show how the neighbor structure and the destination cache are used by a protocol's output function to quickly find the output network interface, the hardware header, and the output transmission function once an output packet is about to be transmitted. We will begin at the point where the destination cache has been checked by the network layer protocol's transmit function when a packet is ready to be transmitted. The destination cache entry is accessed through the socket buffer. To understand how the destination cache works, it is best to examine a specific scenario and we will use the IP protocol's output routine as an example. The `ip` output code can be found mostly in `linux/net/ipv4/ip_output.c`.

In most cases, the final processing step is to transmit the packet out the physical interface. IP output determines what should be done with the packet by checking the `dst` field in the `skb` to see whether the packet knows where it is supposed to go. This is actually a check if the destination hardware addresses has been defined yet for this particular packet.

When the IP protocol is ready to transmit a packet, it checks to see whether there is a known destination for the packet by checking the dst field in the skb. Next, ip_finish_output2 checks to see whether there is an actual hardware address defined for the destination by checking the hh field in the destination cache entry. The hh field is either NULL or points to the hardware header cache entry containing the complete MAC header for the packet.

IP Output and Sending Packets Using the Neighbor Cache and Hardware Header Cache

At this point, one of two things can happen depending on the value in the hh field of the destination cache. First, we will see what happens if there isn't a resolved route to the packet's destination. If so, hh would be NULL. If hh is NULL, we check the neighbor cache by de-referencing the neighbour field of the skb and through this pointer, we get the output function for the neighbor cache entry. In our example, the packet is an IP packet, and neighbour has been previously initialized to point to one of the ARP protocol output functions, either neigh_resolve_output or neigh_compat_output. However, if the address of the destination has already been resolved and the hardware header cache is up to date, output will point to the function dev_queue_xmit. Depending on the destination, the output field in the neighbor will be set to one of the function pointers in the neigh_ops structure: output, connected_output, hh_output, or queue_xmit. For example, if the network interface is an Ethernet device, ops is set to arp_hh_ops during ARP protocol initialization phase. The ops field defines the behavior of a neighbor cache entry. The ops field is shown in the following code snippet. If this neighbor cache entry is for a reachable node, the output field in the neighbor cache entry is set to point to ops->hh_output.

The neigh_ops Structure

The structure neigh_ops used in the previous example is defined in the file linux/include/net/neighbour.h.

```
struct neigh_ops
{
    int         family;
    void        (*destructor)(struct neighbour *);
    void        (*solicit)(struct neighbour *, struct sk_buff*);
    void        (*error_report)(struct neighbour *, struct sk_buff*);
    int         (*output)(struct sk_buff*);
    int         (*connected_output)(struct sk_buff*);
    int         (*hh_output)(struct sk_buff*);
    int         (*queue_xmit)(struct sk_buff*);
};
```

If the next-hop destination is known but its physical address of the neighbor has not been determined, output will point to neigh_resolve_output. The function neigh_resolve_output checks the neighbor cache's entry state to make sure that the neighbor is reachable. The NUD state is in the nud_state field of the neighbor cache. These states are used to see whether there is a need to resolve the destination address. The NUD states are used by the neighbor discovery protocol (NDP) [RFC 2461] and are listed in Table 5.4.

TABLE 5.4 Neighbor Cache Entry NUD States

State	Value	Description
NUD_INCOMPLETE	0x01	Currently, address resolution is being performed for this neighbor entry.
NUD_REACHABLE	0x02	Indicates that the neighbor is reachable. Positive confirmation was received and the path to this neighbor is okay.
NUD_STALE	0x04	More than the configured elapsed time has passed since reachability confirmation was received for this neighbor.
NUD_DELAY	0x08	More than the configured elapsed time has passed since reachability was confirmed for this neighbor. This state allows TCP to confirm the neighbor. If not, a probe should be sent after the next delay time has elapsed.
NUD_PROBE	0x10	A solicitation has been sent and we are waiting for a response from this neighbor.
NUD_FAILED	0x20	Indicates that neighbor reachability state detection failed.
NUD_NOARP	0x40	Pseudo-state indicating that ARP is not used for this neighbor entry.
NUD_PERMANENT	0x80	Pseudo-state indicating that garbage collection should not be performed to remove this entry.
NUD_NONE	0x00	No state is defined.

When the address is resolved, the hh field in the neighbor cache will be updated to point to the hardware header cache entry, which contains the actual link layer destination address. The output function in the neighbor cache entry will be updated to point to the same function as the `queue_xmit` field in the `neigh_ops` part of the `neighbour` structure. This is because `neigh_ops` had been previously initialized by ARP to point to the `dev_queue_xmit` function. In any case, `dev_queue_xmit` is the function that is called to the output packet if the address has already been resolved. If the destination is unreachable, the packet will be dropped. Figure 5.3 shows the sequence for transmitting packets through the destination cache.

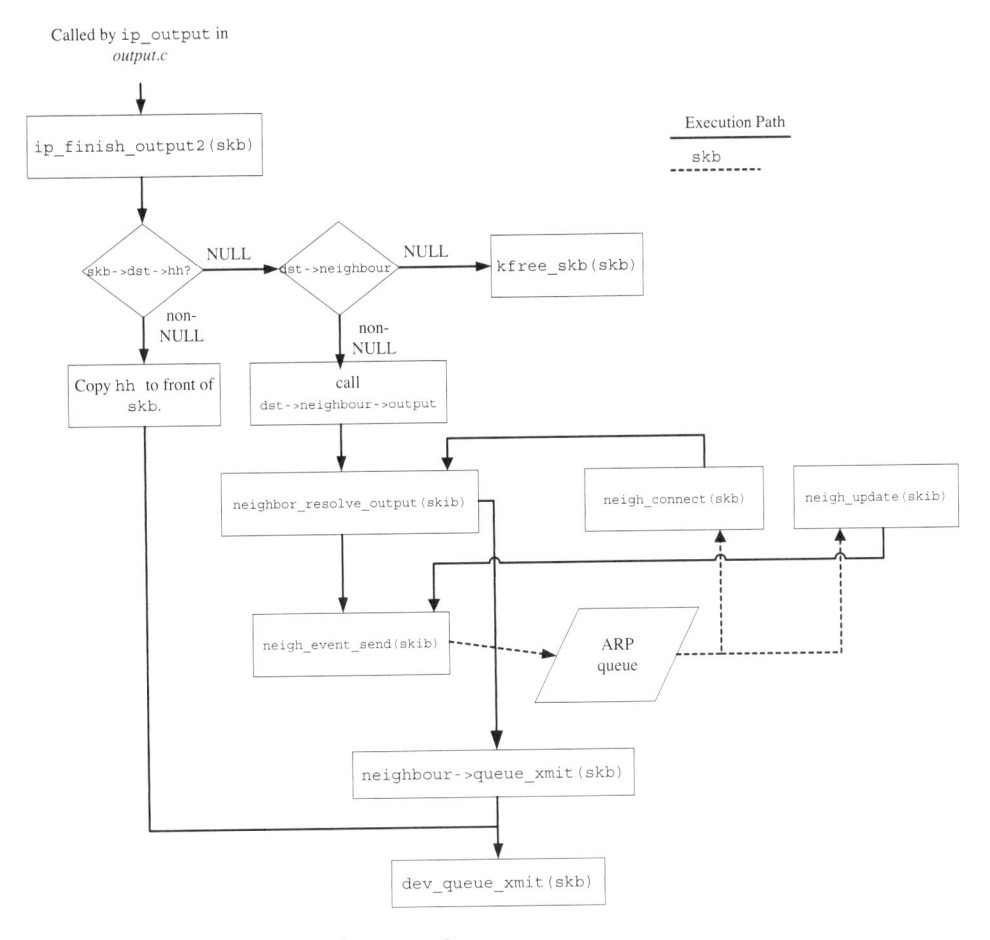

FIGURE 5.3 Destination cache transmit sequence.

If the hh field is not NULL, `ip_finish_output2` gets the link layer header and its length through hh. It reserves space at the head of the sk_buff for the link layer header and copies the header to the front of the packet. The packet is now ready for transmission. Therefore, we call the function pointed to by `hh_output` and in most cases, it has been initialized to point to the `dev_queue_xmit` function.

STRUCTURES AND FUNCTIONS FOR ADDRESS ASSIGNMENT, MULTICAST, AND CONFIGURATION

Any TCP/IP implementation must have configurable options for IP multicasting and multiple network interface address assignment. Linux is no exception and does this through the use of the `in_device` structure. The structure also contains most of the IPv4 tunable parameters. As shown in Chapter 4, most of the `net_device` structure is protocol independent. However, network interface addresses for IPv4 must be kept somewhere, and they are stored in the `in_device` structure. Fields can be set in this structure either via `sysctrl` or `setsockopt` and the `rtnetlink`. The address information is kept here rather than the `net_device` structure because address and Internet configuration information must be kept independent of the device.

The `in_dev_get` Function

The `in_device` structure is defined in the file `linux/include/linux/inetdevice.h`. It is accessed by using the `in_dev_get` or one of the related functions in the same file.

```
static __inline__ struct in_device *
in_dev_get(const struct net_device *dev)
{
    struct in_device *in_dev;
    rcu_read_lock();
    in_dev = __in_dev_get_rcu(dev);
    if (in_dev)
        atomic_inc(&in_dev->refcnt);
    rcu_read_unlock();
    return in_dev;
}
```

The `in_device` Structure

The `in_device` structure includes many fields for managing multiple addresses per network interface driver instance or actually per interface.

```
struct in_device
{
```

`dev` is a pointer back to the `net_device` structure that references this Internet device instance.

```
    struct net_device   *dev;
    atomic_t            refcnt;
    int                 dead;
```

This is where we put IP addresses assigned to the interface. Since multiple addresses are supported, `ifa_list` is implemented as a linked list. `mc_list` holds the list of multicast addresses for the device, `dev`. These multicast addresses are managed by the IGMP protocol covered in Chapter 8. `mr_v1_seen` is used by the IGMP protocol to indicate an incoming IGMP packet.

```
struct in_ifaddr     *ifa_list;
rwlock_t             mc_list_lock;
struct ip_mc_list    *mc_list;
spinlock_t           mc_tomb_lock;
struct ip_mc_list    *mc_tomb;
unsigned long        mr_v1_seen;
unsigned long        mr_v2_seen;
unsigned long        mr_maxdelay;
unsigned char        mr_qrv;
unsigned char        mr_gq_running;
unsigned char        mr_ifc_count;
```

The next field is the general query timer. This is used for IGMP query timeouts.

```
struct timer_list    mr_gq_timer;
```

This field, `mr_ifc_timer`, is the interface change timer.

```
struct timer_list    mr_ifc_timer;
struct neigh_parms   *arp_parms;
struct ipv4_devconf  cnf;
```

For recent 2.6 versions, this structure is put on an RCU list for more efficiency in SMP systems.

```
    struct rcu_head      rcu_head;
};
```

The `ipv4_devconf` Structure

This structure is also defined in the file `linux/include/linux/inetdevice.h`. It is contained in the `cnf` field of the `in_device` structure, shown earlier when the structure is used for IPv4, which it almost always is. `ipv4_devconf` contains configuration values for IPv4, and each field in the structure corresponds to one of the configuration items listed in Table 5.5.

```
struct ipv4_devconf
{
```

```
        int     accept_redirects;
        int     send_redirects;
        int     secure_redirects;
        int     shared_media;
        int     accept_source_route;
        int     rp_filter;
        int     proxy_arp;
        int     bootp_relay;
        int     log_martians;
        int     forwarding;
        int     mc_forwarding;
        int     tag;
        int     arp_filter;
        int     arp_announce;
        int     arp_ignore;
        int     medium_id;
        int     no_xfrm;
        int     no_policy;
        int     force_igmp_version;
        int     promote_secondaries;
        void    *sysctl;
};
```

Table 5.5 shows the configuration items defined in the file `linux/include/linux/sysctl.h`. These variables are associated with the `ipv4_devconf` structure shown previously. Each variable can be set via `sysctl` and some by `ioctl`.

TABLE 5.5 IPv4 Configuration Items

Name	Value	Purpose
NET_IPV4_CONF_FORWARDING	1	IP forwarding is set for this interface.
NET_IPV4_CONF_MC_FORWARDING	2	Multicast forwarding is set for this interface.
NET_IPV4_CONF_PROXY_ARP	3	Respond to proxy ARP requests.
NET_IPV4_CONF_ACCEPT_REDIRECTS	4	Accept ICMP redirects.
NET_IPV4_CONF_SECURE_REDIRECTS	5	Accept secure redirects.
NET_IPV4_CONF_SEND_REDIRECTS	6	Send ICMP redirects.
NET_IPV4_CONF_SHARED_MEDIA	7	Shared media

→

`NET_IPV4_CONF_RP_FILTER`	8	Reverse path filtering. This option is turned on by default if IP forwarding is also enabled.
`NET_IPV4_CONF_ACCEPT_SOURCE_ROUTE`	9	Used for source routing.
`NET_IPV4_CONF_BOOTP_RELAY`	10	DHCP or Bootp relay is configured.
`NET_IPV4_CONF_LOG_MARTIANS`	11	This configuration tells us to log packets with Martian addresses.
`NET_IPV4_CONF_TAG`	12	Not used in core TCP/IP protocol suite.
`NET_IPV4_CONF_ARPFILTER`	13	Configure ARP filtering. ARP filtering can be used to prevent multiple interfaces from responding to an ARP request.
`NET_IPV4_CONF_MEDIUM_ID`	14	This configuration item is not used in the core TCP/IP protocol suite.
`NET_IPV4_CONF_NOXFRM`	15	Bypass route policy checks in Linux transformer (XFRM).
`NET_IPV4_CONF_NOPOLICY`	16	This configuration item turns on the DST_NOPOLICY flag in the destination cache entry as a default value. It also bypasses XFRM policy checks.
`NET_IPV4_CONF_FORCE_IGMP_VERSION`	17	Force IGMP to earlier version. This value doesn't appear to be referenced in the IPv4 code.
`NET_IPV4_CONF_ARP_ANNOUNCE`	18	This value doesn't appear to be referenced in the IPv4 code.
`NET_IPV4_CONF_ARP_IGNORE`	19	This value doesn't appear to be referenced in the IPv4 code.
`NET_IPV4_CONF_PROMOTE_SECONDARIES`	20	This value doesn't appear to be referenced in the IPv4 code.

IPv4 Device Configuration Utility Functions

Several utility functions associated with the `in_device` structure are used widely in the IP protocol and elsewhere.

The Function, `inet_select_address`

The most important of these functions is to select the default destination address from the list of addresses assigned to the device. This function is `inet_select_address`.

```
u32 inet_select_addr(const struct net_device *dev, u32 dst, int scope);
```

The argument, `dev` points to the network interface device, `dst` is the destination address associated with a packet that is lacking a source address. We want to find the appropriate source address to place in a packet that is being sent to the destination address defined by the parameter, `dst`. The parameter, `scope`, is set to either `RT_SCOPE_LINK` or `RT_SCOPE_UNIVERSE`. The complete set of values for `scope` is shown in Chapter 8.

SECURITY, STACKABLE DESTINATION, AND XFRM

IPSec has been the security mechanism of choice for many years. The security features for TCP/IP were first specified in the mid-1990s. The security architecture for IP, known collectively as *IPSec*, was revised in the late 1990s [RFC 2401]. It was revised to include a definition of an Authentication Header (AH) [RFC 2402], an Encapsulating Security Payload (ESP) [RFC 2406], and Internet Key Exchange (IKE) for key management [RFC 2409]. This book won't go into the theory of network security, but we will explore some of the internal structures used to support IPSec. It also supports the concept of Security Associations (SAs). SAs can be thought of as secure connections. The management of SAs involve a three-tuple consisting of a Security Parameter Index (SPI), a destination address, and a security protocol, which can be either ESP or SH. With certain types of SAs, the IP traffic passes through an IP tunnel where an outer IP header specifies the IPSec information and an inner header that is the real IP header. Linux supports the `PF_KEY` key management API version 2 [RFC 2367]. The `PF_KEY` type address family is defined in the file `linux/include/linux/pfkeyv2.h`.

To support these security features, Linux provides a Security Policy Database (SPD), which contains the rules to implement the secure policy. It also provides a Security Association Database (SAD) to manage the secure connections. The destination cache, covered earlier in this chapter, is used to assign a destination to a packet, which could be an external host machine or an internal packet handler. Starting with Linux 2.6, there is a mechanism called the Transformer (XFRM) that transforms destination cache entries based on the security policy. The essentials of the xfrm implementation consist of a policy rule implemented as a structure called `xfrm_policy`. In addition, it defines a transformer with the `xfrm_state` structure definition from the file `linux/include/net/xfrm.h`. The SPD contains the transform rules that are implemented as a list of `xfrm_policy` instances, ordered by priority. The transformer allows the `dst_entry` structures to be accumulated into bundles. In addition, the `dst_entry` structure has a new field, `xfrm_state`, which points to a `xfrm_state` instance.

The `xfrm_lookup` Function

The SPD is accessed when protocol output routines do a lookup in the SPD by calling `xfrm_lookup`, defined in the file `linux/include/net/dst.h`.

```
int xfrm_lookup(struct dst_entry **dst_p, struct flowi *fl, struct sock
*sk, int flags);
```

The function, `xfrm_lookup` finds a match in the SPD and then checks the action in the `xfrm_policy` entry. If the action is `XFRM_POLICY_BLOCK`, it returns an error. If the action is `XFRM_POLICY_ALLOW`, then a bundle of destinations is accumulated and returned. The `xfrm_state` structure is defined in the file `linux/include/net/xfrm.h`.

SOME PRACTICAL CONSIDERATIONS

Most of this chapter focused on the infrastructure of Linux TCP/IP. In this section, we present some hints about debugging Linux kernel code and how to access information about each of the kernel modules associated with the protocols that are members of the Linux TCP/IP suite.

Configuring TCP/IP via `sysctl` and the `/proc` Filesystem

The `/proc` filesystem is a virtual filesystem that contains Linux kernel and networking parameters and statistics. The `sysctl` facility requires the `/proc` file system to be configured in the kernel. The `/proc` file system can be browsed by using the usual filesystem navigation commands such as `cd` and `ls`. Through the course of the book, we list the `/proc` facilities that are relevant to the TCP/IP facility being discussed. Elsewhere in this book, we also show examples of how a protocol can provide support for `/proc` by registering a function that is called while the user browses the virtual filesystem.

`Sysctl` parameters can be read or written by a user with the command `sysctl(8)`. In addition to specifying them dynamically, configuration values can be preloaded into the kernel by putting them in the `sysctl.conf` file, usually in `/etc`. See `sysctl.conf(8)`. The best documentation of the `sysctl` values is in the file `linux/Documentation/networking/ip-sysctls.txt`.

Rate Limiting

One type of configuration parameter that deserves special mention is rate limiting. Rate limiting restricts the timing of various types of packets to provide more predictable real-time performance. This way, rate limiting prevents packets from building up in queues in the device driver or causing system performance bottlenecks elsewhere in TCP/IP. As we have seen in this chapter, the normal Linux clock rate is measured in Hz, the number of ticks per second, and the current time is maintained in the global variable `jiffies`. The rate limit is set to the allowed number of ticks or `jiffies` per packet. Some of the rate limits have defaults. For example, our host has a clock rate of 100 ticks per second, which is typical for x86 systems. The default ICMP rate limits are set to 100, allowing one packet per second for certain types of ICMP packets. This is how we could increase the limit of the number of ICMP echo reply packets to the value of two per second. Since the rate limit for ICMP applies to all types of ICMP packet, we must set the ICMP rate mask to add the additional type. We set the value one into `icmp_ratemask` via the `sysctl(8)` utility to indicate that we want to rate limit echo reply packets. Then, we set `icmp_ratelimit` to 50.

In various places in the book, as the path of packets through the source code is traced, we show how rate limits are checked for different packet types. Linux provides the ability to rate-limit many aspects of packet flow through the TCP/IP stack. All sysctl values including rate limits are documented in the file `linux/Documentation/networking/ip-sysctl.txt`.

SUMMARY

In this chapter, we discussed some of the implementation, or the internal structure, of Linux TCP/IP. We discussed the difference between a protocol and its implementation. We covered the internals of the queuing layer and how packets pass between the network layer protocols and the device drivers. We talked about the mechanism for registering protocol's packet handlers with the stack. We looked at the interface functions available for developers of protocols and discussed some of the internal mechanisms to move packets around within the stack. Next, Chapter 6 covers the Linux system for network buffering in detail. Chapters 7 through 10 look at packets as they are processed—we will follow the packets as they travel through the layers of the TCP/IP stack.

6 Socket Buffers and Linux Memory Allocation

In This Chapter

- A Few Words
- Introduction
- Requirements for TCP/IP Memory Allocation
- Traditional Memory Allocation Schemes
- Slab Allocation
- Linux Socket Buffers
- Socket Buffers, Fragmentation, and Segmentation
- Socket Buffer Allocation and Lists
- Socket Buffer Utility Functions
- Some Practical Considerations

A FEW WORDS

We began with Chapters 1 and 2, which covered general networking topics. Chapter 3 began the detailed discussion of the internal TCP/IP stack in the Linux OS by discussing the network interface drivers. Chapter 4 continued by discussing material on the socket layer, and Chapter 5 discussed some of the network framework and infrastructure in Linux. This chapter continues the detailed discussion of the Linux implementation of TCP/IP by discussing the memory allocation scheme and Linux network buffers.

In this chapter, we focus on Linux memory allocation. During this discussion, we dive into the Linux socket buffer implementation in detail. Linux socket buffers are used to hold network packets, whether they are outgoing packets allocated at the socket interface or are incoming packets allocated by the network interface driver. Like other Unix implementations, Linux places TCP/IP within the kernel and uses a kernel-facility for memory allocation scheme to hold network packets. In this chapter, we look at the Linux kernel memory allocation scheme called Linux *slab cache* and how it is used as the basis for Linux socket buffers. Before we undertake the detailed examination of network packet memory allocation in Linux, we introduce other memory allocation schemes used with TCP/IP implementations and contrast them with Linux. We show how the Linux slab cache has inherent advantages over other methods and how it is appropriate for use in embedded systems' TCP/IP applications.

Memory allocation is a key factor in the performance of any TCP/IP stack. Like other TCP/IP stack implementers before them, the developers of Linux were aware of the importance of memory allocation on network performance. Most other TCP/IP implementations have a memory implementation mechanism that is independent from the OS. However, the Linux implementers took a different approach by using the slab cache method, which is used for most other internal kernel allocation, and in this chapter, we will see how this method has been adapted for socket buffers. We'll see how the Linux scheme has sufficient or better performance than other memory allocation mechanisms used with other TCP/IP stack implementations.

INTRODUCTION

Although a complete discussion of memory allocation in modern OSs is beyond the scope of this book, in this section, we will discuss the basics of memory allocation. Most modern processors provide hardware memory management. Therefore, most operation systems (with the exception of the smallest OSs used in embedded systems) run in processors that provide support for hardware-based virtual memory. Operating systems use memory management hardware to allow user processes to run in protected memory space.

Most virtual memory schemes divide physical memory into small fixed-sized units called *pages*. Paging schemes go back to early OS development and the memory paging support was originally developed was intended for limited physical memory environments. With these schemes, each page can be loaded separately into memory from long term storage or disk. It is important to understanding the allocation scheme behind the socket buffer implementation. Like these early paged systems, the page is the fundamental unit used with slab allocation in the Linux kernel. For a thorough examination of memory allocation used in various flavors of the Unix operation system, see *Unix Internals*, Chapters 12 through 15 [VAHAL96].

For our purposes, we remember that the TCP/IP implementation is in the kernel where the physical and virtual addresses are identical, Therefore we can ignore virtual memory. However, even without considering virtual memory, the Linux slab memory allocation scheme remains a complex topic. The Solaris OS was the first widely used OS to implement slab allocation. For more information about Solaris, refer to Section 12.10 in [VAHAL.96]. In this chapter, we will discuss how the Linux slab allocator is used with socket buffers.

REQUIREMENTS FOR TCP/IP MEMORY ALLOCATION

Networking stacks have certain characteristics that provide a challenge for memory allocation implementers. Network protocols such as TCP/IP receive, transmit, and process data in relatively small independent packets. Moreover, network protocols also have to run continuously with high reliability, and they can't risk any downtime. Yet the OSs must frequently allocate memory buffers for packets as they are received by the computer at wire rates. The OS must also release the buffers at an equally high rate when the stack is done processing the packets. Any latencies associated with memory allocation could have an adverse performance impact. In addition, copying of network buffers should be minimized. Because of the unique needs of network protocols, there are three important requirements for any memory allocator that is to be used with TCP/IP.

Memory should be made available in different sizes to allow for the variable-length packets used in TCP/IP. TCP/IP is constantly processing packets, and this processing involves the frequent pre-pending or removal of headers. The buffering scheme must support this without copying any data. The manipulation of headers should be done by moving pointers while avoiding copying the actual data. It should be easy to place packets on lists or queues, and there should be a way that packets can be consolidated efficiently from multiple buffers. While processing, multiple buffers of data are often gathered into a single logical packet, and packets are frequently placed on queues to wait for processing or transmission. The buffer data structures should support pointers both for queuing of packets and pulling buffers together into a single packet without copying of data.

Therefore, any memory allocation scheme used with TCP/IP must be based on a reliable but flexible dynamic method that can run continuously. The simplest memory allocation method is based on a heap, but heaps are prone to fragmentation. With a scheme like this, buffers are rapidly allocated and returned; the memory space can be quickly broken up into small pieces so the time spent searching for an available buffer eventually degrades.

TRADITIONAL MEMORY ALLOCATION SCHEMES

Other TCP/IP implementations solve the problem of heap fragmentation by using a system of fixed-sized buffers for the TCP/IP stack. In contrast, the Linux implementation of TCP/IP uses the slab memory allocation method also used for allocation by other subsystems in the kernel. The next two sections provide background on earlier buffering schemes used in other TCP/IP stack implementations. The next section covers the Linux slab allocation method and why it is suitable for use by the TCP/IP stack. Later, we will look at the internal structure of `skbuffs`, the shared area, the header cache, and the internal queuing capability, and we will also discuss the `skbuff` API.

Heap-Based Memory Allocation

The first memory allocation method we look at is heap-based memory allocation. In this section, we show why this method is not appropriate for use by TCP/IP or other network protocols. The simplest method of memory allocation is the basic heap. A heap provides varying-sized buffers that are allocated from a logically continuous space. When an application needs a buffer, it calls a function such as `malloc`, which returns the smallest available buffer that is larger than the requested amount. The buffer is returned to the heap by calling the function `free`, which puts the buffer back in the heap. If another user wants a larger buffer, `malloc` has to pass over all the smaller pieces of memory looking for a contiguous hunk of available space that is larger or equal to the requested amount. For example, if a user wants 97 bytes, he calls `malloc(97)`, which returns a buffer of 100 bytes. When this buffer is returned by calling `free`, a 100-byte hole is left in the available memory. Although the 100 bytes is put back on the free list by `free`, it is only available to a subsequent caller that asks for 100 bytes or less.

As discussed in earlier chapters, a typical networking packet such as an Ethernet frame is 1500 bytes or less in length. Commonly used buffer sizes will be 2 K or even 512 bytes or smaller for frequently used small packets. Since a real-world system can have packets arriving on a 1 GB Ethernet connection or higher, packets are being processed at least at rates of one packet every few microseconds or less. At these rates, a heap-based, best-fit memory allocation scheme would fragment very fast if used in a fast networking application. The fragmentation decomposes the available memory into ever smaller holes. It is possible that without some mechanism to coalesce the smaller holes into larger pieces, the protocol could come to a complete stop.

Heaps are often combined with a resource map consisting of a set of address- and size-tuples and a set of policies for answering memory requests. This method is called a *resource map allocator*. The policy may be first fit, best fit, or worst fit.

However, even with the use of one of these policies, the memory pool will fragment over time [KNUTH73]. See Figure 6.1 for an illustration of how the fragmentation could occur.

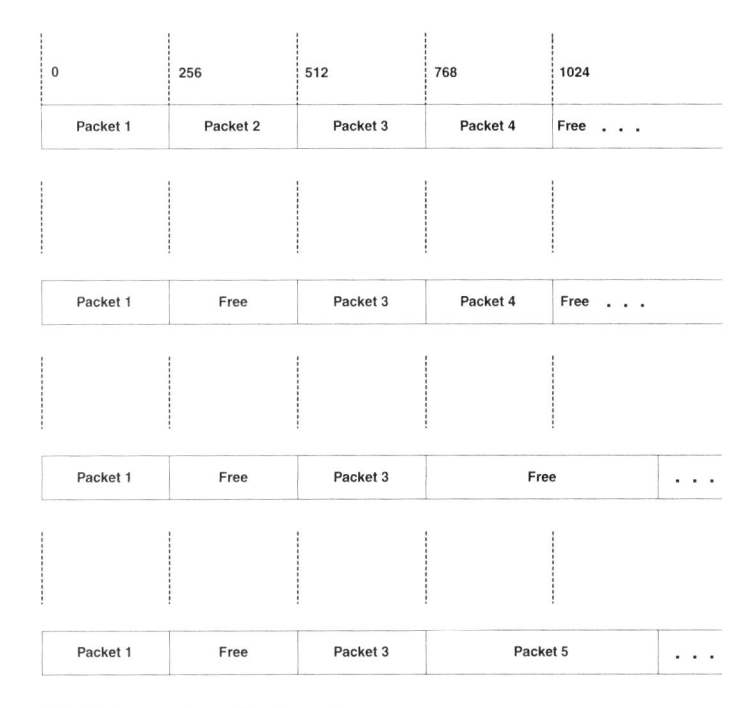

0	256	512	768	1024	
Packet 1	Packet 2	Packet 3	Packet 4	Free	...

Packet 1	Free	Packet 3	Packet 4	Free	...

Packet 1	Free	Packet 3	Free	...

Packet 1	Free	Packet 3	Packet 5	...

FIGURE 6.1 Best-fit allocation.

Pre-Allocated Fixed-Sized Buffers

Because of the limitation of heap-based methods, an alternative method of memory allocation is often used with networking protocols. This method, based on pre-allocated, fixed-sized buffers has better performance and less overhead than a heap-based method. As discussed earlier, a heap-based method of memory allocation is not generally suitable for networking protocols because of its tendency toward fragmentation. Traditionally, in embedded systems it is preferable to have a bounded memory pool; so most traditional TCP/IP implementations used in embedded systems incorporate a fixed-buffer-based method. The buffer quantities are tuned to allow for the expected amount of networking traffic. Of course, if a particular buffer size is unavailable, packets will be dropped or queued until the loading is reduced. An example of the use of fixed-sized buffer allocation can be found in

STREAMS [STREAMS93]. STREAMS is a framework for network protocols original developed by Dennis Ritchie and used widely in some Unix variants and other OSs. STREAMS uses a memory allocation method officially called *message buffers*, but more specifically called *mblocks*. In many implementations, this scheme is based on fixed-sized pre-allocated buffers. Buffers are available in sizes that are powers of two. The service routine `allocb` is called to get a buffer. It will return the next largest-sized buffer, which will hold the requested amount of data. The buffer is taken from the pool of `mblocks`. Since the buffers are fixed sizes, the buffer pool does not fragment the way the heap-based method does. Refer to Figure 6.2 for an illustration of how packets are allocated with `mblocks` in STREAMS.

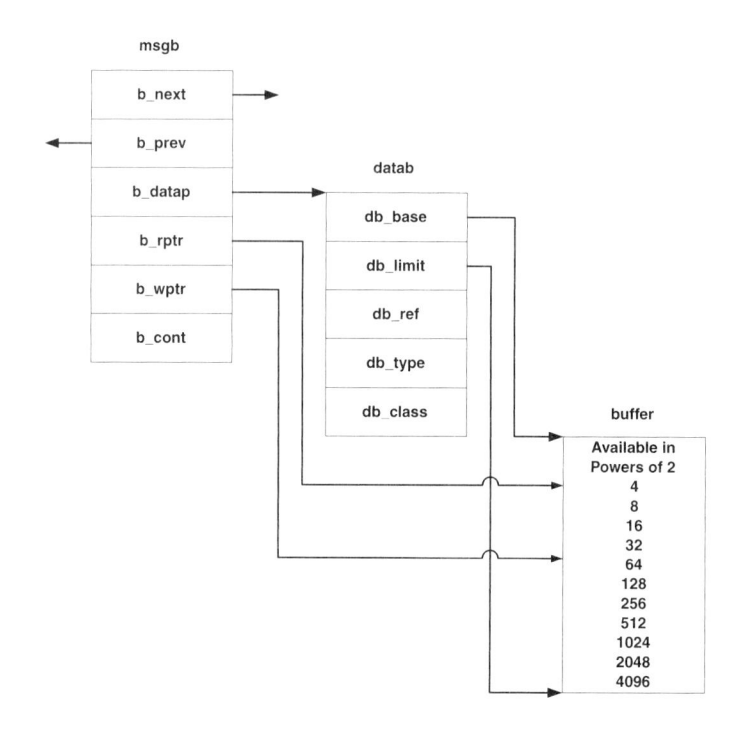

FIGURE 6.2 STREAMS `mblocks`.

Berkeley `mbufs`

Another common example of pre-allocated fixed-sized buffers is called `mbufs`. `Mbufs` are found in the Berkeley-based TCP/IP implementation that is used in BSD Unix and other proprietary OSs for embedded systems. See [MCKUS96] Section 11.3 for a detailed explanation of `mbufs`. As is the case with `mblocks`, `mbufs` are also intended to support variable-length frames needed for protocol stacks such as

TCP/IP. The mbuf data structure is 128-bytes long. It is designed so that the small amounts of data found in short packets or packet headers can be placed in the data area of the mbuf, which is directly below the header. Larger amounts of data are supported by extending the mbufs with clusters.

In many embedded implementations of Berkeley-based TCP/IP, both the mbufs and the clusters are pre-allocated. As with mblocks, clusters are available in sizes that are powers of two. Typical sizes supported can be 64, 128, 256, 512, 1024, and 2048. Generally, 2048 is the most common size. Mbufs can also be chained to support queues of packets. Often in embedded systems, network loading factors are predetermined based on the type of network traffic the system is likely to see. Then parameters are adjusted for the numbers of each size of buffer to be pre-allocated before the system starts up. See Figure 6.3 for an illustration of how the mbuf system works. This presents a challenge for tuners because peak network loads must be anticipated. If the network loading is underestimated, packets can be dropped. Table 6.1 lists the fields in the mbuf structure.

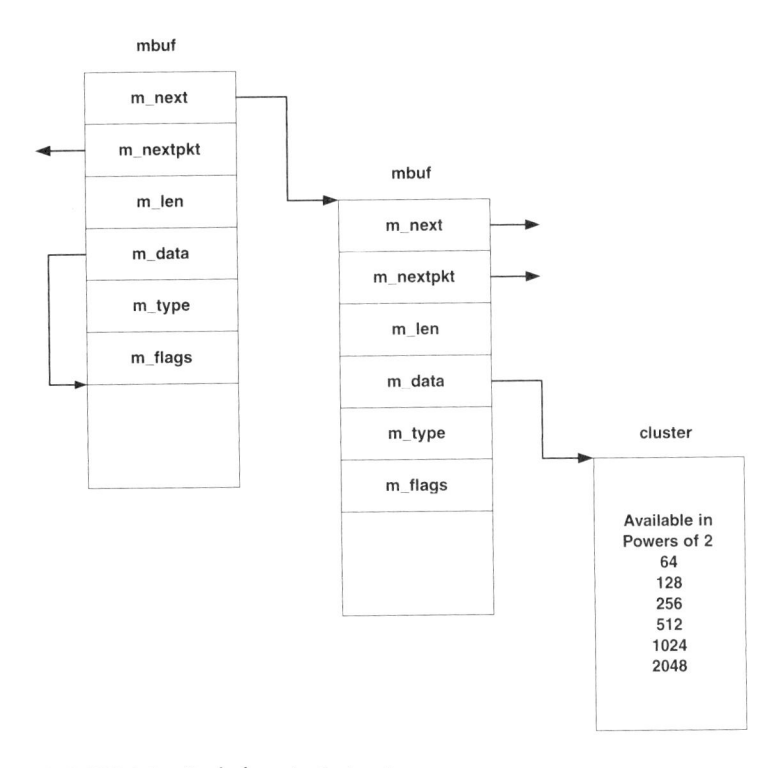

FIGURE 6.3 Berkeley mbuf structure.

TABLE 6.1 mbuf **STRUCTURE**

Field	Purpose
m_next	Next mbuf in chain of mbufs.
m_nextpkt	Next mbuf in a queue of packets.
m_len	This field shows the length of data in the mbuf. It includes the data in the cluster if one is attached.
m_data	Points to the beginning of the usable data. This field can point to the area immediately after the mbuf header, or may point to an address within an attached cluster. This field can be changed to either prepend or remove packet headers.
m_type	Indicates type of mbuf.
m_flags	Indicates whether mbuf is extended with a cluster.
m_pkthdr.len	This location will be the beginning of data if flags field is zero.
m_pkthdr.rcvif	Points to the data structure for interface from which the packet was received.

Mbufs in BSD 4.4

The BSD 4.4 OS also uses mbufs as the core network buffer system [MCKUS96]. However, there are a few important differences from the fixed-size pre-allocated buffer method described earlier. In BSD 4.4, the mbufs are allocated with the standard kernel memory allocator by calling the malloc() function. Instead of initializing separate lists for each of the cluster sizes, only the list of four-Kbyte clusters is pre-allocated. If smaller cluster sizes are requested, they can be obtained from the free page list of the four-Kbyte clusters. If the list of clusters is exhausted while the protocols are processing packets, the backend page allocator will create more four-Kbyte clusters up to a predefined limit. A reference count is maintained in the clusters. When clusters are de-allocated, they are not returned to the memory pool. Instead, the reference count is decremented and the returned clusters are made available for new cluster allocation.

As with the systems described previously, BSD 4.4 does away with fragmentation. It also eliminates the need for precise pre-tuning of buffer requirements because new buffers are grabbed from the page allocator if needed.

SLAB ALLOCATION

The Linux operating system uses a memory allocation method called *slab allocation*. This method was first introduced in the Solaris operating system from Sun Microsystems in version 2.4 [VALHAL96]. The slab allocation method is used for all memory allocation in the Linux kernel, not just networking buffers. The slab allocation system is organized into specific slab caches, one for each major function in the Linux kernel. When used for the allocation of network buffers, slab cache allocation has advantages over a heap-based method. The first advantage is that it is less prone to fragmentation. It also has less overhead and uses hardware cache more efficiently than other methods. As discussed earlier, the pre-allocated fixed-sized buffer mechanisms used with most embedded TCP/IP implementations also solve the fragmentation problem. However, a disadvantage of using pre-allocated fixed-sized buffers is that an area of memory has to be pre-allocated for the buffering mechanism and is not available for any purpose. Another disadvantage of using the fixed-sized buffering methods is that (except in BSD 4.4) in order to avoid starvation, buffer tuning must be done to determine the amount of buffers of each size, and it is not always possible to predict how an embedded system is going to be deployed.

Slab allocation achieves efficiency by organizing all the memory buffers for a specific purpose into a common cache. The slab cache also makes optimum use of hardware caching, and in Linux, each slab cache can be specifically aligned along a cache line for optimum performance. In Linux, when a memory buffer is de-allocated, it is re-assigned to the cache from which it came instead of going back into a generic pool of buffers. Since each cache is specific to a purpose, common fields can be pre-initialized when the buffer is de-allocated. This is quite efficient because as subsequent allocation requests are satisfied from the cache most of the structure initialization will have already been done. Socket buffers are complex and contain spin locks, use counts, and other complex data structures, all of which require initialization. Network buffers are continually allocated and de-allocated at a high rate as the application writes data into a socket when data is received at the network interface, so pre-initialization of structure fields is particularly beneficial to a networking stack such as TCP/IP. There is considerable gain in having these fields pre-initialized when a buffer is allocated. We will see how Linux benefits by this when we discuss socket buffers later in this chapter.

Linux Slab Allocator

The slab allocator can be thought of as having a frontend and a backend. The frontend consists of the functions to allocate and free cache objects, and the backend is the page memory allocator that assigns one additional slab to a particular slab cache if there are no objects left in that slab cache. This is called *growing* the slab cache and actually involves assigning one or more memory mapped pages of the right type for the particular slab.

Table 6.2 shows most of the slab caches used in the TCP/IP protocol suite. The first and most important is the socket buffer cache, which is discussed in detail later in this chapter. The other caches are discussed elsewhere in the book as part of the explanation of the various protocols in TCP/IP. The names in Table 6.2 show up as identifiers in the /proc filesystem under /proc/slabinfo.

TABLE 6.2 Linux TCP/IP Slabs

Name	Purpose	File where the Cache Is Allocated
skbuff_head_cache	Socket buffer cache	linux/net/core/skbuff.c
flow	Generic flow control cache	linux/net/core/flow.c
Table ID	Neighbor table cache	linux/net/core/neighbour.c
sock	Sock structure cache	linux/net/core/sock.c
sock_inode_cache	Socket inode cache	linux/net/socket.c
udp_sock	UDP socket cache for IPv4	linux/net/ipv4/af_inet.c
tcp_sock	TCP socket cache for IPv4	linux/net/ipv4/af_inet.c
raw4_sock	Raw socket cache for IPv4	linux/net/ipv4/af_inet.c
ip_fib_hash	FIB hash table cache for IPv4	linux/net/ipv4/fib_hash.c
ip_fib_alias	FIB alias cache for IPv4	linux/net/ipv4/fib_hash.c
inet_peer_cache	Internet peer structure cache	linux/net/ipv4/inetpeer.c
ip_dst_cache	IPv4 routing table destination cache	linux/net/ipv4/route.c
tcp_open_request	TCP open request cache	linux/net/ipv4/tcp.c
tcp_bind_bucket	TCP bind bucket cache	linux/net/ipv4/tcp.c
tcp_tw_bucket	TCP TIME-WAIT state buckets	linux/net/ipv4/tcp.c
tcp6_sock	TCP socket cache for IPv6	linux/net/ipv6/af_inet6.c
udp6_sock	UDP socket cache for IPv6	linux/net/ipv6/af_inet6.c
raw6_sock	Raw socket cache for IPv6	linux/net/ipv6/af_inet6.c
fib6_nodes	FIB table cache for IPv6	linux/net/ipv6/ip6_fib.c
ip6_dst_cache	IPv6 destination cache	linux/net/ipv6/route.c
bridge_fdb_cache	Layer 2 bridge database cache	linux/net/bridge/br_fdb.c
secpath_cache	XFRM security path cache	linux/net/xfrm/xfrm_input.c
xfrm_dst_cache	XFRM destination cache	linux/net/xfrm/xfrm_policy.c

Cache Utility Functions

Linux provides a set of generic functions to create a slab cache and manipulate the entries in the cache. These functions are defined in the file `linux/include/linux/slab.h`. As discussed earlier, the slab allocator is used by many kernel subsystems, not just TCP/IP. Therefore, these functions are not part of TCP/IP itself, but are widely used in the sources discussed in this book. In addition, they are available for use by any programmer who is implementing her own protocol module in the Linux kernel.

The `kmem_cache_create` function.

The function creates a new slab cache.

```
kmem_cache_t     *kmem_cache_create (const char *,
                 size_t size, size_t offset, unsigned long flags,
                 void (*)(void*, kmem_cache_t *, unsigned long),
                 void (*)(void*, kmem_cache_t *, unsigned long));
```

The first parameter is a string pointer that points to the cache's identifier. Generally, it is a hard-coded string such as shown in Table 6.2. The function returns a pointer to `kmem_cache_t`, which is generically defined as a pointer to the cache structure `kmem_cache_s` in file `linux/mm/slab.c`. However, each call to `kmem_cache_create` generally redefines `kmem_cache_t` to be set to the unique type of the slab cache, which is also the cache name. The `unsigned long` parameter are flags set to one of the values in Table 6.3. The flags are defined in the file `linux/include/linux/slab.h`. The first of the two function arguments points to the constructor function and the second points to the destructor function. Each of these two functions can be NULL or may point to a function implemented to be specific to the cache type.

TABLE 6.3 Slab Cache Flags for `kmem_cache_create` Function

Flag	Value	Purpose
SLAB_DEBUG_FREE	0x00000100UL	Perform debug checks when calling free. This flag does not appear to be used anywhere.
SLAB_DEBUG_INITIAL	0x00000200UL	Perform debug checks when objects are initialized and the constructor is called.
SLAB_RED_ZONE	0x00000400UL	Create a "red zone" around the allocated buffer for overrun checking.
SLAB_POISON	0x00000800UL	Request that a new buffer be initialized with a test pattern, which is `a5a5a5a5`.

→

Flag	Value	Purpose
SLAB_NO_REAP	0x00001000UL	Objects in the cache should never be reaped. This flag does not appear to be used very widely.
SLAB_HWCACHE_ALIGN	0x00002000UL	Specifies that objects in the cache be aligned to a hardware cache line when created. This flag is used by almost all the slab caches in TCP/IP.
SLAB_CACHE_DMA	0x00004000UL	Objects in the cache should be created from DMA memory, type GFP_DMA. This flag is not used in TCP/IP. DMA is used by the network drivers, but data is placed into pages attached to the socket buffer and not directly into the slab cache.
SLAB_MUST_HWCACHE_ALIGN	0x00008000UL	Force alignment to hardware cache line. This flag is not used by TCP/IP.
SLAB_STORE_USER	0x00010000UL	Store the last owner of the object. This flag is used for debugging only.
SLAB_RECLAIM_ACCOUNT	0x00020000UL	Track individual pages to indicate which of them may be reclaimed later. This flag is used by the socket `inode` cache.
SLAB_PANIC	0x00040000UL	This flag says to generic panic if `kmem_cache_create` fails.
SLAB_DESTROY_BY_RCU	0x00080000UL	This flag indicates that destruction should be deferred by RCU list.
		The following three flags are passed to the constructor function when a cache object is allocated.
SLAB_CTOR_CONSTRUCTOR	0x001UL	Indicates that the constructor should be called for object initialization and not the de-constructor, which normally does object initialization.
SLAB_CTOR_ATOMIC	0x002UL	Indicates to the constructor that it must execute atomically.
SLAB_CTOR_VERIFY	0x004UL	If this flag is set, the constructor is being called to verify only.

The constructor function pointed to by the second function argument is called only when new uninitialized slabs are added to the slab cache.

The `kmem_cache_destroy` Function

This function deletes a slab cache.

```
int kmem_cache_destroy (kmem_cache_t *);
```

The parameter points to the slab cache. This function will remove all traces of the slab cache. If a module creates a slab cache that does not need to persist between module loads, this function should be called from the module before it is unloaded. All objects in the cache should be freed before calling this function. The cache must be protected by the caller from allocations while the function is executing.

The `kmem_cache_shrink` Function

```
int kmem_cache_shrink(kmem_cache_t *);
```

This function removes as many slabs as possible. It returns a zero when all slabs in the slab cache have been released.

The `kmem_cache_size` Function

The purpose of this function is to obtain the cache size of the cache.

```
unsigned int kmem_cache_size(kmem_cache_t *);
```

It returns the size of the objects in the cache pointed to by the parameter.

Functions for Allocation and Freeing Slabs from a Slab Cache

The functions in this section are provided for allocation and freeing of slab caches. They are used extensively in the Linux networking code, although sometimes they are hidden behind more specialized functions.

The `kmem_cache_alloc` Function

```
void * kmem_cache_alloc (kmem_cache_t *, gfp_t);
```

`kmem_cache_alloc` returns a pointer to an object allocated from the slab cache pointed to by the first argument. The second parameter, can have one of the values listed in Table 6.4. it is used only when the cache does not contain any objects and it must be grown. The values are the "get free pages" values, which govern the individual page allocation that occurs in the backend of the slab cache.

TABLE 6.4 Values for Flag Argument in Kmem_cache_alloc Function

Flag	Meaning
GFP_USER	Used when memory is allocated for an application in user space.
GFP_KERNEL	Used with normal kernel memory allocation.
GFP_ATOMIC	Used when the caller is an interrupt service routine.
GFP_DMA	States that memory should be allocated from DMA space. This flag is architecture dependent.
GFP_NOFS	Set when wait and re-schedule and physical IO is OK.
GFP_NOIO	Set when wait and re-schedule but no physical IO.

The kmem_cache_free Function

The last function in this section, kmem_cache_free, de-allocates an object from a slab cache.

```
void kmem_cache_free (kmem_cache_t *, void *);
```

The second parameter points to the object to be de-allocated. The first parameter must point to the cache from which the object was originally allocated.

LINUX SOCKET BUFFERS

As discussed earlier in this chapter and others, the socket buffer is the container for a packet traversing the TCP/IP stack. In this section, we discuss the internal architecture of the socket buffers, or sk_buffs, how they are allocated, how they are placed in a header cache when freed, and how the internal sk_buff queuing works. Socket buffers are complex and contain many fields with seemingly obscure purposes such as pointers, counters, and other maintenance items. In this and subsequent sections we try to sort out this information and make sense of all the fields in the sk_buff structure as well as examine the functions to manipulate them. The ≠actual data associated with the socket is in a separate buffer, which is generally allocated directly with a call to kmalloc; however, this is not as simple as it seems. A socket buffer can be either cloned or shared, and the socket buffer structure contains fields that indicate whether the particular buffer is cloned or shared. Linux provides a utility function to clone a socket buffer, and we explain this function along with the other utility functions in a later section in this chapter. However, the fields of the socket buffer structure are shown later in this section. The buffer or data area attached to the socket buffer can be in one of various forms. It may directly contain the whole TCP/IP packet, or it may contain only the TCP/IP header with the rest of the packet content in an attached list of mapped pages. Figure 6.4 shows a picture of a socket buffer in its most general form and how the pointer fields can be used to find various positions in the attached TCP/IP packet.

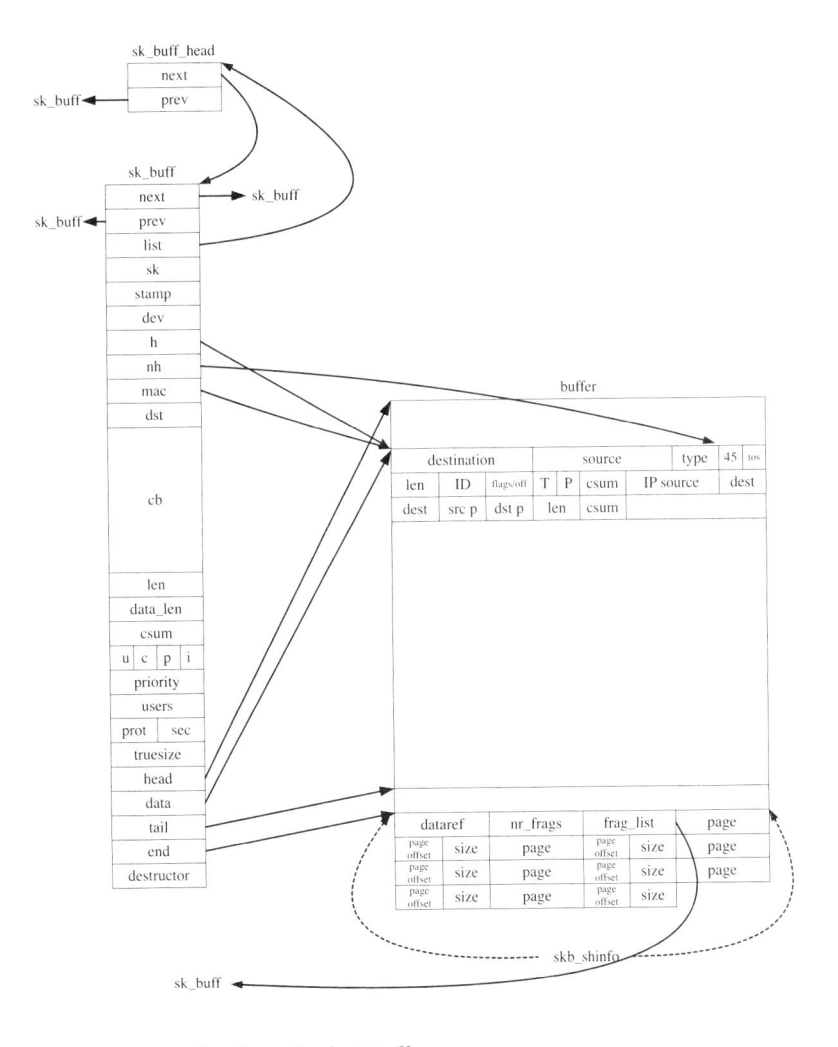

FIGURE 6.4 The Linux Socket Buffer.

254   Linux TCP/IP Networking for Embedded Systems

The Socket Buffer Structure, `sk_buff`

In this section we examine the internal structure of the socket buffer. Refer to Figure 6.4 for a general picture of how the buffers are laid out. The structure defining the Linux socket buffer, `sk_buff`, is defined in the file `linux/include/linux/skbuff.h`.

```
struct sk_buff {
```

The following two fields in the socket buffer must be first. As we will see later in the book, sometimes the socket buffer lists are overloaded as different types. `next` points to the next buffer on the list, and `prev` points to the previous buffer.

```
struct sk_buff      *next;
struct sk_buff      *prev;
```

The next field points to a `sock` structure, and for transmitted packets, it points to the socket from which this packet originated.

```
struct sock         *sk;
```

For received packets, the next field, `stamp`, indicates the time this packet arrived at the interface. For received packets, `dev` shows the device from which this packet was received. `Dev` points to the network interface. In the case where a pseudo-device is involved, `real_dev` points to the actual physical device.

```
struct timeval      stamp;
struct net_device   *dev;
struct net_device   *input_dev;
```

The next three fields are unions that are expanded into specific head type fields. The purpose of these fields is to provide convenient access to all of the header fields in the packet. `h` points to the transport layer header in the packet contained by this buffer, and `nh` points to the network layer header in the packet contained by this buffer. `mac` points to the link layer header.

```
union {
```

These are the transport layer headers, but actually include any protocol that is encapsulated by IP. The first four headers are for TCP, UDP, ICMP, and IGMP, respectively.

```
struct tcphdr   *th;
```

```
            struct udphdr     *uh;
            struct icmphdr    *icmph;
            struct igmphdr    *igmph;
```

ipip is the IP tunneling header, and raw is a generic header pointer and ipv6h is the IPv6 IP header.

```
            struct iphdr      *ipiph;
            struct ipv6hdr    *ipv6h;
            unsigned char     *raw;
        } h;
```

These are the network layer headers. Iph is the IPv4 header, and ipv6h is the IPv6 header.

```
        union {
            sstruct iphdr     *iph;
            struct ipv6hdr    *ipv6h;
```

arph is the ARP protocol header; raw is the generic network layer header; and raw in the mac union is the Ethernet or layer 2 header.

```
            struct arphdr     *arph;
            unsigned char     *raw;
        } nh;
        union {
            unsigned char     *raw;
        } mac;
```

The next field, dst, points to the destination address cache entry for this packet. It could also be the routing cache entry for the packet. We discuss the destination cache extensively elsewhere in the book.

```
        struct dst_entry      *dst;
```

The next field, sec_path, is used with XFRM, the internal kernel implementation of IPSec as part of secure VPNs.

The next field, cb, is the control buffer. It is for private storage of protocol-specific items that must be copied across layers. In TCP/IP, it is primarily used by TCP for the TCP control buffer, which is discussed in Chapter 8. The contents of the cb field are copied to a new buffer when the sk_buff is cloned.

```
        char                  cb[48];
```

The next field, `len`, contains the overall length of the packet including the header and any data in attached buffers. `data_len` is the length of the data part of the packet, and `mac_len` is the length of the Layer 2 header. `csum` holds the IP header checksum. `priority` is the packet queuing priority.

```
unsigned int     len,
                 data_len,
                 mac_len,
                 csum;
```

`local_df` holds the "don't fragment" value. If set, this packet will not be fragmented when it is transmitted. `cloned` indicates that this packet was cloned. The field `ip_summed` indicates whether the output device can calculate IP checksums in hardware. `nohdr` indicates that this buffer contains a packet that does not have a header. `nfctinfo` has information about the connection used by the connection tracking module in `netfilter`. `pkt_type` is the class of the packet and is set to one of the values in Table 6.5 which are all defined in `include/linux/if_packet.h`. The classes shown in the table are used by IP to determine how to internally route a packet. The values are set by decoding the packet's destination address and checking it in the packet's destination and routing caches.

TABLE 6.5 Packet Types in Socket Buffer `pkt_type` Field

PacketType	Value	Purpose
PACKET_HOST	0	Packet is directed to this machine.
PACKET_BROADCAST	1	Broadcast packet.
PACKET_MULTICAST	2	Multicast packet.
PACKET_OTHERHOST	3	Unicast packet for sending to a peer.
PACKET_OUTGOING	4	Outgoing packet.
PACKET_LOOPBACK	5	Any looped back broadcast or unicast packet.
PACKET_FASTROUTE	6	This packet is to be processed in the fast-route path.

```
__u8        local_df:1,
            cloned:1,
            ip_summed:2,
            nohdr:1,
            nfctinfo:3;
__u8        pkt_type:3,
```

fclone indicates whether this instance represents a cloned buffer. The next field, ipvs_property says that this buffer is owned by the Linux virtual server, ipvs. protocol is the value of the protocol field in the packet's MAC header. This field is used to dispatch a packet to the network layer protocol handler.

```
                            fclone:2,
                            ipvs_property:1;
    __be16                  protocol;
```

The next field points to the destructor function for this packet or NULL if there isn't any.

```
    void                    (*destructor)(struct sk_buff *skb);
```

The following fields are used by netfilter if it is configured. netfilter is the kernel facility used with the iptables program for user control of packet filtering.

```
#ifdef CONFIG_NETFILTER
    __u32                   nfmark;
    struct nf_conntrack *nfct;
```

This field, nfct_reasm, is used by the netfilter connection tracking module. It points to the list of sk_buff structures of packet portions necessary to reassemble a fragmented packet.

```
#if defined(CONFIG_NF_CONNTRACK) || defined(CONFIG_NF_CONNTRACK_MODULE)
    struct sk_buff          *nfct_reasm;
#endif
```

The next field is used by the bridge net filter used to control the Linux bridging code.

```
#ifdef CONFIG_BRIDGE_NETFILTER
    struct nf_bridge_info *nf_bridge;
#endif
#endif
```

The next option field is the traffic control index, and the following field, tc_verd is the traffic control verdict.

```
#ifdef CONFIG_NET_SCHED
    __u16                   tc_index;
```

```
#ifdef CONFIG_NET_CLS_ACT
    __u16                   tc_verd;
#endif
#endif
```

The following fields must be at the end of the `sk_buff`. This is necessary because of the way the function `alloc_skb` allocates a new socket buffer. Socket buffers may be followed by pages containing packet data, which are allocated directly from the kernel's paged memory. `truesize` is the actual packet size. `Users` is the packet user count. This field must be implemented atomically.

```
    unsigned int            truesize;
    atomic_t                users;
```

Head points to the start of the attached data buffer. `data` points to the beginning of useable data in the attached data buffer. `tail` points to the end of the useable data in the attached buffer. `end` points to the absolute end of the data. It is also the start of the "shared" portion that is common to all clones of the buffer.

```
    unsigned char           *head,
                            *data,
                            *tail,
                            *end;
};
```

Where Are Socket Buffers Allocated in Linux TCP/IP?

On the transmit side of the TCP/IP stack, socket buffers are generally allocated in the socket layer before data is ready to transmit. However, socket buffers may be allocated anywhere in the protocol stack. Buffers are allocated whenever any internal protocol in the stack needs to send a packet. This can happen within TCP, ARP, IGMP, or elsewhere. If the packet survives error checking and other processing, the socket buffer is not de-allocated until the driver's `hard_start_xmit` network returns, which indicates that the packet was actually physically transmitted. For more details on how a packet is transmitted through a network interface driver, refer to Chapter 3, "Linux Network Interfaces Drivers." On the receive side, socket buffers are allocated by the network interface driver's interrupt service routine as a new packet is received from the physical interface. If the packet is not de-allocated as a result of error checking and processing, it remains until the application code receives the data, and then the socket buffer is de-allocated. If the packet is dropped for any reason, the socket buffer is de-allocated.

More About Socket Buffer Use in TCP/IP

The first three fields in the socket buffer, `sk_buff` described in the previous section are for list maintenance, including the two pointers `next` and `prev`. These two pointers are identical to the fields in the `sk_buff_head` so pointers can be casted, making it easier to process lists and queues of `sk_buffs`. The third field, points back to the socket buffer head. Lists of socket buffers can exist for many reasons and may also be overloaded with similar types such as TIME-WAIT buckets. This is why the socket buffer fields involved with list maintenance are generic and placed in the beginning of the structure. Linux allocates socket buffers from a slab cache called the `skbuff_head_cache`. The slab allocator is described earlier in this chapter. When buffers are de-allocated, they are returned to the slab cache. The next field, `sk`, is relevant for buffers that originate from a transport layer or the socket layer. It points to the socket structure (`struct sock`) of an open socket if there is one associated with the buffer. The `sk` field can be de-referenced anywhere in the protocol stack to access the file descriptor, IO-related parameters, and status associated with the open socket. If the socket buffer contains a received packet, the next field, `stamp`, is set by the device driver to the time when the packet was received at the interface. The field `dev` is also used for received packets. It points to the receiving driver's network device structure. The `h`, `nh`, and `mac` fields are pointers to the transport, network, and link layer header fields of a TCP/IP packet. The `dst` field points to the destination cache entry. As discussed elsewhere in this book, this cache entry can be either the destination cache or neighbor cache. These caches may include information about the hardware address of the next system to receive this packet, routing information, or internal destination information. The neighbor cache and destination caches are described in more detail in Chapter 5, "The Linux TCP/IP Stack." The part of the buffer in `cb` is a private area available to protocol implementers to use as they wish. However, it is generally used by the TCP protocol to contain the TCP control buffer. It is important to note that this buffer is explicitly copied to the new `sk_buff` when a socket buffer is cloned. The `len` field contains the length of the packet. The value of `len` includes both the packet header and the data.

The final socket buffer fields, `head`, `tail`, `end`, and `data` require a little more explanation. The `head` pointer points to the start of the packet, and `tail` points to the end of the packet. The `end` field points to the absolute end of the user data portion of the packet. The application program, device driver, or even the internal protocol stack layers will rarely change these fields directly. Generally, they are accessed through the socket buffer utility functions listed in later sections. As discussed earlier, one of the requirements for any networking buffer system is that headers can be pre-pended or removed without copying the packet contents. A TCP/IP packet grows in length from where it was formed at the socket layer and traverses down the stack to the network interface drivers. The growth occurs as each layer encapsulates the data it receives from the layer above with its own header. Usually, the growth is at the beginning of the packet as headers are put in front of the data received from layers above. It is important to reduce or eliminate the physical copying packets when doing this header manipulation and far better to do the encapsulation by moving pointers. When a socket buffer is allocated at the socket layer, sufficient space is reserved for the total maximize size or MTU of the interface likely to transmit the packet. This is called *reserving headroom*. Then, as the socket buffer travels down the stack, packet headers can be placed in front without copying the data using a set of utility functions that use the `head`, `tail`, `end`, and `data` fields. These fields are provided to enable the API functions to keep track of positions in the buffer where data of interest starts and ends, and these functions use these pointers.

SOCKET BUFFERS, FRAGMENTATION, AND SEGMENTATION

Fragmentation and segmentation is supported with the aid of an additional structure separate from the `sk_buff` structure. A discussion of the socket buffer implementation in Linux is not complete without discussing this structure. It is placed at the end of the data buffer attached to the `sk_buff` and pointed to by the `end` field which also points to the end of the data portion of the packet. However, `end` can be used to find the beginning of `skb_shinfo` in the attached data buffer because it immediately follows the data portion of the regular packet. `Skb_shared_info` has several purposes, including IP fragmentation, TCP segmentation, and keeping track of cloned socket buffers. When used for IP fragmentation, `skb_shared_info` points to a list of `sk_buffs` containing IP fragments. When used for TCP segmentation, this structure contains an array of attached pages containing the segment data. The handling of TCP segments is more efficient than IP fragments. IP fragmentation is not quite as common as it was in earlier days of the Internet. Fragmentation is used when a network segment has a smaller MTU than the packet size. IP fragmentation is necessary if the MTU of the outgoing device is smaller than the packet size. See Chapter 8 for more details about IP fragmentation. TCP segmentation, however, is far more common because it is the underlying mechanism for the transport of streaming data that occurs in most network traffic

The `skb_shared_info` Structure

In this section, we show the shared info structure, `skb_shared_info`, used to support IP fragmentation and TCP segmentation. The shared info structure, also known as `skb_shinfo`, is defined in the file `include/linux/skbuff.h`.

```
struct skb_shared_info {
```

This field contains the reference count for this `skbuff`. It is incremented each time the buffer is cloned.

```
atomic_t          dataref;
```

`nr_frags` is the number of fragments in this packet. This field is used by TCP segmentation.

```
unsigned int      nr_frags;
```

The next two fields are used for devices that have the capability of doing TCP segment processing in hardware. This is the network device feature, `NET_F_TSO`.

```
unsigned short    tso_size;
unsigned short    tso_segs;
```

These three fields are for supporting fragmentation. `ufo_size` is the amount of data included in a fragment, the length of the fragment minus the fragment header. `ip6_frag_id` is the fragment id field in IP version 6. (See Chapter 11.) `frag_list` points to the list of fragments for this packet if it is fragmented.

```
unsigned short    ufo_size;
unsigned int      ip6_frag_id;
struct sk_buff    *frag_list;
```

This is the array of page table entries. Each entry is actually a TCP segment.

```
skb_frag_t        frags[MAX_SKB_FRAGS];
};
```

TCP Segmentation, Fragmentation and the `skb_shared_info` Structure

As discussed earlier, `skb_shared_info` is used for IP fragmentation. It can also be used to hold TCP segments and when used this way, it contains an array of pointers to memory mapped pages containing TCP segments. TCP provides a streaming service that makes the data look like an uninterrupted sequence of bytes even though the data must be split up to fit into IP packets. See Chapter 7, "Sending the Data from the Socket through UDP and TCP," for more information about TCP segmentation. When a socket buffer is cloned, `skb_shared_info` is copied to the new buffer.

A non-zero value in the first field in the shared info structure, `dataref`, indicates that a socket buffer is cloned because it is incremented each time cloning occurs. (The `cloned` field in the socket buffer is also set to one when a socket buffer is cloned.) The next field in the shared info structure, `frag_list`, is used by the IP fragment reassembly facility. This is how each fragment on the list can share the same IP header. The IP headers for each fragment are almost identical. They differ only in the fragment ID field, the fragment offset, and the checksum. When the input processing in the IP protocol discovers that an incoming skb is actually an IP fragment, it places the packet on a special list containing the fragments. IP moves this list (without copying the actual packet data) into a single datagram consisting of a head socket buffer followed by a list of socket buffers, each of which points to a single fragment. The frag_list field in the shared info area points to the list of socket buffers containing the fragments. Although each IP fragment occupies a separate socket buffer, the skb_shinfo structure itself is copied to each socket buffer when it is created. See Figure 6.5 for an illustration of a socket buffer that points to an array of IP fragments.

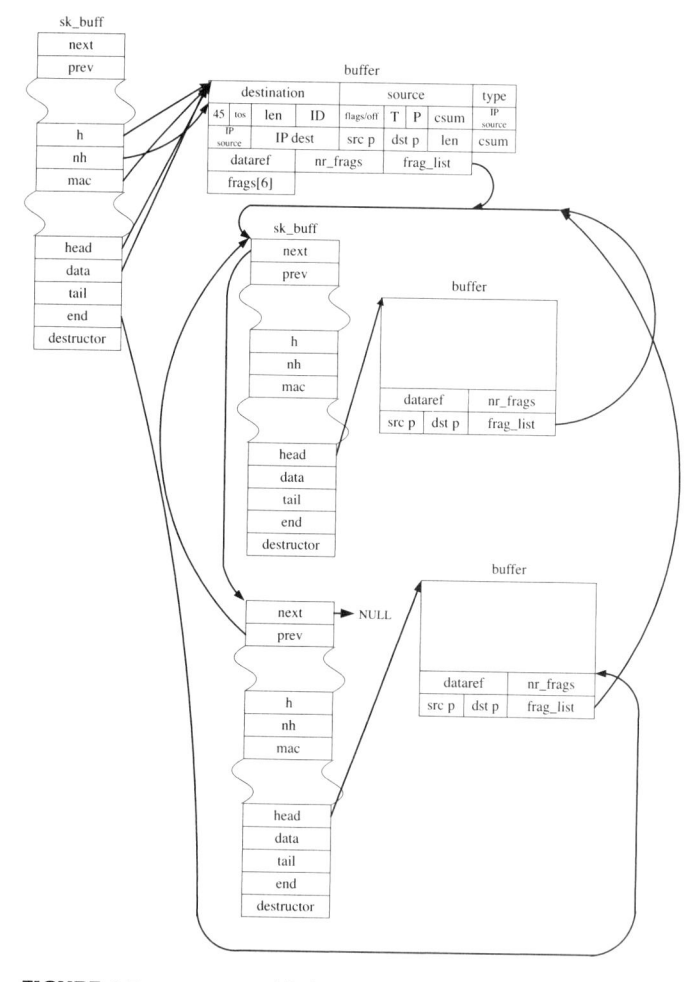

FIGURE 6.5 Sk_buff with fragments.

The `skb_shared_info` Structure and Segmentation

The second field in the shared info structure, `nr_frag`, is not used for IP fragmentation; instead, it is for TCP segmentation. A socket buffer containing segments is indicated when this field contains a non-zero value. The value of `nr_frag` corresponds to the number of segment pages attached to the socket buffer, and the `shared_info` structure contains pointers to the segment pages in the field `frags`. The array of `frags` is placed in memory immediately after the `nr_frag` field. It can contain as many as six pages in the array. The actual number of locations in the array will depend on the hardware architecture and the configured page size, `PAGE_SIZE`. Each of the elements in the `frags` array points to a memory-mapped page in the Linux virtual page table array. Earlier in Chapter 5, we provided more extensive information about Linux slab allocation and virtual page tables. When a socket buffer created by TCP contains a chain of segments, each sequential segment's data is in a separate memory mapped page pointed to by a location in the `frags` array. This is considerably more efficient than maintaining a redundant `sk_buff` structure for each TCP segment. When TCP is in the ESTABLISHED state, the packet headers for subsequent segments are nearly identical so the packet header can be shared among each of the segments. Processing time is saved during processing by not requiring Linux to copy a complete IP header for each segment.

The `skb_frag_t` Structure

Each location in the `frags` array consists of the `skb_frag_t` structure defined in the file `linux/include/linux/skbuff.h`. The size of the `frags` array is calculated to hold a total of 64 Kb of data, which is the maximum packet size defined for IPv4. Of course, the array divides the 64 K hunk of data into individual memory mapped pages.

```
#define MAX_SKB_FRAGS (65536/PAGE_SIZE + 2)
typedef struct skb_frag_struct skb_frag_t;
struct skb_frag_struct {
```

`page` is a pointer to a page table entry. The next field, `offset`, is the offset from the start of the page to where the data begins. `size` is the length of data in page.

```
    struct page    *page;
    __u16          page_offset;
    __u16          size;
};
```

Figure 6.6 is an illustration of a socket buffer containing an array of TCP segments.

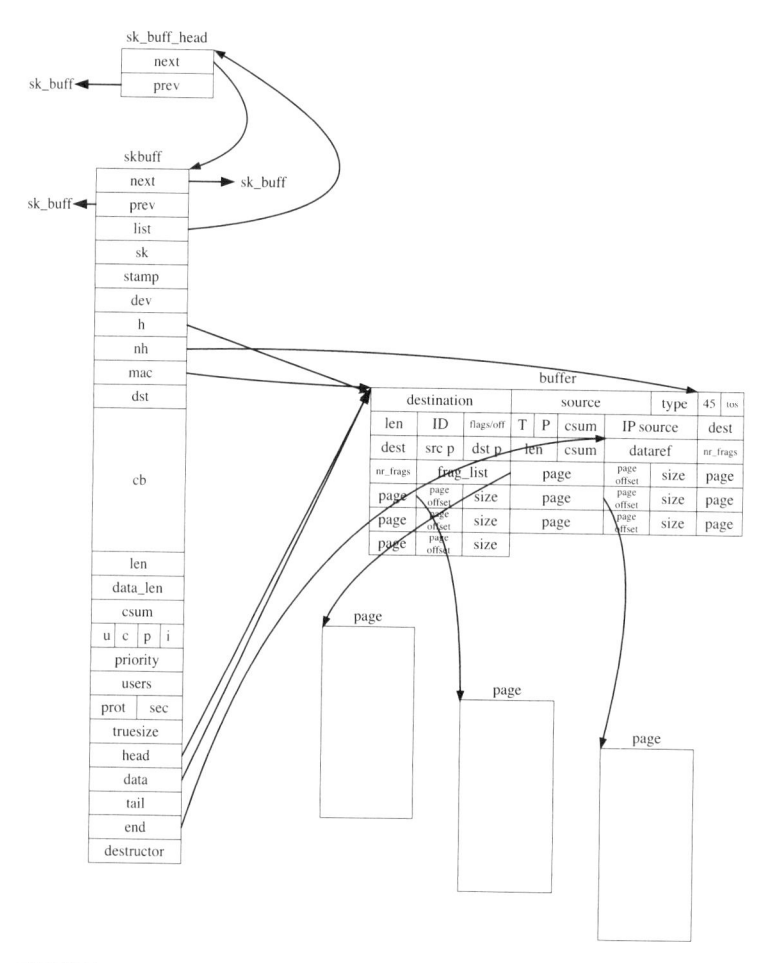

FIGURE 6.6 Sk_buff with segments.

SOCKET BUFFER ALLOCATION AND LISTS

As discussed earlier in this chapter, the Linux slab memory allocation system is suitable for networking protocol stacks because it is efficient and is not prone to fragmentation. The socket buffer header cache also provides a performance enhancement because the socket buffers are not returned to the general kernel memory when they are freed, but instead are placed on a separate header cache. There are multiple header caches, one for each CPU in multiple processor implementations. The buffers are fetched or returned to the header cache for the current CPU. When a sk_buff is created, the allocation function, alloc_skb, allocates socket buffers from the slab cache, `skbuff_head_cache`, both of which are declared in the file `linux/net/core/skbuff.c`. As we saw earlier, if the slab cache does not have any socket buffers, it is grown, by adding pages from the kernel's general memory allocation slab. When a caller frees a socket buffer, the socket buffer is returned to the header cache pool. The `skbuff_head_cache` consists of an array of socket buffer header structures indexed by CPU number. The fields of the socket buffer header structure, `next` and `prev`, correspond to the first two fields of the `sk_buff`.

Socket Buffer Cloning

Cloning is done for efficiency. TCP segments or IP fragments share most header information and we try to avoid copying packet headers that are replicated in packets being sent sequentially. In this section, we will describe the cloning process in more detail to see how cloning results in more efficiency.

When a `sk_buff` is cloned, the `skb_shinfo` is replicated. Cloning allows TCP fragment arrays to share the same socket buffer structure and packet header. Cloned buffers are not the same as shared buffers. Although confusing, it is important to differentiate the two. A shared socket buffer is held by more than one user. Each time the buffer is referenced by another user, the `users` field is incremented to indicate that the buffer is shared. Each time the buffer is de-referenced, the same field is decremented. A cloned `skb` is something entirely different from a buffer with multiple users. This is confusing, because the term *shared* is also sometimes used in the context of buffer cloning. A cloned `sk_buff` points to the same data and packet header information as the `sk_buff` from which it was cloned. It has most of the same fields set as the original buffer. In addition, it has a copy of the control block or `cb` field from the original `sk_buff`. Most important, it has the same attached data buffer, usually consisting of an IP header and the `skb_shinfo`, which immediately follows the data. The original and the clone both contain a list of page table pointers, each of which points to a page with a TCP segment. Figure 6.6 illustrates a cloned buffer with an array of TCP segments.

Socket Buffer Queues

As we saw earlier, socket buffers contain the next and previous pointers as the first two fields. This is done to facilitate the maintenance of queues. The ability to manipulate queues of network buffers is of fundamental importance to any buffer system used in networking. For this reason, Linux provides a group of interface functions for en-queuing, de-queuing, and maintaining lists of socket buffers. For an example of the use of queues of `sk_buffs`, we can look at Chapter 5, which contains more detailed information on the queuing layer.

SOCKET BUFFER UTILITY FUNCTIONS

Linux provides many utility functions to allocate, de-allocate, and manipulate the socket buffers, `sk_buffs`. Some of the socket buffer functions are not interrupt-safe unless used properly, and generally, there are both safe and unsafe versions of these functions. The unsafe functions include the parameter `gfp_mask`, where GFP stands for *get free pages*. `Gfp_mask` must be set to `GFP_ATOMIC` if the functions are called from an interrupt service routine. However, interrupt-safe versions of most of the functions are declared in `linux/include/linux/skbuff.h`. If possible, it is preferable to call the safe versions because the unsafe versions are used only where the caller has already masked interrupts. Most of the functions listed later in this section are the safe versions. The first set of functions controls socket buffer allocation and de-allocation. The next group of functions is for copying and cloning socket buffers. Another group of functions is for the manipulation of the data pointers in the socket buffer to make room for headers in the front of a packet or extend the end of a packet. The final group of socket buffer calls includes functions for manipulating lists and queues of socket buffers. This section explains each of the utility functions in detail.

Functions for Socket Buffer Allocation and De-allocation

This group of functions provide an interface for socket buffer creation and destruction.

The `alloc_skb` Function

The first function, `alloc_skb`, allocates a new socket buffer.

```
extern struct sk_buff *alloc_skb(unsigned int size, gfp_t priority);
```

This function is unsafe. It must be called with `priority` value set to `GFP_ATOMIC` if it is called from an interrupt service routine. It is called with `priority` set to `GFP_KERNEL` when called from elsewhere in the Linux kernel. The first thing `alloc_skb` does after checking `gfp_mask` is try to get the `skb` from the socket buffer header list by calling `skb_head_from_pool`. If there are no more `sk_buffs` available, it allocates a new one by calling `kmem_cache_alloc` to get the buffer from the slab cache. Every `skb` must point to at least one data buffer, so a new data buffer is always allocated from the kernel's general slab cache by calling `kmalloc`. The data buffer must contain at least enough space for the packet header and the `skb_shinfo` structure, so `kmalloc` requests an amount of bytes equal to or greater than the value of the `size` parameter, plus the length of the `skb_shinfo` structure. `alloc_skb` aligns `size` according to the machine's architecture, so if the caller requests an odd size, it will be rounded up.

```
extern struct sk_buff *__alloc_skb(unsigned int size,
                                   gfp_t priority, int fclone);
```

After allocation, `alloc_skb` sets a few fields in the socket buffer structure. Since the socket buffer is allocated from the slab cache, most fields have been pre-initialized. The `truesize` field is set to the length of the attached buffer, plus the length of the socket buffer structure itself. The `head`, `data`, and `tail` pointers are all set to point to the beginning of the actual data buffer, which was allocated with `kmalloc`. End is set to point to the end of the user data part of the buffer, and as discussed earlier, this is where the `skb_shinfo` structure lives. The `len`, `cloned`, and `data_len` fields are all set to zero. These fields are adjusted later to reflect changes in the size of the packet pointed to by this `sk_buff`. The `users` field is set to one to indicate that this is the first reference to the `sk_buff`. Finally, a few fields are initialized in the `skb_shinfo` structure. Because there is neither a fragment list yet or an array of `frag` pages defined for this packet, `dataref` is set to one, and `frag_list` is set to NULL.

The `dev_alloc_skb` Function

`dev_alloc_skb` also allocates a new socket buffer, `sk_buff`.

```
static inline struct sk_buff *dev_alloc_skb(unsigned int length)
...
```

`dev_alloc_skb` is provided for convenience of device driver developers. It is used by Ethernet network interface drivers and other network interface drivers. This function is safe, and internally it calls `alloc_skb` with the `gfp_mask` set to `GFP_ATOMIC`. In addition, it adds 16 bytes to the length field to reserve room for the Ethernet MAC header before calling `alloc_skb` to actually allocate the `sk_buff` and the attached data buffer.

The `kfree_skb` Function

```
static inline void kfree_skb(struct sk_buff *skb)
...
```

Before freeing the buffer, it checks the use count in the `users` field, and if the use count is one, it goes ahead and frees the buffer. Before freeing, it checks to make sure that the `skb` was removed from all lists by checking the `list` field, and if `list` is NULL, it means that the `sk_buff` is not a member of anybody's list. Next, it releases the destination cache entry. This will return the destination cache entry back to the destination cache slab. For details about the destination cache and the neighbor cache system, see Chapter 6. It calls the destructor function if the `destructor` field is not equal to NULL. Next, it cleans up the socket buffer state by setting most of the fields to zero. This prepares the buffer for returning to the slab cache so it can be used later without much initialization. The attached buffer must be freed as well, and after freeing the attached buffer, it calls `skb_head_to_pool` to return the cleaned-up `sk_buff` to the header cache.

Functions to Copy and Clone Socket Buffers

All of the functions in this group copy or clone socket buffers in various ways.

The `skb_cow` Function

`skb_cow` copies the socket buffer and expands its headroom.

    int skb_cow(struct sk_buff *skb, unsigned int headroom);

`skb_cow` copies the header of the `skb` if required. It expands the headroom at the start of the buffer, which is the space between the start of the buffer and the point in the buffer referenced to by the `data` field in `skb`. If the socket buffer does not have enough headroom or its data part is shared, the data is re-allocated and both the `skb` header data and shared info are copied to the new buffer. The `frags` and `frag_list` are copied to the `skb_shinfo` structure in the new `skb`. In the new socket buffer, pointers are adjusted to point to the correct corresponding places in the attached data buffer. `Skb_cow` does not expand the headroom by less than 16 bytes, so headroom is rounded up to the next largest multiple of 16.

The `skb_clone` Function

`skb_clone` duplicates a socket buffer.

    struct sk_buff *skb_clone(struct sk_buff *skb, int priority);

It allocates a new socket buffer structure and returns a pointer to the new `sk_buff`. This call is not safe unless it is called with the `gfp_mask` set to GFP_ATOMIC or GFP_KERNEL. The `prev`, `next`, and `list` fields in the new `sk_buff` are set to NULL because the new socket buffer is not a member of any list. The `destructor` and `sk` fields are set to NULL because the new buffer is not associated with a socket. The `users` field in the new buffer is set to one. It copies the other fields from the old socket buffer to the new one. After cloning, the new `sk_buff` points to the same attached data buffer as the old one. The `dataref` field in the `skb_shinfo` area of the attached buffer is incremented to indicate that there is an additional reference to the attached data buffer.

The `skb_cloned` Function

`skb_cloned` checks to see whether a socket buffer is a clone.

    static inline int skb_cloned(const struct sk_buff *skb);

It returns TRUE if the `dataref` field in the `skb_shinfo` structure in the attached buffer is greater than one and if the `cloned` field is set in `skb`.

The Function, `skb_copy`

`skb_copy` copies a socket buffer.

    struct sk_buff *skb_copy(const struct sk_buff *skb, int priority);

This function copies the socket buffer structure, `skb`, along with the attached data buffer. It returns a pointer to the new socket buffer structure. The new `sk_buff` will be given an attached buffer with enough space to hold all the data in `skb`. A new shared info structure is initialized in the buffer attached to the new `sk_buff`. In addition, the data from any attached fragment list or fragment pages is copied directly into the new buffer. The new buffer is an entirely new copy, so the caller may modify any data pointed to by the new buffer. Header space is reserved in the new buffer by adjusting the data pointer.

The `pskb_copy` Function

`pskb_copy` copies a socket buffer with a private header portion.

A socket buffer and the header part of the attached data buffer are copied into a new `sk_buff`. A pointer to the new `sk_buff` is returned. This function does not copy the fragmented portion of the original socket buffer. It copies `skb_shinfo` only so the fragment list and segment array are shared with the old socket buffer. Header space is reserved in the new buffer by adjusting the data pointer.

The Function `skb_shared`

The function `skb_shared` checks to see whether a socket buffer is shared.

    int skb_shared(const struct sk_buff *skb);

It checks the reference count of the socket buffer by looking at the `users` field in `skb`. It returns TRUE if `users` is not equal to one.

The `skb_share_check` Function

`skb_share_check` checks whether a socket buffer is shared and clones the buffer if it is.

```
struct sk_buff *skb_share_check(struct sk_buff *skb, int pri);
```

First, this function checks to see whether a socket buffer is shared. If it is shared, `skb_share_check` clones the socket buffer by calling `skb_clone`. It drops the reference count to the old socket buffer by one, effectively deleting it by calling `kfree_skb`.

The Function `skb_get`

`skb_get` obtains a new reference to a socket buffer.

```
struct sk_buff *skb_get(struct sk_buff *skb);
```

`skb_get` increments the reference count by adding one to the `users` field of `skb`. This indicates that the socket buffer is shared. It returns a pointer to `skb`.

Functions to Manipulate Socket Buffer Pointer Fields

In this group, we include functions provided by Linux to pre-pend headers in the front of packets or remove headers from a packet. In addition, we have functions for manipulating the amount of space at the end of the packet. All the functions in this group operate without copying the data. Most of the functions included in this section manipulate the `head`, `tail`, `len` and `data` fields in the socket buffer.

The Function `skb_headroom`

The first of the functions in this group, `skb_headroom`, reserves space at the front of the attached buffer.

```
int skb_headroom(const struct sk_buff *skb);
```

It returns the amount of available space between the start of the attached buffer and the start of the data.

The `skb_put` Function

This function extends the user data area of the socket buffer by `len`.

```
unsigned char *skb_put(struct sk_buff *skb, unsigned int len);
```

It extends the user data area of the attached buffer by adjusting the `tail` and `len` fields in `skb`. The entire new length must not exceed the total buffer size.

The Function `skb_tailroom`

`skb_tailroom` gets the amount of space at the end of the buffer.

```
int skb_tailroom(const struct sk_buff *skb);
```

It gets the amount of space at the end of the attached buffer pointed to by skb. It subtracts the value of tail from the value of end in the socket buffer, skb. If skb is not linear, skb_tailroom returns zero. A nonlinear sk_buff is one with attached fragments. A sk_buff with attached fragments has no user data in the attached buffer.

The skb_reserve Function

skb_reserve adjusts the headroom of a socket buffer, skb, by length len.

```
void skb_reserve(struct sk_buff *skb, unsigned int len);
```

It adjusts the headroom of the data buffer attached to skb. It increases the data and tail fields in skb by the desired length.

The skb_push Function

skb_push adds data space to the front of socket buffer, skb.

```
unsigned char *skb_push(struct sk_buff *skb, unsigned int len);
```

skb_push adds data space to the front of a socket buffer by changing the data field in skb to point to the new start of the useable data. It increases len in skb by the new amount of space. It returns a pointer to the new start of the useable data.

The skb_pull Function

skb_pull removes the amount of data space specified by len from the front of a socket buffer.

```
unsigned char *skb_pull(struct sk_buff *skb, unsigned int len);
```

It removes the data space from the front of the data buffer and advances the data field in skb to point to the new start of the useable data. It subtracts the number of bytes of removed space from the len field. It returns a pointer to the new start of the useable data.

The skb_trim Function

The last function in this group, skb_trim, removes space from the end of socket buffer, skb.

```
void skb_trim(struct sk_buff *skb, unsigned int len);
```

`skb_trim` reduces the length of the buffer attached to the socket buffer by setting the `len` field in `skb` to the `length` argument and adjusting the `tail` field to point to the beginning of the data, plus `length`.

Functions to Manage Lists of Socket Buffers

The functions in this group are provided by Linux for the use of writers of protocol and network interface drivers to manage socket buffer lists. Queues of socket buffers are a key part of all the layers and member protocols in Linux TCP/IP. In each of the following functions, the structure `sk_buff_list` is used to hold the head of a list of `sk_buffs`. Every function in this group is safe to call from anywhere in the code because all the functions acquire `irq_spinlock` before manipulating the list of socket buffers.

The `skb_queue_head` Function

The first function in this group, `skb_queue_head`, places the socket buffer, `newsk`, at the beginning of a list pointed to by `list`.

```
void skb_queue_head(struct sk_buff_head *list, struct sk_buff *newsk);
```

The `skb_queue_tail` Function

The next function, `skb_queue_tail`, puts the socket buffer, `newsk`, at the end of a list.

```
void skb_queue_tail(struct sk_buff_head *list, struct sk_buff *newsk);
```

The `skb_dequeue` Function

`skb_dequeue` removes the `sk_buff` from the beginning of the list, pointed to by `list`. It returns a pointer to the removed socket buffer.

```
struct sk_buff *skb_dequeue(struct sk_buff_head *list);
```

The `skb_dequeue_tail` Function

The function `skb_dequeue_tail` removes a socket buffer from the end of a list and returns a pointer to the removed item.

```
struct sk_buff *skb_dequeue_tail(struct sk_buff_head *list);
```

The `skb_append` Function

`skb_append` inserts the socket buffer, `newsk`, anywhere on a list of socket buffers. It puts the new socket buffer after the one pointed to by `old`.

```
void skb_append(struct sk_buff *old, struct sk_buff *newsk);
```

The `skb_insert` Function

As with the previous function, `skb_insert`, also inserts a socket buffer on a list of `sk_buffs`. However, it puts the new `sk_buff` on the list ahead of the socket buffer pointed to by `old`.

```
void skb_insert(struct sk_buff *old, struct sk_buff *newsk);
```

The `skb_queue_empty` Function

This function, `skb_queue_empty`, checks to see whether a list of socket buffers is empty. It does this by checking whether the `next` field in `skb` points back to itself. If the list is empty, it returns TRUE; otherwise, it returns FALSE.

```
int skb_queue_empty(const struct sk_buff_head *list);
```

The `skb_queue_len` Function

This function, `skb_queue_len` returns the length of a list of socket buffers by checking the `qlen` field in the `sk_buff` head structure.

```
__u32 skb_queue_len(const struct sk_buff_head *list_);
```

The `skb_queue_purge` Function

The next function in this group, `skb_queue_purge` removes all socket buffers on a list. Each socket buffer on the list is dropped by calling `kfree_skb`.

```
void skb_queue_purge(struct sk_buff_head *list);
```

The `skb_peek_tail` Function

This function, `skb_peek_tail` returns a pointer to the last `skb` on the list.

```
struct sk_buff *skb_peek_tail(struct sk_buff_head *list_);
```

The `skb_queue_head_init` Function.

Finally, the last function in this group, `skb_queue_head_init`, initializes a queue. It sets up the queue header as well as the `next` and `prev` pointers in the `sk_buff_head` structure pointed to by `list`.

```
static inline void skb_queue_head_init(struct sk_buff_head *list);
```

SOME PRACTICAL CONSIDERATIONS

Slab cache allocation statistics are kept in the /proc file system. They can be examined by executing the command cat/proc/slabinfo. Refer to the man page, slabinfo(5) for more information.

SUMMARY

In this chapter, we covered Linux network memory allocation and the Linux socket buffer structure. Socket buffers are the most fundamental part of Linux network memory allocation, and they should be examined for a complete understanding of the Linux TCP/IP protocol suite. We began by discussing various memory allocation schemes used for allocating packet buffers in network protocol stacks. We contrasted the Linux slab allocation method with other allocation schemes and compared the advantage with slab allocation for efficiency and avoiding memory fragmentation. In addition, we discussed Linux socket buffers, sk_buffs, the primary structure used in Linux to hold network packets. We discussed socket buffer cloning and copying and listed functions for manipulating socket buffer headers and tail space without copying the data. In addition, we covered types of socket buffers and how they can be formed into lists and queues.

7
Sending the Data from the Socket through UDP and TCP

In This Chapter

- A Few Words
- Introduction
- Socket Layer Glue
- Transport Layer Socket Initialization
- Initiating a Connection at the Transport Layer
- Sending Data from a Socket Via UDP
- Sending Data from a Socket Via TCP
- TCP Output
- Some Key TCP Data Structures
- TCP Timers

A FEW WORDS

We began this journey looking at the fundamentals of networking and the basics of the TCP/IP protocol suite. Most of this book focuses on the internal structure of Linux. The middle chapters covered network interface drivers, Linux sockets, Linux infrastructure, and Linux socket buffers. This chapter continues the discussion of the internals of Linux TCP/IP including the implementation of the transport layer protocols, UDP and TCP. Often, the best way to understand a complex system of protocols is to follow the data as it flows through the system. Remember that TCP/IP is a layered protocol implemented as a stack. For transmission, data is prepared when the application writes it into the socket at the top of the stack. It flows down through the transport protocol onto the network layer protocol and out the physical interface. In this chapter, we explain what happens inside the transport protocols by watching the data as it flows from the socket to the IP layer. To explain how this happens, we will follow a packet as it is sent from a socket through either UDP or TCP and arrives ready for processing at the IP protocol level.

INTRODUCTION

In this chapter, we look at what happens in the transport layer as data is transmitted. When a user writes data into an open socket, socket buffers are allocated by the transport layer, and these buffers in effect travel through the transport layer to IP where they are routed and passed to the device drivers for sending. Specifying SOCK_DGRAM in the type field of the socket call invokes the UDP protocol, and specifying SOCK_STREAM invokes the TCP protocol. For SOCK_DGRAM type sockets, the process is relatively simple, but it is far more complicated for SOCK_STREAM type sockets. We will examine both UDP and TCP and look at the functions that interface the protocol to the socket layer. Next, we will focus on the sendmsg function for each of the protocols which is the fundamental function for sending. From this function, we will follow the data as it flows through the transport layer.

SOCKET LAYER GLUE

Before we start looking at the internals of each of the transport layer protocols, we should look at how service functions in the transport layer protocols are associated with the socket layer functions. Through this mechanism, the application program is able to direct the actions of the transport layer for each of the socket types, SOCK_STREAM and SOCK_DGRAM. As explained in Chapter 4, "Linux Sockets," each of the two transport protocols is registered with the socket layer.

The proto Structure

The key to this registration process is the data structure, proto, which is defined in linux/include/net/sock.h. We won't discuss the actual registration mechanism in this chapter, but we will focus on how the two transport protocols utilize each of the fields in this data structure. Most of these fields are function pointers. Each of these point to specific functions for each transport protocol. A transport protocol does not have to implement every function. For example, UDP does not have a shutdown function that cleans up after a connection is terminated and, therefore, is not relevant to UDP. However, both UDP and TCP implement most of the functions in the proto structure.

```
struct proto {
```

Chapter 7 Sending the Data from the Socket through UDP and TCP

The first seven functions in this structure, close through shutdown, are described in later sections in this chapter for both UDP and TCP.

```
void            (*close)(struct sock *sk,
                         long timeout);
int             (*connect)(struct sock *sk,
                         struct sockaddr *uaddr, int addr_len);
int             (*disconnect)(struct sock *sk, int flags);
struct sock *   (*accept) (struct sock *sk, int flags, int *err);
int             (*ioctl)(struct sock *sk, int cmd,
                         unsigned long arg);
int             (*init)(struct sock *sk);
int             (*destroy)(struct sock *sk);
void            (*shutdown)(struct sock *sk, int how);
```

The getsockopt and setsockopt functions are used to set options for both UDP and TCP (as well as other protocols in the AF_INET family). The options for UDP and TCP are covered in detail later in this chapter.

```
int             (*setsockopt)(struct sock *sk, int level,
                         int optname, char *optval,
                         int optlen);
int             (*getsockopt)(struct sock *sk, int level,
                         int optname, char *optval,
                         int *option);
```

The sendmsg function is key to this chapter, and it does different things based on the transport protocol. Later we include detailed discussion of what happens when it is invoked for UDP or TCP.

```
int             (*sendmsg)(struct sock *sk,
                         struct msghdr *msg, int len);
```

This chapter focuses on the send side at least to the extent that the send and receive capabilities can be differentiated. The function recvmsg is associated with packet reception at the socket layer, and it is covered in detail in Chapter 9, "Receiving the Data in the Transport Layer, UDP and TCP."

```
int             (*recvmsg)(struct sock *sk,
                         struct msghdr *msg, int len,
                         int noblock, int flags,
                         int *addr_len);
```

The `bind` function is not implemented by either TCP or UDP within the transport protocols themselves. Instead, it is implemented at the socket layer which is covered in Chapter 4, "Linux Sockets."

```
int             (*bind)(struct sock *sk,struct sockaddr
                        *uaddr, int addr_len);
```

`backlog_rcv` is invoked when a socket layer queue is full. It is implemented by TCP but not UDP. Refer to Chapter 9, "Receiving Data in the Transport Layer, UDP and TCP," to see what happens when it is executed.

```
int             (*backlog_rcv) (struct sock *sk,
                                struct sk_buff *skb);
```

The `hash` and `unhash` functions are for manipulating hash tables. These tables are for associating the endpoint addresses (port numbers) with open sockets. The tables map transport protocol port numbers to instances of `struct sock`. `hash` places a reference to the `sock` structure, sk, in the hash table.

```
void            (*hash)(struct sock *sk);
Unhash removes the reference to sk from the hash table.
void            (*unhash)(struct sock *sk);
```

The next field, `get_port`, points to a function that retrieves the port number associated with the `sock` structure, sk. Generally, the port is obtained from one of the protocol's port hash tables.

```
int             (*get_port)(struct sock *sk,
                            unsigned short snum);
```

The next fields are used for conditions where kernel memory is nearly all allocated known as memory pressure. The first of these fields points to the function called when the kernel is under memory pressure. The next two fields show the amount of memory allocated and the current number of sockets in the system.

```
void            (*enter_memory_pressure)(void);
atomic_t        *memory_allocated;
atomic_t        *sockets_allocated;
```

When the next field is set, it indicates that memory pressure conditions are present and that the system should try to collapse the amount of memory in use.

Chapter 7 Sending the Data from the Socket through UDP and TCP

```
    int             *memory_pressure;
    int             *sysctl_mem;
    int             *sysctl_wmem;
    int             *sysctl_rmem;
    int             max_header;
    kmem_cache_t    *slab;
```

This field is the size of an instance of the sock structure for this protocol.

```
    unsigned int        obj_size;
    atomic_t            *orphan_count;
    struct request_sock_ops     *rsk_prot;
    struct timewait_sock_ops    *twsk_prot;
    struct module       *owner;
```

This field contains the name of the protocol. For our purposes in this chapter, the field will be set to either UDP or TCP.

```
    char                name[32];
    struct list_head            node;
#ifdef SOCK_REFCNT_DEBUG
    atomic_t        socks;
#endif
    struct {
        int inuse;
        u8  __pad[SMP_CACHE_BYTES - sizeof(int)];
    } stats[NR_CPUS];
};
```

Neither UDP nor TCP implement all of the functions in the proto structure. As we saw in Chapter 4, the AF_INET family provides pointers to default functions that get called from the socket layer in the case where the specific transport protocol doesn't implement a particular function. Each of the transport protocols registers a set of functions by initializing a data structure of type struct proto, defined in the file linux/include/net/sock.h.

The msghdr Structure

All the socket layer read and write functions are translated into calls to either rcvmsg or sendmsg, a BSD type message communication method. Internally in the socket layer, all the IO calls in the socket layer are translated into the internal functions that use the msghdr structure, defined in the file linux/include/linux/socket.h, to pass data to and from the underlying protocols. Of course, sendmsg can also be called directly from the application layer, in which case the user-level programmer fills in the fields of the structure.

```
struct msghdr {
```

The msg_name field is also known as the socket name or the fully qualified destination address for this message including the port number. Generally, this field is cast into a pointer to a sockaddr_in instance. The msg_namelen field is the address length of the msg_name.

```
    void *         msg_name;
    int            msg_namelen;
```

The next field, msg_iovec, points to an array of data blocks passed either to the kernel from the application or from the kernel to the application. msg_iovlen holds the number of data blocks pointed to by msg_iov. The msg_control field is for the BSD style file descriptor passing. msg_controllen is the number of messages in the control message structure.

```
    struct iovec *   msg_iov;
    __kernel_size_t  msg_iovlen;
    void *           msg_control;
    __kernel_size_t  msg_controllen;
    unsigned         msg_flags;
};
```

UDP Socket Glue

As we saw in Chapter 4, the transport protocols register with the socket layer by adding a pointer to a proto structure, shown in the previous section. UDP creates an instance of this structure at compile time in the the file linux/net/ipv4/udp.c and initializes it with values from Table 7.1.

The UDP protocol is invoked when the application layer specifies SOCK_DGRAM in the type field of the socket call. SOCK_DGRAM type sockets are fairly simple. Because UDP is connectionless and doesn't support streams of data, there is no connection management or buffering. A call to one of the send functions in the application layer causes the data to be sent out immediately as a single datagram. Table 7.1 shows the UDP protocol functions mapped to each of the fields in the proto structure described earlier in this chapter.

TABLE 7.1 Protocol Block Functions for UDP, Struct proto

Protocol Block Structure Field Name	UDP Function
close	udp_close
connect	udp_connect
disconnect	udp_disconnect
ioctl	udp_ioctl
setsockopt	udp_setsockopt
getsockopt	udp_getsockopt
sendmsg	udp_sendmsg
recvmsg	udp_recvmsg
backlog_rcv	udp_queue_rcv_skb
hash	udp_v4_hash
unhash	udp_v4_unhash
get_port	udp_v4_get_port
obj_size	sizeof(struct udp_sock)

TCP Socket Glue

Like UDP, TCP registers a set of functions with the socket layer. As in UDP, this is done at compile time by initializing tcp_prot with the functions shown in Table 7.2. These functions are defined in the file linux/net/ipv4/tcp_ipv4.c. Tcp_prot is an instance of the proto structure and is initialized with the function pointers shown in Table 7.2.

Socket Options for TCP

In general, TCP is very configurable to the point where it can be confusing. Of course, most users will just use the default options, and it will run fine particularly in embedded systems that don't have the complex load balancing requirements of high volume servers. During the discussion of the internals of the TCP protocol later in this chapter and in Chapter 9, we refer to various options and how they affect the performance or operation of the protocol. In Chapter 7, we showed the TCP options structure that holds the values of many of the socket options. However, in this section, the TCP socket options and ioctl configuration options are gathered together in one place. Although, most of these are covered in some fash-

TABLE 7.2 Protocol Block Functions for TCP, `Struct proto`

Protocol Block Structure Field Name	TCP Function
close	tcp_close
connect	tcp_v4_connect
disconnect	tcp_disconnect
accept	tcp_accept
ioctl	tcp_ioctl
init	tcp_v4_init_sock
destroy	tcp_v4_destroy_sock
shutdown	tcp_shutdown
setsockopt	tcp_setsockop
getsockopt	tcp_getsockop
sendmsg	tcp_sendmsg
recvmsg	tcp_recvmsg
backlog_rcv	tcp_v4_do_rcv
hash	tcp_v4_hash
unhash	tcp_unhash
get_port	tcp_v4_get_port
enter_memory_pressure	tcp_enter_memory_pressure
sockets_allocated	&tcp_sockets_allocated
orphan_count	&tcp_orphan_count
memory_allocated	&tcp_memory_allocated
memory_pressure	&tcp_memory_pressure
sysctl_mem	sysctl_tcp_mem
sysctl_wmem	sysctl_tcp_wmem
sysctl_rmem	sysctl_tcp_rmem
max_header	MAX_TCP_HEADER
obj_size	sizeof(struct tcp_sock)
twsk_prot	&tcp_timewait_sock_ops
rsk_prot	&tcp_request_sock_ops

ion in the `tcp(7)` manpage, this section lists applicable internal constants and internal variables as well as any references to other sections in the text.

Options Typically Set via `setsockopt`

The following options are set via the `setsockopt` system call or read back with the `getsockopt` system call.

The `TCP_CORK` Option

If this option is set, TCP doesn't send out frames until there is enough data to fill the maximum segment size. It allows the application to stop transmission if the route MTU is less than the Minimum Segment Size (MSS). This option is unique to Linux, and application code using it will not be portable to other operating systems (OSs). This option is held in the `nonagle` field in the TCP options structure because the corking is known as the Nagle algorithm. The field is typically set to the number two. `TCP_CORK` is mutually exclusive with the `TCP_NODELAY` option

The `TCP_DEFER_ACCEPT` Option

The application caller may sleep until data arrives at the socket, at which time it is awakened. The socket is also awakened when it times out. The caller specifies the number of seconds to wait for data to arrive. This option is unique to Linux, and application code using it will not be portable to other OSs. The option value is converted to the number of ticks and is kept in the `defer_accept` field of the TCP option structure.

The `TCP_INFO` Option

The caller using this option can retrieve lots of configuration information about the socket. This is a Linux-unique option, and code using it will not necessarily be portable to other OSs. The information is returned in the `tcp_info` structure, defined in the file `linux/include/linux/tcp.h`.

The `tcp_info` Structure

```
struct tcp_info
{
```

The first field, `tcpi,_state`, contains the current TCP state for the connection. The other fields in this structure contain statistics about the TCP connection.

```
    __u8    tcpi_state;
    __u8    tcpi_ca_state;
    __u8    tcpi_retransmits;
    __u8    tcpi_probes;
    __u8    tcpi_backoff;
    __u8    tcpi_options;
    __u8    tcpi_snd_wscale : 4, tcpi_rcv_wscale : 4;
    __u32   tcpi_rto;
    __u32   tcpi_ato;
    __u32   tcpi_snd_mss;
    __u32   tcpi_rcv_mss;
    __u32   tcpi_unacked;
    __u32   tcpi_sacked;
    __u32   tcpi_lost;
```

```
        __u32   tcpi_retrans;
        __u32   tcpi_fackets;
```

The following fields are event time stamps; however, we don't actually remember when an **ACK** was sent in all circumstances.

```
        __u32   tcpi_last_data_sent;
        __u32   tcpi_last_ack_sent;
        __u32   tcpi_last_data_recv;
        __u32   tcpi_last_ack_recv;
```

The last fields are TCP metrics, such as negotiated MTU, send threshold, round-trip time, and congestion window.

```
        __u32   tcpi_pmtu;
        __u32   tcpi_rcv_ssthresh;
        __u32   tcpi_rtt;
        __u32   tcpi_rttvar;
        __u32   tcpi_snd_ssthresh;
        __u32   tcpi_snd_cwnd;
        __u32   tcpi_advmss;
        __u32   tcpi_reordering;
};
```

The TCP_KEEPCNT Option

By using this option, the caller can set the number of keepalive probes that TCP will send for this socket before dropping the connection. This option is unique to Linux and should not be used in portable code. The field keepalive_probes in the tcp_opt structure is set to the value of this option. For this option to be effective, the socket level option SO_KEEPALIVE must also be set.

The TCP_KEEPIDLE Option

With this option, the caller may specify the number of seconds that the connection will stay idle before TCP starts to send keepalive probe packets. This option is only effective if the socket option SO_KEEPALIVE is also set for this socket. This is also a nonportable Linux option. The value of this option is stored in the keepalive_time field in the TCP options structure. The value is normally set to a default of two hours.

The TCP_KEEPINTVL Option

This option, also a nonportable Linux option, is used to specify the number of seconds between transmissions of keepalive probes. The value of this option is stored in the `keepalive_intvl` field in the TCP options structure and is initialized to a value of 75 seconds.

The `TCP_LINGER2` Option

This option may be set to specify how long an orphaned socket in the `FIN_WAIT2` state should be kept alive. The option is unique to Linux and, therefore, is not portable. If the value is set to zero, the option is turned off and Linux uses normal processing for the `FIN_WAIT_2` and `TIME_WAIT` states. One aspect of this option is not documented anywhere: if the value is less than zero, the socket proceeds immediately to the `CLOSED` state from the `FIN_WAIT_2` state without passing through the `TIME_WAIT` state. The value associated with this option is kept in the `linger2` of the `tcp_opt` structure. The default value is determined by the `sysctl`, called `tcp_fin_timeout`.

The `TCP_MAXSEG` Option

This option specifies the maximum segment size set for a TCP socket before the connection is established. The advertised MSS value sent to the peer is determined by this option but won't exceed the interface's MTU. The two TCP peers for this connection may renegotiate the segment size. In a later section we discuss more details about how MSS is used by `tcp_sendmsg`.

The `TCP_NODELAY` Option

When set, this option disables the Nagle algorithm. The value is stored in the `nonagle` field of the `tcp_opt` structure. This option may not be used if the option `TCP_CORK` is set. When `TCP_NODELAY` is set, TCP will send out data as soon as possible without waiting for enough data to fill a segment.

The `TCP_QUICKACK` Option

This option may be used to turn off delayed acknowledgment by setting the value to one, or enable delayed acknowledgment by setting to a zero. Delayed acknowledgment is the normal mode of operation for Linux TCP. With delayed acknowledgment, **ACK**s are delayed until they can be combined with a segment waiting to be sent in the reverse direction. If the value of this option is one, the `pingpong` field in the **ACK** part of `tcp_opt` is set to zero, which disables delayed acknowledgment. The `TCP_QUICKACK` option only temporarily affects the behavior of the TCP protocol. If delayed acknowledgment mode is disabled, it could eventually be automatically re-enabled, depending on the acknowledgment timeout processing and other factors.

The `TCP_SYNCNT` Option

The caller may use this option to specify the number of **SYN** retransmits that should be sent before aborting an attempt to establish a connection. This option is unique to Linux and should not be used for portable code. The value is stored in the `syn_retries` field of the `tcp_opt` structure.

The `TCP_WINDOW_CLAMP` Option

By setting this option, the caller may specify the maximum advertised window size for this socket. The minimum allowed for the advertised window is the value `SOCK_MIN_RCVBUF` divided by two, which is 128 bytes. The value of this option is held in the `window_clamp` field of `tcp_opt` for this socket.

TRANSPORT LAYER SOCKET INITIALIZATION

In this section, we cover how the transport protocols are initialized when a socket is created. The `proto` structure contains the mapping from the socket layer generic functions to the protocol specific functions. Earlier in this chapter, we discussed the proto structure and how it is set for both transport protocols, and in Chapter 4, we discussed how an AF_INET socket of type SOCK_STREAM is created and how the function pointed to by the `init` field is executed by the `inet_create` function. When a socket of type SOCK_DGRAM is created, the `proto` structure is filled in with specific values for UDP.

UDP is relatively simple and provides only a datagram. Since virtually no state information exists with a connectionless service, UDP does not require any protocol-specific socket initialization, and the `proto` structure for UDP does not map any function to the `init` field because no UDP specific socket initialization is done at socket creation time. In contrast, for TCP, a SOCK_STREAM socket, the `init` field of this structure is set to point to a function `tcp_v4_init_sock`, which must do quite a bit of socket layer initialization. In the next section, we will see what happens when this function initializes a TCP socket.

TCP Socket Initialization

In this section, we discuss initialization of a socket for the SOCK_STREAM or TCP protocol. We do the initiialization after the sock structure is created and by then most of the fields have already been set generally to zero by the sock slab allocator before we have a pointer to a new sock structure. For details on the sock structure see Chapter 4.

The tcp_v4_init_sock Function

We do do in TCP socket initialization in the function `tcp_v4_init_sock`, defined in the file *linux/net/ipv4/tcp_ipv4c*.

```
static int tcp_v4_init_sock(struct sock *sk)
{
```

With the last several revisions of the 2.6 kernel, Linux has been generalizing to use common elements between IPv4 and IPv6. The inet_connection_sock shown later is a structure overlaid on the generic sock structure discussed in Chapter 4. It emphasizes the aspects of the structure which are specific to the AF_INET address family. These fields are handled separately because of differences between IPv4 and IPv6. Similarly, the tcp_sock structure overlays the generic sock structure with aspects specific to connection oriented protocols such as TCP.

```
struct inet_connection_sock *icsk = inet_csk(sk);
struct tcp_sock *tp = tcp_sk(sk);
```

The out_of_order_queue is initialized. Unlike the other queues, this queue is unique to TCP and therefore has not been initialized by the socket layer. The transmit timers are initialized by calling tcp_init_xmit_timers. Refer to the section on TCP timers in this chapter for more information.

```
skb_queue_head_init(&tp->out_of_order_queue);
tcp_init_xmit_timers(sk);
tcp_prequeue_init(tp);
```

The retransmit time, rto, and the medium deviation, mdev, which is for Round Trip Time (RTT) measurement, are set to a value of three seconds.

```
icsk->icsk_rto = TCP_TIMEOUT_INIT;
tp->mdev = TCP_TIMEOUT_INIT;
```

The send congestion window, cwnd, is initialized to two and it seems strange that it is not zero, but the source code includes the following comment: "So many TCP implementations out there (incorrectly) count the initial **SYN** frame in their delayed-ACK and congestion control algorithms that we must have the following Band-Aid to talk efficiently to them. - DaveM" Apparently, this allows for proper operation of slow start and congestion control.

```
tp->snd_cwnd = 2;
```

The send slow start threshold, snd_ssthresh, is set to the maximum 32-bit number, effectively disabling the slow start algorithm. The send congestion window clamp, snd_cwnd_clamp, is set to the maximum 16-bit value. The field mss_cache is the minimum segment size for TCP and is initialized to 536 as required [RFC 794].

```
tp->snd_ssthresh = 0x7fffffff;
tp->snd_cwnd_clamp = ~0;
tp->mss_cache = 536;
```

The reordering field of the TCP options structure is initialized to its configured system control value. The function pointers in icsk for congestion control are set to values specific to IPv4. The socket state, kept in the state field in the sock structure, is initialized to the closed state.

```
tp->reordering = sysctl_tcp_reordering;
icsk->icsk_ca_ops = &tcp_init_congestion_ops;
sk->state = TCP_CLOSE;
```

The sk_write_space field of the sock structure, sk, is a pointer to a callback function called when buffers are available in the socket's write queue. It is initialized to point to tcp_write_space. The use_write_queue field of the sock structure is set to one to indicate that this protocol (which is TCP, of course) uses the socket's write queue.

```
sk->sk_write_space = tcp_write_space;
sock_set_flag(sk, SOCK_USE_WRITE_QUEUE);
```

The icsk_af_ops field of the protocol family specific structure is set to a set of functions used by the TCP protocol in IPv4. This is discussed in detail in the next section. tcp_sync_mss is an output function used for advertising the maximum segment size (MSS) on the beginning of TCP connection negotiation.

```
icsk->icsk_af_ops = &ipv4_specific;
icsk->icsk_sync_mss = tcp_sync_mss;
```

The sndbuf and rcvbuf fields of the sock structure hold the socket options SO_SNDBUF and SO_RCVBUF, which determine the size of the socket's send and receive buffers, respectively. They are initialized to the system control values here as the socket is being initialized, but setsockopt may change them later. The field, tcp_sockets_allocated is a global defined in tcp.c that holds the number of open TCP sockets.

```
sk->sndbuf = sysctl_tcp_wmem[1];
sk->rcvbuf = sysctl_tcp_rmem[1];
atomic_inc(&tcp_sockets_allocated);
return 0;
}
```

Table 7.3 shows the initialization of the address family specific sock operations values for AF_INET and TCP. For TCP in IPv4, this initialization occurs in the file `linux/net/ipv4/tcp_ipv4`. The structure itself is defined in the file `linux/include/net/inet_connection_sock.h`.

The `inet_connection_sock_af_ops` Structure for TCP

TABLE 7.3 TCP Specific Values for `inet_connection_sock_af_ops`

Field	TCP Actual Value	Description
queue_xmit	ip_queue_xmit	IPv4 network layer transmit function.
send_check	tcp_v4_send_check	Function to calculate IPv4 TCP checksum.
rebuild_header	tcp_v4_rebuild_header	Obtains IPv4 destination address for IP header.
conn_request	tcp_v4_conn_request	Function to process incoming connection request for IPv4.
syn_recv_sock	tcp_v4_syn_recv_sock	Function to create new child socket after receiving SYNACK from peer.
remember_stamp	tcp_v4_remember_stamp	A function to save the last received timestamp from a particular peer, used for duplicate segment detection.
net_header_len	sizeof(struct iphdr)	Size of network header. Set to IPv4 header length.
setsockopt	ip_setsockopt	The network layer socket option functions for IPv4. They handle IP socket options left over after socket layer and transport layer socket options have been processed.
getsockopt	ip_getsockopt	See setsockopt field above.
addr2sockaddr	inet_csk_addr2sockaddr	Function to generate sockaddr_with type for IPv4.
sockaddr_len	sizeof(struct sockaddr_in)	Size of sockaddr_in for IPv4.

INITIATING A CONNECTION AT THE TRANSPORT LAYER

As we are aware, UDP is a protocol for sending individual datagrams and doesn't actually maintain connections between peer hosts. No state information is maintained between subsequent UDP packet transmissions. In contrast, TCP is connection oriented, and much of the processing associated with TCP is related to the setup and breakdown of connections. Connections are initiated at the client side by calling the connect socket call. As Table 7.2 shows, when connect is called from the application code, the tcp_v4_connect function is executed for TCP.

Even though UDP doesn't support connections, the connect socket call is supported for UDP. For datagram sockets, the function is used to cache the peer address and associate it with the socket so subsequent send calls can omit specifying the destination address. In this section, we discuss the how the connect socket call is processed for both TCP and UDP.

The connect Call and UDP

The connect call can be made for a UDP socket. When the application layer programmer uses this function, she specifies the destination address and the main purpose of connect for UDP is to establish the route to the destination and enter it in the routing cache. After a route is established, subsequent packet transmissions through the UDP socket can use the cached route information. In the Linux sources, this is often called the *fast path* for a connected socket. When connect is called on an open SOCK_DGRAM type socket, the function ip4_datagram_connect, in the file linux/net/ipv4/datagram.c, is called by the socket layer. The sock structure for the open socket is pointed by sk and uaddr is the destination address to which we want to create a route.

```
int ipv4_datagram_connect(struct sock *sk, struct sockaddr *uaddr, int addr_len)
{
```

IPv4-specific address and option information is in the inet_sock structure, which is the IPv4 specific overlaid version of the sock structure.

```
struct inet_sock *inet = inet_sk(sk);
struct sockaddr_in *usin = (struct sockaddr_in *) uaddr;
```

rt is a pointer to a route cache entry. See Chapter 8, "The Network Layer, IP," for more information about the route cache. oif is the index of the output network interface that will carry the packet using the route to the destination.

```
struct rtable *rt;
u32 saddr;
int oif;
int err;
```

First, we make sure that the specified address is in the correct format for an Internet address.

```
if (addr_len < sizeof(*usin))
        return -EINVAL;
if (usin->sin_family != AF_INET)
        return -EAFNOSUPPORT;
```

We call `sk_dst_reset` to free any old destination cache entry pointed to by the dst field in the sock structure, sk.

```
sk_dst_reset(sk);
```

The application code calls bind to set the source address information. Since the socket referred to in this function may be a bound socket, the network interface may already be known. If so, oif will be the index of the outgoing network interface, and if not, it will be zero. Next, we check to see if the destination address in usin is a multicast address. If it is multicast, it doesn't mean that the user is trying to connect to a multicast address; instead, it means that the user will be sending subsequent packets to the same address. In addition, if the destination address is multicast, we get the output interface and source address from the inet_sock part of the sock, sk.

```
oif = sk->bound_dev_if;
saddr = sk->saddr;
if (MULTICAST(usin->sin_addr.s_addr)) {
    if (!oif)
        oif = sk->protinfo.af_inet.mc_index;
    if (!saddr)
        saddr = sk->protinfo.af_inet.mc_addr;
}
```

This is the most important call in this function. `ip_route_connect` gets a route to the destination address in usin and sets rt to point to the new cached route. If it returns a nonzero value, it wasn't able to find a route or add a new one to the routing cache, so we return the error. If it found a broadcast route, we return an error.

```
        err = ip_route_connect(&rt, usin->sin_addr.s_addr, saddr,
                               RT_CONN_FLAGS(sk), oif, sk->sk_protocol,
                               inet->sport, usin->sin_port, sk);
    if (err)
        return err;
    if ((rt->rt_flags&RTCF_BROADCAST) && !sock_flag(sk,
SOCK_BROADCAST)) {
        ip_rt_put(rt);
        return -EACCES;
    }
    if(!sk->saddr)
```

Here, we update the source address and destination address for outgoing packets from the fields in the route cache entry, rt. The destination port is specified by the user.

```
        sk->saddr = rt->rt_src;
    if(!sk->rcv_saddr)
        sk->rcv_saddr = rt->rt_src;
    sk->daddr = rt->rt_dst;
    sk->dport = usin->sin_port;
```

We set the socket state to TCP_ESTABLISHED to indicate that there is a cached route. This value is misleading for a UDP socket, but it is merely to show that the socket has a cached route associated with it. Later, when the user tries to transmit a packet and the source address is missing in the send call, we consider it okay because the state indicates that there is a route established.

```
    sk->state = TCP_ESTABLISHED;
    inet->id = jiffies;
```

Finally, a pointer to the route cache entry is placed in the destination field, dst, of the socket.

```
        sk_dst_set(sk, &rt->u.dst);
        return(0);
}
```

The `tcp_v4_connect` Function, Requesting a TCP Connection

Earlier, we discussed how the sockets are initialized for TCP when the application calls the socket function. Now we will take a look at what happens when a user initiates a connection to a remote server.

Chapter 7 Sending the Data from the Socket through UDP and TCP

Users specify `sock_stream` when opening up a connection-oriented socket for TCP connections. Application using connections are typically thought of as either clients or servers. The client requests connections with a server and the server responds to connection requests. The socket call made by a client to request a connection with a server is `connect`. When `connect` is called by the application on an open socket, inside the kernel, the socket layer executes a function in the transport protocol specific part of the TCP/IP stack to process the connection request. For `SOCK_STREAM` type protocols in the `AF_INET` address family, the function called by the socket layer is `tcp_v4_connect` defined in the file `linux/net/ipv4/tcp_ipv4.c`.

```
int tcp_v4_connect(struct sock *sk, struct sockaddr *uaddr, int
addr_len)
{
```

As with UDP, `inet` points to the `AF_INET` specific portion of the sock structure, and it contains options and functions particular to TCP/IP.

```
struct inet_sock *inet = inet_sk(sk);
```

The next variable, `tp`, points to the TCP options, `tcp_opt`, in the sock structure. The TCP options are discussed later in this chapter. The variable `rt` is a route table cache entry. Later, it will point to the cached route for packets being sent through this socket.

```
struct tcp_opt *tp = &(sk->tp_pinfo.af_tcp);
struct sockaddr_in *usin = (struct sockaddr_in *) uaddr;
struct rtable *rt;
```

This variable, `daddr`, is the IP destination address, and `nexthop` is the IP address of the gateway router for the route if there is one.

```
u32 daddr, nexthop;
int tmp;
int err;
```

After making sure that the specified address is in the correct format, we initialize `nexthop` and the destination address to point to the user-specified destination address. Later, `nexthop` may be changed depending on the route.

```
if (addr_len < sizeof(struct sockaddr_in))
    return(-EINVAL);
```

```
if (usin->sin_family != AF_INET)
    return(-EAFNOSUPPORT);
nexthop = daddr = usin->sin_addr.s_addr;
```

This is a check to see whether the source routing option is set for this socket.

```
if (inet->opt && inet->opt->srr) {
    if (daddr == 0)
        return -EINVAL;
    nexthop = inet->opt->faddr;
}
```

Now we attempt to get a route to the destination address given the destination address, which for now is in nexthop, the source address, and the network interface. The function ip_route_connect will return a zero if successful and will set rt to point to the new cached route if it found one.

```
tmp = ip_route_connect(&rt, nexthop, inet->saddr,
                      RT_CONN_FLAGS(sk), sk->sk_bound_dev_if,
                      IPPROTO_TCP,
                      inet->sport, usin->sin_port, sk);
if (tmp < 0)
    return tmp;
```

We don't allow TCP to connect to nonunicast addresses; therefore, if the route in the route cache is not a unicast route, we return an error. We also set the source address to the address in the cached route, if the source address isn't already defined.

```
if (rt->rt_flags&(RTCF_MULTICAST|RTCF_BROADCAST)) {
    ip_rt_put(rt);
    return -ENETUNREACH;
}
if (!inet->opt || !inet->opt->srr)
    daddr = rt->rt_dst;
if (!inet->saddr)
    inet->saddr = rt->rt_src;
inet->rcv_saddr = inet->saddr;
```

Here, we reset the inherited state. This is in case we are working with a socket that is *dirty* with information about an inherited connection.

Chapter 7 Sending the Data from the Socket through UDP and TCP

```
        if (tp->ts_recent_stamp && inet->daddr != daddr) {
            tp->ts_recent       = 0;
            tp->ts_recent_stamp = 0;
            tp->write_seq       = 0;
        }
        if (sysctl_tcp_tw_recycle &&
            !tp->ts_recent_stamp && rt->rt_dst == daddr) {
            struct inet_peer *peer = rt_get_peer(rt);
```

The next section of code is for implementing the Van Jacobsen algorithm [JACOB88]. Refer to Chapter 9," Receiving Data in the Transport Layer, UDP and TCP," where we discuss all the TCP states for more information about the TIME_WAIT state. The last used timestamp values are saved in the `inet_peer` structure associated with the route entry when the socket is in the TIME_WAIT state. Then, when a new connection is requested, the recent received timestamp and the timestamp fields in the `tcp_sock` structure are restored from the saved values in the `inet_peer` structure. This is a method for detecting duplicate segments when the connection is re-established.

```
        if (peer && peer->tcp_ts_stamp + TCP_PAWS_MSL >= xtime.tv_sec)
    {
            tp->ts_recent_stamp = peer->tcp_ts_stamp;
            tp->ts_recent = peer->tcp_ts;
        }
    }
```

Here, we initialize the destination address, port, the TCP header length, and the TCP options. Note that the TCP header length can vary depending on the presence or absence of options in the header.

```
        inet->dport = usin->sin_port;
        inet->daddr = daddr;
        inet_csk(sk)->icsk_ext_hdr_len = 0;
        if (inet->opt)
            tp->ext_header_len = inet->opt->optlen;
```

The field `mss_clamp` is for maximum segment size (MSS) negotiation. The number 536 is the minimum allowed MSS value.

```
        tp->mss_clamp = 536;
```

Although, we are in the process of doing an active open, the identity of the socket is not known. We don't know the source port, sport, because we have not yet assigned the ephemeral port. However, we put ourselves in the **SYN_SENT** state and enter sk into the TCP connection's hash table. The remainder of the work for initialization the connection will be finished later.

```
tcp_set_state(sk, TCP_SYN_SENT);
```

We call inet_hash_connect to enter the socket in the connect hash table. This assigns an ephemeral port for the connection, and puts it in the sport field of the sock.

```
err = inet_hash_connect(sk);
if (err)
    goto failure;
err = ip_route_newports(&rt, IPPROTO_TCP, inet->sport, inet->dport,
sk);
if (err)
    goto failure;
```

We commit the destination for this connection by setting the dst field of the sock structure, sk, to point to the destination associated with the route. When a route is for a packet sent to an external destination, dst will point to the gateway. However, if the destination is for a directly connect host, dst will point to information about the host.

```
sk_setup_caps(sk, &rt->u.dst);
```

The sequence number in the TCP header helps keep track of the data ordering so the data can be reconstructed in the correct order in the destination machine. Here, we initialize the first sequence number.

```
if (!tp->write_seq)
    tp->write_seq = secure_tcp_sequence_number(inet->saddr,
                                               inet->daddr,
                                               inet->sport,
                                               usin->sin_port);

inet->id = tp->write_seq ^ jiffies;
```

We call tcp_connect to complete the work of setting up the connection including transmitting the **SYN**.

```
    err = tcp_connect(sk);
    rt = NULL;
    if (err)
        goto failure;
    return 0;
failure:
```

If we failed when we attempted to connect with the peer machine, we take the socket out of the hash table for connected sockets and release the local port.

```
    tcp_set_state(sk, TCP_CLOSE);
    ip_rt_put(rt);
    sk->sk_route_caps = 0;
    inet->dport = 0;
    return err;
}
```

SENDING DATA FROM A SOCKET VIA UDP

Now we are ready to actually transmit data. First, we will look at how data is transmitted using UDP. At this point in our discussion, the application program has called the socket function to open a connectionless socket.

In this section, we show how the UDP protocol processes a request from the application layer to send a datagram. When a user program writes data to a SOCK_DGRAM type socket by calling sendmsg or any other application layer sending function, the UDP protocol will process the request. UDP is fairly simple, and mostly consists of a framing layer. It doesn't do much more than pre-pend the user data with the UDP header. Unlike TCP, there is no buffering or connection management. To construct the UDP header, the destination and source port are required. Usually, the destination port and IP address are specified together in the peer socket's name. Generally, when the port is known, the IP address is known, too. If the destination IP address is specified in the socket name, it is saved before the packet is passed to IP. In addition, before passing the packet on to IP, UDP checks to see whether the destination is internal or whether IP must determine a route for the packet. Moreover, the destination address may be a multicast or broadcast address, in which case IP does not need to route the packet. Before UDP is done, the source and destination ports are placed in the UDP header and the IP address is kept for later processing by IP.

The udp_sendmsg Function

When the application calls one of the write functions on an open socket, the socket layer calls the function pointed to by the sendmsg field in the prot structure. See Chapter 4, "Linux Sockets," for detailed information about what happens at the socket layer. This results in a call to udp_sendmsg, which is found in the file linux/net/ipv4/udp.c. This is the sending function that is executed for SOCK_DGRAM type sockets. See Table 7.1 for a list of all the protocol block functions for UDP.

```
int udp_sendmsg(struct sock *sk, struct msghdr *msg, int len)
{
```

We retrieve the protocol specific parts of the sock structure.

```
struct inet_sock *inet = inet_sk(sk);
struct udp_sock *up = udp_sk(sk);
```

The field ulen is set to the parameter len, which is the amount of data sent by the application layer. The next field, ipc, will hold the return from the function ip_cmsg_send discussed later in this chapter..

```
int ulen = len;
struct ipcm_cookie ipc;
struct rtable *rt = NULL;
int free = 0;
int connected = 0;
```

The next statements declare daddr, which is for the destination IP address, and tos for the TOS field of the IP header. The field faddr is to support IP source routing.

```
u32 daddr, faddr, saddr;
u16 dport;
u8  tos;
int err;
int corkreq = up->corkflag || msg->msg_flags&MSG_MORE;
```

Chapter 7 Sending the Data from the Socket through UDP and TCP

The first thing we do in udp_sendmsg is check for an out-of-range value in the len field to see whether the caller is attempting to send a packet greater than 64K bytes, the maximum size for UDP. We also check to see whether the caller has requested any illegal flags for this type of socket. The only illegal flag for UDP is MSG_OOB, which is used only for SOCK_STREAM type sockets.

```
if (len < 0 || len > 0xFFFF)
    return -EMSGSIZE;
if (msg->msg_flags&MSG_OOB)
    return -EOPNOTSUPP;
```

Now, check to see whether there are any pending packets already waiting to be set. The socket lock must be held while the socket is corked for processing the pending frames. This is to prevent the user from sending more data before the pending packets are transmitted.

```
if (up->pending) {
    lock_sock(sk);
    if (likely(up->pending)) {
        if (unlikely(up->pending != AF_INET)) {
            release_sock(sk);
            return -EINVAL;
        }
        goto do_append_data;
    }
    release_sock(sk);
}
```

We add the UDP header length to the length of the user data.

```
ulen += sizeof(struct udphdr);
```

Next in udp_sendmsg, we check to make sure that either there is a valid destination address specified or the socket is in a connected state. For historical reasons, the address of a socket is often called its name. We verify the address by checking the name field in the msghdr structure. The msghdr is defined in the sendmsg(2) manpage. If the application caller invoked the sendto socket API call, then the name field of the msghdr structure will contain the address originally specified in the to field of the sendto call.

```
if (msg->msg_name) {
    struct sockaddr_in * usin = (struct sockaddr_in*)msg->msg_name;
    if (msg->msg_namelen < sizeof(*usin))
```

```
                return -EINVAL;
        if (usin->sin_family != AF_INET) {
                if (usin->sin_family != AF_UNSPEC)
                        return -EINVAL;
        }
```

At this point, we get the destination and source addresses.

```
        daddr = usin->sin_addr.s_addr;
        dport = usin->sin_port;
        if (dport == 0)
                return -EINVAL;
} else {
```

Here, we know that the destination address specified was NULL. However, we can allow the packet to be transmitted if the socket is a connected UDP socket, which is indicated when the state field is set to TCP_ESTABLISHED. If the socket is connected, we can assume that the destination address is already known. Although the socket state name is confusing, this socket is definitely a connectionless UDP socket.

```
        if (sk->state != TCP_ESTABLISHED)
                return -EDESTADDRREQ;
        daddr = inet->daddr;
        dport = inet->dport;
```

If the socket is connected, then routing in the IP layer can use the *fast path*, which bypasses the routing table lookup and uses the destination cache entry directly.

```
        connected = 1;
    }
...
```

If no valid destination address is found, udp_sendmsg returns EINVAL.

The udphdr Structure

The udphdr structure, defined in the file linux/include/linux/udp.h, contains the actual UDP header including the source port, destination port, length, and checksum. In the udp_sendmsg function, the UDP header is a field in ufh, the UDP fake header structure.

```
struct udphdr {
    __u16   source;
```

Chapter 7 Sending the Data from the Socket through UDP and TCP   **301**

```
        __u16    dest;
        __u16    len;
        __u16    check;
};
```

Handling Control Messages in the `udp_sendmsg` Function

Let's continue with the `udp_sendmsg` function to see how it handles the control messages. The next thing `udp_sendmsg` does is determine whether the argument `msg` points to a control message. It checks the field `msg_controllen` for nonzero value. The structure `ipcm_cookie`, pointed to by `ipc`, holds the result of the control message processing. Initially, some fields of `ipc` are initialized, such as the IP options and the interface (if there is one bound to this socket).

```
. . .
    ipc.addr = inet->saddr;
    ipc.oif = sk->bound_dev_if;
    if (msg->msg_controllen) {
```

The control messages are also called *ancillary data* and are part of the expanded IPv6 sockets interface specification. For more information on control messages, see the Linux manual, page `cmsg(3)`, and "Advanced Sockets API for IPv6," [RFC 2292]. If `msg` contains a pointer to a control message, the function `ip_cmsg_send`, defined in the file `linux/net/ipv4/ip_sockglue.c` processes the request. These control messages are a way of setting and retrieving UDP information, such as the address and port. Fields in the `inet` options structure, which contains the addressing information, can be retrieved directly by the control message.

```
        err = ip_cmsg_send(msg, &ipc);
        if (err)
            return err;
        if (ipc.opt)
            free = 1;
        connected = 0;
    }
    if (!ipc.opt)
        ipc.opt = inet->opt;
    saddr = ipc.addr;
    ipc.addr = faddr = daddr;
    if (ipc.opt && ipc.opt->srr) {
        if (!daddr)
            return -EINVAL;
```

```
            faddr = ipc.opt->faddr;
            connected = 0;
    }
...
```

The function `ip_cmsg_send` returns the results in `ipc`, which points to a structure called `ipcm_cookie`, defined in the file `linux/include/net/ip.h`.

The `ipcm_cookie` Structure

```
        struct ipcm_cookie
        {
            u32                 addr;
            int                 oif;
            struct ip_options   *opt;
        };
```

Two types of control messages are processed by UDP. `I_RETOPTS` retrieves the options field from the IP header and returns a pointer to the options in the `opt` field of `ipc`. If `IP_PKTINFO` was specified in the control message, `ip_cmsg_send` returns the interface index in the `oif` field of `ipc` and the interface's IP address in the `addr` field.

The `udp_sendmsg` Function and Packet Output

We continue with our examination of the `udp_msgsend` function. At this point, most of the information needed for the UDP header is established. We could queue the packet to IP, have it prepend its header and pass it to the device driver for transmission. However, we will see that things are not quite this simple. We don't directly transmit a packet, even though we have all the header information; instead, we post the data to a queue held by the socket. In affect, the memory mapped pages are mapped directly from the user space to an array associated with the socket pointed by to the socket, `sk`. Although this may seem complex, it allows IP to handle streamed data, fragmented data, and datagrams in the same way.

First, we will check to see how this packet is to be routed by IP. Of course, we don't actually do the routing here, mostly we are checking to see whether we have a valid cached route, to reduce the workload for IP when it receives the packet.

```
...
    tos = RT_TOS(inet->tos);
    if (sock_flag(sk, SOCK_LOCALROUTE) ||
        (msg->msg_flags & MSG_DONTROUTE) ||
        (ipc.opt && ipc.opt->is_strictroute)) {
        tos |= RTO_ONLINK;
```

```
            connected = 0;
    }
```

In addition, if the packet is for transmission through a connected socket, it is assumed that the destination is already known and there is already a route to the destination address in this packet. If the destination address is a multicast address, there is no need to route the packet either.

```
    if (MULTICAST(daddr)) {
        if (!ipc.oif)
            ipc.oif = inet->mc_index;
        if (!saddr)
            saddr = inet->mc_addr;
        connected = 0;
    }
    if (connected)
        rt = (struct rtable*)sk_dst_check(sk, 0);
    if (rt == NULL) {
```

If we don't have a route, we prepare for a search of the routing table by building a flow information structure, associated with routing. For more details about IP routing refer to Chapter 8.

```
        struct flowi fl = { .oif = ipc.oif,
                            .nl_u = { .ip4_u =
                            { .daddr = faddr,
                              .saddr = saddr,
                              .tos = tos } },
                            .proto = IPPROTO_UDP,
                            .uli_u = { .ports =
                                { .sport = inet->sport,
                                  .dport = dport } } };
```

We call ip_route_output to try to come up with a route. See Chapter 9 for more information about ip_route_output and how the routing table entries are manipulated and searched.

```
        err = ip_route_output_flow(&rt, &fl, sk,
                                    !(msg->msg_flags&MSG_DONTWAIT));
        if (err)
            goto out;
        err = -EACCES;
```

If the routing cache entry indicates broadcast, but the socket did not have the SO_BROADCAST flag set, then it is an error.

```
if (rt->rt_flags&RTCF_BROADCAST &&
    !sock_flag(sk, SOCK_BROADCAST))
    goto out;
```

Now we know we have a good route, so if the socket is connected, we set a pointer to the route in the destination cache. See Chapter 5 for more information about the destination cache.

```
if (connected)
    sk_dst_set(sk, dst_clone(&rt->u.dst));
}
```

Next, udp_msgsend checks whether the application requested routing confirmation by looking for the flag MSG_CONFIRM in the flags field of the msghdr structure. If required, dst_confirm is called to confirm the route.

```
if (msg->msg_flags&MSG_CONFIRM)
    goto do_confirm;
```

At this point, we are routed. We have a destination, and we queue the data to IP. First though, we check to see we are already holding up the socket.

```
back_from_confirm:
    saddr = rt->rt_src;
    if (!ipc.addr)
        daddr = ipc.addr = rt->rt_dst;
    lock_sock(sk);
    if (unlikely(up->pending)) {
```

Check that the sock is already corked. This shouldn't happen at this point because we just checked above.

```
        release_sock(sk);
        LIMIT_NETDEBUG(KERN_DEBUG "udp cork app bug 2\n");
        err = -EINVAL;
        goto out;
}
```

Now, we must cork the socket in order to append additional data to the socket's queue.

Chapter 7 Sending the Data from the Socket through UDP and TCP

```
    inet->cork.fl.fl4_dst = daddr;
    inet->cork.fl.fl_ip_dport = dport;
    inet->cork.fl.fl4_src = saddr;
    inet->cork.fl.fl_ip_sport = inet->sport;
    up->pending = AF_INET;
```

Now we send the data to IP by calling `ip_append_data`, which builds a large datagram from individual pieces of data. The second argument, `ip_generic_getfrag`, is the callback function to fragment the data if what we are appending is too long to fit into the output devices MTU.

```
do_append_data:
    up->len += ulen;
    err = ip_append_data(sk,ip_generic_getfrag,msg->msg_iov, ulen,
                    sizeof(struct udphdr), &ipc, rt,
                    corkreq ? msg->msg_flags|MSG_MORE : msg->msg_flags);
    if (err)
        udp_flush_pending_frames(sk);
    else if (!corkreq)
        err = udp_push_pending_frames(sk, up);
    release_sock(sk);
```

Here, we actually exit the function.

```
out:
    ip_rt_put(rt);
    if (free)
        kfree(ipc.opt);
    if (!err) {
        UDP_INC_STATS_USER(UDP_MIB_OUTDATAGRAMS);
        return len;
    }
    return err;
do_confirm:
```

If there is already is a destination, determined by checking to see whether the neighbor cache has an entry for this route, we call `dst_confirm` to update the timestamp on the entry.

```
    dst_confirm(&rt->u.dst);
```

If the MSG_PROBE flag is set, we don't send the packet; instead we probe for maximum MTU.

```
        if (!(msg->msg_flags&MSG_PROBE) || len)
            goto back_from_confirm;
        err = 0;
        goto out;
}
```

Copying Data from User Space, `ip_generic_getfrag`

This section covers the function that gets pieces of data from user space to append to a datagram, `ip_generic_getfrag`. This function is not just for fragments, it is executed for UDP whether or not the data fits in a single IP datagram. It is defined in `linux/net/ipv4/ip_output.c`. It is a callback from the `ip_append_data` function, also in the same file.

`ip_append_data` is executed whether or not checksums have been disabled. All IO from user space including socket IO has the data organized in one or more buffer pointers referenced by `iov`. For UDP, generally, there is one buffer pointed to by `iov`.

```
int ip_generic_getfrag(void *from, char *to, int offset, int len,
int odd, struct sk_buff *skb)
{
```

The UDP header does not need to be copied from user space to kernel space. It has already been built in kernel space in `udp_msgsend`. We just need to get the data, so we call one of two functions depending on whether the output hardware has hardware checksum capability. The first of the two functions, `csum_partial_copy_fromiovecend`, calculates partial checksums while copying. In the other function, `memcpy_fromiovecend` doesn't calculate the checksum but assumes it is done in hardware later. A UDP checksum includes parts of the IP header. It includes the source and destination IP addresses, IP header protocol, and length fields. Therefore, the checksum calculation is done in three stages: once for the data, again for the actual UDP header, and then a third time with the required fields from the IP header.

```
        struct iovec *iov = from;
        if (skb->ip_summed == CHECKSUM_HW) {
            if (memcpy_fromiovecend(to, iov, offset, len) < 0)
            return -EFAULT;
        } else {
            unsigned int csum = 0;
```

The actual copying is done by the `iovec` utility routine. If required, the checksum is calculated on the data while copying for efficiency. It is important to avoid manipulating the packet contents twice. The data must be copied from user space via the `iov` pointer to a location pointed to by the `sk_buff` in kernel space referenced by the `to` argument.

```
        if (csum_partial_copy_fromiovecend(to, iov, offset, len, &csum)
< 0)
            return -EFAULT;
        skb->csum = csum_block_add(skb->csum, csum, odd);
    }
    return 0;
}
```

SENDING DATA FROM A SOCKET VIA TCP

In this section, we see what happens when we transmit streaming data, and in the remaining part of this chapter, we examine the send-side processing of TCP. The best way to describe the implementation of a complex protocol like TCP is to follow the data as it flows through the protocol. It is important to keep in mind that TCP is probably the most complex part of the TCP/IP protocol suite. It is because TCP provides a connection-oriented service at the transport layer that it is far more complicated than UDP. TCP must manage the relationship between the local host and the remote host, including retransmitting bad and lost packets, managing the connection state machine, buffering the data, and setting up and breaking down the connection. In addition, as we will see, it does much more than this. Linux TCP implements all of the enhancements for security, reliability, and performance that have been developed in more than 20 years since TCP was first specified in RFC 793. This section focuses primarily on the connection with the socket, how data is removed from the application and placed in queues for transmission. In the following section, we talk about the actual packet transmission. Then we cover the data structures used to keep control variables and configuration options, and finally we look at the TCP timers used primarily on the send side of the connection. Figure 7.1 shows the TCP connection state for the sending side.

Let's look at how the send side of the protocol handles write information passed from the socket layer. After an application layer program opens a socket of type SOCK_STREAM, the TCP protocol is invoked to process all write requests for data transfers through the open socket. The transmission of data through TCP is controlled primarily by the state of the connection with the peer and the availability of data in the send buffer. Because of the asynchronous nature of TCP, actual data transmission is independent of the application layer, as it writes data into the socket layer buffers. In general, TCP gathers the data into segments and passes it to the

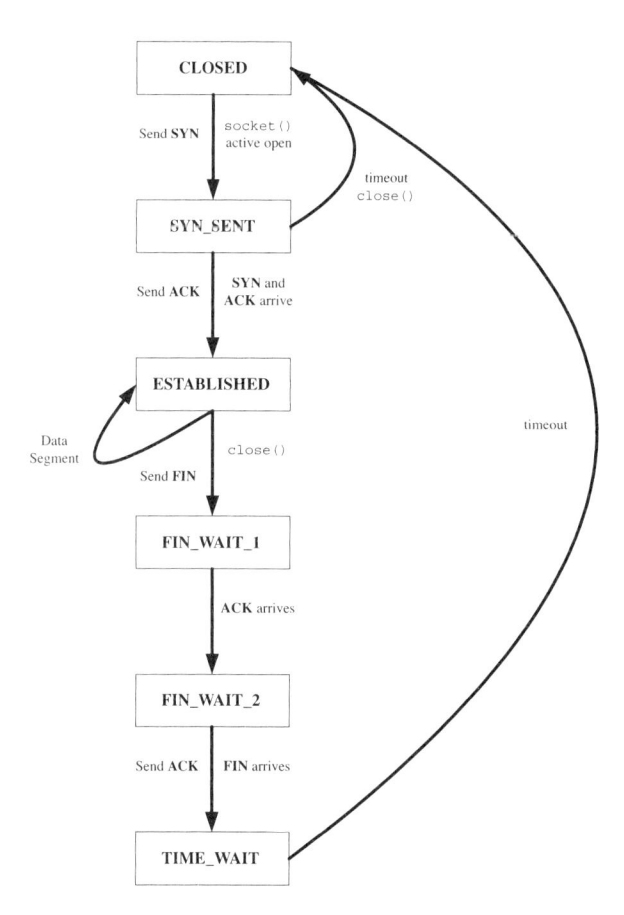

FIGURE 7.1 TCP send state diagram.

peer machine when there is available bandwidth in the network. This is different from UDP where the user-level process controls transmission, because with UDP, a write of data to the socket results directly in the transmission of a datagram. When any of the socket layer write functions are invoked by the application, TCP copies the data into a list of socket buffers, which are queued up for later transmission. Most of the work associated with writing in a socket involves determining the type of socket buffer and managing the queue of buffers. It must be determined whether the transmission interface has scatter-gather capability, otherwise known as *chained DMA*. If the interface has scatter-gather support, TCP sets up a transfer of a chain of buffers to the networking device. In this case, TCP uses the fragment list in the shared info structure of the skbuff. In addition, TCP maintains a queue of socket buffers, so the send function must also determine if there is room for more data in the current socket buffer or if a new one must be allocated.

The `tcp_sendmsg` Function

The `tcp_msgsend` function, defined in the file `linux/net/ipv4/tcp.c`, is invoked when any user-level write or message sending function is invoked on an open `SOCK_STREAM` type socket. All the write functions are converted to calls to this function at the socket layer. The best way to show the operation of TCP on the send side is to examine this function, so we will follow it to see how it processes the data.

The socket layer is able to find `tcp_sendmsg` because it is referenced by the `sendmsg` field of the protocol block structure, `prot`, which is initialized at compile time in the file `linux/net/ipv4/tcp_ipv4.c`. The protocol block functions for TCP are shown in Table 7.2. `tcp_sendmsg` collects all the TCP header information possible, copies the data into socket buffers, and queues the socket buffers for transmission. It makes heavy use of the TCP sock structure. `tcp_sendmsg` also sets many fields in the TCP control block structure, described in in a later section, which is used to pass TCP header information to the transmission side of the TCP protocol.

```
int tcp_sendmsg(struct sock *sk, struct msghdr *msg,
int size)
{
```

The variable `iov` is to retrieve the IO vector pointer in the message header structure in the argument `msg`. The variable, `tp` points to the TCP options that will be retrieved from the sock structure `sk`. `skb` is a pointer to a socket buffer that will be allocated to hold the data to be transmitted. The next variable, `iovlen` is set to the number of elements in the `iovec`.

```
struct iovec *iov;
struct tcp_opt *tp = tcp_sk(sk);
struct sk_buff *skb;
int iovlen, flags;
```

Next we declare `mss_now`, which holds the current maximum segment size (MSS) for this open socket.

```
int mss_now, size_goal;
int err, copied;
long timeo;
lock_sock(sk);
TCP_CHECK_TIMER(sk);
flags = msg->msg_flags;
```

The value of the `SO_SNDTIMEO` option is put in timeo unless the `MSG_DONTWAIT` flag was set for the socket.

```
timeo = sock_sndtimeo(sk, flags & MSG_DONTWAIT);
```

The next thing `tcp_sendmsg` does is wait for a connection to be established before sending the packet. The state of the connection for this open socket is checked, and if the connection is not already in the TCPF_ESTABLISHED or TCPF_CLOSE_WAIT state, TCP is not ready to send data so it must wait for a connection to be established. The value of the timeout set with the SO_SNDTIMEO socket option is passed into the `sk_stream_wait_connect` function.

```
if ((1 << sk->state) & ~(TCPF_ESTABLISHED | TCPF_CLOSE_WAIT))
    if((err = sk_stream_wait_connect (sk, &timeo)) != 0)
        goto out_err;
```

The SOCK_ASYNC_NOSPACE bit in flags is cleared to indicate that this socket is not currently waiting for more memory.

```
clear_bit(SOCK_ASYNC_NOSPACE, &sk->sk_socket->flags);
```

Now we set `mss_now` to the current mss for this socket. The function `tcp_current_mss` takes into account MTU discovery, the negotiated MSS, and the TCP_MAXSEG option. See the section on TCP utility functions for more details.

```
mss_now = tcp_current_mss(sk, !(flags&MSG_OOB);
size_goal = tp->xmit_size_goal;
```

Now, set up to send the data. Get `iov` and `iovlen` from the `msghdr` structure. Get ready to start copying the data into socket buffers.

```
iovlen = msg->msg_iovlen;
iov = msg->msg_iov;
copied = 0;
err = -EPIPE;
```

If the application called `shutdown` with `how` set to one, this means that a socket shutdown on the send side of the socket has been requested, so get out.

```
if (sk->err || (sk->shutdown & SEND_SHUTDOWN))
    goto do_error;
```

The IO vector structure is the mechanism where data is retrieved from user space into kernel space. `iovlen` is the number of `iov` buffers queued up by the socket send call.

Chapter 7 Sending the Data from the Socket through UDP and TCP

```
while (-iovlen >= 0) {
```

Next, `seglen` is the length of each `iov`, and `from` points to the data to be copied.

```
int seglen=iov->iov_len;
unsigned char * from=iov->iov_base;
iov++;
while (seglen > 0) {
    int copy;
    skb = sk->write_queue.prev;
```

If `send_head` is null, there are not yet any segments queued for sending. `size_goal` is the desired MSS.

```
if (!tp->send_head == NULL ||
    (copy = size_goal - skb->len) <= 0) {
```

If `send_head` is NULL, it is necessary to allocate a new segment. `Tcp_alloc_pskb` is used as a TCP-specific wrapper for `alloc_skb`. It allocates a paged socket buffer. This buffer includes the socket buffer shared info and are used for efficient handling of TCP segments and IP fragments. They are particularly suitable for network interfaces that have scatter-gather DMA capability that can send a chain of buffers via DMA with minimum overhead. Next we call `select_size` to round off the requested size to the nearest TCP segment size or page size determined from the MSS. `skb_entail` sets up the flags and sequence numbers in the TCP control block and puts the new `skb` on the write queue. `copy` is the amount of data to copy to the segment. We set it to `mss_now`, the most recent negotiated value of MSS, which is the best indicator of segment size at this point.

```
new_segment:
            if (!sk_stream_memory_free (sk))
                goto wait_for_sndbuf;
            skb = sk_stream_alloc_pskb (sk,
                                        select_size(sk, tp),
                                        0,
                                        sk->allocation);
            if (!skb)
                goto wait_for_memory;
```

We check to see whether we can use the hardware checksum capability.

```
                    if (sk->sk_route_caps &
                        (NETIF_F_IP_CSUM | NETIF_F_NO_CSUM |
                         NETIF_F_HW_CSUM))
                        skb->ip_summed = CHECKSUM_HW;
                    skb_entail(sk, tp, skb);
                    copy = size_goal;
                }
    . . .
```

`tcp_sendmsg` Continues: Copying Data from User Space to the Socket Buffer

If possible, `tcp_sendmsg` tries to squeeze the data into the header portion of the `skb` before allocating a new segment, so it tries to determine the actual address where the data will be copied.

```
    . . .
                if (copy > seglen)
                    copy = seglen;
                if (skb_tailroom(skb) > 0) {
```

`Skb_tailroom` returns the amount of room in the end of the `skb`, and copy is set to the amount of available space if there is any. `Skb_add_data` copies the data to the `skb` and calculates the checksum while it is doing the copy. The partial checksum in progress is placed in the `csum` field of the socket buffer, `skb`. Chapter 6, includes a description of the socket buffer structure.

```
                    if (copy > skb_tailroom(skb))
                        copy = skb_tailroom(skb);
                    if ((err = skb_add_data(skb, from, copy)) != 0)
                        goto do_fault;
                } else {
```

If there was no `tailroom` in the main part of the socket buffer, `skb`, we try to find room in the last fragment attached to `skb`. If there is no room in the fragment, we allocate a new page and attach it by putting a pointer to it at the end of the `frags` array in the shared `info` part of the `skb`. Chapter 6 "Linux Socket Buffers," has a complete discussion of how the `frag` array is laid out in the socket buffers. Merge is set to one if there is any room in the last page, and `i` is set to the number of `frags` already in the socket buffer. Page is declared to point to a memory-mapped page, and `off` is set to the offset to the start of the data to be copied from the `msghdr` structure. `TCP_PAGE` is used several times in the `tcp_sendmsg` function. It is a macro that updates the `sndmsg_page` field in the `tcp_options` structure to hold a pointer to the current page in the `frags` array. The macro, `TCP_OFF`, also defined in `linux/net/`

Chapter 7 Sending the Data from the Socket through UDP and TCP 313

`ipv4/tcp.c`, updates the `sndmsg_off` field with an updated offset into the page. Both these macros also defined in the same file.

```
int merge = 0;
int i = skb_shinfo(skb)->nr_frags;
struct page *page = TCP_PAGE(sk);
int off = TCP_OFF(sk);
```

Now, we check to see that there is space in the last page in the socket buffer by calling `can_coalesce`, which returns a one if there is room. Next, we determine whether a new page is needed or a complete new socket buffer must be allocated. To do this, we check whether the `frag` slots in the `skb` are full or whether the outgoing interface has scatter-gather capability. SG means that the interface hardware can efficiently exploit socket buffers with attached pages by doing segmented DMA.

```
if (can_coalesce(skb, i, page, off) && off
    != PAGE_SIZE) {
    merge = 1;
```

We check to see whether there is any reason why we can't add a new fragment.

```
} else if (i == MAX_SKB_FRAGS ||
        (!i && !(sk->route_caps&NETIF_F_SG))) {
```

Perhaps, all the page slots are used or the interface is not capable of scatter-gather DMA. In any case, we know that we can't add more data to the current segment. Therefore, we call `tcp_mark_push` to set the `TCPCB_FLAG_PSH` flag in the control buffer for this connection. This will mean that the PSH flag will be set in the TCP header of the current `skb`, and then we jump to the `new_segment` label to allocate a new `skb`.

```
    tcp_mark_push(tp, skb);
    goto new_segment;
} else if (page) {
```

If the page has been allocated, `off` is aligned to the page boundary. Then, as an extra error check, we see whether `off` is valid, and if it isn't, we free the page and remove it from the `skb`.

```
if (off == PAGE_SIZE) {
    put_page(page);
    TCP_PAGE(sk) = page = NULL;
    off = 0;
```

```
                     }
             } else
                  off = 0;
             if (copy > PAGE_SIZE - off)
                  copy = PAGE_SIZE - off;
             if (!sk_stream_wmem_schedule(sk, copy))
                  goto wait_for_memory;
```

A new page is allocated if necessary, and `copy`, the length of data, is corrected for the page size.

```
             if (!page) {
```

Allocate the new cache page.

```
                  if (!(page= sk_stream_alloc_page(sk)))
                       goto wait_for_memory;
             }
                  err = skb_copy_to_page(sk, from, skb, page,
                                               off, copy);
```

Finally, in `tcp_sendmsg` we are ready to copy the data from user space to kernel space. We call `tcp_copy_to_page` to do the copying, which in turn calls `csum_and_copy_from_user` to copy the data efficiently by simultaneously calculating a partial checksum. If `tcp_copy_to_page` returns an error, the allocated but empty page is attached to the sock structure for this open socket, `sk`, in the `sndmsg_page` field so the page will be de-allocated when the socket is released.

```
             err = tcp_copy_to_page(sk, from, skb, page, off, copy);
             if (err) {
                  if (TCP_PAGE(sk) == NULL) {
                       TCP_PAGE(sk) = page;
                       TCP_OFF(sk) = 0;
                  }
                  goto do_error;
             }
```

Now that the copy has been done, the `skb` can be updated to reflect the new data. If `merge` is non-zero, it means that the data was merged into the last `frag`, so the size field in that `frag` must be updated. Otherwise, a new page was allocated, so we can call `fill_page_desc`, which updates the `frag` array in the `skb` with information about the new page. We update the `sndmsg_page` field in the `tcp_options` structure to point to the next page, and the `sndmsg_off` field gets an updated offset into the page.

```
            if (merge) {
                skb_shinfo(skb)->frags[i-1].size += copy;
            } else {
                fill_page_desc(skb, i, page, off, copy);
                if (TCP_PAGE(sk)) {
                    get_page(page);
                } else if (off + copy < PAGE_SIZE) {
                    get_page(page);
                    TCP_PAGE(sk) = page;
                }
            }
            TCP_OFF(sk) = off + copy;
        }
. . .
```

`tcp_sendmsg` Completion

At this point, most of the work of `tcp_sendmsg` is done. The data has been copied from user space to the socket buffer. The socket buffer's `frags` array has been updated with a list of pages ready for sending segments. A zero value in the variable `copied` indicates that this is the first time through the `while` loop for the initial segment so the PSH flag in the TCP header is set to zero. As we will see in this section, the TCP header is not set directly at this point. Instead, the intended values are saved in the TCP control block for later when the queued socket buffers are removed for transmission. Stevens has an excellent discussion in Section 20.5 of the use of the PSH flag in TCP [STEV94].

```
    . . .
        if (!copied)
            TCP_SKB_CB(skb)->flags &= ~TCPCB_FLAG_PSH;
```

The `write_seq` field in the TCP options structure is updated with the amount of data processed in this trip through the `while` loop. The `end_seq` field in the TCP control block is also updated with the amount of data that was processed. From, which points to the data source in the `msg` argument, and `copied`, which holds the total number of bytes processed so far, are updated for this iteration. `iovlen` is the number of `iov`s in the `msghdr` structure, and `seglen` was initialized to this value at the start of the function. Each loop through this code processes one `iov`.

```
            tp->write_seq += copy;
            TCP_SKB_CB(skb)->end_seq += copy;
            skb_shinfo(skb)->tso_segs = 0;
            from += copy;
            copied += copy;
            if ((seglen -= copy) == 0 && iovlen == 0)
                goto out;
            if (skb->len < mss_now || (flags&MSG_OOB))
                continue;
```

At this point, we decide whether small segments should be pushed out or held. We call forced_push to check whether we must send now no matter what the segment size is. If so, the PSH flag is set, and the segments are transmitted.

```
            if (forced_push(tp)) {
                tcp_mark_push(tp, skb);
                __tcp_push_pending_frames(sk, tp, mss_now,
                  TCP_NAGLE_PUSH);
            } else if (skb == tp->send_head)
                tcp_push_one(sk, mss_now);
            continue;
```

This is where tcp_sendmsg ends up if there is insufficient number of buffers or pages. It waits until a sufficient number of buffers are available.

```
wait_for_sndbuf:
            set_bit(SOCK_NOSPACE, &sk->socket->flags);
wait_for_memory:
            if (copied)
                tcp_push(sk, tp, flags&~MSG_MORE, mss_now,
TCP_NAGLE_PUSH);
            if ((err = sk_stream_wait_memory (sk, &timeo)) != 0)
                goto do_error;
            mss_now = tcp_current_mss(sk, !(flags&MSG_OOB));
            size_goal = tp->xmit_size_goal;
        }
    }
```

This is the label where we jumped if it was time to push the remaining data and exit the function. We return the value of copied to indicate to the application program how much data was transmitted.

```
out:
    if (copied)
        tcp_push(sk, tp, flags, mss_now, tp->nonagle);
    TCP_CHECK_TIMER(sk);
    release_sock(sk);
    return copied;
```

These last three labels mean that we are at the end of tcp_sendmsg. This is where we finally end up if errors were detected in the process of copying and processing the data.

```
do_fault:
    if (!skb->len) {
        if (sk->sk_send_head== skb)
            sk->send_head = NULL;
        __skb_unlink(skb, &sk->sk_write_queue);
        sk_stream_free_skb(sk, skb);
    }
do_error:
    if (copied)
        goto out;
out_err:
    err = sk_stream_error (sk, flags, err);
    TCP_CHECK_TIMER(sk);
    release_sock(sk);
    return err;
}
```

TCP OUTPUT

The previous discussion about TCP focused primarily on how the TCP protocol was interfaced to the socket and how data was removed from the application and placed in queues for transmission. In this section, we cover the actual packet transmission (see Figure 7.2).

Transmit the TCP Segments, the tcp_transmit_skb Function

Now it is time to transmit the TCP segments, and in the function tcp_Transmit_skb, we do the actual packet transmission. The source code for this function can be found in the file linux/net/ipv4/tcp_output.c. We send the packets that are queued to the socket. This function can be called from anywhere in TCP state processing whenever there is a request to send a segment. Earlier, we saw how

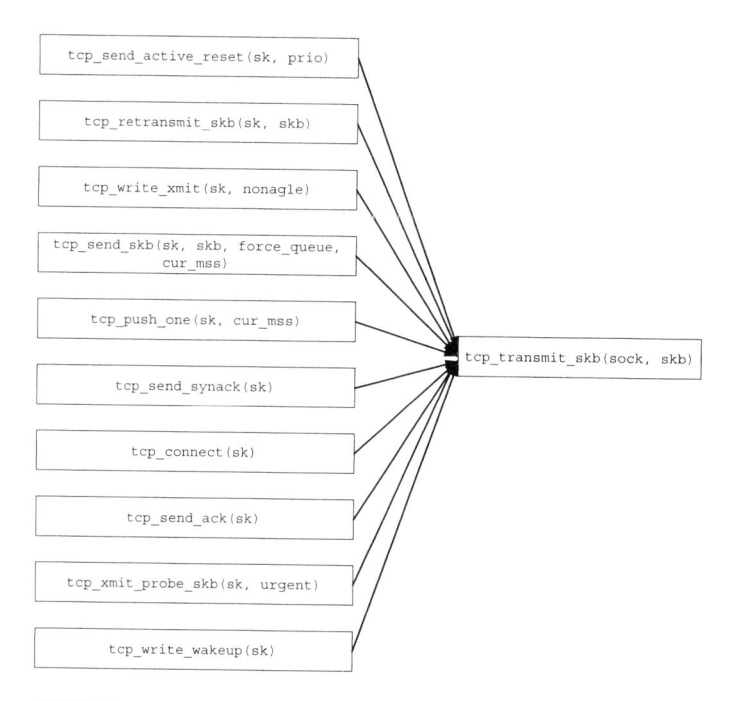

```
              tcp_send_active_reset(sk, prio)

              tcp_retransmit_skb(sk, skb)

              tcp_write_xmit(sk, nonagle)

              tcp_send_skb(sk, skb, force_queue,
                           cur_mss)

              tcp_push_one(sk, cur_mss)
                                                    tcp_transmit_skb(sock, skb)
              tcp_send_synack(sk)

              tcp_connect(sk)

              tcp_send_ack(sk)

              tcp_xmit_probe_skb(sk, urgent)

              tcp_write_wakeup(sk)
```

FIGURE 7.2 TCP transmit sequence.

tcp_sendmsg readied the segments for transmission and queued them to the socket's write queue. and now we will see what happens next.

In tcp_transmit_skb, we build the TCP packet header and pass the packet on to IP.

```
int tcp_transmit_skb(struct sock *sk, struct sk_buff *skb)
{
```

The variable, inet points to the inet options structure, and tp points to the TCP options structure. It is in tcp_opt where the socket keeps most of the configuration and connection state information for TCP. Tcb points to the TCP control buffer containing most of the flags as well as the partially constructed TCP header. Th is a pointer to the TCP header. Later, it will point to the header part of the skb, and sysctl_flags is for some critical parameters configured via sysctl and setsockopt calls.

```
        const struct inet_connection_sock *icsk = inet_csk(sk);
        struct inet_sock *inet;
        struct tcp_sock *tp;
```

Chapter 7 Sending the Data from the Socket through UDP and TCP **319**

```
    struct tcp_skb_cb *tcb;
    int tcp_header_size;
    struct tcphdr *th;
    int sysctl_flags;
    int err;
    BUG_ON(!skb || !tcp_skb_pcount(skb));
    if (icsk->icsk_ca_ops->rtt_sample)
        __net_timestamp(skb);
    if (likely(clone_it)) {
        if (unlikely(skb_cloned(skb)))
            skb = pskb_copy(skb, gfp_mask);
        else
            skb = skb_clone(skb, gfp_mask);
        if (unlikely(!skb))
            return -ENOBUFS;
    }
    inet = inet_sk(sk);
    tp = tcp_sk(sk);
    tcb = TCP_SKB_CB(skb);
    tcp_header_size = tp->tcp_header_len;
#define SYSCTL_FLAG_TSTAMPS0x1
#define SYSCTL_FLAG_WSCALE0x2
#define SYSCTL_FLAG_SACK0x4
    sysctl_flags = 0;
```

Here, we check to see whether this outgoing packet is a **SYN** packet, and if so, we check for the presence of certain TCP options in the flags field of the control buffer structure. This is because the TCP header length may need to be extended to account for certain TCP options, which generally include timestamps, window scaling, and Selective Acknowledgement (SACK) [RFC 2018]

```
    if (unlikely(tcb->flags & TCPCB_FLAG_SYN)) {
        tcp_header_size = sizeof(struct tcphdr) + TCPOLEN_MSS;
        if(sysctl_tcp_timestamps) {
            tcp_header_size += TCPOLEN_TSTAMP_ALIGNED;
            sysctl_flags |= SYSCTL_FLAG_TSTAMPS;
        }
        if(sysctl_tcp_window_scaling) {
            tcp_header_size += TCPOLEN_WSCALE_ALIGNED;
            sysctl_flags |= SYSCTL_FLAG_WSCALE;
        }
        if(sysctl_tcp_sack) {
            sysctl_flags |= SYSCTL_FLAG_SACK;
            if(!(sysctl_flags & SYSCTL_FLAG_TSTAMPS))
```

```
                    tcp_header_size += TCPOLEN_SACKPERM_ALIGNED;
         }
    } else if (unlikely(tp->rx_opt.eff_sacks) {
```

The following processing is for the SACK option. If we are sending SACKs in this segment, we increment the header to account for the number of SACK blocks that are being sent along with this packet. The header length is adjusted by eight for each SACK block.

```
              tcp_header_size += (TCPOLEN_SACK_BASE_ALIGNED +
                                  (tp->eff_sacks *
                                  TCPOLEN_SACK_PERBLOCK));
    }
    if (tcp_packets_in_flight(tp) == 0)
         tcp_ca_event(sk, CA_EVENT_TX_START);
```

Now that we know the size of the TCP header, we adjust the skb to allow for sufficient space.

```
         th = (struct tcphdr *) skb_push(skb, tcp_header_size);
         skb->h.th = th;
         skb_set_owner_w(skb, sk);
```

At this point, the TCP header is built, space for the checksum field is reserved, and the header size is calculated. Some of the header fields used to build the header are in inet_opt structure; some are in the TCP control buffer; and some are in the TCP options structure.

```
              th->source      = inet->sport;
              th->dest        = inet->dport;
              th->seq         = htonl(tcb->seq);
              th->ack_seq     = htonl(tp->rcv_nxt);
              *(((__u16 *)th) + 6) = htons(((tcp_header_size >> 2) << 12) |
                                     tcb->flags);
```

The advertised window size is determined. If this packet is a **SYN** packet; otherwise, the window size is scaled by calling tcp_select_window. [RFC1323]

```
         if (unlikely(tcb->flags & TCPCB_FLAG_SYN)) {
              th->window = htons(tp->rcv_wnd);
         } else {
              th->window = htons(tcp_select_window(sk));
         }
```

If urgent mode is set, we calculate the urgent pointer and set the URG flag in the TCP header.

```
th->check = 0;
th->urg_ptr = 0;
if (unlikely(tp->urg_mode &&
            between(tp->snd_up, tcb->seq+1,
                    tcb->seq+0xFFFF))) {
    th->urg_ptr = htons(tp->snd_up-tcb->seq);
    th->urg = 1;
}
```

Here, we actually build the TCP options part of the packet header. If this is a **SYN** segment, we include the window scale option. If not, it is left out. We check to see whether we have a timestamp, window scaling, or SACK option from the sysctl_flags set earlier. We call tcp_syn_build_options to build the options with window scaling, and we call tcp_build_and_update_options is for non-**SYN** packets and do not include window scaling.

```
if (unlikely(tcb->flags & TCPCB_FLAG_SYN)) {
    tcp_syn_build_options((__u32 *)(th + 1),
                    tcp_advertise_mss(sk),
                    (sysctl_flags & SYSCTL_FLAG_TSTAMPS),
                    (sysctl_flags & SYSCTL_FLAG_SACK),
                    (sysctl_flags & SYSCTL_FLAG_WSCALE),
                    tp->rcv_wscale,
                    tcb->when,
                        tp->ts_recent);
} else {
    tcp_build_and_update_options((__u32 *)(th + 1),
                        tp, tcb->when);
```

We call the TCP_ECN_send to send explicit congestion notification. This TCP modification [RFC3168] changes the TCP header to make it slightly incompatible with the header specified by RFC 793.

```
    TCP_ECN_send(sk, tp, skb, tcp_header_size);
}
```

We calculate the checksum. We check the flags to see whether we are sending an **ACK** or sending data, and we update the delayed acknowledgment status depending on whether we are sending data or an **ACK**. See the sections on timers for information about the delayed acknowledgment timer. If we are sending data, we update the congestion window and mark the send timestamp. In addition, we increment the counter to indicate the number of TCP segments that have been sent.

```
tp icsk->icsk_af_ops->send_check(sk, skb->len, skb);
if (likely(tcb->flags & TCPCB_FLAG_ACK))
    tcp_event_ack_sent(sk, tcp_skb_pcount(skb));
if (skb->len != tcp_header_size)
    tcp_event_data_sent(tp, skb, sk);
TCP_INC_STATS(TCP_MIB_OUTSEGS);
```

Now, we call the actual transmission function to send this segment. The segment will be queued up for processing by the next stage whether the packet has an internal or an external destination.

```
err = icsk->icsk_af_ops->queue_xmit(skb, 0);
if (unlikely(err <= 0))
    return err;
tcp_enter_cwr(sk);
```

A return of a value less than zero tells the caller that the packet is dropped. We return all errors except explicit congestion notification, which doesn't indicate to the caller that the packet was dropped.

```
    return err == NET_XMIT_CN ? 0 : err;
#undef SYSCTL_FLAG_TSTAMPS
#undef SYSCTL_FLAG_WSCALE
#undef SYSCTL_FLAG_SACK
}
```

SOME KEY TCP DATA STRUCTURES

In this section we describe some important structures used in TCP. Most of the data structures are allocated on a per-socket or per-connection basis. The longest and most complicated of these structures is the TCP Options structure. This structure holds the TCP options and most of the variables used to maintain the TCP state machine and is accessed through the sock structure.

TCP Control Buffer

TCP is completely asynchronous. All socket-level writes are insulated from the actual packet transmission. It allocates socket buffers to hold the data as the application writes data into the socket. Each packet requires control information, which is passed from the `tcp_sendmsg` function to the transmission part of TCP. The socket buffer is described in Chapter 6.

The Control Block Structure, `tcp_skb_cb`

The `tcp_skb_cb` structure is defined in the file, `linux/include/net/tcp.h`.

```
struct tcp_skb_cb {
    union {
```

The fields `inet_skb_parm` and `inet6_skb_parm` hold the IP options from an incoming packet; `inet_skb_parm` is for IPv4, and `inet6_skb_parm` are the options for IPv6.

```
        struct inet_skb_parm    h4;
#if defined(CONFIG_IPV6) || defined (CONFIG_IPV6_MODULE)
        struct inet6_skb_parm   h6;
#endif
    } header;
```

The field `seq` is the sequence number for the outgoing packet, and `end_seq` is the ending sequence.

- end_seq = seq + **SYN** + **FIN** + length of the current segment.
- is used for calculating Round Trip Time (RTT).

```
    __u32       seq;
    __u32       end_seq;
    __u32       when;
```

The field, `flags` contains the TCP flags field in the TCP header. The values should match bit for bit the flags in the actual TCP header, and Table 7.3 lists the values. The last two items are for explicit congestion control and are not defined in the original TCP specification [RFC 793]. They actually are taken from the 6-bit reserved area of the TCP header.

```
    __u8        flags;
```

The `sacked` field holds the state flags for the Selective Acknowledge (SACK) and Forward Acknowledge (FACK) states. The possible states and their values are listed in Table 7.4.

```
    __u8        sacked;
```

TABLE 7.4 Sacked State Flags

Flag	Value	Purpose
TCPCB_SACKED_ACKED	1	The data in the segment pointed to by this `skb` has been acknowledged by a SACK block.
TCPCB_SACKED_RETRANS	2	The segment needs to be retransmitted.
TCPCB_LOST	4	The segment is "lost."
TCPCB_TAGBITS	7	This segment is a tagged segment.
TCPCB_EVER_RETRANS	0x80	This is a retransmitted segment for any reason.
TCPCB_RETRANS	(TCPCB_SACKED_RETRANS | TCPCB_EVER_RETRANS)	Combination of the previous three flags.
TCPCB_URG	0x20	The TCP urgent pointer is advanced.
TCPCB_AT_TAIL	(TCPCB_URG)	The TCP urgent pointer is advanced.

The next field, `urg_ptr`, is the value of the TCP header urgent pointer. The `TCPCB_FLAG_URG` must be set when this field is valid. The last field, `ack_seq`, is equivalent to the acknowledgment field in the TCP header.

```
    __u16      urg_ptr;
    __u32      ack_seq;
};
```

The `tcp_sock` and `inet_connection_sock` Structures

The sock structure, discussed in Chapter 4, contains the support necessary to maintain connection state. Linux TCP, however, implements the TCP options structure, `tcp_sock`, which is defined in the file `linux/include/linux/tcp.h` and the `inet_connection_sock` defined in file `linux/include/net/inet_connection_sock.h`. In –addition to the TCP options, they contain the send and receive sequence variables, TCP window management, and everything to manage slow start and congestion avoidance. These data structure are presented in their own section because of inherent complexity of TCP and because the structures contains field to help manage many aspects of the TCP protocol. Together, they are allocated as part of the sock structure for a SOCK_STREAM type socket. We won't cover every field in these structures but will discuss a few key fields and their implications for TCP in IPv4.

The inet_connection_sock Structure

```
struct inet_connection_sock {
```

The fist part of the inet_connection_sock is the inet_sock covered in the next section.

```
    struct inet_sock            icsk_inet;
    struct request_sock_queue   icsk_accept_queue;
    struct inet_bind_bucket     *icsk_bind_hash;
    unsigned long               icsk_timeout;
    struct timer_list           icsk_retransmit_timer;
    struct timer_list           icsk_delack_timer;
    __u32                       icsk_rto;
```

The next field, icsk_pmtu_cookie, is set to the last PMTU (Path Maximum Transmission Unit) for the connection referenced by this socket.

```
    __u32                       icsk_pmtu_cookie;
    const struct tcp_congestion_ops *icsk_ca_ops;
    const struct inet_connection_sock_af_ops *icsk_af_ops;
    unsigned int                (*icsk_sync_mss)(struct sock *sk, u32 pmtu);
```

The next field, ca_state, holds the fast retransmit machine states listed in Table 7.5.

```
    __u8                        icsk_ca_state;
```

TABLE 7.5 tcp_ca_state, Fast Retransmit States

State	Value
TCP_CA_Open	0
TCP_CA_Disorder	1
TCP_CA_CSR	2
TCP_CA_Recovery	3
TCP_CA_Loss	4

The next field, `icsk_retransmits`, contains the number of unrecovered RTOs (Retransmit Timeouts).

```
    __u8            icsk_retransmits;
    __u8            icsk_pending;
    __u8            icsk_backoff;
    __u8            icsk_syn_retries;
    __u8            icsk_probes_out;
    __u16           icsk_ext_hdr_len;
```

The `icsk_ack` structure is for controlling delayed acknowledgment. Delayed acknowledgment is implemented to increase TCP efficiency by holding back on acknowledging received data until there is return data to carry the **ACK**. This reduces the number of **ACK**s transmitted by combining the **ACK** with an outgoing data packet wherever possible. A comprehensive explanation of delayed acknowledgments is in Stevens, Section 19.3 [STEV94]. `pending` contains the quick acknowledge state, shown in Table 7.6. These values are defined in the file `linux/include/net/inet_connection_sock.h`. `quick` is the scheduled number of quick acknowledgments. If the field `pingpong` contains the value one, the normal delayed acknowledgment mode is enabled. When `pingpong` is zero, quick acknowledgment mode is enabled and **ACK**s are set as soon as possible. `blocked` indicates that sending of an **ACK** was blocked for some reason.

```
    struct {
        __u8        pending;
        __u8        quick;
        __u8        pingpong;
        __u8        blocked;
```

TABLE 7.6 TCP Acknowledge State Values, `tcp_ack_state_t`

State	Value
ICSK_ACK_SCHED	1
ICSK_ACK_TIMER	2
ICSK_ACK_PUSHED	4

The next field, `ato`, is the calculated delayed acknowledge timeout interval, and `timeout` holds the actual timeout value for the delayed acknowledgment. `lrcvtime` holds the time the last data packet was received.

Chapter 7 Sending the Data from the Socket through UDP and TCP

```
      __u32         ato;
      unsigned long timeout;
      __u32         lrcvtime;
```

`last_seg_size` is the size of the most recent incoming segment. `rcv_mss` holds the best guess of the MSS received from the peer machine.

```
      __u16         last_seg_size;
      __u16         rcv_mss;
} icsk_ack;
```

The tcp_sock Structure

The fist part of the `tcp_sock` is the `inet_connection_sock` covered in the previous section.

```
struct tcp_sock{
    struct inet_connection_sock   inet_conn;
    int       tcp_header_len;
```

The next field, `pred_flags`, is used to determine whether TCP header prediction should be done. Header prediction is used for fast path TCP reception. This chapter covers the transmit side, so see Chapter 9 for more details about how this field is used.

```
    __u32     pred_flags;
```

The following are the send and receive sequence variables [RFC 793]. These variables govern the sequence numbers exchanged between peers during data exchange through a connection. `rcv_next` is the receive next sequence variable, **RCV.NXT**, in the RFC [RFC793]. It represents the next sequence number that is expected in incoming segments.

```
    __u32    rcv_nxt;
```

Send next sequence variable is SND.NXT. It is the next sequence number to be sent.

```
    __u32    snd_nxt;
```

This is the send unacknowledged sequence variable, **SND.UNA**, the oldest unacknowledged sequence number. It should be the next byte for which we should receive an **ACK**.

```
    __u32    snd_una;
```

The next field, snd_sm1, is the last byte in the most recently transmitted small packet.

```
__u32    snd_sml;
```

rcv_tstamp is the timestamp of the last received acknowledge. It is used for maintaining keepalives when the SO_KEEPALIVE socket option is set and for calculating RTT.

```
__u32    rcv_tstamp;
```

This field, lsndtime, is the timestamp when transmitted data was last sent. This is used for restart.

```
__u32    lsndtime;
```

The ucopy structure holds the prequeue for fast copying of data from packets to application space. For more information, see Chapter 9, "Receiving the Data in the Transport Layer, UDP and TCP," about TCP pre-queue processing.

```
struct {
    struct sk_buff_head    prequeue;
    struct task_struct     *task;
    struct iovec           *iov;
    int                    memory;
    int                    len;
} ucopy;
```

snd_wl1 holds a received window update sequence number; snd_wnd is the maximum sized window that the peer is willing to receive, **SND.WND** variable [RFC 793]. In addition, max_window is the largest window received from the peer during the life of this connection.

```
__u32    snd_wl1;
__u32    snd_wnd;
__u32    max_window;
```

The fields mss_cache and xmit_size_goal, respectively, are the current MSS on the sending side and the sending side MSS target size goal for MSS negotiations.

```
    __u16    mss_cache;
....__u16    xmit_size_goal;
```

This value `window_clamp` is the maximum sized window to advertise and the next field is the current window clamp.

```
__u32    window_clamp;
__u32    rcv_ssthresh;
__u32    frto_highmark;
```

`reordering` is a packet reordering metric representing the maximum distance that a packet can be displaced in the stream.

```
__u8     reordering;
__u8     frto_counter;
__u8     nonagle;
__u8     keepalive_probes;
__u32    srtt;
__u32    mdev;
__u32    mdev_max;
__u32    rttvar;
__u32    rtt_seq;
__u32    packets_out;
__u32    left_out;
__u32    retrans_out;
```

The `tcp_options_received` Structure

Now, we break in the middle of `tcp_opt` to take a look at another data structure because the next field in `tcp_opt` structure holds the TCP options in a `tcp_options_received` structure. This structure is defined in the file `linux/include/net/tcp.h`. The y are also listed in Table 7.7. Some options are received only in **SYN** packets, and others can be found in any data packet.

```
struct tcp_options_received {
```

This value, `ts_recent_stamp`, is where we store the most recent timestamp for aging. It is used for PAWS and Round-Trip Time (RTT) calculations.

```
long     ts_recent_stamp;
__u32    ts_recent;
__u32    rcv_tsval;
__u32    rcv_tsecr;
```

TABLE 7.7 TCP Options

Option	Kind	Length	Description
TCPOPT_EOL	0	0	End of options.
TCPOPT_NOP	1	0	Padding.
TCP_OPT_MSS	2	4	Segment size negotiation.
TCPOPT_WINDOW	3	3	Window scaling.
TCPOPT_SACK_PERM	4	2	Selective acknowledgments are permitted. See RFC 2018.
TCPOPT_SACK	5	variable	Actual selective acknowledgments are included in the options.
TCPOPT_TIMESTAMP	8	10	Sender can include this option in any segment. The sender's timestamp value is echoed back in an ACK packet so sender can calculate RTT.

This flag, saw_tstamp, indicates that a timestamp option, TCPOPT_TIMESTAMP, in the most recent packet was seen and processed.

```
__u16    saw_tstamp : 1,
```

The next field, tstamp_ok, indicates that a timestamp was received in the **SYN** packet. The field, dsack is used for double acknowledgements [RFC 2883]. wscale_ok indicates that the window scale option was received in a **SYN** packet. sack_ok indicates that the TCPOPT_SACK option was received in a **SYN** packet.

```
tstamp_ok : 1,
dsack : 1,
wscale_ok : 1,
sack_ok : 4,
```

The window scale option specifies a shift count, which is the number of bits left to shift the window size. This allows the 16-bit window field in the TCP header to represent a much larger window than 65535. See Stevens, Section 24.4 for a discussion of window scaling [STEV94]. Window scaling increases TCP efficiency by decreasing the number of **ACK**s.

```
        snd_wscale : 4,
        rcv_wscale : 4;
```

The following two fields are for SACKS, and the last two fields contain the user-specified MSS in the `TCP_MAXSEG` option, and the final value, `mss_clamp` is the maximum negotiated MSS allowed.

```
    __u8    eff_sacks;
    __u8    num_sacks;
    __u16   user_mss;
    __u16   mss_clamp;
};
```

Continue with the `tcp_sock` Structure

This field was covered in the previous section.

```
    struct tcp_options_received rx_opt;
```

The following fields are used on the send side and are for slow start and congestion control [KARN91].

```
    __u32 snd_ssthresh;
    __u32 snd_cwnd;
    __u16 snd_cwnd_cnt;
    __u16 snd_cwnd_clamp;
    __u32 snd_cwnd_used;
    __u32 snd_cwnd_stamp;
```

The socket buffer queue, `out_of_order_queue`, holds received out of order segments.

```
    struct sk_buff_head out_of_order_queue;
```

This value, `rcv_wnd`, is the current receive window size, which is the **RCV.WND** variable in RFC 793. `rcv_wup`, receive window update, is the current advertised window size. `write_seq` is the send side sequence number, actually equal to the end of the data in the last send buffer, plus one byte. `pushed_seq` is the last pushed sequence number. `copied_seq` is the position of the start of received data that has not yet been read by the user process.

```
    __u32   rcv_wnd;
    __u32   rcv_wup;
```

```
__u32    write_seq;
__u32    pushed_seq;
__u32    copied_seq;
```

These fields are used for SACK and duplicate sack processing [RFC1383].

```
struct tcp_sack_block duplicate_sack[1];
struct tcp_sack_block selective_acks[4];
struct tcp_sack_block recv_sack_cache[4];
struct sk_buff* lost_skb_hint;
struct sk_buff *scoreboard_skb_hint;
struct sk_buff *retransmit_skb_hint;
struct sk_buff *forward_skb_hint;
struct sk_buff *fastpath_skb_hint;
int      fastpath_cnt_hint;
int      lost_cnt_hint;
int      retransmit_cnt_hint;
int      forward_cnt_hint;
```

advmss is the advertised MSS. and prior_ssthreash holds the slow start threshold value saved from the start of the congestion recovery phase. It is the previous value of the ssthresh. lost_out is the number of lost packets, the number of segments that were sent but not acknowledged. The next value, sacked_out, is the number of segments that were sent by this side and have arrived at the receiver but have been acknowledged with SACKs. Next, fackets_out is the number of transmitted packets that have been Forward Acknowledged (FACKed), and high_seq is set to the value of snd_nxt when congestion is detected or the loss state is entered. For more information on FACKs, see Mathis and Mahdavi's papers on forward acknowledgement [MATH96] and [MATH97].

```
__u16    advmss;
__u16    prior_ssthresh;
__u32    lost_out;
__u32    sacked_out;
__u32    fackets_out;
__u32    high_seq;
```

retrans_stamp is set to the timestamp of the most recent retransmit. It is used in the **SYN_SENT** state to retrieve the time the last **SYN** packet was sent. undo_marker indicates when tracking of retransmits have started; it is set to the snd_una variable. undo_retrans is the number of retransmits that need to be undone if possible. urg_seq is the sequence number of a received urgent pointer, and urg_data contains the number of the saved byte of Out-of-Band (OOB) data, plus the associated control flags. The value, urg_mode indicates that the TCP MSG_OOB flag was set, and snd_up is the urgent pointer to be sent.

```
__u32     retrans_stamp;
__u32     undo_marker;
int       undo_retrans;
__u32     urg_seq;
__u16     urg_data;
__u8      urg_mode;
__u8      ecn_flags;
__u32     snd_up;
__u32     total_retrans;
__u32     bytes_acked;
```

The next field, keepalive_time, is the amount of time the connection is allowed to remain idle before keepalive probes are set. It is initialized to two hours by the constant TCP_KEEPALIVE_TIME in the file linux/include/net/tcp.h. It can be changed with the TCP_KEEPIDLE socket option. Next, keepalive_intvl is the time between each transmission of a keepalive probe and is initialized to 75 seconds. It can be changed via the socket option, TCP_KEEPINTVL. Both of these TCP socket options are unique to Linux and, therefore, are not portable. Also, linger2 holds the value of another unique Linux TCP socket option, TCP_LINGER2. This value governs the lifetime of orphaned sockets in the **FIN_WAIT2** state. It overrides the default value of one minute in the TCP_FIN_TIMEOUT, same as the TCP_TIMEWAIT_LEN constant also in the file linux/include/net/tcp.h.

```
unsigned int    keepalive_time;
unsigned int    keepalive_intvl;
int             linger2;
```

This field in the TCP options structure, last_synq_overflow, is for the support of syncookies, a security feature in Linux TCP. Syncookies consists of a mechanism to protect TCP from a particular type of Denial-of-Service attack (DoS) where an attacker sends out a flood of **SYN** packets. Syncookies are enabled via the tcp_syncookies sysctl value.

```
unsigned long    last_synq_overflow;
```

Finally, the last two fields are data structures. The first one holds the estimated round trip time (RTT). The final one, rcvq_space, determines the amount of receive queue space for a TCP or connection-oriented socket.

```
        struct {
            __u32       rtt;
            __u32       seq;
            __u32       time;
        } rcv_rtt_est;
        struct {
            int         space;
            __u32       seq;
            __u32       time;
        } rcvq_space;
    };
```

TCP TIMERS

In this chapter we discussed the sending side of the transport protocols of the TCP/IP stack. As discussed earlier, TCP maintains the connection state internally; so it requires timers to keep track of events. There are four timers used by TCP to maintain the state on the transmit side in the protocol. These three timer functions could be implemented in one timer, but Linux uses three separate timers. In Chapter 5, we discussed the generic timer facility in Linux. When timers are initialized, there must be an associated function, which is called when the timer goes off. Of course, each timer is completely re-entrant, and each timer function for TCP is passed a pointer to the sock structure. The timer uses the sock to know its context, which connection it is dealing with The four timers are listed in Table 7.8. Two of the timer structures are kept in the inet_connection_sock structure and the keepalive timer is in the generic sock structure and both of these structures are discussed earlier in this chapter.

TABLE 7.8 TCP Transmit Timers

Timer Name	Timer Structure	Timer Function	Purpose
ICSK_TIME_RETRANS	icsk->retransmit_timer	tcp_write_timer	Retransmit Timer
ICSK_TIME_PROBE0	icsk->retransmit_timer	tcp_write_timer	Zero window probe timer
ICSK_TIME_DACK	isck->delack_timer	tcp_delack_timer	Delayed Acknowledgment Timer
ICSK_TIME_KEEPOPEN	sk->sk_timer	tcp_keepalive_timer	Keepalive Timer

TCP Timer Functions

The timer functions can be found in the file linux/net/ipv4/tcp_timer.c. Both the data pointer and the timer function pointer for each of the retransmit timers are maintained in the TCP-specific part of the sock structure, described in more detail earlier in this chapter. The keepalive timer is maintained directly in the sock structure. The sock structure is shown in Chapter 4. In addition, functions to manage the timers, also in the same file create, initialize, and delete all the timers. These functions are declared in the file linux/include/net/tcp.h.

The inet_csk_init_xmit_timers Function

The function inet_csk_init_xmit_timers is defined in the file linux/net/ipvr/inet_connection_sock.c and declared in the file linux/include/net/inet_connection_sock.h. It initializes all the TCP timers

```
extern void inet_csk_init_xmit_timers(struct sock *sk,
                    void (*retransmit_handler)(unsigned long),
                    void (*delack_handler)(unsigned long),
                    void (*keepalive_handler)(unsigned long));
```

The inet_csk_clear_xmit_timers Function

This function, inet_csk_clear_xmit_timers, clears all the TCP timers by resetting the counts.

```
void inet_csk_clear_xmit_timers(struct sock *sk);
```

Functions to Manage Individual TCP Timers

Linux TCP provides two functions to manage the individual retransmit, zero probe, and delayed acknowledgment timers.

The inet_csk_clear_xmit_timer Function

The first function, tcp_clear_xmit_timer, deletes the timer specified by the argument what, which specifies one of the timers from Table 7.8.

```
static inline void inet_sk_clear_xmit_timer(struct sock *sk, int what);
```

The inet_csk_reset_xmit_timer Function

The second function, tcp_reset_xmit_timer, resets the timer to expire at the time specified by the argument when.

```
static inline void inet_csk_reset_xmit_timer(
                                struct sock *sk,
                                const int what,
                                unsigned long when,
                                const unsigned long max_when)
```

The Keepalive Timer Functions

In addition, also in the same file, there are two separate functions to delete and reset the keepalive timers: `tcp_delete_keepalive_timer` and `tcp_reset_keepalive_timer`.

```
extern void inet_csk_delete_keepalive_timer(struct sock *sk);
extern void inet_csk_reset_keepalive_timer(struct sock *sk,
                                unsigned long timeout);
```

TCP Write Timer

The TCP write timer serves two send-side timer purposes. The first purpose is the retransmission timer, which is set to the maximum time to wait for an acknowledgment after sending data. The other purpose is the window probe timer. Window probes are periodically sent from the send side of the connection once a zero window size is received from the peer. The probes are sent periodically to see whether the window size has been increased, and the window probe timer is set to the maximum time to wait for a response to the window probe. The retransmission and zero window conditions do not occur simultaneously; therefore, both functions can be implemented with the same timer. The retransmission timer is set after sending any segment containing data, but the window probe timer is set after receiving an acknowledgment from the receiver with a window size of zero. Stevens devotes considerable time to the explanations of these two timers in two chapters. Chapter 21, "TCP Timeout and Retransmission" discusses the retransmission timer in detail, and Chapter 22, "TCP Persist Timer" discusses the window probe timer [STEV94].

The `tcp_write_timer` Function

When the timer expires, the function `tcp_write_timer` defined in the file `linux/net/ipv4/tcp_timer.c` is executed with the argument, `data`, which points to the socket containing the newly expired timer.

```
static void tcp_write_timer(unsigned long data)
{
```

The variable, `sk` is set to the `sock` structure pointed to by `data`, and `icsk` is set to the `inet` connection-oriented sock structure from within the `sock` structure.

Chapter 7 Sending the Data from the Socket through UDP and TCP

```
struct sock *sk = (struct sock*)data;
struct inet_connection_sock *icsk = inet_csk(sk);
int event;
```

For safety, the socket is locked. See Chapter 4 for details about the socket locking. If the socket is locked, we want to try again later; so we set the timer value to 20 seconds and return.

```
bh_lock_sock(sk);
if (sock_owned_by_user(sk)) {
    sk_reset_timer(sk, &icsk->icsk_retransmit_timer,
                jiffies + (HZ / 20));
    goto out_unlock;
}
```

The socket state sk->sk_state and the quick acknowledgment state icsk->icsk_pending are checked to see whether the socket is closed and there are no outstanding segments that have not yet been acknowledged.

```
if (sk->state == TCP_CLOSE || !tp->pending)
    goto out;
```

If the timeout value is still in the future, the retransmit timer is reset to the value in the timeout field in the options structure. A zero return from mod_timer indicates that the timer was still pending. If the timer was still pending, the socket reference count is incremented and the function returns.

```
if (time_after(icsk->icsk_timeout, jiffies)) > 0) {
    sk_reset_timer(sk, &icsk->icsk_retransmit_timer,
                icsk->icsk_timeout);
    goto out;
}
```

As discussed earlier, the write timer serves two purposes. It is used as the retransmit timer, TCP_TIME_RETRANS, or the window probe timer, TCP_TIME_PROBE0. We determine which role we are performing by looking at the icsk->icsk_pending field. If the current timeout is a retransmission timer expiring, we call the function tcp_retransmit_timer, but if the current timeout is a window prove timer expiring, we call tcp_probe_timer. These timer functions are discussed in the next two sections.

```
event = icsk->icsk_pending;
icsk->icsk_pending = 0;
switch (event) {
```

```
            case TCP_TIME_RETRANS:
                tcp_retransmit_timer(sk);
                break;
            case TCP_TIME_PROBE0:
                tcp_probe_timer(sk);
                break;
        }
        TCP_CHECK_TIMER(sk);
out:
    sk_stream_mem_reclaim (sk);
out_unlock:
    bh_unlock_sock(sk);
    sock_put(sk);
}
```

The `tcp_retransmit_timer` Function

The `tcp_retransmit_timer` function is called when the retransmit timer expires. The timer is used to indicate that an expected acknowledgment was not received. The function is invoked from the general TCP write timer function, `tcp_write_timer`.

```
static void tcp_retransmit_timer(struct sock *sk)
{
    struct tcp_sock *tp = tcp_sk(sk);
    struct inet_connection_sock *icsk = inet_csk(sk);
    if (tp->packets_out == 0)
        goto out;
    BUG_TRAP(!skb_queue_empty(&sk->sk_write_queue));
```

First, we check to see whether the connection should be timed out or the sender has reduced the window size to zero with the socket still in the **ESTABLISHED** state. If a zero window has been received and the timestamp in the received packet indicates that the received packet is older than the maximum retransmit time, the next time the write timer is called it will become a zero window probe timer. The Congestion Avoidance (CA) processing state or loss state is entered by calling `tcp_enter_loss`.

```
        if (!tp->snd_wnd && ! sock_flag(sk, SOCK_DEAD) &&
            !((1<<sk->sk_state)&(TCPF_SYN_SENT|TCPF_SYN_RECV))) {
#ifdef TCP_DEBUG
            if (net_ratelimit()) {
                struct inet_opt *inet = inet_sk(sk);
                printk(KERN_DEBUG "TCP: Treason uncloaked!
```

```
                    Peer %u.%u.%u.%u:%u/%u shrinks window %u:%u. Repaired.\n",
                    NIPQUAD(inet->daddr), htons(inet->dport),
                    inet->num, tp->snd_una, tp->snd_nxt);
        }
#endif
```

If the received timestamp has aged more than two minutes, we indicate a write error, time out the socket, and drop the socket and the connection.

```
        if (tcp_time_stamp - tp->rcv_tstamp > TCP_RTO_MAX) {
            tcp_write_err(sk);
            goto out;
        }
```

The second parameter, now, of tcp_enter_loss is set to zero indicating that the loss state is being entered from a retransmit timeout. This part of congestion avoidance is discussed in more detail in Chapter 9. Next, we call tcp_retransmit_timer to try to retransmit the skb, which is at the head of the write queue by calling tcp_retransmit_skb. At this point, the connection is in a dubious state if the peer hasn't disappeared altogether, so __sk_dst_reset is called to reset the destination cache. Refer to Chapter 5 for information about the destination cache.

```
        tcp_enter_loss(sk, 0);
        tcp_retransmit_skb(sk, skb_peek(&sk->sk_write_queue));
        __sk_dst_reset(sk);
        goto out_reset_timer;
    }
```

Next, we call tcp_write_timeout to see whether there has been a sufficient number of retries and to complete the processing for the last retry attempt.

```
    if (tcp_write_timeout(sk))
        goto out;
```

In the following section of code, we increment the TCP statistics in the /proc filesystem. We check the congestion avoidance state, icsk_ca_state, field in the TCP option structure to see what sort of failure triggered the retransmit timeout. For more information about how to access TCP/IP statistics in /proc, refer to Chapter 5.

```
        if (icsk->retransmits == 0) {
            if (icsk->icsk_ca_state == TCP_CA_Disorder ||
                icsk -> icsk_ca_state == TCP_CA_Recovery) {
```

```
            if (icsk -> icsk_sack_ok) {
                if (icsk -> icsk_ca_state == TCP_CA_Recovery)
                    NET_INC_STATS_BH(LINUX_MIB_TCPSACKRECOVERYFAIL);
                else
                    NET_INC_STATS_BH(LINUX_MIB_TCPSACKFAILURES);
            } else {
                if (icsk -> icsk_ca_state == TCP_CA_Recovery)
                    NET_INC_STATS_BH(LINUX_MIB_TCPRENORECOVERYFAIL);
                else
                    NET_INC_STATS_BH(LINUX_MIB_TCPRENOFAILURES);
            }
        } else if (icsk -> icsk_ca_state == TCP_CA_Loss) {
            NET_INC_STATS_BH(LINUX_MIB_TCPLOSSFAILURES);
        } else {
            NET_INC_STATS_BH(LINUX_MIB_TCPTIMEOUTS);
        }
    }
```

Now, the loss state is entered, congestion avoidance processing is initiated, and a retransmit is attempted.

```
    if (tcp_use_frto(sk)) {
        tcp_enter_frto(sk);
    } else {
        tcp_enter_loss(sk, 0);
    }
    if (tcp_retransmit_skb(sk, skb_peek(&sk->sk_write_queue)) > 0) {
```

If tcp_retransmit_skb returned a value greater than zero, it is because the low-level IP transmit function failed due to a local transmission problem such as a busy network interface driver. The retransmit timer must be reset to try again later.

```
        if (!tp->retransmits)
            tp->retransmits=1;
        tcp_reset_xmit_timer(sk, TCP_TIME_RETRANS, min(tp->rto,
                                TCP_RESOURCE_PROBE_INTERVAL));
        goto out;
    }
```

The retransmit timeout, rto, in the TCP options structure is increased each time a retransmit occurs; it is actually doubled each time. The maximum value of the retransmit timeout is TCP_RTO_MAX, or 120 seconds, which is also the maximum value for RTT. The doubling of the retransmit timer is suggested by Van Jacobson

Chapter 7 Sending the Data from the Socket through UDP and TCP

in his paper on congestion avoidance [JACOB88]. The RTT estimate is not changed by the timeout. If the number of retransmits is greater than TCP_RETR1, which is 3, the destination cache is aged out.

```
        icsk->icsk_backoff++;
        icsk-> icsk_retransmits++;
out_reset_timer:
        icsk->icsk_rto = min(icsk->icsk_rto << 1, TCP_RTO_MAX);
        tcp_reset_xmit_timer(sk, TCP_TIME_RETRANS, tp->rto);
        if (icsk->icsk_retransmits > sysctl_tcp_retries1)
            __sk_dst_reset(sk);
out:;
}
```

The TCP Window Probe Timer

The window probe timer, tcp_probe_timer, also in the file linux/net/ipv4/tcp_timer.c, is called from the generic TCP write-side timer function, tcp_write_timer. As shown earlier, when the pending event is a window probe timeout, tcp_probe_timer is called. The zero window timer is set when this side of the connection sends out a zero window probe in response to a zero window advertisement from the peer. We arrive at this function because the timer expired before a response was received to the zero window probe.

The tcp_probe_timer Function

In this function, we set tp to point to the TCP options structure for the sock structure sk. First, tcp_probe_timer sees whether there is a valid zero window event, which can occur only if the last packet sent was a zero window probe. The packet_out and the sk_send_head are checked for outstanding unacknowledged data or data segments in the process of being sent. If either of these conditions exists, we return because this can't be a valid zero window probe event.

```
static void tcp_probe_timer(struct sock *sk)
{
    struct inet_connection_sock *icsk = inet_csk(sk);
    struct tcp_opt *tp = tcp_sk(sk);
    int max_probes;
    if (tp->packets_out || !sk-sk_send_head) {
        icsk->icsk_probes_out = 0;
        return;
    }
```

We set the maximum number of probes out, `max_probes`, to the value `TCP_RETR2`, which is defined as the number 15 in the file `linux/include/net/tcp.h`. We do a check to see whether the socket is orphaned. Linux does not kill off the connection merely because a zero window size has been advertised for a long time, so we want to see whether we need to keep the connection alive. Therefore, we check to see that the next retransmission timeout value, `rto`, will still be less than the maximum RTO, `TCP_RTO_MAX`. `max_probes` is recalculated for the orphaned socket. A call to `tcp_out_of_resources` checks to make sure that the orphaned socket does not consume too much memory, as it should not be kept alive forever. If the socket is to be killed off, `tcp_probe_timer` returns here.

```
max_probes = sysctl_tcp_retries2;
if (sock_flag(sk, SOCK_DEAD)) {
    int alive = ((icsk->icsk_rto << icsk->icsk_backoff)
                    < TCP_RTO_MAX);
    max_probes = tcp_orphan_retries(sk, alive);
    if (tcp_out_of_resources(sk, alive || icsk->icsk_probes_out
    <= max_probes))
        return;
}
```

Next, we check the number of outstanding zero window probes to see whether it has exceeded the maximum number of probes in `max_probes`, which was a value calculated previously. If so, an error condition is indicated and the function returns. Another window probe is sent only if all the previous checks have passed.

```
    if (icsk->icsk_probes_out > max_probes) {
        tcp_write_err(sk);
    } else {
        tcp_send_probe0(sk);
    }
}
```

Delayed Acknowledgment Timer

The purpose of delayed acknowledgment is to minimize the number of separate ACKs that are sent. The receiver does not send an **ACK** as soon as it can. Instead, it holds on to the **ACK** in the hopes of piggybacking the **ACK** on an outgoing data packet. The delayed acknowledgment timer is set to the amount of time to hold the **ACK** waiting for outgoing data to be ready.

The `tcp_delack_timer` Function

The function, `tcp_delack_timer`, defined in file `linux/net/ipv4/tcp_timer.c` is called when the delayed acknowledgment timer expires, indicating that we have now given up finding an outgoing packet to carry our **ACK**. The timer value is maintained between a minimum value, `TCP_DELACK_MIN`, defined as 1/25 second, and a maximum value, `TCP_DELACK_MAX`, defined as 1/5 second.

As in the other TCP timer functions, `tcp_delack_timer` is called with a pointer to the sock structure for the current open socket.

```
static void tcp_delack_timer(unsigned long data)
{
    struct sock *sk = (struct sock*)data;
    struct tcp_sock *tp = tcp_sk(sk);
    struct inet_connection_sock *icsk = inet_csk(sk);
    bh_lock_sock(sk);
```

If the socket is locked, the timer is set ahead and an attempt is made later.

```
    if (sock_owned_by_user(sk)) {
icsk->icsk_ack.blocked = 1;
NET_INC_STATS_BH(LINUX_MIB_DELAYEDACKLOCKED);
        sk_reset_timer(sk, &icsk->icsk_delack_timer,
                   jiffies + TCP_DELACK_MIN);
        goto out_unlock;
    }
```

By calling `sk_stream_mem_reclaim`, we can account for reclaiming memory from any TCP pages allocated in queues. If the socket is in the **TCP_CLOSE** state and there is no pending acknowledge event, we exit the timer without sending an **ACK**. Next, we check to see whether we got here somehow, even though the timer has not yet expired, in which case we exit.

```
sk_stream_mem_reclaim (sk);
    if (sk->state == TCP_CLOSE || !(icsk->icsk_ack.pending &
                        ICSK_ACK_TIMER))
        goto out;
    if (time_after(icsk->icsk_ack.timeout, jiffies)) {
        sk_reset_timer(sk, &icsk->icsk_delack_timer,
                   icsk->icsk_ack.timeout)
        goto out;
    }
```

Since the delayed **ACK** timer has fired, the pending timer event can be removed from the acknowledgment structure to indicate we are done processing the event.

```
tp->ack.pending &= ~TCP_ACK_TIMER;
```

The field prequeue points to incoming packets that have not been processed yet. Since this timer went off before we could acknowledge these packets, they are put back on the backlog queue for later processing, and failure statistics are incremented for each of these packets.

```
if (!skb_queue_empty(&tp->ucopy.prequeue)) {
    struct sk_buff *skb;
    NET_ADD_STATS_BH(LINUX_MIB_TCPSCHEDULERFAILED);
    while ((skb = __skb_dequeue(&tp->ucopy.prequeue)) != NULL)
        sk->sk_backlog_rcv(sk, skb);
    tp->ucopy.memory = 0;
}
```

Here, we check to see whether there is a scheduled **ACK**.

```
if (inet_csk_ack_scheduled(sk)) {
```

If we have a scheduled **ACK**, it means that the timer expired before the delayed **ACK** could be sent out. We check the current acknowledgment mode in the pingpong field of the icsk_ack structure. If it is zero, we must be in quick acknowledgment mode, so we inflate the value of the Acknowledgment Timeout (ATO) in ato. This increases the amount of time until the next **ACK** timeout expires. However, if we are in delayed acknowledgment mode, we decrease the ATO to the minimum amount, TCP_ATO_MIN. In addition, we switch to fast acknowledgment mode by turning off delayed acknowledgment in pingpong. This will force the next **ACK** to go out as soon as TCP_ATO_MIN time elapses without waiting for an outgoing data segment to carry the **ACK**.

```
if (!icsk->isck_ack.pingpong) {
    icsk->icsk_ack.ato = min(icsk->icsk_ack.ato << 1,
                             icsk->icsk_rto);
} else {
    icsk->icsk_ack.pingpong = 0;
    icsk->icsk_ack.ato = TCP_ATO_MIN;
}
```

Finally, we send the **ACK** and increase the delayed **ACK** counter. Next, we clean up and exit the timer.

```
        tcp_send_ack(sk);
        NET_INC_STATS_BH(LINUX_MIB_DELAYEDACKS);
    }
    TCP_CHECK_TIMER(sk);
out:
    if (tcp_memory_pressure)
        sk_stream_mem_reclaim (sk);
out_unlock:
    bh_unlock_sock(sk);
    sock_put(sk);
}
```

Keepalive Timer

This timer is actually used for two separate purposes. In addition to providing the keepalive timeout function, it is also used as a **SYN** acknowledge timer by a socket in a listen state. The keepalive timer function can serve these two separate purposes because keepalives are only sent for a connection that has already been established, but the **SYN** acknowledge timer is only active for connections in the LISTEN state.

TCP normally does not perform any keepalive function; keepalive polling is not part of the original TCP specification. The keepalive is added outside the TCP specification for the use of some TCP application layer servers for protocols that don't do any connection polling themselves. For example, the telnet daemon sets the keepalive mode. Keepalive is enabled via the socket option SO_KEEPALIVE, and the timeout value associated with the timer is maintained in the keepopen field of the sock structure. It can also be set by using the system control value, sysctl_tcp_keepalive_time. The default value for the keepalive time is in the constant, TCP_KEEPALIVE_INTVL, defined in linux/include/net/tcp.h to 75 seconds.

The tcp_keepalive_timer Function

The keepalive timer function, tcp_keepalive_timer in the file linux/net/ipv4/tcp_timer.c, is called when the keepalive timeout value expires. As with the other TCP timer functions discussed in this section, a pointer to the sock structure is passed in via the parameter data, and tp is set to point to the tcp_sock structure in the sock.

```
static void tcp_keepalive_timer (unsigned long data)
```

```
{
    struct sock *sk = (struct sock *) data;
    struct inet_connection_sock *icsk = inet_csk(sk);
    struct tcp_opt *tp = tcp_sk(sk);
    __u32 elapsed;
```

If the socket is currently in use, there is no need for keepalives; so we reset the timer value to 20 seconds and leave.

```
bh_lock_sock(sk);
if (sock_owned_by_user(sk)) {
    inet_csk_reset_keepalive_timer (sk, HZ/20);
    goto out;
}
```

Next, we must determine the state of the connection to see whether the socket is in the **LISTEN, FIN-WAIT2**, or TCP_CLOSE connection state. This timer function is also used to maintain the **SYN**s and **SYN_ACK**s when a socket is in the **LISTEN** state. If the connection is in the **LISTEN** state, tcp_synack_timer is called to process **SYN** acknowledgments or the lack of them as the case may be.

```
if (sk->state == TCP_LISTEN) {
    tcp_synack_timer(sk);
    goto out;
}
```

If the socket is in the **FIN-WAIT2** state and the keepalive option is set, we want to do an abortive release of the connection when the timer expires instead of letting the connection terminate in an orderly fashion. A positive value in the linger2 field tells us that the TCP_LINGER2 socket option was set for this socket, so we want to maintain the connection, which is in **FIN-WAIT2** in an undead state before terminating the connection. If linger2 is less than zero, we shut down the connection immediately. Otherwise, the connection is aborted by calling tcp_send_active_reset, which sends the peer a **RST** segment.

```
if (sk->sk_state == TCP_FIN_WAIT2 && sock_flag(sk, SOCK_DEAD)) {
    if (tp->linger2 >= 0) {
        int tmo = tcp_fin_time(tp) - TCP_TIMEWAIT_LEN;
        if (tmo > 0) {
            tcp_time_wait(sk, TCP_FIN_WAIT2, tmo);
```

```
                goto out;
        }
    }
    tcp_send_active_reset(sk, GFP_ATOMIC);
    goto death;
}
```

Next, we see whether the connection state is in the **CLOSED** state and the keepalive mode is not set (keepopen field). If not, we get the value of the keepalive timer.

```
if (!sock_flag(sk, SOCK_KEEPOPEN) || sk->sk_state == TCP_CLOSE)
    goto out;
elapsed = keepalive_time_when(tp);
```

We check to see whether the connection is actually alive and sending data. If it is, we just reset the keepalive timer without sending out the keepalive probe.

```
if (tp->packets_out || sk->sk_send_head)
    goto resched;
```

We are ready to send the keepalive as long as the elapsed time since the last probe is greater than the timeout value. The probes_out field is updated, and the probe is sent by calling tcp_write_wakeup, which will wake up the socket and send the queued keepalive probe.

```
elapsed = tcp_time_stamp - tp->rcv_tstamp;
if (elapsed >= keepalive_time_when(tp)) {
    if ((!tp->keepalive_probes && icsk->icsk_probes_out >=
            sysctl_tcp_keepalive_probes) ||
        (tp->keepalive_probes && icsk->icsk_probes_out >=
            tp->keepalive_probes)) {
        tcp_send_active_reset(sk, GFP_ATOMIC);
        tcp_write_err(sk);
        goto out;
    }
```

If tcp_write_wakeup sent the probe out successfully, the probes_out counter is incremented, and the configured keepalive timer value is reset to the configured value.

```
            if (tcp_write_wakeup(sk) <= 0) {
                icsk->icsk_probes_out++;
                elapsed = keepalive_intvl_when(tp);
            } else {
```

If the probe was not sent, the keepalive timer value is reset to 1/2 second.

```
                elapsed = TCP_RESOURCE_PROBE_INTERVAL;
            }
        } else {
            elapsed = keepalive_time_when(tp) - elapsed;
        }
        TCP_CHECK_TIMER(sk);
        sk_stream_mem_reclaim (sk);
```

This is where the timer is reset to get ready for sending the next keepalive probe.

```
resched:
        inet_sk_reset_keepalive_timer (sk, elapsed);
        goto out;
death:
        tcp_done(sk);
out:
        bh_unlock_sock(sk);
        sock_put(sk);
}
```

SUMMARY

Generally, in this book, to see how things work, we have taken the approach of following the data as it is processed through the TCP/IP stack. This chapter was no exception, so we began following the data by looking at the output side of UDP and TCP. We covered each protocol's send function as it receives data from the socket layer for transmission. Of course, this is much simpler in UDP than in TCP. For TCP, we showed the state machine from the viewpoint of the sender and looked at the basic TCP data structures used to keep track of connections in conjunction with the open socket. Finally, we looked at the four TCP timers used to maintain the connection state. Later, in Chapter 9, we look at the receive side in TCP and see what happens when streaming data is received in the peer machine.

8. The Network Layer, IP

In This Chapter

- A Few Words
- Introduction
- Routing Theory
- IPv4 Routing, Routing Cache, and the Routing Policy Database
- IP Protocol Initialization
- The Route Cache
- The RPDB, the FIB, and the FIB Rules
- Routing Input Packets
- Routing Output Packets
- Internet Peers and the IP Header ID Field
- The Address Resolution Protocol
- The Internet Control Message Protocol (ICMP)
- Sending ICMP Packets
- Multicast and IGMP
- Sending Packets from IP
- Receiving Packets in IP

A FEW WORDS

According to the OSI layered model, it is the responsibility of the network layer to do packet addressing and routing, and IP is the network layer in the TCP/IP protocol suite. In Linux, IP does many things. In the Linux implementation of TCP/IP, it is responsible for maintaining the routing tables, called the Routing Policy Database (RPDB.) When a packet is received, IP must decide whether to route a packet so it's transmitted out another interface or whether to deliver locally to one of the transport layer protocols, generally UDP or TCP. When a packet to be transmitted is received by IP from a transport layer protocol, it must determine whether there is a route to the packet's destination and select the outgoing interface. Applying the MAC layer header is the responsibility of the network interface driver. Without knowing the details about how the packet is framed, IP provides the outgoing interface with a pointer to the packet's cached destination address.

The IP layer implements fragmentation and re-assembly for packets that are too large for the physical limitations of the interface hardware. Another thing IP does is maintain the Time-To-Live (TTL) to make sure that packets don't get endlessly routed in the Internet. In addition to all the things mentioned previously, the Internet Control Message Protocol (ICMP) must be included in TCP/IP, as this is an integral part of the protocol suite. In addition to making routing decisions for unicast packets, IP can route multicast packets if multicast routing is configured. Therefore, both ICMP and IGMP are intrinsically linked with IP and can be thought of as part of the network layer adding to the complexity. All these things are indeed a heavy burden, and in this chapter we try to reduce to complexity to a digestible portion.

INTRODUCTION

In this chapter, we introduce a little bit of routing theory and then discuss the Linux IP routing mechanism in much more detail. In addition, we discuss other features of IP such as packet fragmentation. We also discuss ICMP, ARP, and IGMP and how these protocols interact with Linux IP. Generally, we explain things the same way we do elsewhere in the book. First, we follow the packets as they are transmitted from the transport layer protocols, TCP and UDP, through IP. Next, we follow the packets as they are received by IP from the network interface drivers and passed up to the transport layer protocols. Along the way, we look at how the packet routing is done by looking at the RPDB, which holds the routing policy information for Linux, and explain how the RPDB and the route cache interact. We show how IP input and output functions do RPDB lookups and how they access the routes in the cache to implement the routing decisions.

ROUTING THEORY

The essence of routing is deciding to whom to forward a packet. At the simplest level, a machine doing IP routing must determine the next hop for an output packet. It makes a decision based on the packet's destination address. If the sending machine knows that it can reach the destination through a LAN connection, this is a fairly simple matter of mapping the IP destination address to the hardware destination address. If the destination is not directly reachable, IP sends the packet to a gateway machine. This is called *routing* or *packet forwarding*, and the information that is the basis of each packet forwarding decision is stored in the routing table. However, in the modern world of the Internet, things are quite a bit more complicated. Routing decisions can be made based on destination IP address alone, or the decision can also be made on other fields in the IP header such as the source IP address and the IP ToS field. Moreover, routing decisions can use other factors, such as the output networking interface. In addition, the routing can be used with Network Address Translation (NAT) to actually change the destination addresses of the packet. The picture can be complicated with the addition of multicast routing and directed broadcast. Output packets may have multiple destinations, or they could be forwarded to a multicast address or a broadcast address effectively being duplicated and transmitted out one or more network interfaces. Another complication is that routes can be looked up based on traffic-shaping values, and the lookup result used to select a particular queuing discipline for transmission at the queuing layer.

To support the real-world complexity of a configurable router, Linux provides more than a simple routing table and cache. It can be configured with multiple routing tables and a database of rules used to select the routing table for a particular route lookup. Setting up Linux routing configuration is done with application utilities that talk to the kernel through netlink sockets. We cover some of how netlink sockets work from the viewpoint of protocol module implementers. In this book, we concentrate on internal implementation rather than theory or network administration. However, a number of good references provide theoretical background on routing or practical information on how to configure Linux-based routers using the application utilities. One of these is *Policy Routing Using Linux*, by Mathew G. Marsh [MARSH01].

IPV4 ROUTING, ROUTING CACHE, AND THE ROUTING POLICY DATABASE

The Linux IP implementation maintains a routing table that is independent of the address format in IPv4 and IPv6 or other network layer protocols. This routing information is contained in the RPDB. Two major components of the RPDB are the Forwarding Information Base (FIB) and the FIB rules. The FIB stores the routing information and the FIB rules are used to select a particular routing table when multiple tables are configured into the kernel. Linux has a route cache to help it make fast forwarding decisions using cached known routes. This helps the system performance when there is high packet volume and many simultaneous open sockets. The route cache itself is derived from the generic destination cache so it is able to make use of two other caches, the neighbor cache and the hardware header cache. The fundamental infrastructure for implementing the three caches is discussed in Chapter 5, "The Linux TCP/IP Stack." In this section, we will show how the routing cache is used in conjunction with the RPDB to make routing decisions. We will follow this with discussion on the initialization of the IP protocol, including ARP, ICMP, and IGMP initialization.

The RPDB supports both *static routing* and *dynamic routing*. From our internal point of view, there really isn't a difference because either type of routing information is added by external application programs. Static routing is where the RPDB is updated through application configuration programs such as iproute2 [HUBHOW02]. This program could be used either with host systems or gateway machines acting as routers. Dynamic routing adds external routing protocols such as OSPF [RFC 1583] and BGP [RFC 1771] that update the RPDB dynamically with information exchanged with other routers.

Among other things, the IP protocol is responsible for IP forwarding, also known as *packet routing*. For each incoming packet, IP must decide whether the packet is supposed to be consumed locally or sent out one of several network interfaces. In addition, for each outgoing packet, IP must decide through which network interface it should send the packet. Moreover, IP must provide enough information about the next destination of the outgoing packet so lower-layer protocols can construct the packet's link layer header. This is called the *next hop* or *gateway address*. The IP protocol and other Layer 3 protocols store the information used for this decision-making process in a dynamic data structure called a *routing table* or *routing cache*. The routing table implementation must provide the following capabilities:

- The routing table must accept and provide information from an external routing protocol.
- It must provide fast search capability on multiple fields.
- Both dynamic routes and static routes must be maintained.
- A timer is necessary to age out routes when no longer needed.
- A use count must be maintained for routes.
- Network and host routes must be differentiated.
- Direct and indirect routes must be differentiated.
- The routing table must support multiple network interfaces.
- Next-hop or gateway addresses must be kept in the routing table.

The routing table implementation in Linux has two components, a route cache for quick retrieval of temporary routes and a more permanent facility called the RPDB, which is used for lookup when a route can't be found in the cache. Another interesting feature of Linux is that the route cache is based on the generic destination cache. This is implemented in such a way that all packet forwarding decisions are symmetrical. Both output and input packets are routed based on destination cache entries. This implementation has several advantages. One is that routing of input packets to local addresses, loopback addresses, can be handled by lookups in the routing table. After these local routes are in cache, fast internal forwarding decisions can be made. This way, internal messages such as netlink messages can be internally routed using the same mechanisms for routing packets sent to external destinations.

When the IP protocol needs to find the destination for either an outgoing or an incoming packet, it first checks the routing cache. If it can't find a route, it searches the FIB, which is where the routes in the RPDB are stored. The route cache is derived from the generic destination cache facility discussed in Chapter 6. The destination cache has routes in current use and routes that are stale but haven't aged out yet. In most practical host systems, these cached routes may be used to transmit and receive packets through open sockets. The FIB is the basic internal storage and lookup facility for the routing table. It used both for internal routing of packets intended for local consumption and routing of outgoing packets. The FIB also provides a way for applications outside the kernel to retrieve routes from the Linux kernel through routing sockets.

IP PROTOCOL INITIALIZATION

IP protocol initialization begins with the AF_INET family initialization discussed in Chapter 5. This initialization is done by the function inet_init as part of its initialization of TCP, UDP, TCP slab cache, and other items. One of the steps performed by inet_init is to call ip_init to perform the initialization steps specific to the IP protocol.

The ip_init Function

This function is the first step in IP protocol initialization and it is found in the file linux/net/ipv4/ip_output.c.

```
void __init ip_init(void)
{
```

We call ip_rt_init to initialize the routing tables and the FIB.

```
    ip_rt_init();
```

Inet_initpeers initializes the Internet peer structure, inet_peer, which hold long-lasting information about IPv4 destination addresses for other machines. Internet peers generate a unique number for the ID field of the IP packet for outgoing packets. Later in this chapter, we will learn more information about the ID field and how it is used with IP fragmentation. We call `igmp_mc_proc_init` to create an entry in the */proc* filesystem for information about IGMP and multicast routing if multicast is configured. In a later section, we provide more information about multicast routing.

```
    inet_initpeers();
#if defined(CONFIG_IP_MULTICAST) && defined(CONFIG_PROC_FS)
    igmp_mc_proc_init();
#endif}
}
```

THE ROUTE CACHE

When a route is determined, the route entry is placed in the route cache for quick and easy access. This means that packets sent via the same route can be instantly routed after the route is known and placed in cache. We will show how the routing cache is searched for resolved routes before the FIB is checked.

A packet may have a destination within the local machine; its final destination may be at a locally reachable host; or it may be sent to a next-hop machine. Therefore, the route and destination caches are designed so the packet destination is transparent to the actual IP sending processes. The destination cache entry is interchangeable with a routing cache entry. Recall in Chapter 5, we discussed how the destination cache is used to find the link layer header by going through the dst field of the socket buffer. In addition to pointing to the destination cache, dst can also point to the routing table entry. This provides IP with an efficient way to check the destination of an outgoing packet without having to look up the route for the packet or explicitly checking if the destination address has been resolved to a hardware address.

Route Cache Data Structures

The routing cache can be thought of as a frontend to the FIB. It is optimized to provide fast path routing for open sockets with known destinations. The routing cache implementation is derived from the generic destination cache facility, discussed in Chapter 5. It consists of a hash table, each containing routing table entries and is designed for fast search with a simple key. Multiple hits at the same hash table location are known as *collisions*. The hash table implementation allows collisions because each hash table location can hold multiple routes.

rt_hash_table and the rt_hash_bucket Structure

The routing cache in IP is a single array of hash buckets, called the `rt_hash_table`, defined in the file `linux/net/ipv4/route.c`. Each location in the array contains a pointer to a chain of routing table entries and a read-write lock, `lock`, so that each slot in the array can contain multiple routes. Each route that matches a table location is placed on a link list pointed to by `chain`.

```
struct rt_hash_bucket {
    struct rtable *chain;
}
static struct rt_hash_bucket   *rt_hash_table;
static unsigned                 rt_hash_mask;
static int                      rt_hash_log;
static unsigned int             rt_hash_rnd;
```

The Routing Table, `rtable` Structure

The routing table, `rtable`, defined in the file `linux/include/net/route.h`, is the fundamental data structure that holds each route entry in the route cache. Like many data structures in the Linux implementation of IPv4, it is essentially object oriented. The routing cache is derived from the generic destination cache facility. For example, the socket buffer structure, `sk_buff`, contains a pointer to the destination cache entry for an outgoing packet. This entry, `dst`, can contain a pointer to the routing cache entry for the packet. Therefore, the `rtable` structure is defined in such a way that the first few fields are identical to the fields of the destination cache, `dst_entry`.

```
struct rtable
{
```

We use a union so the pointer to the next `rtable` instance can be accessed as either a pointer to a destination cache entry through `dst` or a routing table entry pointer through `rt_next`.

```
union
{
    struct dst_entry    dst;
    struct rtable       *rt_next;
} u;
```

The next entry, `idev` contains a pointer to the network interface driver for this route and related interface information. Following, `rt_flags` contains the routing table flags, which are also used by the application interface to the routing table. These are defined in Table 8.2. Because there are multiple routes in a single hash bucket, the routes can clash. When garbage collection is done on the route cache, routes of lower value are cleaned out more aggressively when they clash with routes of higher value. The value of the routes is determined by the routing control flags.

```
struct in_device    *idev;
unsigned            rt_flags;
```

Next, rt_type is the type of this route. For example, it specifies whether the route is unicast, multicast, or a local route. The values for rt_type are in the file linux/include/linux/rtnetlink.h and are shown in Table 8.1.

```
unsigned            rt_type;
```

TABLE 8.1 Route Types

Route Type	Value	Explanation
RTN_UNSPEC	0	Route is unspecified. This is a gateway or direct route.
RTN_UNICAST	0	This route is a gateway or direct route.
RTN_LOCAL	1	On input, accept packets locally.
RTN_BROADCAST	2	On input, accept packets locally as broadcast packets, and on output, send them as broadcast.
RTN_ANYCAST	3	Accept input packets locally as broadcast, but on output, send them as unicast packets.
RTN_MULTICAST	4	This is a multicast route.
RTN_BLACKHOLE	5	Drop these packets.
RTN_UNREACHABLE	6	The destination is unreachable.
RTN_PROHIBIT	7	This route is administratively prohibited.
RTN_THROW	8	The route is not in this table.
RTN_NAT	9	Translate this address using NAT.
RTN_XRESOLVE	10	Use external resolver to determine this route.

Rt_dst is the IP destination address, rt_src is the IP source address, and rt_iif is the route input interface index.

```
__u32               rt_dst;
__u32               rt_src;
int                 rt_iif;
```

The IP address of the gateway machine or neighbor is in the field rt_gateway.

```
__u32               rt_gateway;
```

The next field, fl, contains the actual hash key. The flowi structure is described later in the text.

```
struct flowi        fl;
```

The next few fields contain some miscellaneous cached information. The next field, rt_spec_dst, is the specific destination for the use of UDP socket users to set the source address. [RFC1122]

```
__u32               rt_spec_dst;
```

Internet peer structures are used for generating the 16-bit identification in the IP header. This is called the *long-living peer information*. Linux calculates the ID by incrementing a number for each transmitted packet for a specific host. The Internet peer information for this route is accessed through the peer pointer.

```
    struct inet_peer    *peer;
};
```

The flowi Structure

Searches of the routing cache are done by locating a slot in the hash bucket array with a simple hash code. Next, a second search is done using a key to match a specific route by walking the list of routes accessed through the slot until rt_next is NULL. The second level of searching is done by looking for an exact match with the fl field in the rtable entry against information obtained from the incoming packet. fl is the flowi structure or generic Internet flow. This structure is defined in the file linux/include/net/flow.h and contains all the information to specifically identify a route.

```
struct flowi {
```

The first two fields identify the input and output interfaces. Iif is the input interface index; it is obtained from the ifindex field of the net_device structure for the network interface device from which a packet was received. Oif contains the index of the output interface. Generally, either iif or oif will be defined for a specific route and the other field will be zero.

```
    int     oif;
    int     iif;
```

This structure is generic, so we use a union to define parts for IPv4, IPv6, and DECnet. The IPv4 parts are explained later in the chapter.

```
union {
    struct {
```

The next two fields, `daddr` and `saddr`, are the IP destination address, and the IP source address, respectively.

```
        __u32           daddr;
        __u32           saddr;
```

The next field, `fwmark`, is for firewall marks. This is part of traffic shaping and provides a way of aggregating different services on different ports so they can be directed through the same firewall.

```
        __u32           fwmark;
```

`tos` is the IP header ToS field. The bits in the ToS field include the precedence bits and three bits for low delay, throughput, and reliability. IP doesn't define bit zero of ToS, but Linux uses it to identify a directly connected host. This bit is used so the same routing table searches functions for different purposes, including searches of the destination cache by the ARP protocol.

```
        __u8            tos;
```

Next, `scope` defines the scope or conceptual distance covered by this route. Values for `scope` are shown in Table 8.2. These values are also from linux/include/linux/rtnetlink.h.

```
        __u8            scope;
    } ip4_u;
```

This is the end of the union for IPv4. Next comes IPv6. See Chapter 11, "Internet Protocol Version 6 (IPv6)," for more information about IPv6 routing.

```
    struct {
        struct in6_addr     daddr;
        struct in6_addr     saddr;
        __u32               flowlabel;
    } ip6_u;
```

TABLE 8.2 Route Scope Definitions

Name	Value	Description
RT_SCOPE_UNIVERSE	0	This value indicates that the destination in the route can be anywhere.
RT_SCOPE_SITE	200	The destination address is within the site.
RT_SCOPE_LINK	253	The address is for a directly attached host, which is any machine that can be reached by a direct physical connection.
RT_SCOPE_HOST	254	This value is for addresses that are one of the local addresses on this host.
RT_SCOPE_NOWHERE	255	Destination address is nonexistent.

The union for decnet, dn_u follows. It is not included because it is beyond the scope of this book.

. . .

These macros are provided for easy access to the IPv6 part of the union.

```
#define fl6_dst         nl_u.ip6_u.daddr
#define fl6_src         nl_u.ip6_u.saddr
#define fl6_flowlabel   nl_u.ip6_u.flowlabel
```

These macros are for easy access to the IPv4 specific fields.

```
#define fl4_dst         nl_u.ip4_u.daddr
#define fl4_src         nl_u.ip4_u.saddr
#define fl4_fwmark      nl_u.ip4_u.fwmark
#define fl4_tos         nl_u.ip4_u.tos
#define fl4_scope       nl_u.ip4_u.scope

    __u8 proto;
    __u8 flags;
    union {
        struct {
            __u16 sport;
            __u16 dport;
        } ports;
```

```
        struct {
            __u8    type;
            __u8    code;
        } icmpt;

        struct {
            __u16   sport;
            __u16   dport;
            __u8    8objnum;
            __u8    objnamel;  /* Not 16 bits since max val is 16 */
            __u8    objname[16]; /* Not zero terminated */
        } dnports;

        __u32           spi;
    } uli_u;
```

These macros are for access to ports, ICMP packet elements, and the IPSec Security Policy Identifier (SPI) fields.

```
#define fl_ip_sport     uli_u.ports.sport
#define fl_ip_dport     uli_u.ports.dport
#define fl_icmp_type    uli_u.icmpt.type
#define fl_icmp_code    uli_u.icmpt.code
#define fl_ipsec_spi    uli_u.spi
};
```

The scope of the route requires some more examination; it is in the scope field of the flowi structure. We can think of the scope as the distance to the destination address. It is used for making decisions about how to route packets and how to classify the routes. The values for scope are shown in Table 8.2 from the file linux/include/linux/rtnetlink.h. They are the same values used in the scope field of fib_result and the nh_scope field in the next-hop structure, fib_nhs. A user creating a special routing table application may define additional values for scope between zero and 199. Currently, however, the values most often used by Linux IPv4 are RT_SCOPE_UNIVERSE, RT_SCOPE_LINK, or RT_SCOPE_HOST. A higher number implies a closer destination except for RT_SCOPE_NOWHERE, which says the destination doesn't exist.

The bit definitions for the tos field in the flowi structure are shown in Table 8.3. These definitions are similar to the definitions for the Type of Service (ToS) field of the IP header. This is to support building a quick hash code based on ToS.

However, one of the bits in the ToS field of the IP header has no counterpart in this structure. This bit is 0x02, IPTOS_MINCOST, which maps into bit 6 of tos in the IP header [RFC 795]. In addition, one bit that is not defined in the IP header is used by Linux for internal purposes, RTO_ONLINK, 0x01. All the IP ToS bit definitions are found in the file linux/include/linux/ip.h, and RTO_ONLINK is defined in the file linux/include/net/route.h.

TABLE 8.3 Bit Definitions for tos in the `flowi` Structure

Definition	Value	Purpose
IPTOS_LOWDELAY	0x10	This is the low delay bit defined by IP.
IPTOS_THROUGHPUT	0x08	Throughput bit defined for IP ToS.
IPTOS_RELIABILITY	0x04	Reliability bit in IP ToS field.
IPTOS_MINCOST	0x02	This bit is defined in the IP header but is not used by Linux.
RTO_ONLINK	0x01	This bit is used to identify a directly connected host reachable by link-level transmission.

Route Cache Utility Functions

In this section, we will examine some kernel utility functions used with the routing table. The first part of each route table entry, rtable, contains a destination cache entry structure, dst_entry, which includes the dst_ops structure with function pointers corresponding to operations for manipulating the cache entry. Each specific routing protocol that uses the destination cache facility implement some or all of these functions. The generic destination cache is discussed in Chapter 5. The destination operation functions specific to IP are all implemented in linux/net/ipv4/route.c and are shown in Table 8.4.

One of the functions in Table 8.4 is the garbage collection function, rt_garbage_collect, which we discuss later in our section on route garbage collection. Another one is the destination check function, ipv4_dst_check, which doesn't do anything for IPv4. Typically, IPv4 code calls dst_release directly. A few of the others deserve a closer look.

TABLE 8.4 Dst_ops Values for IP Route Cache

Field in dst_ops	IP Function or Value	Purpose
family	AF_INET	IPv4 address family.
protocol	ETH_P_IP	Protocol field in link header, 0x0800.
gc	rt_garbage_collect	Garbage collection function.
check	ipv4_dst_check	Releases destination cache entry.
destroy	ipv4_dst_destroy	Destructor function for routing table entries.
if_down	ipv4_dst_ifdown	This function is called if an interface goes down.
negative_advice	ipv4_negative_advice	This function is called if an entry becomes redirected or obsolete.
link_failure	ipv4_link_failure	Sends ICMP unreachable message and expires the route.
update_pmtu	ip_rt_update_pmtu	Update the MTU for the route.
entry_size	sizeof(struct rtable)	Specific size of the route table entry.

The `ipv4_dst_destroy` Function

```
static void ipv4_dst_destroy(struct dst_entry *dst);
```

It deletes the attached internet peer, inet_peer, accessed through the rt field of the rtable structure. This effectively removes information about the destination.

The `ipv4_dst_ifdown` Function

```
static void ipv4_dst_ifdown(struct dst_entry *dst, struct net_device *dev,
                            int how)
```

This function is called if the network interface goes down. It sets the network interface associated with the route table to the loopback device.

The `ipv4_negative_advise` Function

```
static struct dst_entry *ipv4_negative_advice(struct dst_entry *dst);
```

This function removes routes in the cache pointed to by dst. First, it checks to see whether the route is obsolete by checking the obsolete field of the dst_entry. If it is, it calls ip_rt_put to return the route to the slab cache. Otherwise, we want to delete all routes to this destination about which we received negative advice. We do this by checking to see whether the entry has expired by checking the expires field in dst_entry, or the route has been redirected, by the presence of the RTCF_REDIRECTED flag in the rt_flags field. If so, it recalculates the 32-bit hash and calls rt_del to delete all the routes in the matching hash bucket location.

In addition to the operation functions, a few routing cache functions are called directly. It is helpful to understanding the route cache to take a closer look at these functions, some of which are defined in linux/include/net/route.h and others in linux/net/ipv4/route.c.

The ip_rt_put Function

The first function, ip_rt_put, deletes a route by calling the generic dst_release function, which removes a route from the destination cache.

```
static inline void ip_rt_put(struct rtable * rt)
{
    if (rt)
        dst_release(&rt->u.dst);
}
```

The rt_bind_peer Function

```
void rt_bind_peer(struct rtable *rt, int create);
```

This function creates a peer entry for the route. This, in effect, adds information about the destination to the routing table. First, it creates a new inet_peer structure by calling inet_getpeer. Then, it sets the peer field in the rtable structure to the new peer and increments the reference count in the inet_peer structure while locking the route cache.

The ip_route_connect Function

An application using TCP, SOCK_STREAM type sockets will need a connection with a remote peer before sending packets through an open socket. To establish the connection, the application calls connect on an open socket. One of the things done when the connection is established is to set up a route to the destination. In addition, applications using UDP, SOCK_DGRAM type sockets use the connect socket call to set up a route to the destination address before sending data. IP provides the function `ip_route_connect` for both TCP and UDP to establish a route. This function is defined in file `linux/include/net/route.h`.

```
static inline int ip_route_connect(struct rtable **rp, u32 dst, u32 src,
                                   u32 tos, int oif, u8 protocol,
                                   u16 sport, u16 dport, struct sock *sk)
```

Actually, this function is only a frontend for the main route resolving function, `ip_route_output`, which is discussed later when along with IP output and route resolution.

A few other functions used with the routing tables deserve more than a mention. These functions aren't part of the interface to the route cache because they are static functions. However, they are used by route resolving functions such as `ip_route_output`. It will be helpful to look at these functions for understanding how route cache entries are created and used.

The `rt_intern_hash` Function

When a new route is ready to be used for transmitting packets, `ip_route_output` calls this function, defined in file `linux/net/ipv4/route.c`, to enter a route, rt, into the route cache.

```
static int rt_intern_hash(unsigned hash, struct rtable *rt,
                          struct rtable **rp);
```

In this function, we use the `hash` parameter as an index into the route hash table, `rt_hash_table`. The index we get is for a location that most closely matches the new route. This location may contain zero, one, or more routes. Next, `rt_intern_hash` uses the `flowi` part in the `rtable` structure, `rt`, to look for an exact match with one of the routes at the hash table location. If it finds an exact match, it moves the matched route to the front of the list, increments its use count, and frees the new route `rt`. If there is not an exact match with any of the routes at the table location, the new route, rt, is put in the front of the list pointed to by `chain` at the hash table location. However, before the new route is put in the cache, we try to bind it to a neighbor cache location by calling `arp_bind_neighbour`. If it appears that the neighbor cache is full, we call `rt_garbage_collect` to remove routes until there is room for the new route, rt. If `rt_intern_hash` doesn't succeed in finding space, it returns an error.

The `rt_set_nexthop` Function

Both of the two major route resolving functions, `ip_route_output_slow` and `ip_route_input_slow`, need to set up some specific information after they have a route to an external destination that does not point to a directly connected host. For example, IP allows the MTU for a route to be specified, and TCP has an option for negotiating the maximum segment size with the peer. The function called to set up this information is `rt_set_nexthop`.

```
static void rt_set_nexthop(struct rtable *rt, struct fib_result *res,
                           u32 itag);
```

Route Cache Garbage Collection

The route cache includes a GC facility. The GC is based on the generic garbage collection in the generic destination cache. The route GC sets a specific function in the `gc` field of the destination cache operations structure. This is to override the function in the generic destination cache garbage collection. The route GC also has an expiration timer that acts as a fallback to completely delete routes from the cache after they age out. In addition to the GC timer, there is a timer for flush delay that governs the amount of time to wait after requesting that all the routes are flushed. The minimum and maximum values for route aging and some garbage collection values may be configured through `sysctl`. These configuration and control items will generally not be accessed by the typical user but are available for use by a more sophisticated routing application. In addition, the flush delay may be specified when a route flush is requested.

The Garbage Collection Timer

The garbage collection timer is called `rt_periodic_timer` and is defined in the file `linux/net/ipv4/route.c`.

```
static struct timer_list rt_periodic_timer;
```

The function associated with this timer is `rt_check_expire`.

```
static void rt_check_expire(unsigned long dummy)
```

The Route Flush Timer

The flush timer is `rt_flush_timer` defined in the same file.

```
static struct timer_list rt_flush_timer;
```

The timer function for the flush timer is `rt_run_flush`, and it is discussed later in this section.

The `ip_rt_init` Function

Both timers are initialized in the `ip_rt_init` function in the same file, which also initializes the route cache.

```
int __init ip_rt_init(void)
```

The default garbage collection timeout value, `ip_rt_gc_timeout`, is set to the configured value, `NET_IPV4_ROUTE_GC_TIMEOUT`, or a default of five minutes. This value is set in the timer function, `rt_check_expire`, which executes once a minute but is varied slightly to reduce multiple simultaneous hits on the route cache. The timer governs the maximum amount of time that aged-out routes are allowed to remain in the cache.

The `rt_check_expire` Function

```
static void rt_check_expire(unsigned long dummy);
```

This function, checks for expired routes in the route cache, `rt_hash_table`.

In this function, we walk through the hash bucket locations in the route cache. If we find a nonempty location, we traverse the list of routes at that location. For each route found, we check the `expires` field of the destination cache entry to see whether that route has aged out. We free each expired route by calling `rt_free`.

Since `rt_check_expire` is a timer function, it runs in the bottom half or interrupt context so it must be efficient. The age of the route entry is calculated by subtracting the value in the `lastuse` field of `dst_entry` from the current time. We also look for broadcast and multicast routes. These routes have `RTCF_BROADCAST` and `RTCF_MULTICAST` set in the routing control flags, `rt_flags`. Broadcast and multicast routes are cleaned more aggressively, particularly if they clash with more specific routes. High value routes are those with the `RTCF_REDIRECTED` or `RTCF_NOTIFY` flags, and these are given preference over other routes when we have clashes in the route cache. The values for these flags and other routing control flags are shown in Table 8.7.

The `rt_garbage_collect` Function

This is a garbage collection function, accessed through the `gc` field in the `dst_ops` field of the destination cache entry.

```
static int rt_garbage_collect(void);
```

We do garbage collection whenever somebody tries to allocate a route cache entry, and there are already too many routes in the table. Specifically, this happens when someone calls the destination cache allocation route, `dst_alloc`, and the `gc_thresh` value in the `ops` field of the destination cache is exceeded by the number of entries.

The goal of garbage collection is to keep the routing cache at an equilibrium point such that the number of aged-out entries is approximately the same as the number of new entries. The function maintains an internal static variable called `expire` to control the number of expired entries that are allowed to remain in the cache. Garbage collection is expensive, so it should not be run unless really necessary. If the networking load is light, the route cache is allowed to keep a higher number of recent expired entries. As the number of routes comes closer to the size of the cache, fewer expired routes are allowed to remain. This is related to the elasticity value of the garbage collection, and it can be changed through the routing `sysctl` value, `NET_IPV4_ROUTE_GC_ELASTICITY`, from its default value.

Each time `rt_garbage_collect` is executed, it calculates a new goal from the number of entries in the cache and reduces it by an amount calculated by the elasticity value. This goal is not less than the number of entries in the cache, `entries`, minus the garbage collection threshold value, `gc_thresh`. Both of these parameters are from the `dst_ops` structure for the route cache. When the goal is set, `rt_garbage_collect` goes through the cache and frees expired entries until the goal is reached. Because garbage collection is time consuming, the routine is kept from spinning by checking the current time, `jiffies`, to make sure that it hasn't executed for too long. It also checks to see whether it is being called in a bottom half context, from a `softirq`. The number of expired entries freed depends on the goal, how long it has been since the entries have expired, and whether the route cache is near full.

Linux provides a separate timer for flushing the route cache. This is because the amount of time this operation takes could be quite a bit if there are a large number of routes in the cache. If the flush is done in the bottom-half context, it starts a flush timer to delay the route cache flush. However, if the route cache flush is requested from user mode, which would cause it to be run in system call context, it is done immediately. This is a good thing particularly for embedded systems that need a predictable latency value. Real-time systems have latency requirements for other time critical kernel tasks running as `soft_irqs` that would be delayed if flushing the cache took too long.

The `rt_cache_flush` Function

`rt_cache_flush` is the function that does the removal of cache entries. It is also in `linux/net/ipv4/route.c`. The parameter `delay` indicates the amount of time to wait before removing the cache entries. It typically isn't called from one of the timers.

```
void rt_cache_flush(int delay)
{
    unsigned long now = jiffies;
```

User_mode is zero if we are running in the bottom half context, and one otherwise.

```
int user_mode = !in_softirq();
```

If the caller set delay to a negative number, we use the configured minimum delay time.

```
if (delay < 0)
    delay = ip_rt_min_delay;
```

We must acquire the route cache lock because we could get called from different contexts.

```
spin_lock_bh(&rt_flush_lock);

if (del_timer(&rt_flush_timer) && delay > 0 && rt_deadline) {
    long tmo = (long)(rt_deadline - now);
```

If the flush timer is currently running, we reset the timer value to the current time plus the requested delay time. If user_mode is set, we set the delay to zero, which will run the timer function as soon as we exit.

```
        if (user_mode && tmo < ip_rt_max_delay-ip_rt_min_delay)
            tmo = 0;
        if (delay > tmo)
            delay = tmo;
    }
    if (delay <= 0) {
        spin_unlock_bh(&rt_flush_lock);
        rt_run_flush(0);
        return;
    }
    if (rt_deadline == 0)
        rt_deadline = now + ip_rt_max_delay;
    mod_timer(&rt_flush_timer, now+delay);
    spin_unlock_bh(&rt_flush_lock);
}
```

The rt_run_flush Function

The next function, rt_run_flush, is the timer function that actually flushes the cache.

```
static void rt_run_flush(unsigned long dummy)
{
    int i;
    struct rtable *rth, *next;
    rt_deadline = 0;
    get_random_bytes(&rt_hash_rnd, 4);
```

Like the other route cache manipulation functions that update the contents of the route cache hash table, we must acquire the write lock. For each table location, we walk through the routes pointed to by chain and call rt_free to remove each route.

```
for (i = rt_hash_mask; i >= 0; i--) {
    write_lock_bh(&rt_hash_table[i].lock);
    rth = rt_hash_table[i].chain;
    if (rth)
        rt_hash_table[i].chain = NULL;
    write_unlock_bh(&rt_hash_table[i].lock);
    for (; rth; rth = next) {
        next = rth->u.rt_next;
        rt_free(rth);
    }
}
}
```

THE RPDB, THE FIB, AND THE FIB RULES

The RPDB consists of the Forwarding Information Base (FIB) and the FIB rules. The FIB is the core of Linux routing. Linux can be configured to support multiple routing tables, but as a default, it is configured with only two tables. In many common uses of the Linux kernel, there is no need for policy-based routing. This would be the case with most embedded systems.

The FIB Tables

Multiple tables can be configured into the kernel in case Linux is used as the basis for complex routers. If multiple tables are not configured, two predefined global variables are pointing to two tables, the local table and the main table. The local table contains routes to addresses that are locally assigned within the machine, such as addresses assigned to network interface devices and the loopback address. The main table contains routes to external machines. Both of these tables are declared in linux/net/ipv4/fib_frontend.c.

```
struct fib_table *ip_fib_local_table;
struct fib_table *ip_fib_main_table;
```

If multiple tables are configured, an array of FIB table pointers are numbered one through 256 (zero is an undefined FIB table index). Each table is referenced by an ID that serves as an index into the array. When multiple tables are defined, the main table and local table each are represented by two IDs that point to the last two locations in the array. RT_TABLE_MAIN is defined as 254, and RT_TABLE_LOCAL is 255. In addition, a default location exists if no ID is defined, RT_TABLE_DEFAULT, which is 253. The definition of the table locations are in include/linux/rtnetlink.h. When application programs such as routing daemons add and create routes, they are actually passing messages through netlink sockets to the FIB. As a new FIB table is created, it will use an ID numbered between 1 and 252.

```
struct fib_table *fib_tables[RT_TABLE_MAX+1];
```

In addition to multiple FIB tables, Linux supports FIB rules that are used to select among the tables. Application programs will define FIB rules and how the rules will be used to do lookups in particular tables

FIB Internal Data Structures

Each location in the array, fib_tables, contains a pointer to a FIB table structure, fib_table, defined in linux/include/net/ip_fib.h. Fib_table hides most of the complexity of the FIB. It consists largely of pointers to operation functions that are called by front-end functions. These internal operation functions are usually not called directly. The idea is to make the FIB as non-IP specific as possible. Someone implementing a network layer protocol could define his own FIB with its own operation functions that process the routing protocol's unique address format and routing rules. The FIB has what are called frontend functions for network layer protocols like IP to call as the interface to the FIB to create, delete, and otherwise manipulate routing entries. These frontend functions are explained later in this chapter. The application layer interface to the FIB is through rtnetlink sockets (routing sockets). This is how an application layer routing protocol updates the FIB by adding and deleting routes.

The fib_table Structure

The fib_table structure mainly consists of the FIB operation function pointers. These function pointers are initialized when a specific fib_table is created.

```
struct fib_table
{
```

The `tb_id` field is the table ID. If multiple tables are configured, it consists of one of the values between 1 and 255. If multiple tables are not defined, `tb_id` is set to either `RT_TABLE_MAIN` or `RT_TABLE_LOCAL`. Tb_stamp is not used.

```
unsigned char tb_id;
unsigned      tb_stamp;
```

The next three fields, `tb_lookup`, `tb_insert`, and `tb_delete` are pointers to functions that look up, insert, and delete routes from the FIB, respectively.

```
int          (*tb_lookup)(struct fib_table *tb,
                      const struct flowi *flp,
                      struct fib_result *res);
int          (*tb_insert)(struct fib_table *table, struct rtmsg *r,
                      struct kern_rta *rta, struct nlmsghdr *n,
                      struct netlink_skb_parms *req);
int          (*tb_delete)(struct fib_table *table, struct rtmsg *r,
                      struct kern_rta *rta, struct nlmsghdr *n,
                      struct netlink_skb_parms *req);
```

The function `tb_dump` gets all the routes in the table. It called from `inet_dump_fib` and is used with `rtnetlink`.

```
int          (*tb_dump)(struct fib_table *table, struct sk_buff
             *skb,
                      struct netlink_callback *cb);
```

The `tb_flush` operation removes all entries from the `fib_table` referenced by table.

```
int          (*tb_flush)(struct fib_table *table);
```

This operation `tb_select_default` selects the default route.

```
void         (*tb_select_default)(struct fib_table *table,
                          const struct rt_key *key,
                          struct fib_result *res);
```

tb_data is really an opaque pointer to the hash entries for this FIB table. It is manipulated by functions pointed by the other fields in the table. It is not accessed directly.

```
    unsigned char tb_data[0];
};
```

The fib_info Structure

Another data structure used by the FIB is fib_info, also defined in the file linux/include/net/ip_fib.h. It contains the data for routes to external unicast addresses that must go through a gateway. If a FIB entry contains a local or broadcast route, this data structure is not used.

```
struct fib_info
{
    struct hlist_node   fib_hash;
    struct hlist_node   fib_lhash;
    int                 fib_treeref;
    atomic_t            fib_clntref;
    int                 fib_dead;
    unsigned            fib_flags;
    int                 fib_protocol;
```

This field, fib_prefsrc, is the preferred source address. It is used as the *specific destination address* specified by RFC 1122 as part of UDP multihoming. It is used by UDP as the source address for response packets.[RFC1122]

```
    u32                 fib_prefsrc;
    u32                 fib_priority;
    unsigned            fib_metrics[RTAX_MAX];
#define fib_mtu fib_metrics[RTAX_MTU-1]
#define fib_window fib_metrics[RTAX_WINDOW-1]
#define fib_rtt fib_metrics[RTAX_RTT-1]
#define fib_advmss fib_metrics[RTAX_ADVMSS-1]
```

fib_nhs is the number of next hops. It should have the value one if this route has a defined gateway; otherwise, it will be zero. If multipath routing is configured, it can have a value greater than one. The next field, fib_power, is only used if multipath routing is configured.

```
    int                 fib_nhs;
#ifdef CONFIG_IP_ROUTE_MULTIPATH
    int                 fib_power;
#endif
```

The next field, fib_nh, contains information about the next hop or the list of next hops if there are more than one. fib_dev is the network interface device that would be used to send a packet to the next hop.

```
    struct fib_nh        fib_nh[0];
#define fib_dev          fib_nh[0].nh_dev
};
```

The fib_nh Structure

The next data structure of interest is fib_nh, also in file linux/include/net/ip_fib.h. It is accessed by the routing mechanism to extract information about the next hop or gateway machine.

```
struct fib_nh
{
    struct net_device    *nh_dev;
    struct hlist_node    nh_hash;
    struct fib_info      *nh_parent;
    unsigned             nh_flags;
```

This field, nh_scope, is similar to the scope field in the flowi structure. It doesn't really define the scope of the route, but rather the conceptual distance to the destination machine—in this case, the gateway machine.

```
    unsigned char        nh_scope;
#ifdef CONFIG_IP_ROUTE_MULTIPATH
    int                  nh_weight;
    int                  nh_power;
#endif
```

The next field is the traffic class identifier, nh_tclassid, for the gateway and is similar to the tclassid field in the destination cache entry. It is used primarily for traffic shaping.

```
#ifdef CONFIG_NET_CLS_ROUTE
    __u32                nh_tclassid;
#endif
```

Finally, nh_oif is the index number of the output interface that would be used to reach the gateway machine.

```
    int                  nh_oif;
    u32                  nh_gw;
};
```

The FIB Rules

FIB rules are part of the RPDB and are most useful when the FIB is configured with multiple tables. When multiple tables are configured, in effect, we have multiple logical routers, and each router is represented by a FIB table instance. In a practical sense, the routing policy is a way of selecting one of the routing tables. When we are configured with multiple tables, we still have the two default tables, the local table containing local address information, and the main table containing the routing information. However, the other tables are accessed by using the FIB rules.

In this section, we show the `fib_rule` data structure and how FIB rules are used to select among the two permanent default routing tables. We also show how FIB rules are added and deleted and how a new routing table is created.

The fib_rule Structure

The `fib_rule` structure is defined in the source file `linux/net/ipv4/fib_rules.c`. It is not accessed directly from functions in other files.

```
struct fib_rule
{
```

FIB rules are implemented as a linked list through `r_next`, and `r_clntref` is the use count, which must be atomically incremented.

```
    struct fib_rule     *r_next;
    atomic_t            r_clntref;
```

The next field, `r_preference`, contains the route preference value, and `r_table` is the index of the FIB table selected by this rule.

```
    u32                 r_preference;
    unsigned char r_table;
```

This field, `r_action`, has the same values as the route message type in the `rtmsg` structure. These values are defined in Table 8.1.

```
    unsigned char r_action;
    unsigned char r_dst_len;
    unsigned char r_src_len;
```

The next two fields are the source address and its netmask.

```
    u32                 r_src;
    u32                 r_srcmask;
```

These two fields are the destination address and the netmask for the destination.

```
        u32             r_dst;
        u32             r_dstmask;
```

The next field, r_srcmap, contains the address to which to map the source address. It is used where we have an address translation rule.

```
        u32             r_srcmap;
        u8              r_flags;
        u8              r_tos;
#ifdef CONFIG_IP_ROUTE_FWMARK
        u32             r_fwmark;
#endif
```

Next we have the index of the network interface device used in this rule.

```
        int             r_ifindex;
```

The next field is the traffic class identifier for this rule. It is used only if traffic class routing is configured in the kernel.

```
#ifdef CONFIG_NET_CLS_ROUTE
        __u32           r_tclassid;
#endif
```

This field, r_ifname, is the network interface device.

```
        char            r_ifname[IFNAMSIZ];
        int             r_dead;
};
```

The FIB Rule Instances

There are three fib_rule instances to select each of the permanent FIB tables: the main table, the local table, and the default table if no table is specified. As new FIB rules are defined, they will be added to the end of the list.

The Rule for the Default Table, 253

```
    static struct fib_rule default_rule = {
        .r_clntref =    ATOMIC_INIT(2),
        .r_preference = 0x7FFF,
        .r_table =      RT_TABLE_DEFAULT,
        .r_action =     RTN_UNICAST,
    };
```

The Rule for the Main Table, 254

```
static struct fib_rule main_rule = {
    .r_next     =   &default_rule,
    .r_clntref  =   ATOMIC_INIT(2),
    .r_preference = 0x7FFE,
    .r_table    =   RT_TABLE_MAIN,
    .r_action   =   RTN_UNICAST,
};
```

The Rule for the Local Table, 255

```
static struct fib_rule local_rule = {
    .r_next     =   &main_rule,
    .r_clntref  =   ATOMIC_INIT(2),
    .r_table    =   RT_TABLE_LOCAL,
    .r_action   =   RTN_UNICAST,
};
static struct fib_rule *fib_rules = &local_rule;
```

FIB Rule Functions

In this section, we examine some of the functions that are used to enter, delete, and look up rules in the FIB rules database. Many of these functions are called from the rtnetlink protocol, which passes messages to us from user space in the nlmsghdr structure. The nlmsghdr structure is followed in memory by the rtmsg structure, which contains most of the information used to determine what rule to use. Each of the following functions use fields in the rtmsg structure, which is explained later in this chapter. These functions are declared in linux/include/net/ip_fib.h and defined in the file linux/net/ipv4/fib_rules.c.

The inet_rtm_delrule Function

The first function is called from the rtnetlink protocol to delete a rule from the FIB rules database.

```
int inet_rtm_delrule(struct sk_buff *skb, struct nlmsghdr* nlh,
                     void *arg);
```

It searches for a rule to delete in fib_rules by looking at the rtm_type field of the structure pointed to by nlh. The values for rtm_type are shown in Table 8.1. The match criteria is based on the source and destination address lengths, rtm_src_len, rtm_dst_len, which can determine the specificity of the route. rtm_tos and the interface name are used to match the rule.

The `inet_rtm_newrule` Function

```
int inet_rtm_newrule(struct sk_buff *skb, struct nlmsghdr* nlh,
                void *arg);
```

This function adds a new rule to the FIB rules. It creates a new rule based on the `rtm_type` in the `nlmsghdr`. It creates a new FIB rule entry with `kmalloc`. It is important to note that the rules don't use a slab cache because they don't need to be that fast. These functions are not in the data path, and rules don't get added or deleted often. In this function, we create source and destination netmasks from the `rtm_src_len` and `rtm_dst_len` fields, respectively. It gets the `r_action` from the `rtm_type` field and the `r_flags` from the `rtm_flags` field in `nlh`. In addition, it gets the network interface device from its name.

The `fib_rules_tclass` Function

The next function, `fib_rules_tclass`, is used only when traffic class based routing is configured into the Linux kernel.

```
u32 fib_rules_tclass(struct fib_result *res);
```

The `fib_lookup` Function

This function, `fib_lookup`, will be shown in its entirety because it is the primary frontend function to do route searches in the FIB.

```
int fib_lookup(const struct flowi *flp, struct fib_result *res)
{
    int err;
    struct fib_rule *r, *policy;
    struct fib_table *tb;
    u32 daddr = flp->fl4_dst;
    u32 saddr = flp->fl4_src;
FRprintk("Lookup: %u.%u.%u.%u <- %u.%u.%u.%u ",
    NIPQUAD(key->dst), NIPQUAD(flp->fl4_src));
    read_lock(&fib_rules_lock);
```

We search `fib_rules` looking for a rule that most closely matches the source, destination address, ToS (if ToS routing is configured), and network interface device. Our goal is to get the correct table to search for the route.

```
    for (r = fib_rules; r; r=r->r_next) {
        if (((saddr^r->r_src) & r->r_srcmask) ||
            ((daddr^r->r_dst) & r->r_dstmask) ||
            (r->r_tos && r->r_tos != flp->fl4_tos) ||
```

```
#ifdef CONFIG_IP_ROUTE_FWMARK
            (r->r_fwmark && r->r_fwmark != flp->flr_fwmark) ||
#endif
            (r->r_ifindex && r->r_ifindex != flp->iif))
                continue;
```

Now that we have a matching rule, we check the route type. If it is RTN_UNICAST, we have found a rule. If not, we return an error.

```
FRprintk("tb %d r %d ", r->r_table, r->r_action);
        switch (r->r_action) {
        case RTN_UNICAST:
            policy = r;
            break;
        case RTN_UNREACHABLE:
            read_unlock(&fib_rules_lock);
            return -ENETUNREACH;
        default:
        case RTN_BLACKHOLE:
            read_unlock(&fib_rules_lock);
            return -EINVAL;
        case RTN_PROHIBIT:
            read_unlock(&fib_rules_lock);
            return -EACCES;
        }
```

Now we get the FIB table for matching rule, r. If we successfully got a table, we call the FIB table's lookup function, which returns the FIB result in res.

```
        if ((tb = fib_get_table(r->r_table)) == NULL)
            continue;
        err = tb->tb_lookup(tb, flp, res);
```

If there is no error, we look up the rule.

```
        if (err == 0) {
            res->r = policy;
            if (policy)
                atomic_inc(&policy->r_clntref);
            read_unlock(&fib_rules_lock);
            return 0;
        }
```

```
            if (err < 0 && err != -EAGAIN) {
                read_unlock(&fib_rules_lock);
                return err;
            }
        }
    FRprintk("FAILURE\n");
        read_unlock(&fib_rules_lock);
        return -ENETUNREACH;
    }
```

The Function, fib_select_default

```
void fib_select_default(const struct flowi *flp, struct fib_result *res);
```

It selects the default route.

We get the default route by calling tb_select_default through the function pointer in fib_table. First, however, it gets the FIB rule to check a few things. It makes sure that the route type is unicast and that it is reasonable. It ensures that there is a next hop (gateway) associated with the fib_result in res and that the gateway is directly connected. It knows that the gateway is connected if the nh_scope field in the next-hop structure is RT_SCOPE_LINK. If all of these conditions are met, it gets the route, otherwise, it returns.

FIB Initialization

In order to understand the FIB better, we will take a look at the initialization code for IPv4.

The ip_fib_init Function

The initialization of the FIB for IPv4 is done by the function ip_fib_init, defined in the file linux/net/ipv4/fib_frontend.c.

```
void __init ip_fib_init(void)
{
```

If we are configured for multiple tables, we call fib_rules_init to set up the rules part of the RPDB. Otherwise, we call fib_hash_init directly for each of the two tables that are globally defined.

```
#ifndef CONFIG_IP_MULTIPLE_TABLES
    local_table = fib_hash_init(RT_TABLE_LOCAL);
    main_table = fib_hash_init(RT_TABLE_MAIN);
```

```
#else
    fib_rules_init();
#endif
```

Next, we register ourselves with the notifier facility in net device. We put ourselves on the chain of functions to be called when network interface devices change status. We will be informed as devices go up or down so we know to add or delete routes through the device.

```
    register_netdevice_notifier(&fib_netdev_notifier);
    register_inetaddr_notifier(&fib_inetaddr_notifier);
    nl_fib_lookup_init();
}
```

The fib_hash_init Function

The initialization of a specific FIB table is done by the function fib_hash_init, defined in the file linux/net/ipv4/fib_hash.c. We have two interfaces to this function depending on whether or not multiple tables are defined.

```
#ifdef CONFIG_IP_MULTIPLE_TABLES
struct fib_table * fib_hash_init(int id)
#else
struct fib_table * __init fib_hash_init(int id)
#endif
{
```

The variable, tb, will point to the new FIB hash table.

```
    struct fib_table *tb;
```

The first thing we do is create the FIB slab cache. This is the slab cache from which FIB entries, in fib_node structures, will be allocated. The new fib_table is allocated by calling kmalloc. We don't need a slab cache for the fib_table because each system will only have a few routing tables. There are at least two instances of the fib_table structure, RT_TABLE_MAIN and RT_TABLE_LOCAL. If the kernel option, CONFIG_IP_MULTIPLE_TABLES, is configured, there are more fib_table instances.

```
    if (fn_hash_kmem == NULL)
        fn_hash_kmem = kmem_cache_create("ip_fib_hash",
                                    sizeof(struct fib_node),
                                    0, SLAB_HWCACHE_ALIGN,
                                    NULL, NULL);
```

```
        if (fn_alias_kmem == NULL)
            fn_alias_kmem = kmem_cache_create("ip_fib_alias",
                                              sizeof(struct fib_alias),
                                              0, SLAB_HWCACHE_ALIGN,
                                              NULL, NULL);
        tb = kmalloc(sizeof(struct fib_table) + sizeof(struct fn_hash),
                     GFP_KERNEL);
        if (tb == NULL)
            return NULL;
```

Now we initialize the fields of the `fib_table`. First, the `tb_id` field is set to the FIB table number. Then, the operation functions are set.

```
        tb->tb_id = id;
```

The function pointers are initialized to operation function. The following six functions are discussed elsewhere in this chapter.

```
        tb->tb_lookup = fn_hash_lookup;
        tb->tb_insert = fn_hash_insert;
        tb->tb_delete = fn_hash_delete;
        tb->tb_flush = fn_hash_flush;
        tb->tb_select_default = fn_hash_select_default;
        tb->tb_dump = fn_hash_dump;
```

The information in each FIB table entry is kept in a structure called a `fib_node`. The field `tb_data` points to an array of FIB node hash structures, which in turn contain pointers to `fib_node`.

```
        memset(tb->tb_data, 0, sizeof(struct fn_hash));
        return tb;
    }
```

The FIB to Application Interface

Many routing application programs exist. Examples of application programs that need to access and set routes include the route(8) program and routing daemons such as zebra or gated. To aid these application programs, Linux provides an interface to the internal kernel routing information stored in the FIB. Information about the routing tables must be passed back and forth between the kernel and application programs. Generally, in Linux, when an application wants to add or delete a route, it will use the rtmsg structure and pass it through a rtnetlink socket. The rtmsg structure was discussed earlier in this chapter, and the rtnetlink sockets were discussed in Chapter 4, "Linux Sockets."

The rtentry Structure

The structure rtentry, defined in the file linux/include/linux/route.h, is provided to the user interface to retrieve and enter routes into the FIB. This structure is not actually used internally in the FIB. It is similar to the rtentry structure passed in the route ioctls used with the BSD operating systems. Linux includes it for application portability. A pointer to the rtentry structure is passed as an argument by ioctl calls such as SIOCADDRT and SIOCDELRT, which add and delete routing information.

```
struct rtentry
{
    unsigned long      rt_pad1;
```

This field rt_dst holds the target address; rt_gateway is the gateway address; and rt_genmask is the target netmask.

```
    struct sockaddr    rt_dst;
    struct sockaddr    rt_gateway;
    struct sockaddr    rt_genmask;
```

rt_flags holds the routing table entry flags. The values for the flags are shown in Table 8.5.

```
    unsigned short     rt_flags;
    short              rt_pad2;
    unsigned long      rt_pad3;
    void               *rt_pad4;
```

The next field, rt_metric, is used to pass in the routing metric or priority. The user passes a pointer to a device name in rt_dev if he wants to add a route for a specific device.

```
    short              rt_metric;
    char               *rt_dev;
```

This field, rt_mtu, and its equivalent, rt_mss, are set by the application to pass the MTU value to specify a maximum packet or segment size for a specific route.

TABLE 8.5 Routing Table Entry Flags

Name	Value	Purpose
RTF_UP	0x0001	The route is usable.
RTF_GATEWAY	0x0002	The destination is a gateway.
RTF_HOST	0x0004	This route is a host entry, not a net route.
RTF_REINSTATE	0x0008	Flag says to reinstate route after it ages out.
RTF_DYNAMIC	0x0010	This route is created dynamically by a redirect.
RTF_MODIFIED	0x0020	Route is modified dynamically by a redirect.
RTF_MTU	0x0040	There is a specific MTU for this route.
RTF_MSS	RTF_MTU	Route maximum segment size. It is the same as RTF_MTU and is provided for compatibility with the BSD OS.
RTF_WINDOW	0x0080	This indicates that there is window clamping for this route.
RTF_IRTT	0x0100	Initial round-trip time.
RTF_REJECT	0x0200	Says to reject route.

```
     unsigned long       rt_mtu;
#ifndef __KERNEL__
#define rt_mss            rt_mtu
#endif
```

The following two fields can be used to maintain two specific parameters for TCP, the TCP window size clamp and the initial round-trip time.

```
     unsigned long       rt_window;
     unsigned short      rt_irtt;
};
```

Functions and Structures Used by `rtnetlink`

The main method of accessing the FIB is through `netlink` sockets. `Netlink` sockets provide extensions for routing called routing `netlink` sockets, or `rtnetlink`. The `netlink` mechanism is explained in Chapter 4. Here, however, we will show the functions `rtnetlink` uses internally to add or delete entries in the FIB. For example, the following two functions add and delete routes from the FIB. They act as front-ends to the internal FIB functions accessed through the `tb_insert` and `tb_delete` function pointers in the `fib_table` structure. These functions are declared in the file `linux/include/net/ip_fib.h` and defined in `linux/net/ipv4/fib_frontend.c`. Both functions accept a `nlmsghdr` structure as an argument because they are called from the `netlink recvmsg` and `sendmsg` functions. The `nlmsghdr` has an associated `rtmsg` structure, which was shown earlier.

The `inet_rtm_newroute` Function

```
int inet_rtm_newroute(struct sk_buff *skb, struct nlmsghdr* nlh,
                      void *arg);
```

It adds a new route to the FIB.

The `inet_rtm_delroute` function.

This function deletes a route from the FIB.

```
int inet_rtm_delroute(struct sk_buff *skb, struct nlmsghdr* nlh,
                      void *arg)
```

The `rtmsg` Structure

Both of the functions described earlier extract the `rtmsg` structure, which is placed in memory immediately after the `nlmsg` header pointed to by `nlh`. The `rtmsg` structure is defined in file `linux/include/linux/rtnetlink.h`.

```
struct rtmsg
{
    unsigned char     rtm_family;
```

The following two fields are the number of bits to use to create a 32-bit or smaller netmask for `AF_INET` type addresses for both the source and destination.

```
    unsigned char     rtm_dst_len;
    unsigned char     rtm_src_len;
```

This field corresponds to the ToS field in the IP header.

```
    unsigned char     rtm_tos;
```

Next, `rtm_table` contains the routing table ID. If multiple tables are not configured, this would be either `RT_TABLE_MAIN` or `RT_TABLE_LOCAL`.

```
    unsigned char     rtm_table;
```

`rtm_protocol` refers to the routing message protocol from Table 8.6. The next field, `rtm_scope`, is the route message scope and the values for this field are the same as those listed earlier in Table 8.2.

```
char               rtm_protocol;
unsigned char      rtm_scope;
```

TABLE 8.6 Route Message Protocol Field Values

Protocol	Value	Purpose
RTPROT_UNSPEC	0	The value is unspecified.
RTPROT_REDIRECT	1	This route is installed by ICMP redirects. This is not used currently by IPv4.
RTPROT_KERNEL	2	This route is installed by kernel.
RTPROT_BOOT	3	The route is installed during boot.
RTPROT_STATIC	4	Route is installed by the administrator.
RTPROT_GATED	8	Used by the gated routing daemon
RTPROT_RA	9	Used for RDISC/ND router advertisements.
RTPROT_MRT	10	This value is used by Merit MRT.
RTPROT_ZEBRA	11	Used by Zebra routing demon.
RTPROT_BIRD	12	Used by BIRD.
RTPROT_DNROUTED	13	Used by DECnet routing daemon.
RTPROT_XORP	14	Used by XORP.

This field is the routing message type, `rtm_type`. It has the same values as the route types shown in Table 8.1.

```
unsigned char      rtm_type;
```

The next field, `rtm_flags`, can be one of three values: `RTM_F_NOTIFY` or 0x100 says to notify the user of route change; `RTM_F_CLONED` or 0x200 indicates that this route is cloned; and the final value, `RTM_F_EQUALIZE` or 0x400, is not implemented yet but is for a multipath equalizer.

```
    unsigned       rtm_flags;
};
```

The values for the protocol field of the `rtmsg` structure are shown in Table 8.4. The values greater than RTPROT_STATIC are not interpreted by the kernel and are passed between user space and the kernel without modification. They are intended to be used by hypothetical multiple routing daemons. The comments in the code recommend that the values should be standardized to avoid conflicts.

The `ip_route_ioctl` Function

This function handles the IP routing `ioctl` call, and it is declared in the file `linux/include/net/route.h` and defined in `linux/net/ipv4/fib_frontend.c`. This function is another way for an application to add or delete routes from the routing tables. These functions are provided for compatibility to some older legacy applications. However, most applications that want to exchange routing information with the internal routing table will use the */proc* file system `proc(5)`, or the `sysctl` interface, `sysctl(2)`, or `netlink` sockets, `netlink(4)`.

```
int ip_rt_ioctl(unsigned int cmd, void __user *arg);
```

The two `ioctl`s supported by `ip_rt_ioctl` are SIOCADDRT and SIOCDELRT to add and delete a route, respectively. The routing control flags are shown in Table 8.7. They are defined in the `linux/include/linux/in_route.h`.

TABLE 8.7 IPv4 Routing Control Flags

Flag	Value	Purpose
RTCF_DEAD	RTNH_F_DEAD	Dead route.
RTCF_ONLINK	RTNH_F_ONLINK	Indicates a locally reachable destination.
RTCF_NOPMTUDISC	RTM_F_NOPMTUDISC	This is an obsolete flag.
RTCF_NOTIFY	0x00010000	Indicates (in theory) that a notification should be sent every time this route becomes stale.
RTCF_DIRECTDST	0x00020000	The destination is directly reachable. This flag does not appear to be used.
RTCF_REDIRECTED	0x00040000	The source address for this route is directly reachable; it is a local route.
RTCF_TPROXY	0x00080000	Not used.

→

Flag	Value	Purpose
RTCF_FAST	0x00200000	Route has not been redirected (if fast routing is enabled).
RTCF_MASQ	0x00400000	Indicates that the source address is masqueraded.
RTCF_SNAT	0x00800000	Indicates that the source address in this route is actually a translated source address.
RTCF_DOREDIRECT	0x01000000	Generate ICMP redirect.
RTCF_DIRECTSRC	0x04000000	Destination is directly connected.
RTCF_DNAT	0x08000000	The destination address is translated.
RTCF_BROADCAST	0x10000000	Broadcast route.
RTCF_MULTICAST	0x20000000	Multicast route.
RTCF_REJECT	0x40000000	This flag does not appear to be used.
RTCF_LOCAL	0x80000000	Local route.
RTCF_NAT	(RTCF_DNAT|(RTCF_SNAT)	Indicates that either the destination or the source for this route is a translated address.

FIB Internal Kernel Interface

Many internal functions have to access routing information from the FIB. When the routing mechanism needs to determine the route for a packet, it first uses a hash key to search the routing table whose entries are defined by the `rtable` structure, shown earlier. When routes are known, they are cached in the routing table cache. Therefore, the FIB provides several functions to convert to and from the `rtable` entry and the internal FIB representation.

The `kern_rta` Structure

Another data structure is sometimes used to represent routing table entries when they are added or deleted by internal modules. This is the `kern_rta` structure, defined in the file `linux/include/net/ip_fib.h`.

```
struct kern_rta
{
    void        *rta_dst;
```

```
    void        *rta_src;
    int         *rta_iif;
    int         *rta_oif;
    void        *rta_gw;
    u32         *rta_priority;
    void        *rta_prefsrc;
    struct rtattr *rta_mx;
    struct rtattr *rta_mp;
    unsigned char *rta_protoinfo;
    unsigned char *rta_flow;
    struct rta_cacheinfo    *rta_ci;
    struct rta_session      *rta_sess;
    u32         *rta_mp_alg;
};
```

The fib_result Structure

Another data structure used to return the result of a lookup in the FIB. We saw earlier that a pointer to this structure is returned by the fib_lookup function. This data structure is fib_result, defined in the file linux/include/net/ip_fib.h.

```
struct fib_result
{
```

prefixlen is the prefix length. This value is used to construct the netmask for the route and consists of a number from 0 to 32, which indicates how many bits of the address to mask.

```
    unsigned char       prefixlen;
    unsigned char       nh_sel;
```

This could be thought of as the type of the route contained in this entry. It actually can be converted to the flags for the routing table entry, which are defined in Table 8.5. Next, scope is the scope of the route.

```
    unsigned char       type;
    unsigned char       scope;
#ifdef CONFIG_IP_ROUTE_MULTIPATH_CACHED
    __u32               network;
    __u32               netmask;
#endif
```

The fib_info structure is shown earlier in the discussion about the FIB.

```
        struct fib_info      *fi;
```

If multiple routing tables are configured, the following field points to the fib_rule structure used to get this result.

```
#ifdef CONFIG_IP_MULTIPLE_TABLES
    struct fib_rule    *r;
#endif
};
```

FIB Interface Functions

Previously, we introduced the data structures used internally by the FIB and the data structures used to interface to the FIB. Now we describe some of the functions that are commonly used to interface to the FIB. Most of these functions are defined in linux/net/ipv4/fib_frontend.c. However, we will explain some of the FIB utility functions that are accessed through the function pointers in the fib_table structure. The FIB is a generic resource to all protocols, not just IPv4; therefore, it is protocol independent. The external interfaces have no dependency on IPv4 32-bit address formats.

The __fib_new_table Function

The first function we will discuss is __fib_new_table, which creates a new FIB table. This function is defined in the file linux/net/ipv4/fib_frontend.c. Id contains the new table ID, and it must be between 1 and 252. The higher table numbers are used by the permanent FIB tables.

```
struct fib_table *__fib_new_table(int id);
```

It calls fib_get_table to retrieve the FIB table indexed by id.

The ip_dev_find Function

This function returns the output network interface that has been configured with the address, addr. It is declared in linux/include/linux/inetdevice.h and implemented in linux/net/ipv4/fib_frontend.c. It returns a pointer to the net_device structure for the device. It is interesting to examine this structure because it shows how the local table in the FIB is used to keep local address information.

```
struct net_device * ip_dev_find(u32 addr);
{
```

First, we build the `flowi` structure to do the search of the FIB. The only field in `flowi` that we use is the destination address.

```
struct flowi fl = { .nl_u = { .ip4_u = { .daddr = addr } } };
struct fib_result res;
struct net_device *dev = NULL;
#ifdef CONFIG_IP_MULTIPLE_TABLES
    res.r - NULL;
#endif
```

It does the lookup in the local FIB table, `local_table`, which includes all IP address information within this machine. Each FIB table has its own set of service functions. In this example, the lookup routine is called through the `tb_lookup` function field of the `fib_table` structure for the local table. The returned routes must be of type `RTN_LOCAL`, or there is a bogus entry in the table.

```
if (!ip_fib_local_table||
    ip_fib_local_table->tb_lookup (ip_fib_local_table, &fl, &res))
    return NULL;
if (res.type != RTN_LOCAL)
    goto out;
dev = FIB_RES_DEV(res);
```

After we have a reference to the network interface device, we must increment the use count in the `net_device` structure.

```
    if (dev)
        dev_hold(dev);
out:
    fib_res_put(&res);
    return dev;
}
```

The `inet_addr_type` Function

The function `inet_addr_type`, defined in the file `linux/include/net/route.h`, looks up the address, `addr`, in the local FIB table, and returns an address type of unicast, broadcast, or multicast. The return values for this function are shown in Table 8.1.

The `fib_validate_source` Function

The following function, `fib_validate_source`, declared in the file `linux/include/net/ip_fib.h` and implemented in `linux/net/ipv4/fib_frontend.c`, provides a way of verifying the source address. A side effect of this function is that it retrieves the specific destination address and sets `spec_dst` to point to the address. The specific destination address is used as the source address for outgoing UDP packets from multihomed hosts. The function also gets the route tag or traffic class identifier, which is used for traffic shaping. The function sets the parameter, `itag`, to point to the traffic class identifier for the next hop to the destination address.

```
int fib_validate_source(u32 src, u32 dst, u8 tos, int oif,
                struct net_device *dev, u32 *spec_dst, u32 *itag)
{
```

In this function, our purpose is to make sure that there is a route to a source address. For example, if the caller needs to verify the source address in an input packet, it can call `fib_validate_source` to check that the source address is valid.

```
struct in_device *in_dev;
```

We initialize with the information for the FIB table lookup. We set fields in `flowi` based on the arguments, but some of the fields are optional. The only required parameter for a meaningful lookup is the source address, `saddr`.

```
struct flowi fl = { .nl_u = { .ip4_u =
                    { .daddr = src,
                      .saddr = dst,
                      .tos = tos } },
                    .iif = oif };
struct fib_result res;
int no_addr, rpf;
int ret;
```

We get the `inet_device` structure for the interface, `dev`. If `no_addr` is zero, it indicates that the interface does not have an IP address. If `rpf` is one, then the reverse path filtering option is enabled for the interface, `dev`.

```
no_addr = rpf = 0;
rcu_read_lock();
in_dev = __in_dev_get_rcu(dev);
if (in_dev) {
    no_addr = in_dev->ifa_list == NULL;
    rpf = IN_DEV_RPFILTER(in_dev);
}
rcu_read_unlock();
if (in_dev == NULL)
    goto e_inval;
```

Now we call `fib_lookup` to search the FIB. This function returns zero if the lookup succeeds. If the route type is not unicast, then the source address parameter, src, must be Martian because multicast or broadcast source addresses don't make any sense.

```
if (fib_lookup(&fl, &res))
    goto last_resort;
if (res.type != RTN_UNICAST)
    goto e_inval_res;
```

We get the specific destination address from the `fib_info` structure attached to the FIB result, res. The special destination address is used by UDP as the source address for response packets.

```
*spec_dst = FIB_RES_PREFSRC(res);
```

`fib_combine_itag` generates the traffic class tag. In the simplest case, it returns the traffic class identifier of the next hop. If multiple tables are configured and we are doing traffic shaping, it returns the traffic class ID in the `fib_rules` for the route.

```
fib_combine_itag(itag, &res);
```

This is where we check of the validity of the output device. so dev must be the same as the device shown in route entry (unless multipath routing is configured). In other words, the network interface at which the packet arrived should be the same as the network device for the route to the host from which the packet was sent.

```
#ifdef CONFIG_IP_ROUTE_MULTIPATH
    if (FIB_RES_DEV(res) == dev || res.fi->fib_nhs > 1)
#else
    if (FIB_RES_DEV(res) == dev)
#endif
    {
        ret = FIB_RES_NH(res).nh_scope >= RT_SCOPE_HOST;
        fib_res_put(&res);
        return ret;
    }
    fib_res_put(&res);
    if (no_addr)
        goto last_resort;
    if (rpf)
        goto e_inval;
    fl.oif = dev->ifindex;
```

If the test for a network interface failed, we might still have some type of logical device. We do another lookup, and if this lookup is successful, we recalculate the special destination address.

```
    ret = 0;
    if (fib_lookup(&fl, &res) == 0) {
        if (res.type == RTN_UNICAST) {
            *spec_dst = FIB_RES_PREFSRC(res);
            ret = FIB_RES_NH(res).nh_scope >= RT_SCOPE_HOST;
        }
        fib_res_put(&res);
    }
    return ret;
```

We end up here if the FIB lookup failed, so we call `inet_select_addr` to find the specific distribution address. This function will return the address assigned to network interface, `dev`, to be used for the special destination address.

```
last_resort:
    if (rpf)
        goto e_inval;
    *spec_dst = inet_select_addr(dev, 0, RT_SCOPE_UNIVERSE);
    *itag = 0;
    return 0;
e_inval_res:
    fib_res_put(&res);
e_inval:
    return -EINVAL;
}
```

FIB Table Hash Functions

Under the covers, the FIB table is implemented as a multizone hash table. Each location in the hash table is held by a `fib_info` structure, explained earlier in this chapter. The `fib_info` structures are allocated from a slab cache called the FIB node cache, which is defined in the file linux/net/ipv4/fib_hash.c.

```
    static kmem_cache_t * fn_hash_kmem;
```

Next, we will look at the hash functions defined for the `fib_table`. As we know from earlier discussions, the FIB is a generic routing database. The `fib_table` structure consists of a set of pointers to operation functions. Actions affecting the FIB are done through these function pointers, which could be overridden by specific protocol implementations of the FIB. The functions for the IPv4 FIB implementation are defined in linux/net/ipv4/fib_hash.c. Each of the functions performs multizone hash calculations to locate particular FIB entries. The functions that retrieve entries from the FIB store the result in a feb_result structure pointed to by the argument, res. Functions that add entries to the FIB accept a pointer to the kern_rta structure as an argument. Most of the functions return a zero on success and a negative error if unsuccessful.

The fn_hash_lookup Function

The first of these functions, fn_hash_lookup, is the low-level function provided to look up a route entry in the FIB.

```
static int fn_hash_lookup(struct fib_table *tb,
                          const struct flowi *fl,
                          struct fib_result *res);
```

It accepts a pointer to a FIB table, tb, and routing flow information in fl and returns the result of the search in the fib_result structure pointed to by res. In this function, we retrieve the FIB node hash table from the field, tb_data in fib_table. Before doing the lookup, we form a FIB zone key from the destination address in the IPv4 part of the flowi structure, fl4_dst. If we get a match on the address, we set the type, scope, and prefixlen in the fib_result structure pointed to by res.

The fn_hash_insert Function

The next function, fn_hash_insert, adds a new route to the FIB table, tb.

```
static int fn_hash_insert(struct fib_table *tb, struct rtmsg *r,
                          struct kern_rta *rta, struct nlmsghdr *n,
                          struct netlink_skb_parms *req);
```

It accepts information about the route to be added in the rtmsg structure because it is called from the rtnetlink protocol. Information about the result is returned in the kern_rta structure rta.

The fn_hash_delete Function

The next function, fn_hash_delete, deletes an entry from the FIB table, tb.

```
static int fn_hash_delete(struct fib_table *tb, struct rtmsg *r,
                          struct kern_rta *rta, struct nlmsghdr *n,
                          struct netlink_skb_parms *req);
```

The `fn_hash_flush` Function

The next function, `fn_hash_flush`, is much simpler.

    static int fn_hash_flush(struct fib_table *tb);

It removes all entries in the FIB table, `tb`. It returns the number of entries it found or zero if it didn't find any.

The `fn_hash_dump` Function

`fn_hash_dump` dumps the contents of the FIB table, `tb`.

    static int fn_hash_dump(struct fib_table *tb, struct sk_buff *skb,
                    struct netlink_callback *cb);

It calls the callback function `cb` for each entry in the FIB table.

The `fn_hash_select_default` Function

This function, `fn_hash_select_default`, is called as the lowest-level function to find a default route in the FIB table, `tb`.

    static void fn_hash_select_default(struct fib_table *tb,
                        const struct flowi *flp,
                        struct fib_result *res);

This function is usually called from internal kernel routines such as `fib_select_default` and not called directly from `rtnetlink`. It searches for the route indicated by the `flowi` structure. It returns the result in the `fib_result` structure pointed to by `res`.

ROUTING INPUT PACKETS

As we will show later in this chapter, the IP receive packet handler makes a decision of what to do with each valid incoming packet. TCP requests a new route for input packets when the `accept` or `connect` socket calls are issued. There are two stages to this decision process, *fast path routing* and *slow path routing*. The fast path consists simply of a lookup in the routing cache to see whether a route has been used recently. The fast path looks for a match on the incoming interface, the source, and the destination IP addresses to see whether there is a cached route that applies to this packet. The slow path consists of a more time-consuming search of the FIB for the most appropriate applicable match. First, we will discuss the fast path routing in this section. A later section will cover slow path routing.

Routing Input Packets—the Fast Path

Each packet has a destination that at any given time may either be known or unknown. As a packet is transmitted, after the destination is known, the destination cache entry, dst, in the socket buffer structure, sk_buff, is used to quickly extract the link layer header including the hardware destination address. The purpose of fast path routing is to find the entry in the route cache and place a pointer to it in the socket buffer. When we are done, dst is a pointer to an entry in the destination cache for a specific route.

For reasons of efficiency, internally we handle incoming packets the same way as outgoing packets. Therefore, we also consider incoming packets as having a destination. Generally, this destination may be a transport protocol or it may be the packet forwarding routine. In this section, we examine how the destination cache entry is obtained by searching the route cache with a key based on a few fields of the incoming packet. The destination of the incoming packet is in the IP forwarding routine, and if that is the case, IP forward will worry about how to extract the link layer header from the destination cache when the packet is ready to be transmitted.

The ip_route_input Function

Routing information for an incoming packet is obtained during input packet processing. The IP receive routine, after it does some basic validity checking of the incoming IP packet, must decide where to send the packet next. To make this decision, it calls a function to get the destination for an incoming packet. This function, ip_route_input, defined in the file linux/net/ipv4/route.c, gets a route to the destination by first searching for the route table entry in the routing table cache. If there is no matching entry in the cache, it calls ip_route_input_slow to search the FIB. It returns a zero if a route was found.

```
int ip_route_input(struct sk_buff *skb, u32 daddr, u32 saddr,
                   u8 tos, struct net_device *dev, int our)
{
```

The variable rth is a pointer to a route table entry, and hash is the first-level hash code to find a location in the rt_hash_table. We are trying to route an input packet, so we set iif to the incoming network interface index.

```
struct rtable * rth;
unsigned      hash;
int iif = dev->ifindex;
tos &= IPTOS_RT_MASK;
```

We call rt_hash_code to calculate a 4-byte hash code from the source and destination addresses, the type of service field, and the input interface in the incoming packet, skb.

```
hash = rt_hash_code(daddr, saddr ^ (iif << 5), tos);
```

Each location in the hash bucket array, rt_hash_table, has an RCU type read/write lock. As a reader of the table, we read-lock the location before searching the chain. Anyone writing to the table must write-lock the same location because a use count is incremented after a route table entry is used.

```
rcu_read_lock()
```

We use the hash code, hash, to start our search at a location in the hash bucket table. In this location, the field chain points to a linked list of routes. An item on the list can be an entry in the destination cache or a route table entry.

```
for (rth = rcu_dereference(rt_hash_table[hash].chain); rth;
     rth = rcu_dereference(rth->u.rt_next)) {
```

Now we follow the chain of routes to find a precise match by comparing the destination and source addresses, the input interface index, and the IP ToS field.

```
        if (rth->fl.fl4_dst == daddr &&
            rth->fl.fl4_src == saddr &&
            rth->fl.iif == iif &&
            rth->fl.oif == 0 &&
#ifdef CONFIG_IP_ROUTE_FWMARK
            rth->fl.fl4_fwmark == skb->nfmark &&
#endif
            rth->fl.fl4_tos == tos) {
```

If we have a match, we are actually in the fast path for input packets. This means that the route has been resolved and the matching route entry actually points to a destination cache entry, not a route table entry. Both structures begin with a next field so they can be overloaded in the same cache. The dst_entry structure is shown later in this section, and a more detailed explanation of the destination entry cache can be found in Chapter 5.

We have a match, and we know that rth actually points to the destination cache. The destination cache is defined by the structure dst_entry. We can access this structure through the union, u, in the beginning of the rtable structure. We update a few fields in the dst_entry structure now that we have a hit. We mark the time when this destination cache entry was last used by setting `lastuse` to the current time. (The global kernel variable, `jiffies`, holds the current time in ticks.)

```
rth->u.dst.lastuse = jiffies;
```

We increment the reference count, `__refcnt` by, calling `dst_hold`. The use count, `__use`, is incremented also. Cache statistics are updated to indicate that we have a routing cache hit. Finally, the `dst` field of the socket buffer, `skb`, is updated to point to `rth`, which is actually a destination cache entry. We return zero to indicate that we have found a route for this packet. Before returning, we unlock the location in the hash bucket, `rt_hash_table`.

```
            dst_hold(&rth->u.dst);
            rth->u.dst.__use++;
            RT_CACHE_STAT_INC(in_hit);
            rcu_read_unlock();
            skb->dst = (struct dst_entry*)rth;
            return 0;
        }
        RT_CACHE_STAT_INC(in_hlist_search);
    }
```

If we end up here, it means that we did not find a matching route in the route table cache. We could be in the slow path for unicast routes or we may have a multicast destination address. First, we unlock the location in the hash bucket because we are done with the routing cache.

```
rcu_read_unlock();
```

We check to see whether the destination IP address, `daddr`, is a multicast address. The comments in the code indicate that multicast recognition in earlier releases was done in the route cache. However, some types of Ethernet interfaces didn't properly recognize hardware multicast addresses, so the number of entries in the routing cache could explode. To avoid this problem, host multicast address decoding is done here outside the routing cache. Multicast routers will still use the route cache.

```
if (MULTICAST(daddr)) {
```

The first thing we do if `daddr` is a multicast destination address is get the Internet device structure, `in_device`, from the network interface device structure, `dev`. The `in_device` structure contains the multicast address list among other things. The `in_device` structure has a global read/write spin lock so we read lock the structure to protect it.

```
            struct in_device *in_dev;
            rcu_read_lock();
            if ((in_dev = __in_dev_get(dev)) != NULL) {
```

We call `ip_check_mc` to see whether the destination address of the incoming packet, `daddr`, is one of the addresses on the list of multicast addresses for the incoming network interface. If so, our is set to TRUE. This means that the input interface has been added to the multicast group for the address, `daddr`.

```
            int our = ip_check_mc(in_dev, daddr, saddr,
                                skb->nh.iph->protocol);
```

`Ip_route_input_mc` is called to route input multicast packets if a couple of specific conditions are met. It is called if our is not zero, indicating that the incoming network interface has subscribed to the multicast address, `daddr`. Next, we call `ip_route_input_mc` if multicast routing is configured in the kernel and the multicast forwarding option is set for the input interface. However, if `daddr` is a multicast address but none of these other conditions are met, we return an error indicating that the input packet, `skb`, should be dropped.

```
                        if (our
#ifdef CONFIG_IP_MROUTE
                            || (!LOCAL_MCAST(daddr) && IN_DEV_MFORWARD(in_dev))
#endif
                            ) {
                            rcu_read_unlock();
                            return ip_route_input_mc(skb, daddr, saddr,
                                            tos, dev, our);
                        }
                    }
                    rcu_read_unlock();
                    return -EINVAL;
                }
```

This is the slow path. If arrive here, there was no routing cache hit for the incoming packet, `skb` is valid and `daddr` is not a multicast address

```
                return ip_route_input_slow(skb, daddr, saddr, tos, dev);
            }
```

The destination entry cache structure, `dst_entry`, is explained in Chapter 5. This structure is referenced by the `ip_route_input` structure in the case where there is a routing table cache hit. Refer to Chapter 6 for more information about the destination cache as well.

The Main Input Route Resolving Function

In the previous section, we discussed how the routing table cache is accessed for fast path routing of incoming packets. If there is no cache hit in the attempt to route the packet in the fast path, we try to find a route for the incoming packet by accessing the FIB. This is called the slow path.

The Slow Path, the `ip_route_input_slow` Function

The slow path routing function for an incoming packet is `ip_route_input_slow`. This function is called from `ip_route_input` if there is no routing cache hit for the incoming packet, `skb`.

```
int ip_route_input_slow(struct sk_buff *skb, u32 daddr, u32 saddr,
                        u8 tos, struct net_device *dev)
{
```

The first variable, `res`, points to the result of the FIB search. The `fib_result` structure is described earlier in this chapter.

```
struct fib_result res;
```

This variable, `in_dev`, is the Internet device associated with the incoming network interface, `dev`. This structure was also used in the fast path routing described in the previous section. Since we are routing incoming packets, `out_dev` is NULL.

```
struct in_device *in_dev = in_dev_get(dev);
struct in_device *out_dev = NULL;
```

Next, we initialize the flow structure for the FIB search. The fields for addresses and TOS are initialized.

```
struct flowi fl = { .nl_u = { .ip4_u =
                    { .daddr = daddr,
                      .saddr = saddr,
                      .tos = tos,
```

We set the `scope` field in the search key to be as broad as possible. The values for route scope are shown in Table 8.2. Later in the function, as we attempt to narrow the routing decision, this value may be narrowed based on the result of the FIB lookup.

```
                          .scope = RT_SCOPE_UNIVERSE,
#ifdef CONFIG_IP_ROUTE_FWMARK
                          .fwmark = skb->nfmark
#endif
                          } },
                          .iif = dev->ifindex };
```

The values in `flags` are the route control flags, and they are derived from information in the FIB as we determine the route. They help provide instructions to the consumers of this packet as to how to dispose of the packet. The route control flags are shown in Table 8.7.

```
        unsigned        flags = 0;
        u32             itag = 0;
```

Next, `rth` points to a routing table cache entry described in an earlier sectio; `hash` is the hash code; and `spec_dst` is the special destination address.

```
        struct rtable * rth;
        unsigned        hash;
        u32             spec_dst;
        int             err = -EINVAL;
        int             free_res = 0;
```

If `in_dev` is NULL, there is no AF_INET information for the incoming network interface, `dev`, and therefore, no IP address. IP packets are disabled for this input device.

```
        if (!in_dev)
            goto out;
```

Some Martian source addresses are filtered out first because they can't be detected by a lookup of the FIB. These include loopback, multicast, or broadcast source addresses. Afterward, we see whether the incoming packet has been sent to a broadcast address, and if so, we jump to `brd_input` for further processing.

```
        if (MULTICAST(saddr) || BADCLASS(saddr) || LOOPBACK(saddr))
            goto martian_source;
```

We check whether we have a broadcast destination, and we filter out zero source addresses. If the destination IP address does not make any sense, we filter it out. We should not see packets with destination loopback addresses at this point.

```
if (daddr == 0xFFFFFFFF || (saddr == 0 && daddr == 0))
    goto brd_input;
if (ZERONET(saddr))
    goto martian_source;
if (BADCLASS(daddr) || ZERONET(daddr) || LOOPBACK(daddr))
    goto martian_destination;
```

At this point, a fast search of the routing table cache did not yield a hit, but the previous checks indicate that we have valid source and destination unicast addresses. Therefore, we need to find a route for the packet in the FIB, and we do this by calling `fib_lookup`. Fib_lookup does the search using the `flowi` structure. It provides the result in a `fib_result` structure pointed to by res. It returns a zero if the search was successful, or an error if not.

```
if ((err = fib_lookup(&fl, &res)) != 0) {
    if (!IN_DEV_FORWARD(in_dev))
        goto e_hostunreach;
    goto no_route;
}
free_res = 1;
RT_CACHE_STAT_INC(in_slow_tot);
```

The type of the route is returned in the type field of the `fib_result`. If the returned route type is broadcast, we complete processing at the `brd_input` label.

```
if (res.type == RTN_BROADCAST)
    goto brd_input;
```

The returned route type is RTN_LOCAL if the destination matched one of our local addresses.

```
if (res.type == RTN_LOCAL) {
    int result;
    result = fib_validate_source(saddr, daddr, tos,
                                 loopback_dev.ifindex,
                                 dev, &spec_dst, &itag);
    if (result < 0)
        goto martian_source;
    if (result)
        flags |= RTCF_DIRECTSRC;
```

We know now that we have a local route. The packet should not be forwarded. It should be passed to the higher level protocols because the packet was sent to one of our local addresses. The variable `spec_dst` holds the value for the `rt_spec_dst` field of `rtable`. This is the UDP-specific destination address used in certain UDP applications for the source address of an outgoing packet as specified by [RFC 1122]. Finally, we jump to `local_input` to complete processing.

```
        spec_dst = daddr;
        goto local_input;
}
```

At this point, we know we will have to forward the incoming packet. It was rejected for the fast route match by `ip_route_input`, or we wouldn't have ended up here. By failing the previous tests in this function, we know it is not a multicast packet; it is not a broadcast packet; and it is not being sent to one of our addresses. There are a few other tests before we prepare to route the packet. If the input device is not configured for IP forwarding, we have an error condition. If the route type returned from the FIB is not unicast, we assume there is an error condition; the destination address must have been Martian.

```
        if (!IN_DEV_FORWARD(in_dev))
            goto e_hostunreach;
        if (res.type != RTN_UNICAST)
            goto martian_destination;
```

At this point, we know that the incoming packet will be routed. We also know that the destination machine or the gateway is theoretically reachable. Therefore, we call `ip_mkroute_input`; which in turn, calls another function to do multicast routing if the destination address was multicast.

```
        err = ip_mkroute_input(skb, &res, &fl, in_dev, daddr, saddr, tos);
        if (err == -ENOBUFS)
            goto e_nobufs;
        if (err == -EINVAL)
            goto e_inval;
```

Now we are done with routing input packets. We decrement the reference count in the input device `inet_device`, `in_dev` and the reference count in the `fib_info` structure attached to the `fib_res` if there is one. When we return a non-zero value, it tells the caller to drop the input packet it is trying to route. A zero return means we found a route for the packet.

```
done:
    in_dev_put(in_dev);
```

```
        if (out_dev)
            in_dev_put(out_dev);
        if (free_res)
            fib_res_put(&res);
out:    return err;
```

We end up at this label, brd_input, if the packet we are trying to route is a broadcast packet or the FIB search returned a broadcast route. If the packet is okay, we set the routing control flags to indicate it is a broadcast, set the specific destination address, and proceed to local input route processing.

```
brd_input:
    if (skb->protocol != __constant_htons(ETH_P_IP))
        goto e_inval;
```

If the source address of the incoming packet is zero, we must set the specific destination address, spec_dst, so a UDP application will know how to set the source address of a response packet.

```
        if (ZERONET(saddr))
            spec_dst = inet_select_addr(dev, 0, RT_SCOPE_LINK);
        else {
```

If the source address wasn't zero, we validate the source address. While we are at it, we also assign the specific destination address, spec_dst.

```
            err = fib_validate_source(saddr, 0, tos, 0, dev, &spec_dst,
                                        &itag);
            if (err < 0)
                goto martian_source;
            if (err)
                flags |= RTCF_DIRECTSRC;
        }
        flags |= RTCF_BROADCAST;
        res.type = RTN_BROADCAST;
        RT_CACHE_STAT_INC(in_brd);
```

The local input label is used for cases where the packet was sent to our machine and is intended for local consumption. We allocate a route cache entry. This cache entry is also a destination cache entry because a packet using this route will not be sent out any interface. It will be consumed locally.

```
local_input:
    rth = dst_alloc(&ipv4_dst_ops);
    if (!rth)
        goto e_nobufs;
```

We set fields in the routing hash entry. The output function isn't used because we will be consuming these packets, not transmitting them. We set the destination address, tos, and the source address. The dst_entry flags field is set to DST_HOST.

```
        rth->u.dst.output= ip_rt_bug;
        atomic_set(&rth->u.dst.__refcnt, 1);
        rth->u.dst.flags= DST_HOST;
        if (in_dev->cnf.no_policy)
            rth->u.dst.flags |= DST_NOPOLICY;
        rth->fl.fl4_dst    = daddr;
        rth->rt_dst     = daddr;
        rth->fl.fl4_tos    = tos;
#ifdef CONFIG_IP_ROUTE_FWMARK
        rth->fl.fl4_fwmark = skb->nfmark;
#endif
        rth->fl.fl4_src    = saddr;
        rth->rt_src     = saddr;
#ifdef CONFIG_NET_CLS_ROUTE
        rth->u.dst.tclassid = itag;
#endif
```

The destination device is the loopback device. The input interface is set to the networking interface that received the packet we are trying to route. The most important field of the dst_entry structure is the input function pointer, which is set to ip_local_deliver. This function will receive any input packets using this entry in the routing cache. In addition, if the routing control flags, rt_flags, has RTCF_LOCAL set, it indicates that the incoming packet is for local consumption.

```
        rth->rt_iif    =
        rth->fl.iif    = dev->ifindex;
        rth->u.dst.dev    = &loopback_dev;
        dev_hold(rth->u.dst.dev);
        rth->idev = in_dev_get(rth->u.dst.dev);
        rth->rt_gateway    = daddr;
        rth->rt_spec_dst= spec_dst;
        rth->u.dst.input= ip_local_deliver;
        rth->rt_flags = flags|RTCF_LOCAL;
```

The route type in the FIB result is unreachable if we got here from the `no_route` label, and if so, we indicate an error and unset the local flag.

```
if (res.type == RTN_UNREACHABLE) {
    rth->u.dst.input= ip_error;
    rth->u.dst.error= -err;
    rth->rt_flags &= ~RTCF_LOCAL;
}
rth->rt_type  = res.type;
```

Here, we calculate the hash code and set the route, also setting the destination cache entry in the socket buffer. Any more packets arriving with the same destination will go to the internal destination via the fast path covered earlier in this chapter.

```
hash = rt_hash_code(daddr, saddr ^ (fl.iif << 5), tos);
err = rt_intern_hash(hash, rth, (struct rtable**)&skb->dst);
goto done;
```

We came to this label, `no_route`, if the FIB search indicated that the destination of the packet we were trying to route is unreachable.

```
no_route:
    RT_CACHE_STAT_INC(in_no_route);
    spec_dst = inet_select_addr(dev, 0, RT_SCOPE_UNIVERSE);
    res.type = RTN_UNREACHABLE;
    goto local_input;
```

If our previous FIB search indicated that the destination address was Martian (entirely unknown), we log the appropriate errors but we don't cache the route.

```
martian_destination:
    RT_CACHE_STAT_INC(in_martian_dst);
#ifdef CONFIG_IP_ROUTE_VERBOSE
    if (IN_DEV_LOG_MARTIANS(in_dev) && net_ratelimit())
        printk(KERN_WARNING "martian destination %u.%u.%u.%u from "
                    "%u.%u.%u.%u, dev %s\n",
                    NIPQUAD(daddr), NIPQUAD(saddr), dev->name);
#endif
e_hostunreach:
    err = -EHOSTUNREACH;
    goto done;
e_inval:
    err = -EINVAL;
    goto done;
```

```
        e_nobufs:
            err = -ENOBUFS;
            goto done;
```

If the FIB search indicated that the source address was Martian, we also increment the statistics. RFC 1812, Section 5.3.8 has some hints for source address validation based on the reachability of the source addresses through the interface in which the packet came. We do all this in the function ip_handle_martian_source.

```
        martian_source:
            ip_handle_martian_source(dev, in_dev, skb, daddr, saddr);
            goto e_inval;
        }
```

ROUTING OUTPUT PACKETS

In this section, we discuss how IP chooses a route for packets before they are transmitted. If the destination host is directly connected to the sending machine, the destination address can be converted to a link layer address with ARP or another address resolution protocol, and the packet can be sent on its way. This seems to be a fairly simple process. However, if the destination is not directly reachable, things are not as simple. The IP protocol must decide how to route the packet, which means that it must choose an output interface if there is more than one network interface device on the sending machine. In addition, it must choose the gateway or next hop that will receive the packet.

Before UDP sends a datagram, it requests a route to the destination address. TCP, however, has already established the route to the destination by the time it sends a packet. TCP requests the route for output packets when the connect socket call is issued by the application. This is because TCP transmission uses the cached route for all segments sent through an open socket once it is active.

The ip_route_connect Function

Whether TCP or UDP packets are being transmitted, ip_route_connect, defined in file linux/include/net/route.h, is the main function for resolving routes for output packets.

```
        static inline int ip_route_connect(struct rtable **rp,
                                           u32 dst, u32 src,
                                           u32 tos, int oif, u8 protocol,
```

```
                                    u16 sport, u16 dport, struct sock
                                    *sk)
{
```

As with the input route resolving functions, the `flowi` structure, examined earlier, is initialized with the information to try to do a match of routes in the route cache. It is also used for a search of the FIB if the route can't be matched in the cache.

```
        struct flowi fl = { .oif = oif,
                            .nl_u = { .ip4_u = { .daddr = dst,
                                                 .saddr = src,
                                                 .tos   = tos } },
                            .proto = protocol,
                            .uli_u = { .ports =
                                        { .sport = sport,
                                          .dport = dport } } };
        int err;
        if (!dst || !src) {
```

We call one of the fast path routing functions. Afterward, we try to update both the source and destination addresses if one is missing.

```
            err = __ip_route_output_key(rp, &fl);
            if (err)
                return err;
            fl.fl4_dst = (*rp)->rt_dst;
            fl.fl4_src = (*rp)->rt_src;
            ip_rt_put(*rp);
            *rp = NULL;
        }
```

If both the source and destination addresses are defined, we pass in a pointer to the sock in `sk`.

```
        return ip_route_output_flow(rp, &fl, sk, 0);
}
```

The `ip_route_output_flow` Function

The function `ip_route_output_flow` in the file `linux/net/ipv4/route.c` can automatically transform the route if the protocol value in the `flowi` structure is set to NAT or some other non-zero number.

```
int ip_route_output_flow(struct rtable **rp, struct flowi *flp, struct sock
                         *sk, int flags)
{
    int err;
```

We call the fast route resolving function here.

```
    if ((err = __ip_route_output_key(rp, flp)) != 0)
        return err;
```

If we found a route, and the proto info in the `flowi` was not zero, we try to transform the route.

```
    return flp->proto ? xfrm_lookup((struct dst_entry**)rp, flp, sk,
flags) : 0;
}
```

The __ip_route_output_key Function

In the `_ip_route_output_key` function, we do the fast path output routing. First, we try to find a matching route in the route cache. If we can't find the route in the cache, then we look for the route by searching the FIB. We return a zero if we find the route, and a non-zero value if not. If the search is successful, a pointer to the route cache entry, `rtable`, in placed in the parameter, `rp`.

```
int ip_route_output_key(struct rtable **rp, const struct flowi *flp)
{
```

We use a simple 32-bit hash for a first-level search of the hash table. After a slot in the hash table, `rt_hash_table`, is identified, we read-lock the table location and try for an exact match of the routes at that location.

```
    unsigned hash;
    struct rtable *rth;
    hash = rt_hash_code(flp->fl4_dst, flp->fl4_src ^ (flp->oif << 5),
                        flp->fl4_tos);
    rcu_read_lock_bh();
```

This is a second-level search done with the information from the `flowi` structure pointed to by the argument, `flp`. In this search, we try to find an exact match for the route. In many cases, there will be only one `rtable` entry at a hash slot.

```
            for (rth = rcu_dereference(rt_hash_table[hash].chain); rth;
                 rth = rcu_dereference(rth->u.rt_next)) {
                if (rth->fl.fl4_dst == flp->fl4_dst &&
                    rth->fl.fl4_src == flp->fl4_src &&
                    rth->fl.iif == 0 &&
                    rth->fl.oif == flp->oif &&
#ifdef CONFIG_IP_ROUTE_FWMARK
                    rth->fl.fl4_fwmark == flp->fl4_fwmark &&
#endif
```

Let's look at this part of the `if` statement closely. The bit definitions of the `fl4_tos` field in the `flowi` structure are similar to the ToS field of the IP header. Earlier in this chapter, we examined the `flowi` structure. In the `fl4_tos` field, the `RTO_ONLINK` actually refers to bit zero, which is not defined in the real IP packet ToS field. Linux uses it here to identify a route to a directly connected host (reachable via link layer transmission). Generally, when we are called from ARP, `tos` is set to `RTO_ONLINK` to request a route to a directly connected host. Because the routing table is derived from the destination cache, the search of the routing cache returns a destination cache entry pointing to the attached host.

```
                    !((rth->fl.fl4_tos ^ flp->fl4_tos) &
                      (IPTOS_RT_MASK | RTO_ONLINK))) {
```

First, we check to see whether we are looking for a multipath route. If not, we check to see whether the key matches, and if so, we set `lastuse` to the current time to indicate when this destination entry was last used. Also, the use count is decremented. We return a pointer to the new destination cache entry in `rp` and exit from the function.

```
                if (multipath_select_route(flp, rth, rp)) {
                    dst_hold(&(*rp)->u.dst);
                    RT_CACHE_STAT_INC(out_hit);
                    rcu_read_unlock_bh();
                    return 0;
                }
                rth->u.dst.lastuse = jiffies;
                dst_hold(&rth->u.dst);
                rth->u.dst.__use++;
                RT_CACHE_STAT_INC(out_hit);
                rcu_read_unlock_bh();
                *rp = rth;
                return 0;
            }
```

```
            RT_CACHE_STAT_INC(out_hlist_search);
    }
```

If we didn't find a match in the route cache, we unlock the hash table slot and call the slow output route resolving function, `ip_route_output_slow`, with `flp` to search the FIB.

```
        rcu_read_unlock_bh();
        return ip_route_output_slow(rp, flp);
    }
```

The Main Output Route Resolving Function, `ip_route_output_slow`

If the fast path route failed, we continue with the slow path routing. If the fast path routing function can't match the new route in the route cache, it calls the function `ip_route_output_slow` in the file linux/net/ipv4/route.c to search the FIB.

```
    int ip_route_output_slow(struct rtable **rp, const struct flowi
    *oldflp)
    {
```

This variable, `tos`, is built from the `tos` field in the `flowi` structure pointed to by the parameter `oldflp`. It mostly contains the IP ToS field bits, which are used as part of the criteria to determine the route. However, `tos` also includes another bit that is not part if the IP header ToS field. When set in `fl4_tos` field of `flowi`, this bit, `RTO_ONLINK`, defined as bit zero, indicates that the route is to a directly connected host.

```
        u32 tos = RT_FL_TOS(oldflp);
```

In this function, we create a new `flowi` structure, which is created from the input `flowi` pointed to by `flp`. Most of the fields are copied from the old `flp` but a few are calculated.

```
        struct flowi fl = { .nl_u = { .ip4_u =
                                    { .daddr = oldflp->fl4_dst,
                                      .saddr = oldflp->fl4_src,
```

In the `tos` field in the IPv4 part of the `flowi` structure, the `RTO_ONLINK` actually refers to bit zero, which is not defined in the real IP packet ToS field. Linux uses it here to identify a route to a directly connected host (reachable via link layer transmission).

```
                                      .tos = tos & IPTOS_RT_MASK,
                                      .scope = ((tos & RTO_ONLINK) ?
```

```
                                        RT_SCOPE_LINK :
                                        RT_SCOPE_UNIVERSE),
```

The next field, fwmark, is for firewall marks. It is used for traffic shaping if firewall marks are configured into the Linux kernel.

```
#ifdef CONFIG_IP_ROUTE_FWMARK
                                    .fwmark = oldflp->fl4_fwmark
#endif
                                } },
                      .iif = loopback_dev.ifindex,
                      .oif = oldflp->oif };
```

The structure fib_result holds the result of a search of the FIB.

```
struct fib_result res;
unsigned flags = 0;
```

We will use dev_out as a pointer to the input network interface device associated with the route, and in_dev as a pointer to the output network interface.

```
struct net_device *dev_out = NULL;
int free_res = 0;
int err;
res.fi     = NULL;
#ifdef CONFIG_IP_MULTIPLE_TABLES
    res.r  = NULL;
#endif
```

We do some basic checking before looking up the route.

```
if (oldflp->fl4_src) {
```

If the source address is specified by the caller, we check to see whether it is a Martian address.

```
err = -EINVAL;
if (MULTICAST(oldflp->fl4_src) ||
    BADCLASS(oldflp->fl4_src) ||
    ZERONET(oldflp->fl4_src))
    goto out;
```

In this test, we check to see whether the source address is one of our local addresses. If the address is assigned to an interface, `ip_dev_find` returns the network interface device that has that address. This check is functionally similar to calling `inet_addr_type` with source address as an argument to see whether the address is in the local FIB table.

```
dev_out = ip_dev_find(oldflp->fl4_src);
if (dev_out == NULL)
    goto out;
```

Comments in the code say that code was removed to see whether the output interface `oif` was for the same device as the one returned by `ip_dev_find`. This check would have been incorrect because the source address could have been an address different from the device from which the packets are sent.

```
if (oldflp->oif == 0
    && (MULTICAST(oldflp->flr_dst) ||
    oldflp->fl4_dst == 0xFFFFFFFF)) {
```

Comments in the code say this is a special hack so applications can send packets to multicast and broadcast addresses without specifying the IP_PKTINFO IP option. This facilitates applications such as VIC and VAT for video and audio conferencing. We need this hack because these applications bind the socket to the loopback address, set the multicast TTL to zero and send the packets out without doing a join group or specifying the outgoing multicast interface.

```
fl.oif = dev_out->ifindex;
```

Now we are ready to go to the label `make_route` to enter the new route in cache.

```
        goto make_route;
}
```

This is just a cleanup. We decrement the use count of the device we used temporarily, `dev_out`.

```
    if (dev_out)
        dev_put(dev_out);
    dev_out = NULL;
}
```

If the output interface, oif, is specified by the caller, we get the net_device pointer and make sure that it references an in_device structure that contains the AF_INET type address information. The in_device structure is explained in more detail in Chapter 5.

```
if (oldflp->oif) {
    dev_out = dev_get_by_index(oldflp->oif);
    err = -ENODEV;
    if (dev_out == NULL)
        goto out;
    if (__in_dev_get_rtnl(dev_out) == NULL) {
        dev_put(dev_out);
        goto out;
    }
```

Now we check to see whether we are trying to route a multicast destination address, and if so, we get the source address by calling inet_select_addr. This source address will be put in the route information so it can be used later as the source address of outgoing packets sent to the multicast or broadcast address in flp->fl4_dst. Next, since there is no need to do a FIB lookup, we go to make_route to enter the new route in the route cache.

```
    if (LOCAL_MCAST(oldflp->fl4_dst) || oldflp->fl4_dst ==
        0xFFFFFFFF) {
        if (!fl.fl4_src)
            fl.fl4__src = inet_select_addr(dev_out, 0,
                                            RT_SCOPE_LINK);
        goto make_route;
    }
    if (!fl.fl4_src) {
        if (MULTICAST(oldflp->fl4_dst))
            fl.fl4_src = inet_select_addr(dev_out, 0, fl.fl4_scope);
        else if (!oldflp->fl4_dst)
            fl.fl4_src = inet_select_addr(dev_out, 0,
                                           RT_SCOPE_HOST);
    }
}
```

If the destination address in the key is NULL, we assume that we are looking for a local (internal) destination. We set the output network device to the loopback device and set both flags to look for a local route. Therefore, packets using this route will be looped back; they will be sent back up the IP stack. There is no need to do the FIB lookup for this key, so we go straight to make_route, which enters this local route in the route cache.

```
        if (!fl.fl4_dst) {
            fl.fl4_dst = fl.fl4_src;
            if (!fl.fl4_dst)
                fl.fl4_dst = fl.fl4_src = htonl(INADDR_LOOPBACK);
            if (dev_out)
                dev_put(dev_out);
            dev_out = &loopback_dev;
            dev_hold(dev_out);
            fl.oif = loopback_dev.ifindex;
            res.type = RTN_LOCAL;
            flags |= RTCF_LOCAL;
            goto make_route;
        }
```

Now, we call `fib_lookup` to get the route for `fl`. If it finds a route, it returns a zero and puts the result in `res`.

```
        if (fib_lookup(&fl, &res)) {
```

The FIB lookup has failed. We haven't found a route.

```
            res.fi = NULL;
            if (oldflp->oif) {
```

We are here because the FIB lookup failed even though an output interface was specified in the lookup key, `oldkey`. A comment in the code states that the routing tables must be wrong if the lookup failed event even though an output device was specified. We are allowed to send packets out an interface even when there are no routes specifying the interface and no addresses assigned to the interface. Therefore, we assume that the destination is directly connected to the output interface `oif` even though there was no route in the FIB. If the output interface `oif` is specified, the route lookup is only for checking to see whether the final destination is directly connected or reachable only through a gateway.

```
                if (fl.fl4_src == 0)
```

If the source address wasn't specified, we must pick one. We put it in the key, set the route type to multicast, and jump to `make_route` to enter the route into cache.

```
                    fl.fl4_src = inet_select_addr(dev_out, 0,
                                                  RT_SCOPE_LINK);
```

```
                res.type = RTN_UNICAST;
                goto make_route;
        }
```

We arrived here because we couldn't find a route, so we set the error to unreachable and get out.

```
        if (dev_out)
            dev_put(dev_out);
        err = -ENETUNREACH;
        goto out;
}
```

This section of the code is executed if we know that the FIB lookup has given us a route. We do some checks of the route type in the type field before we add the route to the cache.

```
        free_res = 1;
```

We got here because the FIB lookup gave us a local route, which means that the destination address in the key was one of our own addresses. We set the output device to the loopback device, and the route cache flag, flags, to RTCF_LOCAL, indicating that the route is a local route. Next, we go to make_route to enter the route in cache.

```
        if (res.type == RTN_LOCAL) {
            if (!fl.fl4_src)
                fl.fl4_src = fl.fl4_dst;
            if (dev_out)
                dev_put(dev_out);
            dev_out = &loopback_dev;
            dev_hold(dev_out);
            fl.oif = dev_out->ifindex;
            if (res.fi)
                fib_info_put(res.fi);
            res.fi = NULL;
            flags |= RTCF_LOCAL;
            goto make_route;
        }
```

Multipath routing is a kernel option that allows more than one routing path to be defined to the same destination. If the option is configured, we check the fib_nhs field in the `fib_info` structure to see whether it is greater than one. This lets us know that there is more than one "next hop" for the same destination.

```
#ifdef CONFIG_IP_ROUTE_MULTIPATH
    if (res.fi->fib_nhs > 1 && key.oif == 0)
        fib_select_multipath(&key, &res);
    else
#endif
```

Here, we check to see whether we got a `fib_result` with no netmask and no output device. With neither of these things, we get the default route by calling `fib_select_default`. The field `prefixlen` specifies the number of bits to use for the netmask, and if it is zero, there is no netmask. If the output device was specified in the `fib_result`, we would know we are trying to reach a directly connected host, and if the netmask was specified, we would know we have a route to a gateway.

```
    if (!res.prefixlen && res.type == RTN_UNICAST && !fl.oif)
        fib_select_default(&fl, &res);

    if (!fl.fl4_src)
        fl.fl4_src = FIB_RES_PREFSRC(res);

    if (dev_out)
        dev_put(dev_out);
    dev_out = FIB_RES_DEV(res);
    dev_hold(dev_out);
    fl.oif = dev_out->ifindex;
```

At this point, we are done with the FIB lookup. We have a route so we enter it in the route cache after making a few checks for broadcast, multicast, and just plain bad destination addresses. It may seem that some of these checks are redundant at this point, but we may have come to this label by bypassing the FIB lookup. All this stuff is hidden in the `ip_mkroute_output` function.

```
make_route:
        err = ip_mkroute_output(rp, &res, &fl, oldflp, dev_out, flags);
        if (free_res)
            fib_res_put(&res);
        if (dev_out)
            dev_put(dev_out);
out:    return err;
    }
```

INTERNET PEERS AND THE IP HEADER ID FIELD

Internet peers are primarily for generating the value in the identification field (ID) in the IP header of outgoing packets. We know that IP fragments outgoing packets when the packet size exceeds the MTU of the route, so it must provide a way for the receiving machine to identify the packet fragments. The receiving side uses this field in the IP header of the received fragment when reassembling the original packet. Since IP datagrams are not guaranteed to arrive in order, an unique sequential ID is generated for each outgoing fragment so the machine receiving the packets can piece together the original packet from the fragments correctly. Each outgoing packet sent to a specific destination has an ID that is incremented by one from the previously transmitted packet sent to the same destination. Linux IP uses the Internet peer to keep track of each of the known peers so the IDs can be quickly calculated from the route table entry without having to do a separate search of the route cache or the FIB.

The `inet_peer` Structure

The Internet peers are kept on an AVL tree, and each node is an instance of the `inet_peer` structure. This structure is defined in the file `linux/include/net/inetpeer.h`.

```
struct inet_peer
{
```

The two fields, `avl_left` and `avl_right`, position the node in the AVL tree. Next, `unused_next` and `unused_prevp` are to maintain the node in the list of unused nodes.

```
        struct inet_peer    *avl_left, *avl_right;
        struct inet_peer    *unused_next, **unused_prevp;
```

The reference count for this node is in `refcnt` and must be atomically incremented and decremented. Next, `dtime` is the time when this entry was last referenced.

```
        atomic_t            refcnt;
        unsigned long       dtime;
```

The peer's IPv4 address is in `v4daddr`.

```
        __u32               v4daddr;
        __u16               avl_height;
```

The next field, `ip_id_count`, is the value for the identification field in the next IP packet, and `rid` is the fragment reception counter.

```
    __u16           ip_id_count;
    atomic_t        rid;
```

The next two fields, `tcp_ts` and `tcp_ts_stamp`, are used for TCP TIME_WAIT state recycling, where sockets in the TIME_WAIT state can be reused as new connections are requested. Old timestamp values are saved in here for at least the 2MSL interval for the TIME_WAIT state duration. When a new connection is requested, the timestamp values are restored from these values. See Chapter 9 for more information about the TIME_WAIT state in TCP.

```
    __u32           tcp_ts;
    unsigned long   tcp_ts_stamp;
};
```

Each `inet_peer` instance can be reached through the `peer` field of the `rtable` structure. There is exactly one `inet_peer` instance for each peer IP address. The `inet_peer` entry is accessed only when the IP needs to select a value for the identification field of an outgoing IP packet. Normally, `inet_peer` nodes are only removed when the reference count, `refcnt`, becomes zero. The node isn't removed immediately, but only after a certain amount of time has passed since it was last referenced. When a new route cache entry is created, it can find the `inet_peer` by searching the AVL tree. Least recently used entries may be cleaned off the tree if we are out of space or the pool of entries is overloaded. The advantage of using an AVL tree over a hash table is to reduce the risk of successful Denial-of-Service (DoS) attacks. DoS attacks can overload a single hash bucket, causing time to be wasted with linear searches. Unfortunately, since the route cache implementation uses a hash table and there is mostly a one-to-one relationship between route table entries and the `inet_peer` entries, the theoretical advantages of having the `inet_peers` in an AVL tree may not be fully realized.

THE ADDRESS RESOLUTION PROTOCOL

The ARP protocol maps IP addresses to link layer addresses [RFC 826]. It is defined for the Ethernet LAN. When a packet is about to be transmitted, the output routine prepends the link layer header to the output packet. The host contains a lookup table called the *ARP cache* that contains the mapping of the destination IP address and the link layer destination hardware address. When a lookup in the ARP cache fails, an

ARP request message is broadcast on the local area net. When an ARP response message is received, the sender will update its ARP cache.

Any implementation of TCP/IP needs both an ARP cache and a routing table. Some systems implement a separate unique table for the ARP cache that doesn't share any of the structure with the routing table. In Linux, ARP is implemented in the file linux/net/ipv4/arp.c. It uses the generic neighbor cache facility, described in Chapter 5, as the framework for the ARP cache. Some of this framework is shared with the routing cache implementation. Most of the ARP table management is supplied by the neighbor facility, and most of the generic framework for the neighbor cache was discussed in Chapter 5. However, in this section, we will show the parts that are specific to the ARP protocol. We show how the ARP-specific parts are initialized, how ARP processes incoming packets, and how it handles requests to resolve addresses.

ARP Protocol Initialization

The ARP protocol has a few structures that are initialized at compile time in the file linux/net/ipv4/arp.c.

The arp_packet_type

The first of these is the packet_type structure, which registers the handler function, arp_rcv, which will be called when an ARP packet arrives at any network interface device. Chapter 5 has more details about how packet handlers are registered.

```
static struct packet_type arp_packet_type = {
    .type = __constant_htons(ETH_P_ARP),
    .func = arp_rcv,
};
```

The arp_netdev_notifier

Another structure is the net device notifier block for the ARP protocol, arp_netdev_notifier.

```
struct notifier_block arp_netdev_notifier = {
    .notifier_call = arp_netdev_event,
};
```

The function arp_netdev_event will be called with any change in device status.

The `arp_init` Function

The ARP protocol is initialized by the function `arp_init` implemented in the file `linux/net/ipv4/arp.c`. This function is called as part of the main IP initialization process.

```
void __init arp_init(void)
{
```

The ARP cache is initialized by calling `neigh_table_init`. ARP uses the neighbor facility, and it is the neighbor cache initialization function. Here, we are creating a neighbor table instance. The `neig_table` instance for ARP, `arp_tbl`, is initialized at compile time and is shown later in this section.

```
neigh_table_init(&arp_tbl);
```

The ARP protocol is not encapsulated with an IP packet. It is encapsulated directly by the link layer header; therefore, we must call `dev_add_pack` to register our packet type with the queuing layer. As shown earlier, the handler function points to `arp_rcv`, which will be called when a packet of type ETH_P_ARP is received at the network interface

```
dev_add_pack(&arp_packet_type);
```

We call `arp_proc_init` to initialize the ARP directory in the */proc* pseudo filesystem. This is so users can look at the ARP cache and tuning parameters. Chapter 5 contains more information about the */proc* filesystem.

```
arp_proc_init();
```

There are many ARP parameters that can be tuned. We call the following function so that the ARP parameters can be set via `sysctl` if it is configured into the kernel.

```
#ifdef CONFIG_SYSCTL
    neigh_sysctl_register(NULL, &arp_tbl.parms, NET_IPV4,
                          NET_IPV4_NEIGH, "ipv4" , NULL, NULL);
#endif
```

Next, we register with the netdevice notifier so ARP will be informed when the interface address changes. When an interface address changes, the function `arp_netdev_event` will be called. We will see later that we are only interested in the NETDEV_CHANGEADDR notification. We don't use the notification of an interface going down. Instead, the function `arp_ifdown` is called directly to tell about this event.

```
        register_netdevice_notifier(&arp_netdev_notifier);
}
```

The arp_table Structure

Now let's look at how the ARP cache is instantiated. As discussed earlier, Linux uses the neighbor cache as the framework for the ARP cache. See Chapter 6 for more details about the neighbor system and the `neigh_table` structure. Next, we show how an instance, `arp_table`, is initialized at compile time. This structure is the actual ARP cache.

```
struct neigh_table arp_tbl = {
    .family    =   AF_INET,
    .entry_size = sizeof(struct neighbour) + 4,
    .key_len   =   4,
```

The `neigh_table` has a destructor function defined but it is used for ARP. This is because the ARP protocol is a permanent part of IPv4; therefore, the ARP cache will never totally be removed.

```
    .hash       =      arp_hash,
    .constructor =arp_constructor,
    .proxy_redo = parp_redo,
    .id         =      "arp_cache",
```

Here is the initialization of the `neigh_parms` values that contain the timeout values and the garbage collection intervals.

```
    .parms = {
        .tbl =                     &arp_tbl,
        .base_reachable_time =     30 * HZ,
        .retrans_time = 1 * HZ,
        .gc_staletime = 60 * HZ,
        .reachable_time =          30 * HZ,
        .delay_probe_time =  5 * HZ,
        .queue_len =         3,
        .ucast_probes = 3,
        .mcast_probes =      3,
        .anycast_delay =     1 * HZ,
        .proxy_delay =       (8 * HZ) / 10,
        .proxy_qlen =        64,
        .locktime =          1 * HZ,
```

```
        },
        .gc_interval =      30 * HZ,
        .gc_thresh1 =       128,
        .gc_thresh2 =       512,
        .gc_thresh3 =       1024,
};
```

The arp_generic_ops Structure

There are also four neighbor operations structures initialized for ARP: arp_generic_ops, arp_hh_ops, arp_direct_ops, and arp_broken_arps.

These structures contain the operation functions called when we actually must resolve an address. One of these structures, arp_generic_ops, is initialized as follows.

```
static struct neigh_ops arp_generic_ops = {
        .family =           AF_INET,
```

Only the solicit and error_report fields are set to functions unique to ARP. The other fields use the default ones for the neighbor cache.

```
        .solicit =          arp_solicit,
        .error_report =     arp_error_report,
        .output =           neigh_resolve_output,
        .connected_output = neigh_connected_output,
        .hh_output =        dev_queue_xmit,
        .queue_xmit =       dev_queue_xmit,
};
```

The arp_hh_ops Structure

The arp_hh_ops structure is initialized as shown here. Generally, this set of operations is used with Ethernet.

```
static struct neigh_ops arp_hh_ops = {
        .family =           AF_INET,
```

Again, the solicit and error_report functions are unique to ARP. The dev_queue_xmit function will queue the packet for transmission out of a network interface device. It will be called once a neighbor entry is resolved to an actual Ethernet address. The other operations are set to the generic ones for the neighbor cache.

```
        .solicit =          arp_solicit,
        .error_report =     arp_error_report,
        .output =           neigh_resolve_output,
```

```
        .connected_output = neigh_resolve_output,
        .hh_output =        dev_queue_xmit,
        .queue_xmit =       dev_queue_xmit,
};
```

The `arp_direct_ops` Structure

```
static struct neigh_ops arp_direct_ops = {
        .family =           AF_INET,
        .output =           dev_queue_xmit,
        .connected_output = dev_queue_xmit,
        .hh_output =        dev_queue_xmit,
        .queue_xmit =       dev_queue_xmit,
};
```

The `arp_broken_arps` Structure

This structure is used for unreachable destinations.

```
struct neigh_ops arp_broken_ops = {
        .family =           AF_INET,
        .solicit =          arp_solicit,
        .error_report =     arp_error_report,
        .output =           neigh_compat_output,
        .connected_output = neigh_compat_output,
        .hh_output =        dev_queue_xmit,
        .queue_xmit =       dev_queue_xmit,
};
```

Receiving and Processing ARP Packets

Like all protocols registered with an address family, ARP has a receive function that is executed when packets arrive.

The `arp_rcv` Function

This function is implemented in the file linux/net/ipv4/arp.c. It is called when an ARP packet arrives at an Ethernet or other interface that supports ARP.

```
int arp_rcv(struct sk_buff *skb, struct net_device *dev, struct packet_type *pt)
    struct arphdr *arp;
```

First, we make sure that the incoming packet is at least long enough to hold the ARP header. If not, we free the packet and get out.

```
    if (!pskb_may_pull(skb, (sizeof(struct arphdr) +
                       (2 * dev->addr_len) +
                       (2 * sizeof(u32)))))
        goto freeskb;
```

In this function, we check to make sure that the interface through which the packet arrived uses the ARP protocol and that the packet is not a loopback packet.

```
    if (arp->ar_hln != dev->addr_len ||
        dev->flags & IFF_NOARP ||
        skb->pkt_type == PACKET_OTHERHOST ||
        skb->pkt_type == PACKET_LOOPBACK ||
        arp->ar_pln != 4)
        goto freeskb;
```

Next, we check to make sure that the incoming packet is not shared. This would be the case if another protocol had received the packet and was modifying it. This is unlikely, but possible.

```
    if ((skb = skb_share_check(skb, GFP_ATOMIC)) == NULL)
        goto out_of_mem;
```

If all is okay, we call arp_process through the net filter. IP tables can then log the incoming ARP events.

```
    memset(NEIGH_CB(skb), 0, sizeof(struct neighbour_cb));
    return NF_HOOK(NF_ARP, NF_ARP_IN, skb, dev, NULL, arp_process);
freeskb:
    kfree_skb(skb);
out_of_mem:
    return 0;
}
```

The arp_process Function

The next function, arp_process, also implemented in the file linux/net/ipv4/arp.c, handles all arp_request packets. It is called from the low-level packet handler function arp_rcv.

```
int arp_process(struct sk_buff *skb)
    struct net_device *dev = skb->dev;
    struct in_device *in_dev = in_dev_get(dev);
```

Arp points to the ARP header in the incoming packet.

```
struct arphdr *arp;
unsigned char *arp_ptr;
struct rtable *rt;
```

This variable, sha, points to the source hardware address, and tha points to the target hardware address.

```
unsigned char *sha, *tha;
```

The next two, sip and tip, are for the source IP and destination IP addresses specified in the ARP packet.

```
u32 sip, tip;
u16 dev_type = dev->type;
int addr_type;
struct neighbour *n;
```

First, we verify the packet header and make sure that the incoming network interface is an ARP-type interface. We allow for ARP packets from Ethernet, Token Ring, and FDDI.

```
if (in_dev == NULL)
    goto out;
arp = skb->nh.arph;
switch (dev_type) {
default:
    if (arp->ar_pro != htons(ETH_P_IP) ||
        htons(dev_type) != arp->ar_hrd)
        goto out;
    break;
```

This switch contains cases for each of the devices that are defined to support ARP.

```
#ifdef CONFIG_NET_ETHERNET
    case ARPHRD_ETHER:
#endif
#ifdef CONFIG_TR
    case ARPHRD_IEEE802_TR:
#endif
```

```
#ifdef CONFIG_FDDI
    case ARPHRD_FDDI:
#endif
```

In addition, we check for IEEE 802-type headers.

```
#ifdef CONFIG_NET_FC
    case ARPHRD_IEEE802:
#endif
#if defined(CONFIG_NET_ETHERNET) || defined(CONFIG_TR) || \
    defined(CONFIG_FDDI)          || defined(CONFIG_NET_FC)
```

If the framing is IEEE 802 type framing, we accept hardware types of both ARPHRD_ETHER, one, and ARPHRD_IEEE802, six. This is also true for Fibre Channel (FDDI) [RFC 2625]. The ARP hardware types are defined in the file linux/include/linux/if_arp.h.

```
            if ((arp->ar_hrd != htons(ARPHRD_ETHER) &&
                arp->ar_hrd != htons(ARPHRD_IEEE802)) ||
                arp->ar_pro != htons(ETH_P_IP))
                goto out;
            break;
#endif
#if defined(CONFIG_AX25) || defined(CONFIG_AX25_MODULE)
    case ARPHRD_AX25:
            if (arp->ar_pro != htons(AX25_P_IP) ||
                arp->ar_hrd != htons(ARPHRD_AX25))
                goto out;
            break;
#if defined(CONFIG_NETROM) || defined(CONFIG_NETROM_MODULE)
    case ARPHRD_NETROM:
            if (arp->ar_pro != htons(AX25_P_IP) ||
                arp->ar_hrd != htons(ARPHRD_NETROM))
                goto out;
            break;
#endif
#endif
    }
```

We accept only ARP request and ARP reply type messages. This is okay because there really aren't any other ARP message types.

```
        if (arp->ar_op != htons(ARPOP_REPLY) &&
            arp->ar_op != htons(ARPOP_REQUEST))
            goto out;
```

Next, we extract some fields from the ARP header.

```
arp_ptr= (unsigned char *)(arp+1);
sha     = arp_ptr;
arp_ptr += dev->addr_len;
memcpy(&sip, arp_ptr, 4);
arp_ptr += 4;
tha     = arp_ptr;
arp_ptr += dev->addr_len;
memcpy(&tip, arp_ptr, 4);
```

Now we check for strange ARP requests such as requests for the loopback address or multicast addresses.

```
if (LOOPBACK(tip) || MULTICAST(tip))
    goto out;
```

This is a special case in which we must set the Frame Relay (FR) source (Q.922) address.

```
if (dev_type == ARPHRD_DLCI)
    sha = dev->broadcast;
```

At this point, we handle ARP request packets first. First, we handle the special case for duplicate address detection. We check to see whether the source IP address in the request packet is zero and the target IP address is one of our local addresses. If so, we can send the response right away.

```
if (sip == 0) {
    if (arp->ar_op == htons(ARPOP_REQUEST) &&
        inet_addr_type(tip) == RTN_LOCAL)
        arp_send(ARPOP_REPLY,ETH_P_ARP,tip,dev,tip,sha,dev-
>dev_addr,dev->dev_addr);
    goto out;
}
```

Now we handle the general case for the ARP request message type. We validate the address by checking to make sure that we have a route to the address being requested.

```
if (arp->ar_op == htons(ARPOP_REQUEST) &&
    ip_route_input(skb, tip, sip, 0, dev) == 0) {
    rt = (struct rtable*)skb->dst;
    addr_type = rt->rt_type;
```

Next, `neigh_event_ns` does a lookup in the ARP cache for the source hardware address. If found, it updates the neighbor cache entry.

```
if (addr_type == RTN_LOCAL) {
    n = neigh_event_ns(&arp_tbl, sha, &sip, dev);
    if (n) {
        int dont_send = 0;
        if (!dont_send)
            dont_send |= arp_ignore(in_dev,dev,sip,tip);
        if (!dont_send && IN_DEV_ARPFILTER(in_dev))
            dont_send |= arp_filter(sip,tip,dev);
        if (!dont_send)
```

Here is where we send out the ARP reply message if, of course, we found the entry in the ARP cache.

```
            arp_send(ARPOP_REPLY,ETH_P_ARP,sip,dev,tip,sha,
                    dev->dev_addr,sha);
        neigh_release(n);
    }
    goto out;
```

This is a check to see whether we are receiving a proxy ARP request. We check to see whether the input device is configured for IP forwarding and the route is a NAT route. The function `arp_fwd_proxy` is a check whether we can use proxy ARP for a particular route. Rt points to the route cache entry for this packet.

```
} else if (IN_DEV_FORWARD(in_dev)) {
    if ((rt->rt_flags&RTCF_DNAT) ||
        (addr_type == RTN_UNICAST  && rt->u.dst.dev != dev &&
        (arp_fwd_proxy(in_dev, rt) || pneigh_lookup(&arp_tbl,
          &tip, dev, 0)))) {
        n = neigh_event_ns(&arp_tbl, sha, &sip, dev);
        if (n)
            neigh_release(n);
```

Now, we timestamp the incoming packet.

```
        if (NEIGH_CB(skb)->flags & LOCALLY_ENQUEUED ||
            skb->pkt_type == PACKET_HOST ||
            in_dev->arp_parms->proxy_delay == 0) {
```

Here we send out the ARP reply packet.

```
                        arp_send(ARPOP_REPLY,ETH_P_ARP,sip,dev,tip,sha,
                        dev->dev_addr,sha);
                } else {
```

Next, pneigh_enqueue puts skb on the proxy queue and starts the timer in the arp_tbl.

```
                        pneigh_enqueue(&arp_tbl, in_dev->arp_parms, skb);
                        in_dev_put(in_dev);
                        return 0;
                }
                goto out;
            }
        }
    }
```

Now we look for an entry in the ARP table matching the address and the network interface device. The zero in the last argument says to not create a new entry.

```
    n = __neigh_lookup(&arp_tbl, &sip, dev, 0);
```

If we are configured for accepting unsolicited ARPs, we process them. Unsolicited ARPs are not accepted by default.

```
#ifdef CONFIG_IP_ACCEPT_UNSOLICITED_ARP
    if (n == NULL &&
        arp->ar_op == htons(ARPOP_REPLY) &&
        inet_addr_type(sip) == RTN_UNICAST)
        n = __neigh_lookup(&arp_tbl, &sip, dev, -1);
#endif
```

If n is not NULL, it means we found an existing entry in the ARP table.

```
    if (n) {
```

We set the NUD state to reachable. All reachable nodes can have an entry in the ARP cache.

```
        int state = NUD_REACHABLE;
```

Override is set to one if we want to override the existing cache entry with a new one. We try to use the first ARP reply if we have received several back to back.

```
        int override;
        override = time_after(jiffies, n->updated + n->parms->locktime);
```

If the ARP reply was a broadcast, or the incoming packet is not a reply packet, it means that the NUD state for the destination should not be flagged as reachable. We mark it as stale.

```
        if (arp->ar_op != htons(ARPOP_REPLY) ||
            skb->pkt_type != PACKET_HOST)
                state = NUD_STALE;
```

Finally, we call `neigh_update` to update the neighbor cache entry. `neigh_release` decrements the use count in the neighbor cache entry because we are no longer operating on this entry.

```
        neigh_update(n, sha, state,
                     override ? NEIGH_UPDATE_F_OVERRIDE : 0);
        neigh_release(n);
    }
out:
    if (in_dev)
        in_dev_put(in_dev);
    kfree_skb(skb);
    return 0;
}
```

THE INTERNET CONTROL MESSAGE PROTOCOL (ICMP)

The ICMP protocol handles many control functions for IPv4. The protocol is often thought of as part of IP, and ICMP messages are carried inside IP packets. The most common ICMP use is ping, which consists of echo request and echo reply packets. Many different types of ICMP packets exist, each of which requires different actions. Linux ICMP uses an array to dispatch control functions depending on the input packet types.

The `icmp_control` Array

The array, `icmp_control`, is defined in the file linux/net/ipv4/icmp.c.

```
        struct icmp_control {
```

Many ICMP packets require a packet field to be incremented. This structure contains an offset to a statistics counter to be incremented on output and a similar offset for input.

```
int output_off;
int input_off;
```

Next, `handler` points to a function to handle this specific message type. The next field, `error`, is set to one if this particular message is an error message.

```
    void (*handler)(struct sk_buff *skb);
    short    error;
};
```

Table 8.8 lists the ICMP message types that are defined in the file `linux/include/linux/icmp.h`.

TABLE 8.8 ICMP Messages

Message	Value	Handler	Output Counter	Output Counter
ICMP_ECHOREPLY	0	icmp_discard	IcmpOutEchoReps	IcmpInEchoReps
ICMP_DEST_UNREACH	3	icmp_unreach	IcmpOutDestUnreachs	IcmpInDestUnreachs
ICMP_SOURCE_QUENCH	4	icmp_unreach	IcmpOutSrcQuenchs	IcmpInSrcQuenchs
ICMP_REDIRECT	5	icmp_redirect	IcmpOutRedirects	IcmpInRedirects
ICMP_ECHO	8	icmp_echo	IcmpOutEchos	IcmpInEchos
ICMP_TIME_EXCEEDED	11	icmp_unreach	IcmpOutTimeExcds	IcmpInTimeExcds
ICMP_PARAMETERPROB	12	icmp_unreach	IcmpOutParmProbs	IcmpInParmProbs
ICMP_TIMESTAMP	13	icmp_timestamp	IcmpOutTimestamps	IcmpInTimestamps
ICMP_TIMESTAMPREPLY	14	icmp_discard	IcmpOutTimestampReps	IcmpInTimestampReps
ICMP_INFO_REQUEST	15	icmp_discard	dummy	dummy
ICMP_INFO_REPLY	16	icmp_discard	dummy	dummy
ICMP_ADDRESS	17	icmp_address	IcmpOutAddrMasks	IcmpInAddrMasks
ICMP_ADDRESSREPLY	18	icmp_address_reply	IcmpOutAddrMaskReps	IcmpInAddrMaskReps

ICMP Packet Processing

When the AF_INET family is initialized, the initialization function in linux/net/ipv4/af_inet.c calls inet_add_protocol to add ICMP to the list of protocols that will receive IPv4 packets after IP is done.

The icmp_rcv Function

The handler function for ICMP is icmp_rcv, defined in the file linux/net/ipv4/icmp.c. The main purpose of icmp_rcv is to dispatch separate handler functions for all the ICMP message types shown in Table 8.8. It will receive all incoming ICMP packets once they are stripped of their IPv4 headers. These values are defined in the file linux/include/linux/icmp.h.

```
int icmp_rcv(struct sk_buff *skb)
{
```

The first variable, icmph, points to the ICMP header in the incoming packet, and rt is the route cache entry.

```
struct icmphdr *icmph;
struct rtable *rt = (struct rtable *)skb->dst;
ICMP_INC_STATS_BH(ICMP_MIB_INMSGS);
```

Here, we do some basic packet validity checks. First, we check to if the checksums are correct.

```
switch (skb->ip_summed) {
case CHECKSUM_HW:
    if (!(u16)csum_fold(skb->csum))
        break;
case CHECKSUM_NONE:
    skb->csum = 0;
    if (__skb_checksum_complete(skb))
        goto error;
}
```

Now, we check to see that the packet is at least as long as the length of the ICMP header.

```
if (!pskb_pull(skb, sizeof(struct icmphdr)))
    goto error;
```

If the packet is okay, we set a pointer to the ICMP header in the packet.

```
icmph = skb->h.icmph;
```

Now, we check to see whether we got an illegal ICMP packet type. If so, we silently discard it [RFC 1122].

```
if (icmph->type > NR_ICMP_TYPES)
    goto error;
if (rt->rt_flags & (RTCF_BROADCAST | RTCF_MULTICAST)) {
```

An ICMP echo sent to a broadcast address may be silently ignored [RFC 1122]. An ICMP timestamp packet may be silently discarded if it is sent to a broadcast or multicast address. Linux provides a sysctl variable to govern this behavior.

```
    if ((icmph->type == ICMP_ECHO ||
         icmph->type == ICMP_TIMESTAMP) &&
         sysctl_icmp_echo_ignore_broadcasts) {
        goto error;
    }
    if (icmph->type != ICMP_ECHO &&
        icmph->type != ICMP_TIMESTAMP &&
        icmph->type != ICMP_ADDRESS &&
        icmph->type != ICMP_ADDRESSREPLY) {
        goto error;
    }
}
```

Now, we are ready to dispatch one of the control functions listed in Table 8.8 based on the ICMP message type.

```
ICMP_INC_STATS_BH_FIELD(icmp_pointers[icmph->type].input_entry);
icmp_pointers[icmph->type].handler(skb);
```

Finally, we are done.

```
drop:
    kfree_skb(skb);
    return 0;
error:
    ICMP_INC_STATS_BH(ICMP_MIB_INERRORS);
    goto drop;
}
```

The `icmp_unreach` Function

The next function we examine is `icmp_unreach`, which processes the various types of incoming packets sent by a peer or router when a destination is unreachable including unreachable, time exceeded, and quench packets.

```
static void icmp_unreach(struct sk_buff *skb)
    struct iphdr *iph;
    struct icmphdr *icmph;
    int hash, protocol;
    struct net_protocol *ipprot;
    struct sock *raw_sk;
    u32 info = 0;
    if (!pskb_may_pull(skb, sizeof(struct iphdr)))
        goto out_err;
    icmph = skb->h.icmph;
    iph   = (struct iphdr *)skb->data;
    if (iph->ihl < 5);
        goto out_err;
    if (icmph->type == ICMP_DEST_UNREACH) {
```

We decode the `code` field in the ICMP header to see what type of unreachable packet this is. A few of the codes require special handling.

```
        switch (icmph->code & 15) {
        case ICMP_NET_UNREACH:
        case ICMP_HOST_UNREACH:
        case ICMP_PROT_UNREACH:
        case ICMP_PORT_UNREACH:
            break;
        case ICMP_FRAG_NEEDED:
```

If we get a ICMP packet with an `ICMP_FRAG_NEEDED` code, we call `ip_rt_frag_needed` to process the fragment request. This ICMP type is used with the MTU discovery and means that we have to decrease our packet size by performing IP fragmentation.

```
            if (ipv4_config.no_pmtu_disc) {
```

If we are not configured for MTU discovery, we receive this packet type in error.

```
                    LIMIT_NETDEBUG (KERN_INFO "ICMP: %u.%u.%u.%u: "
                                    "fragmentation needed "
                                    "and DF set.\n",
                                    NIPQUAD(iph->daddr));
        } else {
```

We call `ip_rt_frag_needed` to let IP know that it must fragment the packet.

```
            info = ip_rt_frag_needed(iph,
                                    ntohs(icmph->un.frag.mtu));
            if (!info)
                goto out;
        }
        break;
```

This packet type indicates that ICMP source routing failed. We don't support source routing, so we mark an error.

```
        case ICMP_SR_FAILED:
            LIMIT_NETDEBUG(KERN_INFO "ICMP: %u.%u.%u.%u: Source "
                            "Route Failed.\n",
                            NIPQUAD(iph->daddr));
            break;
        default:
            break;
    }
```

We check for packets of illegal codes. If so, we silently discard them.

```
        if (icmph->code > NR_ICMP_UNREACH)
            goto out;
    } else if (icmph->type == ICMP_PARAMETERPROB)
        info = ntohl(icmph->un.gateway) >> 24;
```

We must pass an ICMP parameter problem packet up through the protocol layers and eventually back to the open socket [RFC1122]. We also pass the code up to any open raw socket, but that code snippet isn't shown here. Hash is calculated from the protocol field in the IP header and is used to find the error socket for the protocol.

```
    if (!sysctl_icmp_ignore_bogus_error_responses &&
        inet_addr_type(iph->daddr) == RTN_BROADCAST) {
        if (net_ratelimit())
            printk(KERN_WARNING "%u.%u.%u.%u sent an invalid ICMP "
```

```
                    "type %u, code %u "
                     "error to a broadcast: %u.%u.%u.%u on %s\n",
                    NIPQUAD(skb->nh.iph->saddr),
                    icmph->type, icmph->code,
                    NIPQUAD(iph->daddr),
                    skb->dev->name);
        goto out;
    }
    if (!pskb_may_pull(skb, iph->ihl * 4 + 8))
        goto out;
    iph = (struct iphdr *)skb->data;
    protocol = iph->protocol;
    hash = protocol & (MAX_INET_PROTOS - 1);
    read_lock(&raw_v4_lock);
    if ((raw_sk = sk_head(&raw_v4_htable[hash])) != NULL) {
        while ((raw_sk = __raw_v4_lookup(raw_sk, protocol, iph->daddr,
                                         iph->saddr,
                                         skb->dev->ifindex)) != NULL) {
            raw_err(raw_sk, skb, info);
            raw_sk = sk_next(raw_sk);
            iph = (struct iphdr *)skb->data;
        }
    }
    read_unlock(&raw_v4_lock);
    rcu_read_lock();
    ipprot = rcu_dereference(inet_protos[hash]);
```

Here, we call the registered error handler function for the transport protocol indicated in the `protocol` field so that protocol can be informed of the error condition.

```
    if (ipprot && ipprot->err_handler)
        ipprot->err_handler(skb, info);
    rcu_read_unlock();
out:
    return;
out_err:
    ICMP_INC_STATS_BH(ICMP_MIB_INERRORS);
    goto out;
}
```

Some Other Functions from Table 8.8

The other functions shown in Table 8.8 are called in the same way as `icmp_unreach` described previously. These functions are also found in the file linux/net/ipv4/icmp.c.

The `icmp_redirect` Function

For example, the function `icmp_redirect` is called when an ICMP redirect packet is received. It gets the header of the packet that caused the redirect and calls the function `ip_rt_redirect` to update the routing table.

```
static void icmp_redirect(struct sk_buff *skb)
```

The `icmp_echo` Function

The next function, `icmp_echo`, is called when pings, `ICMP_ECHO` type packets, are received.

```
static void icmp_echo(struct sk_buff *skb);
```

The `icmp_timestamp` Function

This function, `icmp_timestamp`, is the handler for ICMP timestamp requests. It changes the ICMP header type field to `ICMP_ECHOREPLY` and calls `icmp_reply` to send the reply packet [RFC 1122].

It builds a packet of type `ICMP_TIMESTAMPREPLY`, calculates the time in the correct format, and sends the packet by calling `icmp_reply`.

SENDING ICMP PACKETS

The code for constructing and sending ICMP packets is also found in the file linux/net/ipv4/icmp.c.

The `icmp_reply` Function

The main function for sending ICMP packets is `icmp_reply`, which builds and sends ICMP response messages of various types.

```
static void icmp_reply(struct icmp_bxm *icmp_param, struct sk_buff *skb)
{
    struct sock *sk = icmp_socket->sk;
    struct inet_sock *inet = inet_sk(sk);
    struct ipcm_cookie ipc;
```

This function does a few interesting things before sending the packet. Later, it builds a routing table entry, actually the destination cache entry. It needs a pointer to the `dst_entry` structure in the output socket buffer, `skb`.

```
    struct rtable *rt = (struct rtable *)skb->dst;
    u32 daddr;
    if (ip_options_echo(&icmp_param->replyopts, skb))
        return;
    if (icmp_xmit_lock())
        return;
    icmp_param->data.icmph.checksum = 0;
    icmp_out_count(icmp_param->data.icmph.type);
    inet->tos = skb->nh.iph->tos;
    daddr = ipc.addr = rt->rt_src;
    ipc.opt = NULL;
    if (icmp_param->replyopts.optlen) {
        ipc.opt = &icmp_param->replyopts;
        if (ipc.opt->srr)
            daddr = icmp_param->replyopts.faddr;
    }
```

We build a route cache lookup `flowi` structure and get a route cache entry. Then it checks to see whether the ICMP output packets are rate limited and if we should allow this packet to go out.

```
    {
        struct flowi fl = { .nl_u = { .ip4_u =
                                        { .daddr = daddr,
                                          .saddr = rt->rt_spec_dst,
                                          .tos = RT_TOS(skb->nh.iph->tos)
                                        } },
                            .proto = IPPROTO_ICMP };
        if (ip_route_output_key(&rt, &fl))
            goto out_unlock;
```

This is to check to see whether we are doing ICMP rate limiting. ICMP rate limiting is a technique to prevent DoS attacks by flooding a system with ICMP packets.

```
    if (icmpv4_xrlim_allow(rt, icmp_param->data.icmph.type,
                            icmp_param->data.icmph.code))
```

We queue the packet for transmission, release our route cache entry, and go out.

```
        icmp_push_reply(icmp_param, &ipc, rt);
    ip_rt_put(rt);
out_unlock:
    icmp_xmit_unlock();
}
```

The `icmp_push_reply` Function

In this function, we actually send out the ICMP packets. We will recall that an internal socket was created when the ICMP protocol was initialized. In this function, we use that socket as a way to transmit output packets down the protocol stack. The packets are queued for transmission by placing them on the socket's output queue. This function queues completed ICMP packets on the socket for transmission.

```
static void icmp_push_reply(struct icmp_bxm *icmp_param,
                    struct ipcm_cookie *ipc, struct rtable *rt)
{
    struct sk_buff *skb;
```

Here, we append data to the socket. We make sure that there is room on the sockets `write_queue`. We calculate the checksum as we copy the data.

```
    ip_append_data(icmp_socket->sk, icmp_glue_bits, icmp_param,
                icmp_param->data_len+icmp_param->head_len,
                icmp_param->head_len,
                ipc, rt, MSG_DONTWAIT);
    if ((skb = skb_peek(&icmp_socket->sk->sk_write_queue)) != NULL) {
        struct icmphdr *icmph = skb->h.icmph;
        unsigned int csum = 0;
        struct sk_buff *skb1;
        skb_queue_walk(&icmp_socket->sk->sk_write_queue, skb1) {
            csum = csum_add(csum, skb1->csum);
        }
        csum = csum_partial_copy_nocheck((void *)&icmp_param->data,
                            (char *)icmph,
                            icmp_param->head_len, csum);
        icmph->checksum = csum_fold(csum);
        skb->ip_summed = CHECKSUM_NONE;
```

We call `ip_push_pending_frames` to force IP to send the packets.

```
        ip_push_pending_frames(icmp_socket->sk);
    }
}
```

MULTICAST AND IGMP

The Internet Group Management Protocol (IGMP) is for exchanging messages to manage multicast routing and message transmission. Essentially, the purpose of

IGMP is to associate a group of unicast addresses to a specific class D multicast address. The protocol exchanges information about these groups between hosts and routers.

There are three versions of IGMP: version 1 [RFC 1112], version 2, and version 3 [RFC 3376]. All three versions are interoperable. Version 1 specifies two types of messages, a membership query message sent by IGMP routers, and a membership report sent by IGMP hosts. A host sends the membership report to tell multicast routers to forward messages that are sent to the group address. Version 2 adds a leave group message so a host can tell a router when it wants to leave a group and no longer receive packets sent to that particular group address. Version 3 adds source-specific information. Linux supports the host side of IGMP version 3.

In Linux, multicast capability is optional. It can be completely deconfigured from the Linux kernel. Although the Linux TCP/IP implementation supports host-side multicasting, the kernel by itself is not a multicast router. The routing engine knows how to forward multicast messages, but Linux does not support the automatic updating of the routing tables by incoming IGMP reports. An application layer program such as *mrouted* is required to fully implement multicast routing in Linux. Most the functions described in this section are implemented in the file linux/net/ipv4/igmp.c.

The `ip_mreqn` Structure

Two important data structures are used by Linux IGMP. The first of these is the multicast request, `ip_mreqn`, defined in the file linux/include/linux/in.h. It is for communicating join- or leave-group requests between the socket layer and the internal kernel functions that process the requests.

```
struct ip_mreqn
{
```

The first field in this structure is the multicast address for the group that we want to either join or leave.

```
    struct in_addr    imr_multiaddr;
```

This field specifies the IP address of the local interface through which we want to receive datagrams sent to the multicast group address.

```
    struct in_addr    imr_address;
```

This field is the index of the interface through which we want to receive the datagrams.

```
            int          imr_ifindex;
    };
```

The `ip_mc_socklist` Structure

The second data structure we want to consider is the multicast socket list, `ip_mc_socklist`, defined in `linux/include/linux/igmp.h`. It is for holding the list of addresses for membership reports.

```
    struct ip_mc_socklist
    {
        struct ip_mc_socklist    *next;
        struct ip_mreqn    multi;
```

The next field, `sfmode`, is the multicast source filter mode. It says whether to include or exclude this entry.

```
        unsigned int      sfmode;
```

Next we have `sflist`, which is for multicast source filtering.

```
        struct ip_sf_socklist*sflist;
    };
```

Receiving IGMP Packets

As is the case with the other member protocols in the AF_INET family, the handler function for IGMP is registered with the IP protocol to receive IP packets for each protocol type.

This is done during the initialization process by the function `inet_init` in the file `linux/net/ipv4/af_inet.c`.

The `igmp_rcv` Function

The IGMP main receive function registered for IGMP is `igmp_rcv`. This function is in the file `linux/net/ipv4/igmp.c`.

```
    int igmp_rcv(struct sk_buff *skb)
        struct igmphdr *ih;
```

We need to get the `in_device` structure from the network interface device, because this is where the multicast address lists are stored. If `in_dev` is NULL, that means that the network interface can't receive or transmit IP packets.

```
    struct in_device *in_dev = in_dev_get(skb->dev);
    int len = skb->len;
    if (in_dev==NULL) {
        kfree_skb(skb);
        return 0;
    }
```

Here we check to make sure that the incoming packet is at least long enough to hold the IGMP header information. We also validate the checksums.

```
    if (!pskb_may_pull(skb, sizeof(struct igmphdr)))
        goto drop;
    switch (skb->ip_summed) {
    case CHECKSUM_HW:
        if (!(u16)csum_fold(skb->csum))
            break;
    case CHECKSUM_NONE:
        skb->csum = 0;
        if (__skb_checksum_complete(skb))
            goto drop;
    }
    ih = skb->h.igmph;
```

The `type` field is retrieved from the IGMP header.

```
    switch (ih->type) {
    case IGMP_HOST_MEMBERSHIP_QUERY:
```

The function `igmp_heard_query` handles incoming IGMP queries.

```
        igmp_heard_query(in_dev, skb, len);
        break;
    case IGMP_HOST_MEMBERSHIP_REPORT:
    case IGMPV2_HOST_MEMBERSHIP_REPORT:
    case IGMPV3_HOST_MEMBERSHIP_REPORT:
```

We check to see that we are not looking at our own looped-back report by checking to see whether there is no input network driver interface.

```
        if (((struct rtable*)skb->dst)->fl.iif == 0)
            break;
```

The function `igmp_heard_report` handles incoming reports. Make sure that these incoming packets were truly multicast packets. Reports shouldn't be sent out via unicast.

```
            if (skb->pkt_type == PACKET_MULTICAST ||
                skb->pkt_type == PACKET_BROADCAST)
                igmp_heard_report(in_dev, ih->group);
            break;
        case IGMP_PIM:
#ifdef CONFIG_IP_PIMSM_V1
            in_dev_put(in_dev);
            return pim_rcv_v1(skb);
#endif
        case IGMP_DVMRP:
        case IGMP_TRACE:
    case IGMP_HOST_LEAVE_MESSAGE:
        case IGMP_MTRACE:
        case IGMP_MTRACE_RESP:
            break;
        default:
        }
drop:
        in_dev_put(in_dev);
        kfree_skb(skb);
        return 0;
}
```

Handling IGMP Queries

IGMP queries are sent from routers to the all-hosts destination. This means that all reachable IGMP routers should see this query. If we are an IGMP router, we should respond to the query with a membership report.

The `igmp_heard_query` Function

The function `igmp_heard_query` processes incoming IGMP queries. This function is in linux/net/ipv4/igmp.c.

```
    static void igmp_heard_query(struct in_device *in_dev,
                                 struct sk_buff *skb,
                                 int len)
    {
```

The first variable, ih, points to the IGMP header of the incoming packet.

```
struct igmphdr         *ih = skb->h.igmph;
struct igmpv3_query *ih3 = (struct igmpv3_query *)ih;
struct ip_mc_list   *im;
```

Next, group is the multicasting group, which is the same thing as a class D IP address.

```
u32                 group = ih->group;
int                 max_delay;
int                 mark = 0;
```

The first thing we have to do is figure out whether the incoming query is version 1, 2, or 3. Reports are sent out at pseudo-random intervals. We set timers for version 1 and version 2. A packet length of eight means that either we have a version 1 or a version 2 query.

```
if (len == 8) {
    if (ih->code == 0) {
```

A zero value in the code field of the IGMP header means that this is a version 1 query.

```
        max_delay = IGMP_Query_Response_Interval;
        in_dev->mr_v1_seen = jiffies +
            IGMP_V1_Router_Present_Timeout;
        group = 0;
    } else {
        max_delay = ih->code*(HZ/IGMP_TIMER_SCALE);
        in_dev->mr_v2_seen = jiffies +
            IGMP_V2_Router_Present_Timeout;
    }
```

Here, we cancel the interface change timer.

```
    in_dev->mr_ifc_count = 0;
    if (del_timer(&in_dev->mr_ifc_timer))
        __in_dev_put(in_dev);
```

Clear all deleted report items.

```
    igmpv3_clear_delrec(in_dev);
} else if (len < 12) {
```

If the length is greater than 8 but less than 12, this must be a bogus packet. The caller frees it.

```
        return;
    } else {
```

The incoming packet must be a version 3 query. We make sure that the packet is at least as long as the version 3 query header.

```
        if (!pskb_may_pull(skb, sizeof(struct igmpv3_query)))
            return;
```

The variable ih3 points to the version 3 query header. We check that the packet is sufficiently long to hold the source addresses if there are any.

```
        ih3 = (struct igmpv3_query *) skb->h.raw;
```

We check the number of source addresses in the version 3 packet.

```
        if (ih3->nsrcs) {
            if (!pskb_may_pull(skb, sizeof(struct igmpv3_query)
                            + ntohs(ih3->nsrcs)*sizeof(__u32)))
                return;
            ih3 = (struct igmpv3_query *) skb->h.raw;
        }
        max_delay = IGMPV3_MRC(ih3->code)*(HZ/IGMP_TIMER_SCALE);
        if (!max_delay)
            max_delay = 1;
        in_dev->mr_maxdelay = max_delay;
        if (ih3->qrv)
            in_dev->mr_qrv = ih3->qrv;
```

The value in the IGMP group field lets us know whether this is a general query or whether it is a source-specific query.

```
        if (!group) {
```

Number-of-sources must be zero for a general query.

```
            if (ih3->nsrcs)
                return
```

We start the group query timer. Each interface has a timer, which is in the inet_device structure described in Chapter 5. The timer will schedule the next query.

```
            igmp_gq_start_timer(in_dev);
            return;
    }
```

If there are included sources, we indicate that by setting mark.

```
        mark = ih3->nsrcs != 0;
    }
```

Now, we start timers in all of the membership groups to which the query applies for the interface from which we received the query. If a timer is already running, it is reset. We don't start timers for any well-known IGMP groups such as the all hosts group, 224.0.0.1.

```
        read_lock(&in_dev->lock);
        for (im=in_dev->mc_list; im!=NULL; im=im->next) {
            int changed;
            if (group && group != im->multiaddr)
                continue;
            if (im->multiaddr == IGMP_ALL_HOSTS)
                continue;
            spin_lock_bh(&im->lock);
            if (im->tm_running)
                im->gsquery = im->gsquery && mark;
            else
                im->gsquery = mark;
            changed = !im->gsquery ||
                igmp_marksources(im, ntohs(ih3->nsrcs), ih3->srcs);
            spin_unlock_bh(&im->lock);
            igmp_mod_timer(im, max_delay);
        }
        read_unlock(&in_dev->lock);
    }
```

Handling IGMP Reports

IGMP reports are handled by an IGMP router. The Linux multicasting router facility is not implemented in the kernel. The kernel receives the reports but depends on a multicast routing daemon such as *mrouted* to interpret the raw IGMP packets and update the routing tables.

The `igmp_heard_report` Function

This function listens for incoming IGMP reports.

```
static void igmp_heard_report(struct in_device *in_dev, u32 group);
```

It does little more than stop the timer for the group, which is referenced in the membership report packet.

Adding and Leaving Groups

When an application using IGMP version 2 wants to join a group, it calls the `setsockopt` function with the option `IP_ADD_MEMBERSHIP` or `MCAST_JOIN_GROUP`.

The `ip_mc_join_group` Function

If `setsockopt` sees either of these options, it calls `ip_mc_join_group`.

```
int ip_mc_join_group(struct sock *sk , struct ip_mreqn *imr);
```

This function must find the network interface specified by the index in `ip_mreqn`, a data structure discussed earlier. Next, it checks for a match between the multicast address in `ip_mreqn` and the list of multicast addresses assigned to the interface. If it finds a match, it increments the reference count and adds the unicast address to the group. Then, it calls `ip_mc_inc_group`, which will set the timer for that group. Later when the timer expires, the group report will be transmitted.

The `ip_mc_leave_group` Function

If the application using IGMP version 2 is requesting to leave a group, it will call `setsockopt` with either the `MCAST_LEAVE_GROUP` or the `IP_DROP_MEMBERSHIP` option set. In this case, `setsockopt` will call the function `ip_mc_leave_group`.

```
int ip_mc_leave_group(struct sock *sk, struct ip_mreqn *imr);
```

As with the join group function, the second argument, `imr`, points to the multicast request structure shown earlier. The function must find the `inet_device` for the interface. It then removes the specified multicast address from the interface.

SENDING PACKETS FROM IP

In Chapter 5, we explained that IP queues its packet to the output network interface drivers through the queuing layer. Linux provides multiple queuing disciplines that are selected by traffic class. When IP is done forming a packet, it places the packet on one of these queues. However, the IP output routine is not called directly. Instead, it is done indirectly through the `output` operation field in the neighbor cache entry.

In general, all internal packet routing is done through the neighbor cache. For example, if a packet is supposed to be forwarded, the neighbor cache output pointer will point to `ip_forward`. After all the processing of an output packet is complete, and if there is an unresolved route for the packet, the neighbor cache's output operation may point to the function, `ip_output`. If there is a resolved route for the packet, the output function will point to `dev_queue_xmit`. The queuing layer and the lower part of the IP transmit facility was discussed in Chapter 5.

In this section, we discuss the functions called directly from the upper layers to construct an IP datagram from a UDP datagram or a TCP segment. IP provides several functions for this purpose, and they are defined in the file `linux/net/ipv4/ip_output.c`. Some of the functions we will discuss are used by datagram-oriented transport layer protocols, such as UDP or raw sockets. One of the functions builds a single IP datagram from pieces. Another does the same thing but builds the datagram from mapped memory pages. In addition, we will discuss a function used primarily by TCP to make an IP datagram from a TCP segment.

The `ip_append_data` Function

```
int ip_append_data(struct sock *sk,
                int getfrag(void *from, char *to, int offset,
                        int len, int odd,
                        struct sk_buff *skb),
                void *from,  int length,
                int transhdrlen,  struct ipcm_cookie *ipc,
                struct rtable *rt, unsigned int flags);
```

The parameter `getfrag` points to the function called to get the IP fragment contents. Usually, it will point to `ip_generic_getfrag`, which copies the actual data from user space into the kernel buffers while simultaneously calculating the IP checksum. The argument `from` points to the data buffer, and `offset` is an offset into the data buffer. The parameter, `transhdrlen`, is the header length without IP options, and `ipc` points to the control message structure from the `sendmsg` socket call. It contains the IP options to be put in the IP header. The route cache entry for the output packet is in `rt`, and this is where we get the destination address.

The first thing that we do in `ip_append_data` is check to see whether the socket write queue is empty. If so, it builds the corked data that will become the IP header of each outgoing fragment sent through this socket. It calculates a fragment length based on the MTU and the IP header size. Next, it builds a chain of `sk_buff`s and places them on the socket's output queue. If the output device has scatter-gather capability, the output packet is set up as a chain of mapped pages ready for transmission by the network interface hardware. For each socket buffer, we call __skb_queue_tail to place the skb on the socket's pending write queue.

The `ip_append_page` Function

The next function, `ip_append_page`, conceptually does the same thing as `ip_append_data`. It is much simpler, however, because the data to assemble into IP output packets is already in a list of mapped pages.

```
ssize_t ip_append_page(struct sock *sk, struct page *page, int offset,
                       size_t size, int flags)
```

Typically, this function is called by the upper layer's `sendpage` function such as `udp_sendpage`, defined in the file `linux/net/ipv4/udp.c`. It allocates a `sk_buff` if there is room on the socket's write queue. The `skb` holds the IP header. Then the pages in the list pointed to by `page` are appended to the `skb`. Finally, the function `__skb_queue_tail` is called to place the `skb` on the sockets pending write queue.

The `ip_queue_xmit` Function

```
int ip_queue_xmit(struct sk_buff *skb, int ipfragok)
```

The first thing we do in this function is check to see whether there is already a route for the output packet. We do this by checking `dst` field in the `sk_buff`, which points to the route cache entry. If there is no route, we build a flow information structure from the information in `skb` such as the destination address, port, and ToS value. Then, we call `ip_route_output_flow` to resolve the route. After we have a route, we construct the IP header, calculate the IP checksum, and call the function pointed to by the `output` field in the route cache entry, which generally points to `ip_forward` or `ip_output` depending on the route.

RECEIVING PACKETS IN IP

When a packet arrives in IP, a few basic decisions must be made. First, IP must decide whether the packet is a valid IP packet or whether to discard it. The next decision is either to forward the packet out an interface or send it to an internal destination. If it is sent out another interface, IP must figure out who to send the packet to, and whether it is sent to the final destination or to a gateway. Finally, for packets it is keeping, IP must decide which higher level protocol should receive the packet next. The first decision is based on the basic packet integrity. The second decision, to forward or not, is based on a search of the routing tables. Earlier in this chapter we discussed the IP routing mechanism and how forwarding is done based on a search of the routing tables. In this section, we start with an IP packet as it arrives in the IP receive packet handler and follow it as it is processed. Figure 8.1 shows the processing sequence for packets received by the IP receive packet handler.

In Chapter 5, we talked about how packets are removed from the input packet queue and how the `NET_RX_SOFTIRQ` tasklet checks the link layer header type field to determine which packet handler to call for the particular type. In the case of the IP protocol, the packet type has the value `0x0800`.

The IP Input Function `ip_rcv`

As discussed earlier, IP registers the packet handler function `ip_rcv` during its initialization phase. This function is the main input function for the IP protocol, and it is passed the incoming packet in a `sk_buff`, a pointer to the incoming network interface, `dev`, and a pointer to the packet type, `pt`.

```
int ip_rcv(struct sk_buff *skb, struct net_device *dev,
           struct packet_type *pt)
{
```

First, we get a pointer to the IP packet header, `iph`.

```
struct iphdr *iph;
u32 len;
```

The `pkt_type` field of the socket buffer, `skb`, indicates the class of the packet. Later, we check this field to see whether the packet was not sent to this host. Since we are currently executing a receive routine for this host, if the packet was not sent to us, we drop it. This is really a redundant check. Unless the packet was received promiscuously, it wouldn't have been sent to the IP receive routine if it was not intended for our consumption. Values for the packet type field are shown in Chapter 6.

```
if (skb->pkt_type . PACKET_OTHERHOST)
    goto drop;
IP_INC_STATS_BH(IPSTATS_MIB_INRECEIVES);
if ((skb = skb_share_check(skb, GFP_ATOMIC)) == NULL) {
    IP_INC_STATS_BH(IPSTATS_MIB_INDISCARDS);
    goto out;
}
```

This is a check to see whether the packet is at least as long as the IP header, and if not, we discard it.

```
if (!pskb_may_pull(skb, sizeof(struct iphdr)))
    goto inhdr_error;
iph = skb->nh.iph;
```

Now we check the header checksum to see whether the IP version is four and that the header length is at least 20 bytes. If not, we silently discard the packet [RFC 1122]. We check to see that the packet is big enough to hold the header and any IP options.

```
if (iph->ihl < 5 || iph->version != 4)
    goto inhdr_error;
if (!pskb_may_pull(skb, iph->ihl*4))
    goto inhdr_error;
```

We get a pointer to the header and calculate the IP header checksum.

```
iph = skb->nh.iph;
if (unlikely(ip_fast_csum((u8 *)iph, iph->ihl)))
    goto inhdr_error;
len = ntohs(iph->tot_len);
if (skb->len < len || len < (iph->ihl<<2))
    goto inhdr_error;
```

Since the network interface may have padded the end of the buffer holding the packet, __pskb_trim will eliminate the padding so the length of the skb is equal to the packet length field in the IP header.

```
if (pskb_trim_rcsum(skb, len)) {
    IP_INC_STATS_BH(IPSTATS_MIB_INDISCARDS);
    goto drop;
}
```

Next, ip_rcv_finish continues the input packet processing as described in the next section.

```
return NF_HOOK(PF_INET, NF_IP_PRE_ROUTING, skb, dev, NULL,
               ip_rcv_finish);
```

```
inhdr_error:
    IP_INC_STATS_BH(IpInHdrErrors);
drop:
            kfree_skb(skb);
out:
        return NET_RX_DROP;
}
```

The `ip_rcv_finish` Function

This function is defined in the file `linux/net/ipv4/ip_output.c`. It is called by `ip_rcv` to continue processing the input packet, `skb`. At the point where we arrive in this function, we have done some basic input packet filtering. At this point, the main purpose of the input packet processing is to determine the processing path for the input packet. We determine where the packet will be sent next. This is not just for external packet routing; decisions must be made for packets intended for internal processing, too. After we know what is to be done with the input packet, we retrieve the destination information for the packet by setting the `dst` field of the `skb` to point to an entry in the destination cache. In `ip_rcv_finish`, we also extract the IP options from the input packet (if there are any) and process them.

```
static inline int ip_rcv_finish(struct sk_buff *skb)
{
    struct iphdr *iph = skb->nh.iph;
```

Here we set the destination cache (`dst` field of the `skb`) for this packet if it is not already set. We do this by calling `ip_route_input`, which determines the internal route and sets up `dst` to point to the entry in the destination or routing cache.

```
    if (likely(skb->dst == NULL)) {
        int err = ip_route_input(skb, iph->daddr, iph->saddr,
                            iph->tos, dev))
        if (unlikely(err)) {
            if (err == -EHOSTUNREACH)
                IP_INC_STATS_BH(IPSTATS_MIB_INADDRERRORS);
            goto drop;
        }
    }
```

This section of code is for traffic class routing.

```
#ifdef CONFIG_NET_CLS_ROUTE
    if (unlikely(skb->dst->tclassid)) {
        struct ip_rt_acct *st = ip_rt_acct + 256*smp_processor_id();
        u32 idx = skb->dst->tclassid;
        st[idx&0xFF].o_packets++;
        st[idx&0xFF].o_bytes+=skb->len;
        st[(idx>>16)&0xFF].i_packets++;
        st[(idx>>16)&0xFF].i_bytes+=skb->len;
    }
#endif
```

Next, we process the IP options if there are any in this incoming packet. We determine whether we have IP options by looking to see whether the IP header length is greater than the normal length, 20 bytes. The IP header length field indicates the number of 32-bit words, so if it is greater than five, we assume that options are present in the packet. If okay, we call `ip_rcv_options`, which includes all the logic to decode the IP options present in this incoming packet.

```
    if (iph->ihl > 5 && ip_rcv_options(skb)) {
        goto drop;
```

If the incoming packet passed all the initial checks, we pass it on to the next processing step by calling the input function pointer defined for the destination cache in the socket buffer, `dst`. The value of the `dst` field was determined earlier when `ip_route_input` was called. For incoming packets intended for any of the IP family protocols such as UDP, TCP, or IGMP, the input operations field in `dst` will point to the function, `ip_local_deliver`.

```
        return dst_input(skb);
    drop:
        kfree_skb(skb);
        return NET_RX_DROP;
}
```

Delivering Input IP Packets to Higher Level Protocols

After `ip_rcv_finish` is done with the incoming packets, if the packets are for local consumption and we have a local destination within this host, the packets will be passed to another function to handle the distribution of the packet to registered transport layer protocols.

The `ip_local_deliver` Function

The next function we examine is `ip_local_deliver`. In this function we decide which higher layer protocols are to receive the packet next.

```
int ip_local_deliver(struct sk_buff *skb)
{
```

First, `ip_defrag` is called to reassemble IP fragments. The reassembled IP packet is returned in `skb`.

```
if (skb->nh.iph->frag_off & htons(IP_MF|IP_OFFSET)) {
    skb = ip_defrag(skb, IP_DEFRAG_LOCAL_DELIVER);
    if (!skb)
        return 0;
}
```

When the IP packet is complete, we are ready to hand off the packets to the higher level protocols.

```
    return NF_HOOK(PF_INET, NF_IP_LOCAL_IN, skb, skb->dev, NULL,
                   ip_local_deliver_finish);
}
```

The `ip_local_deliver_finish` Function

The function `ip_local_deliver_finish` delivers the input packet to all the protocols that will receive the packet next. It determines whether the input packets are to be sent to a single higher level protocol or to multiple protocols. IP can dispatch packets to multiple protocols under several conditions. For example, if any protocol has asked to receive packets promiscuously, it must receive a copy (actually a clone) of the input packet. If one or more raw sockets are open, each of the raw sockets will receive a clone of the input packet.

```
static inline int ip_local_deliver_finish(struct sk_buff *skb)
{
```

First, `ihl` is the length of the IP header.

```
    int ihl = skb->nh.iph->ihl*4;
```

At this point in our processing of the input packet, we have consumed the IP header, so we call `__skb_pull` to set the `data` field in the `skb` to point to the IP packet payload.

```
    __skb_pull(skb, ihl);
```

The raw header field in the `skb` points to the first byte after the IP header.

```
    skb->h.raw = skb->data;
    rcu_read_lock();
{
```

We retrieve the `protocol` field from the IP header.

```
    int protocol = skb->nh.iph->protocol;
```

Next, `hash` is used as an index into both the `inet_protos` and `raw_v4_htable` protocol tables. Hash is set from the 8-bit protocol field from the IP header. Both `raw_v4_htable` (the raw hash table) and `inet_protos` are sized large enough to hold all the common protocols defined for IP [IAPROT03]. The size of both these arrays is defined by the constant, `MAX_INET_PROTOS`, equal to 32. There isn't a separate slot for every single protocol, and the `inet_protocol` structure pointers are put on a list if the hash lookup generates a conflict. However, the protocol hashing provides a fast decision for the common protocols in TCP/IP, UDP, TCP, IGMP, and ICMP. Earlier, in Chapter 5, we discussed how the member protocols of the `AF_INET` family register their handler functions.

`raw_sk` is a pointer to a `sock` structure for a raw socket. This will be used to point to a slot in the raw socket hash table, `raw_v4_htable`. Each location in the table contains either a pointer to a `sock` structure if there is an open raw socket for this protocol number, or NULL. Hash indexes into the raw socket array to yield a pointer to an open raw socket, or NULL if there isn't one.

```
         int hash;
         struct sock *raw_sk;
         struct inet_protocol *ipprot;
resubmit:
```

If there is a raw socket for `protocol`, we will call `raw_v4_input` to distribute clones of `skb` to each of the raw sockets.

```
         hash = protocol & (MAX_INET_PROTOS - 1);
         raw_sk = sk_head(&raw_v4_htable[hash]);
         if(raw_sk && !raw_v4_input(skb, skb->nh.iph, hash))
             raw_sk = NULL
```

Next, the `inet_protocol` array, `inet_protos`, is indexed by hash, and `ipprot` is set to the first matching protocol.

```
        if ((ipprot = rcu_dereference(inet_protos[hash])) != NULL) {
            int ret;
            if (!ipprot->no_policy)
                if (xfrm4_policy_check(NULL, XFRM_POLICY_IN, skb)) {
                    kfree_skb(skb);
                    goto out;
                }
                nf_reset(skb);
        }
```

Here is where we call the handler function for the upper-layer protocol.

```
            ret = ipprot->handler(skb);
            if (ret < 0) {
                protocol = -ret;
                goto resubmit;
            }
            IP_INC_STATS_BH(IPSTATS_MIB_INDELIVERS);
        } else {
```

If we didn't have a raw socket, we check for unknown protocols. If the destination protocol is unknown, we send an ICMP unreachable message.

```
            if (!raw_sk) {
                if (xfrm4_policy_check(NULL, XFRM_POLICY_IN, skb)) {
                    IP_INC_STATS_BH(IPSTATS_MIB_INUNKNOWNPROTOS);
                    icmp_send(skb, ICMP_DEST_UNREACH,
                                   ICMP_PROT_UNREACH, 0);
                }
            } else
                IP_INC_STATS_BH(IPSTATS_MIB_INDELIVERS);
            kfree_skb(skb);
        }
    }
 out:
    rcu_read_unlock();
    return 0;
}
```

SUMMARY

In this chapter, we covered the IPv4 protocol. Essentially, all internal packet routing in IP is through the neighbor system, which includes the destination cache. Although the framework for the routing cache was discussed in Chapter 5, in this chapter we discussed the routing policy database and the FIB as well as how the IPv4-specific route cache is implemented. We followed input packets as they arrived in IP and were delivered to higher level protocols. We also discussed what happens when the higher level protocols want to transmit a packet through IP. We covered how packets are routed and described the main route resolver functions for input packets and output packets. We also discussed the ICMP and IGMP protocols.

9 Receiving Data in the Transport Layer, UDP, and TCP

In This Chapter

- A Few Words
- Introduction
- Receive-Side Packet Handling
- Receiving Data in TCP
- TCP Receive State Processing
- Processing Data Segments in Established State
- The TCP TIME-WAIT State
- TCP Socket-Level Receive

A FEW WORDS

This chapter is a continuation of Chapter 8. It continues to examine the implementation of the TCP/IP transport layer protocols in Linux. In the previous two chapters, we followed the data as it was written into a socket, passed through the transport layer, and transmitted by the network layer. In this chapter, we will see what happens as data is received in the transport layer from the network layer. We discuss both the UDP and TCP transport layer protocols.

INTRODUCTION

In this chapter, we show what happens when a packet arrives in the transport layer. We cover the UDP protocol, which processes packets for SOCK_DGRAM type sockets, and the TCP protocol, which processes packets for SOCK_STREAM type sockets. As we saw in Chapter 7, "Sending the Data from the Socket through UDP and TCP," UDP is far simpler than TCP because it doesn't handle any state information. As with the earlier chapter, the majority of this chapter is devoted to TCP, but we do discuss the packet handling for both protocols. Because of TCP's additional complexity with comparison to UDP, we discuss the handling of the internal queues and processing of input TCP segments in the various state even though this overlaps Chapter 7 in some respects. We show how each transport layer protocol works by following the data on the receive side as it flows up from the network layer, IP through the transport layer, and up into the receiving socket. The flow of input packets is straightforward for UDP, so we can discuss the input side here independently from the flow of output packets in Chapter 7. UDP is limited to individual packet processing and doesn't have to maintain as much internal state information. However, with TCP, since the received packet flow depends on the internal state of the protocol, it isn't possible to completely separate the discussion of the receive side from the send side. Therefore, the TCP-related sections in this chapter might be easier to swallow if read while occasionally referring to Chapter 7.

As is the case with the send side, which we covered earlier in Chapter 8, all the user-level read functions are converted into a single function at the socket layer. In UDP, the function doing the work is udp_recvmsg, and for TCP, it is tcp_recvmsg. In the bulk of this chapter, we talk about these two functions and their associated processing. UDP is a simpler case because packet reception in UDP essentially consists of little more than checksum calculation and copying of the packet data form kernel space to user space. In later sections we cover the UDP-specific receive packet handling. TCP is far more complex, and the receive side must ensure coordination with the send-side processing, TCP state handling, and keeping track of acknowledgments. Later in this chapter, we will discuss the actual internal processing of received packets in TCP.

RECEIVE-SIDE PACKET HANDLING

The transport layer protocols—TCP, UDP, and other member protocols in the AF_INET protocol family—all receive packets form the network layer, IP. As we saw in Chapter 8, when IP is done processing an input packet, it dispatches the packet to a higher layer protocol's receive function by decoding the 1-byte protocol field in the IP header. It uses a hash table to determine whether TCP, UDP, or some other protocol should receive the packet.

In Chapter 5, we discussed the hash tables, the inet_protocol structure, and how incoming IP packets are de-multiplexed. In Chapter 8, we discussed the flow of incoming packets through the IP input routine. In this chapter, we will start following the packets as soon as they arrive in each of the two transport layer protocols' handler functions.

Receiving a Packet in UDP

In Chapter 6, we saw how protocols register with the AF_INET family by calling the inet_add_protocol function in linux/net/ipv4/protocol.c. This initialization step happens when the AF_INET initialization function, inet_init, in the file linux/net/ipv4/af_inet.c, runs at kernel startup time. In the inet_protocol structure for UDP, the value in the protocol field is IPPROTO_UDP, and the function defined in the handler field is udp_rcv. This is the function that gets called for all incoming UDP packets passed up to us by IP.

The UDP Receive Handler Function, udp_rcv

The function udp_rcv in the file linux/net/ipv4/udp.c is the first function in UDP that sees a UDP input packet after IP is done with it. This function executed when the protocol field in the IP header is IPPROTO_UDP, or the value 17.

```
int udp_rcv(struct sk_buff *skb)
{
```

The variable sk will point to the socket that gets this packet if there is a socket open on this port. Uh points to the UDP header, and rt gets the routing table entry from the destination cache.

```
struct sock *sk;
struct udphdr *uh;
unsigned short ulen;
struct rtable *rt = (struct rtable*)skb->dst;
u32 saddr = skb->nh.iph->saddr;
u32 daddr = skb->nh.iph->daddr;
int len = skb->len;
```

The function pskb_may_pull is called to confirm that there is sufficient space in the socket buffer to hold the UDP header. uh points to the UDP header, and ulen is the value of the length field in the UDP header.

```
if (!pskb_may_pull(skb, sizeof(struct udphdr)))
    goto no_header;
uh = skb->h.uh;
ulen = ntohs(uh->len);
```

We check to ensure that the `skb` is sufficiently long to contain a complete UDP header. `Pskb_trim` checks the packet length in the process of setting `tail` to point to the end of the UDP header.

```
if (ulen > len || ulen < sizeof(*uh))
    goto short_packet;
if (pskb_trim_rcsum(skb, ulen))
    goto short_packet;
```

The UDP checksum is begun. We set the `ip_summed` field in `skb` depending on whether it is necessary to calculate the checksum.

```
udp_checksum_init(skb, uh, ulen, saddr, daddr);
```

We check the routing table entry for this incoming packet to see whether it was sent to a broadcast or multicast address. If so, we call `udp_v4_mcast_deliver` to complete the processing.

```
if(rt->rt_flags & (RTCF_BROADCAST|RTCF_MULTICAST))
    return udp_v4_mcast_deliver(skb, uh, saddr, daddr);
```

Next, we call `udp_v4_lookup` to determine whether there is an open socket on the UDP port in this packet's header by searching the UDP hash table. If there is an open socket, the packet is passed on to the socket's receive queue and we are done.

```
sk = udp_v4_lookup(saddr, uh->source, daddr, uh->dest,
                   skb->dev->ifindex);
if (sk != NULL) {
    int ret = udp_queue_rcv_skb(sk, skb);
    sock_put(sk);
```

If the return value is greater than zero, we must tell the caller to resubmit the input packet.

```
    if (ret > 0)
        return -ret;
    return 0;
}
if (!xfrm4_policy_check(NULL, XFRM_POLICY_IN, skb))
    goto drop;
```

If there is no socket for this packet, the checksum calculation is completed. The packet is dropped silently if there is a checksum error. If it is a valid packet but has been sent to a port for which there is no open socket, it is processed as a port-unreachable packet. This means we must increment the UDP_MIB_NOPORTS count, send an ICMP port-unreachable message back to the sending machine, and free the packet. We are done.

```
if (udp_checksum_complete(skb))
    goto csum_error;
UDP_INC_STATS_BH(UDP_MIB_NOPORTS);
icmp_send(skb, ICMP_DEST_UNREACH, ICMP_PORT_UNREACH, 0);
kfree_skb(skb);
return(0);
```

At this point, all that is left is to process the bad packet errors detected earlier.
short_packet:

```
LIMIT_NETDEBUG(KERN_DEBUG
    "UDP: short packet: %u.%u.%u.%u:%u %d/%d to %u.%u.%u.%u:%u\n",
            NIPQUAD(saddr),
            ntohs(uh->source), ulen, len,
            NIPQUAD(daddr),
            ntohs(uh->dest));
no_header:
    UDP_INC_STATS_BH(UDP_MIB_INERRORS);
    kfree_skb(skb);
    return(0);
csum_error:
```

Even though the packet is discarded silently, we still increment the UDP error statistics.

```
LIMIT_NETDEBUG(KERN_DEBUG
            "UDP: bad checksum. From %d.%d.%d.%d:%d to
            %d.%d.%d.%d:%d ulen %d\n",
            NIPQUAD(saddr),
            ntohs(uh->source),
            NIPQUAD(daddr),
            ntohs(uh->dest),
            ulen));
drop:
    UDP_INC_STATS_BH(UDP_MIB_INERRORS);
    kfree_skb(skb);
    return(0);
}
```

Receiving Multicast and Broadcast Packets in UDP

Multicast and broadcast packets are sent to multiple destinations. In fact, there may be multiple destinations in the same machine. When UDP receives a multicast or broadcast packet, it checks to see whether there are multiple open sockets that should receive the packet.

The `udp_v4_mcast_deliver` Function

When the routing table entry for the incoming packet has the multicast or broadcast flags set, the UDP receive function, udp_rcv, calls the UDP multicast receive function, udp_v4_mcast_deliver in the file linux/net/ipv4/udp.c to distribute the incoming packet to all valid listening sockets.

```
static int udp_v4_mcast_deliver(struct sk_buff *skb, struct udphdr *uh,
                                u32 saddr, u32 daddr)
{
    struct sock *sk;
    int dif;
```

First, we lock the UDP hash table. Then, we select the first socket in the hash table that is open on a port matching the destination port in the header of the incoming packet.

```
    read_lock(&udp_hash_lock);
    sk = sk_head(&udp_hash[ntohs(uh->dest) & (UDP_HTABLE_SIZE - 1)]);
    dif = skb->dev->ifindex;
    sk = udp_v4_mcast_next(sk, uh->dest, daddr, uh->source, saddr,
dif);
    if (sk) {
        struct sock *sknext = NULL;
```

We loop through the hash table checking each potential matching entry. When an appropriate listening socket is found, the socket buffer, skb, is cloned, and the new buffer is put on the receive queue of the listening socket by calling udp_queue_rcv_skb, which is the UDP backlog receive function discussed in a later section. If there is no match, the packet is silently discarded. There is no statistics counter to increment for discarded multicast and broadcast received packets.

```
        do {
            struct sk_buff *skb1 = skb;
            sknext = udp_v4_mcast_next(sk->next, uh->dest, daddr,
                                       uh->source, saddr, dif);
            if(sknext)
```

Chapter 9 Receiving Data in the Transport Layer, UDP, and TCP   **465**

```
            skb1 = skb_clone(skb, GFP_ATOMIC);
        if(skb1)
            int ret = udp_queue_rcv_skb(sk, skb1);
            if (ret > 0)
```

The comments say that we should be reprocessing packets instead of dropping them here. However, as of this kernel revision, we are not.

```
            kfree_skb(skb1);
        }
        sk = sknext;
    } while(sknext);
} else
    kfree_skb(skb);
read_unlock(&udp_hash_lock);
return 0;
}
```

UDP Hash Table

As we know from earlier chapters, an application opens a socket of type SOCK_DGRAM to receive UDP packets. This type of socket may listen on a variety of address and port combinations. For example, it may want to receive all packets sent from any address but with a particular destination port, or it may want to receive packets sent to multicast or broadcast addresses. A packet arriving in the udp_rcv function may be passed on to multiple listening sockets. It is not sufficient for UDP to determine which socket or sockets should receive the packet solely by matching the destination port.

The Hash Table, udp_hash

To determine which socket should get an incoming packet, Linux uses a UDP hash table, udp_hash, defined in the file linux/net/ipv4/udp.c.

```
struct hlist_head udp_hash[UDP_HTABLE_SIZE];
```

The hash table can contain up to 128 slots, and each location in the hash table points to a list of sock structures. The hash value used for the table index is calculated from the lowest 7 bits of the UDP port number.

In linux/net/ipv4/udp.c, udp_v4_lookup is a utility function that looks up a socket in the hash table based on matching source and destination ports, source and destination addresses, and network interface. It locks the hash table and calls udp_v4_lookup_longway to do the real work.

```
__inline__ struct sock *udp_v4_lookup(u32 saddr, u16 sport, u32 daddr,
u16
                                            dport, int dif)
{
   struct sock *sk;
   read_lock(&udp_hash_lock);
   sk = udp_v4_lookup_longway(saddr, sport, daddr, dport, dif);
   if (sk)
       sock_hold(sk);
   read_unlock(&udp_hash_lock);
   return sk;
}
```

The udp_v4_lookup_longway Function

The next function, udp_v4_lookup_longway, is called from udp_v4_lookup. It is declared in the file linux/net/ipv4/udp.c. It tries to find the socket as best it can. Minimally, it matches the destination port number. Then, it tries to refine the choice further by matching the source address, destination address, and the incoming network interface.

```
struct sock *udp_v4_lookup_longway(u32 saddr, u16 sport, u32 daddr, u16
                                   dport, int dif)
{
   struct sock *sk, *result = NULL;
   struct hlist_node *node;
   unsigned short hnum = ntohs(dport);
   int badness = -1;
   sk_for_each(sk, node, &udp_hash[hnum & (UDP_HTABLE_SIZE - 1)]) {
```

Our idea here is to find the best match of the incoming packet with an open socket. First, we check to make sure that it is not an IPv6-only socket. As discussed in Chapter 4, "Linux Sockets," IPv6 sockets may generally be used for IPv4. In this section of code, we find the first matched socket, and this is the one that gets the packet.

```
       struct inet_sock *inet = inet_sk(sk);
       if (inet->num == hnum && !ipv6_only_sock(sk)) {
```

First, we check that the address family matches.

```
           int score = (sk->sk_family == PF_INET ? 1 : 0);
           if (inet->rcv_saddr) {
               if (inet->rcv_saddr != daddr)
```

```
                continue;
            score+=2;
        }
```

Now we check for a matching destination address.

```
        if (inet->daddr) {
            if (inet->daddr != saddr)
                continue;
            score+=2;
        }
```

We check for a matching port.

```
        if (inet->dport) {
            if (inet->dport != sport)
                continue;
            score+=2;
        }
```

Finally, we check to see whether the input network interface matches (but only if it is bound).

```
        if (sk->sk_bound_dev_if) {
            if (sk->sk_bound_dev_if != dif)
                continue;
            score+=2;
        }
        if(score == 9) {
            result = sk;
            break;
        } else if(score > badness) {
            result = sk;
            badness = score;
        }
        }
    }
    return result;
}
```

UDP Backlog Receive

The backlog receive function is called when the socket receive queue is full, probably because the user reading data from the socket is blocked for some reason.

The `udp_queue_rcv_skb` Function

The function, `udp_queue_rcv_skb`, in the file `linux/net/ipv4/udp.c` is the backlog receive function for UDP, called from the bottom half when the socket is held by the user and can't accept any more data. This function is initialized at compile time into the `backlog_rcv` field of the UDP proto structure, `udp_prot`. As we saw earlier, `udp_queue_rcv_skb` is called by `udp_rcv` to complete input packet processing, and its purpose is mainly to place incoming packets on the socket's receive queue and increment the UDP input statistics.

```
static int udp_queue_rcv_skb(struct sock * sk, struct sk_buff *skb)
{
    struct udp_sock *up = udp_sk(sk);
    if (!xfrm4_policy_check(sk, XFRM_POLICY_IN, skb)) {
        kfree_skb(skb);
        return -1;
    }
```

First, we check to see whether this is an encapsulated socket for IPSec.

```
if (up->encap_type) {
```

Here, we have some special handling for Encapsulated Security Protocol (ESP) type packets. If we have an encapsulated socket, the incoming packet must be encapsulated. If it is, we transform the input packet. If not, we assume it is an ordinary UDP packet, and we fall through.

```
    int ret;
    ret = udp_encap_rcv(sk, skb);
    if (ret == 0) {
        kfree_skb(skb);
        return 0;
    }
    if (ret < 0) {
```

Here, we process the ESP packet.

```
        ret = xfrm4_rcv_encap(skb, up->encap_type);
        UDP_INC_STATS_BH(UDP_MIB_INDATAGRAMS);
        return -ret;
    }
```

If we fall through, the packet must be an ordinary UDP packet.

Chapter 9 Receiving Data in the Transport Layer, UDP, and TCP   **469**

Now, we finish calculating the checksum.

```
if (sk->sk_filter && skb->ip_summed != CHECKSUM_UNNECESSARY) {
    if (__udp_checksum_complete(skb)) {
        UDP_INC_STATS_BH(UDP_MIB_INERRORS);
        kfree_skb(skb);
        return -1;
    }
    skb->ip_summed = CHECKSUM_UNNECESSARY;
}
```

Next, we call the socket-level receive function, sock_queue_rcv_skb, covered in Chapter 4, which places the packet on the socket's receive queue and wakes up the socket so the application can read the data. If there is insufficient room on the receive queue, the error statistics are incremented, and the packet is silently discarded.

```
if (sock_queue_rcv_skb(sk,skb)<0) {
```

If the socket returned an error, we increment the statistics and get out.

```
    UDP_INC_STATS_BH(UDP_MIB_INERRORS);
    kfree_skb(skb);
    return -1;
}
```

After we increment the counter, we are done. At this point, the socket-level processing will allow the user-level read to complete.

```
    UDP_INC_STATS_BH(UDP_MIB_INDATAGRAMS);
    return 0;
}
```

UDP Socket-Level Receive

On the send side, internally in the socket layer all the user-level and socket-level send functions converge to call one function to transmit packets. For UDP, this function is udp_sendmsg. As is the case with the send side, when the application calls any of the read functions on an open socket, the socket layer calls the function pointed to by the rcvmsg field in the prot structure.

The `udp_recvmsg` Function

At compile time, the rcvmsg field is initialized to udp_rcvmsg. This function, in the file linux/net/ipv4/udp.c, is the receiving function that is executed for all SOCK_DGRAM type sockets. See Chapter 7 for a description of the protocol block structure for UDP, which shows how UDP and other protocols register with the socket layer.

```
int udp_recvmsg(struct sock *sk, struct msghdr *msg, int len,
                int noblock, int flags, int *addr_len)
{
    struct inet_sock *inet = inet_sk(sk);
    struct sockaddr_in *sin = (struct sockaddr_in *)msg->msg_name;
    struct sk_buff *skb;
    int copied, err;
```

Set the application's address length argument. Check to see whether there are any messages in the error queue of the socket, sk, and if so, process them by calling ip_recv_error and going out.

```
    if (addr_len)
        *addr_len=sizeof(*sin);
    if (flags & MSG_ERRQUEUE)
        return ip_recv_error(sk, msg, len);
```

De-queue packets from the socket sk receive queue by calling the generic datagram receive queue function, skb_recv_datagram, and if it returns without a packet, get out.

```
try_again:
    skb = skb_recv_datagram(sk, flags, noblock, &err);
    if (!skb)
        goto out;
```

Check to see whether the user is asking for more data than the payload in the packet, skb.

```
    copied = skb->len - sizeof(struct udphdr);
    if (copied > len) {
        copied = len;
        msg->msg_flags |= MSG_TRUNC;
    }
```

Chapter 9 Receiving Data in the Transport Layer, UDP, and TCP   **471**

The `ip_summed` field in the socket buffer determines whether checksums are required. If `ip_summed` is not equal to CHECKSUM_UNNECESSARY, checksum calculation must be done, and data is copied from kernel space to user space while calculating a checksum. The copying and checksum calculation is done by `skb_copy_and_csum_datagram_iovec`. However, if a checksum is not required, `skb_copy_datagram_iovec` is the function called to do the copying. It is also possible that a partial checksum was calculated because the data spanned more than one buffer, and in this case, `__udp_checksum_complete` finishes the checksum calculation. A checksum is the amount that makes an integer sum always add up to zero. Checksums can be done partially and finished later.

```
if (skb->ip_summed==CHECKSUM_UNNECESSARY) {
    err = skb_copy_datagram_iovec(skb, sizeof(struct udphdr),
                                    msg->msg_iov, copied);
} else if (msg->msg_flags & MSG_TRUNC) {
    if (__udp_checksum_complete(skb))
        goto csum_copy_err;
    err = skb_copy_datagram_iovec(skb, sizeof(struct udphdr),
                                    msg->msg_iov,
                                    copied);
} else {
    err = skb_copy_and_csum_datagram_iovec(skb, sizeof(struct udphdr),
                                    msg->msg_iov);
    if (err == -EINVAL)
        goto csum_copy_err;
}
if (err)
    goto out_free;
```

Next, the incoming packet is timestamped. If the user supplied a valid buffer, sin, to receive the packet's source address and port, the information is copied from the packet header.

```
sock_recv_timestamp(msg, sk, skb);
if (sin)
{
    sin->sin_family = AF_INET;
    sin->sin_port = skb->h.uh->source;
    sin->sin_addr.s_addr = skb->nh.iph->saddr;
    memset(sin->sin_zero, 0, sizeof(sin->sin_zero));
}
```

Before leaving, `udp_recv` checks the control message flags field, `cmsg_flags`, to see whether any IP socket options are set. For example, certain socket options such as `IP_TOS` require parts of the IP header to be copied into user space. If there are any flags set, `ip_cmsg_recv` retrieves the associated option values.

```
    if (inet->cmsg_flags)
        ip_cmsg_recv(msg, skb);
    err = copied;
    if (flags & MSG_TRUNC)
        err = skb->len - sizeof(struct udphdr);
```

Three error exits are at the end of *udp_rcv*. The most interesting is `csum_copy_err`.

```
out_free:
    skb_free_datagram(sk, skb);
out:
    return err;
csum_copy_err:
    UDP_INC_STATS_BH(UdpInErrors);
```

We arrived here because there was a checksum error. Go back and wait for the next datagram if we are in blocked mode; otherwise exit.

```
    skb_kill_datagram(sk, skb, flags);
    if (noblock)
        return -EAGAIN;
    goto try_again;}
}
```

RECEIVING DATA IN TCP

In an earlier section we looked at how the IP protocol dispatches the UDP receive function based on the protocol field of the IP header, and we have seen this mechanism covered in detail in Chapter 5. As with UDP, TCP also initializes an instance of the `inet_protocol` structure. This structure allows the network layer, IP, to dispatch transport layer handler functions based on the value in the protocol field of the IP header without needing to know anything about the internal structure of each transport layer protocol. It is helpful for a good understanding of TCP to be able to visualize the state management. Figure 9.1 shows the TCP receive-side state machine. See Chapter 7, Figure 7.1, for the send-side TCP state diagram.

Chapter 9 Receiving Data in the Transport Layer, UDP, and TCP

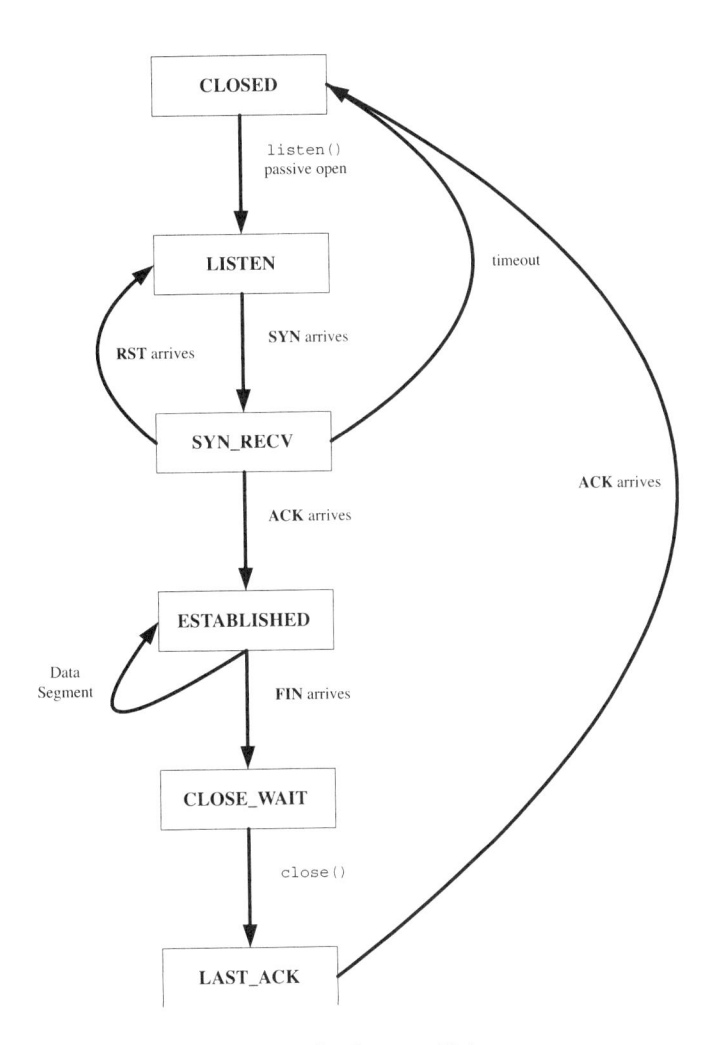

```
                    CLOSED
                      │
                      │ listen()
                      │ passive open
                      ▼
                   LISTEN  ◄──── timeout
                   ▲  │           │
          RST      │  │ SYN arrives
          arrives  │  ▼
                  SYN_RECV
                      │
                      │ ACK arrives
                      ▼
         Data    ESTABLISHED
       Segment      │
                    │ FIN arrives
                    ▼
                 CLOSE_WAIT
                    │
                    │ close()
                    ▼
                 LAST_ACK ────► (ACK arrives → CLOSED)
```

FIGURE 9.1 TCP Receive Process States.

Some key flag definitions are used primarily on the receive side of TCP (see Table 9.1). These definitions, found in the file linux/net/ipv4/tcp_input.c, are primarily used to govern the state processing during the receive side of the TCP connection. The flags are shown in Table 9.1. They are also used as part of the implementation of the slow start and congestion avoidance, selective acknowledgment, and fast acknowledgment, but should not be confused with the flags in the TCP control buffer, which are discussed in Chapter 9.

TABLE 9.1 Receive State Flags

Flag	Value	Description
FLAG_DATA	0x01	Incoming frame-contained data.
FLAG_WIN_UPDATE	0x02	Incoming **ACK** was a window update.
FLAG_DATA_ACKED	0x04	This **ACK** acknowledged new data.
FLAG_RETRANS_DATA_ACKED	0x08	This **ACK** acknowledged new data, some of which was retransmitted.
FLAG_SYN_ACKED	0x10	This **ACK** acknowledged **SYN**.
FLAG_DATA_SACKED	0x20	New SACK.
FLAG_ECE	0x40	The ECE flag is set in this **ACK**.
FLAG_DATA_LOST	0x80	SACK detected data loss.
FLAG_SLOWPATH	0x100	Do not skip RFC checks for window update.
FLAG_ACKED	(FLAG_DATA_ACKED|FLAG_SYN_ACKED)	Combination of previous **ACK** flags.
FLAG_NOT_DUP	(FLAG_DATA|FLAG_WIN_UPDATE|FLAG_ACKED)	Combination of previous flags.
FLAG_CA_ALERT	(FLAG_DATA_SACKED|FLAG_ECE)	Combination of previous notification flags.
FLAG_FORWARD_PROGRESS	(FLAG_ACKED|FLAG_DATA_SACKED)	Previous forward direction flags.

The TCP Receive Handler Function, tcp_v4_rcv

In this section, we will examine the TCP input segment handling and the registered handler function for the TCP protocol in the AF_INET protocol family. Figure 9.2 shows the TCP receive packet flow.

As is the case with all other member protocols in the AF_INET family, TCP associates a handler function with the protocol field value, IPPROTO_TCP, (the value six) by initializing an instance of the inet_protocol structure. This process is described in Chapter 6. The handler field is set to the function tcp_v4_rcv. Therefore,

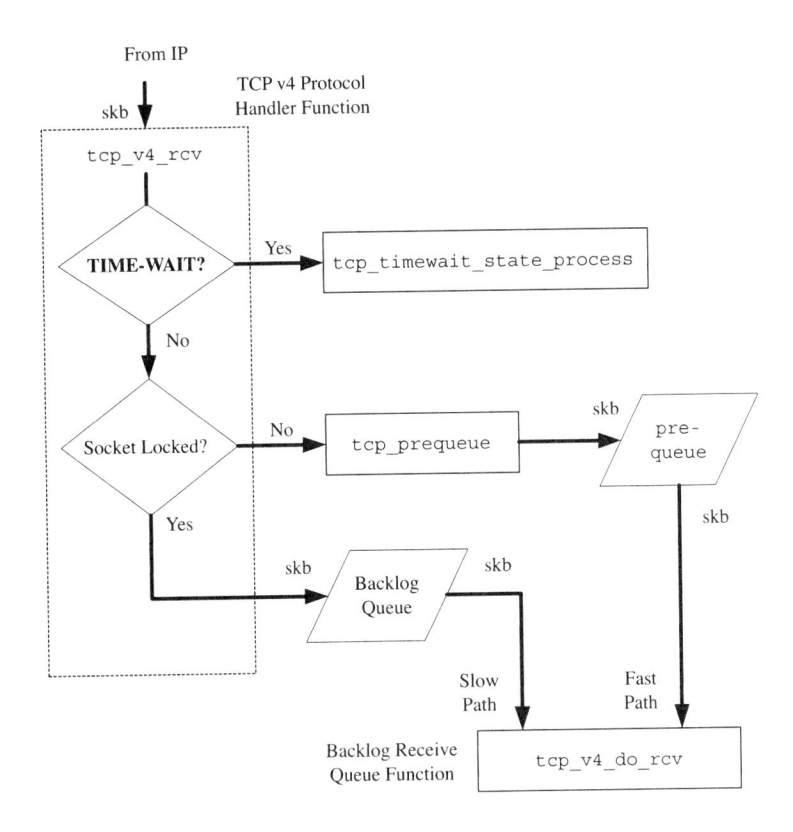

Chapter 9 Receiving Data in the Transport Layer, UDP, and TCP 475

FIGURE 9.2 TCP receive packet flow.

tcp_v4_rcv, defined in file linux/net/ipv4/tcp_ipv4.c, is called from IPv4 when the protocol type in the IP header contains the protocol number for TCP.

```
int tcp_v4_rcv(struct sk_buff *skb)
{
    struct tcphdr *th;
    struct sock *sk;
    int ret;
    if (skb->pkt_type!=PACKET_HOST)
        goto discard_it;
```

TCP counters are incremented before TCP checksums are validated. The next section of code is validating the TCP, checking that it is complete and that the header length field is at least as big as the TCP header without TCP options. As is the case with UDP, we use the socket buffer utility function pskb_may_pull to ensure that the socket buffer, skb, contains a complete header.

```
TCP_INC_STATS_BH(TCP_MIB_INSEGS);
if (!pskb_may_pull(skb, sizeof(struct tcphdr)))
    goto discard_it;
```

This set to point to the TCP header in the SKB. The `doff` field is the 4-bit header length.

```
th = skb->h.th;
if (th->doff < sizeof(struct tcphdr)/4)
    goto bad_packet;
if (!pskb_may_pull(skb, th->doff*4))
    goto discard_it;
```

Here, the checksum is initialized. The TCP header and the IP fake header is used to initialize the checksum. The rest of the checksum calculation is put off until later.

```
if ((skb->ip_summed != CHECKSUM_UNNECESSARY &&
    tcp_v4_checksum_init(skb) < 0))
    goto bad_packet;
```

A few fields are extracted form the TCP header and updated in the TCP control buffer part in the `skb`. TCP will want quick access to these values in the TCP packet header to do header prediction, which chooses incoming packets fast path processing. The fields used for header prediction include the TCP sequence number, `seq` in the control buffer, and the TCP acknowledgment number, `ack_seq`, in the control buffer. The `end_seq` is the position of the last byte in the incoming segment. At this point, it is set to the received sequence number, `seq`, plus the data length in the segment, plus one if this is a **SYN** or **FIN** packet. Two other fields in the control buffer, `when` and `sacked`, are set to zero. `When` is used for RTT calculation, and `sacked` is for selective acknowledgment. The macro `TCP_SKB_CB` is used to get the pointer to the TCP control buffer from the socket buffer. The control buffer structure is covered in Chapter 7.

```
th = skb->h.th;
TCP_SKB_CB(skb)->seq = ntohl(th->seq);
TCP_SKB_CB(skb)->end_seq = (TCP_SKB_CB(skb)->seq + th->syn +
th->fin +
                            skb->len - th->doff*4);
TCP_SKB_CB(skb)->ack_seq = ntohl(th->ack_seq);
TCP_SKB_CB(skb)->when = 0;
TCP_SKB_CB(skb)->flags = skb->nh.iph->tos;
TCP_SKB_CB(skb)->sacked = 0;
```

Now we try to find an open socket for this incoming segment if there is one. As is the case with most functions in Linux, TCP/IP, the double underscore __ before `inet_lookup` means that the caller must acquire the lock before calling the function, which attempts to find the socket based on the incoming network interface, the source and destination IP addresses, and the source TCP port. If we have a socket, `sk` is set to point to the `sock` structure for the open socket, and we continue to process the incoming segment.

```
sk = __inet_lookup(&tcp_hashinfo, skb->nh.iph->saddr, th->source,
                   skb->nh.iph->daddr,
                   ntohs(th->dest), inet_iif(skb));
if (!sk)
    goto no_tcp_socket;
```

We process the incoming packet. If IP security is installed, we do the security transformation. After we have the socket, `sk`, we can check the state of the connection. If the connection is in the TIME-WAIT state, we must handle any incoming segments in a special way. When we are in TIME-WAIT, delayed segments must be discarded and an incoming TCP packet may contain a delayed segment.

```
process:
    if (sk->sk_state == TCP_TIME_WAIT)
        goto do_time_wait;
```

Check for the IPSec security transformation. If there is a security policy in place, and this packet does not match the policy criteria, we discard it.

```
if (!xfrm4_policy_check(sk, XFRM_POLICY_IN, skb))
    goto discard_and_relse;

if (sk_filter(sk, skb, 0))
    goto discard_and_relse;
skb->dev = NULL;
bh_lock_sock(sk);
ret = 0;
```

If the socket is locked by the top-half process, it can't accept any more segments, so we must put the incoming segment on the backlog queue by calling `sk_add_backlog`. If the socket is not locked, we try to put the segments on the `prequeue`. The `prequeue` is in the user copy structure, `ucopy`, which is part of the TCP options structure, discussed in Chapter 7. When segments are put on the `prequeue`, they are processed in the application task's context rather than in the kernel context. This improves the efficiency of TCP by minimizing context switches between kernel and user. If `tcp_prequeue` returns zero, it means that there was no current user task associated with the socket, so `tcp_v4_do_rcv` is called to continue with normal slow path receive processing. The function `tcp_prequeue` is covered in more detail later in this chapter.

```
if (!sock_owned_by_user(sk)) {
    if (!tcp_prequeue(sk, skb))
        ret = tcp_v4_do_rcv(sk, skb);
} else
    sk_add_backlog(sk, skb);
```

Now we can unlock the socket by calling `bh_unlock_sock` instead of `unlock_sock`, because in this function we are executing in the bottom half context. Next, `sock_put` decrements the socket reference count indicating that the `sock` has been processed.

```
bh_unlock_sock(sk);
sock_put(sk);
return ret;
```

The label `no_tcp_socket` is where we end up if there is no current open TCP socket. Again, we check for a match with the IPSec security policy in effect for this connection. Also, we still must complete the checksum to see whether the packet is bad. If the packet had a bad checksum, we increment the error counter. If the packet was good, we are here because the segment was sent to a socket that is not open, so we send out a reset request to bring down the connection. Next, we discard the packet and we are free to go.

```
no_tcp_socket:
    if (!xfrm4_policy_check(NULL, XFRM_POLICY_IN, skb))
        goto discard_it;
    if (skb->len < (th->doff<<2) || tcp_checksum_complete(skb)) {
bad_packet:
        TCP_INC_STATS_BH(TCP_MIB_INERRS);
    } else {
        tcp_v4_send_reset(skb);
    }
```

We arrived here because we need to discard the packet. We decrement the reference count and free the packet.

```
discard_it:
    kfree_skb(skb);
```

```
        return 0;
discard_and_relse:
    sock_put(sk);
    goto discard_it;
```

We jumped here, do_time_wait, because the socket, sk, is in the TIME_WAIT state. The TIME_WAIT state requires a little more discussion because arriving packets require special attention; so we will discuss it in detail in a later section.

```
do_time_wait:
    if (!xfrm4_policy_check(NULL, XFRM_POLICY_IN, skb)) {
        inet_twsk_put((struct inet_timewait_sock *) sk);
        goto discard_it;
}
```

Next, we check to see whether the header length is too short, and we try to complete the checksum. If these tests fail, we get rid of the packet and go out. The function tcp_checksum_complete should return a zero if it is successful.

```
if (skb->len < (th->doff<<2) || tcp_checksum_complete(skb)) {
    TCP_INC_STATS_BH(TCP_MIB_INERRS);
    inet_twsk_put((struct inet_timewait_sock *) sk);
    goto discard_it;
}
```

Next, we call tcp_timewait_state_process to look at the arriving packet, skb, to see whether it is a **SYN**, **FIN**, or a data segment and determines what to do. The states returned by tcp_timewait_state_process are shown in Table 9.2.

```
switch(tcp_timewait_state_process ((struct inet_timewait_sock *)sk,
                                    skb, th)) {
```

TABLE 9.2 TCP TIME_WAIT Status Values

Symbol	Value	Meaning
TCP_TW_SUCCESS	0	Delayed segment or duplicate **ACK** arrived. Discard packet.
TCP_TW_RST	1	Received **FIN**. Send a **RST** to peer.
TCP_TW_ACK	2	Received last **ACK**. Send **ACK** to peer.
TCP_TW_SYN	3	Received **SYN**. Try to re-open connection.

According to RFC 1122, an arriving **SYN** can wake up and re-establish a connection in the **TIME-WAIT** state. In this case, `tcp_v4_lookup_listener` is called to spawn a listener and establish a new connection.

```
case TCP_TW_SYN:
{
    struct sock *sk2 = inet_lookup_listener(&tcp_hashinfo,
                                            skb->nh.iph->daddr,
                                            ntohs(th->dest),
                                            inet_iif(skb));
    if (sk2) {
        tcp_twsk_deschedule((struct inet_timewait_sock *)sk,
                            &tcp_death_row);
        inet_twsk_put ((struct inet_timewait_sock *)sk);
        sk = sk2;
        goto process;
    }
}
```

We received the last **ACK** from the peer, so we must send the final **ACK** to close the connection.

```
case TCP_TW_ACK:
    tcp_v4_timewait_ack(sk, skb);
    break;
```

A **FIN** was received, so we reset the connection by sending an RST, done at the no_tcp_socket label.

```
case TCP_TW_RST:
    goto no_tcp_socket;
```

A duplicate **ACK** or delayed segment was received, so we discard it.

```
    case TCP_TW_SUCCESS:;
    }
    goto discard_it;
}
```

The TCP Slow Path and Fast Path

Linux TCP has two paths for input packet processing, a slow path and a fast path. The slow path is normal input processing. As discussed in Chapter 4, every socket

Chapter 9 Receiving Data in the Transport Layer, UDP, and TCP   **481**

has a two queues, a receive queue and a backlog queue, used if the receive queue is full or the socket is busy. Along the slow path, packets received by TCP are placed on the socket's receive queue only after the packet is determined to be a valid data segment containing in-order segment data. This involves a large amount of processing done in the context of the bottom half of Linux in the context of the network interface receive interrupts. When the packets are on the queue, the socket is awakened, and the scheduler executes the user-level task, which reads the packets from the queue. As part of slow path processing, when the receive queue is full or the user-level task has the socket locked, the packets are placed on the backlog queue.

The TCP Fast Path, the `prequeue`, and the Van Jacobsen Algorithm

In addition to the two queues used in the slow path, Linux TCP has a third queue called the `prequeue`. This third queue is used for fast path processing. Because of the high volume of data that TCP is expected to handle, Linux provides the fast path as a speedups for optimized performance. As we saw in Chapter 5, one of the important performance enhancing aspects of the Linux implementation of TCP/IP is called TCP header prediction also known as the Van Jacobsen algorithm [JACOB93.] This algorithm determines whether a received packet is likely to be an in-order segment containing data and whether it is received while the socket is in the ESTABLISHED state. If these conditions are met, the packet is designated for processing by the fast path. In general, the Van Jacobsen algorithm assumes that at least half of all packets arriving while the connection is established will consist of data segments rather than **ACK** packets. By using header prediction, TCP's low-level receive function tries to determine which of these packets meet the criteria, and those packets are immediately placed on the `prequeue`. When the user task is woken up, TCP processing of the packets on the `prequeue` is done by the user-level task bypassing many of the processing steps that would otherwise occur along the slow path. Fast path processing occurs before the normal processing of any packets on the regular receive queue.

Three functions and one data structure are used with the TCP prequeue. The ucopy structure contains the queue itself. The `tcp_prequeue_init` function in the file linux/net/ipv4/tcp_ipv4.c, initializes the prequeue, and the inline function `tcp_prequeue` in the file linux/include/net/tcp.h puts packets on the queue. A third function, `tcp_prequeue_process` in the file linux/net/ipv4/tcp.c, removes the data while running in the application task's context when the socket receive function is called.

The ucopy Structure

The prequeue is within the ucopy structure also defined in the file linux/include/linux/tcp.h, which is in the TCP sock variant of the sock structure, tcp_sock. See Chapter 7 for more details about the basic sock structure. The field, prequeue, contains the list of socket buffers waiting for processing, and task is the user-level task to receive the data. The iov field points to the user's receive data array, and memory contains the sum of the actual data lengths of all of the socket buffers on the prequeue. Also, len is the number of buffers on the prequeue.

```
struct {
    struct sk_buff_head prequeue;
    struct task_struct  *task;
    struct iovec        *iov;
    int                 memory;
    int                 len;
} ucopy;
```

The tcp_prequeue_init Function

The function tcp_prequeue_init, defined in the file linux/include/net/tcp.h, initializes the elements of the ucopy structure including the list of socket buffers in the prequeue. This initialization occurs whenever a socket of type SOCK_STREAM is open for the AF_INET address family as part of the initialization of socket state information by the function tcp_v4_init_sock.

```
static __inline__ void tcp_prequeue_init(struct tcp_opt *tp)
{
    tp->ucopy.task = NULL;
    tp->ucopy.len = 0;
    tp->ucopy.memory = 0;
    skb_queue_head_init(&tp->ucopy.prequeue);
}
```

The tcp_prequeue Function

Another function, tcp_prequeue, puts socket buffers on the prequeue. It is also defined in the file linux/include/net/tcp.h. It queues up buffers only if there is a user task currently waiting on the socket. This is indicated by a non-NULL value in the task field of the ucopy structure. When the socket is awakened and a read is issued on the socket by the application, tcp_prequeue immediately processes the socket's prequeue before officially calling the socket's receive function through the system call interface.

```
static __inline__ int tcp_prequeue(struct sock *sk, struct sk_buff *skb)
{
```

First, tp is set to the TCP sock structure, which is retrieved from the generic sock structure.

```
        struct tcp_sock *tp = tcp_sk(sk);
```

Here we check to see whether a user task is currently waiting on this socket. If so, we place the socket buffer, skb, on the end of the queue. In addition, the user can control this behavior via sysctl, so we check here.

```
        if (!sysctl_tcp_low_latency && tp->ucopy.task) {
            __skb_queue_tail(&tp->ucopy.prequeue, skb);
            tp->ucopy.memory += skb->truesize;
```

If queuing the current TCP segment, skb, causes the prequeue to grow larger than the size of the socket's receive buffer, the socket buffers on the prequeue are removed, and the socket's backlog receive function, backlog_rcv, is called to put each buffer on the backlog queue until all the buffers on the prequeue are handled. After this, the prequeue is reset to empty by setting the memory field in ucopy to zero.

```
            if (tp->ucopy.memory > sk->sk_rcvbuf) {
                struct sk_buff *skb1;
                BUG_ON(sock_owned_by_user(sk));
                while ((skb1 = __skb_dequeue(&tp->ucopy.prequeue)) != NULL) {
                    sk->backlog_rcv(sk, skb1);
                    NET_INC_STATS_BH(LINUX_MIB_TCPPREQUEUEDROPPED);
                }
                tp->ucopy.memory = 0;
```

When there is only one skb remaining in the prequeue, the socket is awakened. Recall in Chapter 7 in the section about the delayed acknowledgment timer, we discussed how outgoing **ACK**s are held back waiting to be piggybacked on data segments. Therefore, while processing the prequeue, we reset the delayed acknowledgment timer to wait for a send-side segment to carry the **ACK**.

```
            } else if (skb_queue_len(&tp->ucopy.prequeue) == 1) {
```

This is where we wake up the socket so the prequeue will be processed.

```
                wake_up_interruptible(sk->sk_sleep);
                if (!inet_csk_ack_scheduled (tp))
                    inet_csk_reset_xmit_timer(sk, TCP_TIME_DACK,
                                              (3 * TCP_RTO_MIN) / 4,
                                              TCP_RTO_MAX);

            }
```

We return a one if we have placed the packet on the prequeue, and we return a zero if the packet was not queued. The zero return indicates to the caller that the prequeue was full and the packets were put on the backlog receive queue.

```
        return 1;
    }
    return 0;
}
```

TCP Backlog Queue Processing

In this section, we cover the backlog queue processing. When the queue of incoming packets in a TCP socket is full, the backlog takes over to queue packets for further processing.

The `tcp_v4_do_rcv` Function

The function `tcp_v4_do_rcv` is the backlog receive function for TCP. It is set into the `backlog_rcv` field of the `proto` structure at initialization. The function is called when the socket can't accept any more incoming data on its receive queue. It is defined in linux/net/ipv4/tcp_ipv4.c.

```
int tcp_v4_do_rcv(struct sock *sk, struct sk_buff *skb)
{
```

First, we check to see whether we are in the ESTABLISHED state. If so, the skb is a likely candidate for fast path processing. The function `tcp_rcv_established` is called to do the processing of the input packet in the ESTABLISHED state. It does the header prediction to see whether the skb can be processed in the fast path. It returns a one if we must send a reset to the other side of the connection, and on successful processing of the packet, it returns a zero.

```
        if (sk->state == TCP_ESTABLISHED) {
            TCP_CHECK_TIMER(sk);
            if (tcp_rcv_established(sk, skb, skb->h.th, skb->len))
                goto reset;
            TCP_CHECK_TIMER(sk);
            return 0;
        }
```

Here we check to see whether the packet does not have a complete header, and we complete the calculation of the checksum. The function `tcp_checksum_complete` returns a zero if the checksum is okay or it is already done, and a non-zero value if the checksum failed.

```
        if (skb->len < (skb->h.th->doff<<2) || tcp_checksum_complete(skb))
            goto csum_err;
```

If we are in the listening state, we check to see whether the incoming packet, skb, is a **SYN** packet, which would be a connection request. If we receive a valid **SYN**, we must transition to the receive state. This processing is done by tcp_v4_hnd_req, which validates the connection request and returns a sock structure, nsk or NULL. The returned sock will be in the **ESTABLISHED** state.

```
        if (sk->state == TCP_LISTEN) {
            struct sock *nsk = tcp_v4_hnd_req(sk, skb);
            if (!nsk)
                goto discard;
```

Next, tcp_child_process continues with receive state processing on the child socket, nsk. It returns a zero if the skb was processed successfully and returns a nonzero value if we must send a reset to the peer, generally because we received a reset during the brief amount of time the child socket was in the **SYN** received state. After all this has been successfully completed, the new child socket, nsk, will be in the **ESTABLISHED** state, ready to transfer data and we are done processing the incoming packet.

```
            if (nsk != sk) {
                if (tcp_child_process(sk, nsk, skb))
                    goto reset;
                return 0;
            }
        }
```

If we are not in the **LISTEN** state, we proceed with normal state processing by calling tcp_rcv_state_process, which returns a zero if the skb was successfully processed and returns a one if we must send a reset request to the peer.

```
        TCP_CHECK_TIMER(sk);
        if (tcp_rcv_state_process(sk, skb, skb->h.th, skb->len))
            goto reset;
        TCP_CHECK_TIMER(sk);
        return 0;
```

These three exit labels—reset, discard, and csum_err—are for sending a reset to the peer, discarding the skb, and incrementing the TCP input error counter, respectively. The error counter is incremented if a bad packet was detected.

```
reset:
    tcp_v4_send_reset(skb);
discard:
    kfree_skb(skb);
    return 0;
csum_err:
    TCP_INC_STATS_BH(TCP_MIB_INERRS);
    goto discard;
}
```

TCP RECEIVE STATE PROCESSING

In Chapter 7, we discussed the 11 states of TCP and presented a general overview of how and where they are implemented in the Linux kernel. We know that as a TCP packet arrives, TCP must detect whether the packet contains data or whether it contains a signal, which is one of the bits in the TCP header, **SYN, FIN, RST,** or **ACK**. This section explains the code that does the TCP receive processing. This section covers all TCP state processing as mandated by RFC 793 except the **ESTABLISHED** and the **TIME-WAIT** states, which are discussed earlier. [RFC793]

The tcp_rcv_state_process Function

The function tcp_rcv_state_process is in the file linux/net/ipv4/tcp_input.c. It is the function that does most of the work processing the TCP state of the open socket, and generally it follows RFC 793 where it specifies how to process incoming segments (see RFC 793, Section 3.9, page 64). The function returns a zero if the segment was successfully processed and returns a one if the caller must send a reset.

```
int tcp_rcv_state_process(struct sock *sk, struct sk_buff *skb,
                          struct tcphdr *th, unsigned len)
{
    struct tcp_sock *tp = tcp_sk(sk);
    struct inet_connection_sock *icsk = inet_csk(sk);
    int queued = 0;
```

The next variable, saw_tstamp, is set later to a non-zero value if the incoming packet, skb, contains the timestamp option.

```
    tp-> rx_opt.saw_tstamp = 0;
```

First, we handle the CLOSE, LISTEN, and SYN_SENT states. If the state is CLOSED, we discard the incoming segment.

Chapter 9 Receiving Data in the Transport Layer, UDP, and TCP   **487**

```
switch (sk->sk_state) {
case TCP_CLOSE:
    goto discard;
```

If we are in the **LISTEN** state, this socket is acting as a server and is waiting for a connection. If the incoming segment includes an **ACK**, we must send a reset. If the incoming segment contains a **SYN**, we process the connection request. If our connection is in the RST state, we discard the incoming packet.

```
case TCP_LISTEN:
    if(th->ack)
        return 1;
    if(th->rst)
        goto discard;
```

This function is independent of both IPv4 and IPv6. However, where actions taken are specific to an address family, the function in the `af_specific` part of the `tcp_opt` structure is used. Recall that the `tcp_sock`, which was initialized when the socket, sk, was opened for one of the address families, AF_INET or AF_INET6.

```
if(th->syn) {
    if(icsk->icsk_af_ops->af_specific->conn_request(sk, skb) < 0)
        return 1;
    goto discard;
}
```

In the **LISTEN** state, any incoming packets that do not contain a **SYN** or an **ACK** are discarded. There is discussion in the comments of this function about whether we should process any data in the incoming segment based on the behavior of TCP over non-IP network protocols; however, the action in the current kernel release is to discard the segment.

```
        goto discard;
```

If the current state of this socket is **SYN-SENT**, we must check for the **ACK** or **SYN** flags in the incoming segment to see whether we should advance the state to **ESTABLISHED**. The function `tcp_rcv_synsent_state_process` does most of the work for the **SYN-SENT** state as specified in RFC 793, pages 67 through 68.

```
case TCP_SYN_SENT:
    queued = tcp_rcv_synsent_state_process(sk, skb, th, len);
    if (queued >= 0)
        return queued;
```

The comments contain some discussion about how to handle data in received segments while in the **SYN-SENT** state, and tcp_rcv_synsent_state_process can return a negative one if there is data to process. However, other than checking the URG flag, we do nothing with the data. A non-zero return indicates that a reset must be sent.

```
tcp_urg(sk, skb, th);
__kfree_skb(skb);
tcp_data_snd_check(sk);
return 0;
```

Timestamps are checked here before the receive state processing is completed. This is part of the check for wrapped sequence numbers, called Protection Against Wrapped Sequence Numbers (PAWS). Sequence numbers can wrap when the sequence value reaches the maximum integer value and increments to zero. Under conditions of high-speed networks with a high window scaling factor, it is possible for an old retransmitted segment to reappear with the same sequence number as the current wrapped value. To prevent this from happening, timestamps are used. The receiver checks the timestamps for ascending values, and any received segment with an earlier timestamp is thrown out. Refer to Stevens, Section 24.6, for more information on PAWS [STEV94]. The function, tcp_fast_parse_options updates three fields of the tcp_opt structure with the two values in the timestamp TCP option of the incoming packet. The rcv_tsval field is set to the received timestamp, and the rcv_tsecr gets the value of the echo reply timestamp. In addition, saw_tstamp is set, if the timestamp option was detected in the packet. tcp_fast_parse_options returns a zero if skb contains a short TCP header with no options at all. The function, tcp_paws_discard does the PAWS processing by checking the timestamp values and returns a one if it detects a segment that should be discarded. [RFC1323]

```
if (tcp_fast_parse_options(skb, th, tp) && tp-> rx_opt.saw_tstamp &&
                    tcp_paws_discard(sk, skb)) {
```

A reset packet is always accepted even if it flunks the PAWS test; otherwise, tcp_send_dupack enters quickack mode and sends a duplicate selective acknowledgment of the offending segment indicating to the sender that the packet in skb is a duplicate segment.

```
if (!th->rst) {
    NET_INC_STATS_BH(LINUX_MIB_PAWSESTABREJECTED);
    tcp_send_dupack(sk, skb);
    goto discard;
}
}
```

At this point in the `tcp_rcv_state_process` function, we process all the states other than the **SYN-SENT**, **LISTEN**, and **CLOSED** states, which were handled earlier in the function. The steps for processing the remaining eight states are specified starting on page 69 of RFC 793, and in this function, we follow these steps closely. Step one is to validate the sequence number, and `tcp_sequence` does this by seeing whether the sequence number is within the window. It returns a zero if the sequence number is outside of the current window. If we received a bad sequence number, we negatively acknowledge it by calling `tcp_send_dupack` and discard the incoming segment. As specified by RFC 793, page 69, if the incoming packet contains the reset flag, RST, we drop the segment and return.

```
if (!tcp_sequence(tp, TCP_SKB_CB(skb)->seq,
                  TCP_SKB_CB(skb)->end_seq)) {
    if (!th->rst)
        tcp_send_dupack(sk, skb);
    goto discard;
}
```

Step two is to check to see whether the incoming packet is a reset. The **LISTEN** state was already handled earlier in this function. We call `tcp_reset`, which will process the received reset request for all the other states. It sets the appropriate errors in the sock structure, and the socket is destroyed.

```
if(th->rst) {
    tcp_reset(sk);
    goto discard;
}
```

Next, `tcp_replace_ts_recent` stores the timestamp in the `tcp_sock` structure, tp.

```
tcp_replace_ts_recent(tp, TCP_SKB_CB(skb)->seq);
```

Step three on page 71 in RFC 793 is to check security and precedence and is ignored. Step four in the RFC is to check for a received **SYN** in the incoming packet that is inside the current window. A received **SYN** in the window is an error condition so the connection is reset.

```
if (th->syn && !before(TCP_SKB_CB(skb)->seq, tp->rcv_nxt)) {
    NET_INC_STATS_BH(LINUX_MIB_TCPABORTONSYN);
    tcp_reset(sk);
    return 1;
}
```

Step five is to check for an **ACK** in the received packet, skb. This step is fairly complicated in the code, but essentially, if the acknowledge is acceptable, we proceed to the ESTABLISHED state.

```
if (th->ack) {
```

Next, tcp_ack processes incoming **ACK**s, and the FLAG_SLOWPATH argument tells tcp_ack to do comprehensive checking as well as update the window. It returns a one if the **ACK** is acceptable.

```
int acceptable = tcp_ack(sk, skb, FLAG_SLOWPATH);
switch(sk->sk_state) {
```

If the **ACK** was acceptable and the connection is in the **SYN-RECV** state, we most likely are a server in the act of doing a *passive open*. We should move to the **ESTABLISH** state.

```
case TCP_SYN_RECV:
    if (acceptable) {
        tp->copied_seq = tp->rcv_nxt;
        mb();
        tcp_set_state(sk, TCP_ESTABLISHED);
        sk->sk_state_change(sk);
```

Next, sk_wake_async wakes up the socket, but when the socket, sk, has been created with an active open, we receive a **SYN** on the client side of the connection when **SYN** packets are crossed. A socket that is being established with a passive open will not be woken up because the socket field of sk is NULL.

```
if (sk->sk_socket) {
    sk_wake_async(sk,0,POLL_OUT);
}
```

Now we update SND_UNA as specified in RFC 793, page 72. We also update SND_WND with the advertised window shifted by the current scaling factor, snd_wscale, which holds the value in the most recent window scaling option received from the peer. Next, tcp_init_wl updates snd_wl1 to hold the sequence number in the incoming packet.

```
tp->snd_una = TCP_SKB_CB(skb)->ack_seq;
tp->snd_wnd = ntohs(th->window) << tp->
rx_opt.snd_wscale;
tcp_init_wl(tp, TCP_SKB_CB(skb)->ack_seq,
```

Chapter 9 Receiving Data in the Transport Layer, UDP, and TCP   491

```
                    TCP_SKB_CB(skb)->seq);
```

Now that we are moving the socket to the ESTABLISHED state, we must do some housekeeping to make the socket ready to receive data segments. First, `tcp_ack` did not calculate the RTT, so the RTT is determined based on the timestamps if there was a timestamp option in the received **ACK** packet; the RTT value is kept in the `srtt` field of `tcp_opt` structure. The MSS is adjusted to allow for the size of the timestamp option. Next, `tcp_init_metrics` initializes some metrics and calculations for the socket. Next, the received MSS value is set to an initial guess based on the received window size, RCV_WND. Buffer space in the socket is reserved based on the received MSS and other factors. Last, `tcp_fast_path_on` calculates the `pred_flags` field in `tcp_opt`, which determines whether the receive fast path is on, whether header prediction will be used.

```
        if (tp-> rx_opt.saw_tstamp &&
            tp-> rx_opt.rcv_tsecr && !tp->srtt)
            tcp_ack_saw_tstamp(tp, 0);
        if (tp-> rx_opt.tstamp_ok)
            tp->advmss -= TCPOLEN_TSTAMP_ALIGNED;
        icsk->icsk_af_ops->rebuild_header(sk);
        tcp_init_metrics(sk);
        tcp_init_congestion_control(sk);
```

Prevent spurious congestion window restart on the first data packet.

```
        tp->lsndtime = tcp_time_stamp;
        tcp_initialize_rcv_mss(sk);
        tcp_init_buffer_space(sk);
```

We turn on the fast path since we are going to the ESTABLISHED state.

```
        tcp_fast_path_on(tp);
    } else {
```

If the incoming acknowledge packet was not acceptable, we return a one, which tells the caller (`tcp_v4_do_rcv`) to send a reset.

```
        return 1;
    }
    break;
```

If the connection is in the FIN_WAIT_1 state and we receive an **ACK**, we enter the FIN_WAIT_2 state.

```
case TCP_FIN_WAIT1:
    if (tp->snd_una == tp->write_seq) {
        tcp set state(sk, TCP_FIN_WAIT2);
```

Setting shutdown to SEND_SHUTDOWN indicates that a shutdown (a packet containing an RST) should be sent to the peer later when the socket moves to the CLOSED state.

```
sk->shutdown |= SEND_SHUTDOWN;
dst_confirm(sk->sk_dst_cache);
if !sock_flag(sk, SOCK_DEAD))
```

If the socket is not orphaned, we wake it up, which moves it into the FIN_WAIT_2 state.

```
    sk->sk_state_change(sk);
else {
```

Otherwise, we process the Linux TCP socket option, TCP_LINGER2. The value for this option is in the `linger2` field of `tcp_sock`, which controls how long we remain in the FIN_WAIT_2 state before proceeding to the CLOSED state. However, if `linger2` is negative, we proceed directly to CLOSED without passing through the FIN_WAIT_2 and the TIME_WAIT states.

```
int tmo;
if (tp->linger2 < 0 ||
    (TCP_SKB_CB(skb)->end_seq !=
     TCP_SKB_CB(skb)->seq &&
    after(TCP_SKB_CB(skb)->end_seq - th->fin,
        tp->rcv_nxt))) {
    tcp_done(sk);
    NET_INC_STATS_BH(LINUX_MIB_TCPABORTONDATA);
    return 1;
}
```

Next, `tcp_fin_time` checks for the keepalive option, SO_LINGER. It calculates the time to wait in the FIN_WAIT_2 state based on the option value, default settings, and the re-transmit time. The keepalive timer is reset with the calculated timeout value.

```
tmo = tcp_fin_time(sk);
if (tmo > TCP_TIMEWAIT_LEN) {
```

```
                    tcp_reset_keepalive_timer(sk,
                            tmo - TCP_TIMEWAIT_LEN);
            } else if (th->fin || sock_owned_by_user(sk)) {
```

If the incoming **ACK** included a **FIN** or the socket is locked, we reset the keepalive timer. The comment in the code states that if we don't do this, we could lose the incoming **FIN**.

We proceed as if the SO_LINGER option was selected so input state processing for the **FIN** state will resume in the keepalive timer function. Effectively, this should advance the state to TIME_WAIT when the keepalive timer expires. See Chapter 7 for more about the keepalive timer.

```
                    tcp_csk_reset_keepalive_timer(sk,
                                        tmo);
            } else {
                tcp_time_wait(sk, TCP_FIN_WAIT2, tmo);
                goto discard;
            }
        }
    }
    break;
```

Now we continue our processing of the incoming **ACK** packet (Step five, page 72 in RFC 793) by looking at the CLOSING and LAST_ACK states. If we are in the CLOSING state and we receive an **ACK**, we proceed directly to TIME_WAIT provided there is no outstanding data left for the send side of the connection to handle. If we are in the LAST_ACK state, we are in the process of doing a passive close, responding to a close call in the peer. An **ACK** received in this state means that we can close the socket, so we call tcp_done.

```
    case TCP_CLOSING:
        if (tp->snd_una == tp->write_seq) {
            tcp_time_wait(sk, TCP_TIME_WAIT, 0);
            goto discard;
        }
        break;
    case TCP_LAST_ACK:
        if (tp->snd_una == tp->write_seq) {
            tcp_update_metrics(sk);
            tcp_done(sk);
            goto discard;
        }
        break;
```

```
        }
    else
        goto discard;
```

At this point, we are done with processing an incoming **ACK**. The sixth step (RFC 793, page 73) is to process an urgent request, so we check the URG bit in the incoming segment. This check is done in function tcp_urg, which continues with the processing of the urgent data.

```
        tcp_urg(sk, skb, th);
```

Step seven (RFC 793, page 74) is to process segment text.

```
        switch (sk->state) {
        case TCP_CLOSE_WAIT:
        case TCP_CLOSING:
        case TCP_LAST_ACK:
            if (!before(TCP_SKB_CB(skb)->seq, tp->rcv_nxt))
                break;
        case TCP_FIN_WAIT1:
        case TCP_FIN_WAIT2:
```

RFC 793 specifies that we should queue up the received data received in one of these five states. RFC 1122 specifies that we should send a RST, and this is what the BSD operating system does. Starting with version 2.4, Linux does a reset, too.

```
            if (sk->shutdown & RCV_SHUTDOWN) {
                if (TCP_SKB_CB(skb)->end_seq != TCP_SKB_CB(skb)->seq &&
                    after(TCP_SKB_CB(skb)->end_seq - th->fin, tp->rcv_nxt)) {
                    NET_INC_STATS_BH(LINUX_MIB_TCPABORTONDATA);
                    tcp_reset(sk);
                    return 1;
                }
            }
```

Here, we have the normal case where a data segment is received in the ESTABLISHED state; tcp_data_queue is called to continue the processing and put the data segment on the socket's input queue.

```
        case TCP_ESTABLISHED:
            tcp_data_queue(sk, skb);
            queued = 1;
            break;
```

}

The following two functions, `tcp_data_snd_check` and `tcp_ack-snd`, determine whether a data segment or an **ACK**, respectively, needs to be sent to the peer. The comment here states that "tcp_data could move socket to TIME_WAIT," but it is not clear how that can occur.

```
        if (sk->sk_state != TCP_CLOSE) {
            tcp_data_snd_check(sk, tp);
            tcp_ack_snd_check(sk);
        }
        if (!queued) {
discard:
            __kfree_skb(skb);
        }
        return 0;
}
```

PROCESSING DATA SEGMENTS IN ESTABLISHED STATE

Obviously, the purpose of TCP is to transfer data reliably and rapidly. Data is transferred between the peers while the connection is in the ESTABLISHED state. When the socket is in the ESTABLISHED state, the function of the connection is to transfer data between the two sides of the connection as fast as the network and the peer will permit. The `tcp_v4_do_rcv` function covered earlier in the text checks to see whether the socket is in the ESTABLISHED state while processing incoming packets. If so, the function `tcp_rcv_established` in the file `linux/net/ipv4/tcp_input.c` is called to complete the processing. The primary purpose of this function is to copy the data from the incoming segment packets to user space as efficiently as possible. Figure 9.3 shows the Linux TCP ESTABLISHED state processing.

The Linux kernel provides a fast path processing path to speed up TCP data transfer as much as possible during normal conditions where data is being copied through an open socket. It uses a method very similar to Van Jacobson's e-mail about how to do TCP in 30 instructions [JACOB93]. The Linux method differs in that it does header prediction in advance during the early part of the TCP receive path. Although somewhat different from Van Jacobson's method, Linux perhaps improves the method in that the completion of fast path processing happens in the application program's task rather than in the bottom half of kernel processing. Wherever possible, Linux uses header prediction to select the packets that are most likely to be normal data segments for fast path processing. If these packets are in-

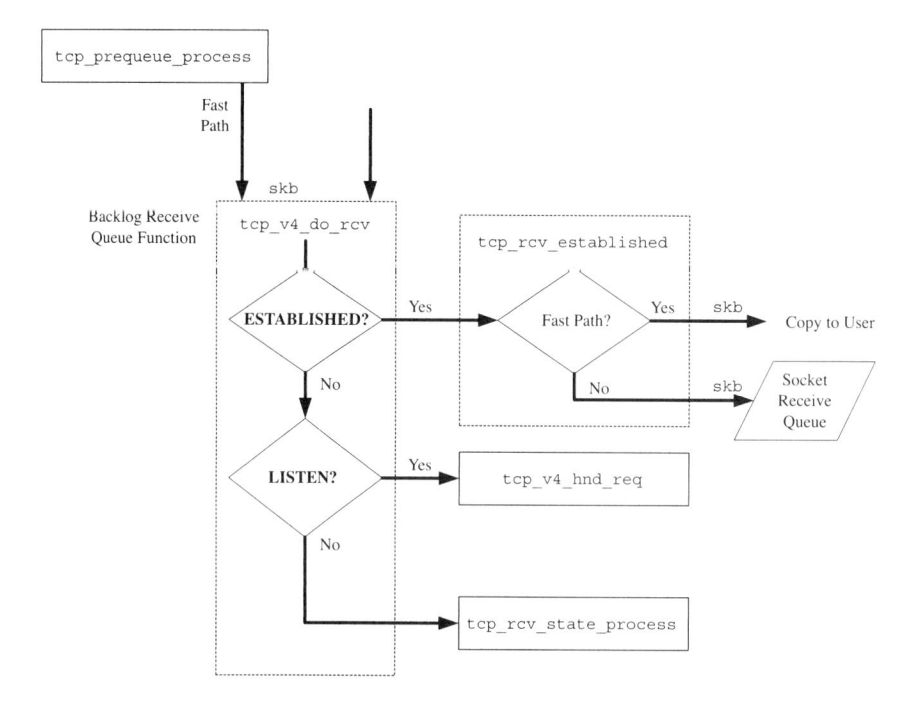

FIGURE 9.3 TCP ESTABLISHED state.

order data segments, they won't require any processing other than copying the data into the application program's receive buffer. Therefore, the fast path processing resumes in the context of the application program task while it is executing one of the socket read API functions.

If all incoming TCP packets were put through the fast path, it would no longer be fast. Therefore, the key to the fast path processing is to choose which packets have a high probability of being normal data segments that don't require any special time-consuming handling. To accomplish this, we do header prediction to quickly mark these candidate packets early in the receive packet path. Prediction flags are calculated, which are later used to direct packets either to the fast path or the slow path.

The Header Prediction Formula

The header prediction value is calculated as follows:

- prediction flags = hlen << 26 ^ ackw ^SND.WND,
- hlen is the header length
- ackw is the BOOLEAN ACK << 20

The preceding formula yields a prediction flags value that is equal to bytes 13 through 20 (in network byte order) of the TCP header expressed as a 32-bit word. Thus, the predication flags will be exactly equal to the third 32-bit word in the header of an input segment that consists of a data segment with an **ACK** but no TCP options. The prediction flags are stored in the TCP options structure `tp->pred_flags`. It is calculated by the `inline` function, `__tcp_fast_path_on`, in the file `linux/include/net/tcp.h`.

Receive-Side ESTABLISHED State Checks for Slow Path

Even though header prediction flags were already calculated, while processing incoming packets in the ESTABLISHED state, there are a few checks that cause packets to be redirected to the slow path.

- Our side of the connection announced a zero window. The processing of zero window probes is only handled properly in the slow path. See Chapter 7 for more information about zero window probes.
- If this side of the connection receives any out-of-order segments, fast path processing is disabled and we proceed with the slow path.
- If urgent data is encountered, fast path processing is disabled until the urgent data is copied to the user.
- If there is no more receive buffer space, the fast path is disabled.
- Any failure of header prediction will divert a particular segment into the slow path.
- The fast path is only supported for unidirectional data transfers; so if we have to send data in the other direction, we default to the slow path processing of incoming segments.
- If there are any options other than a timestamp in the incoming packet, we divert it to the slow path.

The `tcp_rcv_established` Function

The `tcp_rcv_established` function in the file `linux/net/ipv4/tcp_input.c` does the heavy lifting of processing incoming data segments. This function is called only for packets received while the connection is already in the ESTABLISHED state. Therefore, it starts out with the assumption that the packets are to be processed in the fast path. Along the way, if it finds that the incoming packet needs a closer look according to the conditionslisted earlier, it is diverted to the slow path.

```
int tcp_rcv_established(struct sock *sk, struct sk_buff *skb,
                        struct tcphdr *th, unsigned len)
{
```

```
struct tcp_sock *tp = tcp_sk(sk);
tp-> rx_opt.saw_tstamp = 0;
```

Here is where the prediction flags are compared to the incoming segment. We also check to see that the sequence number is in order. The PSH flag in the incoming packet is ignored.

```
if ((tcp_flag_word(th) & TCP_HP_BITS) == tp->pred_flags &&
    TCP_SKB_CB(skb)->seq == tp->rcv_nxt) {
    int tcp_header_len = tp->tcp_header_len;
```

Check to see whether there are any other options other than timestamp, and if so, send this packet to the slow path. The TCP sock field saw_tstamp indicates that the incoming packet contained a timestamp option.

```
if (tcp_header_len == sizeof(struct tcphdr) +
                      TCPOLEN_TSTAMP_ALIGNED) {
    __u32 *ptr = (__u32 *)(th + 1);
```

If the packet contains TCP options, we send it to the slow path.

```
    if (*ptr != ntohl((TCPOPT_NOP << 24) | (TCPOPT_NOP << 16)
                     | (TCPOPT_TIMESTAMP << 8) |
                       TCPOLEN_TIMESTAMP))
        goto slow_path;
    tp-> rx_opt.saw_tstamp = 1;
    ++ptr;
    tp-> rx_opt.rcv_tsval = ntohl(*ptr);
    ++ptr;
    tp-> rx_opt.rcv_tsecr = ntohl(*ptr);
```

Now we do a quick check for PAWS. If the check fails, the packet gets a closer look in the slow path.

```
    if ((s32)(tp-> rx_opt.rcv_tsval - tp-> rx_opt.ts_recent) < 0)
        goto slow_path;
```

Here we check if the header length is too small and if there is any data in the packet.

```
    if (len <= tcp_header_len) {
```

Here we check for the sending-side fast path. Essentially, we see whether we are receiving packets with a valid header but no data, which could indicate that we are doing a one-way data (bulk) transfer in the outgoing direction. Therefore, we acknowledge the packet, free it, and check the send side. We don't checksum the incoming packet, however, because it has been already been done for headerless packets.

```
if (len == tcp_header_len) {
```

The predicted packet is in the window.

```
    if (tcp_header_len == (sizeof(struct tcphdr) +
        TCPOLEN_TSTAMP_ALIGNED) && tp->rcv_nxt ==
        tp->rcv_wup)
        tcp_store_ts_recent(tp);
    tcp_rcv_rtt_measure_ts(sk, skb);
    tcp_ack(sk, skb, 0);
    __kfree_skb(skb);
    tcp_data_snd_check(sk, tp);
    return 0;
```

The header is too small, so throw the packet away.

```
    } else {
        TCP_INC_STATS_BH(TCP_MIB_INERRS);
        goto discard;
    }
} else {
    int eaten = 0;
```

The global `current` always points to the currently running task, which is the task at the head of the list of tasks in the TASK_RUNNING state. We check to see whether we are running in the context of the application task by seeing whether the task structure pointer in ucopy is the same as current, which was saved in the ucopy structure by tcp_recvmsg, the socket-level receive function when it was called by the application program (through the Linux system call interface, of course).

```
    if (tp->ucopy.task == current &&
        tp->copied_seq == tp->rcv_nxt &&
        len - tcp_header_len <= tp->ucopy.len &&
        sock_owned_by_user(sk)) {
        __set_current_state(TASK_RUNNING);
```

Here is where we actually copy the data. If the data was successfully copied, we update rcv_nxt (the variable, RCV.NXT in RFC 793), the next expected receive sequence number. While copying the data, cp_copy_to_iovec also completes the checksum if it wasn't already done by the network interface hardware.

```
            if (!tcp_copy_to_iovec(sk, skb, tcp_header_len)) {
                if (tcp_header_len ==
                    (sizeof(struct tcphdr) +
                     TCPOLEN_TSTAMP_ALIGNED) &&
                    tp->rcv_nxt == tp->rcv_wup)
                    tcp_store_ts_recent(tp);
                tcp_rcv_rtt_measure_ts(sk, skb);
                __skb_pull(skb, tcp_header_len);
                tp->rcv_nxt = TCP_SKB_CB(skb)->end_seq;
                NET_INC_STATS_BH(LINUX_MIB_TCPHPHITSTOUSER);
                eaten = 1;
            }
        }
```

We are here either because there isn't a user task context or the copy to user failed. If the copy to user failed, it is probably because of a bad checksum. We complete the checksum if necessary, and if it is bad, we go out. If there is no room in the socket, we complete processing in the slow path.

```
        if (!eaten) {
            if (tcp_checksum_complete_user(sk, skb))
                goto csum_error;
            if (tcp_header_len ==
                (sizeof(struct tcphdr) + TCPOLEN_TSTAMP_ALIGNED) &&
                tp->rcv_nxt == tp->rcv_wup)
                    tcp_store_ts_recent(tp);
            tcp_rcv_rtt_measure_ts(sk, skb);
            if ((int)skb->truesize > sk->forward_alloc)
                goto step5;
            NET_INC_STATS_BH(LINUX_MIB_TCPHPHITS);
```

This is the receiver side of a bulk data transfer. We remove the header portion from the skb and put the data part of the segment on the receive queue.

```
            __skb_pull(skb,tcp_header_len);
            __skb_queue_tail(&sk->sk_receive_queue, skb);
            sk_stream_set_owner_r (skb, sk);
            tp->rcv_nxt = TCP_SKB_CB(skb)->end_seq;
        }
```

Since we know we received a valid packet, the next few sections of code deal with the sending and receiving acknowledgments. Tcp_event_data_recv updates the delayed acknowledge timeout interval. See Chapter 7 for more about the delayed acknowledgment system. tcp_ack handles incoming **ACKs**.

```
tcp_event_data_recv(sk, tp, skb);
if (TCP_SKB_CB(skb)->ack_seq != tp->snd_una) {
```

If there is no need to send an **ACK**, we jump the next little section.

```
    tcp_ack(sk, skb, FLAG_DATA);
    tcp_data_snd_check(sk, tp);
    if (!inet_csk_ack_scheduled (sk))
        goto no_ack;
}
```

We send an **ACK** if necessary.

```
__tcp_ack_snd_check(sk, 0);
```

There is no need to send an **ACK**.

```
no_ack:
        if (eaten)
            __kfree_skb(skb);
        else
            sk->sk_data_ready(sk, 0);
        return 0;
    }
```

The following code section is the slow path processing of received data segments. This is where we end up if this function was called internally from the kernel's bottom half or if prequeue processing couldn't proceed for some reason.

```
slow_path:
    if (len < (th->doff<<2) || tcp_checksum_complete_user(sk, skb))
        goto csum_error;
```

We do the PAWS check for out-of-order segments by checking for the timestamp TCP option.

```
    if (tcp_fast_parse_options(skb, th, tp) && tp-> rx_opt.saw_tstamp &&
        tcp_paws_discard(tp, skb)) {
```

Even if PAWS checking indicates that we have received an out-of-order segment, we must still check for an incoming RST.

```
    if (!th->rst) {
        NET_INC_STATS_BH(LINUX_MIB_PAWSESTABREJECTED);
        tcp_send_dupack(sk, skb);
        goto discard;
    }
}
```

We resume standard slow path processing of data segments as specified by RFC 793. We must check the sequence number of all incoming packets.

```
    if (!tcp_sequence(tp, TCP_SKB_CB(skb)->seq,
                      TCP_SKB_CB(skb)->end_seq)) {
```

If the incoming segment is not acceptable, send an acknowledgment.

```
    if (!th->rst)
        tcp_send_dupack(sk, skb);
    goto discard;
}
```

If we receive an RST, we silently discard the segment.

```
if(th->rst) {
    tcp_reset(sk);
    goto discard;
}
tcp_replace_ts_recent(tp, TCP_SKB_CB(skb)->seq);
if (th->syn && !before(TCP_SKB_CB(skb)->seq, tp->rcv_nxt)) {
    TCP_INC_STATS_BH(TCP_MIB_INERRS);
    NET_INC_STATS_BH(LINUX_MIB_TCPABORTONSYN);
    tcp_reset(sk);
    return 1;
}
```

The fifth step for the ESTABLISHED state (page 72 in RFC 793) is to check the **ACK** field. The sixth step is to process the URG flag.

```
step5:
    if(th->ack)
        tcp_ack(sk, skb, FLAG_SLOWPATH);
    tcp_rcv_rtt_measure_ts(sk, skb);
    tcp_urg(sk, skb, th);
```

We are in the slow path where we haven't prequalified the segments, so we follow the steps in RFC 793. The seventh step on page 74 in the RFC is to process the segment data. `Tcp_data_queue` queues up data in the socket's normal receive queue. It puts segments that are out of order on the `out_of_order_queue`. For data in the socket's normal receive queue, processing is continued when the application program executes a read system call on the open socket, which will cause `tcp_recvmsg` to be called. The explanation of the socket-level receive is provided in more detail later in this chapter.

```
    tcp_data_queue(sk, skb);
    tcp_data_snd_check(sk, tp);
    tcp_ack_snd_check(sk);
    return 0;
csum_error:
    TCP_INC_STATS_BH(TCP_MIB_INERRS);
discard:
    __kfree_skb(skb);
    return 0;
}
```

THE TCP TIME_WAIT STATE

When one end of a connection receives an active close, it must stay in the TIME_WAIT state for two times the maximum segment lifetime. This section describes the processing of incoming packets when the TCP connection is in this state.

At this point, it is helpful to differentiate an active close from a passive close. An active close is caused by an explicit request by this end of the connection, but a passive close is done when a **FIN** is received from the peer. The TIME_WAIT state serves several purposes. One is to prevent old segments from a closed connection that are hanging around in the network from re-appearing in time to be confused with segments from a new connection. The other purpose is to hold on to the connection for a time that is longer than the maximum retransmission time, long enough to allow the peer to resend a last **ACK** (or **ACK** and data segment combination) when our last **ACK** was lost.

One of the problems of TCP/IP when implemented in large servers is that there could be substantial memory requirements for maintaining many sockets in the TIME_WAIT state. Although this is not a feature of primary importance to embedded systems designers, it illustrates how Linux TCP/IP is designed in part to meet the needs of TCP servers that maintain hundreds or thousands of open connections. The reader will remember that the primary vehicle for holding TCP connections, receive buffers, and connection state is the sock structure. Each instance of a sock structure has memory requirements associated with it, including the sock structure itself and attached data buffers. In a very active server with many connections, it can get very expensive to hold many sockets active waiting for numerous connections to shut down. In the next section, we will see how Linux addresses this problem.

The inet_timewait_sock Structure

To reduce these requirements, the TIME_WAIT state processing used a variant of the sock structure. This data structure is called the inet_timewait_sock, and it is defined in the file linux/include/net/inet_timewait_sock.h. As is the case of the other sock variants, inet_timewait_sock shares the first 16 fields with the sock structure so it can use the same list maintenance pointers and functions.

```
struct inet_timewait_sock {
```

The common part matches the generic sock structure.

```
        struct sock_common    __tw_common;
#define tw_family             __tw_common.skc_family
#define tw_state              __tw_common.skc_state
#define tw_reuse              __tw_common.skc_reuse
#define tw_bound_dev_if       __tw_common.skc_bound_dev_if
#define tw_node               __tw_common.skc_node
#define tw_bind_node          __tw_common.skc_bind_node
#define tw_refcnt             __tw_common.skc_refcnt
#define tw_hash               __tw_common.skc_hash
#define tw_prot               __tw_common.skc_prot
```

Substate holds the states that are possible while processing a passive close, FIN_WAIT_1, FIN_WAIT_2, CLOSING, and TIME_WAIT.

```
        volatile unsigned char   tw_substate;
        unsigned char            tw_rcv_wscale;
```

The following fields are for socket de-multiplexing of incoming packets. These five fields are in the inet_sock structure.

```
    __u16           tw_sport;
    __u32           tw_daddr
                    __attribute__((aligned(TCP_ADDRCMP_ALIGN_BYTES)));
    __u32           tw_rcv_saddr;
    __u16           tw_dport;
    __u16           tw_num;
```

The fields from here to the end are unique to inet_timewait_sock. The following field is for one byte alignment for IPv6.

```
    __u8                    tw_ipv6only:1;
    __u16                   tw_ipv6_offset;
    int                     tw_timeout;
    unsigned long           tw_ttd;
    struct inet_bind_bucket    *tw_tb;
    struct hlist_node       tw_death_node;
};
```

TCP TIME_WAIT State Processing

Linux TCP supports fast time-wait recycling to prevent the number of connections in the TIME_WAIT state from using too many resources. Since the TIME_WAIT state can be maintained for several minutes, there is a possibility that the number of connections in the TIME_WAIT state can grow very large. Therefore, instances of the time-wait socket, tcp_tw_sock structure, are maintained in slots accessed through a hash function. In a busy TCP server, these buckets are recycled depending on the value of the system control value, tcp_tw_recycle.

The tcp_timewait_state_process Function

The function tcp_timewait_state_process is in the file linux/net/ipv4/tcp_minisocks.c. It does most of the work of processing of incoming packets during TIME_WAIT. However, it also does the processing for the FIN_WAIT_2 state, which is part of the active close but before the TIME_WAIT state in the TCP state machine. The function returns an enum, tcp_tw_status, defined in the file linux/include/net/tcp.h, the values of which are shown in Table 9.2. As we examine the function closely, we will observe that it actually repeats most of the steps done by the function tcp_rcv_state_process, described earlier in this chapter, for most of the states, TIME_WAIT, but in abbreviated form. This is probably why this is called *minisocks* in Linux.

```
    enum tcp_tw_status
```

```
tcp_timewait_state_process(struct inet_timewait_sock *tw, struct
sk_buff
                           *skb, struct tcphdr *th)
{
    struct tcp_timewait_sock *tcptw = tcp_twsk((struct sock *)tw);
    struct tcp_options_received tmp_opt;
    int paws_reject = 0;
    tmp_opt.saw tstamp = 0;
```

Here we check to see whether the incoming packet contained a timestamp. If it does, we do the PAWS check for an out-of-order segment.

```
if (th->doff > (sizeof(struct tcphdr)>>2) &&
        tcptw->tw_ts_recent_stamp) {
    tcp_parse_options(skb, & tmp_opt, 0);
    if (tmp_opt.saw_tstamp) {
        tmp_opt.ts_recent = tcptw->tw_ts_recent;
        tmp_opt.ts_recent_stamp = tcptw->tw_ts_recent_stamp;
        paws_reject = tcp_paws_check(&tmp_tp, th->rst);
    }
}
```

Similar to `tcp_rcv_state_process`, we check to see whether we are in the FIN_WAIT2 state. If so, we must check for an incoming **FIN**, **ACK**, or an incoming out-of-order segment. If the earlier PAWS check found that the incoming segment is out of order, we must send an **ACK**.

```
if (tw->tw_substate == TCP_FIN_WAIT2) {
```

RFC 793 on page 69 states that an acknowledgment should be sent for an unacceptable segment if we are in TIME_WAIT, so we return TCP_TW_ACK to tell the caller to send an **ACK**.

```
if (paws_reject ||
        !tcp_in_window(TCP_SKB_CB(skb)->seq,
            TCP_SKB_CB(skb)->end_seq, tcptw->tw_rcv_nxt,
        tcptw->tw_rcv_nxt + tcptw->tw_rcv_wnd))
    return TCP_TW_ACK;
```

If the incoming segment contains an RST, we can finally kill off the connection.

```
if (th->rst)
    goto kill;
```

If we receive a **SYN**, but it is old or out of the window, we send a **RST**.

```
if (th->syn && !before(TCP_SKB_CB(skb)->seq, tcptw-
    >tw_rcv_nxt))
    goto kill_with_rst;
```

We check to see whether the incoming segment has a duplicate **ACK**. If so, we will want to discard the segment.

```
if (!after(TCP_SKB_CB(skb)->end_seq, tcptw->tw_rcv_nxt) ||
    TCP_SKB_CB(skb)->end_seq == TCP_SKB_CB(skb)->seq) {
    inet_twsk_put(tw);
    return TCP_TW_SUCCESS;
}
```

If the arriving segment contains new data, we must send a reset to the peer to kill off the connection. We also stop the **TIME-WAIT** state timer.

```
if (!th->fin ||
    TCP_SKB_CB(skb)->end_seq != tcptw->rcv_nxt+1) {
kill_with_rst:
    tcp_tw_deschedule(tw. &tcp_death_row);
    inet_twsk_put (tw);
    return TCP_TW_RST;
}
```

At this point, we know the arriving segment is a **FIN**, and we are still in the **FIN-WAIT-2** state, so we enter the actual **TIME-WAIT** state. We also process the received timestamp, saving the incoming timestamp value in ts_recent and marking when it was received.

```
tw->tw_substate = TCP_TIME_WAIT;
tcptw->tw_rcv_nxt = TCP_SKB_CB(skb)->end_seq;
if (tmp_opt.saw_tstamp) {
    tcptw->ts_recent_stamp = xtime.tv_sec;
    tcptw->tw_ts_recent = tmp_opt.rcv_tsval;
}
```

Next, we call tcp_tw_schedule to manage the timer, which determines the length of time the connection will remain in the **TIME-WAIT** state. RFC 1122 specifies that the timer should be 2MSL (two times the Maximum Segment Lifetime). If possible, Linux makes an attempt to reduce the time to an amount based on the RTO (Re-Transmission Timeout). The comments contain a note apologizing for the IPv4-specific code, but it is okay because the IPv6 implementation, unlike IPv4, doesn't support fast time wait recycling. If we are part of an IPv6 connection, we pass a constant value of one minute to `tcp_tw_schedule`; otherwise, we pass in the RTO value, which could be less.

```
        if (tw->tw_family == AF_INET &&
            tcp_death_row.sysctl_tw_recycle &&
            tcptw->tw_ts_recent_stamp &&
            tcp_v4_tw_remember_stamp(tw))
                inet_twsk_schedule (tw, &tcp_death_row, tw->tw_timeout,
                                TCP_TIMEWAIT_LEN);
        else
                inet_twsk_schedule (tw, &tcp_death_row, TCP_TIMEWAIT_LEN,
                                TCP_TIMEWAIT_LEN);
        return TCP_TW_ACK;
}
```

Here we enter the real **TIME-WAIT** state. RFC 1122 states in section 4.2.2.13 that if we receive a **SYN** in a connection in the **TIME-WAIT** state, we may re-open the connection. However, we must assign the initial sequence number of the new connection to a value larger than the maximum sequence number used in the previous connection. We must also return to the **TIME-WAIT** state if the incoming **SYN** is a duplicate of an old one from the previous connection.

```
        if (!paws_reject &&
            (TCP_SKB_CB(skb)->seq == tcptw->tw_rcv_nxt &&
            (TCP_SKB_CB(skb)->seq == TCP_SKB_CB(skb)->end_seq || th->rst)))
{
```

The value of zero in `paws_reject` indicates that the incoming segment is inside the window; therefore, it is either a RST or an ACK with no data.

```
        if (th->rst) {
```

It is possible that this incoming RST will result in **TIME-WAIT** Assassination (TWA). The system control, `sysctl_tcp_rfc1337`, can be set to prevent TWA. Linux TCP does not prevent TWA as its default behavior, so if the system control is not set, we kill off the connection [RFC1337].

```
            if (sysctl_tcp_rfc1337 == 0) {
kill:
                    inet_twsk_deschedule (tw, &tcp_death_row);
                    inet_twsk_put (tw);
```

Chapter 9 Receiving Data in the Transport Layer, UDP, and TCP   **509**

```
            return TCP_TW_SUCCESS;
        }
    }
```

The incoming segment must be a duplicate **ACK**, so we discard it. We also update the timer by calling `tcp_tw_schedule`.

```
        inet_twsk_schedule(tw, &tcp_death_row, TCP_TIMEWAIT_LEN,
                        TCP_TIMEWAIT_LEN);
        if (tmp_opt.saw_tstamp) {
            tcptw->tw_ts_recent = tmp_opt.rcv_tsval;
            tcptw->tw_ts_recent_stamp = xtime.tv_sec;
        }
        inet_twsk_put (tw);
        return TCP_TW_SUCCESS;
    }
```

If we reached here, the PAWS test must have failed, so we must have either an out-of-window segment or a new **SYN**. All the out-of-window segments are acknowledged immediately. To accept a new **SYN**, it must not be an old duplicate. The check mandated by RFC 793 only works at slower network speeds, less than 40 Mbit per second. Although, the PAWS checks are sufficient to ensure that we don't really need to check the sequence numbers, we do the mandated sequence number check anyway.

```
    if (th->syn && !th->rst && !th->ack && !paws_reject &&
        (after(TCP_SKB_CB(skb)->seq, tw->tw_rcv_nxt) ||
        (tmp_opt.saw_tstamp && (s32)(tcptw->tw_ts_recent -
                                tmp_opt.rcv_tsval) < 0))) {
        u32 isn = tcptw->tw_snd_nxt + 65535 + 2;
        if (isn == 0)
            isn++;
        TCP_SKB_CB(skb)->when = isn;
        return TCP_TW_SYN;
    }
    if (paws_reject)
        NET_INC_STATS_BH(LINUX_MIB_PAWSESTABREJECTED);
    if(!th->rst) {
```

We reset the TIME_WAIT state timer, but only if the incoming segment was an **ACK** or out of the window.

```
            if (paws_reject || th->ack)
                inet_twsk_schedule(tw, &tcp_death_row, TCP_TIMEWAIT_LEN,
            TCP_TIMEWAIT_LEN);
```

We tell the caller to acknowledge the bad segment.

```
        return TCP_TW_ACK;
    }
```

We must have received a RST, so we kill the connection and return successfully.

```
    tcp_twsk_put(tw);
    return TCP_TW_SUCCESS;
}
```

TCP SOCKET-LEVEL RECEIVE

When the user task is signaled that there is data waiting on an open socket, it calls one of the receive or read system calls on the open socket.

The `tcp_recvmsg` Function

All the socket layer and user-level receive functions eventually result in a call to `tcp_recvmsg`. This function is defined in the file `linux/net/ipv4/tcp.c`. The function copies data from an open socket into a user buffer.

```
int tcp_recvmsg(struct kiocb *iocb, struct sock *sk, struct msghdr *msg,
                int len, int nonblock, int flags, int *addr_len)
{
    struct tcp_sock *tp = tcp_sk(sk);
    int copied = 0;
    u32 peek_seq;
    u32 *seq;
    unsigned long used;
    int err;
```

Target is set to the minimum number of bytes that this function should return.

```
    int target;
    long timeo;
    struct task_struct *user_recv = NULL;
    lock_sock(sk);
```

```
TCP_CHECK_TIMER(sk);
err = -ENOTCONN;
if (sk->state == TCP_LISTEN)
    goto out;
timeo = sock_rcvtimeo(sk, nonblock);
```

If the MSG_OOB flag is set on this socket, urgent data (incoming segments with the URG flag) are handled specially. At entry, seq is initialized to the next byte to be read because the copied_seq field of the tcp_opt structure contains the last byte that has been processed.

```
if (flags & MSG_OOB)
    goto recv_urg;
seq = &tp->copied_seq;
if (flags & MSG_PEEK) {
    peek_seq = tp->copied_seq;
    seq = &peek_seq;
}
```

The number of bytes to read, target, is set to the low-water mark for the socket, or the length of the data len, whichever is less. The MSG_WAITALL flag indicates whether this call will block for target number of bytes.

```
target = sock_rcvlowat(sk, flags & MSG_WAITALL, len);
```

This do while loop is the main loop of tcp_recvmsg. In this loop, we will continue to copy bytes to the user until target bytes is reached or some other exception condition is detected while processing the incoming data segments.

```
do {
    struct sk_buff * skb;
    u32 offset;
```

If after copying some data, we encounter urgent data while processing segments, we stop processing.

```
if (tp->urg_data && tp->urg_seq == *seq)
    if (copied);
        break;
```

Here we check to see whether there is a signal pending on this socket to ensure the correct handling of the SIGURG signal.

```
            if (signal_pending(current)) {
                copied = timeo ? sock_intr_errno(timeo) : -EAGAIN;
                break;
            }
```

We get a pointer to the first buffer on the receive queue, and in the inner `do while` loop, we walk through the receive queue until we find the first data segment. When we find the segment and know how many bytes to copy, we jump to `found_ok_skb`. Along the way, we calculate the number of bytes to copy (using the variable `offset`) from the `skb`.

```
            skb = skb_peek(&sk->sk_receive_queue);
```

In this inner loop, we keep examining packets until we find a valid data segment. Along the way, we check for **FIN** and **SYN**. If we see a **SYN**, we adjust the number of bytes to be copied by subtracting one from `offset`. A **FIN** drops us out of the loop.

```
            do {
                if (!skb)
                    break;
```

Now we check to see that the current byte to be processed is not before the first byte in the most recently received segment to see whether somehow we got out of synchronization while processing the queue of packets. This is actually a redundant check because socket locking and multiple queues should prevent us from getting lost.

```
                if (before(*seq, TCP_SKB_CB(skb)->seq)) {
                    printk(KERN_INFO "recvmsg bug: copied %X seq %X\n",
                            *seq, TCP_SKB_CB(skb)->seq);
                    break;
                }
                offset = *seq - TCP_SKB_CB(skb)->seq;
                if (skb->h.th->syn)
                    offset--;
                if (offset < skb->len)
                    goto found_ok_skb;
                if (skb->h.th->fin)
                    goto found_fin_ok;
                BUG_TRAP(flags&MSG_PEEK);
                skb = skb->next;
            } while (skb != (struct sk_buff *)&sk->sk_receive_queue);
```

Chapter 9 Receiving Data in the Transport Layer, UDP, and TCP 513

If we get here, it means that we found nothing in the socket receive queue. If we have packets in the backlog queue, we try to process that, too.

```
if (copied >= target && sk->backlog.tail == NULL)
    break;
```

Now we must make a few checks to see whether we need to stop processing packets. We check for an error condition in the socket, if the socked is closed, or if we received a shutdown request from the peer (this would be a RST in a received packet as we discussed earlier in this chapter.).

```
if (copied) {
    if (sk->sk_err ||
        sk->sk_state == TCP_CLOSE ||
        (sk->sk_shutdown & RCV_SHUTDOWN) ||
        !timeo ||
        (flags & MSG_PEEK))
        break;
} else {
    if (sock_flag(sk, SOCK_DONE))
        break;
    if (sk->err) {
        copied = sock_error(sk);
        break;
    }
    if (sk->shutdown & RCV_SHUTDOWN)
        break;
    if (sk->state == TCP_CLOSE) {
```

The variable done is set on a socket when a user closes, so normally it is non-zero when the connection state is CLOSED. If done is zero on a CLOSED socket, it means that an application program is trying to read from a socket that has never been connected, which, of course, is an error condition.

```
            if (!sock_flag(sk, SOCK_DONE)) {
                copied = -ENOTCONN;
                break;
            }
            break;
        }
        if (!timeo) {
            copied = -EAGAIN;
```

```
                    break;
                }
                if (signal_pending(current)) {
                    copied = sock_intr_errno(timeo);
                    break;
                }
            }
            cleanup_rbuf(sk, copied);
```

We are here because there are no more segments on the receive queue left to process. We will process any packets on the prequeue that have been prequalified for fast path processing. Previously, header prediction has indicated that there are likely to be data segments received when the connection state is ESTABLISHED. The prequeue packets are processed by the user task instead of in the context of the bottom half. ucopy.task is set to current, which forces the prequeue segments to be copied from the prequeue later by the user task, current.

```
            if (!sysctl_tcp_low_latency && tp->ucopy.task == user_recv) {
```

Here we install a new reader task.

```
                if (!user_recv&& !(flags&(MSG_TRUNC|MSG_PEEK))) {
                    user_recv = current;
                    tp->ucopy.task = user_recv;
                    tp->ucopy.iov = msg->msg_iov;
                }
                tp->ucopy.len = len;
                BUG_TRAP(tp->copied_seq == tp->rcv_nxt ||
                         (flags&(MSG_PEEK|MSG_TRUNC)));
```

If prequeue is not empty, it must be processed before releasing the socket. If this is not done, the segment order will be damaged at the next iteration through this loop. The packet processing order on the receive side can be thought of as consisting of a series of four pseudo-queues, packets in flight, backlog, prequeue, and the normal receive queue. Each of these queues can be processed only if the packets ahead of it have already been processed. The receive queue is now empty, but the prequeue could have had segments added to it when the socket was released in the last iteration through this loop. The prequeue is processed at the do_prequeue label.

```
                if (skb_queue_len(&tp->ucopy.prequeue))
                    goto do_prequeue;
            }
            if (copied >= target) {
```

Now, the backlog is processed to see whether it is possible to do any direct copying of packets on that queue. At this point, we have processed `prequeue`. To do this processing, we call `release_sock` to walk through the packets on the backlog queue, `sk->backlog`, before waking up any tasks waiting on the socket.

```
            release_sock(sk);
            lock_sock(sk);
        } else
```

If there is no more data to copy and absolutely nothing more to do, we sit and wait for more data. The function `tcp_data_wait` puts the socket (and, therefore, the calling task) in the wait state, `TASK_INTERRUPTIBLE`. Daniel Bovet and Marco Cesati have an excellent discussion of Linux process scheduling policy in Chapter 11 [BOVET02].

```
            sk_wait_data (sk, &timeo);
        if (user_recv) {
            int chunk;
```

We account for any data directly copied from the backlog queue in the previous step. We also return the scheduler to its normal state.

```
            if ((chunk = len - tp->ucopy.len) != 0) {
                NET_ADD_STATS_USER (LINUX_MIB_TCPDIRECTCOPYFROMBACKLOG,
                                    chunk);
                len -= chunk;
                copied += chunk;
            }
            if (tp->rcv_nxt == tp->copied_seq &&
                skb_queue_len(&tp->ucopy.prequeue)) {
do_prequeue:
```

This is where we come to process any packets on the `prequeue`. The function `tcp_prequeue_process` does the work and is covered earlier. After calling it, we adjust `chunk` to account for any data copied from the `prequeue`.

```
                tcp_prequeue_process(sk);
                if ((chunk = len - tp->ucopy.len) != 0) {
                    NET_ADD_STATS_USER (
                        LINUX_MIB_TCPDIRECTCOPYFROMPREQUEUE, chunk);
                    len -= chunk;
                    copied += chunk;
                }
            }
        }
```

```
        if ((flags & MSG_PEEK) && peek_seq != tp->copied_seq) {
            if (net_ratelimit())
                printk(KERN_DEBUG
                    "TCP(%s:%d): Application bug, race in
                    MSG_PEEK.\n",
                    current->comm, current->pid);
            peek_seq = tp->copied_seq;
        }
        continue;
```

This is where we jumped to out of the previous inner loop if we found a data segment on the receive queue. We figure out how much data we have to copy from the len field of skb and offset calculated earlier.

```
    found_ok_skb:
        used = skb->len - offset;
        if (len < used)
            used = len;
```

We must check for urgent data. Unless the socket option, SO_OOBINLINE, was set, we skip the urgent data because it was processed separately.

```
        if (tp->urg_data) {
            u32 urg_offset = tp->urg_seq - *seq;
            if (urg_offset < used) {
                if (!urg_offset) {
                    if (!sock_flag(sk, SOCK_URGINLINE)) {
                        ++*seq;
                        offset++;
                        used—;
                        if (!used)
                            goto skip_copy;
                    }
                } else
                    used = urg_offset;
            }
        }
```

This is where we copy the data to user space. If we get an error while copying, we return an EFAULT.

```
        if (!(flags&MSG_TRUNC)) {
            err = skb_copy_datagram_iovec(skb, offset,
```

Chapter 9 Receiving Data in the Transport Layer, UDP, and TCP

```
                                         msg->msg_iov, used);
            if (err) {
```

This is an exception condition.

```
                if (!copied)
                    copied = -EFAULT;
                break;
            }
        }
        *seq += used;
        copied += used;
        len -= used;
        tcp_rcv_space_adjust(sk);
skip_copy:
        if (tp->urg_data && after(tp->copied_seq,tp->urg_seq)) {
            tp->urg_data = 0;
```

Now that we are done processing urgent data, we turn on the fast path (set TCP header prediction). Fast path processing was turned off if input processing encountered a segment with urgent data (URG flag on) and a valid urgent pointer field in the TCP header.

```
            tcp_fast_path_check(sk, tp);
        }
        if (used + offset < skb->len)
            continue;
        if (skb->h.th->fin)
            goto found_fin_ok;
        if (!(flags & MSG_PEEK))
            tcp_eat_skb(sk, skb);
        continue;
```

This is where we jumped if we found a packet containing a **FIN** in the receive queue. RFC 793 says that we must count the **FIN** as one byte in the sequence and TCP window calculation.

```
    found_fin_ok:
        ++*seq;
        if (!(flags & MSG_PEEK))
            tcp_eat_skb(sk, skb);
        break;
    } while (len > 0);
```

We are at the end of the outer while loop, processing socket buffers until we have copied the amount of data, `len`, requested by the caller in the application program. If we dumped out of the loop, leaving any data on the `prequeue`, it must be processed now before getting out.

```
if (user_recv) {
    if (!skb_queue_empty(&tp->ucopy.prequeue)) {
        int chunk;
        tp->ucopy.len = copied > 0 ? len : 0;
        tcp_prequeue_process(sk);
        if (copied > 0 && (chunk = len - tp->ucopy.len) != 0) {
            NET_ADD_STATS_USER (LINUX_MIB_TCPDIRECTCOPYFROMPREQUEUE,
                                chunk);
            len -= chunk;
            copied += chunk;
        }
    }
    tp->ucopy.task = NULL;
    tp->ucopy.len = 0;
}
```

We call `cleanup_rbuf` to clean up the TCP receive buffer. It will send an **ACK** if necessary.

```
cleanup_rbuf(sk, copied);
TCP_CHECK_TIMER(sk);
release_sock(sk);
return copied;
```

We are done, so release the socket and get out.

```
out:
    TCP_CHECK_TIMER(sk);
    release_sock(sk);
    return err;
```

We jumped here if we encountered urgent data while processing segments. We call `cp_recv_urg` to copy the urgent data to the user.

```
recv_urg:
    err = tcp_recv_urg(sk, timeo, msg, len, flags, addr_len);
    goto out;
```

        }

Receiving Urgent Data

Urgent data is data received in a segment that has the URG TCP flag and a valid urgent pointer. Urgent data, also known as *Out-of-Band* (OOB) data, is handled separately from the normal data in the data segments. Theoretically, it is handled as a higher priority and gets passed up to the socket as OOB data.

The `tcp_recv_urg` Function

The function `tcp_recv_urg` in the file `linux/net/ipv4/tcp.c` is called from `tcp_recvmsg` when a segment containing urgent data is encountered while processing the stream of data segments.

```
static int tcp_recv_urg(struct sock * sk, long timeo,
                struct msghdr *msg, int len, int flags,
                int *addr_len)
{
    struct tcp_opt *tp = tcp_sk(sk);
```

The `SOCK_URGINLINE` flag in the `sock` structure is set from the `SO_OOBINLINE` socket option, which states that urgent data should be handled as if it were ordinary segment data. If this socket option was set, it is an error because we are in the function that is supposed to process the urgent data specially.

```
    if (sock_flag(sk, SOCK_URGINLINE)|| !tp->urg_data ||
        tp->urg_data == TCP_URG_READ)
        return -EINVAL;
    if (sk->state==TCP_CLOSE && !sock_flag(sk, SOCK_DONE))
        return -ENOTCONN;
```

Now that we have survived the initial steps, we copy the urgent data into the user's buffer.

```
    if (tp->urg_data & TCP_URG_VALID) {
        int err = 0;
        char c = tp->urg_data;
        if (!(flags & MSG_PEEK))
            tp->urg_data = TCP_URG_READ;
```

Setting the `MSG_OOB` flag tells the application that urgent data has been received. We call `memcpy_toiovec` to do the actual copying.

```
            msg->msg_flags|=MSG_OOB;
            if(len > 0) {
                if (!(flags & MSG_TRUNC))
                    err = memcpy_toiovec(msg->msg_iov, &c, 1);
                len = 1;
            } else
                msg->msg_flags|=MSG_TRUNC;
            return err ? -EFAULT : len;
        }
        if (sk->state == TCP_CLOSE || (sk->sk_shutdown & RCV_SHUTDOWN))
            return 0;
```

We should not block in this call, regardless of the blocking state of the socket. All implementations as well as BSD have the same behavior.

```
        return -EAGAIN;
    }
```

SUMMARY

In this chapter, we discussed the receive side of the transport protocols, TCP and UDP. This chapter is a companion to Chapter 7, where we discussed the sending side of the same protocols. We saw how TCP is much more complicated than UDP because of the necessity of maintaining connection state and buffering for streaming data. We covered the receive-side packet handling in UDP and looked at the socket hash de-multiplexing. We also covered processing of incoming broadcast and multicast packets. For TCP, we discussed input state handling and how TCP header prediction is implemented. Finally, we looked at how received packets are processed while in the **ESTABLISHED** and the **TIME-WAIT** states.

10 A Protocol Family Implementation

In This Chapter

- A Few Words
- Introduction
- The AF_NADA Protocol Family
- Address Family Initialization
- Module Initialization
- Socket Layer Interface
- Receiving Packets in the AF_NADA Family
- Sending Packets from the Socket Layer
- The Test Setup for AF_NADA

A FEW WORDS

Throughout the earlier chapters in this book, we explored the TCP/IP implementation in Linux. We started by looking at networking and communications in general and then we looked at TCP/IP. We followed by diving deeply into the details of TCP/IP and its implementation in Linux. Along this journey, we explored aspects of the framework Linux provides to TCP/IP protocols. Although not always explicit in the remainder of this work, Linux provides an excellent platform to implement protocols or complete protocol families. In this chapter, we will go through a sample kernel module that creates a sample protocol family. All the code presented in this chapter will be included in the CD-ROM accompanying this book. It can be found in the /nada directory. A Makefile is included to build a kernel module that can be loaded with insmod(8). The sources can be found in the nada directory on the CD-ROM. The actual protocol is in one file, nada/af_nada.c, and there are three header files, nada/nada.h, nada/nadasock.h, and nada/nadadebug.h. In addition to the nada protocol itself, we include a test program to transmit and receive packets using the nada protocol and a program to set up tunnel interfaces for testing the AF_NADA protocol family.

521

INTRODUCTION

A protocol family is simply a number that corresponds to the domain argument in the socket() system call. Table 4.1 contains a list of all the registered protocol families. Sometimes, these are also called address families. The address family is the first part of a qualifying address that uniquely identifies an endpoint. Of course, as we have seen in Chapter 4, a qualifying address also includes the network address and the port number.

Currently, there is a maximum of 32 protocol families defined for Linux. All 32 are defined, so we can't really introduce a new protocol family just for the purposes of this book. We will borrow a little used protocol family and equate it to a new type in our code, and we will see how this is done later. For our test code, we will pass packets through dedicated tunnels so we won't pollute the public Internet with bogus packets containing strange protocol numbers. Our main purpose in this chapter is to show how the mechanisms work and not to actually invent a new protocol.

Our protocol family doesn't really do anything useful. It merely exchanges individual packets or datagrams between peer machines. There is a very simple addressing scheme borrowed from the econet protocol family defined in the Linux kernel.

Later in this chapter, we will see how to use the tun/tap driver to set up tunnels that for testing this protocol family. We will provide a simple program to implement the tunnel endpoints using sockets. Figure 10.1 shows our test setup. This test setup is discussed in detail at the end of this chapter.

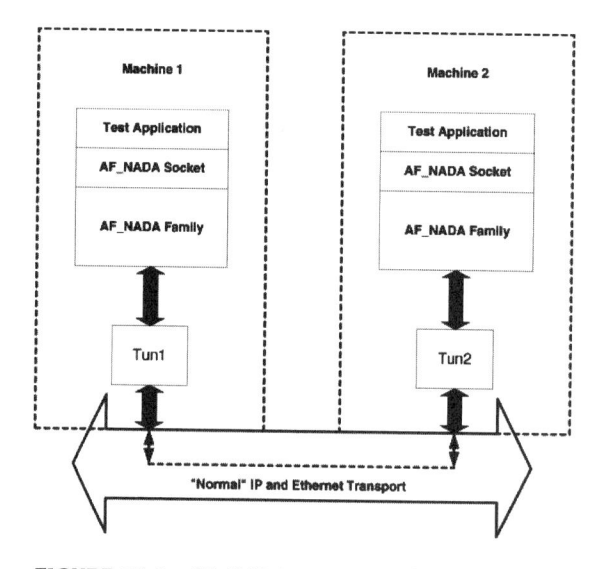

FIGURE 10.1 AF_NADA test network.

THE `AF_NADA` PROTOCOL FAMILY

For our example code, we have invented the `AF_NADA` protocol family. We named it `AF_NADA` because *nada* means nothing in Spanish, and this protocol family does nothing useful other than serve as a simple example. Of course, we hope to show that demonstrating how we utilize the Linux networking infrastructure is useful, even though the protocols don't actually do any packet mangling.

Linux defines a maximum of 32 address families. As of this writing, we didn't request that this number be extended. We borrow a little used protocol family and redefine it in our header file. We will use `AF_SNA` which isn't so widely used of late. Also, to test this protocol, we will run through virtual private networks created with the Linux `tun` driver so we certainly aren't likely to encounter any real SNA packets. Protocol and address families are defined in the file `linux/include/linux/socket.h`. However, we will overwrite the definition in `nada/nada.h`.

```
#ifndef AF_NADA
#define AF_NADA   AF_SNA
#endif
```

In Linux we also equate address families and protocol families.

```
#ifndef PF_NADA
#define PF_NADA AF_NADA
#endif
```

`AF_NADA` Address Type

In our family, things are simple and straightforward. Rather than a complicated addressing scheme, we will merely number each node consecutively. These consecutive numbers will constitute the node addresses.

The `sockaddr_nada` Structure

Each protocol must have a `sock` address type. There is a generic `sockaddr` type defined in `linux/include/linux/socket.h`. This structure is used to communicate address information between kernel and user space via the `sendmsg(2)`, `recvmsg(2)`, `connect(2)`, and `bind(2)` functions. Each address family will generally have an include file with its specific address type definitions in the directory */usr/include/linux*. However, since our address type isn't official, we defined it in our own file *nada/nada.h*.

```
struct sockaddr_nada {
```

First and foremost, we have our family.

```
sa_family_t      nads_family;
```

We follow this by our protocol-specific network layer address and port. The network layer address follows. We use a 1-byte field for our port because this is more than sufficient for our demonstration protocol.

```
    struct nada_address nads_addr
    unsigned char   nad_port
};
```

The nada_address Structure

In this structure, we define our actual network layer address. This address is incorporated in the sockaddr type discussed previously.

```
    struct nada_address {
```

Our addressing structure is similar to Econet. It consists of a simple network identifier and a station address. However, since our simple test environment has only point–to-point connections, pretty much everything sent will be received by the peer anyway. The address only has two bytes, which is enough for purposes of illustration. A real network layer protocol would need a much larger address space.

```
    unsigned char net;
    unsigned char station;
};
```

The Nada Packet Format

The nada packet is very simple. See Figure 10.2 for an illustration of the nada packet structure.

```
    struct nada_hdr {
```

We have a one protocol number followed by the 2-byte source address and the 2-byte destination address.

```
    unsigned char       prot;
    unsigned char       src_net;
    unsigned char       src_station;
    unsigned char       dst_net;
    unsigned char       dst_station;
```

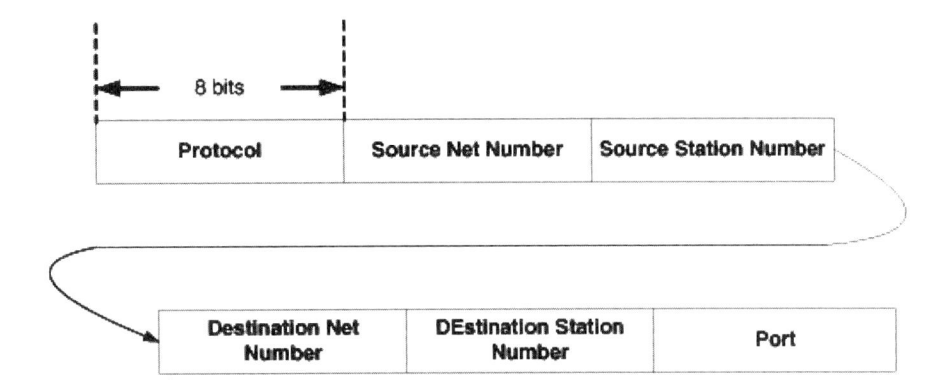

Chapter 10 A Protocol Family Implementation **525**

FIGURE 10.2 Nada header.

The last field in the header is the 1-byte port number.

```
    unsigned char    port;
};
```

ADDRESS FAMILY INITIALIZATION

We have seen in Chapter 5 how the AF_INET family is set up in Linux, and in Chapter 11, we will see a similar setup for IPv6, the AF_INET6 family. In this section, we explore the setup for our demonstration protocol family, AF_NADA. In this section, we will show the data structures and functions used for initialization. As we have seen in earlier chapters, address family initialization primarily consists of introducing our protocol to the socket layer.

The nada_ops Structure

The nada_ops structure contains pointers to all the socket level functions. We will see how a pointer to this structure is passed in when we create the socket. A socket is created when the user calls socket(2). When our protocol family does not define a function, we initialize the pointer to the generic sock_no . . . function.

```
    static struct proto_ops nada_ops = {
```

We set the family to AF_NADA. Also, we must define the release function so we can clean up when a user closes a socket. We define bind so we can respond when the user wishes to define a local address for a AF_NADA socket.

```
.family      = PF_NADA,
.owner       = THIS_MODULE,
.release     = nada_release,
.bind        = nada_bind,
.connect     = sock_no_connect,
.socketpair  = sock_no_socketpair,
.accept      = sock_no_accept,
.getname     = sock_no_getname,
```

This is the generic datagram polling function. We define this function pointer so our protocol family will work with polled sockets. Next, we define our own IO control function so a user-level application can set and get device addresses. We will see how all `ioctl` calls to underlying devices are passed through.

```
.poll        = datagram_poll,
.ioctl       = nada_ioctl,
.listen      = sock_no_listen,
.shutdown    = sock_no_shutdown,
.setsockopt  = sock_no_setsockopt,
.getsockopt  = sock_no_getsockopt,
```

Finally, we define `sendmsg` and `recvmsg` so we can send and receive datagrams at the socket level.

```
.sendmsg     = nada_sendmsg,
.recvmsg     = nada_recvmsg,
.mmap        = sock_no_mmap,
.sendpage    = sock_no_sendpage,
};
```

The `nada_family_ops` Structure

This structure is used for socket registration. Socket registration is done at initialization. Later, when a user calls `socket(2)`, the socket layer will know how to process her request for a AF_NADA type socket.

```
static struct net_proto_family nada_family_ops = {
```

Here, we define our family. Remember that PF_NADA and AF_NADA are the same.

```
.family = PF_NADA,
```

As we have seen in Chapter 4, "Linux Sockets," when socket(1) is called, the following function is accessed through the create pointer. Finally, the owner field is provided to ensure that things will get properly cleaned up if this module is unloaded from the kernel.

```
    .create = nada_create,
    .owner  = THIS_MODULE,
};
```

The nada_proto Structure

The nada_proto structure is used for registering with the socket layer. It lets the socket layer know how much space to reserve for our special variant of the sock structure. Most protocol families will create a sock variant with some protocol family-specific data structures at the end of the generic sock structure to hold state and header information specific to the protocol.

```
static struct proto nada_proto = {
```

When our module is loaded, not only will we be entered in /proc/modules, but we will also show up in /proc/net/protocols with the name NADA.

```
    .name   = "NADA",
    .owner  = THIS_MODULE,
```

Here we announce how much space we need for our sock structure.

```
    .obj_size = sizeof(struct nada_sock),
};
```

MODULE INITIALIZATION

Most of the initialization is done when the module is loaded, and we will discuss the initialization steps in this section. In general in kernel modules, initialization functions are typed __init and are called when a module is loaded into the kernel. Socket registration is done at initialization time.

Protocol Registration

The purpose of protocol registration is to facilitate the socket interface. The socket interface for a protocol family has several purposes. User-level applications can receive and send data encapsulated within the protocol. Also, sockets allow application code to send messages with configuration data intended to be consumed within the kernel.

Finally, protocol families are also used for internal communication between user-level code and the kernel. For example, the AF_KEY family is for passing keying material between the internal Security Data Base (SDB) and a keying daemon such as Internet Key Exchange (IKE) in user space.

There is no absolute requirement that an address family need be as complicated as TCP/IP, which contains member transport protocols, UDP and TCP. For example, the AF_PACKET protocol family is simpler. It exists only so user applications can receive and send raw packets. More germane to our example, in the AF_NADA protocol family created for this chapter, we haven't as yet defined any transport or other member protocols in the family. We register the address family with the socket layer so a user application can receive and send data through AF_NADA type packets. For the reason, the socket address for AF_NADA is quite simple.

The nada_init Function

The nada_init function is called when the module is loaded into the kernel. It is in this function where we do our initial registration with the socket layer and the Linux networking infrastructure.

```
static int __init nada_init(void)
{
    int res;
```

We call proto_register to register our AF_NADA variant of the sock structure. See Chapter 4 for more information about Linux Socket implementation and how the sock structure is used. The nada_proto structure was discussed in an earlier section.

```
    res = proto_register(&nada_proto, 0);
    if (res != 0)
        goto out;
```

Here, we do the socket registration. This is how we tell the socket layer which of our functions correspond to the user level system calls: bind(2), connect(2), sendmsg(2), recvmsg(2), and others. The data structure nada_family_ops contains the function pointers.

```
    res = sock_register(&nada_family_ops);
    if (res != 0)
        goto out;
```

If we want to show any specific information about our protocol family in a special directories and files in the /proc file system, we would call a function to set up our entries here. As of this writing, we didn't put in any special /proc support for our module.

```
#ifdef NADA_PROC_SUPPORT
    if ((res = nada_proc_init()) != 0)
        goto out;
#endif
```

Here is where we register our packet handlers. Packet handlers are functions called when a packet of a matching type is received by the network interface driver. As of this writing, we have not implemented promiscuous packet handling, but if we needed that, we would call a special packet handler.

```
#ifdef NADA_PROMISCUOUS
    dev_add_pack(&nada_packet_prom);
#endif
    dev_add_pack(&nada_packet_eth);
```

Notifier chains are lists of functions that get called when an event is triggered. The most common of these is the net device notifier. After a function is registered with the notifier chain, we will be told when a network interface device status changes. See Chapter 3 for more information.

```
#ifdef NADA_NOTIFIER
    register_netdevice_notifier(&nada_notifier);
#endif
out:
    return res;
}
```

SOCKET LAYER INTERFACE

As discussed earlier, the nada_ops structure contains pointers to NADA-specific functions called in response to user requests through the socket layer. In this section, we discuss several of these functions and some of the associated data structures.

Open Socket List

In our protocol family, we define a socket list to keep track of open sockets. We must also associate address and port numbers with sockets. This is our abbreviated alternative to the more complex transport layer de-multiplexing code used by IPv4 and covered in earlier chapters.

The Socket List Declaration

```
HLIST_HEAD(nada_sockets_list);
```

We also define a lock to control access to the socket list.

```
DEFINE_RWLOCK(nada_sockets_lock);
```

Socket List Utility Functions

Associated with the socket, we have functions to insert and remove a socket from the list.

The nada_insert_socket Function

This function acquires the socket list and places a new socket in the list. It is called from the nada_create function.

```
static void nada_insert_socket(struct hlist_head *sock_list, struct sock *sk)
{
    write_lock_bh(&nada_sockets_lock);
    sk_add_node(sk, sock_list);
    write_unlock_bh(&nada_sockets_lock);
}
```

The nada_remove_socket Function

The remove function acquires the lock and removes a socket from the list. This function is called from nada_release.

```
static void nada_remove_socket(struct hlist_head *sock_list, struct sock *sk)
{
    write_lock_bh(&nada_sockets_lock);
    sk_del_node_init(sk);
    write_unlock_bh(&nada_sockets_lock);
}
```

Socket Creation

In this section, we will explain some of the data structures and functions specifically associated with socket creation. The socket is created when the user executes the `socket(2)` system call.

The `nada_sock` Structure

Generally, each protocol family will define a family-specific or protocol-specific sock structure variant. In our case, it is called `nada_sock`.

```
struct nada_sock
{
```

We note that the first field in the structure is the actual generic sock structure. This allows all sock structures to share the same slab cache for efficiency. Certain fields in the sock structure are pre-initialized when the sock structure is allocated. We will see how this makes our code much simpler.

```
        struct sock         sk;
```

Our sock structure contains the protocol number, network layer address, and port for this open socket.

```
        unsigned char       prot;
        unsigned char       port;
        unsigned char       station;
        unsigned char       net;
        unsigned char       state;
};
```

The `nada_sk` Function

Generally, each protocol family will define a simple inline to get the family-specific variant from the generic sock structure.

```
static inline struct nada_sock *nada_sk(struct sock *sk)
{
        return (struct nada_sock *)sk;
}
```

The nada_create Function

The function nada_create creates a new AF_NADA family socket. It allocates a sock structure and initializes some fields including any protocol-specific private areas. The new socket is put on a list of sockets maintained locally within our protocol.

```
static int nada_create(struct socket *sock, int protocol )
{
    int    ret;
    struct sock *sk;
```

First, we check the type of the socket the user is attempting to open. For simplicity, we only support datagram or connectionless sockets.

```
ret =-ESOCKTNOSUPPORT;
if (sock->type != SOCK_DGRAM)
    goto out;
```

Now, we allocate the socket structure, by calling the function sk_alloc. It uses some fields in proto structure to see which slab cache to use and to keep track of the owner of the new socket. Most of these fields in the proto structure were pre-initialized. We only set a few of them. Since we didn't specify a different slab cache, sk_alloc will use the default slab cache.

```
ret = -ENOBUFS;
sk = sk_alloc(AF_NADA, GFP_KERNEL, &nada_proto, 1);
if (sk == NULL)
    goto out;
```

Here, we initialize some fields in the new sock structure. We set a pointer to the nada_ops structure shown earlier. This way, the socket layer will know which functions to call when the user executes one of the socket-layer system calls.

```
sk->sk_reuse = 1;
sock->ops = &nada_ops;
sock_init_data(sock, sk);
sk->sk_family = PF_NADA;
```

Next, we do some custom initialization of our own variant of the socket.

```
nada_sock_init(sk, protocol);
sock_reset_flag(sk, SOCK_ZAPPED);
```

Finally, we insert the socket on our local list of open sockets.

```
    nada_insert_socket(&nada_sockets_list, sk);
    ret = 0;
out:
    return ret;
}
```

The nada_sock_init Function

This function is called from nada_create. It initializes some fields in the nada variant of the sock structure.

```
static void nada_sock_init(struct sock *sk, int prot)
{
```

We get our special sock variant.

```
    struct nada_sock *nadas;
    nadas = nada_sk(sk);
```

All we do for now is set the protocol number and increment a variable to indicate the number of open sockets in our family.

```
    nadas->prot = prot;
    atomic_inc(&nada_num_socks);
}
```

Other Socket Interface Functions

In this section, we will discuss other aspects of the socket layer interface including functions to bind to the local address, do IO controls, and receive packets. The socket send function will be covered in a later section.

The nada_bind Function

The function, nada_bind, runs when the user calls the bind(2) system call. Its main purpose is to associate a local address with an open socket so our protocol can find which open socket should receive an incoming packet based on the destination address of the packet. In our simple family, we have only simple addresses, and we are testing with point-to-point connections so our main concern will be associating open sockets with network interface drivers.

```
static int nada_bind(struct socket *sock, struct sockaddr *uaddr,
                    int addr_len)
{
```

We define a pointer to the generic `sock` structure and the NADA-specific `sock` structure. We also get a pointer to the address passed in the `my_addr` field of the `bind(2)` system call.

```
struct sock *sk = sock->sk;
struct nada_sock *nadas = nada_sk(sk);
struct sockaddr_nada * nada_adr = (struct sockaddr_nada *) uaddr;
int err;
```

First, we check for a valid address family.

```
err = -EINVAL;
if (addr_len != sizeof(struct sockaddr_nada) ||
            nada_adr->nads_family != AF_NADA)
    goto bye;
```

Next we check for valid address and port. In our case, at least for now, the function `nada_addr_check` merely checks for the family again.

```
err = -EINVAL;
if (nada_addr_check(nada_adr) == 0)
    goto bye;
```

We set the port and address information into the `nada_sock` structure so it will be associated with this open socket.

```
nadas->port = nada_adr->nad_port;
nadas->station = nada_adr->nads_addr.station;
nadas->net = nada_adr->nads_addr.net;
return 0;
bye:
    return err;
}
```

The IO Control Functions

In our example, there are two `ioctl` functions. This is common practice in protocol implementations in Linux. We have a generic `ioctl` function that passes unrecognized commands down to the device layer and intercepts commands intended for local processing by the protocol.

The Generic ioctl Function, nada_ioctl

The function nada_ioctl is referenced in the nada_ops structure. It will be called whenever a user calls ioctl(2) on an open socket of our address family type.

```
static int nada_ioctl(struct socket *sock, unsigned int cmd, unsigned long arg)
{
        struct sock *sk = sock->sk;
```

We get a pointer to the function argument in user space.

```
        void __user *argp = (void __user *)arg;
        switch(cmd) {
                case SIOCGSTAMP:
                        return sock_get_timestamp(sk, argp);
```

Here, we check for commands for interception by our protocol and call nada_specific_ioctl for processing.

```
                case SIOCSIFADDR:
                case SIOCGIFADDR:
                        return nada_specific_ioctl(sock, cmd, argp);
                        break;
```

We pass any unrecognized commands down to the device layer.

```
                default:
                        return dev_ioctl(cmd, argp);
        }
        return 0;
}
```

The nada_specific_ioctl Function

This function processes all local ioctls within our protocol. In our simple example family, we are concerned only with the set and get interface address functions so we can associate nada address with network interfaces.

```
static int nada_specific_ioctl(struct socket *sock, unsigned int cmd,
                               void __user *arg)
{
```

All interface address changes are contained in an ifreq structure.

```
struct ifreq ifr;
struct nada_device *ndev;
struct net_device *dev;
struct sockaddr_nada *naddr;
int ret;
```

We map the argument from user space to kernel space and put it into the `ifreq` structure.

```
ret = -EFAULT;
if (copy_from_user(&ifr, arg, sizeof(struct ifreq)))
    goto err;
```

Next, we check to see whether the user is naming a valid device.

```
ret = -ENODEV;
if ((dev = dev_get_by_name(ifr.ifr_name)) == NULL)
    goto err;
```

Now we set our protocol `sock` address structure to point to the user-specified address.

```
naddr = (struct sockaddr_nada *) &ifr.ifr_addr;
switch (cmd)
{
```

We set a new device address into the network interface device. Typically, each protocol family needs to keep track of protocol-specific addressing and device-related information. The `net_device` structure provides some pointers to store this information. We must do something tricky here since we haven't yet submitted our AF_NADA family to the Linux community. We borrow a little used DECnet pointer by equating `nada_ptr` to `dn_ptr` in the header file `nada/nada.h`.

```
case SIOCSIFADDR:
    ndev = dev->nada_ptr;
    if (ndev == NULL) {
```

If necessary, we create a new `nada_device` structure. This device equates to the `inet_device` structure used for IPv6. In our case, things are much simpler. Our `nada_device` only contains the address information. The structure will be automatically freed when the containing `net_device` structure is freed.

```
            ndev = kmalloc(sizeof(struct nada_device), GFP_KERNEL);
            if (!ndev) {
                goto err_dev;
            }
            memset (ndev, 0, sizeof(struct nada_device));
            dev->nada_ptr = ndev;
        }
```

If there is already a `nada_device` in our device, we update the address information. We maintain a list of devices so we can map outgoing packets. This is a very simple alternative to ARP. We will see later that all we do is decide which outgoing device to use based on the destination address.

```
        else
            nada_dev_list[ndev->net] = NULL;
        ndev->station = naddr->nads_addr.station;
        ndev->net = naddr->nads_addr.net;
        nada_dev_list[ndev->net] = dev;
        if (nada_dev_list[0] == NULL)
            nada_dev_list[0] = dev;
        ret = 0;
        goto out;       case SIOCGIFADDR:
```

Here we get the address of the device and copy it back to the user. We extract the device address from the `nada_device` structure attached to the `net_device`. It is an error if there is no address defined for this device.

```
        ret = -ENODEV;
        ndev = dev->nada_ptr;
        if (ndev == NULL)
            goto err_dev;
        memset (naddr, 0, sizeof(struct sockaddr_nada));
        naddr->nads_addr.station = ndev->station;
        naddr->nads_addr.net = ndev->net;
        naddr->nads_family = AF_NADA;
        ret = -EFAULT;
```

Here, we copy the information back to user space.

```
        if (copy_to_user(arg, &ifr, sizeof(struct ifreq)))
            goto err_dev;
        ret = 0;
        goto out;
```

```
                default:
                        ret = -EINVAL;
                        goto err_dev;
        }
out:
                        dev_put(dev);
                        return 0;
err_dev:
                        dev_put(dev);
err:
        return ret;
}
```

The nada_recvmsg Function

This function, nada_recvmsg runs when the user calls read(2), recvmsg(2), or one of its variants. In this function we read packets from the socket receive queue and map them into user space.

```
static int nada_recvmsg(struct kiocb *iocb, struct socket *sock,
                        struct msghdr *msg, size_t len, int flags)
{
```

First, as with the other socket layer functions, we get a pointer to the sock structure, and we define a pointer to the socket buffer.

```
struct sock *sk = sock->sk;
struct sk_buff *skb;
int copied;
int ret = -EINVAL;
```

First, we check for unsupported flags. These flags are set in the flags argument to the recvmsg(2) call.

```
if (flags & ~(MSG_PEEK|MSG_DONTWAIT|MSG_TRUNC|MSG_CMSG_COMPAT))
    goto out;
```

We recall that a name is really an address. We set the name length to be the length of our sockaddr structure variant. Next, we call the generic datagram receiving function, skb_recv_datagram. This function is also used by UDP and many other protocols because it is an excellent protocol-independent datagram receiving function. It hides much socket locking and queue handling. This makes this protocol code nice and clean.

```
        msg->msg_namelen = sizeof(struct sockaddr_nada);
        skb = skb_recv_datagram(sk, flags, flags & MSG_DONTWAIT, &ret);
        if (skb == NULL)
            goto out;
```

Here we check to see whether the length of the incoming packet minus the header is smaller than the amount of data the user requested when she called `read(2)` or `recvmsg(2)`.

```
        copied = skb->len;
        if (copied > len ) {
            msg->msg_flags |= MSG_TRUNC;
            copied = len;
        }
        skb->h.raw = skb->data;
```

Next, we copy the data from user space to kernel space. If this copy fails, we return the error.

```
        ret = skb_copy_datagram_iovec(skb, 0, msg->msg_iov, copied);
        if (ret)
            goto out_free;
```

Next we get the timestamp to mark when the packet was received.

```
        sock_recv_timestamp(msg, sk, skb);
```

We return the requested length or the actual length passed to the user.

```
        ret = (flags & MSG_TRUNC) ? skb->len : copied;
out_free:
        skb_free_datagram(sk, skb);
out:
        return ret;
}
```

RECEIVING PACKETS IN THE AF_NADA FAMILY

This protocol, as is the case with IP in `AF_INET` and other protocols, has a function registered to receive packets that match the protocol number in the link layer header. Earlier, in the module we looked at the initialization code and saw how our protocol family registered a packet handler function. The packet handler is not called directly by the network interface drivers interrupt service routine, instead it is called from a special kernel thread or `softirq`. In our example, we are testing this code with the pseudo-network interface driver, `tun`, so there really aren't any interrupts involved.

The `nada_rcv_skb` Function

The function `nada_rcv_skb` is called when a packet of matching type is received by the lower layers of the Linux networking infrastructure. For more information about the queuing layer and the Linux network interface drivers, see Chapters 3 and 5.

```
static int nada_rcv_skb(struct sk_buff *skb, struct net_device *dev,
                        struct packet_type *pt)
{
```

First, we define a pointer to a nada packet header, a pointer to the generic `sock` structure, and a pointer to the nada device information structure.

```
struct nada_hdr *nhdr;
struct sock *sk;
struct nada_device *ndev = dev->nada_ptr;
```

We check to make sure that the packet is really headed our way.

```
if (skb->pkt_type == PACKET_OTHERHOST)
    goto drop_free;
if (!dev)
    goto drop_free;
```

We check that the socket buffer holding this packet is shareable.

```
if ((skb = skb_share_check(skb, GFP_ATOMIC)) == NULL)
    goto drop;
```

Next, we ensure that the socket buffer is at least big enough for a nada packet header.

```
if (!pskb_may_pull(skb, sizeof(struct nada_hdr)))
    goto drop_free;
```

We set the header pointer to point to the beginning of the actual packet.

```
nhdr = (struct nada_hdr *) skb->data;
```

We must find which open socket, if any, should receive this packet. The function `nada_find_listener` finds an open socket ready for data.

```
sk = nada_find_listener(nhdr->port, nhdr->src_station,
nhdr->src_net);
if (!sk)
    goto drop_free;
```

Next, if we found a listening socket, we queue up the packet on that sockets receive queue.

```
if (nada_rcv_queue_pkt(sk, skb, ndev->net,nhdr->src_station,
    nhdr->src_net))
        goto drop_free;
```

Finally, we are done. If we must drop the packet, we make sure to free the `skb` we created earlier. When we return 0, the layers below know that we consumed the packet.

```
    return 0;
drop_free:
    kfree_skb(skb);
drop:
```

If we drop the packet, we tell the layers below.

```
    return NET_RX_DROP;
}
```

The `nada_find_listener` Function

This function is called from the packet handler function. It searches our list of open sockets to find one that corresponds to the header information in the current packet. This function implements a very simple version of the transport layer demultiplexing done by UDP or TCP.

```
static struct sock *nada_find_listener(unsigned char port, unsigned char stn,
                                       unsigned char net)
{
    struct sock *sk;
    struct hlist_node *node;
```

The next section of code is our simple de-multiplexer. We loop through all the open sockets on our list, `nada_sockets_list`, and look for matching address and port number.

```
sk_for_each(sk, node, &nada_sockets_list) {
    struct nada_sock *nsk = nada_sk(sk);
```

We match the address in the incoming packet with our local address. We recall how the local address was set in the `nada_sock` structure when the user called `bind`. If there is no local address defined, we will accept all packets with a matching protocol number no matter what else is in the nada header of the packet.

```
    if ((nsk->port == port || nsk->port == 0) &&
        (nsk->station == stn || nsk->station == 0) &&
        (nsk->net == net || nsk->net == 0))
        return sk;
}
return NULL;
}
```

The `nada_rcv_queue_pkt` Function

This function is called from the packet handler function. It queues a packet to a listening socket's receive queue. From there, the packet on the receive queue can fulfill a `recvmsg` request from the user space application.

```
static int nada_rcv_queue_pkt(struct sock *sk, struct sk_buff *skb,
                              unsigned char station, unsigned char net,
                              unsigned char port)
{
```

First, we retrieve a pointer to the nada protocol control block. The control block is a private area of the socket buffer structure. It is reserved for specific protocol to put address and header information. Next, nada is set to the `sock` address kept in the control block.

```
    struct nada_cb *nada_cb = (struct nada_cb *)&skb->cb;
    struct sockaddr_nada *nad = (struct sockaddr_nada *)&nada_cb->nad;
    int ret;
```

We initialize the `sock` address structure to zeros and set the information extracted from the packet header.

```
        memset (nad, 0, sizeof(struct sockaddr_nada));
        nad->nads_family = AF_NADA;
        nad->nad_port = port;
        nad->nads_addr.net = net;
        nad->nads_addr.station = station;
```

Finally, we call the generic socket receive queue function, `sock_queue_rcv_skb`, to put the packet on the socket's receive queue.

```
        ret = sock_queue_rcv_skb(sk, skb);
        return ret;
}
```

The Control Block Structure, `nada_cb`

The control block structure, `nada_cb`, is contained in the private area of the socket buffer. As we will recall, socket buffers contain all the information about a particular packet flowing through the protocol stack including the packet data and headers. For more information on socket buffers, see Chapter 6. In complex protocols like TCP, the control block contains socket state information. In our simple family, it contains only the protocol address information.

```
struct nada_cb
{
    struct sockaddr_nada nad;
};
```

SENDING PACKETS FROM THE SOCKET LAYER

Packet transmission is initiated when the user calls `write(2)`, `sendmsg(2)`, or a similar function from her program. As we know, when these functions are called, the socket layer calls the function through the `sendmsg` pointer in the `proto_ops` structure for the address family associated with the open socket type.

The `nada_sendmsg` Function

This function executes when the socket layer calls it through the `sendmsg` field of the `proto_ops` structure. Since our protocol is quite simple, we do all the processing in this function and queue the packet for transmission through the network interface device driver. As we know from Chapter 5, most protocols don't send the packet directly to the device driver. Instead, they follow a more complicated path depending on whether the packet is sent directly to the peer or sent to an intermediary router. Also, the packet is queued to the device independent queuing layer containing multiple queue disciplines, which schedule it for transmission by the network interface driver.

```
static int nada_sendmsg(struct kiocb *iocb, struct socket *sock,
                        struct msghdr *msg, size_t len)
{
```

First, we set up a pointer to the generic sock structure and the AF_NADA-specific sock structure. We also convert the name of the socket to the nada sockaddr structure. The name corresponds to the to field of the user level sendto(2) system call.

```
struct sock        *sk = sock->sk;
struct nada_sock   *nsk = nada_sk(sk);
struct sockaddr_nada *naddr = (struct sockaddr_nada *)msg->msg_name;
#if 0
    unsigned char eth_addr[ETH_HLEN];
#endif
```

We need a local address structure to construct the address of the outgoing packet.

```
struct nada_address nad;
struct sk_buff    *skb = NULL;
struct net_device *dev;
int                ret = 0;
```

These variables are used to construct the outgoing packet header: `proto`, `port`, `station`, and `net` are calculated from the name or from the local address bound to this socket. The variable `proto` is set to our protocol number.

```
unsigned short proto = htons(ETH_P_NADA);
struct nada_hdr *nhdr;
unsigned char port;
unsigned char station;
unsigned char net;
```

First, we check the message flags. These are set in the flags argument of the sendmsg(2) system call. For now we are not supporting any flags.

```
ret = -EINVAL;
if (msg->msg_flags)
    goto out;
```

Next, we check the validity of the destination address specified by the user in the name. If there is no destination address, we build one from the local address bound to this socket. Since most of our packet flow is point-to-point, this works fine. We don't support any loopback address in our simple protocol ether.

```
if (naddr == NULL) {
    nad.station = naddr->nads_addr.station;
    nad.net = naddr->nads_addr.net;
    port = naddr->nad_port;
} else {
    nad.station = nsk->station;
    nad.net = nsk->net;
    port = nsk->port;
}
```

Now, we must select an output network interface through which to send the packet. We call `nada_dev_list` to find the device based on the network address either specified by the user or calculated as shown earlier in this function.

```
dev = nada_dev_list[nad.net];
```

Here, we do something we borrowed from the Econet code. If there is no output device, we use the default device if there is one. The default output device is set in location zero of `nada_dev_list`, which is an array of network device structures. This is similar to the default router in IP routing where the default network interface device always points to the network has a reachable link to the default gateway.

```
if (dev == NULL) {
    dev = nada_dev_list[0];
    ret = -ENETDOWN;
    if (dev == NULL)
        goto out;
}
```

In this family, we don't support fragmentation. Fragmentation is done by IP when the packet size exceeds the MTU of the device. In this protocol, we simply reject the request if the size exceeds the MTU. In calculating the MTU, we allow for the length of the nada protocol header. Also, we *hold the device*, which means we lock it until we call the transmit function.

```
ret = -EMSGSIZE;
if (len + sizeof(struct nada_hdr) > dev->mtu)
    goto out;
dev_hold(dev);
```

Here, we allocate the socket buffer, `skb`, for the output packet. We allocate enough space in the socket buffer for the nada header.

```
skb = sock_alloc_send_skb(sk, sizeof(struct nada_hdr),
                          msg->msg_flags & MSG_DONTWAIT, &ret);
                          if (skb == NULL)
    goto out_dev;
```

We set the destination address and port from the calculated address we did earlier.

```
port = naddr->nad_port;
station = naddr->nads_addr.station;
net = naddr->nads_addr.net;
```

Now we must decide where to send the packet. Unlike IPv4, which has ARP (at least for Ethernet), and IPv6, which uses Neighbor Discovery (ND), we do something quite a bit simpler. In our test network, we are using the `tun` driver, which supports either `tap` or `tun`, where `tap` contains a fake Ethernet header and `tun` does not contain a header. Here, we construct a fake Ethernet header if required.

```
#if 1
    if (dev->hard_header) {
```

We could call `get_eth_address` to generate an arbitrary fake Ethernet header to arbitrarily insert the destination net and station numbers in the last bytes of the address. However, if we are using a real Ethernet device, the lower layers will use the ARP protocol to determine the destination. In our case, we are primarily testing our little protocol family with tunneling point to point devices. Essentially, we can defer the network layer to link layer address mapping issues.

```
//get_eth_address(eth_addr, &naddr->nads_addr);
```

For Ethernet network interface devices, the `hard_header` pointer in the network device structure points to a generic function to construct an Ethernet header. For headerless, network interfaces like `tun`, it will do nothing.

Chapter 10 A Protocol Family Implementation

```
        ret = dev->hard_header(skb, dev, ntohs(proto), NULL, NULL, len);
        if (ret)
            goto out;
    }
#endif
```

Next, we construct the network header. The variable nhdr already points to the front of the packet in the skb. See Figure 10.2 for the structure of a nada protocol header.

```
nhdr = (struct nada_hdr *)(skb->data);
nhdr->port = port;
nhdr->dst_station = station;
nhdr->dst_net = net;
nhdr->prot = (unsigned char) proto;
```

We set a few fields in the outgoing skb.

```
skb->protocol = proto;
skb->dev = dev;
skb->priority = sk->sk_priority;
```

To build the data part of the packet, we copy the data from user space into the skb. The skb only has space reserved for the packet header. We call the function skb_put to lengthen the space in the skb sufficiently for the actual packet data, which has the length, len. The function memcpy_fromiovec does the address space translation between user space and kernel space when it copies the data. It also will perform checksums, but none are required in our case.

```
ret = memcpy_fromiovec(skb_put(skb, len), msg->msg_iov, len);
if (ret)
    goto out_skb;
```

We make sure that the output device is up.

```
ret = -ENETDOWN;
if (!(dev->flags & IFF_UP))
    goto out_skb;
```

Finally, we transmit the packet.

```
ret = 0;
dev_queue_xmit(skb);
goto out_dev;
```

We have several exit labels, so we can de-allocate the skb and free the device hold as required.

```
out_skb:
    kfree_skb(skb);
out_dev:
    dev_put(dev);
out:
    return ret ? : len;}
```

THE TEST SETUP FOR AF_NADA

In this section, we will show how to set up the private network to test the nada protocol. We don't want the packets created in this example to be flowing all over the public network. Therefore, to test our protocol family, we will create a private network with tunnels using the tun/tap driver. We provide a program, tapif, to create tunnels between two arbitrary machines using the tun driver. The tapif program sources are provided on the accompanying CD-ROM. We also provide a test program to configure the nada module and send and receive packets via the nada protocol family. The file chapter10/README.txt in the CD-ROM provides more information about creating the test setup.

Building and Loading the nada Module

To build the nada code, copy the code from the CD-ROM to any directory. Go to the directory and type Make. The module is created in a file called nadas.ko in the nada directory.

```
[herbert@machine nada]$ make
make -C /lib/modules/2.6.12.3_TFH/build SUBDIRS=/home/herbert/nada modules
make[1]: Entering directory '/usr/src/Linux-2.6.12.3_TFH'
  CC [M]  /home/herbert/nada/af_nada.o
  LD [M]  /home/herbert/nada/nadas.o
  Building modules, stage 2.
  MODPOST
  CC      /home/herbert/nada/nadas.mod.o
  LD [M]  /home/herbert/nada/nadas.ko
make[1]: Leaving directory '/usr/src/Linux-2.6.12.3_TFH'
```

Chapter 10 A Protocol Family Implementation **549**

To load the kernel module, type the following command.

```
# /sbin/insmod ./nadas.ko
```

To check whether the module is actually loaded, you can look in `/proc/modules`, or you may type the following command:

```
[herbert@machine nada]$ /sbin/lsmod | grep nada
```

The `tun/tap` Module

Tun/tap is a pseudo network interface device driver that allows packet data to be read by user space programs using a straightforward character interface. The tun module is part of the standard Linux kernel distribution. The complete Linux kernel used for this book is included in the CD-ROM. To install the tun module, execute the following command as root.

We can pump this data through a normal socket effectively creating a custom tunnel between two machines or within the same machine. Figure 10.1 shows our test setup.

```
# /sbin/modprobe tun
```

You will see the tun driver loaded in the kernel by looking in `/proc/modules` or by using the following command.

```
# /sbin/lsmod | grep tun
tun                    18180  0
```

The `tapif` Program

The tapif program sets up tunnels between two systems using the tun drivers. The tapif program should also be run with root privileges because it sets up network interfaces.

```
% ./tapif -?
./tapif [-b] [[-l] | [-s]] [-c host] [-p port] [-t tun]
 Options:
          -b —      background mode (run as daemon)
          -l
          -a —      Use TAP device (default is TUN)
          -r —      Put protocol number in front of packet
          -s —      run as server (default)
          -c host — Run as client (host is peer system)
```

```
                 -p port - Port number (default is 5010)
                 -t tun  - number of tun device (default is 0)

       examples:
         tapif -b -l -p 5009 Run as server daemon and listen on port 5009
         tapif -b -l -p 5009 -t 1 Run as server daemon, listen on port 5009,
         and
                 use tun1 as the network interface device.
         tapif -c 192.168.1.100 -p 5009 Run as client and
             connect to 192.168.1.100 at port 5009.
```

We use the `tapif` program to create a tunnel between two test systems through which we will pass nada packets. The packet handler function, nada_rcv_skb, discussed earlier is registered to receive packets matching the nada protocol number, 22. When we set up our tunnel we use the -r option to `tapif` to pass the nada protocol number along with the packet. On the receiving side, the tun driver will put the protocol number in the protocol field in the skb so the packet will be matched and our packet handler function will execute.

tapif Receiving Side Setup

The `tapif` program passes the packets through a tunnel constructed with TCP sockets. In the receiving side machine, `tapif` is set up as a server to listen on port 5010 by executing the following command.

```
tapif -l -r
```

tapif Sending Side Setup

On the sending side, the `tapif` program acts as a client. It transmits packets to port 5010 on the receiving machine by executing the following command.

```
tapif -c <receiving machine address> -r
```

The nada Test Program

The nada test program is located in the directory, chapter10/nada/test, in the Companion CD-ROM. We use it to configure the nada protocol, set the address of a network interface device for the nada protocol, and to send and receive nada packets.

Nada Receiving Side Setup

First, we configure the nada protocol and set the local address by executing the following command.

```
nada -c -p 1 -n 2 -d 3
```

Next, we set the nada program to listen on a nada socket for incoming packets.

```
nada -l
```

nada Sending Side Setup

Similarly to the receiving side, we configure the nada protocol and set the local address by executing the following command.

```
nada -c -p 2 -n 3 -d 4
```

Next, we set the nada program to send a message via the nada protocol. As a default, it will send packets through the network interface device tun0.

```
nada -s -p 1 -n 2 -d 3
```

SUMMARY

In this chapter we introduced code for a module that exhibits concepts discussed throughout the book. We discussed the AF_NADA protocol family and its implementation. We covered the module initialization, the protocol family initialization, and registration. We covered the socket layer interface for the AF_NADA family. We also discussed packet sending and receiving packets. We showed how to build and test the protocol, and we discussed the tapif and nada programs provided for configuring the test setup and sending and receiving nada data.

11 Internet Protocol Version 6 (IPv6)

In This Chapter

- A Few Words
- Introduction
- Facilities in IPv6
- IPv6 Addressing
- IPv6 Packet Format
- IPv6 Implementation in Linux
- IPv6 Socket Implementation
- IPv6 Fragmentation and De-fragmentation Implementation
- IPv6 Output
- IPv6 Input
- IPv6 UDP
- IPv6 TCP
- The ICMP Protocol for IPv6, ICMPv6
- IPv6 Neighbor Discovery
- The Multicast Listener Discovery Protocol
- Auto Configuration
- Routing and the IPv6 FIB

A FEW WORDS

In this chapter, we examine IPv6. We introduce some basics about the protocol and how it enhances IPv4. As in the rest of the book, we concentrate on the internals of TCP/IP. We discuss how the IPv6 protocol works in the Linux kernel networking environment. For historical reasons, some of the Linux networking facilities are IPv4-specific, although as the kernel evolves, the networking implementation has become less protocol family specific. This chapter covers the areas where IPv6 has its own separate facilities, even though they are similar to facilities in IPv4. A few features of IPv6 are still implemented separately from those used with IPv4. The companion CD-ROM contains a copy of all the sources referenced in this book, including the IPv6 source discussed in this chapter.

INTRODUCTION

The Internet protocol is 24 years old at the time of this writing. It was originally specified in 1980 [RFC 760]. In the early days of IP, it was never envisioned how popular the Internet would become. The most fundamental limitation associated with IPv4 is its limited address size. IPv4 addresses are 32 bits long, limiting the total number of addresses. Back in the early 1990s, when there began to be dramatic increases in the use of the Internet, it was becoming clear that the address space was too restricted. There were simply not enough addresses available because of the 4-byte address in IPv4. In the early 1990s, people started to think about ways to expand the address space. Most organizations on the Internet were assigned network IDs from the class C address space, and this only made three bytes available. An innovation called Classless Inter-Domain Routing (CIDR) was specified in 1993 [RFC 1519] that freed up more network IDs by removing restrictions of the class-based addressing scheme. IPv4 addressing is covered in more detail in Chapter 2, "TCP/IP in Embedded Systems." In the mid-1990s, IPv6 was specified. [RFC 1883] IPv6 increases the address length to 128 bits, which should be enough for practically every person, place, or thing to have a unique address. As of 2003, the world is still largely running IPv4, but IPv6 is starting to enjoy wider use. Linux IPv6 is becoming the focus of attention for those working on IPv6 protocols and utilities.

FACILITIES IN IPV6

There is much more to IPv6 than a longer address. In this section, we outline some of these significant capabilities. Later as we discuss the IPv6 sources, we will show where in the source code these facilities are implemented.

Besides the 128-bit address, IPv6 includes the ability to autoconfigure addresses. When using IPv4, we have to statically assign an address to a machine before putting it on the network. Another alternative often used with IPv4 is the Dynamic Host Configuration Protocol (DHCP), which can assign an address when the computer comes online. However, IPv6 supports a mechanism called *stateless autoconfiguration* in which a node coming online can be identified directly by its link-local address. (As we will see in later, the link-local address is based on the machine's unique MAC or Ethernet address.) This means that any device can be plugged in to a local IPv6 net without having to use DHCP or other means of pre-configuring an address. This concept allows the Ethernet or other link layer address to be built into IPv6 128-bit addresses.

IPv6 has a method by which hosts and routers can automatically find each other. This mechanism replaces the ARP protocol in IPv4. We know that with IPv6, devices can autoconfigure themselves by self-assigning unique IPv6 addresses (called *link-local addresses*) based on their MAC addresses. Instead of using ARP, IPv6 has a method for routers to find each of the hosts automatically. With this mechanism machines can automatically determine their default router, and hosts can find each other. This mechanism is called *Neighbor Discovery*, (ND). The ND mechanism consists of four message types: router advertisement, router solicitation, neighbor advertisement, and neighbor solicitation [RFC 2461]. In Linux, ND is based on the neighbor cache facility which was discussed in detail in Chapter 6.

Routing based on Quality-of-Service (QoS) routing is done in IPv4 by using traffic class-based routing. With this method, the routing entries in the Routing Policy Database (RPDB) include the packet's IP header ToS field. When a packet arrives at the queuing layer, forwarding decisions are based on the QoS as defined by the route. We covered this process in detail for IPv4 in Chapter 8. In contrast, with IPv6, QoS is built into the protocol specification. The IP header has a Flow Label field intended to be used by routers to make hard routing decisions based on desired QoS and Linux includes support for IPv6 flows.

With IPv4, a machine is tied to its membership in a local network, although DHCP as an add-on protocol has made it relatively easy to introduce a machine into a new network. In contrast, IP mobility is part of IPv6. A node can introduce itself into a new network based on a permanently assigned IPv6 address. It also supports jumbograms, which are very large packets. IPv6 has a much different header format than IPv4. In addition, unlike IPv4, which uses the IPSec family of protocols for security, IPv6 has security built into the protocol family specification.

IPV6 ADDRESSING

IPv6 specifies several basic types of addresses: *unicast*, *anycast*, and *multicast*. With IPv6, addresses are applied to network interfaces, not nodes as is the case with IPv4. An IPv6 unicast address defines a single interface. A packet sent to a unicast address will be delivered to the particular network interface, which corresponds to the address. In contrast, an anycast address defines a set of network interfaces in which generally each network interface belongs to a different machine. A packet sent to an anycast address will be delivered to one of the interfaces, and generally, the closest one as determined by the address scope. Multicast addresses also define a set of nodes. They are similar in concept to IPv4 multicast addresses. A packet sent to a multicast address will be delivered to each interface belonging to the set also known as a group. IPv6 has no broadcast address type. As we shall see, the broadcast address type of IPv4 is superceded by the IPv6 all nodes link-local and node-local scope multicast address.

Expressing IPv6 Addresses

IPv4 addresses are usually expressed in dotted decimal notation. In contrast, IPv6 addresses are expressed in a string of eight hexadecimal values separated by the colon character [RFC 2373].

x:x:x:x:x:x:x.x

Each x represents a 16-bit value. Often, IPv6 addresses will consists of multiple segments of zeros. To make it easier to express, sequential groups of zeros can be represented with a double colon, ::. Only one double colon can appear in an address. Leading zeros on a 16-bit group can be dropped, but trailing zeros cannot be dropped. An example of an address representing a unicast address could be as follows:

1080:0:0:0:8:800:200C:417A

This same address could be written as shown here, where the :: replaces the 0:0:0. This is called the *compressed form*.

1080::8:800:200C:417A

This address with all zeros is the unspecified address.

0:0:0:0:0:0:0:0

It could also be written as:

::

For another example, we can look at this multicast address.

FF01:0:0:0:0:0:0:101

The same address can be written like this.

FF01::101

Expressing IPv4 Addresses in Mixed Notation

There is also a type of notation where IPv4 address can be shown in what is called mixed notation. Each x represents a 16-bit hexadecimal portion, and each D is an 8-bit decimal number [RFC 3493].

X:X:X:X:X:X:D:D:D:D

For example, an IPv4 mapped IPv6 address is as follows.

0:0:0:0:0:FFFF:10.1.5.10

In compressed notation, it would be written like this.

::FFFF:10.1.5.10

Expressing Netmasks.

IPv4 has a way of representing the network portion and the host portion of an address. The network portion can be shown as a netmask or is often shown in CIDR notation. IPv6 has a similar concept. For example, the following address shows a unicast address with its 56-bit netmask.

11AB::DE40:FEDC:BA98:7654:3210/56

The network number for this address is the following.

11AB:0:0:DE00:0:0:0:0

It can be shown a different way in compressed notation.

11AB::DE00:0:0:0:0

The host portion is like this.

40:FEDC:BA98:7654:3210

The Loopback Address in IPv6

IPv6 also defines a loopback address. All but the trailing bit are zeros.

::1

The Unspecified Address

It defines an address called the *unspecified address*, which is all zeros.

::

IPv6 Address Types and the Format Prefix

As discussed in Chapter 2, IPv4 uses the first three leading bits of the address to define the class of the address. Much like IPv4, IPv6 also uses a variable group of leading bits to define the type of address. This leading group is called the *Format Prefix* (FP). Table 11.1 shows the address space allocation according to the format prefixes.

TABLE 11.1 IPv6 Address Type Allocation

Format Prefix	Fraction of in Binary	Address Space Allocation
0000 0000	1/256	Reserved. The unspecified address (all zeros) and the embedded IPv4 addresses are assigned out of this space.
0000 0001	1/256	Unassigned.
0000 001	1/128	Reserved for NSAP allocation.
0000	1/128	Reserved for IPX allocation.
0000 011	1/128	Unassigned.
0000 1	1/32	Unassigned.
0001	1/16	Unassigned.
001	1/8	Aggregatable global unicast Addresses.
010	1/8	Unassigned.
011	1/8	Unassigned.
100	1/8	Unassigned.
101	1/8	Unassigned.
110	1/8	Unassigned.
1110	1/16	Unassigned.
1111 0	1/32	Unassigned.
1111 10	1/64	Unassigned.
1111 110	1/128	Unassigned.
1111 1110 0	1/512	Unassigned.
1111 1110 10	1/1024	Link-local unicast addresses.
1111 1110 11	1/1024	Site-local unicast addresses.
1111 1111	1/256	Multicast addresses.

Link Local Addresses

IPv4 uses the ARP protocol to map IP address to link-layer MAC addresses. In contrast, IPv6 does not use ARP; instead, it uses a concept called *link-local addresses*. The link-local addresses incorporate the 6-byte Ethernet address directly into the IPv6 addresses. The link-local addresses are prefaced by the bits FE8. The address space allocation for link-local addresses is shown in Table 11.1. For example, the 802.11 wireless adapter on this laptop has the following Ethernet address.

```
00-02-2D-84-D1-A1
```

The link-local IPv6 address for the adapter would be as follows.

```
FE80::2:2D84:D1A1
```

By definition, IPv6 addresses are assigned to the network interface, not to the host. An interface might have multiple addresses of any type. However, at least one link-local address must be assigned to each interface.

Multicast Addresses in IPv6

There are a few other specific multicast addresses used with Neighbor Discovery and other protocols. The first is the solicited-node multicast address [RFC 1883]. This address is formed by taking the lower 24 bits of either an unicast or anycast address and applying the following 96-bit prefix, FF02:0:0:0:0:1. This yields a range of multicast addresses between FF02::1:0:0 and FF02::1:FFFF:FFFF. The next is the all-routers multicast address, which is the link-local scoped address for reaching all nodes, FF02::1. Another is the all-nodes multicast address to reach all link-local scoped nodes, FF02::1.

Linux provides a union data structure to represent the IPv6 address type, in6_addr defined in the file linux/include/linux/in6.h.

```
    struct in6_addr
    {
       union
       {
          __u8          u6_addr8[16];
          __u16         u6_addr16[8];
          __u32         u6_addr32[4];
       } in6_u;
    #define s6_addr        in6_u.u6_addr8
    #define s6_addr16      in6_u.u6_addr16
    #define s6_addr32      in6_u.u6_addr32
    };
```

This structure allows the address to be specified as either a sequence of 32-bit words, 16-bit segments, or 8-bit bytes. The following two definitions in the same file, define types for the unspecified address format (wildcard address) and the loopback address, both of which are frequently referenced in the IPv6 sources.

```
#define IN6ADDR_ANY_INIT { { { 0,0,0,0,0,0,0,0,0,0,0,0,0,0,0,0 } } }
#define IN6ADDR_LOOPBACK_INIT { { { 0,0,0,0,0,0,0,0,0,0,0,0,0,0,0,1 } } }
```

IPV6 PACKET FORMAT

Compared to the IPv4, the IPv6 packet is simplified. Many of the fields that were required in the IPv4 header are optional in the IPv6 header. These formally required fields are now in optional headers called *extension headers*. There is a *next header* field in the main IP header and in all the extension headers. The next header field contains a specific value indicating the type of the next extension header if it exists. If there is no next extension header, the next header field contains the type for the first upper-layer header, or as shown in Table 11.2 from the file. the specific value NEXTHDR_NONE if there are no more extension headers. Figure 11.1 shows the IPv6

Version	Traffic Class ID	Flow Label	
Payload Length		Next Header	Hop Limit
Source Address			
Destination Address			

Version - 6 for IPv6
Traffic Class ID -- Similar to Differentiated Service Field of IPv4, Used for QOS Routing
Payload Length - Length of the packet minus the length of this header.

FIGURE 11.1 The Ipv6 Maim Header

TABLE 11.2 Next Header Field Values

Name	Value	Header Description
NEXTHDR_HOP	0	The hop-by-hop option header.
NEXTHDR_TCP	6	The next header is a TCP header.
NEXTHDR_UDP	17	The next header is a UDP header.
NEXTHDR_IPV6	41	The next header is for IPv6 in IPv6 tunnel.
NEXTHDR_ROUTING	43	The next header is the routing header.
NEXTHDR_FRAGMENT	44	Header for fragmentation or reassembly.
NEXTHDR_ESP	50	Header for Encapsulating Security Payload (ESP).
NEXTHDR_AUTH	51	This is for the authentication header.
NEXTHDR_ICMP	58	IPv6 ICMP.
NEXTHDR_NONE	59	This value means that there is no next header.
NEXTHDR_DEST	60	This is the destination options header.
NEXTHDR_MAX	255	This is the maximum value for the next-header.

main header. All the headers are in the same packet as the main header. However, since the extension headers are optional, the overhead is reduced because headers that are not necessary can be left out of the packet.

The extensions headers that follow the IPv6 header have a recommended order, shown here.

- Hop-by-hop options header
- Destination options header
- Routing header
- Fragment header
- Upper-layer header

Table 11.2 shows the values for the next header field in the IPv6 header. These values are defined in the file linux/include/net/ipv6.h. The format for the fragmentation header is shown in Figure 11.2. Its structure, frag_hdr, is defined in the same file.

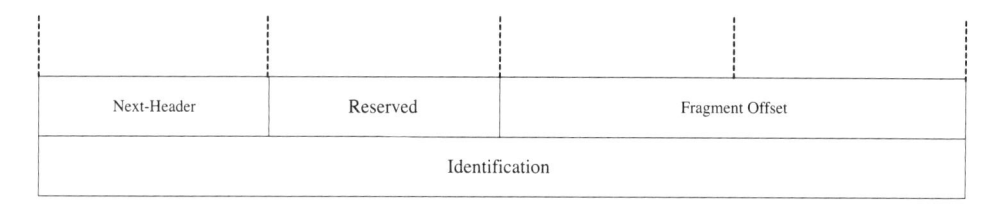

Next-Header	Reserved	Fragment Offset
Identification		

FIGURE 11.2 The fragmentation header.

THE IPV6 IMPLEMENTATION IN LINUX

As with most kernel facilities, the IPv6 protocol is implemented as a module and uses many similar mechanisms to IPv4. The protocol connects with the socket layer in the same way as IPv4 does and it contains a protocol switch table for transport layer de-multiplexing. Therefore, it uses the same method as IPv4 for dispatching incoming packets to UDP, TCP, and other protocols.

The IPv6 Extension Header Field Values

To support IP packet de-multiplexing, each of the next header field values has IPv6 protocol numbers. These numbers are defined in the file linux/include/linux/in6.h.

Hop-by-Hop Options

```
#define IPPROTO_HOPOPTS     0
```

Routing Header

```
#define IPPROTO_ROUTING     43
```

Ipv6 Fragmentation Header

```
#define IPPROTO_FRAGMENT    44
```

ICMPv6 Header

```
#define IPPROTO_ICMPV6      58
```

No Next Header Value

```
#define IPPROTO_NONE        59
```

IPv6 Destination Options

```
#define IPPROTO_DSTOPTS     60
```

The inet6_dev Structure

Linux IPv6 has a structure called the inet6_dev structure. This structure is similar to the inet_dev structure for IPv4 discussed in Chapter 5. This structure, defined in the file linux/include/net/if_inet6.h, contains the non-device-specific information for a particular network interface. This is where the interface address list and the multicast address list is maintained for the network interface device.

```
struct inet6_dev
{
```

Most of the fields are similar to the inet_dev structure for IPv4. The first field, dev, points back to the network interface device. Next, addr_list is the list of addresses for this interface, and mc_list is the list of multicast addresses that this interface has joined.

```
struct net_device    *dev;
struct inet6_ifaddr  *addr_list;
struct ifmcaddr6     *mc_list;
struct ifmcaddr6     *mc_tomb;
rwlock_t             mc_lock;
unsigned long        mc_v1_seen;
unsigned long        mc_maxdelay;
unsigned char        mc_qrv;
unsigned char        mc_gq_running;
unsigned char        mc_ifc_count;
```

The following field is the general query timer, and the next field is the interface change timer.

```
struct timer_list    mc_gq_timer;
struct timer_list    mc_ifc_timer;
struct ifacaddr6     *ac_list;
rwlock_t             lock;
atomic_t             refcnt;
__u32                if_flags;
int                  dead;
```

```
#ifdef CONFIG_IPV6_PRIVACY
    u8                  rndid[8];
    u8                  entropy[8];
    struct timer_list   regen_timer;
    struct inet6_ifaddr *tempaddr_list;
    __u8                work_eui64[8];
    __u8                work_digest[16];
#endif
    struct neigh_parms  *nd_parms;
    struct inet6_dev    *next;
    struct ipv6_devconf cnf;
    struct ipv6_devstat stats;
```

Finally, we have the timestamp for interface table updates.

```
    unsigned long       tstamp;
};
```

IPv6 Family Initialization

The protocol family initialization capabilities are generic in Linux. In Chapter 10, we saw how this might work for a bogus protocol family. Ipv6 is no exception and utilizes the Linux networking framework code for initialization.

The `inet6_init` Function

IPv6 is initialized in the file linux/net/ipv6/af_inet6.c. The functions in this file provide most of the glue for the protocols in the AF_INET6 address family, including socket registration. The main initialization function is inet6_init.

```
    static int __init inet6_init(void);
```

This function is very similar to the function inet_init used for IPv4 initialization, and we essentially follow the same steps as inet_init. First, we create three slab caches for the three socket types: TCP6, UDP6, and RAW. We register the RAW socket type first by calling inet6_register_protosw. This is different from inet_init, which registers all three socket types at one time. Next, we do the basic socket registration of the AF_INET6 family calling sock_register.

```
    (void) sock_register(&inet6_family_ops);
```

Now, applications can create RAW sockets, but hopefully, no one will try to create a UDP or TCP socket before we complete the registration process. Now, we initialize the IPv6 MIBs and register ourselves with the `sysctl` facility if it is configured in this kernel. We initialize the ICMP protocol by calling `icmpv6_init`, the neighbor discovery protocol by calling `ndisc_init`, and the IGMP protocol by calling `igmp6_init`.

Next, we set up our entries in the `/proc` file system. IPv6 uses the standard `/proc` facility like many other facilities and protocols in the Linux kernel. We register with the filesystem in the same way that IPv4 and other protocols do. The following directories in `/proc` are unique for IPv6.

```
if_inet6
raw6
anycast6
ip6_flowlabel
igmp6
mcfilter6
snmp6
rt6_stats
sockstat6
```

Now that `/proc` is set up, we can initialize some of the functionality unique to IPv6. At the end, the `inet6_init` performs the following steps. The next function is called to initialize the IPv6 `notifier` chains. The IPv6 `notifier` chain is built on the generic `notifier` facility discussed in Chapter 3.

```
ipv6_netdev_notif_init();
```

We call this function to register the packet handler function and the link layer protocol type so we can receive IPv6 packets.

```
ipv6_packet_init();
```

We initialize IPv6 routing facility. We discuss the IPv6 routing in a later section in this chapter.

```
ip6_route_init();
```

Next, we call `ip6_flowlabel_init` to initialize flow labels, which are the method in IPv6 of routing packets based on QoS. Next, address auto configuration is initialized when we call `addrconf_init`. Following this, we initialize the Simple Internet Transition (SIT), by calling `sit_init`. The SIT is the IPv6 over IPv4 tunnel network interface pseudo-device.

```
ip6_flowlabel_init();
addrconf_init();
sit_init();
```

Next, by calling the following four functions, we initialize the handlers for the IPv6 extension headers. Earlier, we discussed how IPv6 consists of a basic header and a number of extension headers. Each extension header type has a registered protocol handler just like UDP and TCP.

```
ipv6_rthdr_init();
ipv6_frag_init();
ipv6_nodata_init();
ipv6_destopt_init();
```

Finally, we initialize the two transport protocols, UDP and TCP. Each of these initialization functions registers a protocol handler just like IPv4 UDP and TCP.

```
udpv6_init();
tcpv6_init();
```

The `inet6_protocol` Structure

Earlier in this book, we discussed transport layer de-multiplexing of incoming packets, which we did by calling a protocol handler function through the destination cache entry. The handler functions were placed in a linked list through a registration process. In IPv6, we do the protocol registration in a similar fashion. However, IPv6 adds a `flags` field to its version of the registration structure, `inet6_protocol`, defined in the file `linux/include/net/protocol.h`.

```
struct inet6_protocol
{
```

As is the case with the `inet_protocol` structure used with IPv4, two handler functions are defined: one for incoming error packets and one for incoming normal packets.

```
int   (*handler)(struct sk_buff **skb, unsigned int *nhoffp);
void  (*err_handler)(struct sk_buff *skb,
        struct inet6_skb_parm *opt,
        int type, int code, int offset,
        __u32 info);
```

The `flags` field is unique to IPv6. In recent versions of IPv6, the value in `flags` determines whether a security check is made on the incoming packet. This is a way to see whether packets should be rejected because of a failed security association.

```
    unsigned int   flags;
};
```

The Values in `flags` and IPv6 Security

The values in the `flags` field of the `inet6_protocol` structure are defined as follows. The `FINAL` value says that there is no XFRM policy and therefore there is no need to do a security check of this particular input packet. XFRM is for IP encapsulated packets such as IPSec.

```
#define INET6_PROTO_FINAL    0x2
```

However, the value `NOPOLICY` says that a check should be made in the SADB to see whether there is a transformation policy associated with this incoming packet.

```
#define INET6_PROTO_NOPOLICY  0x1
```

The `ipv6_packet_init` Function

One of the necessary steps in the initialization of the IPv6 protocol is to register the packet handler with the link-layer IPV6 protocol type, `ETH_P_IPV6`, which is defined as `0x86DD`. We do this in the function `ipv6_packet_init` in the file `linux/net/ipv6/ipv6_sockglue.c`.

```
void __init ipv6_packet_init(void)
{
    dev_add_pack(&ipv6_packet_type);
}
```

The `ipv6_packet_type` Structure

The structure `ipv6_packet_type` is initialized in the same file.

```
static struct packet_type ipv6_packet_type = {
    .type = __constant_htons(ETH_P_IPV6),
    .func = ipv6_rcv,
};
```

By setting up the packet type, we set the function `ipv6_rcv` as the registered low-level packet handler for IPv6 packets when they are received at the queuing layer.

IPV6 SOCKET IMPLEMENTATION

To create an IPv6 socket we specify the IPv6 address family, `AF_INET6` in the `socket` call. There were some socket API changes to Linux and other operating systems as IPv6 and other protocol families came into use to make sockets more generic and less specific to IPv4. The IPv6 semantics require that the socket programming API be protocol independent. To support this, Linux sockets are implemented so the definitions of socket addresses are entirely protocol independent. The fact that IPv4 or IPv6 protocols are used through a socket should be entirely transparent to the application programmer. Other than a few updates for version 2.6, there are no implementation changes in the generic socket implementation itself because, as shown in Chapter 5, it is already entirely protocol independent. The socket structure is defined to work with both address families simultaneously.

As we recall from earlier chapters, the `proto_ops` structure maps the transport layer internal functions to the socket function calls. As we see from the following definitions of the function mappings, there is not much change from IPv4. The `proto_ops` structure for IPv6 (`AF_INET6` address family) `SOCK_DGRAM` type sockets are shown next. This structure is initialized in the file `linux/net/ipv6/af_inet6.c`.

The `inet6_dgram_ops` Structure

```
struct proto_ops inet6_dgram_ops = {
        .family =       PF_INET6,
        .owner =        THIS_MODULE,
```

The `release` and `bind` functions are unique to IPv6.

```
        .release =      inet6_release,
        .bind =         inet6_bind,
        .connect =      inet_dgram_connect,
        .socketpair =   sock_no_socketpair,
        .accept =       sock_no_accept,
```

We recall that the *name* of a socket is its associated address specification. The `getname` function is new to support the new address mapping capabilities for IPv6.

```
        .getname =      inet6_getname,
        .poll =         datagram_poll,
```

The `ioctl` function must be different for IPv6.

```
        .ioctl =        inet6_ioctl,
        .listen =       sock_no_listen,
```

```
        .shutdown    =    inet_shutdown,
        .setsockopt  =    inet_setsockopt,
        .getsockopt  =    inet_getsockopt,
        .sendmsg     =    inet_sendmsg,
        .recvmsg     =    inet_recvmsg,
        .mmap        =    sock_no_mmap,
        .sendpage    =    sock_no_sendpage,
};
```

The SOCK_STREAM socket mapping in proto_ops is not much different from IPv4 either. The functions that are not unique to the individual member protocols in AF_INET6 address family, inet6_stream_ops are defined in the file linux/net/ipv6/af_inet6.c.

```
struct proto_ops inet6_stream_ops = {
        .family      =    PF_INET6,
        .owner       =    THIS_MODULE,
        .release     =    inet6_release,
        .bind        =    inet6_bind,
        .connect     =    inet_stream_connect,
        .socketpair  =    sock_no_socketpair,
        .accept      =    inet_accept,
        .getname     =    inet6_getname,
        .poll        =    tcp_poll,
        .ioctl       =    inet6_ioctl,
        .listen      =    inet_listen,
        .shutdown    =    inet_shutdown,
        .setsockopt  =    inet_setsockopt,
        .getsockopt  =    inet_getsockopt,
        .sendmsg     =    inet_sendmsg,
        .recvmsg     =    inet_recvmsg,
        .mmap        =    sock_no_mmap,
        .sendpage    =    tcp_sendpage
};
```

Even though the preceding mappings look like the ones in IPv4, when the user opens an AF_INET6 socket, SOCK_STREAM packets are processed by the IPv6 version of TCP, and SOCK_DGRAM packets are processed by the IPv6 version of UDP. This is because IPv6 registered its own unique versions of the transport protocols with the AF_INET6 layer. Transmitted packets are sent through either IPv4 or IPv6 by the transport layer send message function.

The `ipv6_pinfo` Structure

As we recall from Chapter 5, the `sock` structure contained a union with protocol-specific areas for each of the protocols using sockets. For IPv6, this area is defined by the `ipv6_pinfo` structure defined in the file `linux/include/linux/ipv6.h`.

```
struct ipv6_pinfo {
    struct in6_addr     saddr;
    struct in6_addr     rcv_saddr;
    struct in6_addr     daddr;
    struct in6_addr     *daddr_cache;
    __u32               flow_label;
    __u32               frag_size;
    int                 hop_limit;
    int                 mcast_hops;
    int                 mcast_oif;
```

The following packed structure is for the packet option flags.

```
    union {
        struct {
            __u8    srcrt:2,
            osrcrt:2,
                    rxinfo:1,
                    rxoinfo:1,
                    rxhlim:1,
                    rxohlim:1,
                    hopopts:1,
                    ohopopts:1,
                    dstopts:1,
                    odstopts:1,
                    rxflow:1;
                    rxtclass:1;
        } bits;
        __u8    all;
    } rxopt;
```

The following field is for the socket option flags.

```
    __u8                mc_loop:1,
                        recverr:1,
                        sndflow:1,
                        pmtudisc:2,
                        ipv6only:1;
```

```
    struct ipv6_mc_socklist    *ipv6_mc_list;
    struct ipv6_ac_socklist    *ipv6_ac_list;
    struct ipv6_fl_socklist    *ipv6_fl_list;
    struct ipv6_txoptions      *opt;
    struct sk_buff             *pktoptions;
    struct {
        struct ipv6_txoptions  *opt;
        struct rt6_info        *rt;
        int                    hop_limit;
        int                    tclass;
    } cork;
};
```

IPV6 FRAGMENTATION AND DE-FRAGMENTATION

IPv6 fragmentation is implemented in the file `linux/net/ipv6/ip6_output.c`. Typically, we know that we have to fragment output packets when the next-hop MTU is smaller than the fragment size. This was previously determined by `ip6_output`.

The `ip6_fragment` Function

We can see how this is done by looking at the function `ip6_fragment`.

```
static int ip6_fragment(struct sk_buff *skb, int (*output)(struct sk_buff*))
. . .
```

In this function, we have a slow path and a fast path. The fast path is used if the `sk_buff` for the output packet already points to a list of prepared fragments as determined by the macro `skb_shinfo(skb)->frag_list`.

First we look at the fast path. The fast path would be likely to be used if the MTU for the route was already known at the time the socket was set up for a particular TCP connection. Now, we walk through the list of fragments. Each fragment must be not shared and of sufficient size. If all is okay, we prepare the fragment header in the following code snippet.

```
    . . .
        tmp_hdr = kmalloc(hlen, GFP_ATOMIC);
        if (!tmp_hdr) {
            IP6_INC_STATS(IPSTATS_MIB_FRAGFAILS);
            return -ENOMEM;
        }
```

```
        *prevhdr = NEXTHDR_FRAGMENT;
        memcpy(tmp_hdr, skb->nh.raw, hlen);
        __skb_pull(skb, hlen);
        fh = (struct frag_hdr*)__skb_push(skb, sizeof(struct frag_hdr));
        skb->nh.raw = __skb_push(skb, hlen);
        memcpy(skb->nh.raw, tmp_hdr, hlen);
        ipv6_select_ident(skb, fh);
        fh->nexthdr = nexthdr;
        fh->reserved = 0;
        fh->frag_off = htons(IP6_MF);
        frag_id = fh->identification;
        first_len = skb_pagelen(skb);
        skb->data_len = first_len - skb_headlen(skb);
        skb->len = first_len;
        skb->nh.ipv6h->payload_len =
                htons(first_len - sizeof(struct ipv6hdr));

        for (;;) {
```

Here we prepare the header of the next frame before the previous one is transmitted.

```
            if (frag) {
                frag->ip_summed = CHECKSUM_NONE;
                frag->h.raw = frag->data;
                fh = (struct frag_hdr*)__skb_push(frag,
                            sizeof(struct frag_hdr));
                frag->nh.raw = __skb_push(frag, hlen);
                memcpy(frag->nh.raw, tmp_hdr, hlen);
                offset += skb->len - hlen - sizeof(struct frag_hdr);
                fh->nexthdr = nexthdr;
                fh->reserved = 0;
                fh->frag_off = htons(offset);
                if (frag->next != NULL)
                    fh->frag_off |= htons(IP6_MF);
                fh->identification = frag_id;
                frag->nh.ipv6h->payload_len =
                    htons(frag->len - sizeof(struct ipv6hdr));
                ip6_copy_metadata(frag, skb);
            }
```

This is where we put the skb on the sending queue.

```
                err = output(skb);
                if (err || !frag)
                    break;
                skb = frag;
                frag = skb->next;
                skb->next = NULL;
            }
            kfree(tmp_hdr);
            if (err == 0) {
                IP6_INC_STATS(IPSTATS_MIB_FRAGOKS);
                return 0;
            }
            while (frag) {
                skb = frag->next;
                kfree_skb(frag);
                frag = skb;
            }

            IP6_INC_STATS(IPSTATS_MIB_FRAGFAILS);
            return err;
        }
slow_path:
        . . .
```

Now we won't look at the slow path. The slow path involves splitting the `skb` into fragments before placing each fragment on the output queue.

IPv6 De-Fragmentation

To do de-fragmentation, a queue of input fragments is maintained. In addition, there is a timer associated with each entry on the queue. Orphaned fragments are aged out and discarded if they remain unclaimed on the queue beyond the reasonable lifetime of a packet [RFC 1883]. IPv6 de-fragmentation is implemented in the file `linux/net/ipv6/reassembly.c`.

Since IPv6 fragments are in optional headers that follow the main IPv4 header, we actually register a separate protocol within the `AF_INET6` address family to handle the fragment header type. This protocol is like a transport protocol in the sense that its handler is dispatched when the protocol number, `IPPROTO_FRAGMENT`, is encountered in the next header field of the IP header. Here we show the structure for registering the fragment protocol's handler function with the `AF_INET6` family.

IPv6 Fragment Protocol Initialization

In IPv4, reassembly operations are an integral part of the network layer, or IP protocol. In contrast, in IPv6, reassembly is implemented in a separate protocol. This protocol must be initialized and registered so it will receive input packets.

The *frag_protocol* Structure

Since IPv6 fragments are in optional headers that follow the main IPv4 header, we actually register a separate protocol within the AF_INET6 address family to handle the fragment header type. This protocol is like a transport protocol in the sense that its handler is dispatched when the protocol number, IPPROTO_FRAGMENT, is encountered in the next header field of the IP header. Here we show the structure for registering the fragment protocol's handler function with the AF_INET6 family.

```
static struct inet6_protocol frag_protocol =
{
```

We initialize ipv6_frag_rcv as the handler function and flags to indicate that there is no security check required for this packet type.

```
    .handler    =   ipv6_frag_rcv,
    .flags      =   INET6_PROTO_NOPOLICY,
};
```

The *ipv6_frag_init* Function

The fragment protocol is initialized by ipv6_frag_init.

```
void __init ipv6_frag_init(void)
{
    if (inet6_add_protocol(&frag_protocol, IPPROTO_FRAGMENT) < 0)
        printk(KERN_ERR "ipv6_frag_init: Could not register protocol\n");
. . .
}
```

The *ipv6_frag_rcv* Function

The fragment receive handler, ipv6_frag_rcv, also in the same file, is executed when the IPPROTO_FRAGMENT is encountered in the next header field of the IPv6 packet.

```
static int ipv6_frag_rcv(struct sk_buff **skbp)
. . .
```

Chapter 11 Internet Protocol Version 6 (IPv6)   **575**

After checking the fragment header for validity, we attempt to find a fragment in the existing fragment queue with the same `identification` value.

```
if ((fq = fq_find(fhdr->identification, &hdr->saddr, &hdr->daddr))
    != NULL) {
    int ret = -1;
    spin_lock(&fq->lock);
```

If we can't find a matching fragment, we add the new one to the queue.

```
ip6_frag_queue(fq, skb, fhdr, *nhoffp);
```

Then we call `ip6_frag_reasm` to try to put the fragments together.

```
    if (fq->last_in == (FIRST_IN|LAST_IN) &&
        fq->meat == fq->len)
        ret = ip6_frag_reasm(fq, skbp, nhoffp, dev);
    spin_unlock(&fq->lock);
    fq_put(fq);
    return ret;
}
IP6_INC_STATS_BH(IPSTATS_MIB_REASMFAILS);
kfree_skb(skb);
return -1;
}
```

IPV6 OUTPUT

IP output processing in IPv6 is very similar to IPv4. After a packet is ready to be transmitted, the destination cache entry's `output` field will point to the function `ip6_output`, which is in the file `linux/net/ipv6/ip6_output.c`.

The `ip6_output` Function

This function is the main output function for the network or IP layer in IPv6.

```
int ip6_output(struct sk_buff *skb)
{
```

As we can see, this function does little more than decide whether or not to fragment the packet. This determination is done by checking the route MTU value in the destination cache entry, `dst`.

```
            if ((skb->len > dst_pmtu(skb->dst) || skb_shinfo(skb)->frag_list))
                return ip6_fragment(skb, ip6_output2);
            else
                return ip6_output2(skb);
    }
```

The `ip6_output2` Function

The function `ip6_output2` also in the file `linux/net/ipv6/ip6_output.c` continues the processing of output packets.

```
    int ip6_output2(struct sk_buff *skb);
```

In this function, we don't do much more than check whether the destination is a multicast address, which is not supported yet anyway. If the destination is multicast, the skb is cloned, and a copy is sent to the loopback address. Before we exit, we call `ip6_output_finish` implemented in the same file to finish the processing of output packets.

The `ip6_output_finish` Function

```
    static inline int ip6_output_finish(struct sk_buff *skb)
    {
        struct dst_entry *dst = skb->dst;
        struct hh_cache *hh = dst->hh;
```

At this point, in the output processing, we do something very much like IPv4 output processing. We can see now how the neighbor system in Linux TCP/IP was designed with IPv6 in mind. If the hardware header cache is defined, we call the `hh_output` function, which will queue up the packet to the network interface device. If not, we call the output function defined for the neighbor in the destination cache, dst.

```
        if (hh) {
            int hh_alen;
            read_lock_bh(&hh->hh_lock);
            hh_alen = HH_DATA_ALIGN(hh->hh_len);
            memcpy(skb->data - hh_alen, hh->hh_data, hh_alen);
            read_unlock_bh(&hh->hh_lock);
            skb_push(skb, hh->hh_len);
            return hh->hh_output(skb);
        } else if (dst->neighbour)
            return dst->neighbour->output(skb);
```

```
            IP6_INC_STATS_BH(IPSTATS_MIB_OUTNOROUTES);
            kfree_skb(skb);
            return -EINVAL;
    }
```

IPV6 INPUT

In this section, we will look at the IPv6 input packet processing.

As shown earlier, we register a specific function as a packet handler for IPv6 input packets which gets called when a network interface device receives a packet of type ETH_P_IPV6. This function in some ways is simpler than its equivalent for IPv4 because of the simpler IPv6 header format. The IPv6 header is simpler because, unlike IPv4, all the IPv6 options are in separate headers.

The `ipv6_rcv` Function

The packet handling function, `ipv6_rcv`, defined in the file linux/net/ipv6/ip6_input.c is called from the softirq context, or bottom half in the packet queuing layer.

```
    int ipv6_rcv(struct sk_buff *skb, struct net_device *dev,
            struct packet_type *pt, struct net_device *orig_dev)
    {
        struct ipv6hdr *hdr;
        u32            pkt_len;
        if (skb->pkt_type == PACKET_OTHERHOST)
            goto drop;
        IP6_INC_STATS_BH(IPSTATS_MIB_INRECEIVES);
        if ((skb = skb_share_check(skb, GFP_ATOMIC)) == NULL) {
            IP6_INC_STATS_BH(IPSTATS_MIB_INDISCARDS);
            goto out;
        }
```

Here, we store the index of the incoming network interface device. We don't refer to the actual network interface device, dev, after the packet is queued.

```
        IP6CB(skb)->iif = skb->dst ?
                ((struct rt6_info *)skb->dst)->rt6i_idev->dev->ifindex :
                  dev->ifindex;
```

We must check to make sure that the incoming packet is at least long enough to hold the IPv6 header.

```
if (skb->len < sizeof(struct ipv6hdr))
    goto err;
if (!pskb_may_pull(skb, sizeof(struct ipv6hdr))) {
    IP6_INC_STATS_BH(IPSTATS_MIB_INHDRERRORS);
    goto drop;
}
hdr = skb->nh.ipv6h;
```

We check to make sure that the version field is six for IPv6.

```
if (hdr->version != 6)
    goto err;
```

We get the payload length directly from the packet header. The payload length includes the length of the optional headers if there are any.

```
skb->h.raw = (u8 *)(hdr + 1);
IP6CB(skb)->nhoff = offsetof(struct ipv6hdr, nexthdr);
pkt_len = ntohs(hdr->payload_len);
```

It is possible that the payload length is zero if our input packet is a jumbogram.

```
if (pkt_len || hdr->nexthdr != NEXTHDR_HOP) {
    if (pkt_len + sizeof(struct ipv6hdr) > skb->len)
        goto truncated;
    if (pskb_trim_rcsum(skb, pkt_len + sizeof(struct ipv6hdr))) {
        IP6_INC_STATS_BH(IPSTATS_MIB_INHDRERRORS);
            goto drop;
    }
    hdr = skb->nh.ipv6h;
}
```

If the next header is a hop-by-hop header, then we call `ipv6_parse_hopopts` to extract the hop options from the incoming packet. The hop options are stored back in the socket buffer, `skb`.

```
if (hdr->nexthdr == NEXTHDR_HOP) {
    if (ipv6_parse_hopopts(&skb, IP6CB(skb)->nhoff) < 0) {
        IP6_INC_STATS_BH(IPSTATS_MIB_INHDRERRORS);
        return 0;
    }
    hdr = skb->nh.ipv6h;
}
```

Now we continue processing by calling `ip6_rcv_finish`, which calls `ip_route_input` to set up the destination cache for this incoming packet by setting the `dst` field in the `skb`.

```
        return NF_HOOK(PF_INET6,NF_IP6_PRE_ROUTING, skb, dev,
                       NULL, ip6_rcv_finish);
truncated:
        IP6_INC_STATS_BH(Ip6InTruncatedPkts);
err:
        IP6_INC_STATS_BH(Ip6InHdrErrors);
drop:
        kfree_skb(skb);
out:
        return 0;
}
```

At this point, the processing is very similar to IPv4 input packet processing. Input packets may have a local destination in this machine, or they may need to be forwarded. The packet destination was calculated when the `ip_route_input` function was called during the first stage of input packet processing. For example, if the destination is an internal destination on a machine, the `input` field in the `dst_entry` will point to the function `ip6_input`, which continues the processing of the input packets.

The `ip6_input_finish` Function

Next, `ip6_input` calls `ip6_input_finish` to deliver the packet to the upper-layer protocols. If the destination is a locally reachable host, `output` will point to the function `dev_queue_xmit`, which queues the output packet to the network interface drivers. This process is the same as IPv4 and is covered in earlier chapters.

```
        static inline int ip6_input_finish(struct sk_buff *skb)
        . . .
```

Next, the rest of the processing is done by the input functions for each of the optional headers (other than the hop-by-hop header, which was processed already). The `nexthdr` field may contain the protocol number for an optional header, or it may be UDP, TCP, IGMP, ICMP, or perhaps some other protocol.

```
        hash = nexthdr & (MAX_INET_PROTOS - 1);
if ((ipprot = rcu_dereference(inet6_protos[hash])) != NULL) {
        int ret;
        if (ipprot->flags & INET6_PROTO_FINAL) {
```

```
                    struct ipv6hdr *hdr;
                    nf_reset(skb);
                    skb_postpull_rcsum(skb, skb->nh.raw,
                                       skb->h.raw - skb->nh.raw);
                    hdr = skb->nh.ipv6h;
                    if (ipv6_addr_is_multicast(&hdr->daddr) &&
                        !ipv6_chk_mcast_addr(skb->dev, &hdr->daddr,
                                             &hdr->saddr) &&
                        !ipv6_is_mld(skb, nexthdr))
                        goto discard;
                }
                if (!(ipprot->flags & INET6_PROTO_NOPOLICY) &&
                    !xfrm6_policy_check(NULL, XFRM_POLICY_IN, skb))
                    goto discard;
```

Here is where we call the handler function for the protocol defined in the nexthdr field of the IP header.

```
                ret = ipprot->handler(&skb, &nhoff);
                if (ret > 0)
                    goto resubmit;
                else if (ret == 0)
                    IP6_INC_STATS_BH(IPSTATS_MIB_INDELIVERS);
            } else {
                if (!raw_sk) {
                    if (xfrm6_policy_check(NULL, XFRM_POLICY_IN, skb)) {
                        IP6_INC_STATS_BH(IPSTATS_MIB_INUNKNOWNPROTOS);
                        icmpv6_send(skb, ICMPV6_PARAMPROB,
                                    ICMPV6_UNK_NEXTHDR, nhoff,
                                    skb->dev);
                    }
                } else
                    IP6_INC_STATS_BH(IPSTATS_MIB_INDELIVERS);
                kfree_skb(skb);
            }
            rcu_read_unlock();
            return 0;
        discard:
            IP6_INC_STATS_BH(IPSTATS_MIB_INDISCARDS);
            rcu_read_unlock();
            kfree_skb(skb);
            return 0;
        }
```

IPV6 UDP

IPv6 has its own implementation of the UDP protocol, in the file linux/net/ipv6/udp.c. Although the source code for IPv6 is mostly separate from IPv4, all the socket structures are shared, including the dynamic state information.

The udpv6_init Function

As with IPv4, UDP has an initialization function that is called from the IP initialization function, as shown earlier. The initialization function for UDP is udpv6_init, and it is in the file linux/net/ipv6/udp.c.

```
void __init udpv6_init(void)
{
```

As is the case with the IPv4 function, inet_add_protocol registers the packet handlers.

```
    if (inet6_add_protocol(&udpv6_protocol, IPPROTO_UDP) < 0)
        printk(KERN_ERR "udpv6_init: Could not register protocol\n");
    inet6_register_protosw(&udpv6_protosw);
}
```

The udpv6_protocol Structure

The udpv6_protocol structure is shown here from the file linux/net/ipv6/udp.c. The handler for incoming UDP packets is udpv6_rcv.

```
static struct inet6_protocol udpv6_protocol = {
    .handler      =    udpv6_rcv,
    .err_handler  =    udpv6_err,
```

The flags field is initialized to allow XFRM transformations to be used with incoming UDP packets. This will allow packet security checks with the SDB.

```
    .flags        =    INET6_PROTO_NOPOLICY|INET6_PROTO_FINAL,
};
```

The udpv6_protosw Structure

```
static struct inet_protosw udpv6_protosw = {
    .type         =    SOCK_DGRAM,
    .protocol     =    IPPROTO_UDP,
```

Next, the `prot` and the `ops` structures are initialized also in file `linux/net/ipv6/udp.c`.

```
        .prot       =       &udpv6_prot,
        .ops        =       &inet6_dgram_ops,
```

The next field, `capability`, has to do with permissions. As is the case with IPv4 UDP, everybody has permission to send UDP datagrams.

```
        .capability =       -1,
        .no_check   =       UDP_CSUM_DEFAULT,
        .flags      =       INET_PROTOSW_PERMANENT,
};
```

The `udpv6_prot` Structure

The UDP proto functions for IPv6 are defined as follows. This structure maps the socket calls to the protocol-specific functions. This data structure is initialized in the file `linux/net/ipv6/udp.c`.

```
struct proto udpv6_prot = {
        .name       =       "UDPv6",
        .close      =       udpv6_close,
        .connect    =       ip6_datagram_connect,
```

The following two functions are the only ones shared with IPv4. It is interesting to note that although the socket level `ioctl` is different for `SOCK_DGRAM` type sockets, the protocol level `ioctl` is the same as UDP for IPv4.

```
        .disconnect = udp_disconnect,
        .ioctl      = udp_ioctl,
        .destroy    = udpv6_destroy_sock,
        .setsockopt = udpv6_setsockopt,
        .getsockopt = udpv6_getsockopt,
        .sendmsg    = udpv6_sendmsg,
        .recvmsg    = udpv6_recvmsg,
        .backlog_rcv =udpv6_queue_rcv_skb,
        .hash       = udp_v6_hash,
        .unhash     = udp_v6_unhash,
        .get_port   = udp_v6_get_port,
        obj_size    = sizeof(struct udp6_sock),
};
```

We noted earlier how IPv6 has its own implementation of UDP. The separate sources are required for a couple of reasons. One is that the different address format requires different address comparison logic. Address comparisons are required when doing a lookup to find the destination socket for an incoming packet. A second reason is we need the ability to send and receive messages with AF_INET type destination addresses through IPv6 sockets, and this requires some special handling.

The udpv6_sendmsg Function

The function, udp6_sendmsg is called when the application wants to transmit a message of any type from a SOCK_DGRAM type socket of the AF_INET6 protocol family. Another reason why IPv6 requires a separate set of functions for UDP is to support flow labeling, which is a fundamental feature of IPv6 for supporting QoS. Although some data structures for IPv4 such as flowi are updated for version 2.6, the standard Linux framework does not support flow labeling. We won't look at the whole function. However, we should look at a small section of code in udp6_sendmsg to see how it decides to whether to send packets via IPv4 or IPv6.

```
static int udpv6_sendmsg(struct kiocb *iocb, struct sock *sk, struct msghdr *msg, size_t len)
. . .
```

The variable sin6 points to the name part of the msghdr structure, which is in the form of a sockaddr_in6 structure.

```
if (sin6) {
    if (addr_len < offsetof(struct sockaddr, sa_data))
        return -EINVAL;
    switch (sin6->sin6_family) {
    case AF_INET6:
        if (addr_len < SIN6_LEN_RFC2133)
            return -EINVAL;
        daddr = &sin6->sin6_addr;
        break;
```

Here, we check for the address families showing that it is legal to receive a message sent to an AF_INET type address family destination through an AF_INET6 socket.

```
    case AF_INET:
        goto do_udp_sendmsg;
    case AF_UNSPEC:
        msg->msg_name = sin6 = NULL;
        msg->msg_namelen = addr_len = 0;
```

```
                daddr = NULL;
                break;
            default:
                return -EINVAL;
        }
    } else if (!up->pending) {
        if (sk->sk_state != TCP_ESTABLISHED)
            return -EDESTADDRREQ;
        daddr = &np->daddr;
    } else
        daddr = NULL;
. . .
do_udp_sendmsg:
            if (__ipv6_only_sock(sk))
                return -ENETUNREACH;
```

We call udp_sendmsg, which is the ordinary IPv4 UDP send message function when we are sending datagrams to AF_INET type destinations.

```
        return udp_sendmsg(iocb, sk, msg, len);
```

IPV6 TCP

IPv6 also has its own version of the TCP protocol, which can be found in the file linux/net/ipv6/tcp_ipv6.c. In this section, we will examine the differences between the IPv6 and IPv4 implementations of TCP

IPv6 TCP Initialization

The initialization sequence for TCP is similar to IPv6 UDP and the IPv4 transport layer protocols.

The tcpv6_protocol Structure

This structure is an instance of inet6_protocol for registering member protocols with the IPv6 address family.

```
        static struct inet6_protocol tcpv6_protocol = {
```

First, tcp_v6_rcv is initialized as the handler function for incoming TCP segments.

```
            .handler      =    tcp_v6_rcv,
            .err_handler  =    tcp_v6_err,
```

As with UDP for IPv6, we allow security policy checks of incoming packets using the XFRM security policy mechanism.

```
        .flags        =       INET6_PROTO_NOPOLICY|INET6_PROTO_FINAL,
};
```

The tcpv6_prot Structure

The proto structure for TCP is defined in this section. Most of the fields are mapped to the very same generic functions used with IPv4, but we have noted a few exceptions here.

```
struct proto tcpv6_prot = {
        .name         =       "TCPv6",
        .close        =       tcp_close,
```

The connect function used is unique for IPv6.

```
        .connect      =       tcp_v6_connect,
        .disconnect   =       tcp_disconnect,
        .accept       =       tcp_accept,
        .ioctl        =       tcp_ioctl,
```

Socket initialization and destruction functions also are unique for IPv6. This is because there are a few fields in the sock structure that are initialized differently from IPv4.

```
        .init         =       tcp_v6_init_sock,
        .destroy      =       tcp_v6_destroy_sock,
        .shutdown     =       tcp_shutdown,
        .setsockopt   =       tcp_setsockopt,
        .getsockopt   =       tcp_getsockopt,
        .sendmsg      =       tcp_sendmsg,
        .recvmsg      =       tcp_recvmsg,
```

Finally, the backlog receive function is different from that used for IPv4. All the socket lookup and socket hash functions are different, too. Both the address and port are used to look up a socket, so all these functions must be implemented specially for the longer address format in IPv6.

```
        .backlog_rcv  =       tcp_v6_do_rcv,
        .hash         =       tcp_v6_hash,
        .unhash       =       tcp_unhash,
```

```
        .get_port       =       tcp_v6_get_port,
};
```

In general, TCP for IPv6 is implemented separately from TCP for IPv4. The ability to support IPv6 addressing and to specify IPv4 destinations over IPv6 sockets.

The tcp_v6_connect Function

We will look at a few code snippets from some of the TCP functions to see how IPv6 handles things differently. For example, let's look at the TCP connect function for IPv6, tcp_v6_connect. This is the kernel function invoked when an application layer program calls connect on an open IPv6 socket.

```
static int tcp_v6_connect(struct sock *sk, struct sockaddr *uaddr, int addr_len)
. . .
```

Here, we check to see whether the application has requested any specific flow labeling for this socket. We recall from the earlier discussion that flow labeling is the IPv6 method of QoS. The variable np points to the IPv6 protocol-specific info in the sock structure.

```
if (np->sndflow) {
    fl.fl6_flowlabel = usin->sin6_flowinfo&IPV6_FLOWINFO_MASK;
    IP6_ECN_flow_init(fl.fl6_flowlabel);
    if (fl.fl6_flowlabel&IPV6_FLOWLABEL_MASK) {
        struct ip6_flowlabel *flowlabel;
        flowlabel = fl6_sock_lookup(sk, fl.fl6_flowlabel);
        if (flowlabel == NULL)
            return -EINVAL;
        ipv6_addr_copy(&usin->sin6_addr, &flowlabel->dst);
        fl6_sock_release(flowlabel);
    }
}
```

If the application wants to connect to INADDR_ANY, that means that we really want to connect to the loopback addresses. Therefore, we explicitly set the bit to define the loopback address type.

```
if(ipv6_addr_any(&usin->sin6_addr))
    usin->sin6_addr.s6_addr[15] = 0x1;
addr_type = ipv6_addr_type(&usin->sin6_addr);
```

We don't support multicast addresses for TCP.

```
if(addr_type & IPV6_ADDR_MULTICAST)
    return -ENETUNREACH;
```

Here we check to see whether the address type is link-local.

```
if (addr_type&IPV6_ADDR_LINKLOCAL) {
    if (addr_len >= sizeof(struct sockaddr_in6) &&
        usin->sin6_scope_id) {
```

The field `sin6_scope_id` field is the scope of the link-local address. It is used to specify the network interface device index. If the socket is bound to an interface, we check to see whether the socket is bound to the same interface through which the application is requesting the connection. If not, the request is invalid.

```
        if (sk->sk_bound_dev_if &&
            sk->sk_bound_dev_if != usin->sin6_scope_id)
            return -EINVAL;
        sk->sk_bound_dev_if = usin->sin6_scope_id;
    }
```

Here we check to see whether our socket is bound to an interface. This is because, by definition, a link-local destination requires that an interface be known. We will recall from earlier in this chapter that a link local address is essentially an Ethernet or hardware LAN address expressed as an IPv6 address.

```
    if (!sk->sk_bound_dev_if)
        return -EINVAL;
}
if (tp->rx_opt.ts_recent_stamp &&
    ipv6_addr_cmp(&np->daddr, &usin->sin6_addr)) {
    tp->rx_opt.ts_recent = 0;
    tp->rx_opt.ts_recent_stamp = 0;
    tp->write_seq = 0;
}
ipv6_addr_copy(&np->daddr, &usin->sin6_addr);
np->flow_label = fl.fl6_flowlabel;
```

Now, we handle TCP over IPv4. If the address to which we are trying to connect is an IPv4 mapped address, we want the TCP from IPv4 to handle packets for this socket.

```
            if (addr_type == IPV6_ADDR_MAPPED) {
                u32 exthdrlen = icsk->icsk_ext_hdr_len;
                struct sockaddr_in sin;
                SOCK_DEBUG(sk, "connect: ipv4 mapped\n");
                if (__ipv6_only_sock(sk))
                    return -ENETUNREACH;
                sin.sin_family = AF_INET;
                sin.sin_port = usin->sin6_port;
                sin.sin_addr.s_addr = usin->sin6_addr.s6_addr32[3];
```

We set the backlog receive function to the correct one for IPv4 TCP and then call the IPv4 TCP connect function with the IPv4 portion of the destination address.

```
            icsk->icsk_af_ops = &ipv6_mapped;
            sk->sk_backlog_rcv = tcp_v4_do_rcv;
            err = tcp_v4_connect(sk, (struct sockaddr *)&sin, sizeof(sin));
            if (err) {
                icsk->icsk_ext_hdr_len = exthdrlen;
                icsk->icsk_af_ops = &ipv6_specific;
                sk->sk_backlog_rcv = tcp_v6_do_rcv;
                goto failure;
            } else {
                ipv6_addr_set(&np->saddr, 0, 0, htonl(0x0000FFFF),
                              inet->saddr);
                ipv6_addr_set(&np->rcv_saddr, 0, 0, htonl(0x0000FFFF),
                              inet->rcv_saddr);
            }
            return err;
        }
        . . .
```

THE ICMP PROTOCOL FOR IPV6, ICMPV6

The ICMP protocol for IPv6 is similar to ICMP for IPv4, but it has a few significant changes. The destination unreachable, `echo` request, and `echo` reply messages are similar [RFC 2463]. In addition, the ICMPv6 implementation is similar to ICMPv4 as discussed in Chapter 8.

The `icmpv6_rcv` Function

The function `icmpv6_rcv` is the handler for ICMPv6 packets, `IPPROTO_ICMPV6`. It is implemented in the file `linux/net/ipv6/icmp.c`. As is the case with other functions covered in this chapter, we won't look at the whole function. We will only examine some parts that are unique to IPv6 or are of particular interest.

```
static int icmpv6_rcv(struct sk_buff **pskb, unsigned int *nhoffp)
...
```

We will skip the preliminaries and show how each type of ICMPv6 packet is processed.

```
switch (type) {
case ICMPV6_ECHO_REQUEST:
```

We handle incoming echo request (ping) packets in the same way as IPv4; we simply send an echo reply.

```
    icmpv6_echo_reply(skb);
    break;
case ICMPV6_ECHO_REPLY:
```

We don't need to do anything special for a received echo reply ICMP packet.

```
    break;
case ICMPV6_PKT_TOOBIG:
```

Here, we handle a message saying the peer received a packet that was too big so we initiate MTU discovery. There is a note in the comments that suggests that we should update the destination cache if the packet contained a router header. However, the current version of the destination cache won't support this.

```
    if (!pskb_may_pull(skb, sizeof(struct ipv6hdr)))
        goto discard_it;
    hdr = (struct icmp6hdr *) skb->h.raw;
    orig_hdr = (struct ipv6hdr *) (hdr + 1);
```

We try to do a path MTU discovery, which hopefully will reduce the size of the MTU for this route.

```
    rt6_pmtu_discovery(&orig_hdr->daddr, &orig_hdr->saddr, dev,
                       ntohl(hdr->icmp6_mtu));
```

For each of these error-type packets, we take no action. Instead we drop through to do the notification. By notifying, we will inform the application of the problem via the open socket.

```
case ICMPV6_DEST_UNREACH:
case ICMPV6_TIME_EXCEED:
case ICMPV6_PARAMPROB:
    icmpv6_notify(skb, type, hdr->icmp6_code, hdr->icmp6_mtu);
    break;
```

The next four packet types are neighbor discover packets. These are covered in the next section..

```
case NDISC_ROUTER_SOLICITATION:
case NDISC_ROUTER_ADVERTISEMENT:
case NDISC_NEIGHBOUR_SOLICITATION:
case NDISC_NEIGHBOUR_ADVERTISEMENT:
case NDISC_REDIRECT:
    ndisc_rcv(skb);
    break;
```

In IPv6, the multicast group management reports and queries are defined as ICMP messages [RFC 2710]. When we receive these messages, we forward to the IGMP protocol for IPv6. We discuss these message types in a later section.

```
case ICMPV6_MGM_QUERY:
    igmp6_event_query(skb);
    break;
case ICMPV6_MGM_REPORT:
    igmp6_event_report(skb);
    break;
case ICMPV6_MGM_REDUCTION:
case ICMPV6_NI_QUERY:
case ICMPV6_NI_REPLY:
case ICMPV6_MLD2_REPORT:
case ICMPV6_DHAAD_REQUEST:
case ICMPV6_DHAAD_REPLY:
case ICMPV6_MOBILE_PREFIX_SOL:
case ICMPV6_MOBILE_PREFIX_ADV:
    break;
default:
    LIMIT_NETDEBUG (KERN_DEBUG "icmpv6: msg of unknown type\n");
```

This type is informational.

```
if (type & ICMPV6_INFOMSG_MASK)
    break;
```

We have an unknown error. We will notify the upper layers.

```
icmpv6_notify(skb, type, hdr->icmp6_code, hdr->icmp6_mtu);
. . .
}
```

IPV6 NEIGHBOR DISCOVERY

The ND protocol is used by hosts and routers for mutual discovery on locally connected nets [RFC 2461]. This protocol replaces two protocols in IPv4. One of these protocols, no longer needed in IPv6, is ARP. In IPv4, ARP was used to map an IP address to a link layer address. As we saw earlier in this chapter, this is no longer necessary because IPv6 addresses include a link-local address type in which the link-layer addresses are built in to the IPv6 address itself. Another facility that is sometimes used IPv4 is router discovery [RFC 1256]. Router discovery is a protocol in which routers send out periodic advertisements containing advertised addresses and preferences. Hosts then choose a default gateway from among the advertisements. This protocol is made obsolete by IPv6 ND.

We covered the generic neighbor system in Chapter 5. In that chapter, we discussed how the neighbor system was designed for the ND protocol, even though it also is used for an ARP cache in IPv4. In this section, we will see how the ND protocol makes use of the generic neighbor discovery cache and other facilities. We will also see which parts are unique for IPv6.

The nd_table Structure

We create a local instance of the generic neighbor table to form the neighbor discovery cache. It is in the file linux/net/ipv6/ndisc.c, that the neighbor table nd_tbl is initialized.

```
struct neigh_table nd_tbl = {
. . .
```

The constructor and proxy constructor member functions are set as follows.

```
.constructor   =   ndisc_constructor,
.pconstructor  =   pndisc_constructor,
.pdestructor   =   pndisc_destructor,
.proxy_redo    =   pndisc_redo,
. . .
}
```

The `ndisc_generic_ops` Structure

This structure is also implemented in the file linux/net/ipv6/ndisc.c.

```
static struct neigh_ops ndisc_generic_ops = {
    .family =           AF_INET6,
```

The next two functions are the only ones that are unique for IPv6.

```
    .solicit =          ndisc_solicit,
    .error_report =     ndisc_error_report,
```

The following four functions are the same ones that are used for the IPv4 neighbor cache and the ARP protocol.

```
    .output =           neigh_resolve_output,
    .connected_output = neigh_connected_output,
    .hh_output =        dev_queue_xmit,
    .queue_xmit =       dev_queue_xmit,
};
```

The `ndisc_hh_ops` Structure

This structure contains the operation functions associated with obtaining the MAC address or hardware header for a discovered neighbor.

```
static struct neigh_ops ndisc_hh_ops = {
    .family =           AF_INET6,
```

The following two fields are set to point to IPv6 specific functions. The rest use the generic operational functions. We will recall that the dev_queue_xmit function is the universal generic function that queues a packet for transmission once the MAC address is determined.

```
    .solicit =          ndisc_solicit,
    .error_report =     ndisc_error_report,
    .output =           neigh_resolve_output,
    .connected_output = neigh_resolve_output,
    .hh_output =        dev_queue_xmit,
    .queue_xmit =       dev_queue_xmit,
};
```

Neighbor Discovery Message Types

ND messages are defined as part of the ICMPv6 protocol. Therefore, there is no packet handler registered specifically for ND. The protocol includes four different message types, defined in the file `linux/include/net/ndisc.h`. These values are shown in Table 11.3.

TABLE 11.3 Neighbor Discovery Messages

Message Type	Value
NDISC_ROUTER_SOLICITATION	133
NDISC_ROUTER_ADVERTISEMENT	134
NDISC_NEIGHBOUR_SOLICITATION	135
NDISC_NEIGHBOUR_ADVERTISEMENT	136
NDISC_REDIRECT	137

The `ndisc_rcv` Function

When an ND message is received by ICMP, it calls the function `ndisc_rcv` implemented in the file `linux/net/ipv6/ndisc.c`.

```
int ndisc_rcv(struct sk_buff *skb)
{
. . .
```

In `ndisc_rcv`, we extract the message from the ICMP packet and decode it.

```
switch (msg->icmph.icmp6_type) {
```

In this section, we decode four types of neighbor discovery messages.

```
case NDISC_NEIGHBOUR_SOLICITATION:
    ndisc_recv_ns(skb);
    break;
case NDISC_NEIGHBOUR_ADVERTISEMENT:
    ndisc_recv_na(skb);
    break;
case NDISC_ROUTER_ADVERTISEMENT:
    ndisc_router_discovery(skb);
    break;
```

```
        case NDISC_REDIRECT:
            ndisc_redirect_rcv(skb);
            break;
    };
    return 0;
}
```

The Neighbor Discovery Solicitation Message

The neighbor solicitation message is sent for two reasons. The first is to discover the link-layer address for a connected neighbor. The other is to determine the reachability status of a neighbor.

The `ndisc_recv_ns` Function

The function `ndisc_recv_ns` in the file `linux/net/ipv6/ndisc.c` processes the neighbor solicitation messages.

```
static void ndisc_recv_ns(struct sk_buff *skb);
```

First, we do some validity checks. If the source address is the unspecified address, `IPV6_ADDR_ANY`, then the destination address must be the solicited node multicast address. Next, we parse the neighbor discovery options in the packet. We update the neighbor cache and the unreachability state depending on the message contents. Of course, we also send a neighbor advertisement message in response if the validity checks pass.

The Neighbor Advertisement Message

The neighbor advertisement message is received in response to a neighbor solicitation.

The `ndisc_recv_na` Function

The `ndisc_recv_na` function in the file `linux/net/ipv6/ndisc.c` processes the neighbor advertisement messages.

```
static void ndisc_recv_na(struct sk_buff *skb)
...
```

The main thing we do in this function is look up the advertised neighbor in the neighbor cache. We do this by calling the generic neighbor cache function, `neigh_lookup`. The parameter, `msg` points to the neighbor advertisement message contents and `target` is the advertised address.

```
neigh = neigh_lookup(&nd_tbl, &msg->target, dev);
if (neigh) {
    u8 old_flags = neigh->flags;
    if (neigh->nud_state & NUD_FAILED)
        goto out;
```

If the neighbor cache entry is listed as a router, we must change that entry back to host and try to get the actual default router. Also we update the neighbor cache entry by calling `neigh_update`. This function, discussed in Chapter 5, will update the reachability state and attach the hardware header, so packets can be transmitted using the valid neighbor entry which will supply a MAC header.

```
neigh_update(neigh, lladdr,
            msg->icmph.icmp6_solicited ?
            NUD_REACHABLE : NUD_STALE,
            NEIGH_UPDATE_F_WEAK_OVERRIDE|
            (msg->icmph.icmp6_override ?
                NEIGH_UPDATE_F_OVERRIDE : 0)|
            NEIGH_UPDATE_F_OVERRIDE_ISROUTER|
            (msg->icmph.icmp6_router ?
                NEIGH_UPDATE_F_ISROUTER : 0));
```

Here we are checking the flag bit in the ICMP header of the incoming packet to see whether it is coming from a router. If so, we update the neighbor cache entry and change the router to a host.

```
if ((old_flags & ~neigh->flags) & NTF_ROUTER) {
    struct rt6_info *rt;
    rt = rt6_get_dflt_router(saddr, dev);
    if (rt)
        ip6_del_rt(rt, NULL, NULL, NULL);
}
```

The Router Advertisement (RA) message serves several functions. Primarily, as the name implies, it is simply an RA message. When a node receives an RA message, it can determine which machine is the default or preferred router. In addition, the RA message is used for interface autoconfiguration because it may contain an address to be added to the interface's list of local addresses.

The `ndisc_router_discovery` Function

The function `ndisc_router_discovery` processes an incoming router advertisement message. This function is also defined in the file `linux/net/ipv6/ndisc.c`.

```
static void ndisc_router_discovery(struct sk_buff *skb);
```

THE MULTICAST LISTENER DISCOVERY PROTOCOL

In this section, we discuss the IPv6 multicast group management. Unfortunately, multicast routing is not supported by IPv6 at the time of this writing; only the host side is fully supported.

IPv4 used the Internet Group Management Protocol (IGMP) for multicast routing. In IPv4, IGMP associates a multicast address with a series of addresses called a *group*. If a host wants to receive packets sent to a particular multicast destination address, it *joins* the group by sending a special IGMP report message to the all routers destination address. Routers send out IGMP queries to the all hosts group address and listen to the IGMP reports from the hosts. Then, multicast routers would forward multicast packets that have a destination address which matches the group address to all members of the group [RFC 1112].

Unlike IPv4, IPv6 is a little different. The multicast group management is now called Multicast Listener Discovery (MLD) [RFC 2710]. The IGMP protocol used with IPv4 [RFC 1112] is not defined for IPv6. Instead, the message types are defined as ICMP messages so there is no special packet handler for MLD.

The `igmp6_init` Function

The initialization function for MLD registers with the socket layer, so join and drop group requests from the application can be processed. The initialization function for MLD is called `igmp6_init`, and it can be found in the file `linux/net/ipv6/mcast.c`.

```
int __init igmp6_init(struct net_proto_family *ops)
{
    struct ipv6_pinfo *np;
    struct sock *sk;
    int err;
```

When we initialize, we create a specific socket type for IGMP, `igmp6_socket`. Notice that the protocol is set to `IPPROTO_ICMPV6` because there is no IGMP protocol defined for IPv6. Add and drop group requests are sent to us through this socket.

```
    err = sock_create(PF_INET6, SOCK_RAW, IPPROTO_ICMPV6, &igmp6_socket);
    if (err < 0) {
        printk(KERN_ERR
            "Failed to initialize the IGMP6 control socket (err %d).\n",
            err);
```

```
        igmp6_socket = NULL;
        return err;
    }
    sk = igmp6_socket->sk;
    sk->sk_allocation = GFP_ATOMIC;
    sk->sk_prot->unhash(sk);
    np = inet6_sk(sk);
    np->hop_limit = 1;
```

Here is where we create nodes for IPv6 multicasting in the /proc file system.

```
#ifdef CONFIG_PROC_FS
    proc_net_fops_create("igmp6", S_IRUGO, &igmp6_mc_seq_fops);
    proc_net_fops_create("mcfilter6", S_IRUGO, &igmp6_mcf_seq_fops);
#endif
    return 0;
}
```

Receiving MLD Queries

As discussed earlier, there is no MLD receive handler function so MLD queries are received by ICMP.

The `igmp6_event_query` Function

When ICMP receives an MLD query, it will forward it to the function `igmp6_event_query`.

```
int igmp6_event_query(struct sk_buff *skb);
```

This function updates the timer for the particular group, which is in the `mc_gq_timer` field of the `inet6_dev` structure. When the timer expires, the group report is sent.

The `igmp6_event_report` Function

When ICMP receives an MLD report, it will forward it to `igmp6_event_report`.

```
int igmp6_event_report(struct sk_buff *skb);
```

This function drops all reports that didn't come from a link-local source address. Next, it deletes the timer for the group. However, as of this writing, it doesn't update the routing table with the addresses in the report because IPv6 multicast routing is not supported yet.

AUTO CONFIGURATION

IPv6 has two forms of address autoconfiguration. The first is called *stateless* autoconfiguration, and the second is *stateful* autoconfiguration. It is important to note that IPv6 addresses are assigned to interfaces, not hosts, and unlike IPv4, interfaces can be assigned one or more addresses and can even function with no address at all. Router advertisement, part of ND discussed earlier, is the mechanism used for stateless autoconfiguration [RFC 2462]. A particular interface can self-assign a link-local address. This link-local address is likely to be unique for a link-local scope, but it can be checked using duplicate address detection. This algorithm works by sending out neighbor solicitations and receiving neighbor advertisements. Another aspect of stateless autoconfiguration uses the router advertisement message in the ND protocol [RFC 2462]. A host is informed that it is advised to use stateful autoconfiguration by a flag bit in the router discovery message.

ROUTING AND THE IPV6 FIB

The Linux IPv6 routing implementation is similar to IPv4 and shares some of the Linux networking framework. Like IPv4, route tables are used for both input and output packets because this is a flexible way of determining both machine local and external destinations in a transparent way. Like IPv4, IPv6 contains a routing cache based on the generic destination cache. Unfortunately, though, it does not yet use the same FIB as IPv4. Instead, IPv6 has its own FIB. Another difference is that the IPv4 FIB defines at least two FIB tables, a local table and a main table. IPv4 can use more FIBs if full policy routing is implemented. IPv6 has only a single FIB.

Routing Data Structures for IPv6

In this section, we will look at a few data structures used for IPv6 routing. These structures are similar to their counterparts for IPv4. We will discuss some differences and a few features unique to IPv6.

The rt6_info Structure

The route cache entry is defined by the rt6_info structure, defined in the file linux/include/net/ip6_fib.h.

```
struct rt6_info
{
```

Just like IPv4, this structure is derived from a dst_entry structure.

```
        union {
            struct dst_entry        dst;
            struct rt6_info         *next;
        } u;
        struct inet6_dev            *rt6i_idev;
```

The `dev`, `neighbour` and `expires` fields are in the `dst_entry` structure. These macros allow them to be retrieved easily from a `rt6_info` structure.

```
#define rt6i_dev            u.dst.dev
#define rt6i_nexthop        u.dst.neighbour
#define rt6i_expires        u.dst.expires
        struct fib6_node        *rt6i_node;
        struct in6_addr         rt6i_gateway;
        u32                     rt6i_flags;
        u32                     rt6i_metric;
        atomic_t                rt6i_ref;
        struct rt6key           rt6i_dst;
        struct rt6key           rt6i_src;
        u8                      rt6i_protocol;
};
```

The rt6key Structure

The search key, defined as the `rt6key` structure is defined in the file linux/include/net/ip6_fib.h and is similar in name to the one for IPv4. However, it is much simpler.

```
struct rt6key
{
```

The key contains only an address and a prefix length. The prefix defines the network portion of the address.

```
        struct in6_addr     addr;
        int                 plen;
};
```

Finally, we should show how the IPv6 FIB is implemented. It is much simpler than the IPv4 FIB, which has a complex series of interleaved hash tables. The IPv6 FIB is a relatively simple tree structure. It does have the optional capability of supporting subtrees.

The `fib6_node` Structure

The FIB node structure, `fib6_node`, is shown next. It is defined in the file linux/include/net/ip6_fib.h.

```
struct fib6_node
{
    struct fib6_node    *parent;
    struct fib6_node    *left;
    struct fib6_node    *right;
```

Subtrees are supported if the option is configured into the kernel.

```
    struct fib6_node    *subtree;
```

The actual route is stored here. The data structure is shown above.

```
    struct rt6_info     *leaf;
```

The next field, `fn_bit`, is used for address prefix matching.

```
    __u16               fn_bit;
    __u16               fn_flags;
    __u32               fn_sernum;
};
```

IPv6 Output Routing

In some respects, IPv6 routing is similar to IPv4 routing. We determine the route we output when we are ready to transmit a SOCK_DGRAM packet or when we are trying to establish a connection for a SOCK_STREAM type socket. When either of these events occurs, we call an output routing function to determine to whom to send an output packet with a remote final destination.

The `ip6_route_output` Function

The function `ip6_route_output` routes the output packets. It is defined in the file linux/net/ipv6/route.c.

```
struct dst_entry * ip6_route_output(struct sock *sk, struct flowi *fl);
```

As is the case with IPv4, the specific goal of the routing function is to find a destination cache entry, `dst_entry` which holds a route that meets the search criteria.

This function is slightly different from its IPv4 counterpart because the destination cache entry is returned directly by the function. The caller updates the skb. With IPv4, the routing function returned an error code and updated the routing cache and the skb automatically.

IPv6 Input Routing

As with IPv4, we not only route output packets, but also have to route input packets, even though this doesn't seem to make sense. An input packet can have any number of internal destinations or it may actually need to be forwarded out some interface. The goal of input routing is to determine the destination for a packet if there is no corresponding entry in the destination cache.

The `ip6_route_input` Function

We call the input routing function when we receive an incoming packet in IPv6 and need to determine what to do with it or who should get it next. In IPv6, the input routing function is `ip6_route_input` in the file linux/net/ipv6/route.c, and it is almost identical to the output routing function.

```
void ip6_route_input(struct sk_buff *skb);
```

This function also finds the destination cache entry in the routing table. Generally, however, the destination cache entry will point to the IPv6 input function, the IPv6 forwarding function, or the multicast input function depending on the match in the routing table.

The `fib6_lookup` Function

Both of the routing functions discussed earlier call a FIB lookup function, `fib6_lookup`, to try to locate a route. This function is implemented in the file linux/net/ipv6/ip6_fib.c.

```
struct fib6_node * fib6_lookup(struct fib6_node *root,
                               struct in6_addr *daddr,
                               struct in6_addr *saddr);
```

In this function, we return a pointer to an entry in the FIB based on the destination and source addresses. The function creates a search key as described earlier and looks up the entry in the FIB if there is one.

SUMMARY

In this chapter, we provided an overview of IPv6, including the address formats and header structure. Primarily, we discussed the IPv6 implementation in Linux. We covered how the protocol family was initialized and discussed the transport protocols, UDP and TCP for IPv6. We also discussed the routing table and neighbor cache implementation. We compared some aspects of IPv6 with IPv4. Finally, we talked about some of the member protocols in the IPv6 protocol suite, including ICMP and ND and MLD.

Appendix A: RFCs

Following is a list of all the RFCs referenced in this book. The RFCs may be found at the website, *http://www.faqs.org/rfcs/*. Also, for convenience, all the RFCs listed here are provided on the CD-ROM.

760	DoD standard Internet Protocol
791	Internet Protocol
792	Internet Control Message Protocol
793	Transmission Control Protocol
795	Service Mappings (Type of Service Field in IP Header)
796	Address Mappings
826	Ethernet Address Resolution Protocol: Or converting network protocol addresses to 48-bit Ethernet address for transmission on Ethernet hardware
853	Telnet Protocol Specification
896	Congestion Control in IP/TCP Internetworks (Nagle Algorithm)
917	Internet Subnets
919	Broadcasting Internet Datagrams
922	Broadcasting Internet Datagrams in the Presence of Subnets
950	Internet Standard Subnetting Procedure
1112	Host extensions for IP multicasting (IGMPv1)
1122	Requirements for Internet Hosts—Communication Layers
1256	ICMP Router Discovery Messages
1191	Path MTU Discovery
1323	TCP Extensions for High Performance
1337	TIME-WAIT Assassination Hazards in TCP
1338	Supernetting: an Address Assignment and Aggregation Strategy
1379	Extending TCP for Transactions—Concepts
1380	IESG Deliberations on Routing and Addressing
1518	An Architecture for IP Address Allocation with CIDR

RFC	Title
1519	Classless Inter-Domain Routing (CIDR): an Address Assignment and Aggregation Strategy
1583	OSPF Version 2 (Open Shortest Path First)
1661	The Point-to-Point Protocol (PPP)
1662	PPP in HDLC-like Framing
1663	PPP Reliable Transmission
1771	A Border Gateway Protocol 4 (BGP-4)
1812	Requirements for IP Version Routers
1883	Internet Protocol Version 6 (IPv6) Specification
1884	Ipv6 Addressing Architecture
2001	TCP Slow Start, Congestion Avoidance, Fast Retransmit, and Fast Recovery Algorithms
2018	TCP Selective Acknowledgement Options
2101	IPv4 Address Behavior Today
2292	Advanced Sockets API for IPv6
2367	PF_KEY Key Management API, Version 2
2373	IP Version 6 Addressing Architecture
2401	Security Architecture for the Internet Protocol
2402	IP Authentication Header
2406	IP Encapsulating Security Payload (ESP)
2409	The Internet Key Exchange (IKE)
2460	Internet Protocol, Version 6 (IPv6) Specification
2461	Neighbor Discovery Protocol for IPv6
2463	Internet Control Message Protocol (ICMPv6) for the Internet Protocol Version 6 (IPv6) Specification
2581	TCP Congestion Control
2582	The NewReno Modification to TCP's Fast Recovery Algorithm
2625	IP and ARP over Fibre Channel
2710	Multicast Listener Discovery (MLD) for IPv6
2861	TCP Congestion Window Validation
2883	An Extension to the Selective Acknowledgement (SACK) Option for TCP
2914	Congestion Control Principles
3056	Connection of IPv6 Domains via IPv4 Clouds
3168	The Addition of Explicit Congestion Notification (ECN) to IP
3261	SIP: Session Initiation Protocol
3376	Internet Group Management Protocol, Version 3
3390	Increasing TCP's Initial Window (Obsoletes RFC2414)
3493	Basic Socket Interface Extensions for IPv6

Appendix B: About the CD-ROM

The companion CD-ROM contains all the kernel source code discussed in this book, the sample NADA protocol and test code introduced in Chapter 10, the RFCs referenced, and a copy of the GNU Public License (GPL). All sources on the CD-ROM are covered by the GPL.

FOLDERS

kernel

linux-2.6.16.20

The directory contains the Linux source tree including all files discussed in Chapters 2–9 and Chapter 11. The working kernel version on which this book is based is 2.6.16.20

RFCs

This directory contains each of the RFCs referenced in this book.

Chapter 10

This folder contains the NADA protocol for Linux and test programs. The nada protocol and test programs have been tested in a 2.6.12.13 Linux kernel. For more information, refer to Chapter 10 or see the README.txt file in this directory.

tapif

This directory contains the tapif program for setting up the tun driver for a point to point pseudo-interface for testing the NADA protocol. You may execute the following command for a synopsis of arguments of this program.

```
% tapif -h
```

nada

The nada directory contains the sources for the NADA protocol. See Chapter 10 or the README.txt file for instructions as to how to load and test the protocol.

test

The test program contains the nada test program for receiving and sending messages via the nada protocol. You may execute the following command for a synopsis of arguments of this program.

```
% tapif -h
```

Instructions for Building and Running the Test Programs in Chapter 10

To test the nada protocol discussed in Chapter 10, read the instructions in README.txt in the Chapter10 directory.

SYSTEM REQUIREMENTS

PC and Windows

- CD-ROM drive
- Network interface
- 128 MB RAM
- 250 MB of disk space
- Mouse or compatible pointing device
- Web browser; monitor
- Recent version of Windows such as Windows NT or later
- Cygwin, freely available from *http://www.cygwin.com/*, is recommended. Also, a text and programming editor such as vim available from *http://www.vim.org* is recommended for browsing the source files in the book.

Linux

- Fedora Core 4 or later or any Linux distribution with a gcc revision capable of compiling the 2.6.20 kernel. The NADA protocol and test programs have been tested with a 2.6.13 kernel.
- CD-ROM drive.

Macintosh

All the files in this CD-ROM should be readable in a Macintosh, but this hasn't been tested.

SOURCES ON THE CD-ROM

```
gpl.txt
/linux-2.6.16.20
    <kernel source tree>
chapter10
    README.txt
    tapif
        Makefile
        tapif.c
    nada
        nada.h
        nadasock.h
        af_nada.c
        Makefile
        nada_debug.h
        test
            nada.c
            Makefile
/RFCs
    rfc760.txt*
    rfc791.txt*
    rfc792.txt*
    rfc793.txt*
    rfc795.txt*
    rfc796.txt*
    rfc826.txt*
    rfc853.txt*
    rfc896.txt*
    rfc917.txt*
    rfc919.txt*
    rfc922.txt*
    rfc950.txt*
    rfc1112.txt*
    rfc1122.txt*
    rfc1191.txt*
    rfc1256.txt*
    rfc1323.txt*
```

```
rfc1337.txt*
rfc1338.txt*
rfc1379.txt*
rfc1380.txt*
rfc1511.txt*
rfc1518.txt*
rfc1519.txt*
rfc1583.txt*
rfc1661.txt*
rfc1662.txt*
rfc1663.txt*
rfc1771.txt*
rfc1812.txt*
rfc1883.txt*
rfc1884.txt*
rfc2001.txt*
rfc2018.txt*
rfc2101.txt*
rfc2292.txt*
rfc2367.txt*
rfc2373.txt*
rfc2401.txt*
rfc2402.txt*
rfc2406.txt*
rfc2409.txt*
rfc2460.txt*
rfc2461.txt*
rfc2463.txt*
rfc2581.txt*
rfc2582.txt*
rfc2625.txt*
rfc2710.txt*
rfc2861.txt*
rfc2883.txt*
rfc2914.txt*
rfc3056.txt*
rfc3168.txt*
rfc3261.txt*
rfc3376.txt*
rfc3390.txt*
rfc3493.txt*
```

Bibliography

[ASCII] American National Standards Institute, "Information Systems—Coded Character Sets—7-Bit American National Standard Code for Information Interchange (7-Bit ASCII)." Document Number ANSI INCITS 4–1986 (R2002).

[BOVET02] Bovet, Daniel P., Cesati, Marco, *Understanding the Linux Kernel*, 2nd Edition. O'Reilly Sebastopol, CA; December 2002. (ISBN 0596002130).

[CISCOa] Cisco Systems, *Internetworking Technology Handbook*, Chapter "IBM System Network Architecture Protocols." Cisco Systems, 1993–2003. Available online at *http://www.cisco.com/univercd/cc/td/doc/cisintwk/ito_doc/ibmsna.htm*, accessed March 19, 2004.

[EDWAR00a] Edwards, Terry, *Gigahertz and Terahertz, technologies for broadband communications*, Chapter 1. Artech House, Inc, 2000. (ISBN 1580530680).

[GALENETa] The Gale Group, "Robert M. Metcalfe." *World of Computer Science*. 2 vols. Gale Group, 2002. Reproduced in *Biography Resource Center*. Available online at *http://galenet.galegroup.com/servlet/BioRC*, 2004.

[GALENETb] The Gale Group, "Jean Baptiste Joseph Fourier, Baron." *Encyclopedia of World Biography*, 2nd ed. 17 Vols. Gale Research, 1998. Reproduced in *Biography Resource Center*. Available online at *http://galenet.galegroup.com/servlet/BioRC*, 2004.

[GALL95] Gallmeister, Bill O., *Posix.4: Programming for the Real World*. O'Reilly & Associates, January 1995. (ISBN: 1565920740).

[HAGEN02] Hagen, Silvia, *IPv6 Essentials*. O'Reilly & Associates, July 2002. (ISBN 0-595-00125-8).

[HOUSE] House, Don Robert, "Telegraph Timeline," North American Data Communications Museum. Available online at *http://www.nadcomm.com/timeline.htm*.

[HUBER02] Hubert, Bert, *Traffic Shaping for the User and Developer*. Ottawa Linux Symposium 2002. Available online at *http://ds9a.nl/ols-presentation*.

609

[HUBHOW02] Hubert, Bert, Gregory Maxwell, Remco van Mook, Martijn van Oosterhaut, Paul B. Schroeder, and Jasper Spaans, *Linux Advanced Traffic Control and Routing HOWTO*, Revision 1.1, July 7, 2002, Linux Documentation Project. Available online at *http://www.linux.org/docs/ldp/howto/Adv-Routing-HOWTO/index.html*.

[IAPROT03] Internet Assigned Numbers Authority, *Protocol Numbers*. Updated January, 13, 2003. Available online at *http://www.iana.org/assignments/protocol-numbers*.

[IEEE802.3] "IEEE Std 802.3–2002 Carrier sense multiple access with collision detection (CSMA/CD) access method and physical layer specifications." *IEEE Computer Society*, March 8, 2002.

[ITUTV21] "300 bits per second duplex modem standardized for use in the general switched telephone network," Recommendation V.21 (11/88), Article Number E7179, International Telecommunications Union, ITU. Available online at *http://www.itu.int*.

[JACOB88] Jacobson, V., "Congestion Avoidance and Control," *SIGCOMM '88*. Available online at *http://citeseer.nj.nec.com/jacobson88congestion.html*, August 1988.

[JACOB93] Jacobson, V., "Re: query about TCP header on tcp-ip," September 7, 1993. Reposted by C. Partridge, "Jacobson on TCP in 30 Instructions," Usenet, comp.protocols.tcp-ip Newsgroup, Message-ID <1993Sep8.213239.28992@sics.se>, September 8, 1993. Available online at *ftp://ftp.ee.lbl.gov/email/vanj.93sep07.txt*

[KARN91] Karn, P. and C. Partridge, "Improving Round-Trip Time Estimates in Reliable Transport Protocols." *ACM Transactions on Computer Systems*, Vol. 9, No. 4, November 1991. Available online at *http://citeseer.nj.nec.com/karn01improving.html*

[KFALL96] K. Fall, S. Floyd, "Simulation-based Comparisons of Tahoe, Reno and SACK TCP," *Computer Communications Review*, ACM-SIGCOMM Vol. 26, No. 3, July 1996.

[KNUTH73] Knuth, Donald, E., *The Art of Computer Programming*, Volume 1: Fundamental Algorithms, 3rd Edition, Addison-Wesley. (ISBN 0201896834).

[LISKOV90] Liskov, B., L. Shrira, and J. Wroclawski, *Efficient At-Most-Once Messages Based on Synchronized Clocks*, ACM SIGCOMM'90, September 1990.

[MARSH01] Marsh, Mathew G. *Policy Routing Using Linux*, March 6, 2001; SAMS. (ISBN 0672320525).

[MATH96] Mathis, Matt, and Jamshid Mahdavi, "Forward Acknowledgement: Refining TCP Congestion Control." Proceedings of SIGCOMM 96, August 1996.

[MATH97] Mathis, Matt, and Jamshid Mahdavi, "TCP Rate-Halving with Bounding Parameters." Technical Note, FACKnotes, 1997. Available online at *http://www.psc.edu/networking/papers/FACKnotes/current/*.

[MCDYSO22a] McDyson, David, and Paw, Dave, "ATM & MPLS Theory and Applications: Foundations of Multi-Service Networking." McGraw Hill, 2002:Chapter 8, pp 104–109. (ISBN 0072222565).

[MCDYSO22b] *ibid*. Appendix B, 881–911.

[MCKUS96] McKusick, Marshall Kirk, Keith Bostic, Michael J. Karels, and John S. Quarterman, *The Design and Implementation of the 4.4BSD Operating System*. Addison-Wesley, 1996. (ISBN 0201549794).

[NEWTON98a] Newton, Harry, *Newton's Telecom Dictionary*. Flatiron Publishing, March 1998: pp 4, 5. (ISBN 1-57820-023-7).

[NEWTON98b] *ibid*. pp 537, 538.

[NEWTON98c] *ibid*. pp 99.

[RBHILL] Hill, R. B., "The Early Years of the Strowger System," *Bell Telephone Record* (Volume XXXI No. 3, March, 1953. P. 95 et. seq.). Available online at *http://www.privateline.com/Switching/EarlyYears.html*.

[RUBINI00] Alessandro Rubini, Alessandro and Corbet, Jonathan; *Linux Device Drivers, 2nd Edition*. O'Reilly, June 2001. (ISBN: 0596000081).

[RUBINI00a] *ibid*. Chapter 2, pp 15–50.

[STALL93] Stallings, William, *Networking Standards, A guide to OSI, ISDN, LAN and MAN Standards*. Addison-Wesley, 1993. (ISBN 0-201-56357-6).

[STEV94] Stevens, W. Richard, *TCP/IP Illustrated, Volume 1 The Protocols*. Addison-Wesley, 1994. (ISBN: 0201633469).

[STEV98] Stevens, W. Richard *UNIX Network Programming, 2nd Edition*. Prentice Hall, January 1998. (ISBN: 013490012X).

[STREAM93] UNIX Systems Laboratories, *STREAMS Modules and Drivers Unix SVR4.2*. Prentice Hall, June 1993. (ISBN 0130668796).

[USAGI03] Yoshifuji, Hideaki, Kazunori Miyazawa, Yuji Sekiya, Hiroshi Esaki, and Jun Murai, *Linux IPv6 Networking Past, Present and Future*. Proceedings of the Linux Symposium, July 23–26, 2003. Available online at *http://archive.linuxsymposium.org/ols2003/Proceedings/All-Reprints/Reprint-Yoshifuji-OLS2003.pdf*.

[VAHAL96] Vahalia, Uresh, *UNIX Internals The New Frontiers*. Prentice-Hall Inc., October, 1995. (ISBN 0131019082).

[WIKIPEDa] *Wikipedia*, the Free Encyclopedia, "Telegraphy." *Wikipedia, the Free Encyclopedia.*. Available online at *http://en.wikipedia.org/wiki/Telegraphy*, accessed October 11, 2006.

[WIKIPEDb] Wikipedia, the Free Encyclopedia, "Plain Old Telephone Service." *Wikipedia, the Free Encyclopedia.*. Available online at *http://en.wikipedia.org/wiki/Plain_old_telephone_service*, accessed October 11, 2006.

[WIKIPEDc] Wikipedia, the Free Encyclopedia, "Teleprinter." *Wikipedia, the Free Encyclopedia*. Available online at *http://en.wikipedia.org/wiki/Teleprinter*, accessed October 11, 2006.

[WIKIPEDd] "EBCDIC," *Wikipedia*, the free Encyclopedia. Available online at *http://en.wikipedia.org/wiki/EBCDIC,* accessed October 11, 2006.

[WIKIPEDe] "Baudot Code," *Wikipedia*, the free Encyclopedia. Available online at *http://en.wikipedia.org/wiki/Baudot_code,* accessed October 11, 2006

[WILC03] Wilcox, Matthew, "I'll Do It Later: Softirqs, Tasklets, Bottom Halves, Task Queues, Work Queues and Timers." Presented at Linux Conference Australia, Perth, Australia, January 2003. Available online at *http://www.linux.org.au/conf/2003.*

[X.25] "Interface between Data Terminal Equipment (DTE) and Data Circuit-terminating Equipment (DCE) for terminals operating in the packet mode and connected to public data networks by dedicated circuit," Recommendation X.25 (10/96); International Telecommunications Union, ITU. Available online at *http://www.itu.int.*

Index

A

AAL (ATM Adaptation Layer), 34–35
AAL5 (ATM Adaption Layer 5), 32–33
accept call, socket API, 136
ACK (Acknowledge)
    stop and wait acknowledgement using, 17
    TCP delayed acknowledgment timer, 342–345
    TCP output, 321–322
    TCP processing data segments, 501–502
    TCP receive handler, 480
    TCP receive state processing, 490, 493–494
    TCP values for, 326
    `tcp_info` structure, 284
    `TCP_QUICKACK` option, 285
    `TIME_WAIT` state processing, 506–507, 509
acknowledgement timeout (ATO), TCP, 344
`add_timer` function, 185
address families. *see* protocol families
Address Resolution Protocol. *see* ARP (Address Resolution Protocol)
addressing, IPv6, 555–560
    address types and Format Prefix, 558
    expressing, 556–557
    expressing netmasks, 557
    link-local addresses, 559
    loopback addresses, 557
    multicast addresses, 559–560
    overview of, 555
    unspecified addresses, 557–558
`addrinfo` structure, 149
advertisement message, ND, 594–596
`AF_INET` protocol family
    creating, 160–163
    initialization of, 202
    IP protocol initialization and, 353
    and socket calls, 126

`AF_NADA` protocol family
    address type, 523
    CD-ROM accompanying book and, 605–606
    creating, 523–525
    initialization, 525–527
    module initialization, 527–529
    `NADA` packet format, 524–525
    `nada_address` structure, 524
    receiving packets, 539–543
    sending packets from socket layer, 543–548
    `sock_addr_nada` structure, 523–524
    socket layer interface, 529–539
    test setup, 548–551
AH (Authentication Header), in IPSec, 236
`alloc_etherdev` function
    network device initialization, 71–73
    network device registration, 89
`alloc_netdev` function
    network device initialization, 71
    network device registration, 89
`alloc_skb` function, 266–267
American Standard Characters for Information Exchange (ASCII), 18
ancillary data, 301
anycast addresses, IPv6, 555
API, FIB, 381–387
application layer, OSI
    defined, 12–13
    in TCP/IP, 53–54
ARP (Address Resolution Protocol), 419–431
    cache, 206–207
    initialization, 420–424
    neighbor table, 223–225
    overview of, 419–420
    receiving and processing ARP packets, 424–431
    replaced in IPv6 with Neighbor Discovery, 555
    TCP/IP implementation and, 43
    TCP/IP network layer and, 49–50

`arp_broken_arps` structure, 424
`arp_direct_ops` structure, 424
`arp_fwd_proxy` function, 429
`arp_generic_ops` structure, 423
`arp_hh_ops` structure, 423–424
`arp_ifdown` function, 421
`arp_init` function
    ARP protocol initialization, 224–225, 421–422
    TCP/IP initialization, 175
`arp_netdev_notifier` structure, 420
`arp_netdv_event` function, 421
`arp_packet_type` structure, 420
`arp_proc_init` function, 421
`arp_process` function, 425–431
`arp_rcv` function, 424–425
`arp_table` structure, 422–423
ARPANET, 42
ASCII (American Standard Characters for Information Exchange), 18–19
ASN.1 (Abstract Syntax Notation), 54
Asynchronous data transmission
    measuring speed in baud rate, 9
    in teletype machines, 8
ATM (asynchronous transmission mode), 31–36
    ATM UNI service class definitions, 34–36
    network interfaces, 33–34
    overview of, 31–32
    PHY layer, 33
    stack, 32–33
    vs. synchronous data transmission, 16–17
    TCP as, 322–323
ATM Adaptation Layer (AAL), 34–35
ATM Adaption Layer 5 (AAL5), 32–33
ATO (acknowledgement timeout), TCP, 344
Authentication Header (AH), in IPSec, 236
autoconfiguration, IPv6, 554, 598

613

B

backlog queue, TCP
  overview of, 481
  processing with `tcp_v4_do_rcv` function, 484–486
  TCP socket-level receive and, 514
backlog receive, UDP, 467–469
`backlog_rcv` function, 278, 483
Backward Explicit Congestion Notification (BECN), 31
`base_addr`, `net_device`, 62
baud rate, 9
Baudot code
  and baud rate, 9
  character coded transmission from, 8
  and modems, transmitting digital data, 11
BECN (Backward Explicit Congestion Notification), 31
Berkeley Software Distribution. *see* BSD (Berkeley Software Distribution)
BH (Bottom Half), 181
`bh_unlock_sock` function, 478
`bind` function, 278
bind socket call, 136
B-ISDN (Broadband ISDN), 31
BISYNC (BSC), 18–20
bit definitions, `tos` field in `flowi` structure, 360–361
bit stuffing, 20–21
bit-oriented synchronous transmission, 20–21
Board Support Package (BSP), 186
boot phase, queuing layer initialization, 189–190
`bottom half`, 172
`bottom half`, 180–181
Bottom Half (BH), 181
Broadband ISDN (B-ISDN), 31
broadband networking. *see* WANs (wide area networks)
broadcast packets, receiving in UDP, 463
BSC (BISYNC), 18–20
BSD (Berkeley Software Distribution)
  defined, 42
  `mbufs`, 246
  sockets, 53
BSP (Board Support Package), 186
buffers, in embedded OS, 56
`bus_add_driver`, 81

C

cache
  destination. *see* destination cache
  neighbor. *see* neighbor cache
  overview of, 205–206
  packet transmission using, 228–231
  route. *see* route cache
  slab. *see* slab cache
  types of, 206
capabilities
  `inet_protosw` structure, 128
  security and, 146–147
Carrier Sense Multiple Access with Collision Detect (CSMA/CD), 15, 45
CD-ROM accompanying book
  building and loading `NADA` module, 548–549
  folders, 605–606
  kernel source tree, 4
  license for source code in book, 4
  protocol family code, 521
  source code, 2
  sources, 607–608
  system requirements, 606–607
  `tapif` program, 547
  `tun/tap` module, 549
  X.25, 22
cell, ATM, 31
central office (CO), 9–10, 36–37
`change_mtu`, 94
character coded transmission, 6–8
character-based synchronous data transmission, 18–19
checksums
  calculating IP, 449
  ICMP packet processing, 433, 440
  Linux network interface device features, 64
  packet transmission and, 101
  receiving data in TCP, 476, 479, 484–485
  receiving IGMP packets, 443
  receiving packets in UDP, 462–463, 471–472
  sending data via UDP, 306–307
  sending packets from IP, 450, 452
  socket buffer structure and, 256
  TCP fragmentation, 262
  turning off on UDP packets, 142
CIDR (Classless Interdomain Routing), 48, 554
CIR (Committed Information Rate), 31
classes, IP address, 48
client-server programming, 53
cloning, socket buffers, 265, 268–270
CLOSE state, TCP, 489
`clusters`, extending `mbufs` with, 245

CO (central office), 9–10, 36–37
CO (Connection Oriented) service, 45–46
coded transmission, history of, 6
Committed Information Rate (CIR), 31
Common Object Request Broker Architecture (CORBA), 54
compressed form, IPv6 addresses, 556–557
Computer Systems Research Group (CSRG), 42
concurrency, embedded OS and, 56
`connect` call
  overview of, 136–137
  and UDP, 290–292
Connection Oriented (CO) service, 45–46
connectionless protocols, 13
connection-oriented protocols, 13
control field, in HDLC framing, 25
control messages, in UDP, 301–302
copying
  data from user space, UDP, 306–307
  socket buffers, 268–270
  TCP/IP stack and data, 57
CORBA (Common Object Request Broker Architecture), 54
count-oriented synchronous protocols, 19–20
`cp_copy_to_iovec` function, 499
CSMA/CD (Carrier Sense Multiple Access with Collision Detect), 15, 45
CSRG (Computer Systems Research Group), 42
`csum_copy_err` function, 472

D

DARPA (Defense Advanced Research Projects Agency), 42
data communication
  connectionless protocols, 13
  connection-oriented protocols, 13
  digital data rate hierarchy in public network, 36–37
  introduction, 3–4
  Linux TCP/IP source code, 4–5
  local area networks, 14–15
  networking standards, 37–39
  OSI seven-layer network model, 11–13
  packets and frames, 13–14
  wide area networks. *see* WANs (wide area networks)

Index

data communication, history of, 5–11
 character coded transmission, 6–8
 coded transmission and printing telegraph, 6
 events in, 7
 evolution of, 5–6
 measuring speeds of, 8–9
 multiplexing channels, 10–11
 over telephony voice network, 9–10
data communications equipment (DCE), 21
Data Link Connection Indicator (DLCI), 30
data link layer, OSI
 address translation at, 205
 defined, 12
 flow control and, 17
 LANs at, 14–15
 in TCP/IP, 45–46
 as X.25 protocol stack, 22
data transmission, through UDP and TCP, 275–348
 initiating connection at transport layer, 290–297
 overview of, 275–276
 socket layer glue for. *see* socket layer glue
 transport layer socket initialization, 286–289
 via TCP. *see* TCP (Transmission Control Protocol), data transmission via
 via UDP, 297–307
DCE (data communications equipment), 21
`DECLARE_TASKLET` macro, 184
`DECLARE_TASKLET_DISABLE` macro, 184
Default Table FIB rule, 375
Defense Advanced Research Projects Agency (DARPA), 42
de-fragmentation, IPv6, 573–575
`del_timer` function, 186
delayed acknowledgment timer, TCP
 defined, 342
 functions managing, 335
 other TCP timers vs., 334
 `tcp_delack_timer` function, 342–345
de-multiplexing, transport layer, 203–205
destination cache, 206–214
 defined, 206
 `dst_dev_notifier` structure, 210
 `dst_entry` structure, 206–209

`dst_ops` structure, 210–211
 garbage collection, 214–216
 overview of, 206
 sending packets using, 228–229
 utility functions, 211–214
destination options, IPv6, 563
`destructor` function, 95
`dev_add_pack` function, 177, 179
`dev_alloc_name` function, 83–84
`dev_alloc_skb` function, 267
`dev_boot_phase` global variable, 85
`dev_get_by_name` function, 85
`dev_init_scheduler` function, 84
`dev_open` function, 91–92
`dev_queue_xmit` function, 100–103, 192–193
`dev_remove_pack` function, 177
device registration, defined, 172
DHCP (Dynamic Host Protocol), 554
dial pulses, telephone data transmission, 9
digital data rate hierarchy in public network, 36–37
Digital Subscriber Lines (DSL)
 broadband vs., 14
 using analog modulations, 11
Direct Memory Access (DMA), 15
directories, TCP/IP source code, 4–5
DLCI (Data Link Connection Indicator), 30
DMA (Direct Memory Access), 15
`do_ioctl` function, 94
`do_time_wait` function, 479
dotted decimal notation, IPv4 addresses in, 556
double underscore (__), defined, 477
`driver_register` function, 80–81
drivers, ATM, 32
DSL (Digital Subscriber Lines)
 broadband vs., 14
 using analog modulations, 11
`dst_alloc` function, 212–213
`dst_clone` function, 213
`dst_confirm` function, 214, 305
`dst_destroy` function, 213
`dst_dev_event` function, 215–216
`dst_dev_notifier` structure, 210
`dst_entry` structure
 defining individual entry in destination cache, 206–209
 route table, 361
 routing input packets, 397
`dst_free` function, 213
`dst_hold` call, 397
`dst_hold` function, 213
`dst_link_failure` function, 214
`dst_negative_advice` function, 214

`dst_ops` structure, 210–211
`dst_run_gc` function, 215
DTMF (Dual-Tone Multi-Frequency) tones, 10
Dual-Tone Multi-Frequency (DTMF) tones, 10
Dynamic Host Protocol (DHCP), 554
dynamic routing, defined, 352

E

e100_probe
 calling driver's probe function, 81–82
 device discovery, 77–79
 `net_device` initialization, 72
EBCDIC, 18–19
EEPROM, 76
embedded systems, TCP/IP in, 54–56
Encapsulating Security Payload (ESP), 236
encapsulation, and OSI model, 45
End System (ES), 34–36
ES (End System), 34–36
ESP (Encapsulating Security Payload), 236
ESTABLISHED state, TCP
 backlog queue, 485
 processing data segments in, 495–503
 receive state processing, 490–491, 494
Ethernet, 14–15, 45
extension headers, IPv6
 field values, 562–563
 format, 560–561
 IPv6 family initialization, 566

F

fast path processing
 defined, 395
 header prediction formula for, 496–497
 of input packets, 396–400
 IPv6 fragmentation, 571–573
 Linux TCP vs. Van Jacobsen algorithm for, 495–496
 of output packets, 409–411
 TCP prequeue and, 481
 TCP socket-level receive, 517
 UDP connected sockets?, 290
FDM (Frequency Division Multiplexing), 10
FECN (Forward Explicit Congestion Notification), 31
FIB (Forwarding Information Base)
 API, 381–387
 defined, 351

616 Index

initialization, 379–381
internal data structure, 370–373
internal kernel interface, 331–334, 387–393
routing and IPv6, 598–601
rules, 374–379
table hash functions, 393–395
tables, 369–370
`fib_hash_init` function, 379–381
`fib_info` structure, 372–373, 393
`fib_lookup` function, 377–379, 415
`fib_new_table` function, 389
`fib_nh` structure, 373
`fib_result` structure, 204–205, 388–389
`fib_rule` structure, 374–376
`fib_rules_init` function, 379
`fib_rules_tclass` function, 377
`fib_select_default` function, 379, 417
`fib_table` structure, 370–371, 393–395
`fib_validate_source` function, 390–393
`fib6_lookup` function, 601
`fib6_node` structure, 600
fields, FR header, 30
files, Linux naming conventions, 172
filters, TCP/IP data link layer, 46
FIN, 517
`FIN_WAIT_2` state, 333, 491–492, 506–507
flags
    IPv4 routing, 386–387
    network interface driver, 89–90
    routing table entry, 382–383
flow control, 17
`flowi` structure
    overview of, 357–361
    slow path routing of input packets, 400–402
    slow path routing of output packets, 411
flush timer, 365
`fn_hash_delete` function, 394
`fn_hash_dump` function, 395
`fn_hash_flush` function, 395
`fn_hash_insert` function, 394
`fn_hash_lookup` function, 394
`fn_hash_select_default` function, 395
Format Prefix (FP), IPv6 address types and, 558
formats, HDLC frames, 25–26
Forward Acknowledged (FACKs), 331–334
Forward Explicit Congestion Notification (FECN), 31

Forwarding Information Base. *see* FIB (Forwarding Information Base)
Fourier, Joseph, 10
Fourier series, 10
FP (Format Prefix), IPv6 address types and, 558
FR (Frame Relay Bearer Server), 29–31
`frag_protocol` structure, 574
fragmentation
    IPv6, 571–573
    overview of, 260
    `sk_buff` and, 261–262
fragmentation header, IPv6, 562
Frame Relay Bearer Server (FR), 29–31
frames
    HDLC, 25–26
    packets vs, 13–14
    in TCP/IP data link layer, 45
`free_divert_blk` function, 87
`freeaddrinfo` function, 149
Frequency Division Multiplexing (FDM), 10

G

garbage collection
    destination cache, 214–216
    timer, 365
garbage collection, route cache, 365–369
    `ip_rt_init`, 366
    overview of, 365
    route flush timer,
        `rt_flush_timer`, 365–366
    `rt_cache_flush`, 367–368
    `rt_check_expire`, 366
    `rt_garbage_collect`, 366–367
    `rt_run_flush`, 368–369
    timer, `rt_periodic_timer`, 365
gateway address, 352
`get_stats` function, 94
`getaddrinfo` function, 148–149
`getnameinfo` function, 149
`getsockopt` function, 140–143, 277
GNU Public License (GPL), 4
GPL (GNU Public License), 4
Graphical User Interfaces (GUIs), 54
groups, IGMP, 448
growing slab cache, 247–248
GUIs (Graphical User Interfaces), 54

H

`hard_start_xmit` function, 92–93, 258
hardware header (HH) cache, 206, 229–231

`hash` function, 278
hash table function, UDP, 465–467
HDLCs (High Level Data Link) protocols
    FR and, 29–30
    framing, 25–26
    SDLC as member of, 20
    sliding windows, 26–28
    types and configurations of, 23–24
    variants of, 23
header prediction, TCP
    fast path and, 481
    formula for, 496–497
    overview of, 495–496
    TCP processing data segments, 498–499
headers, IPv6, 560–563
heap-based memory allocation, 242–243
HH (hardware header) cache, 206, 229–231
High Level Data Link. *see* HDLCs (High Level Data Link) protocols
hold the device, defined, 545
hop-by-hop options, IPv6, 562

I

IAB (Internet Architecture Board), 57
IANA (Internet Assigned Number Authority), 58
ICMP (Internet Control Message Protocol)
    `icmp_control` array, 431–432
    for IPv6, ICMPv6, 588–591
    network layer IP and, 431–438
    overview of, 431
    packet processing, 433–438
    sending packets, 438–440
`icmp_echo` function, 438
`icmp_init` function, 175
`icmp_push_reply` function, 439
`icmp_ratemask` function, 238
`icmp_rcv` function, 433–434
`icmp_redirect` function, 438
`icmp_reply` function, 438–439
`icmp_timestamp` function, 438
`icmp_unreach` function, 435–437
ICMPv6 header, 562
`icmpv6_rcv` function, 588–591
IETF (Internet Engineering Task Force), 38, 57
`ifindex`, `net_device`, 63
`iflink`, `net_device`, 63
IGMP (Internet Group Management Protocol), and multicast, 440–450

Index 617

adding and leaving groups, 448
handling IGMP queries, 444–447
handling IGMP reports, 447–448
`ip_mc_socklist` structure, 442
`ip_mreqn` structure, 441–442
overview of, 440–451
receiving IGMP packets, 442–444
replaced with MDL in IPv6, 596–597
`igmp_heard_query` function, 443, 444–447
`igmp_heard_report` function, 444, 448
`igmp_mc_proc_init` function, 354
`igmp_rcv` function, 442–444
`igmp6_event_query` function, 597
`igmp6_event_report` function, 597
`igmp6_init` function, 596–597
IKE (Internet Key Exchange), 236
`in_dev_get` function, 232
`in_device` structure, 232–236
　`in_dev_get` function, 232
　IPv4 configuration utility functions, 234–236
　`ipv4_devconf` structure, 233–234
　overview of, 232–233
individual retransmit timer. *see* write timer, TCP
`inet_add_protocol` function, 203
`inet_addr_type` function, 390
`inet_connection_sock` structure, 325–327
`inet_connection_sock_af_ops` structure for TCP, 289
`inet_create` function, 160–161
`inet_csk_clear_xmit_timers` function, 335
`inet_csk_init_xmit_timers` function, 335
`inet_csk_reset_xmit_timers` function, 335
`inet_del_protocol` function, 203
`inet_init` function
　IP protocol initialization, 353
　IPv4 member protocol registration, 129
　TCP/IP initialization, 175
`inet_initpeers`, 353–354
`inet_peer` structure, 418–419
`inet_protos` array, 201–203
`inet_protosw` structure, 127–129, 130–131
`inet_register_protosw` function, 127
`inet_rt_newroute` function, 384
`inet_rtm_delroute` function, 384
`inet_rtm_delrule` function, 376
`inet_rtm_newrule` function, 377
`inet_select_addr` function, 393, 414
`inet_select_address` function, 236

`inet_sock` structure, 119–121
`inet_timewait_sock` structure, 504–505
`inet_unregister_protosw` function, 127–129
`inet6_dev` structure, 563–564
`inet6_dgram_ops` structure, 568–569
`inet6_init` function, 564–566
`inet6_protocol` structure, 566–567
information format, HDLC frames, 25
information hiding, principle of OSI model, 45
`init` function, 63, 70
`init_completion` function, 81
`init_timer` function, 185
initialization
　`AF_NET` family member protocols, 202
　ARP, 224–225, 420–424
　FIB, 379–381
　`inet_protosw` structure, 130–131
　IP protocol, 353–354
　IPv6 fragment protocol, 574
　Ipv6 protocol family, 564–567
　IPv6 TCP, 584–586
　MLD protocol, 596–597
　neighbor system, 221–223
　protocol family, 525–527
　protocol family module, 527–529
　queuing layer, 189–191
　TCP socket, 286–289
　transport layer socket, 286–289
initialization, network device
　dynamic network interface driver, 77–83
　`net_device`, 72–77
　overview of, 70–72
initialization, socket layer, 124–133
　family values and protocol switch table, 125–126
　member protocol registration/initialization in IPv4, 129–131
　overview of, 124
　protocol switch registration, 127–129
　registration of protocols with socket layer, 131–133
　`sock_init` function, 124–125
initialization, TCP/IP stack, 175–180
　overview of, 175
　packet handler lists, 179–180
　packet handler lists and pseudo protocol types, 177–178
　packet handler registration and de-registration, 176–177
`inode`, 164
input, Ipv6, 577–580
input packet queues, 188–189

input packets, routing, 395–407
　fast path, 396–400
　Ipv6, 601
　main input route resolving function, 400–407
　overview of, 395–396
Integrated Services Digital Network (ISDN), 31
interface functions, FIB, 389–393
Intermediate System (IS), 33
internal kernel interface, FIB
　FIB interface functions, 389–393
　`fib_result` structure, 388–389
　`kern_rta` structure, 387–388
International Telecommunications Union (ITU) specifications, 21–22, 31
Internet Architecture Board (IAB), 57
Internet Assigned Number Authority (IANA), 58
Internet Control Message Protocol. *see* ICMP (Internet Control Message Protocol)
Internet Engineering Task Force (IETF), 38, 57
Internet Group Management Protocol. *see* IGMP (Internet Group Management Protocol), and multicast
Internet Key Exchange (IKE), 236
Internet peers, 418–419
Internet Protocol
　IP. *see* IP (Internet Protocol)
　version 4. *see* IPv4 (Internet Protocol version 4)
　version 6. *see* IPv6 (Internet Protocol version 6)
`ioctl` functions, 386–387, 534–538
`iovec` structure, socket API, 139–140
IP (Internet Protocol)
　forwarding, 352
　history of IPv6, 554
　initialization, 353–354
　packet handler registration, 179–180
　routing packets in, 450–457
　Routing Policy Database in, 351–353
　in TCP/IP, 47
IP addresses
　ARP in, 49–50
　passing through sockets, 133–134
　scheme, 47–49
　translation at OSI data link layer, 205
`ip_append_data` function, 305, 449–450
`ip_append_page` function, 450

618 Index

ip_cmsg_send function, 301
ip_dev_find function, 389–390, 413
ip_fib_init function, 379–380
ip_generic_getfrag, 306–307
ip_init, 175, 353–354
ip_local_deliver function, 455
ip_local_deliver_finish function, 455–457
ip_mc_join_group function, 448
ip_mc_leave_group function, 448
ip_mc_socklist structure, 442
ip_mkroute_input function, 403
ip_mkroute_output function, 417
ip_mr_init function, 175
ip_mreqn structure, 441–442
ip_output function, 191–192
ip_packet_type function, 179–180
ip_queue_xmit function, 450
ip_rcv function, 204, 451–453
ip_rcv_finish function, 453–454
ip_recv_error function, 470
ip_route_connect function
  route cache, 363–364
  routing output packets, 407–408
  and UDP, 291–292
ip_route_input function, 396, 453
ip_route_input_slow function
  finding slow path route, 400
  route cache, 364–365
  routing input packets, 396
ip_route_ioctl function, 386–387
ip_route_output call, 303
ip_route_output flow function, 408–409
ip_route_output_key function, 409–410
ip_route_output_flow function, 408–409, 450
ip_route_output_key function, 409–411
ip_route_output_slow function
  route cache, 364–365
  routing output packets, 411–417
  routing TCP output packets, 411–417
ip_rt_init function, 366
ip_rt_put function, 363
ip6_output function, 575–576
ip6_output_finish function, 576–577
ip6_output2 function, 576
ip6_route_input function, 601
ip6_route_output function, 600–601
ipcm_cookie structure, 302
IPSec, 236
IPv4 (Internet Protocol version 4)
  address conversion functions, 148–149
  directory for, 4
  expressing in dotted decimal notation, 556
  expressing in mixed notation, 556–557
  flowi structure, 357–358
  history of, 554
  in_device structure for, 232–236
  member protocol registration and initialization in, 129–131
  receive routine, 204
  routing, 351–353
ipv4_devconf structure, 233–234
ipv4_dst_check function, 361–362
ipv4_dst_destroy function, 362
ipv4_dst_ifdown function, 362
ipv4_negative_advise function, 362–363
IPv6 (Internet Protocol version 6), 553–602
  address conversion functions, 148–149
  addressing, 555–560
  auto configuration, 598
  defragmentation, 573–575
  directory for, 4
  extension header field values, 562–564
  facilities, 554–555
  flowi structure, 357–361
  fragmentation, 571–573
  history of, 554
  ICMP protocol for, 588–591
  inet6_dev structure, 563–564
  input, 577–580
  Multicast Listener Discovery protocol, 596–597
  Neighbor Discovery protocol, 591–595
  output, 575–577
  packet format, 560–562
  protocol family initialization, 564–567
  routing and IPv6 FIB, 598–602
  sock address type, sockaddr_in6, 147–148
  socket implementation, 568–571
  TCP, 584–588
  UDP, 581–584
ipv6_frag_init function, 574
ipv6_frag_rcv function, 574–575
ipv6_fragment structure, 571–573
ipv6_input_finish function, 579–580
ipv6_packet_init function, 567
ipv6_packet_type structure, 567
ipv6_pinfo structure, 570–571
ipv6_rcv function, 577–579
IS (Intermediate System), 33
ISCK_TIME_DACK, 334
ISCK_TIME_KEEOPEN, 334
ISCK_TIME_PROBE0, 334
ISCK_TIME_RETRANS, 334
ISDN (Integrated Services Digital Network), 31
ITU (International Telecommunications Union) specifications, 21–22, 31

J
jiffies, 186, 238

K
kdst_lock, 214–215
keepalive timer, TCP
  functions managing, 336
  other TCP timers vs., 334
  overview of, 342–345
  receive state processing, 492–493
  tcp_keepalive_timer function, 345–348
kern_rta structure, 387–388
kernel threading, 180–186
  bottom half and, 180–181
  macros for controlling tasklets, 184
  overview of, 180
  softIRQs and, 181–182
  tasklets, 182–183
  timers, 184–186
  utility functions for tasklets, 183–184
kfree_skb function, 267–268
kmem_cache_alloc function, 251–252
kmem_cache_create function, 249–251
kmem_cache_destroy function, 251
kmem_cache_free function, 252
kmem_cache_shrink function, 251
kmem_cache_size function, 251

L
LANs (local area networks)
  overview of, 14–15
  TCP/IP PHY layer, 45
  WANs vs., 14
LAPB (Link Access Protocol Balanced), 22–23
LAPF (Link Access Protocol Frame Relay), 29
latency, 57
layers, link, 56
leased lines, TDM, 37
license, GPL, 4
Link Access Protocol Balanced (LAPB), 22–23
Link Access Protocol Frame Relay (LAPF), 29
link control protocol, SDLC as, 20

Index **619**

link layers, 56
link-local addresses, IPv6, 559
Linux
    for embedded systems, 55, 57
    kernel timer API, 185–186
    kernels, 61
    MAC addresses in, 45
    memory allocation. *see* memory allocation
    network interface drivers. *see* network interface drivers, Linux
    popularity of, 41
    sockets. *see* sockets
    system requirements, 606
    TCP/IP source code, 4–5
    TCP/IP stack. *see* TCP/IP stack
linux, in pathnames, 4
linux/core directory, 4
linux/drivers/net directory, 4
linux/net directory, 4
linux/net/atm, 32
linux/net/ipv4 directory, 4
linux/net/ipv6 directory, 4
listen socket call, socket API, 136
LISTEN state
    TCP backlog queue, 485
    TCP receive state processing, 487, 489
lists
    managing socket buffer, 272–273
    packet handler, 177–180
    socket buffer allocation and, 264–265
local area networks. *see* LANs (local area networks)
Local Table FIB rule, 376
lock_sock function, 163
locks, garbage collection, 214–215
loopback address, IPv6, 557

M

MAC (Media Access Control)
    basic Ethernet Layer 2 interface, 15
    TCP/IP implementation and, 43
    TCP/IP PHY layer, 45
Macintosh, system requirements, 607
macros
    flowi structure, route cache, 359–360
    tasklet, 184
    TIMER_INITIALIZER, 185
Main Table FIB rule, 376
Maximum Transmission Unit. *see* MTU (Maximum Transmission Unit)
mblocks, STREAMS, 244
mbufs, 244–245, 246

Media Access Control. *see* MAC (Media Access Control)
member protocol, 129–131
memcpy_fromiovec function, 547
memory allocation, 239–273
    introduction, 240–241
    overview of, 239–240
    requirements, 241
    slab allocation, 247–252
    socket buffers and. *see* socket buffers
    traditional schemes for, 242–246
message types, ND, 593
minisocks, defined, 505
mixed notation, IPv6 addresses, 556–557
MLD (Multicast Listener Discovery), 596–597
mod_timer function, 186
modems, 11
modules
    driver, 61
    initialization, 527–529
Morse, Samuel, 5–6
Morse Code, 6
MSG_PROBE flag, 305–306
msghdr structure, 138–139, 279–280
MTU (Maximum Transmission Unit)
    defined, 47
    network interface service function, 94
    sending packets from socket layer, 545
multicast addresses, IPv6, 555, 559–560
multicast and IGMP, 440–448
    adding and leaving groups, 448
    handling IGMP queries, 444–447
    handling IGMP reports, 447–448
    ip_mc_socklist structure, 442
    ip_mreqn structure, 441–442
    overview of, 440–451
    receiving IGMP packets, 442–444
Multicast Listener Discovery (MLD), 596–597
multicast packets, receiving in UDP, 463
multipath routing, 416–417
multiplexing data communication channels, 10–11
mutex locking, 83

N

NADA program. *see* AF_NADA protocol family
nada receiving side setup, 550–551
nada sending side setup, 551
nada test program, 550

nada_address structure, 524
nada_bind function, 533–534
nada_cb (control block structure), 543
nada_create function, 532–533
nada_dev_list function, 545
nada_family_ops structure, 526–527
nada_find_listener function, 541–542
nada_init function, 528–529
nada_insert_socket function, 530
nada_ioctl function, 535
nada_ops structure, 525–526
nada_proto structure, 527
nada_rcv_queue_pkt function, 542–543
nada_rcv_skb function, 540–541
nada_recvmsg function, 538–539
nada_remove_socket function, 530
nada_sendmsg function, 543–548
nada_sk function, 531
nada_sock structure, 531
nada_sock_init function, 533
nada_sockets_list function, 530
nada_specific_ioctl function, 535–538
name, net_device, 62
naming conventions, 172
NAT (Network Address Translation), 351
ND (Neighbor Discovery), 216, 592
    advertisement message, 594–596
    defined, 555
    message types, 593
    multicast addresses in IPv6 and, 559–560
    nd_table structure, 591
    ndisc_hh_ops structure, 592
    overview of, 591
    solicitation message, 594
nd_table structure, 591
ndisc_generic_ops structure, 592
ndisc_hh_ops structure, 592
ndisc_rcv function, 593–594
ndisc_recv_na function, 594–595
ndisc_recv_ns function, 594
ndisc_router_discovery function, 595
neigh_add function, 227
neigh_clone function, 226
neigh_compat_output function, 227
neigh_confirm function, 226
neigh_connected_output function, 227
neigh_create function, 225
neigh_delete function, 227
neigh_destroy function, 225–226
neigh_dump_info function, 227

620 Index

neigh_event_send function, 226
neigh_is_connected function, 226
neigh_lookup function, 225
neigh_ops structure, 229–231
neigh_parms structure, 218–219
neigh_parms_alloc function, 219
neigh_parms_release function, 219
neigh_release function, 226
neigh_resolve_output function, 227
neigh_table structure
    ARP initialization of, 223–225
    instantiating ARP cache and, 422
    overview of, 216–218
neigh_table_init function, 221–223
neigh_update function, 227
neighbor cache, 216–228
    defined, 206
    initialization, 221–223
    neigh_parms structure, 218–219
    neigh_table structure, 216–218
    neighbor table and ARP, 223–225
    neighbour structure, 219–221
    overview of, 216
    proxy functions, 227–228
    sending packets using, 229–231
    utility functions, 225–228
Neighbor Discovery. *see* ND (Neighbor Discovery)
neighbor table
    and ARP, 223–225
    structure, 216–218
neighbour structure, 219–221
net_dev_init function, 189–190
net_device, 61–70
    device class information, 70
    implementing Layer 2 bridging, 70
    initialization of, 72–77
    as main driver structure, 61
    overview of, 61–62
    pointers to service routines, 68–69
    private part, 66–68
    public part, 62–65
net_proto_family data structure, 132–133
net_protocol structure, 201–202, 202
net_rx_action function, 195–196
NET_RX_SOFTIRQ, 187–188. *see also* queuing layer, receiving packets in
net_set_todo, 88
NET_TX_SOFTIRQ, 188–189
netdev_boot_setup, 71
netdev_chain, 106–107
netif_receive_skb function, 198–201
netif_rx , 97, 98–99
netif_rx_ni , 97
netlink mutex locking, 83
netlink semaphore, 83–84
netlink sockets, 144–145, 165–168

netlink_ops, 167–168
netlink_proto_init function, 168
netlink_rcv function, 169
netmasks
    IP addressing and, 49
    IPv4 and IPv6 expressing, 557
Network Address Translation (NAT), 351
network interface devices, 61
network interface drivers, Linux, 59–107
    ATM interfaced to Linux IP through, 32
    device discovery and dynamic initialization, 77–83
    directories for, 4–5
    introduction, 60–61
    network device initialization, 70–77
    network device structure, net_device, 61–70
    network interface devices, 61
    network interface registration, 83–89
    NOTIFIER chains and status notification, 103–107
    receiving packets, 95–100
    service functions, 90–95
    state flags, 89–90
    transmitting packets, 100–103
network interface drivers, registration, 83–89
    generic work of, 80–81
    overview of, 83–85
    sequence, 71
    utility functions, 85–89
network layer, IP, 349–458
    ARP, 419–431
    FIB application interface, 381–387
    FIB initialization, 379–381
    FIB internal data structures, 370–373
    FIB internal kernel interface, 387–393
    FIB rules, 374–379
    FIB table hash functions, 393–395
    FIB tables, 369–370
    ICMP, 431–438
    Internet peers and inet_peer structure, 418–419
    IP protocol initialization, 353–354
    IPv4 routing, 351–353
    multicast and IGMP. *see* IGMP (Internet Group Management Protocol), and multicast
    overview of, 349–350
    receiving packets, 450–457
    route cache. *see* route cache

    routing cache, 351–353
    routing input packets. *see* input packets, routing
    routing output packets. *see* output packets, routing
    Routing Policy Database, 351–353
    routing theory, 350–351
    sending ICMP packets, 438–440
network layer, OSI
    defined, 12
    routing at, 205
    in TCP/IP, 47–50
    as X.25 packet layer, 21–22
network queuing layer
    netif_rx , 98–99
    netif_rx_ni , 97
    overview of, 95–97
    softnet_data , 99–100
networking standards, 37–39
Network-to-Network Interfaces (NNI), 32, 33–34
next hop, 352, 354
nlmsghdr structure, 165–167
NNI (Network-to-Network Interfaces), 32, 33–34
no next header value, IPv6, 562
no_tcp_socket function, 478
notifier chains, 105–107
notifier_call, 106–107
notifier_call_chain, 87, 106
notifier_chain_register, 105
notifier_chain_unregister, 105
number assignments, Internet, 58

O

oif (output interface), 414–415
OOB (Out-of-Band) data, 516, 518–520
open function, 91–92
open socket list, 529–530
OSI (Open System Interconnect) seven-layer network model
    lower layers, 11–12
    overview of, 11
    and TCP/IP. *see* TCP/IP, and OSI reference model
    upper layers, 12–13
    X.25 using first three layers of, 21–22
Out-of-Band (OOB) data, 516, 518–520
out-of-band signaling, 31
output
    Ipv6, 575–577
    neighbor cache, 227
    side packet processing, 191–192
    TCP data transmission, 317–322
    UDP data transmission, 302–306

output interface (oif), 414–415
output packets, routing, 407–417
   ip_route_connect , 407–408
   ip_route_output_flow , 408–409
   ip_route_output_key , 409–410
   ip_route_output_slow , 411–417
   Ipv6, 600–601
   overview of, 407

P

packet handlers, TCP/IP stack initialization
   defined, 176
   lists, 179–180
   lists and pseudo protocol types, 177–178
   naming conventions for registration facility, 172
   overview of, 175
   registration and de-registration, 176–177
packet queuing layer. *see* queuing layer
packet sockets, 144
packet transmission
   ICMP, 438–440
   from IP, 448–450
   overview of, 100–103
   queuing disciplines, 100–103, 191–193
   from socket layer, 543–548
   udp_sendmsg function and, 302–306
   using caches, 228–231
packet_type structure, 176–177, 179
packets
   forwarding, 351
   frames vs., 13–14
   IP protocol responsible for routing, 352
   IPv6 format, 560–562
   processing with ICMP, 433–438
   receiving, 95–100
   receiving and processing ARP, 424–431
   receiving IGMP, 442–444
   receiving in protocol family, 529–539
   receiving in TCP. *see* TCP (Transmission Control Protocol), receiving packets in
   receiving in UDP. *see* UDP (User Datagram Protocol), receiving packets in
   recursion, 103
   routing in IP, 450–457
   transport layer de-multiplexing and internal routing of, 201–205

paging schemes, 240
Passive Optical Networks (PONs), 31
pathnames, 4
PAWS (Protection Against Wrapped Sequence Numbers)
   defined, 488
   TCP processing data segments, 498, 501
   TIME_WAIT state processing, 506, 509
PC and Windows, system requirements, 606
PCI devices
   discovering, 77–83
   net_device initialization, 73–75
   network interface driver registration sequence, 71
PCM (pulse code modification), 36
PDU (Protocol Data Unit), 31
Permanent Virtual Circuits. *see* PVCs (Permanent Virtual Circuits)
physical layer (PHY), OSI
   ATM, 33
   defined, 11–12
   FR, 29
   LAN complexity in, 15
   TCP/IP, 45
Plain Old Telephone System (POTS), 11
pneigh_enqueue function, 228
pneigh_lookup function, 228
Point-to-Point Protocol (PPP), 46
Policy Routing Using Linux (Marsh), 351
PONs (Passive Optical Networks), 31
ports, sockets vs., 134
POTS (Plain Old Telephone System), 9–11
PPP (Point-to-Point Protocol), 46
pre-allocated fixed-size buffers, 243–244
prequeue, TCP
   overview of, 481
   TCP receive handler and, 477–478
   TCP socket-level receive and, 514–515
   tcp_prequeue , 482–484
   tcp_prequeue-init , 482
   within ucopy structure, 481–482
presentation layer, OSI, 12–13, 54
printing telegraph, 6
/proc file system
   configuring TCP/IP via, 237
   IPv6 protocol family initialization, 565
   slab cache allocation statistics in, 274
process_backlog function, 196–198

Protection Against Wrapped Sequence Numbers. *see* PAWS (Protection Against Wrapped Sequence Numbers)
proto structure, 161–163, 276–279
proto_ops structure, 122–124
Protocol Data Unit (PDU), 31
protocol families
   initialization of, 125–126, 202
   Ipv6 initialization, 564–567
   list of registered, 111–112
   overview of, 522
   registration with socket layer, 131–133
protocol families, implementing, 521–551
   address family initialization, 525–527
   creating sample AF_NADA protocol family, 523–525
   introduction, 522
   module initialization, 527–529
   receiving packets in AF_NADA family, 539–543
   sending packets from socket layer, 543–548
   socket layer interface, 529–539
   test setup for AF_NADA, 548–551
protocol stack layer, X.25, 22
protocol switch, 127–129
protocol switch table
   defined, 127
   protocol registration facility vs., 203
   socket layer initialization, 125–126
protosw, 203
pseudo protocol types, 177–178
pskb_copy function, 269
pskb_may_pull function, 461, 475–476
pskb_trim function, 462
PSTN (Public Switched Telephone Network)
   ATM for modern, 31
   purpose of VCs in, 21
   WANs evolving from, 13
Public Switched Telephone Network. *see* PSTN (Public Switched Telephone Network)
pulse code modification (PCM), 36
PVCs (Permanent Virtual Circuits)
   defined, 13
   FR managing, 31
   X.25 packet layer managing, 21

Q

Q.931, 31
QoS (Quality of Service)

622   Index

ATM and, 31
IPv4 vs. IPv6 routing, 555
queries
   IGMP, 444–447
   Multicast Listener Discovery, 597
queues
   slow path, 481
   socket buffers, 265
   TCP receive, 481–484
queuing disciplines
   packet transmission, 100–103, 191–193
   receiving packets, 95–100
queuing layer, 186–201
   initialization of, 189–191
   input side packet processing in, 187–188
   network device registration functions in, 85
   output side packet processing in, 188–189
   overview of, 186–187
   queuing transmitted packets, 191–192
   X.25 protocol stack, 22
queuing layer, receiving packets in, 193–201
   `net_rx_action`, 195–196
   `netif_receive_skb`, 198–201
   overview of, 193–195
   `process_backlog`, 196–198

R

RA (Router Advertisement) message, 595
rate limiting, 238
raw socket, 144
`rcu_read_lock` function, 397
`RCV_SHUTDOWN` socket, 115
receive handler function, TCP, 474–480
receive handler function, UDP, 461–463
receive queue, TCP, 481–484
receive state processing, TCP, 486–495
receiving packets in IP, 450–457
`recv` call, socket API, 140
`recvfrom` call, socket API, 140
`recvmsg` call, socket API, 140
`recvmsg` function, 277
references
   FACKs, 332
   history of telecommunications, 6
   Linux kernels, 4, 181
   RFCs, 57, 603–604
   router configuration, 351
`register_netdav` function, 83, 85–86
`register_netdevice` function, 84, 85–86

`register_netdevice_notifier` function, 106
registration
   initialization, 76
   Linux infrastructure for, 173
   member protocol, 129–131
   network interface drivers. *see* network interface drivers, registration
   protocol, 203, 527–529
   protocol family, 131–133
   protocol switch, 127–129
   `rtnetlink`, 169
   TCP/IP stack initialization, 175–180
`release_sock` function, 163
`remove` function, 82
reports
   IGMP, 447–448
   MLD, 597
Request for Comments. *see* RFCs (Request for Comments)
reserving headroom, 260
resource map allocator, 242–243
`resume` function, 82
Re-Transmission Timeout (RTO) value, 507–508
retransmission timer, 336
RFCs (Request for Comments)
   on accompanying CD-ROM, 3
   list of referenced, 603–604
   TCP/IP standards, 38, 57
round trip time (RTT), TCP, 333
route cache, 354–369
   data structures, 354–361
   garbage collection, 365–369
   overview of, 351–353
   searching with `flowi` structure, 357–361
   using with RPDB in routing decisions, 351–352
   utility functions, 361–365
route hash table, 364
`route(8)` program, 381
routing
   handling IGMP reports, 447–448
   header, IPv6, 562
   input packets, 395–407
   internal packet, 201–205
   IPv4, 351–353
   IPv4 vs. IPv6, 555
   IPv6 FIB and, 598–601
   output packets, 407–419
   sockets, 145–146
   theory, 350–351
Routing Policy Database. *see* RPDB (Routing Policy Database)
routing table
   components of, 352

   defined, 352
   entry flags, 382–383
   information stored in, 351
   route types, 356
   as Routing Policy Database, 349
   `rtable` data structure, 355–357
routing table cache, 205
RPDB (Routing Policy Database)
   defined, 349
   FIB application interface, 381–387
   FIB initialization, 379–381
   FIB internal data structures, 370–373
   FIB internal kernel interface, 387–393
   FIB rules, 374–379
   FIB table hash functions, 393–395
   FIB tables, 369–370
   IPv4 routing, 555
   overview of, 351–353
`rt_bind_peer` function, 363
`rt_cache_flush` function, 367–368
`rt_check_expire` function, 365, 366
`rt_flush_timer`, 365
`rt_garbage_collect` function, 366–367
`rt_hash_bucket` structure, 354–355
`rt_hash_code` function, 397
`rt_hash_table` structure
   route cache and, 354–355
   routing input packets, 397
   routing output packets, 409
`rt_intern_hash` function, 364
`rt_periodic_timer`, 365
`rt_run_flush` function, 365, 368–369
`rt_set_nexthop` function, 364
`rt6_info` structure, 598–599
`rt6key` structure, 599
`rtable` data structure, 355–357, 361
`rtentry` structure, 382–383
`rtmsg` structure, 384–386
rtnetlink sockets
   functions and structures used by, 383–387
   `netlink_rcv` function, 169
   `rtnetlink` socket registration, 169
   `rtnetlink_link` structure, 168–169
   from user program, 170
RTO (Re-Transmission Timeout) value, 507–508
RTT (round trip time), TCP, 333
rules, FIB, 374–379

S

SACK (Selective Acknowledgement), TCP, 319–321
SAR (Segmentation and Reassembly), ATM, 32–33, 35–36

Index

SAs (Security Associations), 236
scatter gather IO, 101
scope, route, 358–359
SDLC (Synchronous Data Link Control), 20
security
    and Linux capabilities, 146–147
    TCP receive handler and, 477
    TCP receive state processing and, 489
    TCP syncookies and, 333
Security Associations (SAs), 236
Security Policy Database (SPD), 236
segmentation, TCP
    defined, 260
    overview of, 261–262
    `skb_shared_info` structure and, 263–264
Segmentation and Reassembly (SAR), ATM, 32–33, 35–36
Selective Acknowledgement (SACK), TCP, 319–321
semaphore protection, 56
send call, socket API, 137
`send` function, socket API, 137
`SEND_SHUTDOWN` socket, 115, 492
`sendmsg` function, socket API, 137, 277
`sendsockopt` function, socket API, 140–143
`sendto` function, socket API, 137
service functions
    `net_device` initialization, 73
    network interface driver, 90–95
Service Specific Convergence Function (SSCF), 35
Service Specific Convergence Sublayers (SSCS), 35
Session Initiation Protocol (SIP), 54
session layer, OSI, 12, 53–54
`set_multicast_list` function, 92
`setsockopt` function, 277, 282–286
signaling protocol, FR, 31
Simple Internet Transition (SIT), 565
Simple Network Management Protocol (SNMP), 54
SIP (Session Initiation Protocol), 54
SIT (Simple Internet Transition), 565
`sit_init` function, 565–566
`sk_add_backlog` function, 477
`sk_backlog` function, 117
`sk_backlog_receive` function, 119
`sk_buffs` . *see* socket buffers
`sk_wake_async` function, 490
`skb_append` function, 272
`skb_clone` function, 268
`skb_cloned` function, 269
`skb_copy` function, 269
`skb_copy_and_csum_datagram_iovec` function, 471

`skb_cow` function, 268
`skb_dequeue` function, 272
`skb_dequeue_tail` function, 272
`skb_frag_t` structure, 263–264
`skb_get` function, 270
`skb_headroom` function, 270
`skb_insert` function, 273
`skb_peek_tail` function, 273
`skb_pull` function, 271
`skb_push` function, 271
`skb_put` function, 270
`skb_queue_empty` function, 273
`skb_queue_head` function, 272
`skb_queue_head_init` function, 273
`skb_queue_len` function, 273
`skb_queue_purge` function, 273
`skb_queue_tail` function, 272
`skb_recv_datagram` function, 470
`skb_reserve` function, 271
`skb_share_check` function, 269–270
`skb_shared` function, 269
`skb_shared_info` function, 261, 263–264
`skb_tailroom` function, 270–271
`skb_trim` function, 271–272
`skbuff_head_cache`, 259
slab allocation, 247–252
    cache utility functions, 249–251
    freeing of slab caches and, 251–252
    overview of, 247
    slab allocator, 247–248
slab allocator, 247–248
slab cache, 247–252. *see also* slab allocation
    allocatinon and freeing slabs from, 251–252
    allocation and freeing of, 251–252
    allocation statistics in /proc file system, 274
    creating and manipulating, 249–251
    slab allocation and, 247
    slab allocator and, 247–248
sliding windows, 17, 26–28
slow path processing
    defined, 395–396
    overview of, 400–407
    receiving packets in TCP, 480–481, 497
SMI (Structure of Management Information), 54
SMP (Symmetric Multiprocessing), 181
SNA (Systems Network Architecture), 18, 21
sndmsg call, socket API, 137–138
SNMP (Simple Network Management Protocol), 54
`SO_KEEPALIVE` socket option, 284, 345

`SO_SNDTIMEO` socket option, 309–310
`sock` structure, 113–121
    defined, 113
    `inet_sock` structure, 119–121
    overview of, 113, 114–119
    `sock_common` structure, 114
`sock_addr_nada` structure, 523–524
`sock_alloc` function, 158
`sock_alloc_inode` function, 159–160
`sock_common` structure, 114–115
`sock_create` function, 157–158
`SOCK_DGRAM` sockets. *see also* UDP (User Datagram Protocol), data transmission via
    defined, 135
    `ip_route_connect` , 363–364
`sock_init` function, 124–125
`sock_queue_rcv` function, 116
`sock_queue_rcv_skb` function, 469
`sock_register` function, 131–132
`SOCK_STREAM` sockets. *see also* TCP (Transmission Control Protocol), data transmission via
    defined, 135
    `ip_route_connect` , 363–364
`sock_unregister` function, 132
`SOCK_URGINLINE` flag, 519
`sock_write_queue` function, 116
`sockaddr` structure, 134
`sockaddr_in6`, IPv6 sock address type, 147–148
socket API functions
    accept, 136
    bind socket, 136
    connect, 136–137
    flags argument, 137
    `getsockopt` and `sendsockopt`, 140–143
    `iovec` structure, 139–140
    listen socket, 136
    `msghdr` structure, 138–139
    overview of, 53, 134–135
    `recv`, `recvfrom` and `recvmsg`, 140
    send, sendto and sendmsg, 137
    send and sendto, 137
    sndmsg , 137–138
    socket, 135–136
    socketpair, 137
socket API, implementing system calls, 149–157
    implementing protocol internal socket functions, 155–157
    implementing socket layer internal functions, 153–155
    overview of, 149–151
    socket multiplexor, 151–152
socket buffers, 252–273
    allocation, 258

allocation and de-allocation functions, 266–268
allocation and lists, 264–265
cloning, 265
copying and cloning, 268–270
defined, 113
fragmentation and segmentation, 260–264
managing lists of, 272–273
manipulating pointer fields, 270–272
overview of, 252–253
queues, 265
sk_buff, 254–258
using in TCP/IP, 259–260
socket de-multiplexing, 125
socket function, socket API, 135–136
socket layer glue, 276–286
msghdr structure, 279–280
proto structure, 276–279
TCP, 281
TCP options, 281–286
UDP, 280–281
socket layer initialization, 124–133
family values and protocol switch table, 125–126
member protocol registration/initialization in IPv4, 129–131
overview of, 124
protocol switch registration, 127–129
registration of protocols with socket layer, 131–133
sock_init , 124–125
socket layer interface
facilitating with module registration, 527–529
IO control functions, 534–538
nada_bind, 533–534
open socket list, 529–530
socket creation, 531–533
socket list, 529–530
socket locks, 163
socket state, 159
socket structure, 113
socket_lock_t structure, 163
socket-level receive, TCP
receiving urgent data, 518–520
tcp_recvmsg , 510–518
socket-level receive, UDP, 469
socketpair call, socket API, 137
sockets, 109–170
accommodating IPv6, 147–148
creating IPv6, 568–571
creation of, 157–165
introduction, 110
IO system calls and, 164–165
IP addresses passing through, 133–134

netlink, 144–145, 165–168
overview of, 110–112
packet, 144
ports vs., 134
protocol families. *see* protocol families
raw, 144
routing, 145–146
rtnetlink for routing, 168–170
security and Linux capabilities, 146–147
sending data through UDP/TCP. *see* data transmission, through UDP and TCP
sock structure. *see* sock structure
socket API. *see* socket API functions
socket API system calls, 149–157
socket buffers, 113
socket layer initialization. *see* socket layer initialization
socket structure, 113, 121–124
softirqs
defined, 172
kernel threading and, 181–182
receiving packets, 96–97
softnet_data structure, 99–100, 188–189
solicitation message, ND, 594
source code
on accompanying CD-ROM, 2, 607–608
copies of referenced RFCs, 3
Linux TCP/IP, 4–5
SPD (Security Policy Database), 236
speed measurement, history of, 8–9
SSCF (Service Specific Convergence Function), 35
SSCS (Service Specific Convergence Sublayers), 35
stack, ATM, 32–34
standards, networking, 37–39
standards, TCP/IP, 57
start bits, 8
state, net_device, 63
state flags, network interface driver, 89–90
stateful autoconfiguration, 598
stateless autoconfiguration, 554, 598
static routing, 352
status notification
notifier chains and, 103–105
overview of, 105–107
stop and wait acknowledgement, 17
stop bits, 8
stop function, 93–94
streams, synchronous data transmission, 16–17
STREAMS framework, 244

Strowger Switch, 10
struct nic, 95
struct proto, 281, 282
Structure of Management Information (SMI), 54
subnetting, IP addressing, 49
supervisory format, HDLC frames, 26
suspend function, 82
SVCs (Switched Virtual Circuits)
defined, 13
FR managing, 31
X.25 packet layer managing, 21
Switched Virtual Circuits. *see* SVCs (Switched Virtual Circuits)
switching fabric, ATM, 33
Symmetric Multiprocessing (SMP), 181
SYN, TIME_WAIT state processing, 506, 508
SYN_SENT state, TCP, 487–488, 489
synchronize_net function, 87
Synchronous Data Link Control (SDLC), 20
synchronous data transmission
vs. ATM, 16–17
bit stuffing, 20–21
bit-oriented, 20
character-based, 18–19
count-oriented protocols, 19–20
data transparency problem, 18–19
overview of, 18
syncookies, TCP, 333
sys_socket function, 157
sysctl (System Control)
configuring TCP/IP via, 237
manipulating neighbor table cache entries, 218–219
rate limiting with, 238
sysctl_tcp_rfc1337, 508
system calls, and sockets, 164–165
system calls, implementing, 149–157
system requirements, on CD-ROM accompanying book, 606–607
Systems Network Architecture (SNA), 18, 21

T

T1 interface, 45
tables, FIB
hash functions, 393–395
overview of, 369–370
tapif program, 549–550, 605
TASK_RUNNING state, TCP, 499
tasklet_disable function, 183
tasklet_enable function, 184
tasklet_init function, 183
tasklet_kill function, 183
tasklet_schedule function, 183
tasklet_struct structure, 182

Index

tasklets
  defined, 172
  macros for controlling, 184
  overview of, 182–183
  predefined softIRQs for running, 181–182
  utility functions for, 183–184
TCP (Transmission Control Protocol)
  header and segments, 52
  ip_route_connect, 363–364
  IPv6, 584–588
  IPv6 family initialization, 566
  overview of, 51
  segmentation, 261–262
  sockets, 53, 135
TCP (Transmission Control Protocol), data transmission via, 307–348
  control buffer, 322–324
  inet_connection_sock, 325–327
  initiating connection at transport layer, 282–287
  output, 317–322
  overview of, 307–308
  protocol block functions for, 282
  send state diagram, 308
  socket glue, 281
  socket initialization, 286–289
  socket options for, 281–286
  TCP control buffer, 322–324
  tcp_options_received, 329–331
  tcp_sendmsg, 309–317
  tcp_sock, 327–329, 331–334
  timers. see timers, TCP
TCP (Transmission Control Protocol), receiving packets in, 472–520
  backlog queue processing, 484–486
  fast path, 481–484
  overview of, 472–474
  prequeue, 481–484
  processing data segments in established state, 495–503
  receive handler function, tcp_v4_rcv, 474–480
  receive state processing, 486–495
  socket-level receive, 510–520
  TIME_WAIT state, 503–510
TCP (Transmission Control Protocol), routing output packets, 407–417
  ip_route_connect, 407–408
  ip_route_output_flow, 408–409
  ip_route_output_key, 409–410
  ip_route_output_slow main, 411–417
  Ipv6, 600–601
  overview of, 407
TCP control buffer, 322–334

inet_connection_sock structure, 325–327
  overview of, 322–325
tcp_options_received structure, 329–331
tcp_sock structure, 327–329, 331–334
tcp_ack function, 490
tcp_ack_snd function, 494–495
tcp_checksum_complete function, 479, 484–485
tcp_child_process function, 485
TCP_CORK option, 282–283
tcp_data_queue, 503
tcp_data_snd_check function, 494–495
tcp_data_wait function, 515
TCP_DEFER_ACCEPT option, 283
tcp_delete_keepalive_timer function, 336
tcp_event_data_recv function, 500–501
tcp_fast_parse_options function, 488
tcp_fast_path_on function, 497
tcp_fin_time function, 492
TCP_FIN_WAIT state, 492
TCP_INFO option, 283
tcp_info structure, 283–284
tcp_keepalive_timer function, 345–348
TCP_KEEPCNT option, 284
TCP_KEEPIDLE option, 284
TCP_KEEPINTVL option, 284–285
TCP_LINGER2 socket option, 285, 492
TCP_MAXSEG option, 285
TCP_NODEDELAY option, 285
tcp_options_received structure, 329–331
tcp_prequeue function, 478, 482–484
tcp_prequeue-init function, 482
tcp_probe_timer function, 341–342
TCP_QUICKACK option, 285
tcp_rcv function, 495
tcp_rcv_established function, 497–503
tcp_rcv_state_process function, 485, 486–495
tcp_rcv_synsent_state_process function, 488
tcp_rcv_synsent_state_progress function, 485
tcp_rec_urg function, 519–520
tcp_replace_ts_recent function, 489
tcp_reset function, 489
tcp_reset_keepalive_timer function, 336
tcp_retransmit_timer function, 338–341

tcp_send_dupack function, 488
tcp_sendmsg function, 309–317
  completion of, 315–317
  copying data from user space to socket buffer, 312–315
  overview of, 309–312
tcp_sequence function, 489
tcp_sock structure, 327–329, 331–334
TCP_SYN_SENT, 487–488
TCP_SYNCNT, 285–286
tcp_timewait_state_process function, 505–510
tcp_timewait_state_progress function, 479–480
tcp_transmit_skb function, 309–317
TCP_TW_ACK, 506
tcp_tw_schedule function, 507–509
tcp_v4_connect function, 282–287
tcp_v4_do_rcv function
  processing data segments in ESTABLISHED state, 495
  receive handler, 478
  receive state processing, 491
tcp_v4_hnd_req function, 485
tcp_v4_init function, 175
tcp_v4_lookup_listener function, 480
tcp_v4_rcv function, 474–480
tcp_v6_connect function, 586–588
TCP_WINDOW_CLAMP, 286
tcp_write_timer function, 336–338
TCPF_CLOSE_WAIT state, 310
TCPF_ESTABLISHED state, 310
TCP/IP, 41–58
  assigned numbers, 57–58
  as dominant protocol suite, 41
  in embedded systems, 54–55
  history of, 42
  implementing, 42–43
  not requiring reliable or sequenced packet delivery, 17
  RFCs for, 38
  sliding windows, 27
  specific requirements for, 55–57
  standards, 57
TCP/IP, and OSI reference model, 43–54
  application layer, 53–54
  data link layer, 45–46
  network layer, 47–50
  overview of, 43–44
  PHY layer, 45
  presentation layer, 54
  session layer, 53–54
  transport layer, 50–53
TCP/IP stack, 171–238
  caches. see cache

Index

configuring via `sysctl` and `/proc` filesystem, 237
infrastructure, 173
initialization, 175–180
internal packet routing, 201–203
introduction, 172
kernel threading. *see* kernel threading
link layer protocol values, 174
memory allocation requirements, 241
as part of Linux kernel, 3
protocol registration and protocol switch table, 203
queuing disciplines, 191–193
queuing layer initialization, 189–191
queuing layer, packet processing, 186–189
queuing layer, receiving packets in, 193–201
rate limiting and, 237
security, 236–237
stackable destination, 236
transport layer de-multiplexing, 203–205
`xfrm_lookup` function, 237
`tcpv6_prot` structure, 585–586
`tcpv6_protocol` structure, 584–585
TCs (Transmission Convergence) sublayers, 33
TDM (time division modulation), 36–37
telegraph, 5–7
telephony voice network
  history of, 9–10
  modems evolving from, 11
  signaling and call management terms from, 21
  WANs evolving from, 13
teletypes, 8
test setup, for `NADA` program, 548–551, 606
`tfp_transmit_skb` function, 317–322
time division modulation (TDM), 36–37
TIME_WAIT state, TCP, 503–510
  `inet_timewait_sock` structure, 504–505
  overview of, 503–504
  receive handler, 479–480
  receive state processing, 492
  `tcp_timewait_state_process`, 505–510
`TIMER_INITIALIZER` macro, 185
`timer_list` structure, 184–185
timers
  API functions for, 184–186

defined, 184
embedded OS requirement, 56
garbage collection, 365–369
initialization of, 75
timers, TCP, 334–348
  delayed acknowledgment timer, 342–345
  functions for, 335–336
  keepalive timer, 345–348
  overview of, 334
  window probe timer, 341–342
  write timer, 336–341
time-sharing, 54
timestamps
  TCP receive state processing, 488
  UDP socket-level receive, 471
Time-To-Live (TTL), 350
TIME-WAIT Assassination (TWA), 508
TLI (Transport Layer Interface), 53. *see also* socket API functions
`tos field`, `flowi` structure, 360–361
traffic engineering, FR, 31
Transformer (XFRM), 236–237
Transmission Control Protocol. *see* TCP (Transmission Control Protocol)
Transmission Convergence (TCs) sublayers, 33
Transport Layer Interface (TLI), 53. *see also* socket API functions
transport layer, OSI
  defined, 12
  de-multiplexing and internal routing of packets in, 201–205
  initiating connection at, 290–297
  receiving packets in, 459–460
  receiving packets in TCP. *see* TCP (Transmission Control Protocol), receiving packets in
  receiving packets in UDP. *see* UDP (User Datagram Protocol), receiving packets in
  socket initialization, 286–289
  in TCP/IP, 50–53
trunks, 10
TTL (Time-To-Live), 350
tun/tap module, 549
TWA (TIME-WAIT Assassination), 508

U

`ucopy` structure, 481–482
UDP (User Datagram Protocol)
  `ip_route_connect`, 363–364
  IPv6, 566, 581–584
  routing output packets. *see* output packets, routing
  sockets, 53, 134–135
  TCP/IP implementation and, 43

TCP/IP transport layer and, 50
UDP (User Datagram Protocol), data transmission via, 297–307
  copying data from user space, 306–307
  handling control messages in `udp_sendmsg`, 301–302
  initiating connection at transport layer, 290–292
  not requiring socket initialization, 286
  overview of, 297–298
  protocol block functions for, 281
  socket glue, 280
  `udp_sendmsg`, 298–300
  `udp_sendmsg` and packet output, 302–306
  `udphdr` structure, 300–301
UDP (User Datagram Protocol), receiving packets in
  backlog receive, 467–469
  hash table, 465–467
  multicast and broadcast packets, 464–465
  overview of, 461
  receive handler, `udp_rcv`, 461–463
  socket-level receive, 469–472
`udp_hash` function, 465–466
`udp_mcast_deliver` function, 462
`UDP_MIB_NOPORTS` count, 463
`udp_queue_rcv_skb` function, 464–465, 468–469
`udp_rcv` function, 461
`udp_recvmsg` function, 470–472
`udp_sendmsg` function
  handling control messages, 301–302
  overview of, 298–300
  packet output, 302–306
  socket-level receive, 469
`udp_v4_lookup` function, 462
`udp_v4_lookup_longway` function, 466–467
`udp_v4_mcast_deliver` function, 464–465
`udphdr` structure, 300–301
`udpv6_init` function, 581
`udpv6_prot` structure, 582–583
`udpv6_protocol` structure, 581
`udpv6_protosw` structure, 581–582
`udpv6_sendmsg` function, 583–584
`unhash` function, 278
UNI (User-to-Network Interfaces), ATM, 32–36
unicast addresses, IPv6, 555
`uninit` function, 92–93
Universal Test and Operations PHY Interface (UTOPIA) bus, 33

Index

Unix
  embedded systems and, 55
  history of, 42
  Linux compatibility with, 3
Unix Network Programming (Stevens), 53
unnumbered format, HDLC frames, 26
unregister_netdev function, 86–88
unregister_netdevice function, 86–88
unregister_netdevice_notifier function, 107
unspecified address, IPv6, 557–558
urgent data, receiving, 516, 518–520
User Datagram Protocol. *see* UDP (User Datagram Protocol)
user program, using rtnetlink from, 170
user space, copying data from, 306–307
User-to-Network Interfaces (UNI), ATM, 32–36
UTOPIA (Universal Test and Operations PHY Interface) bus, 33

V
Van Jacobsen algorithm
  implementing TCP connection with, 295

TCP fast path and, 481
TCP fast path in Linux vs., 495–496
VCs (virtual circuits)
  connection-oriented protocols and, 13
  Frame Relay Bearer Server and, 29–30
  introduced in X.25 protocol, 21

W
WANs (wide area networks), 15–36
  asynchronous transmission mode (ATM), 31–36
  asynchronous vs. synchronous data transmission, 16–17
  connection oriented protocols, 13
  evolving from PSTN, 13
  flow control and reliable transmission, 17
  Frame Relay Bearer Server, 29–31
  high level data link protocol, 23–26
  overview of, 15–16
  sliding windows, 26–28
  synchronous data transmission, 18–21
  TCP/IP PHY layer, 45
  types of interfaces, 16
  X.25 protocol, 21–22

watchdog timer, 75
whohas, 43
wide area networks. *see* WANs (wide area networks)
WIFI 802.11, 14–15
wildcard address, IPv6 multicast, 560
window probe timer, TCP
  functions managing, 335
  other TCP timers vs., 334
  TCP write timer and, 336
  tcp_probe_timer function, 341–342
Windows, system requirements, 606
write timer, TCP, 336–341
  functions managing, 334
  other TCP timers vs., 334
  overview of, 336
  tcp_retransmit_timer function, 338–341
  tcp_write_timer function, 336–338

X
X.25 protocol, 21–22, 29–31
XFRM (Transformer), 236–237
xfrm_lookup function, 237
XML (Extensible Markup Language), 54